The Handbook of
Group
Research
and
Practice

The Handbook of
Group
Research
and
Practice

Susan A. Wheelan
GDQ Associates

SAGE Publications
Thousand Oaks ▪ London ▪ New Delhi

For information:

Sage Publications, Inc.
2455 Teller Road
Thousand Oaks, California 91320
E-mail: order@sagepub.com

Sage Publications Ltd.
1 Oliver's Yard
55 City Road
London EC1Y 1SP
United Kingdom

Sage Publications India Pvt. Ltd.
B-42, Panchsheel Enclave
Post Box 4109
New Delhi 110 017 India

Printed in the United States of America on acid-free paper.

Library of Congress Cataloging-in-Publication Data

The handbook of group research and practice / edited by Susan A. Wheelan.
    p. cm.
Includes bibliographical references and index.
ISBN 0-7619-2958-4 (cloth)
  1. Social groups—Research. 2. Social groups—Research—Methodology.
3. Intergroup relations. 4. Social group work. 5. Group psychotherapy.
6. Group work in education. I. Wheelan, Susan A.
HM716.H35 2005
302.3′072—dc22   2004029459

05   06   07   08   09   10 9 8 7 6 5 4 3 2 1

Acquisitions Editor:	Al Bruckner
Editorial Assistant:	MaryAnn Vail
Production Editor:	Diane S. Foster
Copy Editor:	Jacqueline A. Tasch
Typesetter:	C&M Digitals
Proofreader:	Scott Oney
Indexer:	Molly Hall
Cover Designer:	Janet Foulger

Contents

Introduction

The study of human groups is inherently multidisciplinary. Facilitating individual growth in a group context or group productivity in the workplace is as well. Group researchers and practitioners emerge from a variety of academic disciplines. Researchers continue to study groups, and practitioners apply what they've learned to help groups and their members achieve goals in contexts too numerous to mention. However, group researchers and practitioners do not work very well together.

Paradoxically, the reasons for this state of affairs can be found in some of the topics that group researchers investigate and the situations that group practitioners encounter in the field. Intergroup conflict among disciplines or professional organizations, perceived status differences among the disciplines and professions involved, and the norms of the larger institutions in which the various professions and disciplines are embedded reduce opportunities for intergroup contact and collaboration. Each discipline and profession has its own conferences, journals, reward structures, and modus operandi, and this severely inhibits discourse and collaboration among the disciplines, between researchers and practitioners, and among the different professions that work with groups. In addition, language is not consistent. Different words are used to describe what is studied or methods used to help groups or group members. For example, some disciplines refer to *group* research as *groups* research. Psychoeducational groups are called training groups by some, and group

consultation is referred to as group facilitation by others.

This sorry situation cannot be allowed to continue. We need all hands on deck if we are to make significant progress in understanding how groups operate, how conflict among groups around the world can be ameliorated, how groups can be used to improve workplace productivity, and how groups can be structured to facilitate individual human growth and learning more effectively. These are urgent and important questions and will require sustained collaboration over an extended period of time if we are to find answers.

Efforts to move the disciplines that study groups from isolation to collaboration have already begun. Some multidisciplinary work has occurred, but more is needed. Additional ideas about increasing collaboration are outlined in Chapters 2 and 29 of this book. This book itself is designed to stimulate dialogue among and across the disciplines and professions. People who represent eight academic disciplines and an equivalent number of subdisciplines authored chapters in *The Handbook of Group Research and Practice*. One quarter of the authors are full-time practitioners. Finally, the majority of academic authors work in the field, and the majority of practitioner authors teach, conduct research, and write from time to time. The hope is that this "motley crew," and the readers of their work, will learn from each other, inspiring further collaboration and teamwork. To that end, this handbook is divided into five sections that are briefly described next. The conclusion, Chapter 29, suggests additional ways to increase collaboration.

Part I: Group Research and Practice: Then and Now

This section focuses on the history of group research and practice, describes the current state of these two areas, and identifies key issues that need to be addressed to move forward.

In Chapter 1, Donelson Forsyth and Jeni Burnette explore the fascinating history of group research. The scientific study of groups began in earnest in the early 20th century, as intellectual, social, and political factors combined to shift scientists' attention away from physical processes to social ones. Researchers in a variety of emerging social sciences (psychology, anthropology, sociology) began to ask questions about the nature of groups and developed methods to study groups empirically. Much of the research during this period was conducted with naturally existing groups in applied settings. This steady progress in the first half of the century set the stage for a period of confluence, amplification, and productivity in the 1950s and 1960s, with much of the growth traceable to Kurt Lewin and his colleagues. The authors conclude by noting that although growth slowed during the 1970s, methodological, statistical, theoretical, and societal developments signal a renewed interest in groups that will continue to increase in the future.

In Chapter 2, Jennifer Berdahl and Kelly Bouas Henry propose that the major challenge facing group researchers is the need to integrate multiple overlapping and complementary perspectives on groups. These perspectives have developed largely in isolation from each other as a result of disciplinary preferences and pressures. This has led researchers to conceptualize groups as relatively simple entities, and it has led to a fragmented set of "facts" about groups. In reality, groups are complex and dynamic systems. Therefore, conceptualizing and studying groups as complex and dynamic systems is essential if we are to increase our understanding of how groups function. To do so,

integrative theory development is needed across the multiple perspectives. The authors propose computational modeling and multilevel longitudinal studies of groups as theoretical and empirical tools in this endeavor. They end by discussing the infrastructural challenges that will need to be overcome in order to support collaborative research of this nature.

Chapter 3, by Sally Barlow, Gary Burlingame, and Addie Fuhriman, explores the past century of research on group psychotherapy and group counseling. Studies spanning 100 years are reviewed. Group psychology and group psychotherapy research help us to understand *how*, *why*, and *when* this intervention form works. The authors conclude that therapeutic groups work for a variety of patients, in a variety of settings, encompassing a variety of problems. However, some underlying processes in groups have yet to be identified or connected to certain outcomes.

In Chapter 4, Janice DeLucia-Waack and Cynthia Kalodner describe how group interventions have changed significantly in the past two decades. The focus of groups has expanded to include psychoeducational or training groups focused on skill building as well as counseling and therapy. This chapter describes the current state of group practice as well as key issues related to group theory, research, and practice. Contemporary issues related to group theory and research include the relative efficacy of therapeutic factors, group leadership behaviors and interventions, and accurate assessment of group process and dynamics.

Part II: Theoretical Perspectives on Groups

This section contains seven different theoretical perspectives on how groups develop a unique culture and structure, change and adapt to accomplish goals, and relate to, adapt to, or influence the environment.

Chapter 5, by Marvin Geller, offers an overview of the variety of psychoanalytic perspectives that have been applied to the understanding of both group and organizational life. Although psychoanalytic theory and thinking are in flux and conceptual muddles arise due to conflicts created by differing perspectives, there is a basic theme that runs through all psychoanalytic thinking, differentiating it from nonpsychoanalytic points of view. The core concept that unifies all psychoanalytic thinking is the conviction that individuals, groups, and organizations behave both rationally and irrationally and are driven by unconscious thoughts and feelings that in turn evoke a variety of defense mechanisms. It is also a firmly held conviction that for groups, organizations, and societies to function more effectively in pursuit of their stated conscious objectives, they need to have access to the covert and unconscious process that can undermine their efforts. The goal and ideal of psychoanalytic thought and practice is not to eliminate irrational forces in groups but to make them conscious, with the hope that awareness of these forces will lead to more rational behavior, thereby increasing the possibility of achieving desired goals.

In Chapter 6, Jonathon Cummings and Deborah Ancona review the functional perspective, which is a normative approach to describing and predicting group performance that focuses on the functions of inputs and/or processes. Several principles of the functional perspective are presented, including shared goals, group adaptation, group composition and norms, group culture, and the external environment. The role of interdependence in the functional perspective, distinguishing between member interdependence and contextual interdependence, also is discussed. Finally, concepts (transactive memory, psychological safety, and structural diversity) currently being studied and those concepts (interpersonal trust, formal interventions, and virtual teams) that remain to be explored are outlined.

Chapter 7, by Susan Wheelan, presents the developmental perspective on groups. From this perspective, the overall goal of group development is to create an organized unit capable of working effectively and productively to achieve specific ends. To accomplish the goal, groups move through stages that can be specifically demarcated and described. The chapter describes these changes across time and explores a substantial body of research that supports this perspective. The chapter concludes by suggesting questions for future research.

In Chapter 8, Michael Hogg describes the historical development, metatheoretical background, and current state of the social identity approach. Although originally an analysis mainly of intergroup relations among large-scale social categories, and more recently an analysis with a strong social cognitive emphasis, the social identity approach is a general analysis of group membership and group and intergroup processes. It focuses on the generative relationship between collective self-conception and group phenomena. A number of core conceptual components are compatible but focus on different aspects of social identity and group life. These components are described in detail. The chapter concludes with a section describing some developments, extensions, and applications of the social identity approach to understanding group phenomena.

Chapter 9, by Lawrence Frey and Sunwolf, presents the communication perspective on groups. The communication perspective offers a unique and important approach to the study of groups that views groups as communication sites. From such a perspective, communication demonstrates both a constitutive role, with groups emerging from communication, and a functional purpose, with groups using communication to accomplish important goals. A review of group communication theory, methods used to study group communication, and research conducted about group communication predispositions, practices, processes, and products reveals the significance of communication in creating and sustaining group life, making groups, ultimately, a communication phenomenon.

In Chapter 10, Yvonne Agazarian and Susan Gantt describe the systems perspective on groups and present Agazarian's theory of living human systems and its systems-centered practice. Defining groups as living human systems has had important implications and impact on group practice. Thinking systems instead of just people offers an alternative to the dichotomy of individual-centered or group-centered approaches by introducing the systems-centered approach, which uses functional subgrouping to simultaneously influence both the individual and the group. The essential methods for developing a systems-centered group are described. Applications of the theory and methods are illustrated with examples from therapy groups, training groups, and organizational work groups.

Chapter 11, by Holly Arrow, describes the nonlinear dynamics perspective, which considers how processes in groups unfold over time at multiple levels, from the individual who becomes a group member to the ecology of groups that compete for members within society. This perspective draws on concepts from chaos theory, catastrophe theory, and complexity science to explain the emergence and evolution of dynamic structures and activity patterns that stabilize, evolve, and change, sometimes abruptly. It has been applied to a broad variety of groups, including families, therapy groups, work teams, friendship groups, and voluntary organizations, investigating outcomes such as cooperation, creativity, membership stability, and therapeutic effectiveness. Strategies for developing and testing theory include computer simulations, mathematical models, longitudinal studies, and experiments.

Part III: Methods in Group Research and Practice

Studying groups presents its own set of unique problems. It can be more time-consuming and labor intensive than research on individuals. Study design and data analysis can be challenging as well. This section focuses on four research methods employed to study groups.

In Chapter 12, Rick Hoyle describes experimental research methods. He states that research on groups is motivated by the goal of documenting a causal relation between an aspect of group life and one or more outcomes of relevance to individual group members or the group as a whole. Experiments are studies in which one or more putative causes are manipulated, groups or group members are randomly assigned to levels of the manipulated variables, and one or more control conditions are included. These features allow for satisfaction of the criteria for drawing a causal inference when an association between two variables is detected. Experimental research on groups is complicated by the fact that observations often are nonindependent by virtue of the frequent aggregation of individuals into groups. Although group researchers traditionally have not managed such nonindependence in optimal ways, accessible treatments of random coefficient models have made possible the relatively routine management of nonindependence without loss of potentially important information regarding individual group members' responses to causal factors. In this chapter, the primary characteristics of experimental designs are described, illustrated, and compared with alternative research designs. The second major section provides several examples of intragroup and intergroup research questions addressed using experimental designs. The next section offers a formal presentation of experimental designs and a conceptual presentation of data-analytic concerns specific to experiments involving groups. The chapter concludes with a summary of the strengths and limitations of the experimental method for research on groups and recommendations for expanding basic experimental designs to allow for documentation of the richness and complexity of group life.

Chapter 13, by Maria Riva and Maximillian Wachtel, focuses on methodological and practical considerations in conducting group research in field settings. This chapter takes a broad-based and multidisciplinary approach to group field studies, highlighting strengths, limitations, and examples from such areas as social psychology, social work, business, and psychotherapy. The many different research methodologies used in field studies are discussed, with *field* taken to mean the environment where the behavior naturally occurs (e.g., neighborhoods, work sites, psychotherapy clinics). By definition, the naturalistic environment as a setting for research poses myriad problems, as well as advantages over other types of research designs that are conducted in the laboratory. Therefore, the difficulties and advantages of group field studies have been outlined, and the authors discuss the importance of increasing the collaboration between research and practice when designing and implementing group studies that occur in settings where groups are conducted. This chapter concludes with recommendations for conducting group field studies.

In Chapter 14, Stephen Guastello describes how hypotheses in nonlinear dynamics can be tested with relatively short time series such as those that are commonly encountered in social science data, especially group dynamics. Relationships among the fractal dimension, Lyapunov exponent, chaos, self-organization, and catastrophes have been exploited to produce a compact system of statistical analysis that relies on polynomial regression or nonlinear regression. A procedure based on symbolic dynamics is presented for the dynamical analysis of variables that represent sets of categorical states. The statistical methods provide stronger and more specific tests of hypotheses than techniques based on phase portraits or other approaches.

Chapter 15, by Damon Centola and Michael Macy, describes how sociologists traditionally have studied social life as a structured system of institutions and roles that shape individual behavior from the top down. In contrast, agent-based computational modeling formalizes the social interactionist idea that much of social life emerges from the bottom up, out of local interactions. As in game theory, the intent is to understand the set of assumptions about individual behavior required for a given social phenomenon to emerge at a higher level of organization. However, these new computational tools allow researchers to overcome methodological constraints imposed by the analytical methods in classical game theory. Researchers can now systematically explore the complex interactions of structurally embedded individuals to understand the dynamics and stability of social systems. A burgeoning literature shows how this complexity can often produce surprising global consequences from changes in the rules of local interaction.

Part IV: Applied Group Research

This section focuses on efforts to apply what is known about groups to real-world situations in order to understand the consequences and effects of group dynamics in different contexts.

In Chapter 16, for example, Tjai Nielsen, Eric Sundstrom, and Terry Halfhill concentrate on work groups and the dynamic factors that lead to their success. The authors briefly review the history of applied group research conducted in the field, discuss various theoretical perspectives central to this area of study, and summarize selective empirical research from the past five years. This chapter attempts to address 5 key questions: (1) How have researchers operationally defined work groups? (2) How has the study of work groups in the field been approached? (3) What factors have been examined in an effort to predict success, using what sources of data? (4) What criteria have been used to assess work group effectiveness, using what sources of data? (5) What trends emerge from this body of research? The authors suggest ideas for future research based on answers to these questions.

In Chapter 17, R. Scott Tindale, Amanda Dykema-Engblade and Erin Wittkowski write that conflict, both within and between groups, is a natural outgrowth of living and working in group settings. As groups work to reach their goals, differences in member efforts, preferences, and goals will strain interpersonal relations and can inhibit goal attainment. Thus, a natural function in almost all groups is conflict management or maintenance. Conflict can serve a positive function if managed appropriately, but it can also cause damage to the group and inhibit its ability to function. Conflict between groups is also a naturally occurring phenomenon and, much like intragroup conflict, can have both positive and negative, sometimes catastrophic consequences. In this chapter, the authors discuss the major theoretical and empirical research on the nature of intra- and intergroup conflict, including the antecedents and potential consequences of both types of conflict in different group settings.

Chapter 18, by Dominic Abrams, Daniel Frings, and Georgina Randsley de Moura, outlines some key concepts and evidence in research on group identity and self-definition. The authors describe different theoretical and metatheoretical perspectives on group identity, outline some central questions, and briefly recount how conceptions of the relationship between individuals and groups have changed over time. They describe social identity and self-categorization theories, along with theories that use different assumptions about the self, including evolutionary and cultural influences. Evidence about the relationship between group identity and self-definition as it relates to deindividuation, identity in the workplace, multiple identities, and the role of identity in social dilemmas and collective action also is discussed. Next, the authors consider intragroup dynamics such as how groups deal with deviant members and how group identity affects leadership. They conclude by noting some areas of current controversy and important avenues for future research.

In Chapter 19, Randy Magen and Eugene Mangiardi examine the relationship between groups and individual change with particular focus on groups as the context, medium, or method by which groups help to achieve change in individuals. The chapter addresses one central question: What knowledge and skills are essential

to leading groups in the service of individual change? The answer to this question is explored by examining purposes, composition, cohesiveness, development, and communication in treatment groups. The history of research on group therapy is also discussed, and key findings about the prerequisites for training and supervision are identified. The authors conclude that although there is documented consensus about core practice knowledge and skills in group treatment, the specific mechanisms by which groups effect individual change remain elusive.

Chapter 20, by Marshall Scott Poole and Huiyan Zhang, focuses on virtual teams. The emergence of the virtual team has interested both academics and practitioners, who attempt to map out what makes virtual teams work and how to make them effective. This chapter attempts to organize what we know about virtual teams in terms of the factors that influence how they work and key processes in virtual-team effectiveness. It starts with a definition of team outcomes and then summarizes thinking and evidence on key inputs that influence virtual teams and on processes that occur in virtual teams. Throughout the chapter, the impact of inputs and processes on outputs is discussed. Future directions and trends in research on virtual teams are considered in the conclusion.

Part V: Group Practice: Methods and Outcomes

This section describes how practitioners use the group context to facilitate individual change or learning or implement strategies to improve group effectiveness and productivity. The section also explores methods designed to mediate conflict, improve group performance, and facilitate group communication. Finally, research evidence that supports or does not support these methods is reviewed.

For example, in Chapter 21, Gary Burlingame, Suad Kapetanovic, and Steven Ross focus on group psychotherapy. They present three main facets that help define group treatment as opposed to other forms of treatment: formal theory of change, patient population, and structural features. They use the first facet (formal theory of change) to describe the most common group methods. The second facet (patient population) is used to present the current state of the evidence for the effectiveness of these methods when employed with individuals in the following diagnostic categories: mood disorders, eating disorders, anxiety disorders, substance-related disorders, and several special populations. The authors conclude the chapter by reflecting on the clinical and research implications of the current state of the evidence and use the third facet of group therapy (structural features) to discuss the commonalities between empirically validated group methods.

Chapter 22, written by Dana Sims, Eduardo Salas, and C. Shawn Burke, focuses on team building and training. Work teams have become embedded in the workplace. Work teams help organizations to remain competitive in a society that constantly demands higher productivity, better performance, and greater profits. Teams offer more complex, innovative, adaptive, and comprehensive solutions than any other working structure. However, research has concluded that not all teams are successful or achieve the degree of performance that is expected of them. One solution to ensuring that teams have the knowledge, skills, and attitudes to be effective and meet performance goals is for organizations to provide team training. This chapter discusses the factors that influence the design, delivery, and evaluation of team training strategies. First, the authors discuss the construct of teamwork. Then, using the framework of the three stages of teamwork (i.e., defining the training content, implementing the training, and evaluating the training), they provide a number of literature-based tips that ensure effective team training. They conclude by discussing the effectiveness of several team training strategies.

In Chapter 23, Felice Tilin and Joanne Broder Sumerson discuss team consultation.

The chapter defines and describes the team consultation process and outlines the goals of that process as well. Next, the steps in the consultation process are provided, and a case study helps to bring that process to life. The chapter ends with a discussion of the problems that researchers encounter in attempting to study the effectiveness of team consultation and recommends collaboration between practitioners and researchers as one way to improve the quality and quantity of team consultation research.

Chapter 24, by David Johnson and Roger Johnson, focuses on learning groups. Learning groups have been used as long as humans have existed. Not all groups, however, are effective. The use of learning groups requires that members have joint goals that are positively correlated. This cooperative structure results in achieving three interrelated goals: increasing the achievement of each student, creating positive relationships among students, and increasing students' psychological health. The rich history of the use of learning groups throughout human history has resulted in an interaction among theory, research, and practice rarely found in the social sciences. Three major theoretical perspectives, social interdependence, cognitive developmental, and behavioral, underlie the use of cooperative learning groups. Of the three, social interdependence theory has most completely subsumed the existing research, inspired the most new research, and been used most closely to develop teaching practices. Cooperative learning tends to be effective to the extent that positive interdependence, individual accountability, promotive interaction, appropriate use of social skills, and group processing are all implemented in the procedure. There are a multitude of ways in which cooperative learning has been implemented, but only eight have been systematically evaluated. All eight methods, even though they are quite diverse, result in greater student achievement than do competitive or individualistic learning. These results provide strong validation for the effectiveness of learning groups, indicating that the use of learning groups is one of the most successful and widespread applications of group dynamics theory and research.

In Chapter 25, Tricia Jones describes how organizations are increasingly dependent on effectively functioning groups and well-coordinated actions between groups. But both processes are undermined by unresolved or poorly managed conflict. One tool for effective intragroup and intergroup conflict management is mediation, a form of third-party intervention. However, there is little theory explaining the critical factors that impact successful mediation in these contexts. This chapter provides an initial overview of mediation and discusses the challenges inherent in intragroup and intergroup conflicts. These challenges require distinct mediation strategies, which are presented in the chapter. Directions for future research are discussed as well.

Chapter 26, by Sunwolf and Lawrence Frey, explores methods to facilitate group communication. Groups often need facilitation to enact effective communication processes and practices. This chapter provides an overview of facilitation procedures that are designed to structure and improve group communication. After providing a brief historical overview of group communication facilitation, the chapter concentrates on the research conducted on procedures that are designed to facilitate two types of communication: relational group communication (facilitating group formation, relationships in diverse groups, social support, and group conflict management) and task group communication (facilitating structure, analysis, creativity, agreement, and teams). The chapter concludes by identifying gaps in the research literature and suggesting directions for future research on facilitating group communication.

In Chapter 27, Nina Brown reviews more than 100 studies of psychoeducational groups. Categories for these groups were personal development, support and therapy-related, and life transitions. Significant findings were the global use of psychoeducational groups, a broad

application for a variety of topics and conditions, and the many strengths that such groups seem to possess. Although almost all studies reported positive results for participants, little empirical evidence was available to support this conclusion. Other areas lacking sufficient empirical evidence are assessment of learning, training for group leaders, and significant verifiable impact on participants.

Chapter 28, by Miguel Quiñones and Kelly de Chermont, draws on the published literature on skills training groups to examine their use and effectiveness and explore avenues for future research. Skills training is defined as a group-based method of instruction aimed at giving participants basic life skills that allow them to function more effectively in social contexts, including work and home. Skills taught usually fall under the category of interpersonal or social skills and involve various target populations. Although the literature generally supports the effectiveness of this training method, little research has examined the specific design factors that contribute to its success. Factors such as the mix of participant skill levels, group size, and training content are discussed, and areas in need of further research are identified.

Conclusion: Charting the Future

This final section returns the reader to the introduction's theme of collaboration among and between researchers and practitioners from diverse disciplines and professions. George Anderson and Susan Wheelan authored the sole chapter in this section. Chapter 29 focuses on integrating group research and practice and encouraging collaborative endeavors.

Acknowledgment

I want to formally recognize the contribution of Barbara Bradley to this work. She is an excellent editor, organizer, calming influence, and friend.

PART I

Group Research and Practice: Then and Now

1

The History of Group Research

Donelson R. Forsyth

Jeni L. Burnette

The study of groups cannot be traced back to some single watershed event that can be identified by all concerned as *The Beginning* of research into groups and their processes. Plato, Aristotle, and other classical scholars frequently discussed the nature of groups and group-level processes, and they went so far as to suggest that humans are fundamentally group-living rather than solitary creatures (Ettin, 1992). Shakespeare's plays are filled with recommendations and analyses of groups, including vivid descriptions of shifting coalitions, leadership styles, and interpersonal trust (Corrigan, 1999). Centuries ago, political savants, such as Niccolo Machiavelli and Lord Acton, offered insightful analyses of how leaders could use their power to influence their followers (Jinkins & Jinkins, 1998). In the 1800s, scholars like Craik (1837), Mackay (1841/ 1932), and Le Bon (1895/1960) published major treatises examining the intriguing tendency for people, when part of large groups, to act in atypical and unusual ways.

But the scientific study of groups is scarcely a century old. Scholars and sages of long ago may have puzzled over the nature of groups and their dynamics, but it was the last 100 years or so that witnessed the emergence of a science of groups. In 1900, there were scarcely any scholarly books dealing with leadership, group performance, or social influence; no centers or institutes devoted to the scientific study of groups; no standardized or well-tested methods that investigators could use to examine group processes; no journals that specialized in research papers describing tests of specific hypotheses about groups; no departments or educational programs at colleges and universities that focused on scholarship related to groups; and certainly no scientists who, when asked what they studied, answered "groups." Today, in contrast, groups are studied by scholars in laboratories and research centers located throughout the world.

This chapter reviews the emergence of the scientific study of groups, albeit briefly, by examining the origins of group research and changes that have influenced the course of the field's development. Contemporary group research did not emerge a scant 10 years ago but instead has roots in the work and thought of scholars who published their work from the 1900s to the 1960s. Even though the contemporary researcher may rarely cite these investigators, their findings, and their publications, their work shaped the paradigm and traditions that continue to guide the study of groups. The championing of one theory over another, the choice of one method of study rather than another, the separation of the psychological study of groups from the sociological, or the shift toward one topic of study and away from another—all these aspects of the field's current state are manifestations of events and actions that occurred long ago in the discipline's past. Investigators, by studying the history of group research, can grasp how the field has changed over time and gain insight into the factors that caused those changes.

An awareness of historical antecedents also offers researchers protection against one of the gravest of scientific sins: reinventing the wheel. Researchers, in the rush to conduct their next study, concoct the next theory, or solve yet another practical problem, may ignore their past, but they do so at their own risk. As Shaw (1976) concludes, the history of group research, like all history, is an intriguing catalog of the missteps and mistakes of earlier investigators who sought to expand the field's base of knowledge about groups. Those who are familiar with these misadventures are more likely to avoid them in their own work. To spin Santayana's (1905/1924) oft-quoted warning, "Those who cannot remember the past are condemned to repeat it" (p. 284) in a positive direction, those who know their discipline's history are more likely to become a part of that history. The scientific study of groups, like all things, has a past, and that past shapes its present and its future.

Although it is tempting to trace the growth of group research from the philosophy of classical scholars up to the present day, this analysis is primarily limited to the last century or so. Recognizing, too, that many of the other chapters in this handbook will provide generous descriptions of contemporary issues in group research, more attention is given to the classic studies in groups, with the identification of such studies guided by prior analyses of the history of group research. These include, within the field of social psychology, Allport (1968), Cartwright (1979), Cartwright and Zander (1968), Festinger (1980), McGrath (1997), McGrath and Kravitz (1982), Levine and Moreland (1990, 1998), Pepitone (1981), and Zander (1979). Other excellent resources include Gouran (1999), who provides an analysis of the history of group research within the field of communication; Golembiewski's (2001) handbook of groups and organizational behavior; and Austin, Scherbaum, and Mahlman (2002), who provide a detailed analysis of the history of research into groups in organizational contexts (with a particular focus on quantitative and statistical techniques).

The Origins of Group Research

Why were group researchers so slow to sit down at the table of science? As Cartwright and Zander (1968) suggest in their review of the field's historical roots, some scholars believed that collecting data about human behavior was misguided, for it would lead to public scrutiny of mysteries that should remain undisturbed. Others felt that group behavior was too complex to be studied scientifically, particularly during an era when psychologists were struggling to understand the acquisition of conditioned reflexes, the functioning of the nervous system, and the relationship between mental states and motor activities. Still others suggested that such group-level processes as group mind, social ideas, and collective mind are scientifically suspect and can, in any case, be understood entirely by studying the psychology of the individual.

A number of intellectual, social, and political factors combined to counter these tendencies and, in so doing, stimulated the growth of research into groups. As research into human behavior proliferated across a number of emerging social science concentrations (e.g., psychology, sociology, organizational behavior, and communication), investigators in these newly defined areas realized their analyses would be incomplete if they did not understand group behavior. Specific methodological advances also served to stimulate research into group processes by removing barriers that had stymied investigators' efforts to measure group processes or design studies that would test their hypotheses adequately. World events also influenced the study of groups, for the use of groups in manufacturing, warfare, and therapeutic settings stimulated the need to understand and improve such groups. These societal influences, as noted below, stimulated research into group-level questions of social behavior, work and organizational behavior, and the use of groups to promote adjustment and positive change.

Group Dynamics and Social Science

The earliest scientists concentrated their studies on the physical world rather than the social one. As they learned to develop hypotheses, organize these hypotheses in theoretical systems, and then test these hypotheses by collecting data, they focused on the physics of motion, matter, and energy; the chemistry of compounds and elements; the mechanics of the stars and planets; and the biological systems of flora and fauna. The scientific study of human beings, in contrast, emerged more slowly. By 1850, scientists had already supplied answers to some very basic questions about the natural world and its processes, but the social world was known only through speculation, intuition, and conjecture. As Thomas (1896) noted, "man constructed a science of numbers, of the stars, of molar and molecular masses, of plants, of stones, and of creeping things, before he realized that he was himself an object capable of receiving scientific attention" (p. 434).

This selectiveness in the subjects examined by scientists began to be redressed in the late 1800s as the idea of a *social* science emerged from the grand arguments of such social philosophers as Hobbes, Locke, Hume, and Rousseau. These writers often speculated about the nature of humans and their societies, but it remained for the pioneering social scientists of the 19th and 20th centuries to seek out data to test the validity of their conjectures. Each of the new disciplines in social science—economics, sociology, psychology, political science, and anthropology—pinched off a particular area of human behavior and institutions as its specific subject for scientific study. The early economists were observers of vast changes in national and international systems of commerce and began raising questions about the relationships among income, labor, employment, and production. Political scientists watched as one revolution after another swept over Europe and America, prompting them to reexamine assumptions about government and forms of social organization. Early psychologists were fascinated by the way individuals in large groups or organizations seemed to change in fundamental ways, and sociologists began to explore how mass movements, mobs, and "the public" formed preferences and inclinations.

Researchers within all these disciplines studied, to some degree, groups and individuals' connections to those groups. Anthropologists and sociologists, trying to explain how religious, political, economic, and educational systems function to sustain society, highlighted the role groups played in maintaining social order. Durkheim (1897/1966), for example, linked differences in the suicide rates of individuals with the types of groups to which they belonged, concluding that those who belong to close-knit groups are more likely to internalize those groups' norms and rules. Anthropologists discovered that in many cases, the study of ancient humans was the study of small tribal groups. Political scientists began to explore how political parties and other organized systems of social influence formed and evolved over time, and in many cases, their analyses led them to the study of small groups of closely networked individuals. Michels (1911/1999), for example, offered up his Iron Law of Oligarchy after observing that political associations tend to drift away from democratic decision making toward more centralized oligarchies and autocratic decisional procedures. The early psychologists also studied groups, but especially large groups such as mobs and crowds. In 1895, the French psychologist Le Bon (1895/1960) published his book *Psychologie des Foules* (Psychology of Crowds), which describes how individuals are transformed when they join a group. Wundt (1916), the recognized founder of a scientific psychology, also studied groups extensively. His folk psychology (*Volkerpsychologie*) combined elements of anthropology and psychology by examining the conditions and changes displayed by elementary social aggregates and describing how group memberships influence virtually all cognitive and perceptual processes.

Methods for Studying Groups

By the beginning of the 20th century, such scholars as Cooley, Durkheim, Simmel, McDougall, Ross, and Wundt were seeking answers to fundamentally important questions about the nature of groups and their processes: Why do humans affiliate with others in groups? How do leaders hold sway over the rest of the group? How do groups achieve social control over their members? To what extent is human behavior determined by instincts rather than reflection and choice? How do groups shape the personalities and beliefs of their members? What factors give rise to a sense of community with the in-group and distrust for the out-group? But these early

group researchers were limited by the lack of the tools and methods needed for measuring social phenomena and conducting rigorous scientific tests of hypotheses. They relied, initially, on the merest of data in their studies, often basing their conclusions on everyday experience, informal observations, and the arguments of authorities on the subjects they examined. But in time, their methods became more rigorous and empirical as they borrowed the template of the better-developed natural sciences for their own uses. Although uncertain if the methods developed in the natural sciences were appropriate ones to use in studying humans, researchers nonetheless turned to these sciences as a model for their own work.

Measurement of Individuals and Groups

Progress in the natural sciences was hastened, in nearly all cases, by the development of better methods for measuring the phenomena of interest. Better telescopes, microscopes, scales, meters, and gauges all contributed to better data, which in turn led to more precise descriptions and more comprehensive theory. Similarly, the science of groups required the development of methods for measuring more precisely not only the qualities of individuals who were in groups but also the characteristics of groups and the processes that occurred within them. Although turn-of-the-century theorists spoke of both individual-level qualities—attitudes, values, beliefs, traits, leadership skills, and the like—and such group-level qualities as imitation, contagion, group beliefs, and solidarity, reliable and valid methods for measuring these qualities of people and groups were not yet widely available.

Measurement of human characteristics expanded rapidly in the first third of the 20th century, and each new method was quickly applied to the study of individuals in groups. In 1916, Terman published his remarkably successful and enduring measure of intelligence, and soon, differential psychologists were generating various measures of individual differences that were relevant to group behavior (e.g., leadership skills, communication ability). In 1928, Thurstone published his seminal paper, "Attitudes Can Be Measured," and subsequent investigators used the method to develop Thurstone scales of various group-level processes, including leadership and various national and social groups. In 1932, Likert introduced a simplified scaling procedure that could be used to measure more easily a range of group members' attitudes, opinions, and perceptions. Other measurement scales, focusing on such group-relevant characteristics as ascendance and submissiveness (Allport, 1928), personal values (Vernon & Allport, 1931), attitudes toward other racial and social groups (Bogardus, 1933), introversion-extroversion (Guilford & Braly, 1930), leadership traits (Cowley, 1931), and moral character (Hartshorne, May, & Shuttleworth, 1930), were used by investigators in the 1920s and 1930s to quantify aspects of individuals when in groups.

Once they could measure individual-level qualities, researchers turned their attention to techniques for measuring group-level processes, primarily through the use of observational methods. Scholars had been watching groups for centuries, but their methods were informal and accidental rather than structured and deliberate. In many cases, individuals encountered groups during the course of their normal activities and noted what happened within these groups, but rarely did they deliberately seek out groups or describe the actions of these groups systematically and objectively (Cartwright, 1959). In the 1930s, Goodenough (1928), Olson and Cunningham (1934), and Parten (1932) pioneered the development of structured systems for observing multiple individuals interacting with one another, and these systems began to include all the components required of contemporary observational methods: focus on observable actions, restricted focus on a priori specified types of behavior, sampling of data across time and settings, and the use of trained observers (McGrath & Altermatt, 2001). Bales's (1950) interaction process analysis represents the culmination of these developments, providing the basis for methods of observation for the next 60 years.

Early researchers also began to explore ways to measure structural aspects of groups, such as leadership hierarchy, status relations, and patterns of attraction and disliking within groups. At the forefront of these advances was Moreno's sociometric method, which he developed as early as 1932 in his work with groups of women living in 16 adjacent cottages at the New York Training School for Girls (Hare & Hare, 1996). To reduce conflict in the community, Moreno regrouped the women into more compatible units by giving the women a confidential questionnaire that asked them to indicate those in the community they liked the most. Thus, Moreno had developed the technique for measuring social relationships that he called sociometry. This method involves collecting, from all members if possible, choices of friends and nonfriends and then organizing this information in a sociomatrix of choices or a visual representation called a sociogram. Although a relatively simple method, it provides the basis for subsequent methods for assessing group structure, including social network analyses.

Research Procedures

As researchers became increasingly confident in their measurement methods, they began to adapt the procedures of the natural sciences to the study of groups. Initially, researchers relied heavily on case study and description in their studies. Scholars had used this method to study groups for centuries, but in the hands of a group researcher, the method became more rigorous and more informative. Investigators such as Wirth (1928), Zorbaugh (1929), Thrasher (1927), and Shaw (1930) used this method in studies of a variety of naturally forming groups, including families, crowds, communities, gangs, and unions. Thrasher, for example, collected information about hundreds of inner-city gangs before concluding that these groups form for the same reasons that most groups form: As young men who live in close physical proximity come together in the course of their day's activities, similarities in interests and aptitudes promote the development of a group, which becomes a gang through intergroup conflict processes. Whyte's (1943) study of street corner gangs in Boston serves as the prototype for such studies, for he integrated his detailed, objective records of each day's events in a conceptually rich framework that highlighted the key role groups played in the lives of the individuals he studied. Whyte also included a detailed analysis of the methods he used in his research in an expanded edition of his initial report. Cartwright and Zander (1968, p. 17) trace the substantial impact of Whyte's study back to three factors: (a) its objectivity, (b) its focus on the meaning of the interactions among group members, and (c) its consistent focus on group-level processes, such as leadership, status, obligations, and group cohesion.

Case study designs are still used by researchers, but experience led researchers to supplement case studies with nonexperimental designs that sought to describe relationships among variables and experimental studies conducted in both laboratory and field situations. Nonexperimental studies grew in popularity when advances in statistical procedures, and the correlational coefficient in particular, allowed researchers to index more precisely the strength of relationships among quantitatively assessed variables. Rather than drawing qualitative conclusions from their interpretations of the cases they examined, researchers could use correlational studies to provide more information about the relationship between both individual- and group-level variables. A number of investigators described the level of association between variables statistically, but the work of Hartshorne, May, and their colleagues (Hartshorne & May, 1928; Hartshorne et al., 1930) was particularly influential due to its scope and precision. These researchers measured a variety of characteristics of children with respect to morality, including moral knowledge, moral conduct, cooperativeness, reputation, deceitfulness, and so on. They discovered that even though moral knowledge was not related to moral conduct at the individual level ($r = .116$), at the group level these two variables were correlated at .841.

A second landmark study that used correlational procedures was reported by Newcomb in his 1943 Bennington study. In this work, Newcomb measured the social and political attitudes and social standing of a substantial number of college students attending the relatively progressive Bennington College. When he examined the relationships among these variables, he discovered that attitude was closely related to the amount of time spent in the group, with first-year students displaying conservative political attitudes and graduating students reporting more liberal ones. Newcomb explained this shift in terms of the greater influence of the older, higher status, and more liberal students. New students who were "both capable and desirous of cordial relations with the fellow community members" (p. 149) tended to become more liberal due to the "informational environment of the community and the status structure embedded in that environment" (Alwin, Cohen, & Newcomb, 1991, p. 52). As Cartwright and Zander (1968) explain, whereas "most of these points had been made in one form or another by writers in the speculative era of social science, this study was especially significant because it provided detailed, objective, and quantitative evidence" (p. 17).

Studies of groups using a true experimental design, although relatively rare, were also appearing in the scientific literature at this time. Ringelmann, a French agricultural engineer, conducted some of the earliest experiments in group productivity in the 1880s. He created groups of varying sizes and carefully measured their efficiency before noting the reduction of productivity in groups that now carries his name: the Ringelmann effect. His study, however, remained largely unknown at the time, for Ringelmann (1913) was more concerned with productivity per se than with group processes (Kravitz & Martin, 1986). By the turn of the century, researchers in the United States began studying—experimentally and in earnest—two basic group processes: the facilitative effects of others on performances and the impact of group discussion on attitudes. In 1898, for example, Triplett published the results of a laboratory study of competition confirming that other people, by their mere presence, can change us. He arranged for 40 children to play a game that involved turning a small reel as quickly as possible. He found that those who played the game in pairs turned the reel faster than those who were alone, experimentally verifying the impact of one person on another. F. H. Allport extended these studies throughout the 1920s (e.g., Allport, 1924).

The accumulating advances in methodological sophistication were punctuated in the 1930s by two particularly influential experimental studies: Sherif's (1936) study of conformity to group norms and Lewin, Lippitt, and White's (1939) study of leadership styles. Both of these studies created ad hoc groups in laboratory-like settings; both studied multiple groups to determine the replicability of their results; and both systematically manipulated aspects of the situation while measuring participants' responses. Sherif arranged for groups of three to make judgments, aloud, about the distance a dot of light appeared to move in an otherwise darkened room. Sherif discovered that group members' judgments tended to converge in the group setting, suggesting the group was guided by a social norm. Significantly, this norm also guided members' responses when they made decisions alone, suggesting that this social norm was not completely dependent on the interpersonal setting—individuals had internalized the group product and used it as a frame of reference when making individual judgments.

In 1937, Lewin, Lippitt, and White conducted an equally influential experimental study by randomly assigning a specific type of leader to artificial groups working in a laboratory-like setting (Lewin et al., 1939; White, 1990; White & Lippitt, 1968). Their subjects, young boys, worked on various projects in five-person groups led by an adult who adopted one of three styles of leadership: autocratic, democratic, or laissez-faire. The researchers observed the groups as they worked with each type of leader, measuring group productivity and aggressiveness. They discovered that the autocratic groups spent more time working than the democratic groups, which in turn spent more time working than the laissez-faire groups, but hostility and aggression were highest in the groups working with an autocratic leader.

These studies signaled a transition away from a reliance on studies of naturalistic groups and studies that focused on individuals rather than groups. Both studies succeeded in creating group-level process in a laboratory setting, with Sherif (1936) creating norms and Lewin and his colleagues (1939) manipulating leadership. The groups studied were artificial ones, but the use of experimental techniques with these groups "gave the findings a generality not ordinarily achieved by naturalistic research" (Cartwright & Zander, 1968, p. 16). Lewin's study, in particular, was lauded as the first to create a political system in the microcosm of the small group laboratory.

These studies also laid to rest a conceptual challenge that had nagged early group researchers. Even though interest in group research surged during the early 1900s, some investigators remained skeptical about the value of developing group-level explanations of interpersonal behavior. Allport, for example, argued in 1924 that groups should never be studied by psychologists because they did not exist as scientifically valid phenomena. Allport believed that "the actions of all are nothing more than the sum of the actions of each taken separately" (p. 5), so he felt that a full understanding of the behavior of individuals in groups could be achieved simply through studying the psychology of the group members. But studies conducted by Sherif (1936) and Lewin and his colleagues (1939) convinced most researchers that the behavior of individuals in groups might be significantly influenced by potent group-level processes, such as norms, leadership, and cohesiveness. Allport (1961) eventually amended his position on groups and himself conducted extensive studies of such large group phenomena as rumors and morale during wartime (Allport & Lepkin, 1943) and how norms can cause a skewness in the distribution of social behaviors (the J-curve hypothesis; Allport, 1934).

Groups and Applied Professions

The efforts of researchers working in the first half of the 20th century resulted in the gradual accumulation of a set of procedures for studying groups scientifically, but not all of the research conducted during this period was motivated by scientific curiosity about the nature of groups. Group researchers were, from the outset, as much motivated by the quest for useful, practical information about groups as by the quest for scientific understanding. From Cartwright and Zander (1968): Some "of the most influential early systematic writing about the nature of groups came from the pens of people working in the professions, people whose motivation has often been said to be purely practical" (p. 8).

Groups in Industrial/ Organizational Settings

In the early decades of the 20th century, analyses of work motivation and performance in industrial and business settings adopted a scientific-management orientation popularized by Taylor (1911). Employees were considered to be egoistically motivated and so worked to earn the pay they needed to support themselves and

their families. Productivity was assumed to be tied closely to supervision, payment, and training, with Taylor cautioning against reliance on groups in the workplace. He believed that in some cases, workers conspired to work as little as possible. In others, groups contributed to a loss in productivity by masking each individual's contribution to the product: Motivation dwindles when people are "herded into gangs instead of being treated as separate individuals" (Taylor, 1911, p. 72).

Studies conducted in the 1920s and 1930s by Münsterberg (1913), Mayo (1933), and other early organizational psychologists challenged Taylor's emphasis on individuality. Münsterberg agreed that individuals should be carefully selected and trained, but he felt that groups could contribute to productivity by increasing "solidarity amongst the laborers and their feelings of security" (p. 234). But it was the work of Mayo and his colleagues at the Hawthorne plant of the Western Electric Company, conducted from 1927 to 1932, that signaled a transition away from scientific management to a human relations paradigm (Landsberger, 1958; Mayo, 1945; Roethlisberger & Dickson, 1939). These researchers systematically manipulated features of the work situation, such as the lighting in the room and the duration of rest periods, while measuring output. They were surprised when all the changes led to improved worker output, and after further study, they realized that the change was being produced by group-level influences: The workers were now "members of a working group with all the psychological and social implications peculiar to such a group" (Roethlisberger & Dickson, 1939, p. 86; cf. Bramel & Friend, 1981; Franke, 1979; Franke & Kaul, 1978).

These studies altered both the course of research into organizational behavior and the methods of management used in business and industry (Cartwright & Zander, 1968; Haire, 1956). Researchers who were interested in organizational behavior, no matter what their professional identity, considered groups to be of central importance in their analysis, and this emphasis continues to increase even now (Levine & Moreland, 1995). Those who were responsible for managing organizations and businesses also increasingly adopted approaches that fully recognized the importance of groups and interpersonal relations. Indeed, "the emergence of group dynamics in the late 1930s came, then, at the very time when administrators and organization theorists were beginning to emphasize the importance of groups and of 'human relations' in administration" (Cartwright & Zander, 1968, p. 10). This influence remains strong, as organizational specialists continue to stress the importance of group-level approaches to productivity and performance.

Groups and Interpersonal Change

During the first half of the 20th century, social workers, physicians, educators, public health workers, and therapists became increasingly interested in using group methods to achieve their professional goals. Linking all these disciplines was a shared interest in group work and interpersonal skill training, which included understanding the forces at work in groups, learning how to work effectively in groups, and promoting individual adjustment and change through interventions that are conducted in groups. Busch (1934), Coyle (1930), and other early leaders in the emerging field of social work recommended using social clubs and societies, summer camps and community centers, athletic and recreational programs, and other social groups to promote desired changes in communities. Groups became increasingly important both in the classroom and in schools in general, as educators recommended using active forms of learning in response to Dewey's (1910) broadened conceptualization of teaching and learning. Curriculums were revised to teach leadership, cooperation, and interpersonal sensitivity, and schools increasingly incorporated groups (student government, clubs) into their activities.

In addition, mental health professionals used groups to achieve therapeutic goals during this period. As early as 1905, Pratt (1922), a physician, arranged for patients to gather in groups for instruction, social support, and "thought control." Burrow (1927), even though he was trained as a psychoanalyst and was a founding member of the American Psychoanalytic Association, turned to group approaches to explore problems that sprang from interpersonal rather than intrapsychic processes. Moreno (1932) made use of group activities in treatment as early as 1910, when he asked group members to reenact specific turbulent episodes from their lives or events that happened within the group. Moreno believed that such psychodramas were more involving than discussion and that the drama itself helped members overcome their reluctance to discuss critical issues.

These applications of group research to achieve practical goals emerged as one of the foundational principles of the field of group dynamics. Although in most sciences a line is drawn between basic and applied research, group research emerged from a tradition that blurred this distinction.

Group Research Across Time

Just as groups pass through stages as they mature from a newly formed aggregate into a unified group, so group research has progressed through a series of stages, with some periods marked by more rapid progress than others. Throughout the first half of the 20th century, group research expanded in step with the tremendous growth of the social sciences and vast improvements in the quality of social science methods. As the social sciences exploded into such new fields as psychology, sociology, and anthropology, so did interest in small groups. Methodological advances also stimulated group research: They provided investigators with the means of measuring individual and group-level processes accurately, and they offered templates for case, correlational, and experimental research designs. But complementing these theoretical and methodological developments was an increased concern about having a practical understanding of groups in manufacturing, warfare, and therapeutic settings.

The slow but steady progress in theory and methods of the first half of the century set the stage for a period of confluence, amplification, and productivity: a heyday of group research (Steiner, 1974). By the late 1940s, centers for the study of groups were founded in colleges and universities across the country. The publication rate of papers dealing with groups jumped by 200% (Zander, 1979). Academics and the general lay public felt that the study of groups held the key to important scientific and practical problems, and researchers were able to secure support for their work from both federal and private sources. The relatively narrow focus of earlier years was broadened to include a wide range of topics. Group research had passed through the forming and norming stages of its development and was ready to perform.

Lewin's Legacy

Cartwright (1979), when searching for the cause of the unprecedented increase in group research that occurred in the period from 1945 to 1965, highlights one factor in particular: World War II. The war stimulated studies of leadership, community morale, intergroup relations, and other group topics, and for the first time, researchers were funded to carry out their studies (Johnson & Nichols, 1998). Hitler's rise to power also forced many European researchers and intellectuals to emigrate to America, where they contributed in all areas of psychology. One of these individuals, in particular, had a pronounced impact on group research, for he is generally regarded as the field's founder: Kurt Lewin.

Lewin shaped the field's paradigm through his theoretical work, his research, his teaching and collaborations, and his social and political activism. Born in Prussia in 1890, Lewin studied

and taught in Freiberg, Munich, and Berlin before growing anti-Semitism forced him to move to the United States in 1932. For the next decade, he taught at the Child Welfare Research Station at the University of Iowa, where he refined field theory, his psychological model of human behavior. The approach argued that at any point in time, a group exists in a social and psychological field of forces, and those forces interact dynamically to determine the behavior of groups and the individuals in them. To predict the productivity of a group, for example, one must consider not only the personalities of the individuals in the group but also the type of tasks the group is attempting, the way the leaders interact with followers, and the aspirations of the group's members. To predict the unity of a group, one must study the way members interact with one another, their degree of similarity in general attitudes and values, and their location relative to one another (Lewin, 1947). Lewin's famous formula, B = f (P, E), summarizes the assumption that the interplay of both personal factors and environmental factors determines the actions and reactions of individuals in any social setting, including groups. Interactionism remains one of the central assumptions of research into group processes (Lewin, 1951).

Lewin also spawned, and occupied the central position in, an extensive network of students, researchers, and practitioners who were drawn to the study of groups (Festinger, 1980; Marrow, 1969). That network included not only individuals who worked directly with Lewin on research, including Bavelas, Festinger, French, Lippitt, and White, but also individuals who were affiliated with the Research Center for Group Dynamics. Lewin founded this center in 1944 at the Massachusetts Institute of Technology, and its staff and students were a "who's who" of group researchers, including Back, Cartwright, Deutsch, Kelly, and Schachter. When Lewin died in 1947, the center moved to the University of Michigan, where it continues to fulfill its mission of studying groups scientifically. This group of scholars is responsible for much of the theoretical and empirical work on groups in the 1950s and 1960s, including Festinger's (1954, 1957) social comparison theory and dissonance theory; Schachter's (1951, 1959) analysis of communication and cohesion in groups and of affiliation; Thibaut and Kelley's (1959) exchange theory; Back's (1972) analyses of groups as agents of change; Festinger, Schachter, and Back's (1950) analysis of attitude change in groups; Newcomb's (1961) studies of the acquaintance process and social networks; French's (1956) analysis of power; Zander's (1971/1996) studies of motives and goals in groups; Cartwright's (1968) conceptualization of group cohesion; Deutsch's (1949) work on conflict; and Zajonc's (1965) synthesis of the social facilitation literature.

Lewin also solidified the field's emphasis on research of practical significance with his conception of *action research*. Lewin (1943) argued in favor of intertwining basic and applied research, for he firmly believed that there "is no hope of creating a better world without a deeper scientific insight into the function of leadership and culture, and of other essentials of group life" (p. 113). To achieve this goal, he assured practitioners that in many instances, "there is nothing so practical as a good theory" (Lewin, 1951, p. 169), and he charged basic researchers with the task of developing theories that can be applied to important social problems. Lewin and his students conducted studies of executive leadership, productivity in the workplace, organizational development, the use of group discussion to promote attitude change, and the impact of training in group process on self-development. He was instrumental in creating the National Training Laboratory in Group Development, which continues to hold workshops designed to help individuals improve their relationship and group skills (Highhouse, 2002).

Contemporary Group Research: Rise, Decline, and Renewal

The work of Lewin and his colleagues set the foundation for the research themes and advances in the second half of the 20th century. Group research became paradigmatic (Kuhn, 1970) as researchers used increasingly agreed-upon methods to examine emerging theoretical principles and hypotheses pertaining to a wide range of group processes. The young field of group dynamics transitioned into "normal science," with a focus on three themes noted by McGrath (1984, 1997): influence, interaction, and performance. Researchers who viewed groups as sources of social influence examined such topics as conformity (Asch, 1955), obedience (Milgram, 1963), normative influence (Deutsch & Gerard, 1955), compliance and conversion (Kelman, 1961), social comparison (Latané, 1966), affiliation (Schachter, 1959), and deviance (Schachter, 1951). Those who viewed groups as social systems that pattern interactions studied group structures such as roles and norms (Biddle & Thomas, 1966), interpersonal attraction (Newcomb, 1963), interaction process analysis (Bales, 1950), and communication networks (Shaw, 1964). And those who viewed groups as systems for influencing task performance launched programmatic studies of productivity (Davis, 1969), performance (Hackman & Morris, 1975), group tasks (Steiner, 1972), risky decision making (Wallach, Kogan, & Bem, 1962), faulty decision making (Janis, 1972), leadership (Fiedler, 1964), and bargaining and negotiation (Blake & Mouton, 1964).

The three themes—influence, interaction, and performance—remain the core of a social psychological approach to groups, but by no means do they summarize the variety, creativity, or interdisciplinary scope of research work during this period. In the 1960s and 1970s, for example, interest surged in a number of specific group topics, such as shifts of opinion following group discussion, coalition formation, the Prisoner's Dilemma game, and juries. In the 1970s and 1980s, researchers studied perceptions of leaders, conflict resolution, and minority influence. In the 1990s, such topics as intergroup relations, social identity, cognition in groups, social networks, and team-based processes drew the interest of group researchers. These areas of intense study were complemented by increased interest in groups in many other social sciences, such as organizational and clinical psychology, political science, and communication studies.

By the mid-1970s, however, the field's growth had slowed, signaling to some a period of doldrums and waning interest. Steiner (1974), for example, asked, "Whatever happened to the group in social psychology?" and suggested that studies of groups were disappearing at an alarming rate. McGrath (1997), in reflecting on that period, suggested that small group research, "weighed down by excess conceptual, methodological, and perhaps ideological baggage, simply faded from the mainstream social psychological scene" (p. 12).

Trends emerging at the end of the century, however, suggest a renewed interest in groups. This rise in interest is due, in part, to the increase in research conducted outside of social psychology. As many social psychologists lost interest in groups, researchers in other fields such as organizational behavior, political decision making, education, and family studies increased their investigation of these processes. The interdisciplinary approach blended ideas from the three distinct schools of influence, structure, and performance and, in doing so, offered novel conceptualizations for studying groups. As Moreland, Hogg, and Hains (1994) conclude, groups were still being actively studied, but by researchers from a wide variety of disciplines.

This increase in research was due, as well, to a groundswell of interest in all things cognitive that was sweeping psychology. In step with the waxing of interest in perceptual and cognitive processes in virtually all the social sciences, group researchers expanded their studies of how groups organize and process information (Hinsz, Tindale, & Vollrath, 1997). Studies of transactive memory, information exchange, group memory, and group decision making all highlight the cognitive bases of interpersonal processes in groups, but much of this research also focuses on perceptions of individuals who are members of different groups. Indeed, the rise in the number of publications dealing with

groups (Moreland et al., 1994; Sanna & Parks, 1997) in the final decade of the 20th century was due, in large part, to an upswing of interest in intergroup relations and social identity. Although the study of intergroup relations reaches back to Sumner (1906), in the 1990s, intergroup processes returned as the dominant topic in the study of groups.

Future of Group Research

Nostradamus made astoundingly accurate predictions about future events, but the same cannot be said for those who make predictions about the future of group research. During a dinner meeting of the Society for the Psychological Study of Social Issues in 1942, Lewin predicted that the field of group dynamics would soon be "one of the most important theoretical and practical fields" in the social sciences (quoted in Zander, 1979, p. 418). In 1954, Bogardus predicted that researchers would soon develop extensive measures of group personality and that "groupality" would become as important a concept as personality. In 1974, Steiner predicted a tremendous upswing of research into groups in the 1980s.

Will the study of groups increase in the 21st century? Despite the field's failure to live up to the expectations of past prognosticators, we cannot resist offering an optimistic prediction about the future of groups. Our optimism is based not only on the field's prior record of achievement, but also on methodological, statistical, theoretical, and societal developments that may change the way research is conducted and the value attached to such research.

At the methodological level, advances in statistics and revised attitudes about the value of nonexperimental research have combined to ease some of the labor and time costs of conducting group research. The increasing use of sophisticated statistical approaches to grouped data, such as hierarchical linear modeling, has helped the field effectively deal with group-level data. Although group-level research once posed thorny problems of analysis, as Sadler and Judd (2001) note, "There is nothing inherently difficult to the analysis of group data, once one appreciates the multiple sources of variation that exist in group data structures and treats groups as the effective unit of analysis" (p. 523). Similarly, advanced methods for handling nonexperimental data, such as structural equations modeling, have dethroned experimentation as the gold standard for scientific research, liberating researchers to use a wider variety of research methods (e.g., network analyses, bona fide group studies, ethnography). These advances in methodological sophistication are complemented by an increased theoretical sophistication. Simplistic box-and-arrow conceptualizations of groups, which yielded bivariate predictions that ignore recursiveness and process, are giving way to more complex models that take into account a wider array of neurological, evolutionary, cognitive, and interpersonal processes (e.g., Arrow, McGrath, & Berdahl, 2000).

The field of groups will also change as the people who study groups change. As researchers become more diverse in terms of their ethnicity, sex, race, and cultural backgrounds, the field's theories, methods, and applications will also diversify. Minorities and women will offer a new perspective on groups, stimulating the analysis of issues both overlooked and understudied.

The future of group research also depends, fundamentally, on the role groups play in contemporary and future society. Human behavior is more often than not group behavior, but the importance of groups in shaping human behavior is only beginning to be recognized by researchers and laypeople alike. Although Western countries such as the United States and Great Britain traditionally stress the individual over the group, this cultural norm will change with increased contact between individualistic cultures and collectivistic cultures. Corporations will continue to evolve into multinational organizations, and with that global perspective will come increased exposure to collectivistic values. This general increase in collectivism at the societal level will stimulate the acceptance of a collectivistic, Gestalt view of groups and interpersonal processes as researchers recognize that the sum is, in fact, greater than its parts. As society adjusts to a more technological and united world, and as economic success is determined more by group decisions and work team efforts, the focus on group research will become increasingly relevant, practical, and important (Forsyth, 2000).

References

Allport, F. H. (1924). *Social psychology.* Boston: Houghton Mifflin.

Allport, F. H. (1934). The J-curve hypothesis of conforming behavior. *Journal of Social Psychology, 5,* 141–183.

Allport, F. H. (1961). The contemporary appraisal of an old problem. *Contemporary Psychology, 6,* 195–197.

Allport, F. H., & Lepkin, M. (1943). Building war morale with news-headlines. *Public Opinion Quarterly, 7,* 211–221.

Allport, G. W. (1928). A test for ascendance-submission. *Journal of Abnormal Psychology, 23,* 118–136.

Allport, G. W. (1968). The historical background of modern social psychology. In G. Lindzey & E. Aronson (Eds.), *The handbook of social psychology* (2nd ed., Vol. 1, pp. 1–80). New York: Addison-Wesley.

Alwin, D. F., Cohen, R. L., & Newcomb, T. M. (1991). *Political attitudes over the life span: The Bennington women after fifty years.* Madison: University of Wisconsin Press.

Arrow, H., McGrath, J. E., & Berdahl, J. L. (2000). *Small groups as complex systems: Formation, coordination, development, and adaptation.* Thousand Oaks, CA: Sage.

Asch, S. E. (1955). Opinions and social pressure. *Scientific American, 193*(5), 31–35.

Austin, J. T., Scherbaum, C. A., & Mahlman, R. A. (2002). History of research methods in industrial and organizational psychology: Measurement, design, analysis. In S. G. Rogelberg (Ed.), *Handbook of research methods in industrial and organizational psychology* (pp. 3–33). Malden, MA: Blackwell.

Back, K. W. (1972). *Beyond words: The story of sensitivity training and the encounter movement.* New York: Russell Sage.

Bales, R. F. (1950). *Interaction process analysis: A method for the study of small groups.* Reading, MA: Addison-Wesley.

Biddle, B. J., & Thomas, E. J. (1966). *Role theory: Concepts and research.* New York: Wiley.

Blake, R. R., & Mouton, J. S. (1964). *The managerial grid.* Houston, TX: Gulf.

Bogardus, E. S. (1933). A social distance scale. *Sociology and Social Research, 17,* 265–271.

Bogardus, E. S. (1954). Group behavior and groupality. *Sociology and Social Research, 38,* 401–403.

Bramel, D., & Friend, R. (1981). Hawthorne, the myth of the docile worker, and class bias in psychology. *American Psychologist, 36,* 867–878.

Burrow, T. (1927). The group method of analysis. *Psychoanalytic Review, 10,* 268–280.

Busch, H. M. (1934). *Leadership in group work.* New York: Associations Press.

Cartwright, D. (1959). A field theoretical conception of power. In D. Cartwright (Ed.), *Studies in social power* (pp. 183–220). Ann Arbor, MI: Institute for Social Research.

Cartwright, D. (1968). The nature of cohesiveness. In D. Cartwright & A. Zander (Eds.), *Group dynamics: Research and theory* (3rd ed., pp. 91–109). New York: Harper & Row.

Cartwright, D. (1979). Contemporary social psychology in historical perspective. *Social Psychology Quarterly, 42,* 82–93.

Cartwright, D., & Zander, A. (Eds.). (1968). *Group dynamics: Research and theory* (3rd ed.). New York: Harper & Row.

Corrigan, P. (1999). *Shakespeare on management: Leadership lessons for today's managers.* London: Kogan Page.

Cowley, W. H. (1931). The traits of face-to-face leaders. *Journal of Abnormal and Social Psychology, 26,* 304–313.

Coyle, G. L. (1930). *Social process in organized groups.* New York: R. R. Smith.

Craik, G. L. (1837). *Sketches of popular tumults: Illustrative of the evils of social ignorance.* London: C. Knight.

Davis, J. H. (1969). *Group performance.* Reading, MA: Addison-Wesley.

Deutsch, M. (1949). A theory of cooperation and competition. *Human Relations, 2,* 129–152.

Deutsch, M., & Gerard, H. B. (1955). A study of normative and informational social influences upon individual judgment. *Journal of Abnormal and Social Psychology, 51,* 629–636.

Dewey, J. (1910). *How we think.* New York: Heath.

Durkheim, E. (1966). *Suicide.* New York: The Free Press. (Original work published 1897)

Ettin, M. F. (1992). *Foundations and applications of group psychotherapy: A sphere of influence.* Needham Heights, MA: Allyn & Bacon.

Festinger, L. (1954). A theory of social comparison processes. *Human Relations, 7,* 117–140.

Festinger, L. (1957). *A theory of cognitive dissonance.* Stanford, CA: Stanford University Press.

Festinger, L. (Ed.). (1980). *Retrospections on social psychology.* New York: Oxford University Press.

Festinger, L., Schachter, S., & Back, K. (1950). *Social pressures in informal groups.* New York: Harper.

Fiedler, F. E. (1964). A contingency model of leadership effectiveness. *Advances in Experimental Social Psychology, 1,* 150–190.

Forsyth, D. R. (2000). The social psychology of groups and group psychotherapy: One view of the next century. *Group, 24,* 147–155.

Franke, R. H. (1979). The Hawthorne experiments: Re-view. *American Sociological Review, 44,* 861–867.

Franke, R. H., & Kaul, J. D. (1978). The Hawthorne experiments: First statistical interpretation. *American Sociological Review, 43,* 623–643.

French, J. R. P., Jr. (1956). A formal theory of social power. *Psychological Review, 63,* 181–194.

Golembiewski, R. T. (Ed.). (2001). *Handbook of organizational behavior* (2nd ed.). New York: Marcel Dekker.

Goodenough, F. L. (1928). Measuring behavior traits by means of repeated short samples. *Journal of Juvenile Research, 12,* 230–235.

Gouran, D. S. (1999). Communication in groups: The emergence and evolution of a field of study. In L. R. Frey (Ed.), D. S. Gouran, & M. S. Poole (Associate Eds.), *The handbook of group communication theory & research* (pp. 3–36). Thousand Oaks, CA: Sage.

Guilford, J. P., & Braly, K. W. (1930). Extroversion and introversion. *Psychological Bulletin, 27,* 96–107.

Hackman, J. R., & Morris, C. G. (1975). Group tasks, group interaction process, and group performance effectiveness: A review and proposed integration. *Advances in Experimental Social Psychology, 8,* 47–99.

Haire, M. (1956). *Psychology in management.* New York: McGraw-Hill.

Hare, A. P., & Hare, J. R. (1996). *J. L. Moreno.* Thousand Oaks, CA: Sage.

Hartshorne, H., & May, M. (1928). *Studies in the nature of character: Vol. 1. Studies in deceit.* New York: Macmillan.

Hartshorne, H., May, M., & Shuttleworth, F. (1930). *Studies in the nature of character: Vol. 3. Studies in the organization of character.* New York: Macmillan.

Highhouse, S. (2002). A history of the T-group and its early applications in management development. *Group Dynamics, 6,* 277–290.

Hinsz, V. B., Tindale, R. S., & Vollrath, D. A. (1997). The emerging conceptualization of groups as information processes. *Psychological Bulletin, 121,* 43–64.

Janis, I. L. (1972). *Victims of groupthink.* Boston: Houghton-Mifflin.

Jinkins, M., & Jinkins, D. B. (1998). *The character of leadership: Political realism and public virtue in nonprofit organizations.* New York: John Wiley.

Johnson, B. T., & Nichols, D. R. (1998). Social psychologists' expertise in the public interest: Civilian morale research during World War II. *Journal of Social Issues, 54,* 53–77.

Kelman, H. C. (1961). Processes of opinion change. *Public Opinion Quarterly, 25,* 57–78.

Kravitz, D. A., & Martin, B. (1986). Ringelmann rediscovered: The original article. *Journal of Personality and Social Psychology, 50,* 936–941.

Kuhn, T. S. (1970). *The structure of scientific revolutions* (2nd ed., enlarged). Chicago: University of Chicago Press.

Landsberger, H. A. (1958). *Hawthorne revisited.* Ithaca, NY: Cornell University Press.

Latané, B. (Ed.). (1966). Studies in social comparison. *Journal of Experimental Social Psychology,* Suppl. 1.

Le Bon, G. (1960). *The crowd.* New York: The Viking Press. (Original work published 1895)

Levine, J. M., & Moreland, R. L. (1990). Progress in small group research. *Annual Review of Psychology, 41,* 585–634.

Levine, J. M., & Moreland, R. L. (1995). Group processes. In A. Tesser (Ed.), *Advanced social psychology* (pp. 419–465). New York: McGraw-Hill.

Levine, J. M., & Moreland, R. L. (1998). Small groups. In D. T. Gilbert, S. T. Fiske, & G. Lindzey (Eds.), *The handbook of social psychology* (4th ed., Vol. 2, pp. 415–469). Boston: McGraw-Hill.

Lewin, K. (1943). Forces behind food habits and methods of change. *Bulletin of the National Research Council, 108,* 35–65.

Lewin, K. (1947). Frontiers in group dynamics. *Human Relations, 1,* 143–153.

Lewin, K. (1951). *Field theory in social science.* New York: Harper.

Lewin, K., Lippitt, R., & White, R. (1939). Patterns of aggressive behavior in experimentally created "social climates." *Journal of Social Psychology, 10,* 271–299.

Likert, R. (1932). A technique for the measurement of attitudes. *Archives of Psychology, 140,* 5–53.

Mackay, C. (1932). *Memoirs of extraordinary popular delusions.* New York: L. C. Page. (Original work published 1841)

Marrow, A. J. (1969). *The practical theorist: The life and work of Kurt Lewin.* New York: Basic Books.

Mayo, E. (1933). *The human problems of an industrial civilization.* Cambridge, MA: Harvard University Press.

Mayo, E. (1945). *The social problems of an industrial civilization.* Cambridge, MA: Harvard University Press.

McGrath, J. E. (1984). *Groups: Interaction and performance.* Englewood Cliffs, NJ: Prentice Hall.

McGrath, J. E. (1997). Small group research, that once and future field: An interpretation of the past with an eye to the future. *Group Dynamics, 1,* 7–27.

McGrath, J. E., & Altermatt, T. W. (2001). Observation and analysis of group interaction over time: Some methodological and strategic choices. In M. A. Hogg & S. Tindale (Eds.), *Blackwell handbook of social psychology: Group processes* (pp. 525–556). Malden, MA: Blackwell.

McGrath, J. E., & Kravitz, D. A. (1982). Group research. *Annual Review of Psychology, 33,* 195–230.

Michels, R. (1999). *Political parties: A sociological study of the oligarchical tendencies of modern democracies.* New Brunswick, NJ: Transaction. (Original work published in German, 1911)

Milgram, S. (1963). Behavioral study of obedience. *Journal of Abnormal and Social Psychology, 67,* 371–378.

Moreland, R. L., Hogg, M. A., & Hains, S. C. (1994). Back to the future: Social psychological research on groups. *Journal of Experimental Social Psychology, 30,* 527–555.

Moreno, J. L. (1932). *Who shall survive? Foundations of sociometry, group psychotherapy, and sociodrama.* Beacon, NY: Beacon House.

Münsterberg, H. (1913). *Psychology and industrial efficiency.* Boston: Mifflin.

Newcomb, T. M. (1943). *Personality and social change.* New York: Dryden.

Newcomb, T. M. (1961). *The acquaintance process.* New York: Holt, Rinehart & Winston.

Newcomb, T. M. (1963). Stabilities underlying changes in interpersonal attraction. *Journal of Abnormal and Social Psychology, 66,* 376–386.

Olson, W. C., & Cunningham, E. M. (1934). Time sampling techniques. *Child Development, 5,* 41–58.

Parten, M. B. (1932). Social participation among preschool children. *Journal of Abnormal and Social Psychology, 27,* 243–269.

Pepitone, A. (1981). Lessons from the history of social psychology. *American Psychologist, 36,* 972–985.

Pratt, J. H. (1922). The principle of class treatment and their application to various chronic diseases. *Hospital Social Services, 6,* 401–417.

Ringelmann, M. (1913). Research on animate sources of power: The work of man. *Annales de l'Institut National Agronomique, 2e serié, 12,* 1–40.

Roethlisberger, F. J., & Dickson, W. J. (1939). *Management and the worker.* Cambridge, MA: Harvard University Press.

Sadler, M. S., & Judd, C. M. (2001). The analysis of group data. In M. A. Hogg & S. Tindale (Eds.), *Blackwell handbook of social psychology: Group processes* (pp. 497–524). Malden, MA: Blackwell.

Sanna, L. J., & Parks, C. D. (1997). Group research trends in social and organizational psychology: Whatever happened to intragroup research? *Psychological Science, 8,* 261–267.

Santayana, G. (1924). *The life of reason or the phases of human progress: Reason in common sense* (2nd ed.). New York: Charles Scribner's Sons. (Original work published 1905)

Schachter, S. (1951). Deviation, rejection, and communication. *Journal of Abnormal and Social Psychology, 46,* 190–207.

Schachter, S. (1959). *The psychology of affiliation.* Stanford, CA: Stanford University Press.

Shaw, C. (1930). *The jack-roller: A delinquent boy's own story.* Chicago: University of Chicago

Shaw, M. E. (1964). Communication networks. *Advances in Experimental Social Psychology, 1,* 111–147.

Shaw, M. E. (1976). *Group dynamics: The psychology of small group behavior* (2nd ed.). New York: McGraw-Hill.

Sherif, M. (1936). *The psychology of social norms.* New York: Harper & Row.

Steiner, I. D. (1972). *Group process and productivity.* New York: Academic.

Steiner, I. D. (1974). Whatever happened to the group in social psychology? *Journal of Experimental Social Psychology, 10,* 84–108.

Sumner, W. G. (1906). *Folkways.* New York: Ginn.

Taylor, F. W. (1911). *The principles of scientific management.* New York: Harper.

Terman, L. (1916). *The measurement of intelligence.* Boston: Houghton Mifflin.

Thibaut, J. W., & Kelley, H. H. (1959). *The social psychology of groups.* New York: Wiley.

Thomas, W. I. (1896). The scope and method of folk-psychology. *American Journal of Sociology, 1,* 434–445.

Thrasher, F. M. (1927). *The gang.* Chicago: University of Chicago Press.

Thurstone, L. L. (1928). Attitudes can be measured. *American Journal of Sociology, 33,* 529–554.

Triplett, N. (1898). The dynamogenic factors in pacemaking and competition. *American Journal of Psychology, 9,* 507–533.

Vernon, P. E., & Allport, G. W. (1931). A test for personal values. *Journal of Abnormal and Social Psychology, 26,* 231–248.

Wallach, M. A., Kogan, N., & Bem, D. J. (1962). Group influence on individual risk taking. *Journal of Abnormal and Social Psychology, 65,* 75–86.

White, R. K. (1990). Democracy in the research team. In S. A. Wheelan, E. A. Pepitone, & V. Abt (Eds.), *Advances in field theory* (pp. 19–26). Thousand Oaks, CA: Sage.

White, R. K., & Lippitt, R. (1968). Leader behavior and member reaction in three "social climates." In D. Cartwright & A. Zander (Eds.), *Group dynamics: Research and theory* (3rd ed., pp. 318–335). New York: Harper & Row.

Whyte, W. F. (1943). *Street corner society.* Chicago: University of Chicago Press.

Wirth, L. (1928). *The ghetto.* Chicago: University of Chicago Press.

Wundt, W. M. (1916). *Elements of folk psychology: Outlines of a psychological history of the development of mankind* (E. L. Schaub, Trans.). New York: Macmillan.

Zajonc, R. B. (1965). Social facilitation. *Science, 149,* 269–274.

Zander, A. (1979). The psychology of group research. *Annual Review of Psychology, 30,* 417–451.

Zander, A. (1996). *Motives and goals in groups.* New Brunswick, NJ: Transaction. (Original work published 1971)

Zorbaugh, H. W. (1929). The Gold Coast and the slum: A sociological study of Chicago's near North Side. Chicago: University of Chicago Press.

2

Contemporary Issues in Group Research

The Need for Integrative Theory

Jennifer L. Berdahl

Kelly Bouas Henry

hen asked to write a chapter about contemporary issues in group research, we discussed two possible interpretations of this charge. One is to write about the substantive issues that contemporary groups researchers focus on and to identify and describe recent results. The second is to write about common issues that arise as groups researchers, regardless of their particular topic focus, go about their work. In this volume, the former interpretation seemed redundant, given what other chapters offer. The second interpretation seemed to offer something unique.

Similar issues arise regardless of one's substantive area of study in small group research. This chapter adds to the chorus of like-minded others (e.g., Arrow, Poole, Henry, Wheelan, & Moreland,

2004) who identify and understand the major conceptual issues that confront groups researchers today. Explication of these issues will necessarily lead to the methodological challenges these issues pose. We begin by describing what many might argue is *the* major issue facing groups scholars: The conceptual and empirical fragmentation of different perspectives on what groups are and how best to study them. We argue that this fragmentation is largely a consequence of the dominant methodological tools in our field. We identify possible solutions to these issues, which require a substantial shift in our thinking and practice. Finally, we discuss what is required of groups scholars and the academic field in which they operate to facilitate such a shift.

Authors' Note: We thank Holly Arrow, Virginia Kwan, and Joseph E. McGrath for helpful comments on earlier drafts of this chapter.

The Current State of Group Research

The current state of group research is conceptually fragmented. Several different theoretical perspectives on groups have been identified (Poole, Hollingshead, McGrath, Moreland, & Rohrbaugh, 2004; Wheelan, Chapter 7, this volume). These include the (1) psychoanalytic, (2) social identity, (3) communications, (4) functional, (5) developmental, (6) systems, (7) nonlinear dynamics, (8) socioevolutionary, (9) power-conflict, and (10) feminist perspectives. In this chapter, we address the first seven of these because they are the focus of this volume. Our purpose here is not to provide a review or analysis of each perspective. The other chapters of this volume accomplish that. Rather, we aim to briefly describe the perspectives and how they are fragmented both conceptually and empirically. This fragmentation inhibits building an integrative body of knowledge about groups.

Seven Perspectives

The psychoanalytic perspective on groups, as described by McLeod and Kettner-Polley (2004) and Geller (Chapter 5, this volume), assumes that humans are by nature "groupish" and that group processes have biological bases. The overarching theme of this perspective is that groups are bounded but open systems with internal structures and dynamics. Through the group's internal dynamics, individual members will be able to overcome "dark" processes through rational analysis and emotional expression (Bion, 1961).

The social identity perspective emphasizes the interface of social and individual processes (Hogg, Abrams, Otten, & Hinkle, 2004; Hogg, Chapter 8, this volume). It assumes that individuals categorize both themselves and others according to salient social distinctions. This results in intercategory differentiation and intracategory assimilation. Social comparisons are then made between and within categories. Individual group members are motivated to find an evaluative mechanism that will establish positive in-group distinctiveness.

The communications perspective, elsewhere called the symbolic-interpretive perspective (Frey & Sunwolf, 2004, and Chapter 9, this volume), has a dual emphasis. It examines the ways in which group members use symbols to construct interpretations of their group experience. It also focuses on how groups and their members are products of this symbolic activity. This perspective has been applied to a variety of clinical settings, including work with terminally ill AIDS patients (Adelman & Frey, 1997).

The functional perspective is a normative approach to describing and predicting group performance. It focuses on the functions of group inputs and (occasionally) processes for the outcome of group performance (Cummings & Ancona, Chapter 6, this volume; Wittenbaum et al., 2004). With this emphasis on function, it differs from the prior perspectives' emphasis on social processes. Groups are assumed to be goal oriented, and group performance is evaluated.

The developmental perspective (Wheelan, Chapter 7, this volume), also called the temporal perspective (Arrow et al., 2004), has as its focus how groups change over time. Those adopting a developmental perspective may focus on any of a number of group processes and outcomes over time, including communication patterns, status and influence structures, conflict, and performance. This perspective focuses on identifying the temporal patterns of variables of interest as groups develop.

The systems perspective of groups (Agazarian & Gantt, Chapter 10, this volume) argues that groups are embedded in a hierarchy of interdependent systems that import and use energy to maintain their structure and purpose. Practitioners use this understanding of groups to develop interventions that target midlevel systems in the hierarchy to maximize impact. Emphasis is given to understanding and using the flow of influence among levels in the hierarchy.

The nonlinear dynamics perspective (Arrow, Chapter 11, this volume), like the developmental perspective, emphasizes change over time in groups. Like the systems view, it views groups as multileveled entities. Its defining feature is a focus on how group processes unfold at multiple levels of analysis over time, with both predictable and discontinuous changes (Arrow, Chapter 11, this volume). Local (or micro) group dynamics are thought to be largely unpredictable, although coherent and predictable global outcomes and patterns are believed to rise out of them.

These seven perspectives clearly overlap. The nonlinear dynamics perspective contains within it both the developmental and systems perspectives. These three perspectives do not emphasize any particular substantive group topic, so they could incorporate the psychoanalytic, social identity, communications, and functional perspectives. The latter four perspectives also overlap. The social identity perspective examines intercategory competition, which may also be of interest from a psychoanalytic perspective. The communications perspective can be used to study how psychoanalytic and social processes take on symbolic form and define groups and their members. The perspectives are loosely connected and overlapping, not mutually exclusive.

One might argue that multiple theoretical perspectives within a field are a powerful advantage—they invite the critical thinking that accompanies pluralistic dialogue and help us to avoid doctrinaire assumptions about groups. Yet, once seven (or eight or ten) perspectives have been identified, we are intellectually obligated to trace conceptual connections among them in a larger "frame" theory (von Cranach, 1996). In spite of a high degree of overlap among the perspectives, they remain largely fragmented within the literature. Authors within perspectives read and cite each other's work as they build research programs, but citations across perspectives are few in number. This fragmentation is both conceptual and empirical in nature.

Fragmentation of the Perspectives

Conceptual fragmentation. Disciplinary boundaries fragment these perspectives. The psychoanalytic perspective typically appears in the counseling literature, with emphasis on research dealing with the formation, development, process, and outcomes of therapeutic groups. It is neither surprising nor undesirable that the psychoanalytic perspective takes interest in mental health applications of groups. What is problematic is that research on groups in this tradition rarely connects to research in other traditions that might inform, or be informed by, this approach. A psychoanalytic perspective may have much to offer a functional one, for example, as psychoanalytic processes may well affect group performance. Similarly, the functional approach may well have methods that could inform the psychoanalytic approach, but this conversation rarely occurs in the literature.

The functional perspective is largely housed in organizational psychology and management departments. Again, this is not surprising, given that these departments are interested in group performance. Although the conceptual framework of the functional perspective could be adapted to many different types of groups (e.g., therapeutic, social, or political groups all "perform" one task or another), theory and progress within the functional perspective is rarely reaped for the purposes of studying anything but organizational work teams. At the same time, the functional groups literature rarely draws on other perspectives that might enhance an understanding of processes that may initially seem unrelated to performance but may well be—such as symbolic communication, psychoanalytic and social identity dynamics, and developmental processes in groups.

Each perspective has its disciplinary niche. The communications perspective is rarely cited outside the field of communications. Social identity approaches have primarily appeared in social psychology and organizational behavior group literatures during the past 10 years. The power-conflict perspective (Sell, Lovaglia, Mannix, Samuelson, & Wilson, 2004) resides mainly in the political science and sociology literatures. The feminist perspective is often marginalized into women's studies journals and departments (Meyers, et al., 2005).

Conceptual fragmentation inhibits groups scholars from building an integrated body of knowledge. Rather than understanding how different aspects of group life interrelate, the groups literature resembles a disconnected set of facts. Groups research at present lacks a widely accepted "frame theory" (von Cranach, 1996) to show how different theories, concepts, and findings fit together and have meaning in a larger context. This problem is not unique to groups research but characteristic of several academic disciplines, such as psychology (Fiske, 2003; Sternberg, 2005). If we can unite these disparate approaches to the study of groups, such a plurality of views may well prove valuable. To start, we need to understand why the perspectives have remained conceptually fragmented for so long.

Empirical fragmentation. Fragmentation is a result of more fundamental issues than simply what substantive content is valued by different disciplines. A deeper, more serious reason for fragmentation in groups research is found in our general approach to science. The vast majority of research in general, and research on groups in psychology in particular, has been and continues to be dominated by a positivist philosophy of science and experimental methodology that flows from that understanding of the world (e.g., McGrath & Johnson, 2003). The positivist understanding has led to a reductionist, analytical, and quantitative paradigm as we approach research. Although the topic of groups offers fertile ground for big questions, our paradigmatic assumptions break the big questions down into little questions more suitable to the experimental method and the analysis tools designed to accompany it (e.g., general linear

models). As we continue to do this over time, we have more scholars studying less. The big questions get divided repeatedly until they involve almost nothing of consequence.

McGrath and Johnson (2003) argue that we have reached the limits of what we can learn about human systems (including groups) by exclusive use of the positivistic paradigm. Although some perspectives of groups (e.g., the psychoanalytic and communications perspectives) are not as heavily invested in the positivistic paradigm, the problem remains that the method of preference tends to be confounded with the perspective of preference. The present challenge to groups researchers is to try to integrate different perspectives on groups, as well as methods for studying them. Integration will promote a fuller understanding of groups, articulate gaps in our ability to answer big questions, and perhaps even illuminate some questions yet to be asked.

This movement toward integration requires at least two, perhaps three, significant changes. First and foremost, groups researchers must begin to work toward an integrative theory that helps connect the ostensibly separate perspectives. Second, groups researchers need to move toward a more balanced approach to studying groups that comprises both reductionist and constructionist methodologies. Third, to reward and encourage this integration effort, changes in the disciplinary infrastructure in which groups research takes place may be required. This third point relates to the broader academe beyond groups scholars, and it may prove the most difficult challenge of all.

Toward an Integrative Theory of Groups

Groups are complex systems. They are not made up of a few simple parts that one can draw boxes around and unidirectional arrows between. They comprise several components that are themselves complex and interact in nonlinear ways over time. Every group undergoes psychodynamic processes, has functions it must meet, develops over time, and has members with multiple social identities that shape interaction within and between groups. Each group engages in symbolic-interpretive communication, is embedded in a social context, and provides an embedding context for its members. Interactions between group members give rise to global outcomes and patterns that may be stable or unstable, may change in response to environmental feedback, and may affect the interactions from which they sprung. By attending to more than one aspect of groups, we quickly see that groups are not simple mechanical systems as implied by a positivist approach. Pulling various perspectives together readily reveals the complex causal patterns that are likely to characterize groups.

The Case for Integration

There are at least two problems with focusing on and building theory for only a small aspect of group interaction: We miss the big picture and may even get our small part of it wrong. Focusing on only a part of the whole is reminiscent of the classic Indian tale of the seven blind men and the elephant. One man touched only the elephant's ear and concluded the elephant was a fan; one man touched only its tail and concluded it was a rope; one man touched only its leg and concluded it was a column, and so on. The men could not reconcile their different perspectives to realize it was an elephant. Only when one man ran up and down and all over the elephant, examining all of its parts as a whole, did he understand what it was.

By focusing on only a small aspect of group interaction, we come away with a very limited—and possibly entirely incorrect—understanding of groups. Treating relations between variables (and people) as simple and linear ignores the possible interactions between variables of interest and many others. If other aspects of groups

besides those we attend to play an important role in the story, our predictions and conclusions about the outcomes and processes that are our primary interest may receive seemingly random support. They can be plagued by "mixed results," in which some studies support our theories, others run counter to our predictions, and some do neither.

As an illustration, let's say we're researchers operating within a functional perspective who wish to understand how group efficacy affects group performance. We would put these two variables together in hypotheses and, at most, address one or two additional or intervening variables. We might be creative and draw on literature outside the immediate domain of efficacy and performance, but we would largely limit our conception to these two aspects of groups. To test our hypotheses, we would vary group efficacy (probably sorting groups into *high* and *low*) and examine how efficacy affects performance on a given task. We would probably hold the task constant and ignore the effects of task type on the relationship between efficacy and performance. Let's say we're interested in effects of task type, however, and examine two different tasks. With this simple picture, we have a four-celled design, which we would hope to test with, say, 30 groups in each cell. With a minimum of three people per group, this requires 360 research participants. Finding all these participants would be difficult for most researchers, and this study may take a long time to complete.

This is a familiar story, and the primary way in which small group research in psychology is conducted. What is wrong with this picture? It is a very limited view of groups and may lead to dead ends in our understanding of them. Logistics pressure us to make this view even more limited by ignoring task type to drop our participant requirement down to 180, for example, or by studying individuals instead of actual interacting groups by having participants "interact" with preprogrammed "others" on a computer. Even our original study design ignores the developmental perspective by studying a single iteration of group efficacy and performance, when efficacy and performance are likely to change over time. The design also limits the causal direction of the relationship by manipulating group efficacy and then measuring group performance, even though they are likely to involve recursive cause (i.e., performance affects group efficacy, which affects group performance). But that is too complicated for our experiment, and we choose to ignore it, both empirically and theoretically.

This hypothetical design also ignores the social identities of the group members (in addition to other member characteristics), although much research on the demographic composition (or diversity) of groups demonstrates this can greatly affect group interaction processes and performance (Williams & O'Reilly, 1998). For simplicity's sake, we assume the social identities of group members are randomly distributed and can be factored out as error. But what if, for example, low group efficacy brings members of homogeneous groups together to try harder but tears members of heterogeneous groups apart with conflict and blame? What if high group efficacy benefits groups of women but has no effect on groups of men? By ignoring these potentially important social dynamics, our study and its results may be a "wash," providing inconclusive, insignificant, or equivocal findings.

Our view also ignores psychoanalytic dynamics in the groups. Members may have different emotional associations with and reactions to working with others in a group, based on their individual histories (Moreland & Levine, 2002). High group efficacy might remind some members of a very positive experience in a group (e.g., when their soccer team won the playoffs) and other members of a very negative experience in a group (e.g., when their team of hikers overestimated its abilities, resulting in a tragic accident). As with the social identities of group members, this part of the story would be ignored in our study and assumed to vary randomly and not to affect our results.

Ignoring the other perspectives of groups hinders our understanding of the relationship between group efficacy and performance. We could include the other perspectives by locating our study within a broader theoretical space that contains them. This would still allow us to statistically test our hypotheses by controlling for variables that these perspectives view as important. What is ultimately needed to fully and accurately understand groups as complex systems is an integration of different perspectives to avoid creating an increasingly crowded cemetery of minitheories and "facts." How well we accomplish this rests on our ability to overcome methodological, empirical, and theoretical barriers and to develop strategies to achieve this integration. This may well be the most significant issue facing contemporary groups scholars.

Necessary Ingredients to an Integrative Theoretical Framework of Groups

As complex systems, groups have several characteristics that are largely overlooked in current research. First, groups are dynamic. They change, develop, and mature over time. Second, far from operating in isolation from the world, groups are open systems that adapt to changes in their environment and sometimes effect change in it. Third, groups have complex causal patterns characterized by multiple variables that are likely to interact in nonlinear ways and to be subject to bidirectional cause. These characteristics of groups are the focus of the developmental, systems, and nonlinear dynamics perspectives, respectively. These perspectives are generally not adopted by researchers focusing on particular group content (e.g., psychoanalytic, functional, social identity, and communications perspectives). As such, a starting point for integrating the different perspectives is to combine the systemic and temporal views of groups—developmental, systems, and nonlinear dynamics—into a foundational framework that can be "filled in" with particular substantive relations proposed by the other perspectives (e.g., psychoanalytic, functional, social identity, and communications).

Groups are dynamic. An integrative theory of groups needs to recognize that groups are dynamic and change, develop, and mature over time. Most groups research is static and looks at only a cross section of group life, not the dynamic patterning of the variables of interest (e.g., the relationship between group efficacy and performance over time). A group's position in its own history is also often overlooked. How long the group has been in existence, how long its members have known and interacted with each other, and how long it plans to continue operating are usually ignored by researchers. Research has shown, however, that groups often undergo developmental patterns (Gersick, 1988, 1989; Tuckman, 1965; Tuckman & Jensen, 1977; Wheelan, 1994) as a function of their own histories and as they adapt to changes in their embedding contexts.

Returning to our earlier example, researchers may come to very different conclusions about the relationship between group efficacy and performance, depending on when they study the group in its own history. Factors to consider would be if the group has just formed and its sense of efficacy is likely based on superficial cues or wishful thinking, or if the group has existed a long time and its sense of efficacy is based on much experience and familiarity between group members. Similarly, recent changes in and adaptations to the group's embedding context should be considered, such as whether the group's membership or task, or the way in which the group's performance is evaluated or rewarded, have recently changed.

Groups are open. Second, it is important to recognize that groups are open systems—embedded in multiple contexts with which they interact. This, too, is rarely acknowledged. Instead, the context and its influence on the group (and the group's influence on the context) is ignored, making it difficult to compare results across different studies of groups or to identify relevant contextual parameters. This is also done in research on individuals. If it is difficult to keep track of how individuals' contexts influence average behavior (and vice versa), it is exponentially difficult to do so with groups. Groups contain multiple individuals, each with unique and different embedding contexts. In addition, groups themselves have embedding contexts that are likely to shape their interaction and, in turn, to be shaped by it. But rather than being daunted by this fact and choosing to ignore it, it would be better to place particular research studies and programs within this broader context so that we can locate them in a theoretical grid, make comparisons between them, and perhaps begin to learn how their contexts relate to outcomes of interest. Even better, we could be actively aware of group contexts and take them into consideration in developing theories, designing studies, and interpreting results.

Groups are complex. Third, we must recognize that groups have complex causal patterns. A simple relationship between A and B, whereby A is predicted to lead to B in a linear and unidirectional relationship, is drawn from a mechanical notion of cause that has sometimes proven useful for predicting average individual behavior. It is unlikely, however, to be valid for many relationships between variables in groups. For example, self-efficacy may, on average, lead to improved performance in individuals. Even at the individual level, this gets complex: Instead of a linear relationship, there may be a curvilinear one in which very low and very high levels of self-efficacy depress effort and performance, but medium levels of self-efficacy enhance it. There is also likely to be a bidirectional relationship between self-efficacy and performance, whereby self-efficacy affects performance, which then, in turn, affects self-efficacy. Bringing this relationship to the group level, we suddenly have multiple players, social dynamics, and other processes

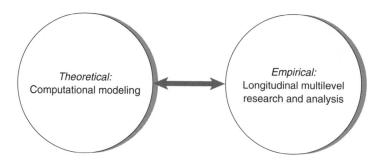

Figure 2.1   A Complementary Approach to Developing Integrative Theory

and variables to consider. Thus, any integrative theory of groups needs to acknowledge the complex causal patterns that are likely to occur in groups and that do not conform to simple, linear, and unidirectional relationships among a small handful of variables.

By keeping these aspects of groups in mind—their dynamic, open, and complex natures—we can build a richer and more accurate theory of groups. Many barriers exist to the development of a metatheoretical integration of small groups, however. Given the current methods, theoretical tools, and infrastructural reward system in our field, it is not hard to see why this kind of progress has been hindered.

Facilitating the Development of Integrative Theory

To build an integrative theory of groups and to study them as dynamic, open, and complex systems, we need new theoretical and empirical approaches to studying groups. We recommend computational modeling for developing theory and longitudinal in-depth studies and multilevel analysis for gathering data. We envision these approaches to theorizing and studying groups as complementary in an ongoing research program (see Figure 2.1). As we shall see, the approaches we recommend to study groups as complex

systems often require more time and investment than traditional approaches. They are theoretically more rigorous and empirically more difficult to conduct.

Building Integrative Theory: Computational Modeling

The suggestion that computational modeling may be the best tool for developing an integrative theory of groups is usually met with a pronounced lack of enthusiasm. The reaction runs from curiosity from those unfamiliar with the method to skepticism from those trained and invested in other paradigms. At best, the response is "yes, but not me"—agreement that computational modeling could be a useful and even profound theoretical tool, but an immediate disclaimer that it would require too much start-up cost to learn and do. Although several good examples of such models exist (e.g., Carley, 1991; Carroll & Harrison, 1998; Hanish, Hulin, & Seitz, 2001; Latané, 2000; Stasser, 1988), this work often falls on deaf ears or does not get read or cited.

A computational model is an interlocking set of theoretical statements that have been translated into logical and/or mathematical terms. The output of one statement becomes the input of the next. In this way, it is possible to build dynamic theory that involves recursive cause and nonlinear relationships between multiple

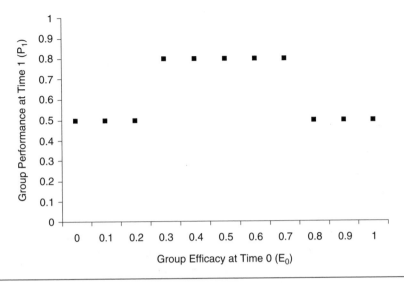

Figure 2.2   A Discrete Relationship Between Group Efficacy and Performance

variables at different levels and to readily explore the implications of this theory. This would be difficult, if not impossible to do with traditional verbal theory alone.

The best way to illustrate the concept and power of computational modeling is with an example. We return to our attempt to study the effects of group efficacy on group performance. To computationally model the relationship, we begin by translating our verbal theory into mathematical or logical terms. Let us say we believe that low levels of group efficacy and very high levels of group efficacy lead to low group performance, reasoning that both discourage effort. This is expressed in the following logical statement:

If group efficacy is very low or very high, then group performance is low; otherwise, group performance is high.

Using symbolic terms, we represent initial group efficacy with E_0 and resulting performance as P_1. We will make them both range from 0 to 1 and choose 0.2 and lower to represent *low* group efficacy, 0.8 and higher to represent *high* group efficacy, 0.5 and lower to

represent *low* performance, and 0.8 and higher to represent *high* performance. Our logical statement above can thus be expressed as follows:

If $0.2 > E_0 > 0.8$, then $P_1 = 0.50$; else $P_1 = 0.80$.

See Figure 2.2 for a mapping of the relationship. This closely mimics the logic behind many verbal theories: Comparative statements of the effects of different conditions (e.g., low versus high group efficacy). Now that we have examined this comparative statement in its bare form, however, we might notice how simplistic and discrete it is and imagine other possibilities.

Perhaps a finer-grained continuous relationship exists between group efficacy and performance. Let's say we envision their relationship as curvilinear instead (see Figure 2.3 and Table 2.1). We write the following mathematical statement to represent a quadratic relationship between group efficacy (E) and performance (P):

$$P_1 = 4 * (E_0 - E_0^2)$$

This relatively simple function between E and P is already more complex than our first logical statement derived from our verbal theory and

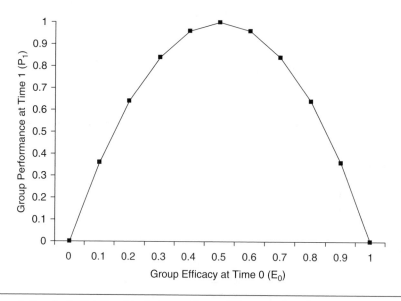

Figure 2.3 A Quadratic Relationship Between Group Efficacy and Performance

Table 2.1 A Spreadsheet Model of the Relationship Between Group Efficacy and Group Performance

$E_{0}:$	$P_{1}:$	$E_{1}:$	$P_{2}:$	$E_{2}:$	$P_{3}:$	$E_{3}:$	$P_{4}:$	$E_{4}:$
	$4 *$ $\{E_0 - (E_0)^2\}$	$(E_0 + P_1)/2$	$4 *$ $\{E_1 - (E_1)^2\}$	$(E_1 + P_2)/2$	$4 *$ $\{E_2 - (E_2)^2\}$	$(E_2 + P_3)/2$	$4 *$ $\{E_3 - (E_3)^2\}$	$(E_3 + P_4)/2$
0.00	0.00	0.00	0.00	0.00	0.00	0.00	0.00	0.00
0.10	0.36	0.23	0.71	0.47	1.00	0.73	0.78	0.76
0.20	0.64	0.42	0.97	0.70	0.84	0.77	0.71	0.74
0.30	0.84	0.57	0.98	0.78	0.70	0.74	0.78	0.76
0.40	0.96	0.68	0.87	0.78	0.70	0.74	0.78	0.76
0.50	1.00	0.75	0.75	0.75	0.75	0.75	0.75	0.75
0.60	0.96	0.78	0.69	0.73	0.78	0.76	0.73	0.75
0.70	0.84	0.77	0.71	0.74	0.77	0.76	0.74	0.75
0.80	0.64	0.72	0.81	0.76	0.72	0.74	0.76	0.75
0.90	0.36	0.63	0.93	0.78	0.68	0.73	0.78	0.76
1.00	0.00	0.50	1.00	0.75	0.75	0.75	0.75	0.75

could more closely approximate the relationship between efficacy and performance. Making it even more realistic, let's say we believe that performance is not entirely determined by group efficacy. We can add random error (e) to our equation to represent this:

$$P_1 = 4 * \{E_0 - (E_0)^2\} + e$$

We make E normally distributed with a small standard error around 0 and range from −1 to +1 so that performance is a function of efficacy and other unspecified forces that have random effects.

The ability to handle stochastic elements is a powerful theoretical advantage that computational modeling has over traditional theory. In addition to allowing for other nonspecified variables to have random effects, it includes the possibility of random sampling. For example, we could randomly sample group members from a population with characteristics (e.g., skills, motives, and demographics) whose distributions are defined by the theorist building the model. In this way, theoretical predictions can be based on random samples just as empirical data are. This represents a dramatic improvement in our ability to assess what we should actually expect to observe in random empirical samples if our theory is correct. Logically thinking through the implications of a theory for the average group (i.e., a group whose members all have average characteristics, work on a task of average difficulty, etc.)—the typical method of verbal theory—may yield a very different prediction than a computational model of the same theory, which randomly staffs groups with members drawn from a population distribution (Berdahl, 1999).

Adding the temporal dimension to our model of group efficacy and performance, let's say we believe performance is likely to influence subsequent group efficacy. If we assume groups have perfect information about their performance and that performing well increases group efficacy and performing poorly decreases it, we

can define group efficacy in the next round (E_1) as an average of initial group efficacy (E_0) and performance at Time 1 (P_1):

$$E_1 = (E_0 + P_1) / 2$$

We could play around with how prior group efficacy and performance are weighed in the equation. For example, performance might be weighed more heavily than efficacy if group members believe performance is accurately measured and reflects their true abilities. On the other hand, group efficacy might be weighed more heavily than performance if members believe the opposite. There are, of course, many other possibilities for the function: Group efficacy could simply be a function of prior performance; it might be impervious to performance feedback; it might be based only on the most memorable performances (e.g., the best and the worst); it might be a function of the slope of the change in performance in a given window of time (i.e., higher despite the same absolute level of performance if performance has been increasing, rather than decreasing).

We could introduce a random term into the deterministic equation above to simulate stochastic forces or other events that shape group efficacy. We might decide our assumption of perfect information about group performance is unrealistic and build in the possibility that groups are more or less accurate depending on random error. This could be tied to theory based on the task itself (e.g., some tasks imply a larger random error in performance feedback than others) or features of the group's context, such as whether group performance is directly assessed by the group or evaluated by an outside source (e.g., a manager). The feedback could be delayed, so that it comes after three iterations of performance instead of one, in which case there would be a time lag for the effect of performance on group efficacy.

We could move beyond the two group-level variables of efficacy and performance and model the group members as well. Group efficacy

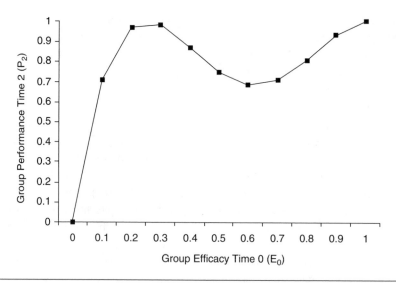

Figure 2.4 The Relationship Between Group Efficacy at Time 1 and Performance at Time 2

could be an aggregate function of members' assessments of the group and its members, which in turn might be based on group dynamics and member characteristics. We could also make group efficacy a function of the task the group is working on: For example, groups working on tasks in which poor performance leads to catastrophic results (e.g., medical teams) may focus on past failures, whereas groups working on tasks with potentially high payoffs (e.g., a team of bank robbers) may focus on past successes.

Whew! This is getting complicated. We hope this illustrates how quickly the exercise of modeling raises issues and possibilities that may not have otherwise been considered. Let us stick to our simple, deterministic, and two-variable (group efficacy and group performance) model to keep our example manageable. Assuming the effect of group efficacy on group performance remains the same over time (as defined earlier, $P_T = 4 * \{E_{T-1} - (E_{T-1}^2)\}$), we plug in the value of group efficacy at Time 1 (E_1, where $E_1 = (E_0 + P_1)/2$) to predict performance in the next round:

$$P_2 = 4 * \{E_1 - (E_1)^2\}$$

Mapping group performance at Time 2 (P_2) to initial group efficacy (E_0), we now see that predictions for performance at Times 1 and 2 are very different between Figures 2.3 and 2.4, respectively, for the same initial values of efficacy. This raises another probably unforeseen issue: The apparent function between group efficacy and performance depends on how far apart in time they are measured. If we empirically measured group efficacy and then waited to measure performance after a few rounds of task completion, we would assume the relationship between group efficacy and performance resembled the function in Figure 2.4. We would not realize the underlying causal relationship was actually that found in Figure 2.3, which would be difficult to derive from our data based on E_0 and P_2 alone.

Running this very simple and deterministic model through a few more iterations (see Table 2.1), we observe the following: All groups that begin with nonzero levels of initial group efficacy converge on performance and group efficacy levels of 0.75 by the sixth iteration of the model and stay there. Thus, our seemingly simple and reasonable theory—that group performance is a curvilinear function of group efficacy and that group efficacy, in turn, adjusts in response to group performance—leads to predictions we probably would not have made with our initial verbal theory. We could investigate the possibility that all groups beginning with nonzero efficacy eventually reach the same levels of efficacy and performance, or we may conclude this is an unreasonable prediction and that we need to further refine our theory.

We hope this brief example makes apparent that the process of trying to create even a simple computational model quickly reveals the lack of precision in most verbal theory and opens up a host of questions that may not have otherwise emerged. Formalizing theory into an integrated set of interrelated equations makes it possible to consider multiple variables, multiple levels of analysis, and their relationships at the same time. Any attempt to do this with paper and pencil quickly gets out of hand when one tries to model a complex system, particularly when stochastic processes and nonlinear and recursive relationships are part of the theory.

Even if the end result is not a computational model, the process of trying to develop one can further refine theory, fill gaps, and provide a kind of rigorous intuition that may not be available without it. Researchers need not immediately go to the highest and most complex forms of modeling. A simple model can be built in a spreadsheet program, for example, in which the output of equations representing the first iteration become the input of equations representing the second, and so forth, as in our example above (see, e.g., Latané, 2000). Researchers can then continue to build the model from this basic engine, adding refinements, stochastic elements, and other variables and theories as they go along. Despite their belief otherwise, most researchers have the basic skills (e.g., math and spreadsheet) required to take the first steps toward building a simple model. If they wish their models to become more complex, they can move them to more flexible and powerful languages with the help of programmers.

The output of a computational model is theoretical data. It can be used to identify weaknesses or problems in the theory informing the model, as when outcomes are impossible or are unlikely to happen in the real world (e.g., a group that performs a difficult task perfectly every time). If the theory is sound, it can be used to simulate likely real-world results that would be impossible or unethical to do otherwise. It can also be used to design empirical studies by identifying those parameter values that should be most important to investigate or are predicted to differ the most widely. For example, a computational model might suggest that 10 group conditions will yield similar levels of efficacy or performance over time (as in groups beginning with nonzero levels of efficacy in our example), but that one condition will differ from these 10 (as in groups beginning with zero efficacy). So instead of comparing 11 different conditions, we can compare 2, greatly reducing the requirements of conducting the empirical research.

Conducting Integrative Research: Longitudinal Multilevel Research and Analysis

To study groups as complex systems, we need to add new research strategies to our box of tools. Laboratory and cross-sectional research may be useful for some questions, such as those limited to phenomena that are by nature temporally robust or fleeting (e.g., research assessing stereotypes or cognitive response times to stimuli). But most social phenomena involve social systems that are complex, multilevel, and longitudinal (cf. Kozlowski & Klein, 2000), such as groups. We therefore should study them as such.

Perhaps the first step is expanding our scope of groups by including more than a handful of variables in our theories and studies of them. Rather than studying only group efficacy and performance, for example, we could also examine the social identities, skills, and personalities of group members; group processes such as conflict and blame in the face of negative performance feedback; and other group outcomes such as group morale. We also need to consider aspects of the groups' environments—the organizations in which they are embedded and their context vis-à-vis other groups, for example. Finally, we need to study groups over time, tracing the development and the bidirectional relationships between their multiple variables. We therefore need to study multiple group variables at multiple levels and times. But doing any one of these, let alone all three, quickly moves us beyond the typical 2×2 experiment in which we can conduct statistical significance tests comparing multiple conditions. So what are we to do?

We can still test our data with simple 2×2 designs, controlling for (or making sure to hold constant) other variables of interest. An awareness of the larger theoretical space in which relations between variables of interest reside— provided by integrative theory—would be a step in the right direction. If major contextual and other parameters are likely to affect the relationships of interest, then researchers can guard against unexplainable mixed results. And by addressing the values of other variables of interest to other groups scholars, researchers interested in other areas can contribute to this broader endeavor.

Moving beyond the typical experimental design, however, we suggest three strategies: in-depth case studies of groups in their real environments over time (e.g., Hackman, 1990), longitudinal laboratory and field experiments, and collaborative research across disciplines studying groups.

In terms of the first strategy, case studies are an ideal method for studying groups in their real contexts over time. Rich data collection techniques, including observation on the part of researchers of multiple group dynamics over time, allow for more ecologically valid and complex treatments of groups as systems. Using such techniques can also be an important strategy

for inductive and integrative theory building. In-depth qualitative case studies can tell us what is possible and provide intuition for how things fit together. Studies involving multiple comparative case studies would be particularly useful, as this allows for consideration of the role of context and other variables that may be unique to different groups. Good examples of this type of research include work on group development, such as Tuckman's (1965) review of therapy groups over time and Gersick's (1988) study of project teams. These studies, which involved intensive case observations over time, yielded very influential theories of group development.

The second strategy, longitudinal laboratory or field experiments, also involves studying groups over time. Using these techniques, researchers can collect similar information (e.g., multiple variables from multiple levels) but also have more control over some of the variables of interest to allow for clearer causal inferences from the data. Good exemplars of this strategy are the JEMCO studies published by McGrath and his colleagues (McGrath, 1993; McGrath & Arrow, 1996) in which groups met weekly for a semester as part of an organizational psychology course to work on projects related to the course content. Longitudinal field experiments in particular would be ideal as they most closely approximate ecologically valid groups, although they are more difficult to conduct because they involve manipulating aspects of extant groups that exist for reasons other than research.

Data from case studies and longitudinal experiments may pose some problems for the researcher wishing to conduct typical linear and causal analyses between variables. Of course, researchers could ignore all but a few variables and relate them to each other as their values exist in snapshots of time, but the approach may not be suitable to the analysis of data such as these. Instead, we suggest extending our logic of inquiry from one that merely compares average values of groups at one point of time (e.g., comparisons of group performance between groups with different levels of efficacy) to include strategies that trace the development of a given group's variables over time, attempting to understand their changes in the context of that particular group. For example, developing an understanding of each group's change in group efficacy and performance over time would be valuable, particularly if the study examined how members related to each other via processes unique to the group as well as those common across groups. This is similar to emic and etic approaches to the study of cross-cultural psychology (cf. Triandis, 1994).

This approach to group research implies another strategy: the collaboration of researchers from different disciplines or perspectives of small groups. With more researchers involved in a given project, more data can be collected. This not only makes statistical hypothesis testing more feasible, but also makes it possible for projects to have more depth and larger, more integrative scope. This, too, is similar to work in cross-cultural psychology, which also often involves multiple researchers in different countries collecting data and comparing them across cultural contexts (e.g., Chirkov, Ryan, Kim, & Kaplan, 2003; Glick et al., 2004).

Supporting Integrative Work: Infrastructural Issues

The groups literature is not without calls for the strategies we have outlined above (e.g., Arrow, McGrath, & Berdahl, 2000; Berdahl, 1998; Poole, Van de Ven, Dooley, & Holmes, 2000; Zaheer, Albert, & Zaheer, 1999). Yet, in spite of calls for a richer, more integrated understanding of group processes, the typical templates used are the laboratory experiment and the cross-sectional field study of extant groups. When rich alternatives exist—computational modeling, longitudinal experimental simulations, and so on—and when those alternatives have been successfully published as a small part of this body of literature, why are groups scholars (ourselves included in this indictment) so slow to embrace

these more integrative and ecologically valid tools in their research programs?

Perhaps the most significant reason is that groups scholars, like many scholars in other fields, operate primarily in contexts that inhibit these approaches to research. The present reward contingencies faced by most groups scholars are part of the broader academe's tenure/promotion system, which typically involves a 4- to 6-year probationary period, followed by an up-or-out promotion/tenure decision. Researchers have at least 4 and at most 6 years to demonstrate to their home institutions that they are capable of productivity and impact and can secure external funding to support future productivity.

The requirements for demonstrating productivity may vary slightly from institution to institution, depending on whether it emphasizes undergraduate training, graduate training, or both. However, nearly all promotion/tenure evaluations heavily weigh the number of publications a scholar has produced. Quality is also measured, of course, but this is a more time-consuming and controversial process, particularly in interdisciplinary committees like promotion/tenure ones. Conducting longitudinal research puts a groups scholar at a distinct disadvantage when it comes to generating a large number of publications. Longitudinal and in-depth research, by its very nature, takes much more time and effort in the data collection process. Analyses of longitudinal data, especially process data, require hours of coding before data can even be entered for analysis. And the analyses themselves may be more complex than the more common general linear methods that typically correspond to one-shot experimental designs. A scholar building a traditional experimental program may collect study data in an hour and be able to produce two or more publications in top-tier journals annually, but a newly formed longitudinal groups program would be hard-pressed to average one empirical publication annually over the probationary period.

The reference to journal quality raises another issue in the present infrastructure. Each particular discipline has its preferred publication outlets. In social psychology, for example, a publication in *Journal of Personality and Social Psychology* is considered outstanding, as is a publication in *Administrative Science Quarterly* for organizational behavior scholars. Interdisciplinary or specialized journals tend to receive lower quality ratings because their citation index within a given field is likely to be lower than a mainstream disciplinary journal. Promotion and tenure committees want evidence of a junior colleague's impact on the discipline. Higher citation indices are typically taken as evidence of impact, leading disciplinary publication outlets to be perceived as higher quality than interdisciplinary or specialized outlets in many departments.

Yet, many interdisciplinary journals publish excellent research relevant to a variety of fields. For example, *Journal of Occupational Health Psychology* draws submissions from medicine, public health, ergonomics, industrial-organizational psychology, clinical psychology, labor and industrial relations, and other fields. Yet, in spite of its wide appeal, or perhaps because of it, this journal is not typically considered the top-tier journal in any of the specific fields from which its submissions come.

Journals that specialize in groups research tend to be interdisciplinary rather than housed in a single field. In fact, some discipline-oriented mainstream journals prefer not to publish interdisciplinary groups work that treats groups as complex systems because that work does not look like "science" as we know it. The focus on hypothesis testing and statistical significance in many fields (e.g., psychology) places undue emphasis on small designs having few variables, designs that analyze data at the individual level rather than rich, qualitative, or theoretical work that examines group-level dynamics and outcomes. A paper presenting a computational model may face more of a challenge finding an outlet (and qualified reviewers) than one based on traditional techniques. A computational model is a tool for building theory, but it is not the traditional type of theory published in a mainstream outlet like *Psychological Review*. On the other hand, *Journal of Personality and Social Psychology* may be less interested in a computational model than a multistudy sequence of experiments because of the former's lack of empirical data. Papers that acknowledge complexity rather than trying to mask it are more likely to be published in interdisciplinary journals, which are open to a variety of methodological and analysis tools.

Although not true of all departments, many would prefer to see publications in top-tier, high-impact journals proprietary to that particular field (*Journal of Experimental Social Psychology*) than to see good interdisciplinary research in a journal like *Small Group Research*. So, in addition to the productivity issue, the quality issue may also work against integrative groups research, as the outlets that would be the most natural fit for such work are likely to be judged as lower in quality and prestige than the narrower, within-field outlets. We as groups scholars who will be tenure candidates, or who will write external peer evaluations for such candidates, need to become more adept at making the case for interdisciplinary groups research and publication outlets to our local peers and administrators making promotion/tenure decisions.

Finally, the scope of the integrative problem itself has inhibited integrative theory as well. The issues involved in integration are enormous. Integration not only requires learning to incorporate new methods into an existing research program but also involves stepping outside of our comfort zone in the literature we read. It involves familiarizing ourselves with perspectives that may have been marginal to our existing work. Researchers find it daunting just to keep up with literature in their own preferred perspectives; finding time to develop expertise in other areas can seem downright impossible.

Collaboration is essential to the challenge that now faces us. Conducting more multiauthored work, where people from many disciplines or perspectives are engaged in collecting data from many different variables, is an achievable state of affairs, and one that would force us to move to a more integrative perspective. Such a state, however, will require significant changes in the way we conduct our business. Rather than a small number of authors working on a small study with a few variables, we need an infrastructure that will support large numbers of scholars studying many variables in larger, shared data sets. Our practitioner colleagues likely have such rich data sets readily available. Why has groups research, of all areas of study, failed to realize how inherently valuable these collaborations could be?

Perhaps it is because our authorship norms create a political disincentive to have multiple authors on a publication. At present, the custom is for first authors to receive most of the credit and additional authors to receive some credit, which weakens with the total number of authors on a piece. Fields like mathematics and physics have developed an alphabetical authorship norm. Five-author teams, for example, collaborate with relatively little freeloading and authorship disputes. It is in all authors' interest to contribute as much as possible and make the work as strong as possible. Promotion is based on collaborators' appraisals of one's contributions to joint work, reducing the incentive to take advantage of coauthors and hope that the rest of the field will not find out. Another alternative is to move to a system similar to that used often in sociology: Many individuals collaborate to collect large data sets, but then write papers with single (or few) authors on different aspects of the data. In either case, it seems that a reconsideration of our collaboration and authorship norms would be a helpful step to design an incentive system that would not discourage integrative multiauthored efforts.

The technology necessary to support collaboration is now available. With the wide availability in the scholarly community of e-mail, cell phones, and other communication media, coordinating collaboration across nations is not as challenging as it once was. By developing new collaborations across perspective lines, and by placing these collaborations into new methodological contexts that include constructionist methodologies, we can begin to move forward in learning more about what each perspective has to offer in context and how it illuminates our understanding of the complex, dynamic processes that characterize life in groups.

Conclusion

The study of human groups is a basic topic in many disciplines interested in human behavior. All human behavior takes place in a social context, and much of it takes place in small groups. Researchers have studied psychoanalytic processes, social identity dynamics, symbolic communication, task performance, socioevolutionary forces, power-conflict, and political aspects of groups, and they have conceptualized them as dynamic and open systems. Unfortunately, researchers have typically done only one of those things while ignoring the others. As a result, the state of groups research is fragmented despite the fact that all human groups are characterized by each of these different qualities.

In this chapter, we reviewed the conceptual and empirical fragmentation of group research and explored its possible causes. We argued for the need for integrative theory and presented theoretical, empirical, and infrastructural strategies for articulating and developing a more unified approach to studying groups. We hope that this chapter, and the other chapters in this volume, aid in this endeavor. Wouldn't it be nice if, 10 years from now, interdisciplinary research and theory on groups was the norm, rather than the exception? We believe this would greatly enrich our understanding of groups and our ability to maximize group interactions and interventions.

References

Adelman, M. B., & Frey, L. R. (1997). *The fragile community: Living together with AIDS.* Hillsdale, NJ: Lawrence Erlbaum.

Arrow, H., McGrath, J. E., & Berdahl, J. L. (2000). *Small groups as complex systems.* Thousand Oaks, CA: Sage.

Arrow, H., Poole, M. S., Henry, K. B., Wheelan, S. A., & Moreland, R. (2004). Time, change, and development: The temporal perspective on groups. *Small Group Research, 35,* 73–105.

Berdahl, J. L. (1998). The dynamics of composition and socialization in small groups: Insights gained from developing a computational model. In M. A. Neale, E. A. Mannix, & D. H. Gruenfeld (Eds.), *Research on managing in groups and teams* (Vol. 1, pp. 209–227). Greenwich, CT: JAI Press.

Berdahl, J. L. (1999). *Perception, power, and performance in small groups: Insights from a computational model.* Doctoral dissertation, University of Illinois, Urbana-Champaign.

Bion, W. (1961). *Experiences in groups.* New York: Basic Books.

Carley, K. M. (1991). A theory of group stability. *American Sociological Review, 56,* 331–354.

Carroll, G., & Harrison, J. R. (1998). Organizational demography and culture: Insights from a formal model and simulation. *Administrative Science Quarterly, 43,* 637–667.

Chirkov, V., Ryan, R. M., Kim, Y., & Kaplan, U. (2003). Differentiating autonomy from individualism and independence: A self-determination theory perspective on internalization of cultural orientations and well-being. *Journal of Personality and Social Psychology, 84,* 97–110.

Fiske, S. T. (2003). *Social beings: A core motives approach to social psychology.* Hoboken, NJ: John Wiley.

Frey, L. R., & Sunwolf. (2004). The symbolic-interpretive perspective on group dynamics. *Small Group Research, 35,* 277–306.

Gersick, C. J. G. (1988). Time and transition in work teams: Toward a new model of group development. *Academy of Management Journal, 31,* 9–41.

Gersick, C. J. G. (1989). Marking time: Predictable transitions in task groups. *Academy of Management Journal, 32,* 274–309.

Glick, P., Lameiras, M., Fiske, S. T., Eckes, T., Masser, B., Volpato, C., Manganelli, A., Pek, J., Hunag, L., Castro, Y., Perita, M., Willemsen, T., Brunnet, A., Materna, I., Wells, R., & Sallall, N. (2004). Bad but bold: Ambivalent attitudes toward men predict gender inequality in 16 nations. *Journal of Personality and Social Psychology, 86,* 713–728.

Hackman, J. R. (1990). *Groups that work (and those that don't): Creating conditions for effective teamwork.* San Francisco: Jossey-Bass.

Hanish, K. A., Hulin, C. L., & Seitz, S. T. (2001). Temporal dynamics and emergent properties of organizational withdrawal models. In M. Erez, U. Kleinbeck, et al. (Eds.), *Work motivation in the context of a globalizing economy* (pp. 293–312). Mahwah, NJ: Lawrence Erlbaum.

Hogg, M. A., Abrams, D., Otten, S., & Hinkle, S. (2004). The social identity perspective: Intergroup relations, self-conception, and small groups. *Small Group Research, 35,* 246–276.

Kozlowsi, S. W. J., & Klein, K. J. (2000). A multilevel approach to theory and research in organizations: Contextual, temporal, and emergent processes. In K. J. Klein & S. W. J. Kozlowski (Eds.), *Multi-level theory, research, and methods in organizations* (pp. 3–90). San Francisco: Jossey-Bass.

Latané, B. (2000). Pressures to uniformity and the evolution of cultural norms: Modeling dynamic social impact. In D. R. Ilgen & C. L. Hulin (Eds.), *Computational modeling of behavior in organizations: The third scientific discipline* (pp. 189–220). Washington, DC: American Psychological Association.

McGrath, J. E. (1993). Introduction: The JEMCO workshop—Description of a longitudinal study. *Small Group Research, 24,* 285–306.

McGrath, J. E., & Arrow, H. (1996). Introduction: The JEMCO-2 study of time, technology, and groups. *Computer-Supported Cooperative Work, 4,* 107–126.

McGrath, J. E., & Johnson, B. A. (2003). Methodology makes meaning: How both qualitative and quantitative paradigms shape evidence and its interpretation. In P. M. Camic, J. E. Rhodes, & L. Yardley (Eds.), *Qualitative research in psychology: Expanding perspectives in methodology and design* (pp. 31–48). Washington, DC: American Psychological Association.

McLeod, P. L., & Kettner-Polley, R. (2004). Contributions of psychodynamic theories to understanding small groups. *Small Group Research, 35,* 333–361.

Meyers, R. A., Berdahl, J. L., Brashers, D., Considine, J. R., Kelly, J., Moore, C., Peterson, J., & Spoor, J. R. (2005). Understanding groups from a feminist perspective. In M. S. Poole & A. B. Hollingshead (Eds.), *Theories of small groups: Interdisciplinary perspectives.* Thousand Oaks, CA: Sage.

Moreland, R. L., & Levine, J. M. (2002). Socialization and trust in work groups. *Group Processes & Intergroup Relations, 5,* 185–201.

Poole, M. S., Hollingshead, A. B., McGrath, J. E., Moreland, R. M., & Rohrbaugh, J. (2004). Interdisciplinary perspectives on small groups. *Small Group Research, 35,* 3–16.

Poole, M. S., Van de Ven, A. H., Dooley, K., & Holmes, M. E. (2000). *Organizational change and innovation processes: Theory and methods for research.* New York: Oxford University Press.

Sell, J., Lovaglia, M. J., Mannix, E. A., Samuelson, C. D., & Wilson, R. K. (2004). Investigating conflict, power, and status within and among groups. *Small Group Research, 35,* 44–72.

Stasser, G. (1988). Computer simulation as a research tool: The DISCUSS model of group decision making. *Journal of Experimental Social Psychology, 24,* 393–422.

Sternberg, R. J. (2005). *Unity in psychology: Possibility or pipedream?* Washington, DC: American Psychological Association.

Triandis, H. C. (1994). *Culture and social behavior.* New York: McGraw-Hill.

Tuckman, B. W. (1965). Developmental sequence in small groups. *Psychological Bulletin, 63,* 384–399.

Tuckman, B. W., & Jensen, M. A. C. (1977). Stages in small group development revisited. *Group and Organizational Studies, 2,* 419–427.

von Cranach, M. (1996). Toward a theory of the acting group. In E. Witte & J. H. Davis (Eds.), *Understanding group behavior: Small group processes and interpersonal relations* (pp. 147–187). Hillsdale, NJ: Lawrence Erlbaum.

Wheelan, S. (1994). *Group processes: A developmental perspective.* Boston: Allyn & Bacon.

Williams, K. Y., & O'Reilly, C. A. (1998). Demography and diversity in organizations: A review of 40 years of research. In B. Staw & L. Cummings (Eds.), *Research in organizational behavior* (Vol. 20, pp. 77–140). Connecticut: JAI Press.

Wittenbaum, G. M., Hollingshead, A. B., Paulus, P. B., Hirokawa, R. Y., Ancona, D. G., Peterson, R. S., Jehn, K. A., & Yoon, K. (2004). The functional perspective as a lens for understanding groups. *Small Group Research, 35,* 17–43.

Zaheer, S., Albert, S., & Zaheer, A. (1999). Time scales and organizational theory. *Academy of Management Review, 24*(4), 725–741.

3

The History of Group Practice

A Century of Knowledge

Sally H. Barlow

Gary M. Burlingame

Addie J. Fuhriman

The history of group practice follows the history of humans. Human primates, nonhuman primates, and many other species congregate for the purpose of survival based on sociality. But what makes an aggregate of humans participating in group psychotherapy or a group of undergraduates participating in a group social psychology experiment different from a woop of gorillas; or for that matter, a gaggle of geese, an exaltation of larks, and a pride of lions? Of course, the answer is obvious, but at a far more subtle level, we must examine the uniquely human quality of written history based on words; how humans communicate with each other, both in the written and spoken forms. This linear view of history has its advantages and its disadvantages. On the one hand, we are able to line up chronological events in order

and examine them (e.g., with literature searches of empirical studies over a century); on the other hand, the deconstructionists remind us that this can be a fairly compressed and sometimes inaccurate view of true historicity. Scholars remind us that there are alternate views of reality (Abbott, 1884/1984). In addition, these forays into history are clearly bounded by the Western world. No doubt, we could learn much from other traditions, cultures, and countries (often aggregated under the appellation Eastern world). With these limitations in mind, we will proceed with an accounting of the facts culled from articles and the empirical literature over the last century and into the present regarding the many types of group practice. Sources included but were not limited to Medline, PsycLIT, ERIC, and Social Science Index, from the beginning of the 20th century to the beginning of the 21st century. Although not exhaustive, these reviews are representative.

History's View

When the physician Dr. John Pratt treated his tubercular patients in a group class in 1905 and subsequently published the findings about his "Thought Control Classes," the written history of group practice most likely got its start. Certainly, philosophers, scientists, and literary authors had written about the power of human groups through the ages (i.e., Plato's societal groups; Le Bon's dangerous "crowd"; Ibsen's contrast of external and internal groups in "Ghosts"; even Abbott's clever mathematical tale of two-dimensional groups). What distinguishes Dr. Pratt's writing is that it represents an early attempt to explain how the unique properties of the group, not simply the traditional medical treatment of doctor and individual patient, could actually have healing properties. The interdependence of these patients contributed to the quality of their care and recovery from tuberculosis. Forsyth (1999, p. 6) reminds us that although interdependence is the key, other words also help to describe groups: communication, influence, interaction, interrelations, psychological significance, shared identity, and structure.

A number of other contributing authors to this text may cite different beginnings, reflecting the great variety of an emerging discipline. Perhaps by the *fin de siècle* of the 1800s, the combination of the refinement of science and society's growing self-reflection allowed curiosity about the nature of individual humans operating in social groups. For whatever reason, the study of groups appears to have popped up in several places and disciplines at the same time (Ruitenbeek, 1969). Since these early beginnings in medicine, sociology, politics, theater, and psychology, the study of group dynamics has spread to business, criminal justice, anthropology, sports, and many other systems (Anthony,

1968; Forsyth, 1999, p. 19; Fuhriman & Burlingame, 1994, p. 3). The application of groups to a variety of human issues continues to grow. No longer viewed as simply a "second best" way to educate, treat, or consult with people, group practice is seen as a potent change agent in global politics, ethnic strife, religious differences, and almost all majority/minority group struggles. The amazing scope of group treatments has been amplified by our entrance into the Internet age. Although they are controversial, virtual groups on the Internet may in fact possess many of the qualifying attributes of real groups (although the face-to-face interaction is clearly missing). Only time will tell.

Generally, group practice is used to address issues in psychotherapy such as group treatments for depression, eating disorders, and so on where the purpose is to reduce troubling symptomatology. Group practice also deals with group dynamics (group interventions in such areas as business, education, and politics, where the purpose is to raise awareness or improve group functioning). These groups range in duration from brief to long term and occur in a variety of settings from hospitals to corporate boardrooms. In this chapter, we will review the individuals who were early group vanguards. The "conglomerate, complex, confabulatory, and conflictual" theoretical and empirical developments (Anthony, 1971, p. 4) will be discussed as well. Finally, the efficacy of group practice as a change agent is explored. After all, what's all the enthusiasm about if groups don't really work?

Early Group Pioneers

Just who garners the title "father or mother" of group practice remains debatable. It would be easy to assign it to Sigmund Freud and his Wednesday night meetings in Vienna, or perhaps to Alfred Adler (although he would strongly object, as he did not see himself primarily as a group therapist), or Jacob Moreno, whose entire body of work promoted interpersonal dynamics, or perhaps Samuel Slavson, considered by many to be the father of modern group psychotherapy. Each in turn made substantial contributions, both to the literature and to application, regarding the underlying properties of group dynamics: Freud's beliefs about the role of the conscious and unconscious in compromise formations and his training in medicine; Adler's unshakable belief that humans seek to belong to mediate inferiority and his background in psychiatry; Moreno's active psychodrama techniques and his training in theater; Slavson's belief in activity group therapy for children.

Gazda (1968, p. 7) reminds us that many definitions of group psychotherapy existed in the early years, and that may be one of the reasons we cannot quite settle on one father. Even so, this multifaceted view created a rich background from which group dynamics emerged as a discipline. Thus, psychoanalytic tenets, interpersonally goal-directed belonging, role-playing theatric interventions, and individual and group processes with children, to name just a few, all became part of group dynamics' patchwork theoretical background.

Group practice forged ahead with the continuing work of Dreikurs (1932, 1956), Marsh (1931), and Lazell (1921). Syz (1928) broadened the growing field to include the power of member influence, the psychoeducation approach, the milieu treatment, and a here-and-now focus. Moreno and Whitin eventually applied the term *group therapy* to these endeavors in their 1932 publication, *Application of the Group Method to Classification.*

Kurt Lewin's (1936) field theory made group dynamics (a term he coined) available to many segments of the population, not just to mental health professionals. Wender (1936), Schilder (1937), Slavson (1940), and Wolf (1949) added re-creation of the primary group, group treatment of children, and credentialing. As noted by Fuhriman and Burlingame (1994) in their seminal textbook, *Handbook of Group Psychotherapy: An Empirical and Clinical Synthesis,*

Contributors themselves came from diverse origins. Traces of theory emanate from such diverse areas as personality theory, field theory, and systems theory, thus influencing our intra-, inter-, and contextual focus. Theoretical orientations also left their mark at various times and to differing degrees, but with lingering influence. Traces of psychoanalytic, group dynamics, existential-experiential, and behavioral theories can be found today in the way group therapy is defined, conceptualized, implemented, and evaluated. Current theory and practice contain threads from multiple disciplines, including psychiatry, psychology, education, social work, and organizational behavior. (p. 6)

This sheer array of diverse origins reflects the complexity of the group phenomenon we are addressing. No wonder many early observers asked: Is this a singular (client or group member), dyadic (subgroup), cumulative (passage of time), or collective (the group-as-a-whole) phenomenon? Well, it is all of them. That is exactly why group researchers can sometimes quake in their boots—dealing with error terms alone causes understandable fear! Still, over the last century, the examination of group processes has continued to improve. Current research has reached a level of sophistication the early researchers would envy (thanks to innovative statistical analyses and advanced methodologies). And what does 100 years of empirical research tell us? Groups work.

Efficacy

The science historian Thomas Kuhn (1977) reminds us that when we look back on earlier forms of thinking, we must be careful not to gaze on them with chronologically biased eyes. That is, we must not assume that ideas of the past constitute quaint notions in view of what we know now. In fact, many theories and applications of theories were contextually quite sound, given the context at the time. This also is true of group research. It would be easy to dismiss the early forays into examining the efficacy of group practice, given the level of sophistication we have reached at the beginning of the 21st century. But a careful reading of those early studies gives us the rich background of curiosity about humans working together. These findings give us a rare glimpse into the early researcher's questions about the group phenomenon, their take on what variables were worthy of study, and their fledgling attempts to explain multilevel phenomena. They were curious about the same basic questions in the 1900s that we are in the 2000s: Do groups work? and if so, How?

Do the same basic group principles that manifest positive outcomes exist consistently across all the diverse applications of group practice? Currently, there are a number of competing theories about how and why groups work, but we may be on the brink of a unified theory. Burlingame, MacKenzie, and Strauss (2004) suggest underlying unifying variables that may be much like the work of Nobel prize–winning physicist Edward Witten. It seems science has been grappling with the problem of unifying the four known forces in physics. String theory (or M theory as it is now dubbed) may be the unifying theory. But there was a problem: Five string theories existed! In 1995, at the international meeting of string theorists, Witten provided the mathematical evidence that there really was just one theory. The five previous theories were but different reflections in a mirror of one underlying phenomenon. What underlies the immense power of group phenomena likely has profoundly simple roots as well. Burlingame and his colleagues (2004) invite us to consider this with regard to group practice.

What allowed Burlingame and others like him to build such a theory were the scores of studies that have been conducted since the beginning of the 20th century. Table 3.1 presents those studies in the second half of the century that helped us know what kinds of interventions at the level of different models (e.g., cognitive behavioral, psychodynamic) worked for what kinds of group members; whereas, the first half

of the century involved studies that mainly catalogued group studies (Burchard, Michaels, & Kotkov, 1948; Thomas, 1943).

For instance, in Burchard et al. (1948), the researchers essentially catalogued 15 scientifically oriented studies and developed a seven-factor descriptive framework to handle the wide variety of orientations, methods, interventions, and goals that were apparent across the disparate studies. The factor they labeled evaluation, which examined success of treatment, had the least amount of information of all the other factors. It is no wonder it was difficult to do anything but catalogue the 15 group treatments. However, from the 1960s on, reviews of group practice efficacy were much more likely to include equal amounts of information in several important areas: treatment orientation, number of studies, characteristics of the group members involved, overall conclusions, and the research methods employed to examine all of this (WLC—wait list control or comparable control group; OT—other group treatment comparison including pharmacotherapy; I—individual therapy comparison groups; COM—combined treatment group). Instead of basic descriptions and cataloging, calculating was occurring, a kind of statistical calculation that allowed for all sorts of important comparisons. Table 3.1 includes 30 reviews of overall efficacy, 22 from the original Fuhriman and Burlingame (1994) text; the remaining reviews cover those articles published from 1993 to 2003.

Group Therapy Outcomes

In the 1960s

Several important characteristics dominate the data included in the reviews of group research from the 1960s. First, a great deal of diversity existed in the various treatment models. Remember that in the first half of the century, researchers' studies mainly focused on anecdotal reports and case or group studies. By the 1960s, empirical investigations were under way, including

(Text continues on page 49)

Table 3.1 Group Psychotherapy Review Articles

Author	Treatment Orientation	Number of Studies	Comparison WLC	OT	IO	CM	Sample	Conclusions
Rickard (1962)	Nondirective, psychoanalytic, psychodrama	22	X	X	X	X	Mixed inpatient and outpatient	Too much variability among patients, therapists, and measures for comparison to be more than tentative. Efficacy of group remains to be empirically validated.
Pattison (1965)	Psychodrama, milieu, analytic	U					Inpatient, prison, addict, delinquent	Group activity is therapeutic using behavioral criteria, disappointing with psychometric criteria, and promising with construct criteria. Notes that the research on individual psychotherapy and small group research has yet to be effectively incorporated into group psychotherapy research.
Stotsky & Zolik (1965)	Psychodrama, round table, and heterogeneous group	U	X	X	X	X	Psychotics	The results of controlled experimental studies do not offer clear support for using group therapy as an independent modality, but they do support group as an adjunctive or helpful intervention when combined with other treatments (drugs, individual, etc.).
Mann (1966)	Psychodrama, nondirective	41	X	X		X	Mixed diagnosis, adult and children, most institutionalized	Group therapy produces change in behavior, attitude, and personality regardless of orientation, method of comparison, or instruments.
Anderson (1968)	Counseling groups	6	X	X		X	Elementary students	Group counseling associated with higher grade point average and personality change when compared with control. No difference when compared with other treatment combined.

(Continued)

Table 3.1 (Continued)

Author	Treatment Orientation	Number of Studies	Comparison WLC	OLT	IC	OM	Sample	Conclusions
Meltzoff & Kornreich (1970)	Heterogeneous, expressive, nondirective, systematic desensitization, behavior, analytic	6	X		X	X	Hospitalized adults, adult outpatients, children	80% of adequately controlled studies reviewed showed primarily positive results with both individual and group therapy. Six studies that made direct comparisons between group and individual therapy found equivalent outcomes, with a slight tendency for individual to be more effective.
Bednar & Lawlis (1971)	Heterogeneous, group psychotherapy, self-help, activity, milieu, work, insight	38	X	X	X	X	Mixed inpatient, seven outpatient, delinquents, alcoholics, sex offenders, students	Group therapy is valuable in treating neurotics, psychotics, and character disorders. It is a two-edged sword that can facilitate client deterioration.
Luborsky, Singer, & Luborsky (1975)	Heterogeneous	12	X		X	X	Unspecific	Majority of comparisons showed no significant differences between group and individual treatment. There was a tie in nine comparisons, group was better in two comparisons, and individual was better in two comparisons.
Grunebaum (1975)	Unspecified	U			X		Heterogeneous	Only meager data exist comparing group and individual therapy, and the evidence suggests that they are equally effective in most instances. Some findings suggest that benefits may be disorder specific: for example, individual therapy better for phobias, and group more effective for schizophrenic outpatients.
Emrick (1975)	Heterogeneous	384	X		X	X	Alcoholics	Found a general trend for both individual and group to be effective in treating alcoholism.

Study	Type of groups	N					Population	Findings
Lieberman (1976)	Heterogeneous, psychotherapy, and personal growth groups	47	X		X		College students, adults	Group consistently produced favorable outcome over controls. Rported no outcome differences in studies that compared group with individual format. Noted that the indices used to measure outcome are relatively insensitive to the potentialities of different treatment contexts such as group and individual psychotherapy.
Parloff & Dies (1977)	Heterogeneous, psychotherapy groups	39	X	X	X	X	Psychoneurotic, schizophrenic, addiction, legal offenders	Group has no unique advantage over other treatments with schizophrenic patients, no firm conclusions can be drawn with psychoneurosis, and limited support for effectiveness with addicts.
Bednar & Kaul (1978)	Heterogeneous, behavioral, transactional analysis, unspecific group therapy, and encounter groups	21		X	X	X	College students, delinquents, prisoners, psychiatric patients	Group treatments have been more effective than no treatment, placebo, and other recognized psychological treatments.
Solomon (1983)	Psychodynamic, aversion	2		X	X	X	Alcoholics	Combined individual and group therapy are related to poorest outcome while individual and group as independent treatment showed equivalent outcomes.
Kanas (1986)	Heterogeneous	32	X	X			Outpatient and inpatient schizophrenic	Group therapy proved to be superior to controls in 67% of inpatients and 80% of outpatients studied, with long-term therapy being the best.
Kaul & Bednar (1986)	Experimental psychotherapy groups	17	X	X			Primarily adult mixed diagnosis	Mixed but favorable outcomes for the efficacy of group psychotherapy.

(Continued)

Table 3.1 (Continued)

Author	Treatment Orientation	Number of Studies	Comparison W L C	O T	I	C O M	Sample	Conclusions
Toseland & Siporin (1986)	Heterogeneous	32	X		X		Heterogeneous	Results of this review indicated that group treatment was as effective as individual treatment in 75% of the studies included and was more effective in 25%. In the 32 studies reviewed, there was no case in which individual treatment was found to be more effective than group treatment.
Bostwick (1987)	Unspecified	13			X	X	Unspecified	Individual treatment had less premature termination than group while combined individual and group treatment proved superior in reducing dropouts over either modality.
Oesterheld, McKenna, & Gould (1987)	Heterogeneous (e.g., behavioral, insight, cognitive behavioral, dynamic)	18	X	X	X		Bulimia	Group seems to be helpful but methodological limitations preclude robust conclusions.
Zimpfer (1987)	Heterogeneous (e.g., group counseling, multimodal, growth, insight)	19	X	X			Elderly	Group seems to be helpful but methodological limitations preclude robust conclusions.
Freeman & Munro (1988)	Cognitive behavioral, eclectic, supportive, didactic	13	X	X	X	X	Bulimia	Neither drug nor group therapy are as effective as individual, but all are more effective than placebo. Group is most cost-effective and combined group and individual are most effective of all treatment.

Study	Orientation	N					Population	Findings
Cox & Merkel (1989)	Heterogeneous	32		X	X	X	Bulimia	In a review of 15 groups and 17 individual studies (only one study provided a comparison between the two modalities, the rest were inferential), it was concluded that there was no support for the two treatments having any differential effectiveness.
Zimpfer (1990)	Cognitive behavioral, psychoeducational behavior	31			X	X	Bulimia	Regardless of treatment type and outcome criteria, group was shown to be an effective treatment.
Piper & McCallum (1991)	Self-help, consciousness, cognitive restructuring, behavioral skills, dynamic	5	X	X	X	X	Grief	Group treatment has not been adequately tested to determine its efficacy.
Vandervoort & Fuhriman (1991)	Cognitive behavioral, psychodynamic, cognitive	12			X	X	Outpatient, depression	Group is efficacious in treating depression with little evidence for differences between individual and group.
Piper & Joyce (1996)	Behavior 30%, cognitive behavior 26%, interpersonal/psychodynamic 14%, didactic 1%	86	X	X	X	X	Lifestyle problems, medical conditions, mixed psychiatric disorders, mostly adults	Preview of a variety of patient problems treated in interactive therapy groups for 6 months or less were examined for evidence of efficacy, applicability, and efficiency of time-limited, short-term group therapy (TSGT). Strong evidence for all three factors was found. Of 50 studies that had TSGT versus control comparison, 48 provided evidence of benefit of group treatment. A difference in benefit was found for the 6 studies that used TSGT versus individual.

(Continued)

Table 3.1 (Continued)

Study	Treatment models	N					Population	Findings
Hoag & Burlingame (1997a)	60% behavioral or cognitive behavioral	56	X	X	X	X	Male and female children and adolescents (4–18), primarily problems of disruptive behavior, self-esteem	Review of studies from 1974 to 1997 of group interventions for children and adolescents (including preventative, psychotherapy, guidance) revealed that treatments occurred mostly in school setting and groups were beneficial.
Marotta & Asner (1999)	Psychoanalytic, cognitive behavioral, self-help, psychoeducational	21	X	X	X	X	Adult females	Review of studies from 1978 to 1995 of group interventions for women with incest histories (using a wide array of treatment models)—categorized by six criteria: design, sample, inclusion criteria, replicability, analysis, and outcome. Fourteen were descriptive or case studies. Some support for group treatment was provided. Minimal adequacy of research designs was noted.
Harney & Harvey (1999)	Cognitive behavioral, interpersonal transaction (Yalom), information processing, psychodynamic	5	X	X		X	Male and female adults	Review of studies of trauma survivors assessed important variables along eight domains: authority over memory, integration of memory with affect, affect tolerance, symptom mastery, self-esteem/self-care, self-cohesion, safe attachment, meaning-making. Multidimensional, stage-oriented approaches worked best.
Shechtman (2002)	Educational, counseling, psychotherapy (multitheoretical and cognitive behavioral)	U	X	X	X	X	Male and female children and adolescents	Review of studies of group interventions for children found that all three types of groups were effective as long as suitable goals were set. Findings regarding process in children's groups showed that very little research exists.

SOURCE: Fuhriman & Burlingame, 1994. Adapted with permission.

NOTE: WLC = wait list control or comparable control group, OT = other group treatment comparison including pharmacotherapy, I = individual therapy comparison groups, COM = combined treatment group, e.g., group plus individual or group plus inpatient ward treatment, U = unstated.

permutations of the combinations allowed, with many kinds of comparison groups. Researchers used control groups (no-treatment condition), alternative treatments (rival group treatments), individual therapy, and combined treatment conditions (e.g., conjoint individual and group therapy). The only problem was the population under study was captive (institutionalized participants). In addition, comparisons were often made simply for convenience—for instance, two wards in the same hospital, which Cook and Campbell (1979) remind us constitute non-equivalent comparison groups.

Methodological problems aside, the studies provided tentative support for the efficacy of group treatment. Rickard (1962) essentially repeated the claims of Burchard and his colleagues from 1948 that enormous variability of patients, therapists, and treatment models leads to questionable findings. Pattison's (1965) work reported modest behavioral support for success with institutionalized patients. However, he was one of the first researchers to point out the problem with selecting dependent measures that did not match the hypotheses. The work of Stotsky and Zolik (1965) suggested that group therapy was an adequate adjunct to individual and/or psychopharmacological therapy, although their findings were far from enthusiastic. Mann (1966) and Anderson (1968) independently concluded in their reviews that groups do work; but each of these authors emphasized the nature of the reviews. Mann had used 11 of the studies reviewed by Rickard in 1962, when he examined a total of 40 "diversely conceived and executed studies" (Fuhriman & Burlingame, 1994). Mann's findings suggested that improvement was uniform across these diverse studies but that it was still not clear if one particular group treatment was superior to another.

In the 1970s

More rigorous research methods were employed in the major group reviews of the 1970s. These seven reviews offered a most optimistic picture. In this decade, some of the giants of group research got under way in what became a lifelong love for studying psychotherapy phenomena. Bednar and Kaul (1978), Lieberman (1976), Yalom (1975, 1985), and others added not only to the more rigorous research methodology but also to the growing maturity of the underlying theoretical components. More representative populations also were being studied (e.g., inpatient and outpatient). These researchers were joined by Emrick (1975) and Meltzoff and Kornreich (1970) in their general conclusion that group psychotherapy was effective, and actually superior, to alternate treatments in many cases.

Another result of the reviews from the 1970s was the growing awareness of the importance of matching. Matching refers to the fact that certain disorders warranted certain kinds of treatment (Bednar & Lawlis, 1971; Grunebaum, 1975; Parloff & Dies, 1977). Still, researchers were unclear about the underlying curative factors operating in groups that might explain positive outcomes. However, this curiosity only was possible because certain other variables had been better controlled.

In the 1980s

One of the by-products of the initial matching studies of the 1980s was the specificity that researchers invoked. They carefully examined specific kinds of patient diagnosis such as depression, eating disorders, bereavement, old age, schizophrenia, and so on. In this decade, carefully controlled comparison groups were de rigueur for researchers. This included multiple comparison groups of both inert and active treatment conditions. Such rigor allowed the researchers to make more definitive statements about general and differential efficacy (Cox & Merkel, 1989; Freeman & Munro, 1988; Kanas, 1986; Kaul & Bednar, 1986; Oesterheld, McKenna, & Gould, 1987; Solomon, 1983; Toseland & Siporin, 1986; Zimpfer, 1987), although Bostwick (1987) drew our attention to the problem of premature termination or dropouts, which continues to wreak havoc with group findings.

In the 1990s and Beyond

Piper and McCallum (1991) began a fruitful examination into complicated bereavement and the differences in supportive versus psychodynamic group therapy, although their initial findings suggested that effectiveness could not be determined, given the flawed methodology. The reviews of Vandervoort and Fuhriman (1991) and Zimpfer (1990) strengthened the growing empirical claim that groups work. Hoag and Burlingame (1997a, 1997b) and Shechtman (2002) branched into groups with children, whereas others (Harney & Harvey, 1999; Marotta & Asner, 1999) reviewed particular problem areas such as trauma and incest.

Into the Twenty-first Century

Forsyth (2000) devoted an entire journal to the advances in group research methodology, detailing the impact of carefully controlled group studies that yielded reliable findings. This advancement alone will encourage many more complex research designs as group psychotherapy is studied into the 21st century. By examining the 750 or so studies over the past 100 years, we are able to state that the group format produces positive effects with a number of disorders using a variety of treatment models. Future studies will likely refine these empirical claims.

Special Concerns: Comparing Individual and Group; Combining Individual and Group

This vast literature provides us with a reputable foundation on which to base our confidence that groups really do work. Nevertheless, several concerns have cropped up. First, recent meta-analyses have shown group to be inferior to other active treatments and comparable to inactive treatments. The second concern surrounds the practice of combining group therapy with other treatments. Understandably, this makes it more difficult to determine which effects can be attributed to group and which to the other treatments.

Meta-analysis

As this large data set of group effectiveness accumulated, Smith and Glass (1977) introduced a new statistical method (meta-analysis) into research designs as a way to estimate the average amount of change one could expect in a given treatment. The resulting effect size (ES), or single index, contrasts with the box score method that had dominated research methodology to that point. This latter method sorted studies according to positive or negative findings. Many researchers and clinicians believe that meta-analysis, in contrast to the box score method, is a much more reliable method. Still, others (Mullen, Driskell, & Salas, 1998) raise concern that our heavy reliance on such a statistical method may be premature. For example, Barlow, Fuhriman, and Burlingame (2004) wrote,

> With the 1977 Smith and Glass publication, the statistical method of meta-analysis burst onto the empirical scene and offered researchers a way to essentially compare oranges and apples. As long as studies included means and standard deviations, comparisons could be made that yielded an effect size. This rendered previously disparate pieces of information comprehensible at an overall level. Still, having an estimate of the average amount of change one could expect from a given treatment has both negative and positive consequences.

On the one hand, it allows researchers and consumers to directly compare certain kinds of treatments. On the other hand, a number of excellent qualitative studies and/or N-of-1 studies are generally left out of the database. In addition, as scientific journals generally only publish statistically significant results, even studies that included traditional methods of statistical analysis but confirmed the null hypothesis are generally excluded from research journals. Thus it has been argued by some that meta-analyses represent only a certain type of investigation. A harsh evaluation of meta-analysis as "junk science" has been leveled at researchers by some authors. (p. 10)

Only time will tell. At present, meta-analysis is the only way researchers have of examining what essentially amounts to comparing apples to oranges.

Nine meta-analyses in Table 3.2 compare the relative effectiveness of group with individual format or compare group format with inert or inactive treatments. Although the resulting effect sizes reflect a convenient, often powerful bottom line, such single indexes may eclipse the rich data available (Dush, Hirt, & Schroeder, 1983; Miller & Berman, 1983; Nietzel, Russel, Hemmings, & Gretter, 1987; Robinson, Berman, & Neimeyer, 1990; Shapiro & Shapiro, 1982; Smith, Glass, & Miller, 1980; Tillitski, 1990). In addition, the various studies may contradict each other.

Horne and Rosenthal (1997) have attempted to understand this state of affairs. They conclude that although individual treatment has been shown to be superior to group, this was true *only* in studies where group formats were used as a convenient and economic way to offer psychotherapy. None of the curative factors unique to group process had apparently been highlighted by the leaders or singled out for examination. Those meta-analyses conducted on studies that directly measure therapeutic factors in groups, as separate from individual factors,

yield larger and, hence, significant effect sizes (Hoag & Burlingame, 1997a; McRoberts, Burlingame, & Hoag, 1998).

The meta-analyses conducted by de Jong and Gorey (1996) and Reeker, Ensing, and Elliott (1997) did not include a direct comparison between group and individual formats. Rather, they were comparing long-term versus short-term group formats and different kinds of specific formats. What they found was that groups were effective regardless of length and regardless of specific format. In research parlance, these studies that compare one treatment modality with another modality have been dubbed "horse races." The horse races in group psychotherapy research appear to yield about the same findings as the horse races in individual psychotherapy research. Years ago, when researchers first noticed this, Luborsky and his colleagues dubbed this the "Dodo" phenomenon (Luborsky, Singer, & Luborsky, 1975)—that although most treatments were effective, no one treatment was superior to another—recalling the *Alice in Wonderland* race. Much has been made of these issues, especially as consumers demand the best treatment, and insurance companies more selectively reimburse only empirically supported treatments (ESTs.) Both individual and group psychotherapy researchers are hoping to find answers to this question: What is it precisely that accounts for the variance?

Beutler (personal communication, November 15, 2003) suggests that as researchers, we must avoid the tendency to pit one treatment against another in a "dogma-eat-dogma" competition and that we must look for the principles (not the treatment packages and manuals) that address *all* the aspects that help people change. This is because even if we could accurately determine what portions of the therapeutic pie were enhanced by treatment method, therapist interventions, and so on, we still would face the sobering issues that a great deal of the variance is still unaccounted for and that some variables may be inevitably uncontrollable. The patients go home to families, jobs, and other environments, which

(*Text continues on page 56*)

Table 3.2 Group Versus Individual Meta-Analyses

Author	Treatment Orientation	Group Characteristics	Sample	Conclusions
Smith, Glass, & Miller (1980)	Heterogeneous	Variable	Heterogeneous	The mode in which therapy was delivered made no difference in its effectiveness. Indeed, the average effects for group and individual therapy are remarkably similar. The average effect size was 0.87 for individual therapy and 0.83 for group therapy. Of the studies reviewed, 43% were individual, and 49% were group.
Shapiro & Shapiro (1982)	Heterogeneous	Average time spent in therapy was 7 hours.	Heterogeneous	This refined meta-analysis of the one conducted by Smith and Glass (1977) reported that although individual therapy appeared the most effective mode ($M = 1.12$), it was closely followed by the predominant group mode ($M = 0.89$), and the only striking treatment mode finding was for couple/family therapy ($M = 0.21$).
Miller & Berman (1983)	Cognitive behavioral	Duration of treatment relatively short.	Adolescents and adults, student/ community volunteers and outpatients, anxious and/or depressed	This meta-analysis of 48 studies reported that cognitive behavioral treatment was equally effective in group and individual formats when compared with a nontreatment group (individual 0.93, group = 0.79) and when compared with other treatment controls (individual = 0.31, group = 0.18); it should be noted that none of the studies in the review directly compared individual with group treatment within a single study.

Dush, Hirt, & Schroeder (1983)	Cognitive behavioral self-statement modification	Mean weeks of treatment were 5.9 with a range of 1 to 26.	About one fourth of studies used outpatients, one fourth used community volunteers, and half used undergraduate depressed and anxious volunteers.	Treatment modality was highly influential, with the mean effect for individual therapy nearly double that of group therapy across all comparisons. When compared with no-treatment controls, the effect size was 0.93 for individual and 0.58 for group; when compared with placebo controls, it was 0.71 for individual and 0.36 for group.
Nietzel, Russel, Hemmings, & Gretter (1987)	Cognitive, behavioral, and other	Mean number of hours in treatment was 16.3, with a range of 3 to 69 (distribution between group and individual hours not made).	Individuals with unipolar depression, adults	Reports a reliable difference between individual and group treatment, with group treatment being less effective. Clients treated with group ($M = 12.47$) reported more depressive symptoms than clients receiving individual treatment ($M = 0.06$).
Robinson, Berman, & Neimeyer (1990)	Included treatments with a prominent verbal component (i.e., cognitive, cognitive behavioral, behavioral, and general verbal therapy)	Number of clients per group ranged from 3 to 12 ($M = 7$).	Depressed individuals	Analysis indicated that both group and individual therapy produced more improvement than no treatment and that the effects of the two approaches were comparable. The 16 studies that compared individual and group therapy with a wait-list control, and the 15 studies that compared group with a wait-list control produced nearly equal effect sizes (0.83 and 0.84 respectively).

(Continued)

Table 3.2 (Continued)

Author	Treatment Orientation	Group Characteristics	Sample	Conclusions
Tillitski (1990)	Therapy, counseling, psychoeducational	Heterogeneous	Adults, adolescents, children diagnostically heterogeneous	In this reexamination of a subset of the studies looked at by Toseland and Siporin (1986), Tillitski reports finding the same average effect size for both group and individual treatment (1.35) and states that this effect was consistently greater than that of controls (0.18). Also, group counseling was found to be almost twice as effective as either therapy or psychoeducation. Recent studies produced larger effect sizes, and group tended to be better for adolescents, whereas individual tended to be better for children.
Hoag & Burlingame (1997a & b)	60% behavioral or cognitive/behavioral	79% took place in school groups (focused primarily on disruptive behavior, social skills, self-esteem). Average group size was 5 to 9. Average treatment length: 14 sessions.	Male and female children and adolescents (4 to 18)	56 outcome studies from 1974 to 1997 of group interventions (including preventative, psychotherapy, guidance) revealed effect size of 0.61 for group treatment over wait list and placebo controls.
McRoberts, Burlingame, & Hoag (1998)	Cognitive, behavioral, dynamic, supportive, eclectic	Average groups of 16 sessions, lasting 90 minutes each, 44% had cotherapists.	Adult outpatients with heterogeneous diagnoses	In this meta-analysis of group versus individual therapy, the general finding was overall equivalence (0.01), although under certain circumstances, individual therapy fared better (depression, cognitive behavioral approach, 0.16); in other circumstances, group fared better (with circumscribed problems, researcher's allegiance to format, attendance of member).

McDermut, Miller, & Brown (2001)	95% behavioral or cognitive behavioral; 5% interpersonal, psychodynamic, or nondirective	Highly diverse clinical settings, typical group lasted 12 sessions, once a week, variety of therapists.	Male (30%) and female (70%) outpatient adults with diagnosis of depression (mean age 44)	48 studies from 1970 to 1998 examined group therapy for depression. Patients showed clinically meaningful improvement compared with untreated controls, although their scores on Beck's Depression Inventory were still higher than normals. Of studies that compared group with individual therapy, slightly more reported individual to be superior.
Burlingame, Fuhriman, & Mosier (2003)	Cognitive, behavioral, dynamic, supportive, eclectic	University, correctional, and outpatient mental health settings	Adult outpatients with heterogeneous diagnoses	Examining 20 years of studies, the report found that patient diagnosis resulted in differential effects, homogeneous groups outperformed those in groups with mixed symptoms, and behavioral fared better than eclectic orientation.

SOURCE: Fuhriman & Burlingame, 1994. Adapted with permission.

influence their overall ability to get better or not. Here is where group therapy just might be ahead of individual psychotherapy research. The social environment is being replicated in the very treatment strategy. In some ways, generalization is more likely to take place because the patient has already practiced in other social settings. Only time will tell how these particular issues in group psychotherapy will be resolved.

Researchers also compare group treatments with other kinds of treatments such as milieu therapy (inpatient treatment that includes an array of interventions), psychopharmocotherapy (some form of psychotropic medication), and so on. Obviously, differential effectiveness would be difficult to determine. Did a patient become healthier because of the milieu therapy, the group therapy, the individual therapy, or the medication? This represents a real conundrum.

One of the most robust findings of these studies found ways to tease apart effects from several lugubrious sources, with the conclusion that combined group and individual therapy resulted in superior outcomes when compared with the independent outcomes of either treatment alone (Amaranto & Bender, 1990; Bostwick, 1987; Freeman & Munro, 1988; Pattison, Brissenden, & Wohl, 1967), although there were dissenting opinions (cf. Anderson, 1968; Stotsky & Zolik, 1965).

Such different combinations of treatments, matched by research methodologies that allow researchers to isolate one effect from another, have led to expanding conceptual models of efficacy. Potential patients benefit from this because clinicians are armed with good data that allow them to tailor a treatment protocol. For instance, in some cases, it is clear that group treatment is the main treatment—the format of choice (Burlingame et al., 2002; Piper, Rosie, Joyce, & Azim, 1996; Taylor et al., 2001). In other cases, however, the combination of one format with another is more helpful to the patient. In 1978, when Ormont and Strean suggested this innovative idea, little did they know it would lead to an explosion of alternatives and further delineate

combined from conjoint therapy. In summary, as more data are analyzed, we will know more clearly both the impact of complicated statistical analyses and permutations of treatment combinations.

The Evolution of Group Psychotherapy and Group Psychology Research: Content Complexity and Sophisticated Methodology

Recall that the origins of research on the small group phenomenon come from diverse fields. In particular, two somewhat independent although interacting domains—group psychology and group psychotherapy—constitute the two main contributors to the research (Back, 1979; Fuhriman & Burlingame, 1994). Group psychology research is subsumed within general social psychological research. Probably, an in-depth examination of the 100 years of research would be less helpful than an overview of themes or topics of research (see Tables 3.3 and 3.4).

In group psychology, the topics have focused on group characteristics and dynamics and how these influence the completion of the particular group tasks at hand. Data are typically collected based on analogue groups. Other issues of structure and communication were addressed in the 1940s (Zander, 1979a, 1979b). Researchers expanded to include such topics or themes as the development and maintenance of norms, the effect of member composition, the operation of member roles, the growing awareness of different developmental stages in groups, and finally, the impact of leaders.

In contrast, group psychotherapy researchers initially borrowed from the individual research literature. Understandably, data were derived from actual therapy groups. Although some topics overlap with group psychology (e.g., structure, format), in the main, group psychotherapy researchers were interested in different areas of

Table 3.3   Small Group Psychology: Thematic Evolution

	1900–1910	1911–1920	1921–1930	1931–1940	1941–1950	1951–1960	1961–1970	1971–1980	1981–1990	1991–2003
Models/approaches						X	X	X		X
Interpersonal influence	X				X	X	X	X	X	X
Problem solving/ decision making	X		X	X	X			X	X	X
Group structure				X	X		X	X	X	X
Group climate				X	X	X	X	X	X	X
Leadership						X	X	X	X	X

SOURCE: Fuhriman & Burlingame, 1994. Adapted with permission.

Table 3.4   Group Psychotherapy: Thematic Evolution

	1900–1910	1911–1920	1921–1930	1931–1940	1941–1950	1951–1960	1961–1970	1971–1980	1981–1990	1991–2003
Formats/theories/ models	X	X	X	X	X	X	X	X	X	X
Patient/client populations	X	X	X	X	X	X	X	X	X	X
Therapeutic relationship			X	X	X	X	X	X	X	X
Therapist variables							X	X	X	X
Therapeutic factors	X	X	X	X	X	X	X	X	X	X
Structure							X	X	X	X
Interaction analysis							X	X	X	X
Client outcomes						X	X	X	X	X
Ecosystem	X	X	X		X		X	X	X	X

SOURCE: Fuhriman & Burlingame, 1994. Adapted with permission.

examination such as models, therapeutic relationship, ecosystem, therapeutic factors, and the mentally ill, across the entire life span (child, adolescent, adult, elderly). In the early years, the study of psychodynamic and psychodrama models dominated the research. Interest broadened to include more models, different populations, and an array of settings. This research shaped conceptual explanations of group therapy as investigators examined three main foci: interpersonal, intrapersonal, and integral; that is, between members, within members (their intrapsychic dynamics), and group as a whole. By the 1980s, researchers were convinced that all three areas were critical to examine.

Eventually, researchers from the two camps began to take note of each other's research. For instance, by the 1970s, both camps were examining leadership. Table 3.4 highlights the diversity of interests that continued to grow over the decades, until by the end of the century, virtually every relevant topic was under scrutiny. Certain topics gained ascendancy and then faded (leadership), whereas others remained steady (therapeutic factors) throughout the decades as researchers' questions were answered and curiosity drove them toward other topics. Although each camp followed divergent interests, it is impossible to think of group psychology and group psychotherapy researchers as not having influenced each other (Tables 3.3 and 3.4). The sheer number of group articles in the latter half of the 20th century as compared with the first half is an impressive manifestation of burgeoning interest in diagnosis, treatments, members, leaders, therapeutic factors, structure, process, and outcome.

Researchers were aided in their search for relevant variables by changes in research methodology as well. What were once simple tallies turned eventually into advanced statistical methodology and carefully controlled experimental designs. In fact, so many advances have been made that an entire issue of the group journal published by Division 49 (Group Psychology and Group Psychotherapy, American Psychological Association) was dedicated to these advances (Forsyth, 1998). But just how did we arrive at this sophistication? Ideally, we hope to find rich idiographic data (e.g., $N = 1$ case studies) as well as the nomothetic data of carefully controlled empirical studies. Early-century investigations were often based on single-group studies using mostly descriptions. As research

methodology matured, preexperimental or pseudoexperimental studies were added to the earlier studies. By the late 1970s, thanks to a wide acceptance of Cook and Campbell (1979), most studies used one of five accepted empirical designs: experimental, quasi-experimental, correlational, survey, and descriptive. In this way, decreasing levels of rigor could be employed depending on such things as (a) feasibility of random assignment into at least two treatment groups with a control; (b) manipulation of an independent variable without random assignment; (c) relationship between certain variables; (d) use of survey methods; and finally, (e) use of case studies, one-group pretest/posttest designs, and nonequivalent comparisons. Thus, rich, in-depth single-case studies complemented carefully controlled empirical studies, balancing the necessary demands of relevance and rigor.

Often, the limits of certain populations, settings, and models determined the number of studies in any given decade that used one type of design over another. Studies that were focused on efficacy (e.g., examining various models with particular patients, such as those with eating disorders) often employed quasi-experimental and experimental designs, whereas those focused on process variables (e.g., comparing therapeutic factors with patient diagnosis) relied heavily on correlational designs. Finally, unusual or emergent models (e.g., alternative treatments such as drama or dance therapy) were likely to be studied with single-case methods.

The Future of Group Research

It makes intuitive sense that the last 100 years of research include methods and models that have become increasingly broad (examining an array of populations, settings, etc.) and deep (using complex methods of inquiry). Does the past predict the future? After reviewing about 500 studies from the last two decades—and if these studies are typical—we can expect more studies dominated by treatment of depression, children and adolescents, criminal offenders, physical and mental illnesses, eating disorders, and inpatient populations (Fuhriman & Burlingame, 1994). If the future of research is more than the "same old thing," we might also expect examinations of Internet groups, even though certain characteristics fail to meet traditional standards (e.g., face-to-face interaction). Other areas of inquiry, equally as intriguing, also may emerge.

In Table 3.5, we have added one more view of the many research studies reviewed thus far. Substantive themes were crossed by the principal characteristic of members for each study. This highlights once again major themes and client populations, although studies that concentrated on as-yet-understudied populations (e.g., stutterers, pathological gamblers) were eliminated for the sake of brevity, as were studies on certain topics for the same reason. If we take a closer look at these mainstream models and group members, we may notice several interesting trends.

Cognitive-behavioral models dominate, as do short-term treatment strategies (these two often go together). The more traditional process groups à la Yalom (1975, 1985) are much less prevalent, as are those that are longer term. Are these longer-term, open-ended process groups a thing of the past, even though there is substantial data to support their efficacy? Do the ascent of cognitive behavioral models and the descent of long-term process models reflect growing budget concerns, HMO pressures for shortened treatment strategies, or the dwindling expert group professionals who are less and less likely to take group courses as part of their curriculum?

Therapists, as a unit of observation, also may be dwindling. Of these 500 or so studies from the last few decades, only those that specifically manipulated or measured a therapists variable were included in Table 3.5. Of these, most of them measured the therapist effect post hoc. However, therapeutic factors still are widely examined. A large number of studies work across patient population categories. Still, therapeutic factors (i.e., curative factors) are generally measured using client self-report. Lambert and Hill (1994) remind us that relying on only one source is clearly problematic. We must, instead, use a multisource strategy that includes expert raters and therapist input, along with client input.

What catches our attention next as we examine Table 3.5 might be the number of studies interested in structure or lack of structure. Far fewer studies looked at such things as pregroup training (clearly related to positive outcome) and development. Finally, it is obvious that measuring verbal and nonverbal interaction—those process analysis systems that allow a researcher to carefully track interactions between member and member or leaders and members—are on the rise. This is a good thing. Perhaps the increased awareness of, and training for, analyzing process is helping (Beck & Lewis, 2000; Benjamin, 1993). Finally, the "not specified" column has far too many Xs. In other words, we still need researchers to detail all the important aspects of their group studies.

Conclusion

Humans gather. They have been doing so since the dawn of time. A very specific group gathering in the 19th and 20th centuries is group psychotherapy, which has a set of recognizable factors: appropriately referred group members, skilled leaders, and defined goals. Group psychology and group psychotherapy research helps us understand *how, why,* and *when* this intervention form works, and it generally finds that groups work for a variety of patients, in a variety of settings, encompassing a variety of problems. Studies spanning 100 years inform us about the powerful process of group. Still, our optimism must be tempered. Burlingame et al. (2004) remind us that we have yet to identify some

Table 3.5   Substantive Themes by Clinical Populations

	Child/ Adolescent	Medical	Depressed	Eating Disorder	Substance Abuse	Criminal	Inpatient	Family/ Marital	Elderly	Outpatient	Schizophrenic	Sexual Abuse	Personality Disorder	Not Specified	Other[a]
Models/ Approaches															
Cognitive behavioral	X	X	X	X	X	X	X	X	X	X	X	X	X	X	X
Short-term	X	X	X		X		X	X	X	X	X	X	X	X	
Rogerian										X					X
Gestalt											X				
Personal growth						X								X	
Psychodrama	X					X	X								
Therapist variables	X	X	X	X	X	X	X	X	X	X	X		X	X	X
Directiveness			X									X		X	
Interpretation												X		X	
Therapeutic factors	X	X	X	X	X	X	X	X	X	X	X	X	X	X	X
Structure	X	X	X	X	X	X	X		X	X		X		X	
Development						X				X				X	
Pregroup training								X		X				X	
Interaction			X		X	X	X	X	X	X	X	X		X	X

SOURCE: Fuhriman & Burlingame, 1994. Adapted with permission.

NOTE: The topical and methodological themes of the 1980s and 1990s were derived from roughly 500 articles about group psychotherapy. A bibliographic listing of the selected literature may be obtained from the authors.

a. Various nontherapeutic designations.

underlying processes in groups *and* connect these processes to certain outcomes.

Initial studies examined a variety of group variables in a fairly nonsystematic way. By mid-century, statistical and methodological sophistication allowed us to know more about group processes and outcomes in a much more systematic way, yielding rewarding and sometimes perplexing findings. What will the next century bring? Perhaps the combination of adequate methodologies and statistics—coupled with the continued curiosity of group researchers, who are attempting to understand all the variables involved in outcome and process research, how they relate to each other, and how they inform an overall theory—might bring us ever closer to understanding this powerful process.

References

Abbott, E. (1984). *Flatland: A romance of many dimensions.* New York: Penguin. (Original work published 1884)

Amaranto, E., & Bender, S. (1990). Individual psychotherapy as an adjunct to group psychotherapy. *International Journal of Group Psychotherapy, 40*(1), 91–101.

Anderson, A. (1968). Group counseling. *Review of Educational Research, 33,* 209–226.

Anthony, E. J. (1968). Reflections on twenty-five years of group psychotherapy. *International Journal of Group Psychotherapy, 18,* 277–301.

Anthony, E. J. (1971). The history of group psychotherapy. In H. Kaplan & B. Sadock (Eds.), *Comprehensive group psychotherapy* (1st ed.). Baltimore, MD: Williams & Wilkins.

Back, K. W. (1979). The small group: Tightrope between sociology and personality. *Journal of Applied Behavioral Science, 15*(3), 283–294.

Barlow, S., Fuhriman, A., & Burlingame, G. (2004). The history of group counseling and psychotherapy. In J. DeLucia-Waack, D. Gerrity, C. Kalodner, & M. Riva (Eds.), *Handbook of group counseling and psychotherapy* (pp. 3–22). Thousand Oaks, CA: Sage.

Beck, A., & Lewis, C. (2000). *The process of group psychotherapy: Systems for analyzing change.* Washington, DC: APA Press.

Bednar, R., & Kaul, T. (1978). Experiential group research: Current perspectives. In A. Bergin & S. Garfield (Eds.), *Handbook of psychotherapy and behavior change* (2nd ed., pp. 769–815). New York: John Wiley.

Bednar, R., & Lawlis, G. (1971). Empirical research in group psychotherapy. In A. Bergin & S. Garfield (Eds.), *Handbook of psychotherapy and behavior change* (pp. 812–839). New York: John Wiley.

Benjamin, L. (1993). *Interpersonal diagnosis and treatment of personality disorder.* New York: Guilford.

Bostwick, G. (1987). Where's Mary? A review of the group treatment dropout literature. *Social Work With Groups, 10*(3), 117–132.

Burchard, E., Michaels, J., & Kotkov, B. (1948). Criteria for the evaluation of group therapy. *Psychosomatic Medicine, 10*(3), 257–274.

Burlingame, G. M., Earnshaw, D., Hoag, M., Barlow, S. H., Richardson, E. J., Donnell, A. J., & Villani, J. (2002). A systematic program to enhance clinician group skills in an inpatient psychiatric hospital. *International Journal of Group Psychotherapy, 52*(4), 555–587.

Burlingame, G., Fuhriman, A., & Mosier, J. (2003). The differential effectiveness of group psychotherapy: A meta-analytic perspective. *Group Dynamics: Theory, Research, and Practice, 7*(1), 3–11.

Burlingame, G., MacKenzie, K. R., & Strauss, B. (2004). Small group treatment: Evidence for effectiveness and mechanisms of change. In M. Lambert (Ed.), *Handbook of psychotherapy and behavior change* (pp. 213–249). New York: John Wiley.

Cook, T., & Campbell, D. (1979). *Quasi-experimentation: Design and analysis issues for field settings.* Boston: Houghton Mifflin.

Cox, G., & Merkel, W. (1989). A qualitative review of psychosocial treatments for bulimia. *The Journal of Nervous and Mental Disease, 177*(2), 77–84.

de Jong, T. L., & Gorey, K. (1996). Short-term versus long-term group work With female survivors of childhood sexual abuse: A brief meta-analytic review. *Social Work With Groups, 19*(1), 19–27.

Dreikurs, R. (1932). Early experiments with group psychotherapy. *American Journal of Psychotherapy, 13,* 882–891.

Dreikurs, R. (1956). The contribution of group psychotherapy to psychiatry. *Group Psychotherapy, 9*(2), 115–125.

Dush, D., Hirt, M., & Schroeder, H. (1983). Self-statement modification with adults: A meta-analysis. *Journal of Consulting and Clinical Psychology, 94,* 408–422.

Emrick, C. (1975). A review of psychologically oriented treatment of alcoholism. *Journal for the Study of Alcoholism, 36*(1), 88–108.

Forsyth, D. (Ed.). (1998). Special issue: Research methods. *Group Dynamics: Theory, Research, and Practice, 4*(2).

Forsyth, D. (1999). *Group dynamics* (3rd ed.). New York: Brooks-Cole.

Forsyth, D. (Ed.). (2000). Special issue: 100 years of research. *Group Dynamics: Theory, Research, and Practice, 4*(1).

Freeman, C., & Munro, J. (1988). Drug and group treatments for bulimia/bulimia nervosa. *Journal of Psychosomatic Research, 32*(6), 647–660.

Fuhriman, A., & Burlingame, G. (1994). Group psychotherapy: Research and practice. In A. Fuhriman & G. M. Burlingame (Eds.), *Handbook of group psychotherapy: An empirical and clinical synthesis* (pp. 3–40). New York: John Wiley.

Gazda, G. M. (Ed.). (1968). *Innovation to group psychotherapy.* Springfield, IL: Charles C. Thomas.

Grunebaum, H. (1975). A soft-hearted review of hard-nosed research on groups. *International Journal of Group Psychotherapy, 25*(2), 185–197.

Harney, P., & Harvey, M. (1999). Group psychotherapy: An overview. In B. Young & D. Blake (Eds.), *Group treatment for post traumatic stress disorder* (pp. 1–15). Philadelphia: Bruner-Mazel.

Hoag, M., & Burlingame, G. M. (1997a). Child and adolescent group psychotherapy: A narrative review of effectiveness, a case for meta-analysis. *Journal of Clinical Child Psychology, 7*(2), 51–68.

Hoag, M., & Burlingame G. M. (1997b). Evaluating the effectiveness of child and adolescent group treatment: A meta-analytic review. *Journal of Clinical Child Psychology, 26,* 234–246.

Horne, A. M., & Rosenthal, R. (1997). Research in group work: How did we get where we are? *The Journal for Specialists in Group Work, 22,* 228–240.

Kanas, N. (1986). Group psychotherapy with schizophrenics: A review of controlled studies. *International Journal of Group Psychotherapy, 36,* 339–351.

Kaul, T., & Bednar, R. (1986). Experimental group research: Results, questions, and suggestions. In S. Garfield & A. Bergin (Eds.), *Handbook of psy-chotherapy and behavior change* (pp. 671–714). New York: John Wiley.

Kuhn, T. (1977). *The essential tension: Selected studies in scientific tradition and change.* Chicago: University of Chicago.

Lambert, M., & Hill, C. (1994). Assessing psychotherapy outcomes and processes. In A. Bergin & S. Garfield (Eds.), *Handbook of psychotherapy and behavior change* (4th ed., pp. 72–113). New York: John Wiley.

Lazell, E. W. (1921). The group treatment of dementia praecox. *Psychoanalytical Review, 8,* 168–179.

Lewin, K. (1936). *Principles of topological psychology.* New York: McGraw-Hill.

Lieberman, M. (1976). Change induction in small groups. *Annual Review of Psychology, 27,* 217–250.

Luborsky, L., Singer, B., & Luborsky, L. (1975). Comparative studies of psychotherapy: Is it true that "everyone has won and all must have prizes," *Archives of General Psychiatry, 32,* 995–1008.

Mann, J. (1966). Evaluation of group psychotherapy. In J. Moreno (Ed.), *The international handbook of group psychotherapy* (pp. 129–148). New York: Philosophical Library.

Marotta, S., & Asner, K. (1999). Group psychotherapy for women with a history of incest: The research base. *Journal of Counseling and Development, 77*(3), 315–323.

Marsh, L. C. (1931). Group treatment for the psychoses by the psychological equivalent of the revival. *Mental Hygiene, 15,* 328–349.

McDermut, W., Miller, I. W., & Brown, R. A. (2001). The efficacy of group psychotherapy for depression: A meta-analysis and review of the empirical research. *Evidence-Based Mental Health, 4*(3), 82–101.

McRoberts, C., Burlingame, G., & Hoag, M. (1998). Comparative efficacy of individual and group psychotherapy: A meta-analytic perspective. *Group Dynamics: Theory, Research, and Practice, 2,* 101–117.

Meltzoff, J., & Kornreich, M. (1970). *Research in psychotherapy.* New York: Atherton.

Miller, R., & Berman, J. (1983). The efficacy of cognitive behavior therapies: A quantitative review of research evidence. *Psychological Bulletin, 94,* 39–53.

Moreno, J., & Whitin, E. (1932). *Application of the group method to classification.* New York: National Commission on Prison and Prison Labor.

Mullen, B., Driskell, J., & Salas, E. (1998). Meta-analysis and the study of group dynamics. *Group Dynamics: Theory, Research, and Practice, 2,* 213–229.

Nietzel, M., Russel, R., Hemmings, K., & Gretter, M. (1987). Clinical significance of psychotherapy for unipolar depression: A meta-analytic approach to social comparison. *Journal of Consulting and Clinical Psychology, 55*(2), 156–161.

Oesterheld, A., McKenna, M., & Gould, N. (1987). Group psychotherapy of bulimia: A critical review. *International Journal of Group Psychotherapy, 37*(2), 163–187.

Ormont, L., & Strean, H. (1978). *The practice of conjoint therapy: Combining individual and group treatment.* New York: Human Science Press.

Parloff, M., & Dies, R. (1977). Group psychotherapy outcome research. *International Journal of Group Psychotherapy, 27,* 281–319.

Pattison, E. (1965). Evaluation studies of group psychotherapy. *International Journal of Group Psychotherapy, 15*(3), 382–397.

Pattison, E., Brissenden, A., & Wohl, T. (1967). Assessing specific effects of inpatient group psychotherapy. *International Journal of Group Psychotherapy, 17,* 283–297.

Piper, W., & Joyce, A. (1996). A consideration of factors influencing the utilization of time-limited, short-term group therapy. *International Journal of Group Psychotherapy, 46*(3), 311–328.

Piper, W., & McCallum, M. (1991). Group interventions for persons who have experienced loss: Description and evaluative research. *Group Analysis, 24,* 363–373.

Piper, W., Rosie, J., Joyce, A., & Azim, H. (1996). *Time-limited day treatment for personality disorders: Integration of research and practice in a group program.* Washington, DC: American Psychological Association.

Reeker, J., Ensing, D., & Elliott, R. (1997). A meta-analytic investigation of group treatment outcomes for sexually abused children. *Child Abuse and Neglect, 21,* 669–680.

Rickard, H. (1962). Selected group psychotherapy evaluation studies. *Journal of General Psychology, 67,* 35–50.

Robinson, L., Berman, J., & Neimeyer, R. (1990). Psychotherapy for the treatment of depression: A comprehensive review of controlled outcome research. *Psychological Bulletin, 108*(1), 30–49.

Ruitenbeek, H. (1969). *Group therapy today.* New York: Atherton Press.

Schilder, P. (1937). Analysis of ideologies as a psychotherapeutic method especially in group treatment. *American Journal of Psychiatry, 93,* 601–615.

Shapiro, D., & Shapiro, D. (1982). Meta-analysis of comparative therapy outcome studies: A replication and refinement. *Psychological Bulletin, 92,* 581–604.

Shechtman, Z. (2002). Child group psychotherapy in the school at the threshold of a new millennium. *Journal of Counseling and Development, 80*(3), 293–299.

Slavson, S. (1940). Group psychotherapy. *Mental Hygiene, 24,* 36–49.

Smith, M., & Glass, G. (1977). Meta-analysis of psychotherapy outcome studies. *American Psychologist, 32,* 752–760.

Smith, M., Glass, G., & Miller, T. (1980). *The benefits of psychotherapy.* Baltimore, MD: Johns Hopkins University Press.

Solomon, S. (1983). Individual versus group therapy: Current status in the treatment of alcoholism. *Advances in Alcohol and Substance Abuse, 2*(1), 69–86.

Stotsky, B., & Zolik, E. (1965). Group psychotherapy with psychotics. *International Journal of Group Psychotherapy, 15*(3), 321–344.

Syz, H. C. (1928). Remarks on group analysis. *American Journal of Psychiatry, 85,* 141–148.

Taylor, N. T., Burlingame, G. M., Fuhriman, A., Kristensen, K. B., Johansen, J., & Dahl, D. (2001). A survey of mental health care provider and managed care organization attitudes toward, familiarity with, and use of group interventions. *International Journal of Group Psychotherapy, 51*(2), 243–263.

Thomas, G. (1943). Group psychotherapy: A review of recent literature. *Psychosomatic Medicine, 5,* 166–180.

Tillitski, L. (1990). A meta-analysis of estimated effect sizes for group versus individual versus control treatments. *International Journal of Group Psychotherapy, 40*(2), 215–224.

Toseland, R., & Siporin, M. (1986). When to recommend group treatment. *International Journal of Group Psychotherapy, 36,* 172–201.

Vandervoort, D., & Fuhriman, A. (1991). The efficacy of group therapy for depression. *Small Group Research, 22*(3), 320–338.

Wender, L. (1936). Dynamics of group psychotherapy and its application. *Journal of Nervous and Mental Diseases, 84,* 54–60.

Wolf, A. (1949). The psychoanalysis of groups. *American Journal of Psychotherapy, 3,* 525–558.

Yalom, I. D. (1975). *The theory and practice of group psychotherapy* (2nd ed.). New York: Basic Books.

Yalom, I. D. (1985). *The theory and practice of group psychotherapy* (3rd ed.). New York: Basic Books.

Zander, A. (1979a). The psychology of group processes. *Annual Review of Psychology, 30,* 417–451.

Zander, A. (1979b). The study of group behavior during four decades. *Journal of Applied Behavioral Science, 15*(3), 272–282.

Zimpfer, D. (1987). Groups for the aging: Do they work? *Journal for Specialists in Group Work, 12,* 85–92.

Zimpfer, D. (1990). Group work for bulimia: A review of outcomes. *Journal for Specialists in Group Work, 15,* 239–251.

4

Contemporary Issues in Group Practice

Janice L. DeLucia-Waack

Cynthia R. Kalodner

Current group counseling theory and practice has its roots in two divergent events, Freud's famous Wednesday night meetings at his house in Vienna and John Pratt's treatment of tuberculosis patients in group "classes" in the United States. Many theoretical approaches and applications have emerged from these early beginnings to create an efficient and empirically validated treatment in psychology today. As more research examined the effectiveness of groups, the focus moved from establishing that groups are more effective than no treatment at all to establishing that groups for certain populations and problems are as effective or even more effective than other active treatments (Barlow, Fuhriman, & Burlingame, 2004). Groups today include psychoeducational, counseling, and therapy groups; they provide treatment for a great array of problems and issues for children, adolescents, adults, and senior citizens. Group techniques have expanded to include skill building, creative arts, and naturalistic healing methods. Research has begun to systematically identify the kinds of behaviors exhibited by group members and interventions by leaders that lead to positive client change and growth. This chapter describes the current state of group practice as well as key issues related to current group theory, research, and practice.

The Current State of Group Practice

A Broader Focus

The term *group therapy* can be applied to a variety of practices, starting with the traditional process group described by Yalom (1975), which has been parodied in TV situation comedies. Today, there are dozens of models for group therapy, "tapping myriad applications and treating an enormous array of human issues, from medical 'self-help' groups to the more traditional psychotherapy groups for adults" (Barlow et al., 2004, p. 3).

To aid in the selection of the appropriate type of group for different populations with different goals, the Association for Specialists in Group Work (ASGW; 2000) delineated four types of groups based on goals and interactional processes: task/work, psychoeducational/guidance, counseling, and therapy groups. Counseling groups "address personal and interpersonal problems of living and promote personal and interpersonal growth and development" (p. 331), whereas therapy groups "address personal and interpersonal problems of living, remediate perceptual and cognitive distortions or repetitive patterns of dysfunctional behavior, and promote personal and interpersonal growth and development" (p. 331). Both counseling and therapy groups use "group-based cognitive, affective, behavioral, or systemic intervention strategies" (p. 331). Although, by definition, counseling and therapy groups have a different focus, these terms often are used interchangeably, and the two kinds of groups may be difficult to differentiate in practice. Examples of counseling and therapy groups include general interpersonal groups and groups directed at the amelioration of specific problems such as depression, eating disorders, or sexual abuse.

In contrast, task/work groups focus on "efficient and effective accomplishment of group tasks" (ASGW, 2000, p. 330), and psychoeducational/guidance groups focus on skill development to prevent problems. Task/work and psychoeducational/guidance groups use "group-based educational and developmental strategies" (ASGW, 2000, p. 330). Examples of task and work groups include committees, clubs, and classrooms that have a common goal. Psychoeducational/guidance groups teach specific skills and coping strategies in an effort to prevent problems (such as anger management, social skills, self-esteem, assertiveness, and friendship skills).

In further contrast, counseling and therapy groups tend to be of longer duration and smaller in size than psychoeducational groups, which often last only 6 to 10 sessions and may consist of 10 or more members. Whereas psychoeducational/guidance groups tend to use educational strategies and practice to teach new skills, the emphasis in counseling and therapy groups is on the use of group process and dynamics to help members identify interpersonal difficulties, develop new ways of thinking and behaving to solve interpersonal problems, practice new behaviors, and learn coping skills from other group members. The major premise inherent in counseling and therapy groups is that group members eventually act in group as they behave in their relationships with others (significant others, friends, co-workers). Thus, as behaviors are enacted, group members can evaluate (with the help of other group members) the effectiveness of these behaviors and their impact (both positive and negative) on their relationships. Members then have the opportunity to practice and try out new behaviors and receive feedback from others about the perceived impact of the new behaviors. A recent survey of 54 co-leadership pairs (Bridbord, 2003) indicated a range of groups: 72.2% of the co-leaders led therapy groups; 13% counseling groups; 11.1% psychoeducational groups; and 14.8% support groups.

Settings and Populations

Psychoeducational, counseling, and psychotherapy groups are a standard treatment modality in a variety of settings. Schools are where the majority of research is conducted on groups with children and adolescents (Prout & Prout, 1998; Riva & Haub, 2004). In schools, groups address social competence deficits, adjustment to parent divorce, behavior problems, and learning disabilities and are most often behavioral

or cognitive behavioral, brief, structured, and homogeneous (Dagley, Gazda, Eppinger, & Stewart, 1994; Hoag & Burlingame, 1997).

Groups are often used with offenders and mandated clients (Morgan, 2004) and in inpatient settings (Emer, 2004). In the Veterans Administration, groups have shifted away from more psychodynamically oriented approaches and toward cognitive behavioral techniques in theme-focused groups. Group approaches are used in health care settings because they are time- and cost-efficient (Spira, 1997). The flexibility of group formats can be used advantageously to address a wide array of concerns specific to a health condition or unique to a given population (Roback, 1984). Groups often are conducted in a variety of health care settings including certain inpatient units, outpatient clinics, community centers, schools, and churches. In most of these groups, participation is voluntary, but in some programs, groups are an integral part of the treatment program, and attendance may be expected (e.g., pain rehabilitation programs).

Group Practice Standards and Guidelines

The ASGW has created three important documents that have major implications for the field of group leadership. "Professional Standards for the Training of Group Workers" (ASGW, 2000) delineates and defines four types of groups and presents core and specialty training guidelines. The knowledge, skills, and experiences for each type of group are identified in this document. Specifically, core training requires coursework in group work, group membership or leadership, and specific knowledge such as the types of groups, theories of group development, assessment of group functioning, and group process and observational skills. Knowledge and leadership skills specific to each type of group also are identified.

"Principles for Diversity-Competent Group Workers" (ASGW, 1999) provides guidance about the complicated issues inherent in conducting groups with diverse populations. Counselor self-knowledge and knowledge of other cultural worldviews and diversity-appropriate group interventions are discussed. A section in the *Handbook of Group Counseling and Psychotherapy* (DeLucia-Waack, Gerrity, Kalodner, & Riva, 2004) also provides guidelines for leading a variety of diverse groups. Specifically, group leaders need to be aware of their own biases, possible racism, and assumptions about mental health and counseling, and they must possess specific knowledge and skills to be effective with different cultures and lifestyles, such as Indigenous Peoples, African Americans, Asian Americans, Latinos, gay/lesbian/bisexual/transgendered people, and people with physical, mental/emotional, and/or learning disabilities.

In "Best Practice Guidelines" (ASGW, 1998), the *Code of Ethics and Standards of Practice* developed by the American Counseling Association (ACA; 1997) is specifically applied to group work. These guidelines address planning, performing, and processing groups, and they form the basis for the section of this chapter on practical issues in group practice. Planning focuses on pregroup decision-making and planning as well as selection and preparation of both members and leaders. Performing focuses on group leadership skills, provision of effective interventions, and assessment of effectiveness. Processing focuses on using interventions to help members learn, as well as evaluating group interventions to assess effectiveness, supervising, and following up with group members.

Key Theoretical and Research Issues in Contemporary Group Practice

The face of groups has certainly changed over the years, and evidence overwhelmingly suggests that groups are an efficacious treatment modality.

Yet, there are still many unanswered questions related to the theoretical underpinnings of how groups work, which generates much research. The major theme in this section is to answer Yalom's (1995) lingering question:

> How does group therapy help patients? If we can answer this seemingly naive question with some measure of precision and certainty, we shall have at our disposal a central organizing principle by which to approach the most vexing and controversial problems of psychotherapy. (p. 1)

While current group practice now includes psychoeducational as well as counseling and therapy groups, the question still holds. This section highlights the major issues currently facing group theorists and researchers as they struggle to answer this question. Several theoretical constructs will be discussed. These are designed to better understand the underlying mechanisms of effective group work: therapeutic factors, leadership behaviors, and interventions. In addition, assessment issues will be described as they relate to current issues in the field of groups.

Therapeutic Factors

In 1975, Yalom hypothesized what he considered to be a comprehensive list of the operations and mechanisms that led to therapeutic change in groups; these were originally called curative factors (and later renamed therapeutic factors): altruism, catharsis, cohesiveness, existentiality, family reenactment, guidance, hope, identification, interpersonal learning input (feedback), interpersonal learning output (new behavior), self-understanding, and universality. Bloch and Crouch (1985) defined a therapeutic factor as "an element of group therapy that contributes to improvement in a patient's condition and is a function of the actions of the group therapist, the other group members, and the patient himself"

(p. 4). Many studies have supported Yalom's contention that these therapeutic factors are essential to effective groups, but more than 25 years later, there is still no consensus about the relative importance of each in relation to client change and the potential differential emphasis of these factors in connection with different types of groups and clients.

Several instruments have been designed to assess therapeutic factors in groups: Therapeutic Factors Scale (Yalom, 1985), Curative Factors Scale–Revised (Lieberman, Yalom, & Miles, 1973; Stone, Lewis, & Beck, 1994), Critical Incidents Questionnaire (Kivlighan & Goldfine, 1991), and Therapeutic Factors Inventory (Lese & McNair-Semands, 2000). Client population (inpatient versus outpatient), type of group (support, counseling, therapy), client gender, and client age all have been hypothesized to impact the importance of different therapeutic factors, but research supporting these hypotheses has been inconsistent. In an effort to make sense of the inconsistent findings, Kivlighan and Holmes (2004) used a cluster analysis of 24 studies that ranked or rated the importance of therapeutic factors. Four clusters emerged from the analysis based on the therapeutic factors that were highest and lowest in each cluster. Cluster 1, *affective insight groups,* rated acceptance, catharsis, interpersonal learning, and self-understanding as the most valued factors. These groups also rated both guidance and vicarious learning as relatively unimportant. Cluster 2, *affective support groups,* rated acceptance, installation of hope, and universality as the most important group factors. Like members of Cluster 1, members of the groups in Cluster 2 rated guidance and vicarious learning as relatively unimportant. Cluster 3, *cognitive support groups,* rated vicarious learning and guidance as highly valued while self-understanding was rated much lower. Cluster 4, *cognitive insight groups,* rated interpersonal learning, self-understanding, and vicarious learning as the most valued therapeutic factors. Kivlighan and Holmes then concluded:

There was no relationship between the type of population study (inpatients, outpatients, prisoners, students, and incest survivors) and group type . . . no relationships between factors such as treatment length, source of ranking data (client vs. therapist), client gender, or client age; and the group types derived from the cluster analysis. (p. 32)

It seems safe to conclude that the 12 therapeutic factors Yalom (1975) hypothesized are essential components of the therapeutic process. In addition, it appears that different types of groups may need different combinations of therapeutic factors to be effective. The next step is to study interventions designed to elicit those therapeutic factors desired in a particular type of group. Kivlighan and Holmes (2004) also called for group member matching based on the type of group and suggested two potential selection criteria:

Client affiliation (friendly vs. unfriendly) is an important concept for distinguishing between clients that will benefit from an affective or cognitive approach to group therapy. The control (dominant vs. submissive) dimension is important for distinguishing between clients who will benefit from a supportive or insight-oriented group therapy experience. (p. 33)

Future practice and research must continue to examine how leaders can best facilitate these therapeutic factors. Following from this, Kivlighan and Holmes (2004) suggested that

identifying the underlying structure of therapeutic factors rankings allows researchers to ask and attempt to answer more interesting and therapeutically meaningful questions. Specifically, attempting to identify which clients will benefit the most from affective support groups, affective insight groups, cognitive support groups, and

cognitive insight groups is an important question for researchers to tackle. Alternatively, it also will be important for researchers to identify group leader characteristics and behaviors that are related to clients experiencing affective support groups, affective insight groups, cognitive support groups, and cognitive insight groups. (p. 33)

In addition, it appears that stage of group development may both call for and influence the relative importance of therapeutic factors, and this interaction has yet to be fully understood.

Leadership Behaviors

Following from the theoretical question of what combination of therapeutic factors facilitates effective group work is its logical extension: What leadership behaviors facilitate the creation of therapeutic factors that in turn facilitate client change and growth? Based on a review of literature on leadership, Riva, Wachtel, and Lasky (2004) suggested that "an essential component related to the effectiveness of therapeutic groups is the leadership. The leader plays a vital role both in the dynamics of the group and the outcomes of its members" (p. 37).

Several types of group leadership behaviors have been identified consistently as correlated with client progress and change. Dies (1994) concluded, based on a review of 135 studies, that group members benefited from positive leader behavior such as warmth, support, and genuine interest. In addition, he suggested that "as leaders become more actively negative, they increase the possibility that participants will not only be dissatisfied, but potentially harmed by the group experience" (p. 139). In addition, researchers have found that leaders who are less controlling, who exhibit warmth/caring, and who set and reinforce clear norms are more likely to have cohesive groups. Increased cohesiveness, in turn, has been found to be positively related to a variety of group treatment outcomes.

Morran, Stockton, and Whittingham (2004) highlighted 10 specific group interventions with research and clinical support. The first category, protecting group members and promoting safety, includes protecting, blocking, and supporting. These interventions are typically most useful in the leader's efforts to provide a group climate that is conducive to trust, openness, and cohesion. Research has indicated that members who are dissatisfied with their group experience often see the group leader as negligent in providing adequate protection. Protecting can sometimes be indirect and might include member selection/exclusion procedures, the establishment of appropriate group norms, or the modeling of caring for group members. More direct protecting interventions might take the form of intervening to stop a member who is self-disclosing too much or at a level that is significantly more intimate than the rest of the members. Blocking is a specific type of protection that is used to stop a member from storytelling, rambling, or inappropriately probing, gossiping, or invading the privacy of others. Research suggests that group members frequently attributed their damaging experiences to undue confrontation, criticism, and pressure to self-disclose by other members. Thus, it is essential that group leaders use blocking to protect potentially vulnerable group members. Supportive interventions help to reassure, reinforce, and encourage members to participate in group and try out new behaviors.

The second category, energizing and involving group members, includes drawing out, modeling, linking, processing, and feedback (Morran et al., 2004). These interventions are most often used to stimulate forward progress, increase member participation, and enhance interpersonal learning. Drawing out occurs when the leader directly invites comments or involvement to encourage participation from members who find it hard to share with others or from members who share on a surface level but avoid deeper issues. Modeling occurs when leaders demonstrate the skills, attitudes, and other characteristics

they hope to engender within group members, such as respect and caring for others, appropriate self-disclosure, giving and receiving feedback, and openness. Many group theorists suggest that modeling is a common factor in nearly all interventions because members naturally observe group leaders and other members and tend to imitate what they see demonstrated. Research has found that behaviors displayed by the therapist, including interpersonal behaviors, feedback delivery and acceptance, and here-and-now communications, lead to increases in those same behaviors by group members. Linking connects what one group member is saying or doing with the concerns of one or more other members and has been shown to be particularly useful in promoting member interaction, cohesion, trust, and universality among group members.

Interpreting involves offering possible explanations for events, behaviors, thoughts, and feelings at a deeper level to be considered as part of the change process. Members typically experience interactions that provide the opportunity to learn more about themselves. Research suggests that leader interpretations helped members to integrate complex personal and group-related events and facilitated generalization from group experiences to personal experiences outside the group. Interpretations about the clients' impact on the environment and their patterns of behavior were most associated with client change.

In addition to specific leadership behaviors, several more general and broad-based leader interventions are essential to creating effective groups. These are providing structure, encouraging feedback, conceptualizing group events, and processing activities and critical incidents.

Providing structure. A certain level of structure is necessary, particularly in early group sessions, to encourage self-disclosure and self-exploration (Burlingame & Fuhriman, 1994; Dies, 1994; Gazda, Ginter, & Horne, 2001; Stockton, Rohde, & Haughey, 1992). Yalom (1985) described four leadership behaviors, one directly related to structure. Executive functions focus on setting limits and providing norms and directions the group can use to operate. Coche, Dies, and Goettelman (1991) concluded that a moderate level of executive function is beneficial.

Encouraging feedback. Morran, Stockton, Cline, and Teed (1998) found that corrective feedback from leaders and other group members may be extremely important in that it provides a different perspective, but it is also generally hard for group members to hear. Stage of group appears to influence what kind of feedback is needed and the probability of it being well-received (Morran et al., 1998). In initial sessions, positive feedback should be emphasized. During later sessions, a balance of positive and corrective feedback is more useful. In addition, both group member and leader feedback is useful (Flowers, 1979; Morran et al., 1998; Morran, Robison, & Stockton, 1985). The Corrective Feedback Self-Efficacy Instrument (Page & Hulse-Killacky, 1999) can be used to assess group leaders' self-efficacy for giving corrective feedback within counseling groups. The instrument is based on the premise that "by giving corrective feedback in groups, the giver learns to communicate honestly and openly with others as well as to provide opportunities for receivers to learn about themselves" (p. 38). However, group leaders may also have significant anxiety about giving feedback.

Conceptualizing group events. Hines, Stockton, and Morran (1995) found that novice and expert group leaders think differently about their groups. Group leaders with more experience interpreted group process, asked internal questions abut members, and interpreted member behavior more often than less experienced leaders, who tended to make more therapeutic value judgments. In addition, the less experienced the leader, the more thoughts he or she had about whether a group transaction was therapeutic. Interpretation of group process was the single most important thought category to predict the experience level of leaders.

Processing of critical events and activities. One of the most common mistakes group leaders make is not to process an activity. Indeed, most books and group exercises involving activities do not include the direction or guidance necessary for effective processing of activities (Kees & Jacobs, 1990). Processing can be described as

> capitalizing on significant happenings in the here-and-now interactions of the group to help members reflect on the meaning of their experience; better understand their own thoughts, feelings and actions; and generalize what is learned to their life outside of the group. (Stockton, Morran, & Nitza, 2000, p. 345)

Effective processing requires that members engage in a process of sharing and exploring among themselves to make sense of what happened, establish what they have learned from the incident, and begin to plan and practice new behaviors to be used outside of group sessions.

Assessment

The focus in group research has shifted from the question of whether groups work to the question of what makes groups effective. Leading group theorists have long hypothesized that process variables such as group climate, dynamics, and therapeutic factors contribute to change in group member behavior. Only recently have researchers begun to systematically study the process of group counseling and therapy. One slowdown in group process research has been the lack of reliable and valid measures. More reliable and valid outcome measures (e.g., anxiety, depression, social skills) exist than group process instruments. DeLucia-Waack and Bridbord (2004) identified a total of 15 instruments used in group process and practice research, with established reliability and validity in the following areas: screening and selection (4), group leadership skills (2), group climate

(2), therapeutic factors (3), and ratings of in-session behavior (4).

Measures with demonstrated reliability and validity have only begun to be consistently used. Typically, researchers have constructed their own measures of group process (Riva & Smith, 1997). Several issues have contributed to the difficulties of creating reliable and valid measures of group process. One is a lack of definitional consensus. For example, what exactly is group cohesiveness? Another issue relates to the reliability of the measure used. Group process is a dynamic construct, and instruments used to assess process variables need to be sensitive to small and large changes within and across group sessions. Furthermore, with only a limited number of reliable and valid measures of group process, it is difficult to establish convergent validity for new measures. The next step is to develop clearly established norms that can be used to compare specific samples and a baseline for future studies. Norms must go beyond college students to adults, children, and adolescents seeking counseling, and they must be applicable to the array of groups, from task to psychoeducational, counseling, and therapy.

Key Practical Issues Facing Group Practice

Group practice involves all the variations of how counselors may work with groups: task/work groups, psychoeducational groups, counseling groups, and therapy groups. Groups may also occur in a variety of settings; they may require different planning and leader skills; they may have different intended outcomes. In this section, the "Best Practice Guidelines" (ASGW, 1998) will guide discussion of planning, performing, and processing groups.

Planning

Planning, as defined by the ASGW (1998), focuses on pregroup decision-making and planning as well as selection and preparation of both members and leaders.

Assessment. It is important to begin with an assessment of "community needs, agency or organization resources, sponsoring organization mission, staff competency, attitudes regarding group work, professional training levels of potential group leaders regarding group work; client attitudes regarding group work, and multicultural and diversity considerations" (ASGW, 1998, p. 238). After a complete assessment, group leaders can decide the purpose, population, and goals of the group, which determine whether the group will be a psychoeducational, counseling, or therapy group. To make this decision, group facilitators should ask organizing questions: Who will be members? What is the reason for forming this group? Are there symptom(s) being treated? What are the severity levels? Is this a prevention or treatment intervention? What is the intended outcome? How long are the group interventions? Are the goals realistic for the length of the group? The answers to these questions will allow leaders to consider the needs of the individuals being served and choose group content and format that appropriately address these needs (Kalodner & Coughlin, 2004). Planning the appropriate type of group involves consideration of many different factors, including group members' developmental maturity, group members' history, group size, leadership style, and settings (Fleckenstein & Horne, 2004).

Group size is dependent on the type and purpose of the group. Psychoeducational groups may be larger than counseling groups. Many school-based psychoeducational programs operate in classrooms and include more than 20 students, but when groups include interaction in addition to didactic presentations, the group size should be reduced to 5 to 10 participants (Smead, 1995). For counseling and therapy groups, the magic number seems to be 6 to 8 participants; this allows sufficient interaction and diversity in perspectives between members to create group cohesion and a supportive environment where feedback can be given and new behaviors and skills tried out.

Different settings are conducive to different types of groups. A review of the literature suggested that psychoeducational groups are the predominant groups in community mental health centers and HMOs (Clifford, 2004). A similar situation exists in the schools, where the goal of most groups is psychoeducational: to teach new skills and prevent potential problems. In college counseling centers, mental health agencies, and hospitals, the converse is true, with counseling and therapy groups the predominant group modality. In contrast, in the workplace, task/work and psychoeducational groups predominate (Wheelan, 2004).

Selection of group members. The ACA (1997) *Code of Ethics and Standards of Practice* states that group leaders "select group members whose needs and goals are compatible with the goals of the group, who will not impede the group process, and whose well-being will not be jeopardized by the group experience" (p. 2). Yet, little has been written about which variables aid in the identification of clients who might benefit from group counseling, or for that matter, which type of group format is the best option. Riva, Lippert, and Tackett (2000) reported that group leaders almost exclusively used clinical judgment to determine whether the potential group member fit the group theme, rather than focusing on specific personality characteristics or behaviors that would increase the likelihood of a successful group experience.

Riva et al. (2004), based on a review of the literature, suggested two areas of attention in selecting group members: interpersonal and intrapersonal characteristics. Piper and McCallum (1994) emphasized as inclusion criteria a moderate amount of social ability and frustration tolerance and a commitment to changing interpersonal behaviors. Intrapersonal variables that have promise as selection criteria are psychological mindedness and the potential group member's expectations about the benefits of group treatment. Lower levels of psychological mindedness (McCallum & Piper, 1990) and hostility (MacNair-Semands, 2002) have been shown to predict dropouts. Moreover, there is support for a positive relationship between a client's expectation that group will be beneficial and the actual benefits gained (Pearson & Girling, 1990).

To assess intrapersonal and interpersonal variables, group leaders may ask questions during the selection process that address potential members' relationships with others (e.g., Describe your behavior and participation in past or current social or therapeutic groups.), their expectations that the group will help them (e.g., How much do you expect this group to be beneficial to you?), and the ability to be self-reflective or psychologically minded (e.g., Describe some of your behaviors that you find difficult to understand.).

Two measures may also be useful in the selection process to assess inter- and intrapersonal skills and expectations about groups. The Group Psychotherapy Evaluation Scale (Kew, 1975) was designed to assess whether potential group members have the necessary skills to participate successfully in group psychotherapy, based on an interview using the following categories: amount of communication, quality of relatedness and communication, quality of content in communication and relatedness, capacity for change, involvement, client willingness to discuss problems openly, client-stated commitment to change, client identification of goals, and specificity of goals. The Group Therapy Survey (Carter, Mitchell, & Krautheim, 2001; Slocum, 1987) assesses misperceptions about group counseling and therapy.

Preparing members for group interventions. As part of the screening and pregroup preparation process, leaders should provide a professional disclosure statement that describes group goals, theoretical orientation, group services, member and leader roles, leader qualifications, confidentiality, and exceptions to confidentiality (ASGW, 1998). The "Best Practice Guidelines" (ASGW, 1998) suggests that planning a group requires that group leaders know the ethical guidelines, state laws, and insurance requirements relevant for group work. An issue that is especially important in group intervention is confidentiality and its limits. Group leaders have the responsibility to inform all group participants of the need for and limits of confidentiality and the potential consequences of breaching it, both verbally and in writing, before group members agree to participate.

In addition to specific procedural information about how the group will operate, it is important to provide potential group members with information about how groups work in terms of the process. "Pregroup preparation sets treatment expectations, defines group rules, and instructs members in appropriate roles and skills needed for effective group participation and group cohesion" (Burlingame, Fuhriman, & Johnson, 2001, p. 375). Pregroup preparation, sometimes called pregroup training, has been shown to be related to the development of group cohesion, group member satisfaction, decreased risk of dropout, and positive group member behaviors (Bednar & Kaul, 1994).

From a practical standpoint, leaders can use the preparation time to address much of the procedural information prior to the first session and help all group members begin with more or less the same knowledge about how the group will function. There is no standard method of preparation, yet Couch (1995) suggested a helpful four-step model: identify the clients' needs, expectations, and commitment; challenge any myths and misconceptions; convey information; and screen the person for group fit. Bowman and DeLucia (1993) suggested a three-step multimodal approach: a cognitive component (a handout summarizing how group works, typical group topics and activities, and helpful group member behaviors), a vicarious component where potential group members view a videotape of a working group (e.g., Stockton, 1996), and an experiential component consisting of role-plays that emphasize helpful group member behaviors.

Preparation for group leaders. To prepare for the group, leaders need to think about it from several different perspectives. How will they prepare for the group personally and professionally? How will they prepare others for the group, specifically their school or agency (including administrators), parents, and group members? Group leaders need to have a sense of their beliefs about the issues to be addressed, the needs of group members, and how best a group can help these members. Second, they must examine the current counseling and group literature to determine what themes, interventions, and structure are most effective with their type of group and with people the age of the group members. To begin to establish trust and cooperation, co-leaders and supervisor should meet before the group starts to discuss theoretical orientation, leadership style, and goals and interventions for the group. Each leader should assess his or her strengths and weaknesses as a leader of the particular group that is being planned. Assessment of the leadership skills needed for this group should include experience with this type of group (psychoeducational or counseling), the age of group members, and the focus and goals of the group.

Co-leadership. The benefits of using a co-leadership model in groups include better management of the group's many (and sometimes conflicting) needs, strong affects, complicated dynamics, and concurrent events; pooling of resources and abilities of both therapists, broadening the range of transferential reactions; increased validity and intensity of therapist interpretations; potential to break a therapeutic impasse; balance of challenge and support; utility in training novice therapists; simulation of a family unit; group continuity of care; and mutual support of co-leaders (Bernard, Drob, & Lifshutz, 1987; Concannon, 1995; Dubner, 1998; Pearlman & Saakvitne, 1995; Roller & Nelson,

1991). Anecdotally, it is believed that the group cannot achieve a higher level of development than the relationship between co-leaders (Dugo & Beck, 1997).

Co-leadership is preferable, specifically a male-female co-leadership team (DeLucia-Waack, 2001). For children and adolescent groups, a male-female co-leadership team models collaboration between male and female adults and provides contact with supportive and caring adults of both sexes. A male presence in such a group is particularly important because many of the children may have little contact with an adult male. Although such a model of co-leadership may be time-intensive and difficult to arrange, it is highly valuable and worth the effort. If the group is psychoeducational in nature and meets in school, one co-leader could be a teacher. In agencies, it may be possible to recruit a youth worker or a caseworker who works with children but who is not trained as a counselor. However, it is important that the co-leader can be empathic and supportive and can provide structure to the group.

Regardless of their skills and experience, co-leaders must commit to weekly planning and supervision sessions to prepare for their group and to process what has happened; an hour a week is recommended (ASGW, 2000) to assess the goals of individual group members and group interventions, review session events and group process, and plan future sessions. Bridbord (2003) found that co-leader relationship satisfaction was best predicted by perceived compatibility of behavior during sessions, theoretical compatibility, and similarities in confrontation style. She suggested using the Leadership Characteristics Inventory (Makuch, 1997) and the Co-therapy Relationship Questionnaire (Bernard et al., 1987) to assess these constructs. The Co-facilitator Inventory (Pfeiffer & Jones, 1975) is a resource for leaders to examine their own style of leadership. It provides a structured format for discussions between co-leaders and between group leader(s) and supervisor.

Performing

The "Best Practices Guidelines" (ASGW, 1998) suggests that performing focuses on provision of effective interventions, evaluation of group leadership skills, and assessment of effectiveness. Supervision is an integral part of this process.

Effective interventions. Specific effective leadership behaviors and interventions were discussed earlier in the Current State of Group Practice section. This section will focus more on activities and creative arts interventions that may be used in groups.

Activities. Activities are often used in task, work, psychoeducational, and guidance groups, and less frequently in counseling and therapy groups. Counseling groups often focus on the group process, and leaders sometimes fear that the use of activities may interfere with the group process, although Yalom (1995) has suggested that activities may sometimes be useful in counseling and therapy groups. This section will focus on the use of activities in both psychoeducational and counseling groups. In psychoeducational groups, activities are an essential part of the group structure focusing on teaching and practicing new behaviors and skills. In counseling and therapy groups, activities are used mainly when a specific need to learn new behaviors becomes apparent for one or more group members (e.g., learning skills related to assertiveness, communication, and expression of feelings) or to accelerate the group past a particularly slow or stuck phase of the group (Yalom, 1995).

Group leaders should tailor activities to the main task inherent in the stage the group is currently working through. From the very beginning of the first group session, all group activities, processing of group activities, and group discussions should emphasize group goals and group norms such as self-disclosure, self-exploration, and the importance of feedback. Activity in the initial stage focuses on building trust and introducing members to the group and to each other. Icebreaker activities need to be focused on two areas: (1) identification of the individual group members' goals within the context of the overall group goals, and (2) introduction of the norms of self-disclosure, self-exploration, and feedback. For introductory activities, the purpose should be getting oriented to the group, building cohesiveness and connection among group members, and promoting the norms of self-disclosure and self-exploration. Group members need structure and guidance in the beginning stage to help figure out how to get the most out of their group experience. Beginning the process of self-disclosure and self-awareness, key elements in counseling and therapy groups, also needs to occur in the introductory group sessions. Any activity that asks members to tell a little about themselves includes self-disclosure. Thus, if an activity is followed up with processing questions that focus on what it is like to self-disclose, the impact of self-disclosure on other members, and similarities and differences between members, then processing self-awareness has begun as well. The *autobiography* activity (Bridbord, 2002) and the *getting to know you—now and then* activity (Conroy, 2002) encourage members to self-disclose and get to know other members while emphasizing safety.

Activities of the working stage focus on assisting members to identify behaviors and cognitions that are negatively affecting their affect and relationship and to identify, learn, and practice potentially new and more effective skills. In psychoeducational groups, most working group sessions will use role-playing, problem-solving, and decision-making interventions to teach and practice new skills. In counseling and therapy groups, similar activities may be used when relevant to a group member's issue or group dynamics.

The termination stage of group is the other stage where structure is important. Activities in the ending stage assist members in termination and bringing what they have learned to use, once the group has ended. Group members need

to leave group with a clear sense of what they have learned from group, how they have learned what they have learned, and who was influential in the learning. They need to identify what changes they will make on leaving group, specifically based on what they have learned in group. The *where in the world can I be?* (Johnson, 2002), *paper quilt* (Paisley, 2002), and *feedback as poetry* activities (Wilson, 2002) can be used in closing sessions to help members say good-bye, summarize what they have learned, and make plans for future change.

Activities are often used to provide structure in groups with children and adolescents. Younger group members seem less able to make the transition from one group session to the next. It is helpful and creates a sense of trust to have a structure for each group session that is expected and predictable. Psychoeducational group sessions typically include four parts. A review or warm-up reviews material from a previous session, discusses homework efforts, and/or introduces the topic for this session. Working activities focus on the goals of the group, allowing discussion and interaction around a specific topic or skill to identify, learn, and/or practice potentially effective behaviors. Processing activities typically include questions to help make sense of the working activities and apply them to life outside of group. Closing activities help group members prepare to leave group.

Such a structure also works well for older adolescents. Beginning each session with a short activity, maybe 15 to 20 minutes at the most, helps members to generate some insight into their personal issues and perhaps introduces a framework within which to work on personal issues. It also helps members focus on the group topic and get ready to work on a topic related to group and individual goals.

Supervision. Self-knowledge is identified as critical to effective group leadership and focuses on the continual evaluation of the group leader's impact on the individual group members and the group as a whole. Supervision is essential to becoming competent at group leadership (Yalom, 1995). Leading effective groups demands continual evaluation of leader skills and interventions, group development, and individual progress of group members. Ebersole, Leiderman, and Yalom (1969) reported that without supervision, group therapists were not able to identify mistakes and generate new plans of action; instead, they became stuck in a cycle of repeated ineffective interventions. It is essential for the supervisor and the leaders of a group to recognize the unique characteristics of the group in order to engage in effective supervision. The skills necessary to conduct a group and the focus of a group differ depending on the type of group; therefore, the emphasis and content of supervision differs as well (ASGW, 2000). Much attention has been paid to how to conduct and structure supervision sessions for group leaders (Conyne, 1999; DeLucia-Waack, 2002). The ASGW (2000) "Professional Standards for the Training of Group Workers" suggests a minimum of one hour a week of planning time, typically supervision, for group leaders, either individually or with a co-leader. The ASGW (1998) "Best Practice Guidelines" emphasizes the importance of supervision and consultation with other group leaders as an integral part of effective and ethical group work. Specifically, group leaders must "process the workings of the group with themselves, group members, supervisors or other colleagues, as appropriate. This may include assessing progress on group and member goals, leader behaviors and techniques, group dynamics and interventions, developing understanding and acceptance of meaning" (ASGW, 1998, p. 4).

Processing group work is much more complicated (ASGW, 1998; Conyne, 1999) than processing individual counseling because of all the potential topics and interactions. Content issues include case conceptualization of both individual member and group goals and the current stage of the group, assessment of interventions on individual group members and the group as a whole, and transference and countertransference (Christensen & Kline, 2001; DeLucia, Bowman, & Bowman, 1989; DeLucia-Waack, 1999). Process topics include the relationships between group members, co-leaders, and the supervisor.

Several variations of supervision occur for group workers. Group supervision is cost-efficient in that several students can be supervised at one time, with the added benefit of having multiple viewpoints and counselors learning from each other. Group supervision is conducted in about 65% of predoctoral psychology training sites approved by the American Psychological Association (Riva & Cornish, 1995) with counselors working both individually with clients and in groups. Co-leaders of a group often meet weekly to plan, process, and prepare for future group sessions and essentially "supervise" each other. Group leaders may meet regularly as a small group to provide supervision and consultation for each other or consult with other group leaders when needed about a particular group member, issue, or intervention. Thus, these variations of the supervision of group work must be taken into consideration when describing a model of supervision for group workers.

Furthermore, Leszcz and Murphy (1994) found the quality of the supervision relationship was the most important variable associated with training satisfaction. Specifically, dissatisfied group leader trainees reported feeling "unheard," "criticized," and "unhelped," whereas satisfied trainees reported feeling "supported" and "empathized with" (p. 100). More recently, Marshall (1999), through a survey of group leaders, noted four important variables: acceptance and support (e.g., I can talk about mistakes and it is OK), play (e.g., we have a lot of fun), tolerance and enjoyment of primary process (e.g., when I could feel and act as dysfunctional as the client, the whole case turned around), and resolution of intergroup conflict (e.g., when we have our differences, we are able to talk about them).

DeLucia et al. (1989) presented a model for supervising co-leaders that was based on the developmental tasks proposed by a group stage model and that emphasized the parallel processes that occur in the development of the group and co-leader relationships. They suggested that for group leaders to facilitate the attainment of tasks by group members at each group stage, they must have first worked through those tasks as a dyad. For example, as group leaders learn how to give each other constructive feedback, they are more encouraging of similar behavior in their group members. Specifically, DeLucia et al. suggested,

> [The] stages of group process are parallel to stages of co-leadership development; thus, successful resolution of issues and tasks for the leaders result[s] in heightened ability to help group members resolve similar issues and facilitates movement through the stages of group development. Counselors are able to facilitate resolution of similar tasks with their clients to the extent they have addressed those tasks in the supervisory relationship. (p. 233)

DeLucia-Waack (2002) extended DeLucia et al.'s (1989) model with suggestions for facilitating the developmental tasks of each stage in supervision with group co-leaders. Supervision tasks and interventions are identified as the co-leader relationship progresses in supervision. Three major tasks for supervisors are identified for a new supervisory relationship: (1) revisit major sources of information about supervision and group leadership, (2) gather information about the specific type of group, and (3) examine the supervisor's specific beliefs, theoretical orientation, and expectations about supervision in order to be able to articulate these to new supervisees. According to DeLucia-Waack (2002), the middle stage of supervision is focused on the evaluation of the effectiveness of group interventions. Co-leaders reflect on what happens in group sessions in terms of critical events, interventions, leader and member reactions, and member progress in an effort to evaluate effective

leader behaviors, plan for future sessions, and explore new behaviors, interventions, and strategies. At this stage, case conceptualization, techniques and interventions, and personal reactions are the foci.

DeLucia-Waack (2002) suggested a format for each supervision session that allows time for discussion, planning, and processing. She included the following five steps: (1) *reporting* of what specifically happened in the last session in terms of critical events, member behavior, and leader interventions; (2) *reflection* on what happened in the last session, specifically in terms of what worked and what did not work and what produced emotional reactions from co-leaders and members; (3) *integration* of events in group sessions with theoretical perspectives on group stages, therapeutic factors, leader interventions, member psychosocial development, and progress toward member goals; (4) *planning* for what needs to happen in the next session in terms of content and process, group interventions, and interventions directed at specific members; and (5) *evaluation* of what was learned during the supervision session and how it will be applied. The format is postulated to provide structure and reduce anxiety for group leaders as well as to allow them to reflect on what was effective (and what was not), in order to plan for future group sessions. Conyne (1999) and Brown, Spenser, and Dlin (1990) have also suggested similar outlines for supervision sessions of group leaders.

Several authors have suggested formats for written notes used by co-leaders as part of the supervision process. DeLucia-Waack (2002) suggested the use of Planning and Processing Sheets to guide reflection on group sessions. Brown et al. (1990) suggested a similar schema, titled the Group Recording Form. Bloch, Brown, Davis, and Dishotsky (1975) also emphasized the use of a written summary of each group session, dictated by co-leaders as a narrative account of the meeting; its goal is to provide the supervisor with more time to focus on particularly striking elements of a group session, including critical process events, dynamics of patients, and intervention strategies. Aveline (1986) advocated the use of written reports in brief group psychotherapy training, focusing on the following questions: (1) What themes were present in the session? (2) How would these themes be tackled in the group? (3) How were these themes tackled by the leader? and (4) How were members involved in the session?

Evaluation of effectiveness. Although it is critical to evaluate the effectiveness of groups in terms of their ability to meet specific goals (e.g., decrease depression and anxiety, increase interpersonal skills), it is also essential to assess the process of the groups and how these contributed to group member learning and change. Assessment of process is valuable for two reasons. First, it adds to the body of knowledge related to therapeutic factors and effective leadership behaviors and group interventions. Second, it helps group members to understand how they can best learn and change and perhaps use such strategies in the future. DeLucia-Waack and Bridbord (2004) suggested several measures that may be useful in the evaluation process. The Skilled Group Counseling Scale (Smaby, Maddux, Torres-Rivera, & Zimmick, 1999) and the Trainer Behavior Scale (Bolman, 1971) can be used for group members to provide feedback about group leadership behaviors. The Group Climate Questionnaire–Short (MacKenzie, 1990) and the Group Environment Scale (Moos, 1986) assess group climate. The Critical Incidents Questionnaire (Kivlighan & Goldfine, 1991) and the Therapeutic Factors Inventory (Lese & McNair-Semands, 2000) can be used to assess the presence of therapeutic factors.

Processing

The final section of the "Best Practice Guidelines" (ASGW, 1998) refers to group processing, which is defined as "assessing progress on group and member goals; leader behaviors and techniques, group dynamics and interventions;

developing understanding and acceptance of meaning" (p. 243). Processing may occur within sessions, before and/or after sessions, at the end of group, and at follow-up with group members.

Processing to develop understanding and meaning. As stated earlier, one of the most common mistakes group leaders make is not to process an activity. Simply experiencing events in group is not sufficient for growth but must be augmented by processing to provide a framework for retaining, integrating, and generalizing the experience. Effective processing of critical incidents requires that members engage in a process of sharing and exploring among themselves to make sense of what happened, establish what they have learned from the incident, and begin to plan and practice new behaviors to be used outside of group sessions.

Several conceptual frameworks for group leaders to use to guide their processing of group events have been suggested. Kees and Jacobs (1990) identified three critical elements involved in processing activities: good questioning skills, advanced accurate empathy, and an awareness of the focus of the group with the ability to hold, shift, and deepen the focus. It is important to note, however, that the focus will differ according to the leadership and membership at any given point in time. Hammel (1986) divided processing skills into concrete (knowledge, comprehension, and application) or abstract (analysis, synthesis, and evaluation) thought processes. Concrete processing questions aim to review and describe events, feelings, thoughts, and problems. Abstract processing questions aim to identify patterns, make comparisons, relate learning to daily life, propose solutions, and examine values.

Stockton et al. (2000) created a conceptual map to provide general guidelines for effective processing. Specifically, they conceptualize processing into four stages that are interrelated: identifying critical incidents of importance to group members, examining the event and member reactions, deriving meaning and self-understanding from the event, and applying new understandings toward personal change. Some potential indicators of critical incidents include heightened emotional or behavioral reactions from group members, conflict in the group, emotional self-disclosure, or body language that suggests unspoken reaction to an event or activity. Stockton et al. suggest examining the event and member reactions in a here-and-now discussion by helping clarify reactions to critical incidents and encouraging members to address each other directly. Deriving meaning and self-understanding from the event involves helping group members apply the critical incident that occurred in group to their personal lives, interactions, and experiences. For example, a group member who has just challenged the leader may learn that despite his or her previous experience, authority figures will not respond with hostility but rather with empathy to questioning. Such insights that occur in the here-and-now of the group's life are often how real change begins to happen. Stockton et al. encourage group leaders to use feedback as a way of helping members see themselves as they are. Leaders also model giving and receiving feedback. Most important, when other members are not directly involved in the critical incident, it is important to engage them in a conversation in which they share their learning as a result of the incident. Finally, promoting change involves helping members apply what they have learned in the here-and-now interactions of group to their everyday lives. Stockton et al. also suggest several strategies for promoting change, including journaling, members' restating their goals and clarifying their learning, and role-playing.

Processing should be included from the outset of groups so that the leader(s) can model its significance and teach members how to facilitate it themselves. One of the goals of the group leader is to discourage the group's initial tendency to expect an authoritative leader and move the group toward a more dynamic interpersonal approach in which member-to-member interaction is encouraged. Examples of such activities include *looking*

at process (Brown, 2002), which encourages members to focus on group process while deciding on a get-acquainted activity, or *power line* (Comstock, 2002), which helps group members examine sources of privilege and/or marginalization in a person's life that impact an individual's sense of agency and relational mutuality, as well as how these experiences impact group dynamics.

Evaluation and follow-up. After the group is over, group leaders should provide an evaluation of the group, including a focus on both the process and outcomes. In the earlier section Evaluation of Effectiveness, assessment measures were suggested that would be useful after group ends and in subsequent follow-up evaluations. Results are used for ongoing program planning, to improve and revise current group, and/or to contribute to professional research literature. It is also important during follow-up sessions to establish if the group member needs additional help and support and to make appropriate referrals for further counseling.

Discussion and Conclusions

Much research has been conducted about counseling groups, but there is still much more to be known about how to effectively facilitate groups. Several considerations are important in leading effective counseling groups. First, sufficient training is needed in the type of group to be facilitated. ASGW provides specific guidelines for training and supervision of task, psychoeducational, counseling, and therapy groups (2000) as well as specific guidelines for diversity-competent group workers (1999) and best practices (1998).

Research has suggested that without supervision, group therapists were not able to identify mistakes and generate new plans of action; instead, they became stuck in a cycle of repeated ineffective interventions. Co-leadership is also recommended to use as a training tool and, in general, to enhance group effectiveness.

Group counseling has been shown to be effective with various populations, settings, and specific problem areas. Research clearly shows that group goals must be clearly defined; leaders require specific leadership training and skills and must take into consideration member expectations about group, willingness to participate, and cultural expectations and values when designing a group and implementing specific interventions.

References

American Counseling Association (ACA). (1997). *Code of ethics and standards of practice.* Alexandria, VA: Author.

Association for Specialists in Group Work (ASGW). (1998). Association for Specialists in Group Work: Best practice guidelines. *Journal for Specialists in Group Work, 23,* 237–244.

Association for Specialists in Group Work (ASGW). (1999). Association for Specialists in Group Work: Principals for diversity-competent group workers. *Journal for Specialists in Group Work, 24,* 7–14.

Association for Specialists in Group Work (ASGW). (2000). Association for Specialists in Group Work: Professional standards for the training of group workers. *Journal for Specialists in Group Work, 25,* 327–354.

Aveline, A. (1986). The use of written reports in a brief group psychotherapy training. *International Journal for Group Psychotherapy, 36,* 477–482.

Barlow, S. H., Fuhriman, A. J., & Burlingame, G. (2004). The history of group counseling and psychotherapy. In J. L. DeLucia-Waack, D. A. Gerrity, C. R. Kalodner, & M. T. Riva (Eds.), *Handbook of group counseling and psychotherapy* (pp. 3–22). Thousand Oaks, CA: Sage.

Bednar, R. L., & Kaul, T. K. (1994). Experiential group research: Can the cannon fire? In A. E. Bergin & S. L. Garfield (Eds.), *Handbook of psychotherapy and behavior change* (4th ed., pp. 631–663). New York: John Wiley.

Bernard, H. S., Drob, S. L., & Lifshutz, H. (1987). Compatibility between co-therapists: An empirical report. *Psychotherapy, 24,* 96–104.

Bloch, S., Brown, S., Davis, K., & Dishotsky, N. (1975). The use of a written summary in group psychotherapy supervision. *American Journal of Psychiatry, 132,* 1055–1057.

Bloch, S., & Crouch, E. (1985). *Therapeutic factors in psychotherapy.* Oxford, UK: Oxford University Press.

Bolman, L. (1971). Some effects of trainers on their T-groups. *Journal of Applied Behavioral Science, 7,* 309–325.

Bowman, V., & DeLucia, J. L. (1993). Preparation for group therapy: The effects of preparer and modality on group process and individual functioning. *Journal for Specialists in Group Work, 18,* 67–79.

Bridbord, K. H. (2002). Autobiography. In J. L. DeLucia-Waack, K. H. Bridbord, & J. S. Kleiner (Eds.), *Group work experts share their favorite activities: A guide to choosing, planning, conducting, and processing* (pp. 26–27). Alexandria, VA: Association for Specialists in Group Work.

Bridbord, K. H. (2003). *Co-therapy teams: The effect of personality, temperament, compatibility, and therapeutic/leadership style on co-therapy relationship satisfaction.* Unpublished doctoral dissertation, SUNY Buffalo.

Brown, B. (2002). Looking at process. In J. L. DeLucia-Waack, K. H. Bridbord, & J. S. Kleiner (Eds.), *Group work experts share their favorite activities: A guide to choosing, planning, conducting, and processing* (pp. 28–30). Alexandria, VA: Association for Specialists in Group Work.

Brown, R. A., Spenser, A., & Dlin, R. (1990). Formulation in groups, or understanding what is going on. *Group, 14*(2), 69–79.

Burlingame, G. M., & Fuhriman, A. (1994). Epilogue. In A. Fuhriman & G. M. Burlingame (Eds.), *Handbook of group psychotherapy: An empirical and clinical synthesis* (pp. 559–562). New York: John Wiley.

Burlingame, G. M., Fuhriman, A., & Johnson, J. E. (2001). Cohesion in group psychotherapy. *Psychotherapy, 38,* 373–379.

Carter, E. F., Mitchell, S. L., & Krautheim, M. D. (2001). Understanding and addressing clients' resistance to group counseling. *Journal for Specialists in Group Work, 26,* 66–80.

Christensen, T., & Kline, W. (2001). Anxiety as a condition for learning in group supervision. *Journal for Specialists in Group Work, 25,* 385–396.

Clifford, M. (2004). Group counseling and group therapy in mental health settings and health maintenance organizations. In J. L. DeLucia-Waack,

D. A. Gerrity, C. R. Kalodner, & M. T. Riva (Eds.), *Handbook of group counseling and psychotherapy* (pp. 414–426). Thousand Oaks, CA: Sage.

Coche, E., Dies, R. R., & Goettelman, K. (1991). Process variables mediating changes in intensive group therapy training. *International Journal of Group Psychotherapy, 41,* 279–397.

Comstock, D. (2002). Learning from the margin power line. In J. L. DeLucia-Waack, K. H. Bridbord, & J. S. Kleiner (Eds.), *Group work experts share their favorite activities: A guide to choosing, planning, conducting, and processing* (pp. 107–110). Alexandria, VA: Association of Specialists in Group Work.

Concannon, C. (1995). The senior-senior team. *Group, 19,* 71–78.

Conroy, K. (2002). Getting to know you—now and then. In J. L. DeLucia-Waack, K. H. Bridbord, & J. S. Kleiner (Eds.), *Group work experts share their favorite activities: A guide to choosing, planning, conducting, and processing* (pp. 31–34). Alexandria, VA: Association of Specialists in Group Work.

Conyne, R. (1999). *Failures in group work: How we can learn from our mistakes.* Thousand Oaks, CA: Sage.

Couch, R. D. (1995). Four steps for conducting a pre-group screening interview. *Journal for Specialists in Group Work, 20,* 18–25.

Dagley, J. C., Gazda, G. M., Eppinger, S. J., & Stewart, B. (1994). Group psychotherapy research with children, preadolescents, and adolescents. In A. Fuhriman & G. M. Burlingame (Eds.), *Handbook of group psychotherapy: An empirical and clinical synthesis* (pp. 340–369). New York: John Wiley.

DeLucia, J. L., Bowman, V. E., & Bowman, R. L. (1989). The use of parallel process in supervision and group counseling to facilitate counselor and client growth. *Journal for Specialists in Group Work, 14,* 232–238.

DeLucia-Waack, J. L. (1999). Supervision for counselors working with eating disorder groups: Countertransference issues related to body image, food, and weight. *Journal of Counseling and Development, 77,* 379–388.

DeLucia-Waack, J. L. (2001). *Using music in children of divorce groups: A session-by-session manual for counselors.* Alexandria, VA: American Counseling Association.

DeLucia-Waack, J. L. (2002). A written guide for planning and processing group sessions in anticipation of supervision. *Journal for Specialists in Group Work, 27,* 341–357.

DeLucia-Waack, J. L., & Bridbord, K. (2004). Measures of group process, dynamics, climate, leadership behaviors, and therapeutic factors: A review. In J. L. DeLucia-Waack, D. A. Gerrity, C. R. Kalodner, & M. T. Riva (Eds.), *Handbook of group counseling and psychotherapy* (pp. 120–135). Thousand Oaks, CA: Sage.

DeLucia-Waack, J. L., Gerrity, D. A., Kalodner, C. R., & Riva, M. T. (Eds.). (2004). *Handbook of group counseling and psychotherapy.* Thousand Oaks, CA: Sage.

Dies, R. R. (1994). Therapist variables in group psychology research. In A. Fuhriman & G. M. Burlingame (Eds.), *Handbook of group psychotherapy: An empirical and clinical synthesis* (pp. 114–154). New York: John Wiley.

Dubner, M. A. (1998). Envy in the group-therapy process. *International Journal of Group Psychotherapy, 48,* 519–531.

Dugo, J. M., & Beck, A. P. (1997). Significance and complexity of early phases in the development of the co-therapy relationship. *Group Dynamics: Theory, Research and Practice, 1,* 294–305.

Ebersole, G., Leiderman, P., & Yalom, I. D. (1969). Training the non-professional group therapist: A controlled study. *Journal of Nervous Mental Disorders, 149,* 294–302.

Emer, D. (2004). The use of groups in inpatient facilities: Needs, focus, successes, and remaining dilemmas. In J. L. DeLucia-Waack, D. A. Gerrity, C. R. Kalodner, & M. T. Riva (Eds.), *Handbook of group counseling and psychotherapy* (pp. 351–366). Thousand Oaks, CA: Sage.

Fleckenstein, L. B., & Horne, A. M. (2004). Anger management groups. In J. L. DeLucia-Waack, D. A. Gerrity, C. R. Kalodner, & M. T. Riva (Eds.), *Handbook of group counseling and psychotherapy* (pp. 547–562). Thousand Oaks, CA: Sage.

Flowers, J. V. (1979). Behavioral analysis of group therapy and a model for behavioral group therapy. In D. Upper & S. M. Ross (Eds.), *Behavioral group therapy: An annual review* (pp. 5–37). Champaign, IL: Research Press.

Gazda, G. M., Ginter, E. J., & Horne, A. M. (2001). *Group counseling and group psychotherapy: Theory and application.* Needham Heights, MA: Allyn & Bacon.

Hammel, H. (1986). How to design a debriefing session. *Journal of Experiential Education, 9,* 20–26.

Hines, P. L., Stockton, R., & Morran, D. K. (1995). Self-talk of group therapists. *Journal of Counseling Psychology, 42,* 242–248.

Hoag, M. J., & Burlingame, G. M. (1997). Evaluating the effectiveness of child and adolescent group treatment: A meta-analytic review. *Journal of Clinical Psychology, 26,* 234–246.

Johnson, V. M. (2002). Where in the world could I be? In J. L. DeLucia-Waack, K. H. Bridbord, & J. S. Kleiner (Eds.), *Group work experts share their favorite activities: A guide to choosing, planning, conducting, and processing* (pp. 162–163). Alexandria, VA: Association for Specialists in Group Work.

Kalodner, C. R., & Coughlin, J. (2004). Psycho-educational and counseling groups to prevent and treat eating disorders and disturbances. In J. L. DeLucia-Waack, D. A. Gerrity, C. R. Kalodner, & M. T. Riva (Eds.), *Handbook of group counseling and psychotherapy* (pp. 481–496). Thousand Oaks, CA: Sage.

Kees, N. L., & Jacobs, E. (1990). Working with groups: Conducting more effective groups: How to select and process group exercises. *Journal for Specialists in Group Work, 15,* 21–29.

Kew, C. E. (1975). A pilot study of an evaluation scale for group-psychotherapy patients. *ETS Test Collection (Set A)* (Tests in Microfiche No. 004944). Princeton, NJ: Educational Testing Services.

Kivlighan, D. M., Jr., & Goldfine, D. C. (1991). Endorsement of therapeutic factors as a function of stage of group development and participant interpersonal attitudes. *Journal of Counseling Psychology, 38,* 150–158.

Kivlighan, D. M. Jr., & Holmes, S. E. (2004). The importance of therapeutic factors: A typology of therapeutic factor studies. In J. L. DeLucia-Waack, D. A. Gerrity, C. R. Kalodner, & M. T. Riva (Eds.), *Handbook of group counseling and psychotherapy* (pp. 23–36). Thousand Oaks, CA: Sage.

Lese, K. P., & McNair-Semands, R. R. (2000). The Therapeutic Factors Inventory: Development of a scale. *Group, 24,* 303–317.

Leszcz, M., & Murphy, L. (1994). Supervision of group psychotherapy. In S. E. Greben & R. Ruskin (Eds.), *Clinical perspectives on psychotherapy supervision* (pp. 99–120). Washington, DC: American Psychiatric Press.

Lieberman, M. A., Yalom, I. D., & Miles, M. B. (1973). *Encounter groups: First facts.* New York: Basic Books.

MacKenzie, K. R. (1990). *Introduction to time-limited group therapy.* Washington, DC: American Psychiatric Press.

MacNair-Semands, R. R. (2002). Predicting attendance and expectations for group therapy. *Group Dynamics: Theory, Research, and Practice, 6,* 219–228.

Makuch, L. M. (1997). *Development and validation of the Leadership Characteristics Inventory.* Unpublished doctoral dissertation, Indiana University.

Marshall, R. J. (1999). Facilitating cooperation and creativity in group supervision. *Modern Psychoanalysis, 24,* 181–186.

McCallum, M., & Piper, W. E. (1990). A controlled study of effectiveness and patient suitability for short-term group psychotherapy. *International Journal of Group Psychotherapy, 40,* 431–452.

Moos, R. H. (1986). *Group environment scale manual.* Palo Alto, CA: Consulting Psychologists Press.

Morgan, R. D. (2004). Groups with offenders and mandated clients. In J. L. DeLucia-Waack, D. A. Gerrity, C. R. Kalodner, & M. T. Riva (Eds.), *Handbook of group counseling and psychotherapy* (pp. 388–400). Thousand Oaks, CA: Sage.

Morran, D. K., Robison, R. F., & Stockton, R. (1985). Feedback exchange in counseling groups: An analysis of message content and receiver acceptance as a function of leader versus member delivery, session and valence. *Journal of Counseling Psychology, 32,* 57–67.

Morran, D. K., Stockton, R., Cline, R. J., & Teed, C. (1998). Facilitating feedback exchange in groups: Leader interventions. *Journal for Specialists in Group Work, 23,* 257–268.

Morran, D. K., Stockton, R., & Whittingham, M. (2004). Effective leader interventions for counseling and therapy groups. In J. L. DeLucia-Waack, D. A. Gerrity, C. R. Kalodner, & M. T. Riva (Eds.), *Handbook of group counseling and psychotherapy* (pp. 3–22). Thousand Oaks, CA: Sage.

Page, B. J., & Hulse-Killacky, D. (1999). Development and validation of the corrective feedback self-efficacy instrument. *Journal for Specialists in Group Work, 24,* 37–54.

Paisley, P. (2002). The paper quilts. In J. L. DeLucia-Waack, K. H. Bridbord, & J. S. Kleiner (Eds.), *Group work experts share their favorite activities: A guide to choosing, planning, conducting, and processing* (pp. 164–165). Alexandria, VA: Association for Specialists in Group Work.

Pearlman, L. A., & Saakvitne, K. (1995). *Trauma and the therapist.* New York: Norton.

Pearson, M. J., & Girling, A. (1990). The value of the Claybury Selection Battery in predicting benefit from group psychotherapy. *British Journal of Psychiatry, 157,* 384–388.

Pfeiffer, J. W., & Jones, J. E. (1975). Co-facilitating. In J. W. Pfeiffer & J. E. Jones (Eds.), *The 1975 annual handbook for group facilitators* (pp. 219–225). Iowa City, IA: University Associates.

Piper, W. E., & McCallum, M. (1994). Selection of patients for group interventions. In H. S. Bernard & K. R. MacKenzie (Eds.), *Basics of group psychotherapy* (pp. 1–34). New York: Guilford.

Prout, S. M., & Prout, H. (1998). A meta-analysis of school-based studies of psychotherapy. *Journal of School Psychology, 36,* 121–136.

Riva, M. T., & Cornish, J. A. E. (1995). Group supervision practices at psychology predoctoral internship programs: A national survey. *Professional Psychology: Research & Practice, 26,* 523–525.

Riva, M., & Haub, A. (2004). Group counseling in the schools. In J. L. DeLucia-Waack, D. A. Gerrity, C. R. Kalodner, & M. T. Riva (Eds.), *Handbook of group counseling and psychotherapy* (pp. 309–321). Thousand Oaks, CA: Sage.

Riva, M. T., Lippert, L., & Tackett, M. J. (2000). Selection practices of group leaders: A national survey. *Journal for Specialists in Group Work, 25,* 157–169.

Riva, M. T., & Smith, R. D. (1997). Looking into the future of group research: Where do we go from here? *Journal for Specialists in Group Work, 22,* 266–276.

Riva, M. T., Wachtel, M., & Lasky, G. B. (2004). Effective leadership in group counseling and psychotherapy. In J. L. DeLucia-Waack, D. A. Gerrity, C. R. Kalodner, & M. T. Riva (Eds.), *Handbook of group counseling and psychotherapy* (pp. 37–48). Thousand Oaks, CA: Sage.

Roback, H. (1984). *Helping patients and their families cope with medical problems.* San Francisco: Jossey-Bass.

Roller, B., & Nelson, V. (1991). *The art of co-therapy: How the therapists work together.* New York: Guilford.

Slocum, Y. S. (1987). A survey of expectations about group therapy among clinical and non-clinical populations. *International Journal of Group Psychotherapy, 37,* 39–54.

Smaby, M. H., Maddux, C. D., Torres-Rivera, E., & Zimmick, R. (1999). A study of the effects of a skills-based versus a conventional group counseling training program. *Journal for Specialists in Group Work, 24,* 152–163.

Smead, R. (1995). *Skills and techniques for group work with children and adolescents.* Champaign, IL: Research Press.

Spira, J. L. (1997). *Group therapy for medically ill patients.* New York: Guilford.

Stockton, R. (Producer/Director). (1996). *Developmental aspects of group work* (Motion picture). Alexandria, VA: Association for Specialists in Group Work.

Stockton, R., Morran, D. K., & Nitza, A. G. (2000). Processing group events: A conceptual map for leaders. *Journal for Specialists in Group Work, 25,* 343–355.

Stockton, R., Rohde, R. I., & Haughey, J. (1992). The effects of structured group exercises on cohesion, engagement, avoidance, and conflict. *Small Group Research, 23,* 1555–1568.

Stone, M. H., Lewis, C. M., & Beck, A. P. (1994). The structure of Yalom's Curative Factors Scale. *International Journal of Group Psychotherapy, 44,* 239–245.

Wheelan, S. A. (2004). Groups in the workplace. In J. L. DeLucia-Waack, D. A. Gerrity, C. R. Kalodner, & M. T. Riva (Eds.), *Handbook of group counseling and psychotherapy* (pp. 401–413). Thousand Oaks, CA: Sage.

Wilson, F. R. (2002). Feedback as poetry. In J. L. DeLucia-Waack, K. H. Bridbord, & J. S. Kleiner (Eds.), *Group work experts share their favorite activities: A guide to choosing, planning, conducting, and processing* (pp. 167–171). Alexandria, VA: Association of Specialists in Group Work.

Yalom, I. D. (1975). *The theory and practice of group psychotherapy* (2nd ed.). New York: Basic Books.

Yalom, I. D. (1985). *The theory and practice of group psychotherapy* (3rd ed.). New York: Basic Books.

Yalom, I. D. (1995). *The theory and practice of group psychotherapy* (4th ed.). New York: Basic Books.

PART II

Theoretical Perspectives on Groups

5

The Psychoanalytic Perspective

Marvin H. Geller

Those not familiar with the extensive body of psychoanalytic thinking devoted to the understanding of groups and organizations might wonder how a psychology historically focused on the study of individuals has much relevance for the study of groups. I hope that by the end of this chapter, readers will come to understand and appreciate what the psychoanalytic perspective, or more accurately perspectives, have to offer to the study of both groups (large and small) and organizational life in general.

Because psychoanalytic thinking comprises multiple schools, the first question to be addressed is what is meant by the psychoanalytic perspective of groups. Psychoanalytic thinking itself is in flux, with much of its basic theory (metapsychology) in serious question. Classical Freudian drive theory, applied by Freud to his own thinking about groups, gave way to ego psychology in the 1950s. This was followed by the emergence of the British object-relations school, with a strong focus on the theories of Melanie Klein, theories used by Bion in his theoretical

work on group dynamics. In America, the development of ego psychology and Sullivan's interpersonal school were followed by Kohut's self-psychology and the intersubjective perspective. Practitioners and theorists of each of these points of view have applied a particular psychoanalytic perspective to thinking about groups and their dynamics, each emphasizing different aspects of human development and motivation.

Aside from thinking about the various schools' emphasis on different aspects of development and motivation, we also must consider how a shift in focus from intra- to intersubjective psychology in psychoanalysis informs the psychoanalytic perspective on group dynamics. Freud's traditional drive theory is a "one-person" psychology, positing that individuals relate to others to satisfy intrinsic or basic instinctual needs. The object-relations, interpersonal, and intersubjective perspectives are "two-person" psychologies where human development is seen as occurring in a matrix of relationships with others, that matrix itself being embedded in the matrix of society and culture.

An added complexity, aside from integrating the multiple psychoanalytic perspectives, is the challenge to psychoanalysis itself. Psychoanalysis, especially its metapsychology, has been challenged from both postmodern and hermeneutical perspectives. In addition to these challenges, there is a muddle in conceptual clarity that exists because of the proliferation of the many schools of psychoanalysis. Despite these challenges and the questions that they raise, questions well beyond the scope of this chapter, we can think of the variety of psychoanalytic perspectives as lenses, lenses through which we can explore and examine group behavior and dynamics. Given the variety of views, we need to find a common thread that runs through all of them, a thread that can be considered the core that differentiates psychoanalytic from nonpsychoanalytic perspectives. Within this multiplicity of perspectives, there is a common theme. The theme relates to the view of people as both rational and irrational, driven by unconscious thoughts, feelings, and fantasies that stir deep fears and anxieties. These fears and anxieties in turn evoke a variety of defense mechanisms. Thus, unconscious processes (processes that are irrational or in conflict with accepted individual or collective norms and values) and the defenses against them are at the core of every psychoanalytic perspective. Transference and countertransference feelings and thoughts are the primary mechanisms through which our unconscious processes and defenses can be made conscious. These fundamental concepts, common to the various schools, provide the basis for the psychoanalytic study of groups.

What Is the Psychoanalytic Perspective?

Eisold (1995), exploring the current state of psychoanalysis and its implications for studying group and organizational behavior in general, believes that the future unifying factor and focus in psychoanalytic thinking will be "the domain of irrational behavior that cannot be accounted for by consciously understood motives, the domain of the unconscious" (p. 13). Mechanisms such as projective identification, displacements, transference, and basic assumption behaviors are concepts that allow us to explore more deeply irrational "behaviors that put us at cross purposes with our conscious articulated goals, whether in the realms of personal relationships or work" (p. 11). Hunt and McCollum (1994), writing about the use of psychoanalytic theory in organizational studies, sum the issue up by stating that "we will take as a starting point the idea that psychoanalytically grounded organizational consultation has as one of its goals the illumination of unconscious processes" (p. 2).

Freud brought his psychoanalytic perspective to the study of groups. In his classic study, *Group Psychology and the Analysis of the Ego*, Freud (1959) took the position that there was no real dichotomy between individual and group psychology. He said,

In the individual's mental life someone else is invariably involved, as a model, as an object, as a helper, as an opponent, and so from the very first individual psychology, in this extended but entirely justifiable sense of the word, is at the same time social psychology as well. (p. 1)

Scheidlinger (1980) labeled Freud's treatise an "armchair essay," speculating that Freud's work on groups was kindled by a desire to develop his concept of the ego-ideal rather than by his intrinsic interest in group dynamics. Others, including Roth (1991), have speculated that the motivation behind Freud's group essay was related to his direct experience with the complex group dynamics that emerged in his own Psychoanalytic Society Group in Vienna. My perception of the driving force in Freud's essay was his desire to use psychoanalytic theory to explain the changes that occurred in individuals "when they entered or became under the influence of a psychological group other than family or those closely connected to them" (Freud, 1959, p. 7). Freud was impressed with LeBon's (1895/1960) graphic description of crowd or mob behavior. In it, he saw the opportunity to affirm his notion of the unconscious and his belief that beneath the surface of civility and rationality lie more primitive irrational forces. Freud also saw an opportunity to deepen LeBon's limited explanations of the forces that led rational individuals to behave as they did in a crowd or mob. It was an opportunity to use both libido theory and oedipal dynamics to explain the observed behavior in psychoanalytic terms.

Freud (1959) thought that LeBon's "brilliant" description of group behavior underscored its primitive, irrational, childlike, and neurotic character, which contained many of the features of Freud's concept of *primary process thinking*, in contrast to the more rational, ego-dominated *secondary process thinking*. In summing up his feelings about LeBon's work, Freud says, "we have made use of LeBon's description by way of introduction because it fits in so well with our own psychology in the emphasis it lays upon unconscious mental life" (p. 14).

Freud (1959) felt certain that there were group dynamics other than those postulated by LeBon that needed to be understood in order to explain the changes that occurred in individuals when they became group members. Freud hypothesized that in a *primary group*, each member surrenders his ego-ideal (projects it) onto the idealized leader, who loves all group members equally. The common bond created when each member projects his ideal onto the same person ties the group members together. The definition of a primary group "is a number of individuals who have put one and the same object in the place of their ego-ideal and have consequently identified themselves with one another in their ego" (Freud, 1959, p. 48). As to the question of why individuals would do this, Freud replaces LeBon's concept of "suggestibility" with his own concept of libido and Eros. He says, "a group is clearly held together by a power of some kind and to what power could this feat

be better ascribed than to Eros, which holds together everything in the world" (p. 24). Freud emphasizes, as Bion did later, the need to belong or to be part of something as a core dynamic in the human psyche. Freud goes on to say,

> If an individual gives up his distinctiveness in a group or lets its members influence him by suggestion, it gives the impression that he does it because he feels the need of being in harmony with them rather than in opposition to them—so perhaps after all he does it *ihnen zu liebe* (for love of them). (p. 25)

In his essay on groups, Freud (1959) portrays the individual as a rational being who reverts to primary process thinking when in the thrall of group process. For Freud, it is *organization* that allows the group to regain its rationality. At this point in his thinking, he does not believe groups are capable of creatively solving problems in the way that individuals can. Individuals alone make great contributions; Freud does not see the fact that even the individual, functioning alone, is in some fashion linked to the group of other thinkers.

Underpinning Freud's (1959) work is the issue that runs through all psychoanalytic perspectives of group dynamics; beneath the surface rationality of groups lies the inevitable irrationality, which can be made rational by leadership, task, and structure. The theme of groups oscillating between the rational and irrational will be more clearly explicated by the work of Wilfred Bion through his concepts of *work group* and *basic assumption group* mentalities.

Bion's (1961) work is also considered to be a major theoretical advance in applying psychoanalytic theory to groups. Bion, a British psychoanalyst and an analysand of Melanie Klein, brought the Kleinian object-relations perspective to his thinking about groups. His initial observations and subsequent theory were developed from his work with therapy groups during and after World War II at Northfield Army

Hospital. Bion uses Kleinian object-relations theories to help illuminate the "obscurities" inherent in group dynamics. In contrast to Freud's perspective, Klein's view in psychoanalytic parlance is referred to as *pre-oedipal*, meaning that its focus on psychic development emphasizes early mother-child dynamics in contrast to Freud's oedipal focus.

Reading Klein's (1948) work requires us to imagine a newly born infant with limited developmental capacity, trying to cope with frustrations, inner destructive impulses, and a potentially comforting breast (concretely and symbolically) that comes and goes and that may be experienced as either good or bad. Klein calls this chaotic, psychotic-like world the *paranoid-schizoid position*. It is a position where the defenses of splitting, projection, and introjection dominate existence. As infants develop and mature, with the aid of a reliable environment, they can move into the more stable *depressive position*. However, under threatening and frustrating circumstances, people may vacillate between the two positions and can fall back into the earlier state. In fact, Klein holds that even as adults, under circumstances of deep distress and frustration, we are vulnerable to experiencing the paranoid-schizoid position, a frightening, disorganizing state.

This early paranoid-schizoid state is the core from which Bion (1961) builds his theory of group dynamics, using his observations of a small therapy group. He writes

> I hope to show that in his contact with the complexities of life in the group the adult resorts, in what may be a massive regression, to a mechanism described by Melanie Klein as typical of the earliest phases of mental life. The adult must establish contact with the emotional life of the group in which he lives; this task would appear to be as formidable to the adult as the relationship with the breast appears to be to the infant, and the failure to meet the demands of the task is revealed in his regression. The

belief that a group exists as distinct from an aggregate of individuals, is an essential part of the regression, as are also the characteristics with which the supposed group is endowed by the individual. (p. 175)

For Bion, group is "mother," before mother was experienced as a separate and whole person, distinct from self. Groups are inherently frustrating because the individual wants to belong and find need satisfaction, while at the same time primitive fears aroused by the group inhibit efforts to do so.

Bion's (1961) work on groups is perhaps best known because of his dual concepts of work group and basic assumption group life. The work group (any group of individuals meeting together for work) shows mental activity designed to further the task of the group. The work group can mobilize its resources, relate to external realities, think clearly, and make decisions. In basic psychoanalytic terms, this is the ego-function. At the same time as work is going on, basic assumption life exists and can break through and obstruct or derail the work mentality of the group. Bion identified three basic assumptions: BAd (dependency), BAf (fight-flight), and BAp (pairing). Basic assumption mentality is opposite from work mentality. In the basic assumption group, there is no belief in work; problems aren't solved through investigation; and planning, thought, and learning are not possible. In the dependency state, the group behaves as if it is bereft of needed support and nourishment, which can only be provided by the leader. In the fight-flight state, the group operates as if there is a danger that needs to be engaged or fled from. In the pairing frame of mind, the group is hopeful with the feeling of well-being stimulated by the fantasy that a pair will emerge to bring new life and hope to the group.

Basic assumption is a group state of mind. It is instantaneous and instinctive, making no demands on the individual for cooperation. Basic assumption life depends on an individual's valency (i.e., a capacity for the instantaneous involuntary combining of one individual with another for sharing and acting on basic assumptions). Basic assumption phenomena, as Bion (1961) perceives them, are defenses against the deep-seated fear of the psychotic anxieties of the paranoid-schizoid state, which are always unconsciously experienced as a potential threat. The emergence of basic assumption phenomena must mean that something in the life of the group is arousing underlying anxiety, even if it is not experienced directly or consciously. Bion's conceptualization of the group has given us a "binocular vision," which keeps one eye on the surface and the other at the unity under the surface, where the need to belong is crucial and members try to find a common method of defending against their anxieties. Bion is implying that we are dealing not with two different kinds of groups but rather with two different states of mental activity coexisting in the same group.

Bion's (1961) concept of basic assumption life is predicated on the notion of defensive splitting and the projective identification that follows splitting. Both concepts are crucial to our understanding of group formation. Freud understood these defensive processes when he suggested that in the formation of groups, each group member projects his ego-ideal into the leader. For Bion, each member of the group is subject to projective identifications from every other member, and the leader becomes the focus of projections from all the members.

Bion (1961) is in touch with how difficult it is for individuals in groups to relate to one another in a consistently productive way. He sees human beings as group animals who cannot do without the group but who also have trouble getting along within the group. Despite this dilemma, people must find a way to establish cooperation in the joint pursuit of a task. Understanding this basic dilemma and the anxieties associated with it is essential to working with groups from a psychoanalytic perspective. This understanding allows us to make sense of group tensions and difficulties so that they may be ameliorated, clearing the way for group goals to be accomplished. In contrast to Freud, Bion believes that groups have creative capacity and that by bringing to awareness the existence of underlying basic assumptions, the group may be able to resume its work state. However, bringing basic assumption life to awareness will not permanently prevent it from emerging again because groups will always vacillate between work and basic assumption mentalities.

To What Kind of Groups Does This Perspective Apply?

Psychoanalytic perspectives have been applied to a broad range of group settings and structures. Freud applied his theoretical perspective to groups in general, as well as major institutions (i.e., the military and the church). Bion's theoretical advances stem from work with small face-to-face psychotherapy groups—groups with a psychotherapist in the role of leader. The object-relations, interpersonal, intersubjective, and self-psychological approaches have all been extensively applied to the area of group psychotherapy (e.g., Nitsun, 1996; Scheidlinger, 1980; Titman, 1991). Analytic group therapists have used concepts from these perspectives to help them compose groups, to guide the way they take up their therapeutic role, to shape their interpretations, and to develop insights about group process that will be illuminating and healing for members.

At the Tavistock Institute of Human Relations in London following World War II, a group of psychoanalysts and social scientists began working systematically at applying both psychoanalytic (primarily Bion's work) and social systems concepts to the study of organizations. A major outgrowth of these approaches to consulting with organizations was the group relations training program (GRTP), which is described in detail by A. K. Rice (1965) in his book, *Learning for Leadership*. These training events provided people working in organizations with the opportunity to study the dynamics of small groups, large groups, intergroups, and institutions as a whole in a context that more readily allowed the unconscious irrational aspects of group life to emerge. In a minimally structured setting, members had the opportunity to experience more clearly those dynamic factors that underlie life in all groups but are less visible when task, structure, and leadership are present. GRTP was introduced in the United States in 1965 under the leadership and guidance of Margaret J. Rioch. In 1970, the A. K. Rice Institute was started, and it has grown and continued to flourish with numerous centers in this country and around the world (functioning under different names), all devoted to the study of group relations from both a psychoanalytic and a systems theory perspective. For basic theoretical and practical writings related to this work, see Colman and Bexton's (1975) *Group Relations Reader* and Colman and Geller's (1985) *Group Relations Reader 2.*

The post–World War II work, begun at Tavistock, of applying social systems and psychoanalytic theory to the study of groups and organizations has attracted a steady stream of scholars and practitioners who apply these perspectives to their work. For basic writings in the area, see Obholzer and Roberts (1994) as well as the collection of papers edited by Gabriel (1999). In 1990, the International Society for the Psychoanalytic Study of Organizations (ISPSO) was started by a group of scholars and practitioners devoted to advancing the impact of psychoanalytic theory in the area of organizational studies. This group has grown significantly, and its members work at applying psychoanalytic thinking to a wide variety of organizations and organizational issues.

While Bion's theoretical advances stemmed from his work with small psychotherapy groups, his ideas have been expanded to groups of varying sizes (large and small) as well as to organizations with varied tasks or functions. In fact, Bion (1961) himself argued that group phenomena (unconscious, irrational basic assumption life) existed in society at large. However, he recognized that a group could become so large that one could no longer make cogent observations about the existence of basic assumption life. Therefore, Bion was concerned with what constitutes an "intelligible field of study," and although he was intrigued with the issue of how society as a whole manages basic assumption life, he never pursued this line of discourse.

Robert Gosling (1985) studied the "very small group" (groups of no more than four individuals) by applying Bion's theoretical perspective to try to ferret out some unique dynamics of groups of that size. Operating from the same frame of reference and similar context, Turquet (1975) wrote a paper titled "Threats to Identity in the Large Group." Turquet says that he "seeks to describe a consultant's personal experience of working with groups of 40–80 people, and attempts to explicate some of the phenomena which lie behind the structures usually deployed in such groups, such as chairman, rules and procedures, and fixed topics for debate" (p. 87). Turquet focuses on the underlying vulnerability of individuals in a large group and their attempts both to be in the group and to maintain a sense of individual self in comparison with other individuals. Members of such a group are always managing the tension and terror of identity loss.

Finally, we can speculate that the psychoanalytic perspective is applicable to all groups, including society at large. Khaleelee and Miller (2000) explore the expansion of Bion's (1961) observations to large groups, within a group relations training model. They conclude that the unconscious dynamics explicated by Bion in small groups also render the large group an "intelligible field of study." In fact, an underlying hypothesis about small group behavior in general is that it can be a microcosm of society at large. Khaleelee and Miller agree that a group of 1,000 (for example) would probably not be a viable field of study; however, the authors do feel that extrapolation from small groups to society at large is possible. They state, "By defining a task boundary, it is possible to evoke, experience and observe societal dynamics in a group of 10–12. Society is present in the group; society and the group are present in the individual" (p. 381). I believe this sentiment is a core belief held by those working with groups and organizations, especially from the psychoanalytic perspective put forth by Bion.

The Individual and the Group

Freud acknowledged, despite his emphasis on individual psychology, that man is a social animal reared in a group setting, the family. He was reluctant, however, to posit a basic irreducible group instinct as he had done with sex and aggression. He preferred to think of our "groupishness" as a derivative of our early family life. Freud did not generally attend to the complex interweaving of individual and group identities. Instead, he focused on the question of how individuals' rational thinking and moral concerns could be diminished through their mutual identification with a leader and the sense of unity this identification provides. Basically, he believed that the group diminished both an individual's ego and super-ego functioning. It was the structure, task, and leadership of an organized group that countered this regression, helping the group to behave more rationally (ego-oriented).

Bion (1961) stated that there is a psychology of the group, but its origins lie solely with the individuals in the group. The existence of the group evokes *group psychology*. The group is an illusion of the individuals, and the group created by this illusion has effects on individuals so that they are then under the thrall of group psychology. In the same vein, Menzies Lyth (1989), paraphrasing Fenichel's (1946) work, says that he believes "social institutions arise through the efforts of human beings to satisfy their needs, but then become external realities comparatively independent of individuals that nevertheless affect the structure of the individual" (p. 26). For Menzies Lyth, this is a profound statement because it underscores that institutions, once established, can be very difficult to change in their essentials but, no matter their impact (positive or negative), can have a crucial effect on the personality of the individual. From this perspective, change in the individual may well be contingent on change in the institution or group.

Bion's (1961) observation of the nature of work group and basic assumption mentality provides a lens for exploring the complex boundary between the individual and the group. In his work with psychotherapy groups, Bion became aware of a common group mentality, the basic assumptions, that seemed to belong to the group-as-a-whole. All members were defending against the underlying anxieties generated by their effort to make emotional contact with the group and get their needs met. Bion said, "the individual is a group animal at war not simply with the group, but with himself for being a group animal and with those aspects of his personality that constitute his 'groupishness'" (p. 149).

For Bion (1961), groups arouse primitive fears and wishes that foster regression, while the group-as-a-whole stirs archaic fantasies about the contents of mother's body: the "group as mother." It is essential to remember that the anxieties leading to basic assumption mentality exist not only in unorganized or therapy groups but also in highly functioning work groups as well; the work group itself is suffused with basic assumption elements.

Bion's (1961) concept of *valency* helps explore the interaction and relationship between the individual and the group. Valency is conceived of as an individual's tendency to combine with other group members to establish or maintain a given basic assumption. It is a relatively stable aspect of personality that leads individuals to react in a given way to a particular group situation. For example, a group moving into a fight-flight pattern is unconsciously in search of a leader who will lead it in that direction. The individual or individuals who are selected or volunteer for the role would be those members whose valency is such that they respond themselves to the fight-flight modality. That person can then carry the fight-flight energy for the group as a whole, allowing those who either cannot mobilize that part of themselves, or are frightened of it, to be passively represented. Each individual in the group, each with his or her own special valency, can be considered a resource to be used when his or her valency fits the needed emotional role. (Just as during its work mentality phase, the group can call on individuals with special skills to help in the accomplishment of task activity.)

Projective identification is a core conceptual tool used to help us understand the complex relationship between the individual and the group. The process starts with one person projecting (out of awareness) a part of him- or herself into others. In a completed projective identification, the target of the projection is, in a sense, captured by the projected material and may behave in ways that do not feel ego-syntonic or characteristic. It is most probable that the basic assumptions of Bion's theory, or the *common group tension* described by Ezriel (1980), which suffuse all group members, come about through the mechanism of projective identification, with each member having the capacity to put certain mental contents into other members.

The nature of the relation between the individual and the group is the topic of an ongoing discussion in the analytic group psychotherapy literature. Historically, there has been tension between those who have held to the importance of focusing on individuals in the group and those who have emphasized what is called the group-as-a-whole approach. According to Ettin (2000), this term was first coined by Trigant Burrow (1928), who recommended "the analysis of the immediate group in the immediate moment" (Burrow, p. 120). Currently, a perspective that emphasizes both the individual and the group-as-a-whole has gained major currency.

The question of the relation between the individual and the group is best summarized by the title of an article published by Malcolm Pines (1998): "The Self as a Group: The Group as a Self." In this article, Pines emphasizes the aspect of identity that is formed in the crucible of the social (family, culture, religion, politics, etc.) and the intertwined boundaries where group and self shade into one another. He says, "If we grasp the complexity of the individual both constituted from and functioning as a group, it becomes less problematic to look at the contrasting notion of the 'group as a self'" (p. 25). It is the individual in the group and the group in the individual that captures the imagination of current psychoanalytic thinkers.

This perspective implies that an individual expressing a feeling, perhaps anger at the leader, a member, or the state of the group, is speaking not only for him- or herself but is representing group feelings or thoughts. Feelings and thoughts that may not be consciously experienced by the group are being projected into an individual or subgroup. In fact, this may escalate to the point where the group wants to expel the angry member, believing this will free the group of angry feelings. Experience shows, however, that extrusion of one scapegoat (Scheidlinger, 1980) typically leads to the emergence of another because at least some members have not yet discovered the underlying unconscious dynamic. However, if a consultant or a therapist can offer an interpretation or some data that results in some members' finding their own negative feelings, then there is a high probability that the member identified as "the angry one" may be freed of feelings he or she may be carrying for the group.

Speaking to this issue, Ettin (2000) says

To locate responsibility for a group event in the therapist creates a dependent or counterdependent culture. To locate responsibility in a lone member creates a hero or a villain. In either case, the group itself is disempowered when the membership-at-large fails to acknowledge its active and vicarious contribution or collusions. Recognition of the nature of one's personal investment in a group is necessary in the reclamation of projections and the reintegration of disowned parts, as a step toward group and self-transformation. (p. 142)

This quotation expresses what I believe is the essential idea concerning the individual/group relationship. If either individuals or groups are to make desired changes, the group must come to see that there exists a group-as-a-whole dynamic in which each individual, either consciously or unconsciously, has a part that must be acknowledged and retrieved in order for growth to occur. Both Fenichel (1946) and Menzies Lyth (1989) emphasize how the individual and group impact one another to foster change. For example, the primary task of group psychotherapy is individual change through the medium of the group. Change may occur as the evolving group culture becomes independent of the individuals, but the created culture now impacts and transforms those individuals. Thus, the culture must be a constructive one in the sense that it leads to productive individual change. If it is not constructive, then the culture needs to be modified—a difficult task—to be therapeutic to the individual.

In the world of group and organizational behavior, the issue of the individual in the group is a vital concern in diagnosing and shaping change strategies. From the group-as-a-whole perspective, psychoanalytically oriented organizational consultants attend closely to individuals or subgroups in an organization that may be carrying or expressing larger group or institutional issues; issues not owned or expressed by the organization. If an individual or subgroup continues to be seen as the sole cause of the dysfunction, it is unlikely that any genuine transformation will occur.

An objection to the group-as-a-whole perspective is that, at its extreme, it appears to eliminate the notion of individual independent action or responsibility. If an individual, even one who has the appropriate valency for a given dysfunctional behavior, is always at some level acting on behalf of the group, then how do we ever hold any individual responsible? Although, for the most part, those theorists and practitioners holding the group-as-a-whole perspective always struggle to find the group or organizational issue in the individual, they also pay special attention to the power of the individual, especially the individual or individuals in the leadership role or roles.

Kets de Vries and Miller (1984), for example, a proponent of the group-as-a-whole perspective, place strong emphasis on the impact that the personality of the leader can have on the organization, as a whole. They write

> Corporate executives, like the rest of us, are not always rational beings; they may be driven by emotions, aspirations, or fantasies that influence the way they run their companies on a day-to-day basis. [Leaders' irrational feelings] can infiltrate the entire corporate culture and management structure . . . leading to effective organizations losing their way and becoming dysfunctional. (p. xiv)

Kernberg (1985), focusing on the regressive processes in groups and organizations, which includes the group-as-a-whole perspective, also holds as a core issue to his approach to studying organizations "a psychoanalytic focus on the personality features of the leader" (p. 90). It is the movement between the group-as-a-whole perspective and the individual perspective that Kernberg feels provides the most powerful lens with which to understand organizational difficulties and to help bring about the needed change. Even from a group-as-a-whole perspective, where a leader's difficulties can be viewed as an expression of organizational issues projected into him or her compromising ability to function, it is also acknowledged that the leader may be the primary cause of the organization's difficulty.

In conclusion, it is clear that the group-as-a-whole perspective is a core concept for those theorists and practitioners who operate within a psychoanalytic framework. It is a firmly held perception that groups use individuals to express unconscious elements of group life through mechanisms like projective identification. The individual member who at any given time is being shaped by the group to carry a needed role is not selected on a random basis. Some aspect of that individual's personality makes him or her a good candidate for a given role. However, the potential power of a "completed projective identification" can make the selected individual feel that he or she is behaving in a fashion not consonant with who she or he is. Often, the goodness of fit makes it easier for others to project and disown their unwanted parts, making it more difficult for the group to acknowledge its projections. Although we have pointed to the powerful influence the individual leader can have, it is equally important to attend to the interaction between leaders and the led.

Group Culture and Structure

In large part, the interest in group and organizational culture, from both a research and a pragmatic perspective, seems to have emerged as a field of study as a reaction to the pre-1990s success of Japanese corporations. At that time, there was a focus on the values inherent in Japanese society that worked to bind workers' allegiance, increase worker satisfaction, and as a result increase efficiency and profitability. These ideas about Japanese culture led us to study our own corporate cultures.

In the broader organizational studies literature related to culture, efforts were made to categorize different types of culture, to understand their origins, and to discover how organizations

maintained and transmitted culture. Much of this work was aimed at an underlying search for a "magic bullet." This magic bullet would create a better culture, one capable of transforming organizations and groups into satisfied, successful, and effectively functioning organizations, as their culture apparently did for Japanese groups and organizations.

Although the study of group and organizational culture did not produce the sure-fire recipe for corporate success, it did shed light on organizations as living, breathing organisms. Different from families, crowds, or mobs, but like all gatherings of human beings into some group form, organizations were filled with tensions, conflicts, and irrational dynamics that often interfered with their stated tasks and goals. The psychoanalytic perspective, however, did not emerge from an effort to find an ideal structure or culture. Instead, psychoanalytic thinking, as it frequently does, started from the dysfunctional and worked toward an understanding of that dysfunction. It sought to understand how dysfunctional structures and cultures form, maintain themselves, and interfere with the espoused goal of the group or organization. Clearly, this search is not to reveal the ideal but to uncover the covert and unconscious dynamics in order to help generate a change strategy.

The psychoanalytic view takes as a basic assumption that all organizations and groups are driven by multiple dynamics existing at multiple levels (overt or covert, conscious or unconscious). Group culture and structure are shaped by leadership style and personality, task demands, risk factors, and environmental contexts. The interaction of these elements, alongside of observable cultural structures, norms, and values, creates underlying dynamics—dynamics that can be uncovered by attending to the meaning of the spoken, the unspoken, the symbols, stories, and myths that abound in any organization.

The impact of leadership style and personality on organizational culture and structure has received a good deal of attention by psychoanalytic writers. Kernberg (1985) writes explicitly about the positive or negative impact that varying kinds of character styles and pathology in a leader has on organizational culture and functioning. For example, obsessive features in a leader may have the positive effect of creating a culture and structures that emphasize "orderliness, precision, clarity, and control, which may foster good, stable delegation of authority and clarity in the decision making process" (p. 97). This can lead to an organization that functions well, with high morale and efficiency, where clarity and decisiveness are encouraged and rewarded. However, serious problems may also be created by some obsessive personalities, especially those "with unconscious unresolved sadism," often an underlying issue in obsessive personalities. These leaders may "need to sadistically control subordinates which may have devastating effects on the functional structure of the organization" (p. 98). The end result of this dynamic, as Kernberg sees it, could be the development of a "chronic passivity, a pseudo-dependency derived from a fear of authority rather than from an authentic 'dependent group'" (p. 99). In this environment, authoritarian and dictatorial methods of dealing with staff are likely to run throughout the entire organization. Cooperation will be based on fear rather than on commitment to task or positive feelings about the organization. Stories will abound, myths will develop, and new employees will soon learn how the organization functions. Kernberg discusses other personality types and how they impact the group or organizational structure and culture. For example, narcissistic leadership is a key concern because narcissistic people are often drawn to positions of power and authority as a way of bolstering their self-esteem by finding continuous sources of admiration and approval.

An example of Kernberg's perspective was apparent in his consultation to a firm that had as its stated goal the desire to engage in a "re-engineering project." It quickly became clear through meetings, interviews, and reading of reports and memos that he was dealing with a culture very much dominated by an authoritarian, obsessive, blame-avoidant leadership style that created fear and pseudo-compliance throughout the organization. Efforts at establishing a new computer system with an "open architecture" were actually being covertly sabotaged out of both rebellion and fear. Although the overt reason for the system change was to increase organizational transparency, enabling a more effective work environment, workers at all levels believed that the "boss" wanted to have data with which to threaten and intimidate them. This culture was deeply embedded. A statement the leader made about his management team after a difficult work meeting summed up his attitude toward his employees: "I feel like I'm throwing pearls before swine." It was clear that not much change could occur unless the blame-avoidant leader could find a space in which to examine his style and its impact on the organization.

Besides leadership, the task of a group also is a factor that impacts group culture. Armelius and Armelius (2000), in their efforts to quantify some of Bion's concepts using Q-sort methodology, state that "group culture is dependent on the task that the group is working with" (p. 262). The authors consider the task to be a "motivating force that puts pressure on the group to do certain things and which evokes feelings and phantasies among the members of the group" (p. 264). They see task requirements as creating a group culture, where culture is defined as "a pattern of actions, feelings, phantasies, etc., summarized by the basic assumption" (p. 265).

Armelius and Armelius (2000) used a research design that simulated two tasks, one that was likely to stimulate competition, the other needing a greater degree of cooperation and sharing. In the first group (task requiring competition), a fight culture developed, with some individuals faring better than others (perhaps because they had the appropriate valency). In the group requiring cooperation, a dependency culture emerged, again with some individuals in the ascendancy. Some tasks require specific activities, often done in specific ways, whereas others provide more flexibility or more individual discretion, which itself can be anxiety provoking. Some tasks are inherently dangerous, putting the individual or group at high risk. Rescue workers, such as firefighters, are constantly performing in high-risk situations. If we studied their organizations closely, we would find attitudes, behaviors, and structures (a culture) that emerged to help them manage the life-threatening work they do. Some structures would be adaptive (aiding and supporting task accomplishment); others might be defensive, interfering with task accomplishment, but perhaps functioning to deny or reduce or avoid the anxiety involved, anxiety that might be better dealt with in a more direct fashion.

There are many examples from organizational life where the impact of leadership, task, and environment on group culture can be seen clearly. For example, much attention was paid to the culture of NASA following the fatal Challenger disaster. In discussing that culture, Schwartz (1999) points to a culture in which leadership sees itself as open, encouraging, and available to listen to concerns or problems. However, a different picture of the organization emerges when employees speak about it. They describe an organization requiring conformity and enforced silence, one that muffles employees and prevents open honest discussion or criticism, a culture of silence in which genuine concerns about safety could not be heard. Schwartz asks which one of these reflects the reality, pointing to the fact that leadership believed what it said and may not have been disingenuous; they may have been in a state of denial about the culture that they had really created. From a psychoanalytic perspective, one could create a hypothesis about how this state of affairs might come about.

From Schwartz's (1999) perspective, NASA is engaged in a very high risk situation where life and death continuously hang in the balance. Risk-taking, pioneering personality types, those most likely to be attracted to the space program, must be able to minimize or successfully deny the dangers inherent in their work. They put their faith and belief in the power of their technology. In addition, NASA is a highly visible organization, carrying the mantle of our nation's technological superiority and initially established to help us recover from the narcissistic wound inflicted by Sputnik. Given the nature of the task, the personalities involved, and the environmental pressures, it is not difficult to imagine that powerful defenses against the anxiety of catastrophic failure would be erected. A consciously open culture would threaten the defensive need that protected its belief in the omnipotence of its technology. Given the external pressures to accomplish their mission, NASA would also have to develop a culture that would prevent any serious challenge to their progress, a challenge that could be both a political threat and a threat to NASA's survival. The reality of the weakness and flaws in the program would be threatening and anxiety provoking on multiple levels.

The concept of a *social defense system*, first put forth by Jacques (1955) and further illuminated by Menzies Lyth (1992) in her classical study of a nursing service in a teaching hospital, has become a crucial lens through which to study and understand organizational culture and structure. The nursing service, a place of high stress, low morale, and a high student drop-out rate, invited Menzies Lyth, a British psychoanalyst and member of the Tavistock Institute group, to consult.

Through her contact with nurses, Menzies Lyth (1992) came to understand the psychic stress, both conscious and unconscious, that the work of nursing evokes. Dealing with illness, death, loss, and intimacy, both emotional and physical, stirs up early and primitive anxieties. If these anxieties are not managed productively, they can lead to increased stress and personal difficulties. Menzies Lyth recognized that the structure and culture of the institution itself was designed around three main themes that served to avoid dealing directly with the anxiety inherent in nursing. However, this avoidance actually led to increased distress, lower morale, and an increased drop-out rate. The work structures were designed to prevent nurses from becoming too intimate with any one patient by frequently moving them from ward to ward. Patient individuality was minimized; patients were referred to by bed number while nurses carried out routine orders whether or not they made practical sense at the time. Individual decision-making authority was minimized, which led to a stressful system of checking and counter-checking. Passing decisions up the ladder helped reduce any sense of individual decision-making responsibility.

It was Menzies Lyth's (1992) contention that these structures were understandable as unconscious defenses and that they had good overt work rationales. Nevertheless, they interfered with the potential growth possibilities inherent in dealing directly with these inevitable anxieties. The defenses not only prevented potential growth but also added to the stress that led to low morale and high turnover rates. This concept of social defense has become a major conceptual perspective that has found a very firm foothold with psychoanalytically oriented group and organizational thinkers and consultants.

In conclusion, the question of group culture and structure, as seen from a psychoanalytic perspective, is clearly a complex one. To fully understand the elements that shape any group or organization's culture, it is essential to focus on the overt and covert (things known but not expressed), as well as the conscious and unconscious forces at play. The forces generated by the task, the demands it makes on leaders and followers, the environment in which it functions, and the individual personality quirks of those in leadership are all key elements that shape the culture and structure of groups and organizations. Any significant change effort must attend to the complex interplay of these forces.

Group Productivity

The previous section on group culture and group structure is directly related to the issues of productivity and adaptation because group culture and structure are crucial to the effective functioning of any group or organization. Thus, the factors that impact culture also impact group functioning and effectiveness.

Both group productivity and adaptation clearly have to be considered in relationship to group task. Task accomplishment is the primary yardstick by which to measure the productivity of any work group, be it an entrepreneurial, educational, or therapeutic group. Much of the group psychotherapy literature, for example, has as its underlying aim the understanding and elucidation of dynamics, conscious and unconscious, with the goal of increasing the group's effectiveness in providing individuals opportunities to learn about their personal and social selves. Group composition (i.e., the mix of individual personality styles) may interfere markedly with productivity. In addition, therapist skill and personality can be a major force in shaping a safe environment that helps the group to work through its early phases of development toward a place where the group can be productive or therapeutic. As is the case with therapy groups, it is essential that organizational leadership help establish a *group culture* that supports self-exploration, which in turn leads to a productive environment supportive of the group or organization's task. Winnicott's (1965) concept of a *facilitating environment* may be useful in establishing such a culture. A facilitating environment is one that is "good enough" (not perfect, but sufficient to facilitate healthy growth) to allow genuine growth and development to take place through openness and freedom. The task of leadership is to identify and maintain those dynamics, conscious and unconscious, that support a facilitating environment.

When exploring the factors that enhance or interfere with productivity in work groups and organizations, those working within the psychoanalytic perspective also have found it essential to integrate open-systems thinking into their work. The early work at the Tavistock Institute of Human Relations combined psychoanalysis and open-systems perspectives, and that integration of perspectives continues to guide and inform group and organizational work today. Together, these two approaches have been far more productive and heuristic than either one alone.

Working with this integrated model, Miller and Rice (1967) focused on the core concepts of leadership, authority, primary task, boundary management, and intergroup relations, all within the group-as-a-whole context. With a systems model that looked at groups and organizations from an input-throughput-output perspective, they focused on boundary management within each subsector as well as across subsectors. The exercise of leadership and authority were also core concepts that allowed them to explore the dynamics of groups and organizations in an effort to determine what factors might be interfering with group productivity and effectiveness. Confusion or conflict about primary task, for example, would inevitably lead to difficulties that interfered with organizational productivity. Group and organizational boundaries were explored in terms of rigidity and permeability. Rigid boundaries, often established for defensive reasons, could prevent important communications and minimize an organization's flexibility, impairing its ability to deal with rapidly changing environments.

Emery and Trist (1997), writing about organizational environments, explored the interaction between internal environmental structure and the larger environment surrounding the group or organization. They were able to show how both awareness of the external world and internal flexibility allow organizations to deal more effectively in ever-increasing "turbulent environments," environments subject to many complex forces and rapid change.

Leadership and authority and the potential dilemmas surrounding their exercise are also crucial foci for Miller and Rice (1967). They defined *authority* as the right to do work, with the people in authority being authorized from above and hopefully from below. Problems in delegation of authority, problems in taking up one's own authority, and problems in dealing with authority are all important lenses through which to explore group and organizational productivity.

Psychoanalytic consultants approach groups and organizations with one eye on the work group functions (including task, boundary, leadership, structure, authority, delegation of responsibility, and clarity of role) and the other eye on the emotional forces beneath the surface. In addition, consultants are aware that individuals (especially those who lead) and the group-as-a-whole dynamics have the potential to undermine and divert the organization's ability to effectively accomplish its primary task. The consultant's goal is to diagnose the situation so that a change strategy can be developed. The strategy has to take account of resistance and involve leadership if it is to succeed. In my experience, if leadership is unable to see or acknowledge the underlying difficulties, the organization may survive, but it probably will not be able to adapt in a constructive way to a changing environment.

The Group in Context

The issue of relating to or influencing the environment (i.e., the world surrounding the group) is not a major issue for theorists writing about analytic psychotherapy groups. However, it might well be an important issue for the individuals in the group. In fact, relating to and influencing their environment could be one major factor that leads people to join such groups. For therapy groups, the question might be, how does the group experience enable individuals to better relate to and influence their environments? This topic is beyond the scope of this chapter, but we could say that one measure of an effective group therapy experience would be the individuals' increased ability to make changes in themselves and in the social and work world around them.

From the psychoanalytic perspective, a central issue in a group's ability to relate to or influence the outer world is its internal dynamics, especially unconscious dynamics that shape the group's view of the world around it. For example, a group that contained a strong fight-flight component, fueled by unacknowledged internal dangers, might well manage these tensions by viewing the outside world as hostile and aggressive. This view might foster rigid boundaries that negatively affect its relations with other groups by limiting the information the group can take in and projecting its own hostility outward. The balance and fixedness between work group and basic assumption mentalities in a group, along with the defensive aspects of its structure, are core factors in a group's ability to relate across its boundaries with the environment. A politically right-wing militant group, for example, viewing its government as predatory, may manage its internal conflicts and paranoia by finding an external enemy that unites the group and establishes loyalty to its leader. The group's ability to assess its inner dynamics and external environment realistically will be compromised because the underlying threats and anxieties are managed by projecting them onto the world around it. External events are interpreted as hostile in the light of the group's fight-flight basic assumption life, which perpetuates its internal dilemma. The group continues to project its own hostility outward, evoking reactions from the environment that confirm its internal perceptions of the outer world; a vicious cycle is established.

Fundamentally, the more pervasive and powerful the basic assumption mentality of a group is, the more likely its social defenses will be structured around denial and distortion of the external world. Its ability to be open to and interact with the environment in a productive way will be very limited. In fact, there is a strong

likelihood that what the group allows itself to take in will reinforce its internal structure, and what it gives out will reflect—and be experienced by others as determined by—the inner dynamics rather than the broader reality of the complex environment. Conversely, a group able to explore its inner dynamics and social defenses in a productive way will be better able to take in a wider variety of information, which will be useful in the accomplishment of its primary task. The group's openness and flexibility will be experienced by the world with which it interacts, and therefore, it will be more likely to join effectively with others in ways that might be beneficial to those in the group and those in the environment around it. The following anecdote is illustrative.

The owner of a successful small manufacturing firm in the United States had been losing business because his customers were moving abroad and competitors were manufacturing products more inexpensively in the Far East. This was a company under siege, fighting for its survival, but recognizing that it was a losing battle. One solution that had been put forth was the possibility of partnering with a foreign firm that produced the same or similar products. The U.S. firm had leading-edge technology, and if it partnered with a foreign firm that had significantly lower labor costs, together, they could produce more efficiently and thereby maximize profitability.

In the process of exploring with management the possibility of inviting executives from an identified foreign company to visit, management's suspicion and fear of the unethical business practices of "foreign" firms emerged. The company leaders were apprehensive about exposing their technology, fearing it would be stolen, and that any potential joint venture possibility would be abandoned. This fear, while not expressed directly, was revealed through their concerns about how to manage a visit from representatives of the foreign firm. What equipment should they let them see, how much should they reveal about their current business climate, should they share proposed technical innovations, and should they allow them to take photographs? As their anxiety crystallized and their fears were more clearly exposed, the managers began to question the wisdom of inviting the identified foreign firm to visit—they decided to scrap this course of action. They still, however, felt that their survival was at risk and created an alternate plan that would have them travel to the "foreign firm" instead. In addition, they decided to find a broker whom they felt they could trust, a person who could effectively vet the firm, as well as find other firms that they could visit while abroad.

It is difficult to assess the reality of the group's anxiety in terms of the pitfalls of doing business in a "foreign culture" with differing values and a different legal structure. While they didn't have hard data, the possibility that foreign companies might pirate technology was to be seriously considered. In addition, the managers' siege mentality—the fact that foreign companies were seen as enemies who undercut their market share—and their fear about survival all added to their fears and suspicions. They also recognized that they were not proud of some things they had done in their own struggle for growth and success. All these factors, coupled with the belief that the only solution available for survival was to "go to bed with their enemy," fueled their suspicions. This was not the most comfortable of solutions.

This vignette demonstrates the dilemma of separating projection from the realistic assessment of external reality. Although the pirating of technology is a reality, this firm's siege mentality and its potential dependence on "strangers" with different values and standards aroused enough fear and anxiety to make its managers apprehensive about doing business with the "unknown foreigner."

Conclusions

Despite the variety of psychoanalytic perspectives and their individual emphasis on different factors, both internal and external, that shape group structure, culture, and group life in general, there is an overarching issue that is the cornerstone of all psychoanalytic thinking. Human beings live on at least two levels (conscious and unconscious) and with at least two core-motivating forces, thought and feeling; each of these is suffused with rationality and irrationality. The unconscious, the emotional, and the irrational are, and have been, the central concern of much psychoanalytic thinking applied to individuals and groups. Although the metapsychological principles of psychoanalytic theory have come under scrutiny and criticism, the existence of the unconscious emotions that create anxiety in our lives and of the defenses we use against them is not in serious doubt, at least not among those who apply this perspective to their daily work with individuals and groups.

If the above core elements of all psychoanalytic theories can be the focus and the defining domain of all psychoanalytic perspectives, as Eisold (1995) has suggested, and if we can agree to define psychoanalysis as the "domain of the unconscious" (in its broadest aspects), then differing perspectives can be mined for the unique light that each casts on the unconscious, the covert, and the irrational aspects of life in groups.

The complexity of our individual lives and the remnants of our earlier and primitive past can create a darker and more frightening side that can be acted on or defended against in ways that may be out of our awareness. These forces can and do undermine our rational goals or desires, creating tensions, anxieties, and unhappiness for those caught in the underlying dynamics of difficult groups and organizations.

Kernberg (2003) aptly illuminates the fragility of our defenses in his recent article about social violence from a psychoanalytic perspective. Kernberg is a keen observer of the regressive forces in group life, especially in unstructured groups (such as those in a group relations training event) or in groups where tasks and structure begin to break down. He says,

> The rapidity of onset, the intensity, the surprisingly universal nature of group regression under unstructured conditions points to a persistent, unmetabolized core of primitive aggression, primitive object relations and primitive defensive operations as an important, perhaps even essential part of the make-up of the individual. (p. 688)

By focusing on both the paranoid and narcissistic aspects of this regressive pull, Kernberg elucidates its relationship to violence. His subsequent statement coincides with the basic psychoanalytic view put forth by Bion (1961) about the binocular perspective we must adopt when looking at (on the surface and beneath it) groups. To this issue, Kernberg (2003) says, "Our normal, civilized stance is poised perilously on a continuum between the two potential threats of the narcissistic and the paranoid dimensions" (p. 690).

Although structural change, task clarification, leadership change, and group composition are concrete actions that may bring about change, often, they are not enough to lead to lasting change. Those holding the psychoanalytic perspective believe that the observable difficulties are, almost always, driven by deeper, more complex, emotional concerns that need to be illuminated and addressed if more lasting and stable change is to occur. Ultimately, our efforts to "make sense of" the irrational forces that drive us rest on the belief that we can ameliorate the impact that unconscious forces have on group life, thereby enabling individuals to accomplish their goals without a destructive toll on others, either inside or outside the group.

Illumination through insight (cognitive and emotional) is the major tool we possess in our efforts to transmit what we see in our attempts to foster the change process. Although it is clear that unconscious forces within us influence our behavior, we are also affected by forces outside of ourselves, namely the group and the environment. We resist knowing and seeing these group forces because acknowledging their power over us challenges our sense of being separate and independent beings whose actions and emotions are solely of our own making. However, it is essential to find methods of overcoming our resistance so that we can make the changes necessary for groups to function more productively and with greater degrees of freedom from unconscious forces.

Gemmill (2002) takes the position that these resistances remain intact because we have "not systematically provided people with the knowledge and tools they could use to discover and learn about these hidden driving forces in their daily lives" (p. 57). He points out that the language we use may itself bolster resistance. Words like *unconscious, irrational, primitive,* or *psychotic* have the potential to both frighten and mystify, leading people to flee and defend against the anxiety such language arouses. Gemmill also feels that the use of these words implies that these underlying forces are "inaccessible to anyone without highly specialized knowledge and tools" (p. 57). He would use words that evoke a less negative reaction and emphasize that there are emotional forces affecting us "but not obvious, lying just below the threshold of awareness" (p. 57).

The import of this perspective is that it raises awareness of our use of language, sometimes quite dramatic language, that may undermine our goal of providing insight or, perhaps more important, sensitizing people to the awareness of unconscious emotional life and its import in our lives. Although I am not sanguine that new language would solve the problem, and I do feel that expertise is valuable, nevertheless, I do think Gemmill's point deserves attention. Any approach that turns our attention to a serious and consistent effort at finding methods to overcome our resistance to exploring our unconscious emotional lives—and the major impact (for better or worse) they have in our daily lives, as individuals, as group members, and as members of society at large, and in our international behaviors in the world—is an approach worth pursuing.

In conclusion, I believe it is reasonable to state that the varying psychoanalytic perspectives referred to in this chapter have all contributed, each in its own way, to an understanding of the unconscious forces at play in our group lives. If we can view these perspectives not as competing views but as differing observations and insights about the complexities of unconscious processes, then we could value each for the contribution it makes to our understanding of the irrational forces at play in our group and organizational worlds.

If we can maintain this focus, we would continuously add to our storehouse of knowledge about unconscious processes and their evolution (evolution in the sense that environmental changes—technological, social, and political—inevitably create underlying and unconscious emotional issues that need to be understood and managed). We would then have an ongoing project, the goal of which would be to acknowledge the dual aspect of our existence (conscious and unconscious) while striving to improve our ability to work with the resistances and defenses against knowing and seeing these forces. Ultimately, we need to accept the inevitability of the irrational in our lives, acknowledge its power, and value its possibilities (for better and worse) while, at the same time, trying to understand and work with it.

References

Armelius, K., & Armelius, B. A. (2000). Group personality: Task and group culture. In M. Pines (Ed.), *Bion and group psychotherapy* (Vol. 1, pp. 255–273). London & Philadelphia: Jessica Kingsley.

Bion, W. (1961). *Experiences in groups.* New York: Basic Books.

Burrow, T. (1928). The basis of group analysis or the analysis of normal and neurotic individuals. *British Journal of Medical Psychology, 8,* 198–206.

Colman, A., & Bexton, H. W. (Eds.). (1975). *Group relations reader.* Sausalito, CA: GREX.

Colman, A., & Geller, M. H. (Eds.). (1985). *Group relations reader 2.* Washington, DC: A. K. Rice Institute.

Eisold, K. (1995, July 7–9). *Psychoanalysis today: Implications for organizational applications.* Paper presented at the International Society for the Psychoanalytic Study of Organizations International Symposium.

Emery, F., & Trist, E. (1997). The causal texture of organizational environments. In E. Trist, F. Emery, & H. Murray (Eds.), *The social engagement of social science* (Vol. 3, pp. 53–65). Philadelphia: University of Pennsylvania Press.

Ettin, M. F. (2000). From identified patient to identifiable group: The alchemy of the group as a whole. *International Journal of Group Psychotherapy, 50*(2), 137–162.

Ezriel, H. (1980). A psychoanalytic approach to group treatment. In S. Scheidlinger (Ed.), *Psychoanalytic group dynamics* (pp. 109–146). New York: International Universities Press.

Fenichel, O. (1946). *The psychoanalytic theory of neurosis.* New York: Norton.

Freud, S. (1959). *Group psychology and the analysis of the ego.* London: Hogarth Press.

Gabriel, Y. (Ed.). (1999). *Organizations in depth.* London: Sage.

Gemmill, G. (2002). Leadership in the shadow of 9/11. *ephemera, 2*(1), 53–60. Retrieved October 10, 2003, from http://www.ephemeraweb.org

Gosling, R. (1985). A study of very small groups. In A. D. Colman & M. H. Geller (Eds.), *Group relations reader 2* (pp. 151–161). Washington, DC: A. K. Rice Institute.

Hunt, J., & McCollum, M. (1994). Using psychoanalytic approaches in organizational consulting. *Consulting Psychology Journal, 46*(2), 1–11.

Jacques, E. (1955). Social systems as a defense against persecutory and depressive anxiety. In M. Klein, P. Heimann, & R. Money-Kyrle (Eds.), *New directions in psycho-analysis* (pp. 478–498). New York: Basic Books.

Kernberg, O. F. (1985). Regression in organizational leadership. In A. D. Colman & M. H. Geller (Eds.),

Group relations reader 2 (pp. 89–107). Washington, DC: A. K. Rice Institute.

Kernberg, O. F. (2003). Sanctioned social violence: A psychoanalytic view. *International Journal of Psychoanalysis, 84,* 683–698.

Kets de Vries, M. F., & Miller, D. (1984). *The neurotic organization.* London: Jossey-Bass.

Khaleelee, O., & Miller, E. (2000). Beyond the small group: Society as an intelligible field of study. In M. Pines (Ed.), *Bion and group psychotherapy* (pp. 354–385). London & Philadelphia: Jessica Kingsley.

Klein, M. (1948). *Contributions to psychoanalysis 1921–1945.* London: Hogarth Press.

LeBon, G. (1960). *The crowd: A study of the popular mind.* New York: Viking Press. (Original work published 1895)

Menzies Lyth, I. (1989). *The dynamics of the social: Selected essays* (Vol. 2). London: Free Association Books.

Menzies Lyth, I. (1992). *Containing anxiety in institutions: Selected essays* (Vol. 1). London: Free Association Books.

Miller, E. J., & Rice, A. K. (1967). *Systems of organization.* London: Tavistock.

Nitsun, M. (1996). *The anti-group: Destructive forces in the group and their creative potential.* London and New York: Routledge.

Obholzer, A., & Roberts, V. Z. (Eds.). (1994). *The unconscious at work.* London: Routledge.

Pines, M. (1998). The self as a group: The group as a self. In I. N. Harwood & M. Pines (Eds.), *Self experiences in groups.* London: Jessica Kingsley.

Rice, A. K. (1965). *Learning for leadership.* London: Tavistock.

Roth, B. E. (1991). Some of the origins of Freud's paper on group psychology: A psychohistorical exploration. In S. Tuttman (Ed.), *Psychoanalytic group theory and therapy: Essays in honor of Saul Scheidlinger* (pp. 287–308). Madison, CT: International Universities Press.

Scheidlinger, S. (1980). Groups: A psychoanalytic perspective. In S. Scheidlinger (Ed.), *Psychoanalytic group dynamics: Basic readings* (pp. 1–6). New York: International Universities Press.

Schwartz, H. S. (1999). Introduction: Psychoanalysis and organization. In Y. Gabriel (Ed.), *Organizations in depth* (pp. 1–12). London: Sage.

Titman, S. (Ed.). (1991). *Psychoanalytic group theory and therapy: Essays in honor of Saul Scheidlinger.* Madison, CT: International Universities Press.

Turquet, P. (1975). Threats to identity in the large group. In L. Kreeger (Ed.), *The large group* (pp. 87–144). Itasca, IL: F. E. Peacock.

Winnicott, D. W. (1965). *The maturational process and the facilitating environment.* London: Hogarth Press and the Institute of Psycho-analysis.

6

The Functional Perspective

Jonathon N. Cummings

Deborah G. Ancona

A primary objective of this chapter is to illustrate how relevant the functional perspective is for understanding task-performing groups in organizations today. The functional perspective is defined as a "normative approach to describing and predicting group performance that focuses on the functions of inputs and/or processes" (Wittenbaum et al., 2004, p. 17). In other words, this is an approach that asserts that teams can be more effective to the extent that they are designed well, are composed of people with the requisite skills and knowledge, and have members who can work well with each other and with others outside of the group. Although the functional perspective has been around since at least Chester Barnard's (1938) *The Functions of the Executive,* we argue that the key ideas are still relevant. Even as work becomes more complex and nonroutine, and the environment more dynamic and uncertain, groups continue to thrive on the principles of the functional perspective. Topics in group theory and research also reflect these exciting changes taking place in

organizations, and we address current and future concepts at the end of this chapter.

We define a group in the classical sense: Three or more individuals who need to work interdependently to accomplish a task (McGrath, 1984; Steiner, 1972). These individuals view themselves as a group, and people on the outside also view them as a group. Consistent with previous authors who take an explicitly functional perspective (e.g., Hackman & Walton, 1986), we bound the definition to exclude those groups not performing a task within an organization. Our assumption is that groups meeting our definitional criteria are goal oriented, they vary in performance and can be evaluated, and performance is a function of the group inputs and/or interaction process (Wittenbaum et al., 2004).

Although group inputs can have a direct impact on performance, here we focus primarily on the conditions under which the interaction process can be adjusted to improve performance. For example, one way of improving decision

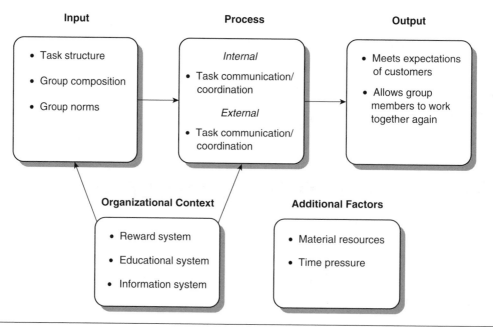

Figure 6.1 Input-Process-Output Model of Group Effectiveness

SOURCE: Figure adapted from Hackman (1987) and Hackman & Morris (1975).

making is to make sure that group members engage in problem analysis, goal setting, identification of alternatives, and evaluation of both the positive and negative consequences of those alternatives (Hirokawa, 1985, 1988).

According to this perspective, a successful and productive group is one that (1) carries out the task in a way that meets expectations of customers efficiently and effectively and (2) allows them to work together again (Hackman, 1987). The factors that contribute to effective groups include inputs such as task structure (e.g., how work is organized), group composition (e.g., the right mix of knowledge and skills), and group norms (e.g., level of member effort), as well as group interaction processes such as internal and external task communication and coordination (Hackman & Morris, 1975).

Organizations can also provide a supportive context for groups to work in, including reward systems (e.g., to reinforce achievement), educational systems (e.g., to provide training), and information systems (e.g., to assess alternatives)

(Hackman, 1987). Additional factors are also critical, such as material resources (e.g., money, space, equipment) and time pressure (e.g., task deadlines, market demands). A classic representation of group effectiveness from the functional perspective is the input-process-output model (see Figure 6.1).

Principles of the Functional Perspective

Shared Goals

First, adapting to changed goals may be accomplished by changing the membership of the group. For example, if members agreed that a shift in focus was required to complete the task successfully and that certain members were no longer needed in the group, then the membership would change to reflect this shift. In one product development team design, engineers were replaced with manufacturing people as the goals changed from innovative product design to production excellence (Ancona & Caldwell, 1992). Second, adaptation can be accomplished by changing the structure of the group, including the division of labor and assignment of tasks. For instance, a group member could discover a new way to approach the work such as creating subgroups or mixing together specialists who had always been separated before. Third, the timing of the group's activities could change, accelerating some and decelerating others. An example is deciding to finish a prototype immediately while delaying further research for a later point in time. If the group is responsive to internal and external feedback, then change is inevitable for effective groups. Groups that adapt through changing their structures and process should perform better than groups that remain rigid.

Group Composition and Norms

Depending on the goals of the group, individuals are usually selected based on the knowledge, expertise, or experiences they bring to the group. It is important to find the right mix or balance of membership to maximize chances of success for the group. How members contribute to carrying out the task successfully determines their standing in the group, and individuals are accountable to the group for their contribution to the task. Groups often ostracize members who do not do their share of the work (referred to as shirking or free-riding) or who work significantly harder than other group members (referred to as rate busting). In many situations, individual efficacy and satisfaction are contingent on group performance, so individuals' motivation to contribute is high.

Group Culture

By focusing on the task at hand, groups often develop a unique culture. Whether it is through

strategies that leaders set early on in the group, experiences members have had on previous and concurrent groups, or the dynamics of the group due to membership characteristics, groups develop their own culture (Schein, 1985). Often, the routines of the group become habitual (Gersick & Hackman, 1990), and group members find themselves behaving in recurring patterns over time. In one famous study of a group, Roy (1960) found group members structured their day around eating different kinds of food at specific times of the day (e.g., banana time and peach time). Different activities often accompanied these "times." Whenever a new member is added to a group, or a new group re-forms entirely, the process does not necessarily have to begin from scratch. Rather, depending on the strength of the leadership, past experiences, or group dynamics, the habitual routines can be reestablished at a faster or slower rate.

External Environment

The external environment also plays an important part in the life of task-performing groups (Ancona, 1993; Homans, 1950; Lewin, 1951); this environment includes the managers who assign members to groups, the resources made available to them, and the clients who evaluate their effectiveness. The group can also influence the environment—through outputs the group generates, conversations members have with external constituents, and the people in the organization to whom group members report. Groups must understand the environment to know when changes are necessary but not be so engrossed in the environment that productivity is stifled.

What Is Not Covered

It is critical to keep in mind that a functional perspective focuses on one aspect of group activity: task performance as influenced by

Table 6.1   Group Focus by Degree of Member Interdependence and Contextual Interdependence

		Contextual Interdependence	
		Low	*High*
Member Interdependence	*Low*	(1) Groups focused on brainstorming or idea generation tasks (e.g., nominal group technique)	(2) Groups focused on scanning environment or seeking external feedback (e.g., business analysis and forecasting)
	High	(3) Groups focused on task execution while buffered from outside (e.g., software program coding)	(4) Groups focused on complex tasks with uncertainty in environment (e.g., new product development)

NOTE: Emphasis in this chapter is on groups in cell 4 (High Member Interdependence—High Contextual Interdependence).

inputs and processes. While doing so, it leaves out other important aspects, including social and interpersonal aspects. Furthermore, groups do not always behave in rational and goal-oriented ways, thus making the functional perspective less valuable in these situations. Sometimes, groups behave in unexplainable ways and produce outputs that are difficult to justify based on the inputs and interaction processes. However, the functional perspective offers researchers a chance to test hypotheses about the success or failure of groups, including linkages to the input and interaction process. For organizations, the functional perspective offers an important approach to improving the effectiveness of task-oriented groups.

The Role of Interdependence in the Functional Perspective

We emphasize the role of interdependence in effective group processes—interactions among members as well as with others in the context. We do this because in organizations today, group members are more dependent on one another and their context than ever before.

Group members are often asked to work closely with other members who not only have different training, knowledge, and skills but also have information and expertise that is needed to get the job done. The tasks are sometimes not well defined and have tight budgets and deadlines. The context includes senior managers responsible for the changing direction of the group, the client whom the group constantly aims to satisfy, and the rhythms and chaos of organizational life that guide group member interactions.

To highlight the key role of member interdependence and contextual interdependence within the realm of task-performing groups in organizations, we illustrate task-performing groups that fit within the scope of the functional perspective. Table 6.1 characterizes the focus of groups by their degree of member interdependence and contextual interdependence. *Member interdependence* is the extent to which members depend on one another to do their work. Groups with high member interdependence often have more member interaction, communication, and meetings about their work than groups with low member interdependence. *Contextual interdependence* is the extent to which members depend on their context to do their work. Groups with high contextual interdependence often have more outside interaction, communication, and meetings about their work than groups with low contextual interdependence.

In the first cell (Low Member Interdependence–Low Contextual Interdependence), not much interaction is required among group members or with others outside of the group. For example, groups in this cell could engage in brainstorming or idea generation tasks that benefit from a large number of unique ideas contributed by members, including problem solving through the nominal group technique (Delbecq & Van de Ven, 1971). In the second cell (Low Member Interdependence–High Contextual Interdependence), little interaction is required among group members, but a lot is required with others outside of the group. For example, groups in this cell could be charged with tasks that rely on scanning the environment and seeking external feedback, such as teams conducting business analysis and forecasting.

In the third cell (High Member Interdependence–Low Contextual Interdependence), interaction is required among group members, but not with others outside of the group. For example, groups in this cell could have tasks geared toward execution while being buffered from outside, as is often the case when software teams have to meet an impending deadline for a program code. Finally, in the fourth cell (High Member Interdependence–High Contextual Interdependence), interaction is required among group members and with others outside of the group. Groups in this cell could work on complex, specialized, and nonroutine tasks with greater uncertainty, change, and reliance on the external environment. For example, new product development typically requires input from team members, from their colleagues in engineering, marketing, and manufacturing, and from top management and the customer. It is groups in this cell that we emphasize throughout the remainder of this chapter, as this is the focus of much of the new research in the functionalist perspective.

A number of concepts at the cutting edge of group research and theory development follow the functionalist perspective and further our understanding of group member and contextual interdependence. The current concepts we cover are transactive memory, psychological safety, and structural diversity, each of which has supporting empirical research from field studies in organizations. The future concepts include interpersonal trust, formal interventions, and virtual teams, which are supported by either laboratory or exploratory research. For each current or future concept, we address the main idea of the topic, how it links to the functional perspective, and the implications for practice (see Table 6.2).

Current Directions

Transactive Memory

Originally conceived to explain how two people in a close relationship are able to coordinate their actions effectively (e.g., Wegner, Erber, & Raymond, 1991), the concept of *transactive memory* has been extended to the group level of analysis. For a group to coordinate members' actions effectively, it helps if all members know what other members know (Hollingshead, 1998). Researchers have examined transactive memory in the lab and found that groups with members trained together outperform groups with members trained alone (Liang, Moreland, & Argote, 1995). Additional lab research suggests that the benefits are due not to improved communication but rather to transactive memory systems in the group, which enable people to act on their awareness of other members' knowledge and skills (Moreland & Myaskovsky, 2000). For example, one team member can send economic data to another team member with the greatest understanding of economics. In the field, research has shown that there are reliable scales for measuring transactive memory (Lewis, 2003) and that the stronger the transactive

Table 6.2   Current and Future Concepts for Group Research and Theory Development

	Main Idea	*Link to Functional Perspective*	*Implications for Practice*
Current concepts			
Transactive memory (Austin, 2003)	Value from knowing what others know	Suggests it is not enough to have expertise; rather, the identification and use of expertise also matters	Select members who know what's what and then train people to learn to identify areas of expertise inside and outside the team
Psychological safety (Edmondson, 1999)	Groups can create a safe environment for risk-taking and learning	In addition to having knowledge and expertise, members must be willing to share it, bring it to the group's attention, and learn from it	Encourage people to recognize and report errors, and create an environment in which group members are not punished for bringing up bad news
Structural diversity (Cummings, 2004)	Member differences in organizational affiliations, roles, or positions shape access to unique information	The right mix of people can facilitate new ideas and perspectives and sources of knowledge	Create teams in which members represent different affiliations, roles, and positions within the organization
Future concepts			
Interpersonal trust (Dirks, 1999)	Trust moderates the relationship between input and output by focusing effort and energy toward task	Addresses interpersonal feelings usually left out and is associated with dysfunction in groups	If possible, allow team members enough time to develop trust
Formal interventions (Okhuysen, 2001)	Activities influence what group members attend to during the execution of the task and can be disruptive or beneficial for performance	Interventions can be designed to influence the effectiveness of the group interaction process	Managers can take corrective actions with groups during the interaction process
Virtual teams (Cramton, 2001)	Information and communication technologies are used to accomplish work across geographic distance	Inputs to support virtual teams are critical, given the high coordination costs	Provide virtual teams with the communication technologies they need to work together, and facilitate face-to-face interaction when possible

memory system, both within and outside of the group, the better goal-oriented groups perform (Austin, 2003). From a functional perspective, this is important because it suggests that having experts in the group is most effective when others can identify them. This also applies to experts in other parts of the organization. Knowing where expertise lies can help a team manage high levels of interdependence as it cuts down on search time (finding the right people) and allocates work to the person who is most qualified to do it. Moreover, in terms of inputs, it suggests that members can be selected for groups based on their prior knowledge of what other members know and that training can be used to improve the interaction process.

Psychological Safety

A group with *psychological safety* is one in which members feel safe taking interpersonal risks and are comfortable being themselves (Edmondson, 2003). Psychological safety is an important contributor to team learning behavior, which is linked to performance through acknowledgment of mistakes, allowing for negative feedback and providing a supportive environment for considering alternatives. Field research has shown how teams with higher levels of psychological safety, due in part to their learning behaviors and capability to change, perform better than teams with lower levels of psychological safety (Edmondson, 1999; Edmondson, Bohmer, & Pisano, 2001). From a functionalist perspective, this research suggests that teams need more than diverse perspectives to do their work effectively; they need an environment that encourages members to express their opinions and raise honest concerns with the group. The ramifications of creating psychological safety in groups include improving their ability to adapt to the context and recognize change when it is needed. Psychological safety is also a key ingredient in enabling people who are interdependent to work together effectively

as they are more likely to share essential information and ideas.

Structural Diversity

The flow of knowledge within and outside of groups is shaped by the roles, positions, and affiliations members have in the broader organization: Members reside in different geographic locations, they perform different functions, they report to different managers, and they are members of different business units. Together, these features of the group's structure are considered *structural diversity* (Cummings, 2004). Members of structurally diverse groups are exposed to unique task information and ideas throughout the organization, and the exchange of this knowledge has been shown in field studies to be linked with performance (Ancona & Caldwell, 1992; Hansen, 1999). From a functional perspective, understanding how to compose groups with the right mix of members for the task is a critical step on the input side, and supporting the interaction process by which disparate sources of knowledge are integrated is necessary for effective group process. From a practical standpoint, groups need to think about the kinds of information and ideas that they need and then staff the group with the people who have access to that information and those ideas (Ancona & Caldwell, 2000). In an important way, managers need to understand that they may not be able to staff a group with individuals who themselves have all the information that the group needs, so they need to think more about at least having access to that additional information.

Future Directions

Interpersonal Trust

Interpersonal trust can take many forms, such as cognition based (e.g., make decisions about one's trustworthiness based on prior experiences) and affect based (e.g., have emotional ties to the other person) (McAllister, 1995). At the group level of analysis, trust is the level of vulnerability group members have with one another, especially when they are part of a temporary group where prior experiences and emotional ties are absent (Meyerson, Weick, & Kramer, 1996). In a laboratory study, Dirks (1999) found that trust moderated the relationship between inputs and outputs by focusing effort and energy toward the task—when group members trusted one another, their interaction processes were more effective. From a functional perspective, interpersonal trust is important because it addresses feelings and emotions that are often left out of the discussions about group performance. In situations where group members do have the answers they need and time is limited, trust may be necessary to pull them together. In trying to manage high levels of interdependence with outsiders, interpersonal trust is particularly important in gauging the extent to which relationships outside of the group can be solicited for help and advice.

Formal Interventions

Groups must contend with the timing of change when they work together to complete their tasks (Ancona & Chong, 1996). Issues arise such as the order in which tasks are completed, when certain members work on parts of the task, and how long it takes for the entire process to unfold; it is especially important to ensure that team members are ready to change when the clients want it. For example, one organization created groups during a massive reorganization in September and then asked those groups' members to help school districts reform their curricula. But the new groups could not function effectively. The reason for their lack of early success was that these school districts were entrained or synchronized with the academic year and textbook publishers, and they only ordered new materials in April. Thus, the groups

were ready to provide help in September when the client was simply not interested. A key formal intervention would have been to schedule the reorganization effort in March.

Formal interventions are defined as planned events that remove groups from their entrainment patterns or create new entrainment patterns. They can shift members' attention to topics like task discussion instead of social concerns. Laboratory research has demonstrated a link between formal interventions and performance, which in part is due to interruptions that can focus member attention on the task discussion and activities that facilitate knowledge integration (Okhuysen, 2001; Okhuysen & Eisenhardt, 2002). A functional perspective considers the opportunity to change behavior as a result of direct intervention to be a critical step in understanding performance in groups. The implications include timing the interventions appropriately so that they reduce the wrong kinds of entrainment and focus members on the task when it is needed, in particular when the group is drifting off course. Formal interventions could also be used to better manage interdependencies within and outside of the group by aligning the cycles, timing of activities, and timing of change across entities that must work together.

Virtual Teams

Research on groups has seen some conflict around the topic of *virtual teams,* members who use information and communication technologies to accomplish work across geographic distance (Townsend, DeMarie, & Hendrickson, 1998). Although some are optimistic that this form of organizing will improve the efficiency with which groups can operate, much of the early work has highlighted the difficult interaction process that groups face, such as problems establishing mutual knowledge among members (Cramton, 2001). Ethnographies and exploratory research have identified issues facing virtual teams: adapting to new technologies (Majchrzak, Rice, Malhotra, King, & Ba, 2000), establishing a rhythm for operating through distance and time (Maznevski & Chudoba, 2000), and figuring out how to build trust (Jarvenpaa, Knoll, & Leidner, 1998).

From a functional perspective, it is important to understand the inputs that create virtual teams as well as the interaction process that can make them effective. For example, managers should consider the level of interdependence necessary to successfully accomplish a distributed task, including how often face-to-face interaction is needed. Managers should also take into account the amount of cohesiveness on a virtual team, in case structured management is required for facilitating communication (Kiesler & Cummings, 2002). Having groups working effectively together at a distance can be a competitive advantage for firms with global operations, which do not have employees located in the same place. When all goes well, groups can take advantage of member skills and expertise located in different parts of the organization.

Conclusion

In this chapter, we describe group theory and research from the functionalist perspective. This perspective takes a goal-oriented approach, assuming that teams can be designed and operated to be more or less effective. In particular, it asserts that by trying to identify how a group should be structured, how members should be chosen, and how members should interact with each other and with outsiders, groups can become more effective. According to this perspective, group members need clear goals and need to adapt to changing conditions. They need to create a culture and an approach to the work that fits the particular task demands that they face. They need to focus within the group and on the external environment. Throughout there is an assumption of rationality; the right design and process can be found and applied.

Although many of the core assumptions and findings of the functionalist perspective remain relevant today, new research often focuses on those structures and processes needed to cope with tasks that are more complex, information that is more distributed, and an external environment that is more dynamic than ever before. Under these conditions, interdependence often increases, both across team members and with individuals outside the team. To manage this interdependence, groups may need to develop transactive memory, psychological safety, structural diversity, high levels of interpersonal trust, and formal interventions, and they may need more virtual interactions. The challenge is to help them to do this.

References

Ancona, D. (1993). The classics and the contemporary: A new blend of small group theory. In J. Murnighan (Ed.), *Social psychology in organizations: Advances in theory and research* (pp. 225–243). Englewood Cliffs, NJ: Prentice Hall.

Ancona, D., & Caldwell, D. (1992). Demography and design: Predictors of new product team performance. *Organization Science, 3*(3), 321–341.

Ancona, D., & Caldwell, D. (2000). Compose teams to assure successful boundary activity. In E. Locke (Ed.), *The Blackwell handbook of principles of organizational behavior* (pp. 199–210). New York: Blackwell Press.

Ancona, D., & Chong, C. (1996). Entrainment: Pace, cycle, and rhythm in organizational behavior. *Research in Organizational Behavior, 18*, 251–284.

Austin, J. (2003). Transactive memory in organizational groups: The effects of content, consensus, specialization, and accuracy on group performance. *Journal of Applied Psychology, 88*(5), 866–878.

Barnard, C. (1938). *The functions of the executive.* Cambridge, MA: Harvard University Press.

Cramton, C. (2001). The mutual knowledge problem and its consequences in dispersed collaboration. *Organization Science, 12*(3), 346–371.

Cummings, J. (2004). Work groups, structural diversity, and knowledge sharing in a global organization. *Management Science, 50*(3), 352–364.

Delbecq, A., & Van de Ven, A. (1971). A group process model for identification and program planning. *Journal of Applied Behavioral Sciences, 7,* 466–492.

Dirks, K. (1999). The effects of interpersonal trust on work group performance. *Journal of Applied Psychology, 84*(3), 445–455.

Edmondson, A. (1999). Psychological safety and learning behavior in work teams. *Administrative Science Quarterly, 44,* 350–383.

Edmondson, A. (2003). Managing the risk of learning: Psychological safety in work teams. In M. West & K. Smith (Eds.), *International handbook of organizational teamwork* (pp. 255–275). London: Blackwell.

Edmondson, A., Bohmer, R., & Pisano, G. (2001). Disrupted routines: Team learning and new technology implementation in hospitals. *Administrative Science Quarterly, 46,* 685–716.

Gersick, C., & Hackman, R. (1990). Habitual routines in task-performing groups. *Organizational Behavior and Human Decision Processes, 47,* 65–97.

Hackman, J. (1987). The design of work teams. In J. Lorsch (Ed.), *Handbook of organizational behavior.* Englewood Cliffs, NJ: Prentice Hall.

Hackman, J., & Morris, C. (1975). Group tasks, group interaction process, and group performance effectiveness: A review and proposed integration. In L. Berkowitz (Ed.), *Advances in experimental social psychology* (Vol. 8, pp. 45–99). New York: Academic Press.

Hackman, J., & Walton, R. (1986). Leading groups in organizations. In P. Goodman (Ed.), *Designing effective work groups* (pp. 72–119). San Francisco: Jossey-Bass.

Hansen, M. (1999). The search-transfer problem: The role of weak ties in sharing knowledge across organization subunits. *Administrative Science Quarterly, 44,* 82–111.

Hirokawa, R. (1985). Discussion procedures and decision-making performance: A test of a functional perspective. *Human Communication Research, 12*(2), 203–224.

Hirokawa, R. (1988). Group communication and decision-making performance: A continued test of the functional perspective. *Human Communication Research, 14*(4), 487–515.

Hollingshead, A. (1998). Retrieval processes in transactive memory systems. *Journal of Personality and Social Psychology, 74,* 639–671.

Homans, G. (1950). *The human group.* New York: Harcourt Brace Jovanovich.

Jarvenpaa, S., Knoll, K., & Leidner, D. (1998). Is anybody out there? Antecedents of trust in global virtual teams. *Journal of Management Information Systems, 14*(4), 29–64.

Kiesler, S., & Cummings, J. (2002). What do we know about proximity and distance in work groups? In P. Hinds & S. Kiesler (Eds.), *Distributed work* (pp. 57–80). Cambridge: MIT Press.

Lewin, K. (1951). *Field theory in social science: Select theoretical papers* (D. Cartwright, Ed.). New York: Harper & Row.

Lewis, K. (2003). Measuring transactive memory systems in the field: Scale development and validation. *Journal of Applied Psychology, 88,* 587–604.

Liang, D., Moreland, R., & Argote, L. (1995). Group versus individual training and group performance: The mediating role of transactive memory. *Personality and Social Psychology Bulletin, 21,* 384–393.

Majchrzak, A., Rice, R., Malhotra, A., King, N., & Ba, S. (2000). Technology adaptation: The case of a computer-supported inter-organizational virtual team. *MIS Quarterly, 24*(4), 569–600.

Maznevski, M., & Chudoba, C. (2000). Bridging space over time: Global virtual team dynamics and effectiveness. *Organization Science, 11*(5), 473–492.

McAllister, D. (1995). Affect- and cognition-based trust as foundations for interpersonal cooperation in organizations. *Academy of Management Journal, 38*(1), 24–59.

McGrath, J. (1984). *Groups.* Englewood Cliffs, NJ: Prentice Hall.

Meyerson, D., Weick, K., & Kramer, R. (1996). Swift trust and temporary groups. In R. Kramer (Ed.), *Trust in organizations* (pp. 166–195). Thousand Oaks, CA: Sage.

Moreland, R. L., & Myaskovsky, L. (2000). Exploring the performance benefits of group training: Transactive memory or improved communication? *Organizational Behavior & Human Decision Processes, 82,* 117–133.

Okhuysen, G. (2001). Structuring change: Familiarity and formal interventions in problem-solving groups. *Academy of Management Journal, 44*(4), 794–808.

Okhuysen, G., & Eisenhardt, K. (2002). Integrating knowledge in groups: How formal interventions enable flexibility. *Organization Science, 13*(4), 370–386.

Roy, D. (1960). Banana time: Job satisfaction and informal interaction. *Human Organization, 18,* 158–168.

Schein, E. (1985). *Organizational culture and leadership.* San Francisco: Jossey-Bass.

Steiner, I. (1972). *Group process and productivity.* New York: Academic Press.

Townsend, A., DeMarie, S., & Hendrickson, A. (1998). Virtual teams: Technology and the workplace of the future. *Academy of Management Executive, 12*(3), 17–29.

Wegner, D., Erber, R., & Raymond, P. (1991). Transactive memory in close relationships. *Journal of Personality and Social Psychology, 61*(6), 923–929.

Wittenbaum, G. M., Hollingshead, A., Paulus, P. B., Hirokawa, R., Ancona, D., Peterson, R. S. Jehn, K. A., & Yoon, K. (2004). The functional perspective as a lens for understanding groups. *Small Group Research, 35*(1), 17–43.

7

The Developmental Perspective

Susan A. Wheelan

The fact that groups change across time is obvious to the most casual observer. Our experience as group members leads us to expect groups that have been meeting for several months to be more organized and to have more defined goals, norms, and values than new groups. We expect that as time passes, groups will change from simple to complex systems, from limited to diverse capabilities, and from dependent to interdependent cultures. We also expect that whereas most groups will develop across time, some groups, like some people, will not mature, and others may regress due to internal or external factors that inhibit group development.

This populist view of group development became the subject of social science inquiries more than 50 years ago. Since that time, impressionistic studies that relied on experiences and reflections of observers (e.g., Bennis & Shepard, 1956; Caple, 1978; Rogers, 1970; Slater, 1966) and empirical studies using observational systems and questionnaires (e.g., Dunphy, 1964; Hill, 1974; Mills, 1964; Wheelan, Davidson, & Tilin, 2003; Wheelan & McKeage, 1993) have

been conducted. Although these studies vary with regard to the number of stages of group development, and the order in which stages occur, the concept of group development across time has garnered significant support.

Reviews of group development research (Tuckman, 1965; Tuckman & Jensen, 1977; Wheelan, 1994) have attempted to reconcile differences among the studies concerning the number of stages and the sequence in which those stages occur. These reviewers came to similar conclusions about the process of group development.

The initial stage of development focuses on issues of inclusion and dependency, as members attempt to identify behavior acceptable to the leader and other group members (Bennis & Shepard, 1956; Bion, 1961; Mann, Gibbard, & Hartman, 1967). These early group meetings also are characterized as a time of member anxiety (Slater, 1966; Stock & Thelen, 1958). The next phase is described as a period of counterdependency (Bennis & Shepard, 1956; Mann et al., 1967) and conflict (Bennis & Shepard, 1956; Braaten, 1974/1975; Miles, 1971; Tuckman, 1965;

Yalom, 1995). Issues of power, authority, and competition are debated at this stage (e.g., Mills, 1964; Slater, 1966).

A number of theories suggest that these early struggles regarding authority and status are prerequisites for subsequent increases in cohesion and cooperation (Dunphy, 1968; Mann, 1966; Mann et al., 1967; Mills, 1964; Slater, 1966; Tuckman, 1965; Tuckman & Jensen, 1977). Confrontations with the leader serve to establish intermember solidarity and openness (Lundgren, 1971; Mills, 1964; Slater, 1966). In addition, if conflicts are adequately resolved, member relationships with the leader and each other become more trusting and cohesive (Coser, 1956; Deutsch, 1971; Northen, 1969). The phase also provides the opportunity to clarify areas of common values, which increases group stability (Theodorson, 1962).

The third phase is devoted to the development of trust, along with more mature and open negotiation regarding goals, roles, group structure, and division of labor (Lundgren & Knight, 1978; Mills, 1964; Slater, 1966; Wheelan, 1990). A work phase follows, characterized by an increase in task orientation and more open exchange of ideas and feedback (Bennis & Shepard, 1956; Slater, 1966; Tuckman, 1965).

Groups that have a distinct ending point experience a fifth phase. Impending termination may cause disruption and conflict (Farrell, 1976; Mann et al., 1967; Mills, 1964). Increased expression of positive feelings may also occur (Lundgren & Knight, 1978), and separation issues are discussed (Braaten, 1974/1975; Dunphy, 1964; Gibbard & Hartman, 1973; Miles, 1971; Mills, 1964; Slater, 1966; Yalom, 1995).

Some models of group development propose that groups develop through an orderly, invariant sequence of stages (e.g., Bennis & Shepard, 1956; Hill & Gruner, 1973; Tuckman, 1965; Tuckman & Jensen, 1977; Zurcher, 1969). Other models describe group development as both sequential and cyclic, where progression may result in regression or recycling (Bradford, Gibb, & Benne, 1964; Burnand, 1990; Mann et al.,

1967; Wheelan, 1994). These life cycle models describe group development in ways that are reminiscent of individual human development (e.g., Mennecke, Hoffer, & Wynne, 1992). Developmental psychology describes the stages of individual human development across time and the tasks associated with each stage (e.g., Erikson, 1950, 1978). Stages of individual human development are sequential and assume developmental maturation across time. However, smooth passage through the stages is not assumed. Although most people eventually mature, not all individuals are successful in accomplishing developmental tasks. Some percentage of people experience developmental delays or failures. Others may regress temporarily or for long periods of time. Groups can be described in this way as well. Like people, some groups either do not develop fully, regress to earlier stages, or experience developmental delays and difficulties (Gabarro, 1987; Goodacre, 1953; Kuypers, Davies, & Glaser, 1986; Zurcher, 1969).

Of course, sequential and life cycle models of group development are not universally accepted. The cyclic models, for example, support the notion of change in groups but reject the idea of an orderly progression of developmental stages (e.g., Bion, 1961; Hare, 1976; Parsons, 1961; Schutz, 1958). Adaptive/nonsequential models agree that groups change across time but assert that how they change, and the rate of change, is dependent on internal contingencies and external demands (e.g., Arrow, McGrath, & Berdahl, 2000; Poole & Roth, 1989; Steiner, 1972). Other models reject the idea that groups develop. These equilibrium models propose a brief period of fluctuation in the beginning that settles into a stable pattern that persists across time (e.g., Bales, 1955; Carley, 1991).

This chapter will focus on the life cycle model of group development because it is the most compelling and enduring model and the one most in tune with how individual group participants view group processes. In addition, a growing body of evidence supports the life cycle model, as opposed to the sequential model, of group development (Wheelan, 2004).

The developmental perspective is most clearly illustrated by the life cycle approach to group development. With regard to theory building, the developmental perspective is underdeveloped. The following sections will attempt to fill in some theoretical gaps, to link the developmental perspective with other group perspectives, and to explore research findings, questions, and future research directions.

The Individual and the Group

Luft's (1984) definition of a group is consistent with the developmental perspective. He stated that a group is

> a living system, self-regulating through shared perception and interaction, sensing and feedback, and through interchange with the environment. Each group has unique wholeness qualities that become patterned by way of members' thinking, feeling, and communicating, into structured subsystems. The group finds some way to maintain balance while moving through progressive changes, creating its own guidelines and rules, and seeking its own goals through recurring cycles of interdependent behavior. (p. 2)

This definition assumes that groups form to achieve goals that cannot be achieved by an individual alone. It also implies that individuals are influenced by, and influence, the groups to which they belong. The idea that group members and the group create a mutual influence system is not new. Lewin (1951) and Mills (1959) were among the first to discuss this mutual influence process. Evidence for this view can be found in the social identity perspective (see Hogg, Chapter 8, this volume; Abrams, Frings, & Randsley de Moura, Chapter 18, this

volume), which states that groups influence the way group members feel, think, and act (Asch, 1955; Brewer & Brown, 1998; Hogg, 2001).

Of course, individuals influence group processes as well. However, the amount of influence exerted by individuals and groups is not equal. Groups have the upper hand in that regard (Abrams, Ando, & Hinkle, 1998; Sampson, 1989; Terry & Hogg, 1998). Most of us are aware that our behavior changes depending on the group we are in at the moment. Each of us is a complex profile of group and social identities (Abrams, 1994; Oakes, 1987), and we express different aspects of ourselves in different group contexts. We behave differently in work groups, for example, than in social or community groups.

Clearly, group membership influences member thoughts, feelings, and actions. However, individuals can and do influence the groups to which they belong, albeit to a lesser extent. Individual members can do many things to facilitate the development and well-being of groups. For example, people who express liking for, respect for, and trust in others facilitate social interaction and cohesion in groups (Keyton, 1999; Sorrentino & Sheppard, 1978). Group members who are willing to interact and communicate with other members contribute to group success (McCroskey, Hamilton, & Weiner, 1974). Individuals who use effective communication skills have a positive influence on group outcomes (Allen & Bourhis, 1996). Members who are assertive and prominent in groups and encourage other members to participate also influence group development and well-being (Salazar, Hirokawa, Propp, Julian, & Leatham, 1994). Emotionally stable members with positive self-concepts also facilitate group functioning (Bass, Wurster, Doll, & Clair, 1953; Buck, Miller, & Caul, 1974; Haythorn, 1953; Leonard, 1975). Acting in a responsible manner in relation to the group promotes effectiveness as well (Mitchell, 1975).

Conversely, expressing anxiety or defensiveness reduces group effectiveness (Kogan & Wallach, 1967; Ryan & Lakie, 1965; Teichman, 1974).

Expressing dislike, distrust, or competitiveness has negative effects on group functioning (Deutsch, 1990; Jehn, 1995). Social loafing also negatively affects many aspects of group functioning (Karau & Williams, 1993). In short, the behavior of individual group members can influence group dynamics and development.

What the developmental perspective adds to this discussion is evidence that the ways in which members' thoughts, feelings, and actions change are related to developmental changes at the group level. For example, the kinds of statements that group members make are related to the length of time that the group has been meeting. Members of groups of longer duration make fewer dependency and fight statements and more work statements (e.g., Wheelan, Davidson, et al., 2003; Wheelan & Williams, 2003). Also, members of older groups perceive those groups to be in the higher stages of group development than members of newer groups (Wheelan, Davidson, et al., 2003; Wheelan & Williams, 2003).

Group Culture and Structure

Descriptions of group development reported in the literature are quite similar. This suggests that group members, either innately or as a result of a historical and personal learning process, interact with each other and with the external environment in ways that produce similar patterns of interaction, patterns that change across time in similar ways. Hogan (1975) concluded on the basis of anthropological evidence that

> [human] survival was promoted by the quality of the group rather than the accomplishments of individuals. Specifically, an adaptive advantage was conferred on those groups that developed an efficient social organization defined in terms of leadership, structure, division of labor, communication systems, transmission of knowledge

[and the like] . . . man seems to have evolved as a group-living, culture-bearing, norm-respecting animal." (p. 537)

This line of reasoning leads to the conclusion that group development is a product of social evolution, and the patterns of development we observe in groups today are those that have been most successful to this point in time. Furthermore, it suggests that the culture and structure of a particular group is not entirely unique. In fact, much of a group's culture and organizational structure is not unique at all. Of course, each group has to cope with its particular problems and the demands of its local environment. However, at the level of group development, groups are much more similar than they are different. This appears to be true even in different cultures. Japanese, Mexican, and U.S. work groups, for example, have been found to be similar with regard to developmental processes (Buzaglo & Wheelan, 1999; Wheelan, Buzaglo, & Tsumura, 1998).

From the developmental perspective, the overall goal of group development is to create an organized unit capable of working effectively and productively to achieve specific ends (Wheelan, 1999). Each stage also has goals, which contribute to the achievement of the overall goal. During the first stage (dependency and inclusion), the goals, appropriately, focus on creating a sense of belonging and the beginnings of predictable patterns of interaction. If the group is to remain intact, developing a sense of loyalty to the group among members will be required as well. Finally, during the first stage, members work to create an environment in which they feel safe enough to begin to contribute ideas and suggestions.

The second stage of group development is referred to as a period of counterdependency and fight. At this stage, members disagree among themselves about group goals and procedures. Conflict is an inevitable part of this process. The group's goal at this stage is to develop a unified set of work goals, values, and operational procedures, a process that inevitably generates some conflict. Conflict also is necessary for the establishment of trust and a climate in which members feel free to disagree with each other.

If the group manages to work through the inevitable conflicts of Stage 2, member trust, commitment to the group, and willingness to cooperate increase. Communication becomes more open and task-oriented. The goals of the third stage of group development (trust and structure) are to solidify positive working relationships among members and to engage in more mature negotiations about roles, organization, and procedures. Members of Stage 3 groups spend their time fine-tuning the components of group culture and structure to ensure that the group is capable of accomplishing its real-world goals.

As its name implies, the fourth or work stage of group development is a time of intense team productivity and effectiveness. Having resolved many of the issues of the previous stages, the group can focus most of its energy on goal achievement and task accomplishment. The goals of Stage 4 include making informed decisions, remaining cohesive while encouraging task-related conflicts, getting the job done well, and maintaining high performance over the long haul.

From the developmental perspective, the elements of group culture, such as values, norms, and ideologies, should support both group goal achievement and group development. Some aspects of group culture will be unique to a group because the group must respond to external and internal demands and problems. However, some aspects of group culture will be similar from group to group because they relate to the developmental process.

With regard to group structures, such as communication, goals, and roles, and group processes, such as conformity, deviation, cohesion, and conflict, the developmental perspective assumes that these change across time to facilitate group development and group goal achievement. For example, interactions between members and the leader will be different at different stages of group development. Division of labor, patterns of communication, and the like will be different as well.

The developmental perspective postulates that although there may be false starts and periods of stagnation or regression, most groups will move in the direction of increased effectiveness and productivity. Some groups, like some people, will not mature. However, the majority of groups will develop cultures, structures, and processes that facilitate goal achievement. The majority of groups also will reach the higher stages of group development. If these propositions are accurate, research studies should find relationships among the length of time that a group has been meeting, group stage, and group productivity. In addition, studies should find differences in group culture, structure, and processes that are consistent with these propositions.

With regard to group culture, structure, and processes, what evidence is there to support the widely held view that these components develop across time? A strong source of support for theories of group development can be found in the hundreds of studies that have been generated in the past 50 years. This literature has been reviewed three times, and the reviewers came to similar conclusions (Tuckman, 1965; Tuckman & Jensen, 1977; Wheelan, 1994). The fact that three reviewers came to similar conclusions could be dismissed easily. However, the fact that so many researchers in different locations came to such similar conclusions is extremely difficult to dismiss. Although those researchers' methods varied and the proposed sequence of development varied to some extent, the majority concluded that groups develop across time.

Over the past two decades, my colleagues and I have attempted to explore changes in group culture more systematically. In a series of investigations of 16 experiential learning groups that met for a minimum of 4½ hours and a maximum of 7½ hours over the course of a week, researchers classified each of the 55,931 statements made by members of these various groups. Raters were trained in the use of the Group Development Observation System, which places each complete thought into one of eight categories (Wheelan, Verdi, & McKeage, 1994). The categories are based on the work of Bion (1961), which was extended by Thelen (1954), Stock and Thelen (1958), and Wheelan (1994). The categories represent the types of verbal statements associated with the various stages of group development outlined in the research literature (Wheelan et al., 1994). The eight categories are briefly described next.

Dependency statements (D) are those that show the inclination to conform with the dominant mood of the group; to follow suggestions made by the leader and, generally, to demonstrate a desire for direction from others.

Counterdependency statements (CD) are those that assert independence from and rejection of leadership, authority, or member attempts to lead.

Fight statements (FI) are those that convey participation in a struggle to overcome someone or something and imply argumentativeness, criticism, or aggression.

Flight statements (FL) are those that indicate avoidance of task and confrontation.

Pairing statements (P) are those that include expressions of warmth, friendship, support, or intimacy with others. Pairing statements are similar to positive maintenance statements as outlined by Bales (1970).

Counterpairing statements (CP) are those that indicate an avoidance of intimacy and connection, and a desire to keep the discussion distant and intellectual.

Work statements (W) are those that represent purposeful, goal-directed activity and task-oriented efforts.

Unscorable statements (US) include unintelligible, inaudible, or fragmentary statements.

What follows are examples of statements that would be classified in a particular category. "I like you" would be classified as pairing. "I'm not interested in collaborating" is an example of counterpairing. "I don't know what to do" is a dependent statement. "That's a bad idea, boss" is a counterdependent statement. "Did you watch the ball game last night?" is a flight statement. "Fred, why don't you ever have any ideas" is a fight statement. "Let's focus on the task at hand" is an example of a work statement (Verdi & Wheelan, 1992).

The proportion of statements in the various categories changed across time in similar ways in all of the groups. Although there were some differences in the quantity of statements within a category based on group size and task, the patterns of verbal communication across time were similar and consistent with groups in the early stages of development (Verdi & Wheelan, 1992; Wheelan & Kaeser, 1997; Wheelan & McKeage, 1993). These studies provided solid evidence that group communication patterns change across time in consistent ways. However, the groups that were studied were short-term learning and project groups functioning in a graduate school setting. The logical next step, then, was to investigate workplace groups.

Communication patterns in work groups have been investigated previously. For example, communication among members of Stage 4 groups is significantly different from communication among members of groups at other stages. Bales (1970) proposed that in highly effective groups, 60% of member communications are work- or task-oriented. More recent research found the percentage of work statements in Stage 4 groups to be on average 76% (Wheelan & Williams, 2003).

In contrast, members of groups in the early stages of group development generate half the work statements generated by Stage 4 groups (see Table 7.1). Also, members of groups in the early stages of development generate significantly more fight, flight, and dependency statements (Verdi & Wheelan, 1992; Wheelan & McKeage,

Table 7.1   Communication Patterns in Groups at Different Developmental Stages

	Stage 1 and 2	Stage 3	Stage 4
Work	38.20%	63.90%	75.70%
Fight	3.60%	0.35%	0.24%
Flight	28.30%	9.20%	3.0%
Dependency	6.36%	2.40%	1.50%

1993; Wheelan & Williams, 2003). Differences also are apparent between Stage 3 and 4 groups. Members of Stage 3 groups generate significantly fewer work statements than members of Stage 4 groups, for example (Wheelan & Williams, 2003).

About 17% of the statements made by members of groups at any stage of group development are supportive or positive maintenance statements (Verdi & Wheelan, 1992; Wheelan & McKeage, 1993; Wheelan & Williams, 2003). Positive, encouraging communications have been described as key to establishing a supportive, as opposed to a defensive communication climate (Gibb, 1961). Group members see a defensive or negative communication climate as a barrier to group effectiveness and productivity (Broome & Fulbright, 1995). However, because the proportion of supportive statements does not seem to increase or decrease significantly at different stages of development, it may be that decreases in fight, flight, and dependency statements are responsible for the creation of a supportive communication climate at the higher stages of group development.

Recently, the relationship between the length of time that work groups had been meeting and the verbal behavior patterns and perceptions of group members about their groups was investigated (Wheelan, Davidson, et al., 2003). The verbal behavior patterns and perceptions of 180 members of 26 work groups were examined. In addition, the perceptions of 639 people in 88 work groups were explored. The researchers noted that how members communicated and how they perceived their group's functioning

varied based on the length of time that the group had been meeting. For example, members of groups that had been meeting longer made significantly fewer dependency and fight statements and significantly more work statements. They also perceived their groups to be functioning at higher stages of group development. Members in groups that had been meeting for longer periods of time were more likely to perceive their groups to be functioning at the higher stages of development. On average, groups that were perceived to be in Stage 1 had been meeting for 2.6 months, Stage 2 groups for 3.7 months, and Stage 3 and 4 groups for at least 4.6 months.

Finally, the verbal behaviors of 12 work groups perceived by members to be in Stage 3 were compared with the verbal behaviors of 12 work groups perceived by members to be in Stage 4. Significant differences were noted in the percentage of flight and counterdependent statements. Members of Stage 3 groups made more flight and counterdependent statements than members of Stage 4 groups. On average, the Stage 3 groups had been meeting for 5.2 months, and the Stage 4 groups had been meeting for 8.5 months. A link between group development and time was supported by these results.

Group Productivity

Previous research concluded that task performance and work activity occur at higher levels later in a group's development. Group members require sufficient time together to develop a mature working unit capable of accomplishing goals. Hare (1967, 1982) found this to be the case in a variety of groups, including an anthropological expedition, factory work groups, and experiential groups. Other researchers have found the same pattern (Bales & Strodtbeck, 1951; Borgatta & Bales, 1953). Therapy and personal growth groups follow suit as well (Hill, 1974; Hill & Gruner, 1973; Stiles, Tupler, & Carpenter, 1982). Even the productive outcomes of the Camp David Summit on the Middle East were accomplished near its end (Hare & Naveh, 1984).

During the past decade, my colleagues and I set out to investigate the relationship between work group members' perceptions of their group's developmental stage and their group's actual and perceived productivity. Insurance underwriting teams, elementary and secondary faculty groups, college student cohort groups, intensive-care staff groups, hotel work groups, and work groups operating in six Japanese companies were investigated. In total, 92 work groups have been investigated. Members completed the Group Development Questionnaire (GDQ), which contains four scales that correspond to the first four stages of group development (Wheelan & Hochberger, 1996). In all cases, groups that were perceived by members to be functioning at the higher stages of group development were more productive than groups that were perceived to be functioning at the lower stages of group development. Productivity was measured by organizational criteria, which included profit, cycle time, customer service, student standardized test scores, grade point averages, and patient outcomes in intensive care units (Wheelan, Burchill, & Tilin, 2003; Wheelan & Kesselring, in press; Wheelan & Lisk, 2000; Wheelan, Murphy, Tsumura, & Fried Kline, 1998; Wheelan & Tilin, 1999). A strong link between group development and group productivity has been established by these findings.

The Group in Context

Group development does not occur in a vacuum. Most groups function within the boundaries of organizations and institutions (Ancona & Caldwell, 1988; Levine & Moreland, 1990; McGrath, 1991). Groups operate within a particular society and can be influenced by macrolevel phenomena that transcend national boundaries. World events, international economic and social conditions, alternative ideologies, and the like are just some of the macrolevel phenomena that can influence small groups.

Group behavior is a function of the group and its psychological environment (Lewin, 1951). That is, how a group operates is affected by intragroup factors such as its developmental level, cohesion, communication structure, and the like. However, the environment in which a group is operating also affects these processes. Thus, a group's internal processes and its external context affect group development and productivity (Ancona & Caldwell, 1992; Campion, Medsker, & Higgs, 1993; Campion, Papper, & Medsker, 1996; Guzzo & Dickson, 1996).

A number of studies have investigated the impact of organizational variables on group processes and performance. Work group effectiveness, for example, is enhanced when the organization of which it is a part has a clear sense of the group's mission and purpose within the organization (Galagan, 1986; Shea & Guzzo, 1987). Clear objectives for good performance are helpful as well (Hackman, 2002). Groups also need sufficient autonomy to do their jobs (Manz & Sims, 1987). The design of the group task is another important factor. Working on a project from beginning to end, for example, increases effectiveness (Cummings, 1981). Working on tasks that are important and require skill also improves results (Hackman, 2002). The design and maintenance of technologies necessary to the task are additional factors related to group effectiveness (Goodman, Devadas, & Hughson, 1988). Organizational responsiveness to group needs for decisions, information, and resources is crucial as well (Guzzo & Dickson, 1996).

Groups need ongoing feedback concerning their performance (Ketchum, 1984; Pritchard, Jones, Roth, Stuebing, & Ekeberg, 1988).

Recognition of a group's contribution to the organization is equally important. Group rather than individual reward systems appear to enhance performance (Pritchard et al., 1988). Access to technical and interpersonal training also improves performance (Hackman, 2002; Salas, Dickinson, Converse, & Tannenbaum, 1992). An organizational culture that values innovation and quality can enhance group effectiveness (Schein, 1992). Finally, an organization that is open to being influenced by a group and gives that group consistent messages about its work can facilitate group performance.

These research findings tell us that the total organization has another kind of influence on its member groups. The organizational context can affect a group's functioning and productivity by providing or withholding resources, training, rewards, feedback, autonomy, goal clarity, appropriate technologies, and other types of support necessary for group goal achievement (Ancona & Caldwell, 1992; Guzzo & Dickson, 1996).

In the final analysis, then, groups have less control over their environment than members might like. However, they do have some control. First, groups that manage their internal processes and development well, and that function at higher levels of development, will be in a position to respond more appropriately to the external environment. Groups engaged in internal conflict or those that develop isolationist norms will have difficulty managing their relationships with the outside. If there is little internal trust, groups may not be able to delegate authority or responsibility to individual members to act on the group's behalf with outsiders. Second, groups that consciously attempt to manage their external relationships will enhance the probability of goal achievement and high performance.

Discussion and Conclusions

The developmental perspective provides a framework for understanding how group patterns and member behaviors change across time. It has generated a sizable body of research, albeit slowly and laboriously. However, much more research is needed to comprehensively map the life cycle of groups. Finally, this perspective has practical implications for consulting with groups in the real world. Each of these points will be discussed in this section.

The developmental perspective provides insights into the macrolevel dynamics of groups as they move through the life cycle. However, it does more than that. This perspective sheds light on microlevel processes as well, such as changes in member behaviors and perceptions as the group moves through the stages of group development. The influence of the environment is taken into account as well. It could be called a comprehensive approach, in that it allows for the examination and integration of individual, interpersonal, group, and environmental processes under one theoretical umbrella. Aspects of all the theoretical perspectives described in this book can be found in this perspective. This chapter, for example, incorporates concepts and research from each of these perspectives.

Theory building and research in this perspective is not complete, however. There is much more to learn. For example, when my colleagues and I began our studies 20 years ago, no one knew whether groups developed across time and, if they did, how long the developmental process took. There was a sizable body of research, but most of it was case studies or impressionistic. Very few systematic observational studies had been undertaken for understandable reasons. Systematic observation of real groups is labor-intensive, is extremely time-consuming, and asks real people to allow researchers to audiotape or videotape their group as they discuss product development, finances, policies, and rival organizations. Developing relationships between participant groups and researchers that were beneficial to both groups often took months and even years. The only way to sustain such an effort is to create a team of researchers and to carve out smaller projects that meet university requirements for publications and dissertations and contribute to the overall long-term goals of the endeavor.

When we began, we thought that groups that met intensively for only one week could move through all the stages of group development. Now, it is clear that is not the case. We now know that there is development within each stage that parallels macrolevel developmental patterns. There are also phases within stages. Phases share some commonalities with stages, and stages share commonalities with the overall developmental process.

At present, there is a rudimentary map of the developmental process that covers the first year of a group's life span. Much detail on that map remains to be filled in, and other questions remain to be asked. What happens next? How long can groups that reach Stage 4 sustain that high level of performance? What can be done to assist groups that have difficulty with development?

This last question has received attention and brings us to the discussion of the practical implications of the developmental perspective for consulting with groups in the real world. Two studies have been conducted that begin to answer this question (Buzaglo & Wheelan, 1999; Wheelan & Gerlach-Furber, 2005). In both cases, the consulting process provided work groups with education about group development, examples of what other groups did to facilitate their group's development and productivity, and an accurate assessment of their group's developmental level; the process also allowed the group to decide which of the issues that emerged in the assessment should be worked on in order to facilitate group development and productivity. Positive changes in developmental level and productivity, as measured by the organization, were evident in both studies. It's a beginning. Given the importance of groups to the economy, education, health care, and, in these times, peace and war, we must learn more and do more to assist groups to be effective, productive, and ethical in their intragroup and intergroup interactions. The developmental perspective has proven to be not only a fertile research area but also a practical approach to consulting with groups. As Kurt Lewin (1951) wrote, "there is nothing so practical as a good theory" (p. 169).

References

Abrams, D. (1994). Social self-regulation. *Personality and Social Psychology Bulletin, 20,* 473–483.

Abrams, D., Ando, K., & Hinkle, S. W. (1998). Psychological attachment to the group: Cross-cultural differences in organizational identification and subjective norms as predictors of workers' turnover intentions. *Personality and Social Psychology Bulletin, 24,* 1027–1039.

Allen, M., & Bourhis, J. (1996). The relationship of communication apprehension to communication behavior: A meta-analysis. *Communication Quarterly, 44,* 214–226.

Ancona, D. G., & Caldwell, D. F. (1988). Beyond task and maintenance: Defining external functions in groups. *Group and Organization Studies, 13,* 468–494.

Ancona, D. G., & Caldwell, D. F. (1992). Bridging the boundary: External activity and performance in organizational teams. *Administrative Science Quarterly, 37,* 634–665.

Arrow, H., McGrath, J. E., & Berdahl, J. L. (2000). *Small groups as complex systems: Formation, coordination, development, and adaptation.* Thousand Oaks, CA: Sage.

Asch, S. E. (1955). Opinions and social pressures. *Scientific American, 193*(5), 31–35.

Bales, R. F. (1955). Adaptive and integrative changes as sources of strain in social Systems. In A. P. Hare, E. F. Borgatta, & R. F. Bales (Eds.), *Small groups: Studies in social interaction* (pp. 127–131). New York: Knopf.

Bales, R. F. (1970). *Personality and interpersonal behavior.* New York: Holt, Rinehart and Winston.

Bales, R. F., & Strodtbeck, F. L. (1951). Phases in group problem solving. *Journal of Abnormal and Social Psychology, 46,* 485–495.

Bass, B. M., Wurster, C. R., Doll, P. A., & Clair, D. J. (1953). Situational and personality factors in leadership among sorority women. *Psychological Monographs, 67,* 16.

Bennis, W., & Shepard, H. (1956). A theory of group development. *Human Relations, 9,* 415–437.

Bion, W. (1961). *Experiences in groups.* New York: Basic Books.

Borgatta, E. F., & Bales, R. F. (1953). Task and accumulation of experience as factors in the interaction of small groups. *Sociometry, 16,* 239–252.

Braaten, L. J. (1974/1975). Developmental phases of encounter groups: A critical review of models and a new proposal. *Interpersonal Development, 75,* 112–129.

Bradford, L., Gibb, J., & Benne, K. (1964). *T-group theory and the laboratory method.* New York: John Wiley.

Brewer, M. B., & Brown, R. J. (1998). Intergroup relations. In D. T. Gilbert, S. T. Fiske, & G. Lindzey (Eds.), *The handbook of social psychology* (Vol. 2, pp. 554–594). New York: McGraw-Hill.

Broome, B. J., & Fulbright, L. (1995). A multistage influence model of barriers to group problem solving: A participant-generated agenda for small group research. *Small Group Research, 26,* 25–55.

Buck, R., Miller, R. E., & Caul, W. F. (1974). Sex, personality, and physiological variables in the communication of affect via facial expression. *Journal of Personality and Social Psychology, 30,* 587–596.

Burnand, G. (1990). Group development phases as working through six fundamental human problems. *Small Group Research, 21,* 255–273.

Buzaglo, G., & Wheelan, S. (1999). Facilitating work team effectiveness: Case studies from Central America. *Small Group Research, 30*(1), 108–129.

Campion, M. A., Medsker, G. J., & Higgs, A. C. (1993). Relations between work group characteristics and effectiveness: Implications for designing effective work groups. *Personnel Psychology, 46,* 823–850.

Campion, M. A., Papper, E. M., & Medsker, G. J. (1996). Relations between work group characteristics and effectiveness: A replication and extension. *Personnel Psychology, 49,* 429–452.

Caple, R. (1978). The sequential stages of group development. *Small Group Behavior, 9,* 470–476.

Carley, K. (1991). A theory of group stability. *American Sociological Review, 56*(3), 331–354.

Coser, L. (1956). *The functions of social conflict.* New York: Free Press.

Cummings, T. G. (1981). Designing effective workgroups. In P. C. Nystrom & W. Starbuck (Eds.), *Handbook of organizational design* (Vol. 2, pp. 250–271). Oxford, UK: Oxford University Press.

Deutsch, M. (1971). Toward an understanding of conflict. *International Journal of Group Tensions, 1,* 42–54.

Deutsch, M. (1990). Forms of social organization: Psychological consequences. In H. T. Himmelweit & G. Gaskell (Eds.), *Societal psychology* (pp. 157–176). Newbury Park, CA: Sage.

Dunphy, D. C. (1964). Social change in self-analytic groups. In P. J. Stone, D. C. Dunphy, M. S. Smith, & D. M. Ogilvie (Eds.), *The general inquirer: A computer approach to content analysis.* Cambridge: MIT Press.

Dunphy, D. C. (1968). Phases, roles, and myths in self-analytic groups. *The Journal of Applied Behavioral Science, 4,* 195–225.

Erikson, E. (1950). *Childhood and society.* New York: W. W. Norton.

Erikson, E. (Ed.). (1978). *Adulthood.* New York: W. W. Norton.

Farrell, M. P. (1976). Patterns in the development of self-analytic groups. *The Journal of Applied Behavioral Science, 12,* 523–542.

Gabarro, J. J. (1987). The development of working relationships. In J. W. Lorsch (Ed.), *Handbook of organizational behavior* (pp. 172–189). Englewood Cliffs, NJ: Prentice Hall.

Galagan, P. (1986). Work teams that work. *Training and Development Journal, 11,* 33–35.

Gibb, J. R. (1961). Defensive communication. *Journal of Communication, 11,* 141–148.

Gibbard, G., & Hartman, J. (1973). The Oedipal paradigm in group development: A clinical and empirical study. *Small Group Behavior, 4,* 305–354.

Goodacre, D. M. (1953). Group characteristics of good and poor performing combat units. *Sociometry, 16,* 168–178.

Goodman, P. S., Devadas, R., & Hughson, T. L. G. (1988). Groups and productivity: Analyzing the effectiveness of self-managing teams. In J. P. Campbell & R. J. Campbell (Eds.), *Productivity in organizations* (pp. 295–327). San Francisco: Jossey-Bass.

Guzzo, R. A., & Dickson, M. W. (1996). Teams in organizations: Recent research on performance and effectiveness. *Annual Review of Psychology, 47,* 307–338.

Hackman, J. R. (2002). *Leading teams: Setting the stage for great performances.* Boston: Harvard Business School Press.

Hare, A. P. (1967). Small group development in the relay assembly testroom. *Sociological Inquiry, 37,* 169–182.

Hare, A. P. (1976). *Handbook of small group research* (2nd ed.). New York: Free Press.

Hare, A. P. (1982). *Creativity in small groups.* Beverly Hills, CA: Sage.

Hare, A. P., & Naveh, D. (1984). Group development at the Camp David Summit, 1978. *Small Group Behavior, 15,* 299–318.

Haythorn, W. (1953). The influence of individual members on the characteristics of small groups. *Journal of Abnormal and Social Psychology, 48,* 276–284.

Hill, W. F. (1974). Systematic group development— SGD therapy. In A. Jacobs & W. Spradlin (Eds.), *The group as agent of change* (pp. 97–120). New York: Behavioral Publications.

Hill, W. F., & Gruner, L. (1973). A study of development in open and closed groups. *Small Group Behavior, 4,* 355–382.

Hogan, R. (1975). Theoretical egocentrism and the problem of compliance. *American Psychologist, 30,* 533–539.

Hogg, M. A. (2001). Social categorization, self-categorization, depersonalization, and group behavior. In M. A. Hogg & S. Tindale (Eds.), *Blackwell handbook of social psychology: Vol. 3. Group processes* (pp. 56–85). Oxford, UK: Blackwell.

Jehn, K. A. (1995). A multimethod examination of the benefits and detriments of intragroup conflict. *Administrative Science Quarterly, 40,* 256–282.

Karau, S. J., & Williams, K. D. (1993). Social loafing: A meta-analytic review and theoretical integration. *Journal of Personality and Social Psychology, 65,* 681–706.

Ketchum, L. (1984). How redesigned plants really work. *National Productivity Review, 3,* 245–254.

Keyton, J. (1999). Relational communication in groups. In L. R. Frey, D. S. Gouran, & M. S. Poole (Eds.), *The handbook of group communication theory and research* (pp. 251–287). Thousand Oaks, CA: Sage.

Kogan, N., & Wallach, M. A. (1967). Group risk taking as a function of members' anxiety and defensiveness. *Journal of Personality, 35,* 50–63.

Kuypers, B., Davies, D., & Glaser, K. (1986). Developmental arrestations in self-analytic groups. *Small Group Behavior, 17,* 269–302.

Leonard, R. L., Jr. (1975). Self-concept and attraction for similar and dissimilar others. *Journal of Personality and Social Psychology, 31,* 926–929.

Levine, J. M., & Moreland, R. L. (1990). Progress in small group research. *Annual Review of Psychology, 41,* 585–634.

Lewin, K. (1951). *Field theory in social science* (D. Cartwright, Ed.). New York: Harper.

Luft, J. (1984). *Group processes: An introduction to group dynamics.* Palo Alto, CA: Mayfield.

Lundgren, D. (1971). Trainer style and patterns of group development. *The Journal of Applied Behavioral Science, 7,* 689–709.

Lundgren, D., & Knight, D. (1978). Sequential stages of development in sensitivity training groups. *The Journal of Applied Behavioral Science, 14,* 204–222.

Mann, R. (1966). The development of member and member-trainer relationships in self-analytic groups. *Human Relations, 19,* 85–115.

Mann, R., Gibbard, G., & Hartman, J. (1967). *Interpersonal style and group development.* New York: John Wiley.

Manz, C. C., & Sims, H. P. (1987). Leading workers to lead themselves: The external leadership of self-managing work teams. *Administrative Science Quarterly, 32,* 106–128.

McCroskey, J. C., Hamilton, P. R., & Weiner, A. N. (1974). The effect of interaction behavior on source credibility, homophily, and interpersonal attraction. *Human Communication Research, 1,* 42–52.

McGrath, J. E. (1991). Time, interaction, and performance (TIP): A theory of groups. *Small Group Research, 22,* 147–174.

Mennecke, B. E., Hoffer, J. A., & Wynne, B. E. (1992). The implications of group development and history for group support system theory and practice. *Small Group Research, 23,* 524–572.

Miles, M. (1971). *Learning to work in groups.* New York: Teachers College Press.

Mills, C. W. (1959). *The sociological imagination.* London: Oxford University Press.

Mills, T. (1964). *Group transformations: An analysis of a learning group.* Englewood Cliffs, NJ: Prentice Hall.

Mitchell, R. R. (1975). Relationships between personal characteristics and change in sensitivity training groups. *Small Group Behavior, 6,* 414–420.

Northen, H. (1969). *Social work with groups.* New York: Columbia University Press.

Oakes, P. J. (1987). The salience of social categories. In J. C. Turner, M. A. Hogg, P. J. Oakes, S. D. Reicher, & M. S. Wetherell (Eds.), *Rediscovering the social group: A self-categorization theory* (pp. 117–141). Oxford, UK: Blackwell.

Parsons, T. (1961). An outline of the social system. In T. Parsons, E. Shils, K. D. Naegele, & J. R. Pitts (Eds.), *Theories of society* (pp. 30–79). New York: Free Press.

Poole, M. S., & Roth, J. (1989). Decision development in small groups V: Test of a contingency model. *Human Communication Research, 15,* 549–589.

Pritchard, R. D., Jones, S., Roth, P., Stuebing, K., & Ekeberg, S. (1988). Effects of group feedback, goal setting, and incentives on organizational productivity. *Journal of Applied Psychology, 73*(2), 337–358.

Rogers, C. (1970). *Carl Rogers on encounter groups.* New York: Harper & Row.

Ryan, E. D., & Lakie, W. L. (1965). Competitive and noncompetitive performance in relation to achievement motive and manifest anxiety. *Journal of Personality and Social Psychology, 1,* 342–345.

Salas, E., Dickinson, T. L., Converse, S. A., & Tannenbaum, S. I. (1992). Toward an understanding of team performance and training. In R. W. Swezey & E. Salas (Eds.), *Teams: Their training and performance* (pp. 3–29). Norwood, NJ: ABLEX.

Salazar, A. J., Hirokawa, R. Y., Propp, K. M., Julian, K. M., & Leatham, G. B. (1994). In search of true causes: Examination of the effect of group potential and group interaction on decision performance. *Human Communication Research, 20,* 529–559.

Sampson, E. E. (1989). The debate on individualism: Indigenous psychologies of the individual and their role in personal and societal functioning. *American Psychologist, 43,* 15–22.

Schein, E. (1992). *Organizational culture and leadership* (2nd ed.). San Francisco: Jossey-Bass.

Schutz, W. (1958). *FIRO: A three dimensional theory of interpersonal behavior.* New York: Holt, Rinehart & Winston.

Shea, G. P., & Guzzo, R. A. (1987). Groups as human resources. In K. M. Rowland & G. R. Ferris (Eds.), *Research in personnel and human resources management* (Vol. 5, pp. 256–323).Greenwich, CT: JAI Press.

Slater, P. (1966). *Microcosm.* New York: John Wiley.

Sorrentino, R. M., & Sheppard, B. H. (1978). Effects of affiliation-related motives on swimmers in individual versus group competition: A field experiment. *Journal of Personality and Social Psychology, 36,* 704–714.

Steiner, I. D. (1972). *Group process and productivity.* New York: Academic Press.

Stiles, W. B., Tupler, L. A., & Carpenter, J. C. (1982). Participants' perceptions of self-analytic group sessions. *Small Group Behavior, 13,* 237–254.

Stock, D., & Thelen, H. (1958). *Emotional dynamics and group culture.* New York: New York University Press.

Teichman, Y. (1974). Predisposition for anxiety and affiliation. *Journal of Personality and Social Psychology, 29,* 405–410.

Terry, D. J., & Hogg, M. A. (Eds.). (1998). *Attitudes, behavior, and social context: The role of norms and group membership.* Mahwah, NJ: Lawrence Erlbaum.

Thelen, H. A. (1954). *Dynamics of groups at work.* Chicago: University of Chicago Press.

Theodorson, G. A. (1962). The function of hostility in small groups. *Journal of Social Psychology, 256,* 57–66.

Tuckman, B. W. (1965). Developmental sequence in small groups. *Psychological Bulletin, 63,* 384–399.

Tuckman, B. W., & Jensen, M. A. C. (1977). Stages in small group development revisited. *Group and Organizational Studies, 2,* 419–427.

Verdi, A. F., & Wheelan, S. (1992). Developmental patterns in same-sex and mixed-sex groups. *Small Group Research, 23,* 256–278.

Wheelan, S. A. (1990). *Facilitating training groups: A guide to leadership and verbal intervention skills.* New York: Praeger.

Wheelan, S. (1994). *Group processes: A developmental perspective.* Boston: Allyn & Bacon.

Wheelan, S. (1999). *Creating effective teams.* Thousand Oaks, CA: Sage.

Wheelan, S. (2004). *Group processes: A developmental perspective* (2nd ed.). Boston: Allyn & Bacon.

Wheelan, S., Burchill, C., & Tilin, F. (2003). The link between teamwork and patients' outcomes in intensive care units. *American Journal of Critical Care, 12*(6), 527–534.

Wheelan, S., Buzaglo, G., & Tsumura, E. (1998). Developing assessment tools for cross cultural group research. *Small Group Research, 29*(3), 359–370.

Wheelan, S., Davidson, B., & Tilin, F. (2003). Group development: Reality or illusion? *Small Group Research, 34*(2), 223–245.

Wheelan, S., & Gerlach-Furber, S. (2005). Facilitating team development, communication, and productivity. In L. Frey (Ed.), *Innovations in group facilitation: Applications in natural settings* (pp. 95–116). Thousand Oaks, CA: Sage.

Wheelan, S., & Hochberger, J. (1996). Validation studies of the group development questionnaire. *Small Group Research, 27,* 143–170.

Wheelan, S., & Kaeser, R. M. (1997). The influence of task type and designated leaders on developmental patterns in groups. *Small Group Research, 28*(1), 94–121.

Wheelan, S., & Kesselring, J. (in press). The link between faculty group development and the performance of elementary students on standardized tests. *Journal of Educational Research.*

Wheelan, S., & Lisk, A. (2000). Cohort group effectiveness and the educational achievement of adult undergraduate students. *Small Group Research, 31,* 724–738.

Wheelan, S., & McKeage, R. (1993). Developmental patterns in small and large groups. *Small Group Research, 24,* 60–83.

Wheelan, S., Murphy, D., Tsumura, E., & Fried Kline, S. (1998). Member perceptions of internal group dynamics and productivity. *Small Group Research, 29,* 371–393.

Wheelan, S., & Tilin, F. (1999). The relationship between faculty group effectiveness and school productivity. *Small Group Research, 30,* 59–81.

Wheelan, S., Verdi, A., & McKeage, R. (1994). *The group development observation system: Origins and applications.* Philadelphia: GDQ Associates.

Wheelan, S., & Williams, T. (2003). Mapping dynamic interaction patterns in work groups. *Small Group Research, 34,* 443–467.

Yalom, I. (1995). *The theory and practice of group psychotherapy* (4th ed.). New York: Basic Books.

Zurcher, L. A. (1969). Stages of development in poverty program neighborhood committees. *Journal of Applied Behavioral Science, 5,* 223–251.

8

The Social Identity Perspective

Michael A. Hogg

The social identity approach is a set of interconnected concepts that provide a unified social psychological explanation of group membership, group behavior, and intergroup relations. These concepts address cognitive, social interactive, and macrosocial dimensions. The approach is explicitly framed by an interactionist metatheory, and the group is defined cognitively in terms of people's self-conception as group members. A group exists psychologically to the extent that three or more people define and evaluate themselves in terms of attributes they share and that distinguish them from other people.

Historically, the social identity approach has focused on large-scale intergroup relations and the analysis of prejudice, discrimination, social conflict, and social change (see Tajfel & Turner's 1979 classic statement of social identity theory). These remain an important focus, but over the past 10 or 15 years, a focus on social interactive phenomena within and between small groups has also developed (for overviews, see Abrams, Hogg, Hinkle, & Otten, in press; Hogg, Abrams,

Otten, & Hinkle, 2004). The approach is now genuinely an analysis of group membership and group life, which addresses both intra- and intergroup phenomena and ranges from small interactive groups to large-scale social categories. Originating in the work of Henri Tajfel at the start of the 1970s, the social identity approach has attracted many collaborators and followers, and since the mid-1990s, it has become a familiar part of the landscape of mainstream social psychology—one that continues to develop conceptually and to spawn a huge literature.

This chapter describes the concepts that form the social identity approach. Although some empirical research is referenced in passing, this is a theory chapter. Research findings related to social identity and collective self-conception are described later in this volume by Dominic Abrams and colleagues (see Abrams, Frings, & Randsley de Moura, Chapter 18, this volume). The notion of an integrated social identity *approach* (or perspective) is not new. This idea was explicit in Hogg and Abrams's (1988) overview of social identity theory and research and in their and others' subsequent research; it is consistent with Tajfel's original vision. The idea of an integrated social identity approach has also been echoed by Turner (1999), and it frames a number of recent overviews and reviews of social identity theory and research (e.g., Abrams & Hogg, 2001; Hogg, 2001b, 2003; Hogg & Abrams, 2003).

The chapter opens with a short history of the development of the social identity approach and a description of its metatheoretical background. I then describe each of the conceptual components or subtheories of the approach and go on to deal briefly with some developments, extensions, and applications of the social identity approach, most of them conceptual.

History and Development

For recent accounts of the history and meta-theoretical background of the social identity approach, see Turner (1999), Hogg (2000a), Hogg and Williams (2000), and Abrams and Hogg (2004). The social identity approach has its scientific origins in research by Henri Tajfel on perceptual accentuation effects of categorization (Tajfel, 1959), cognitive aspects of prejudice (Tajfel, 1969), effects of minimal intergroup categorization (Tajfel, Billig, Bundy, & Flament, 1971), and social comparison processes and intergroup relations (Tajfel, 1974). The emotional drive for its development was, however, very personal: Tajfel's experiences as a Polish Jew in Europe during the rise of the Nazis, the Second World War, the Holocaust, and the postwar relocation of displaced Europeans.

Tajfel had an overwhelming personal passion to understand prejudice, discrimination, and intergroup conflict. His explicit metatheoretical goal (Turner, 1996) was to develop an explanation that (a) did not reinterpret the phenomena as reflecting personality traits or individual personality differences and (b) did not reinterpret large-scale collective phenomena as simply the expression of individual or interpersonal

processes among a large number of people (see Billig, 1976). In resisting reductionism, Tajfel set himself up in opposition to the dominant paradigm in social psychology; this is one reason why, from the outset, social identity research was sometimes conducted as though it were a social movement, and social identity theorists were an "active minority" (cf. Moscovici, 1976).

From the late 1960s through to his death in 1982, Tajfel—in collaboration with John Turner, who joined him in the early 1970s—integrated his social categorization, ethnocentrism, social comparison, and intergroup relations research around the concept of social identity. Drawing on work by Berger (1966; Berger & Luckmann, 1971), Tajfel (1972) first defined social identity as "the individual's knowledge that he belongs to certain social groups together with some emotional and value significance to him of this group membership" (p. 292). Groups, as collections of people sharing the same social identity, compete with one another to be distinctive in ways that are evaluated positively. The strategies that groups use to compete for positive distinctiveness depend on people's beliefs about the nature of intergroup relations. This analysis, which became known as social identity theory and later the "social identity theory of *intergroup behavior*" (Turner, Hogg, Oakes, Reicher, & Wetherell, 1987, p. 42), was laid out by Tajfel (1974) and published by Tajfel and Turner in their classic 1979 article.

From the end of the 1970s through the mid-1980s, Turner and his students refocused attention on and elaborated the role and operation of the categorization process. These ideas were formalized as self-categorization theory (Turner, 1985; Turner et al., 1987), also called "the social identity theory of the group" (Turner et al., 1987, p. 42). Self-categorization theory, as the cognitive component of the social identity approach (see Farr, 1996), describes precisely how social categorization of self and others underpins social identification and associated group and intergroup phenomena. During this period, an analysis of the social influence process associated with group membership and social identity was also developed (Turner, 1982): People construct group norms from appropriate in-group members and in-group behaviors and internalize and enact these norms as part of their social identity. The early and mid-1980s also witnessed growing interest in the motivational bases of social identity processes; self-enhancement seemed to be involved, but researchers hoped to describe precisely how (Abrams & Hogg, 1988).

By the mid-1980s, social identity research had become relatively diverse, conceptually and empirically, and the field was in need of integrative focus. This was provided by Hogg and Abrams (1988), who promoted the idea of a social identity approach (or perspective, or analysis) within which were embedded specific concepts, theories, or analyses dealing with different aspects of social identity processes and phenomena.

Since the late 1980s, there has been an explosion of research and publication on social identity processes. The social identity approach plays a central role in the continuing revival of social psychological research on group processes and intergroup relations (Abrams & Hogg, 1998; Hogg & Abrams, 1999; Moreland, Hogg, & Hains, 1994). Much of this work can be characterized as theoretical or empirical consolidation. However, there have also been more substantial and concerted developments. For example, work on stereotyping (e.g., Leyens, Yzerbyt, & Schadron, 1994; Oakes, Haslam, & Turner, 1994), self-conception (e.g., Abrams, 1996; Brewer & Gardner, 1996; Hogg, 2001c; Reid & Deaux, 1996), motivation (e.g., Abrams & Hogg, 1988; Hogg, 2000b; Rubin & Hewstone, 1998), collective processes (e.g., Reicher, 2001; Reicher, Spears, & Postmes, 1995), norms and social influence (e.g., Terry & Hogg, 1996; Turner, 1991), multiple categorization and diversity (e.g., Crisp, Ensari, Hewstone, & Miller, 2003; Wright, Aron, & Tropp, 2002), and intragroup phenomena mainly in small groups (see Abrams et al., in press; Hogg et al., 2004).

Metatheoretical Background

The social identity approach has always been characterized by an explicit metatheoretical commitment—what the approach should and should not do or deal with, what its explanatory scope and range are, what level of explanation is appropriate, and so forth. The social identity approach was developed within the metatheoretical framework of postwar European social psychology, and although the approach is no longer tied to Europe, it retains this metatheoretical heritage.

European social psychology was decimated by World War II, and for many years after 1945, it was effectively an outpost of American social psychology. However, by the 1960s, it had become clear to European social psychologists that they had a common and distinctive European perspective, emphasis, or agenda in social psychology, which differed from mainstream American social psychology in that it was more sharply focused on the "wider social context" of social behavior (e.g., Jaspars, 1980, 1986).

This European emphasis on a more *social* social psychology (e.g., Taylor & Brown, 1979) is exemplified by *The Social Dimension: European Developments in Social Psychology*, a two-volume, 700-page book edited by Tajfel (1984). The book was intended to capture the essence of a distinctive European social psychology over the 20 years since the birth of postwar European social psychology in the early 1960s. In their introduction to Volume 1, Tajfel, Jaspars, and Fraser (1984) noted that amid the diversity of European social psychology,

there seems to exist a very general common denominator: in a phrase, it can be referred to as *the social dimension* of European social psychology. This is simply described: in much of the work—whatever its background, interests, theoretical approach or research direction—there has been a constant stress on the social and interactive aspects of our subject. Social psychology in

Europe is today much more *social* than it was 20 years ago. (p. 1)

Later, they defined the social dimension as a

view that social psychology can and must include in its theoretical and research preoccupations a direct concern with the relationship between human psychological functioning and the large-scale social processes and events which shape this functioning and are shaped by it. (Tajfel et al., 1984, p. 3)

European social psychology adopted an interactionist metatheory that attended closely to levels of explanation and proscribed reductionism (e.g., Doise, 1986). The goal was to develop concepts and theories that were appropriate to the level of explanation being sought and then to articulate these concepts and theories within a wider conceptual framework. Together, the social dimension and the interactionist metatheory have promoted a keen interest among European social psychologists in the study of groups and, in particular, relations between large-scale social categories. The study of intergroup relations is tightly linked to a distinctive European perspective that focuses on people's interaction with one another not as unique individuals but as members of social groups (Manstead, 1990). The focus is on the collective self, not the autonomous individual self.

The social identity approach was deliberately and systematically developed within this intellectual milieu; its genealogy is European. Until the late 1980s, social identity theory, along with research on minority influence and social representations (Moscovici, 1976, 1980, 1988), epitomized the distinctively European approach to social psychology and was sometimes seen as a vehicle for the promotion of a European metatheory. The metatheory remains important, but key social identity researchers, most of them Europeans, are now spread around the world. Although social identity theorists are still

passionate, the missionary zeal of the early years is less strident, and the approach is now more inclusive and diverse.

Social Identity, Collective Self, and Group Membership: Conceptual Architecture

In this section, the social identity approach is described in terms of its conceptual components (Hogg, 2003; also see Hogg et al., 2004), each of which is not only described but also discussed in terms of any qualifications, debates, or controversies. The components serve different explanatory functions and focus on different aspects of group membership and group life. They fit together and articulate smoothly with one another to provide an integrative middle-range social psychological theory of the relationship between self-conception and group processes. This way of characterizing the social identity approach and its conceptual building blocks is consistent with Tajfel's original vision of an interactionist theory linking individual cognition, social interaction, and societal processes in a nonreductionist manner.

Social Identity and Personal Identity

A social group is a collection of more than two people who share the same social identity: They identify themselves in the same way and have the same definition of who they are, what attributes they have, and how they relate to and differ from specific out-groups or from people who are simply not in-group members. Group membership is a matter of collective self-construal—*we, us,* and *them.* Social identity is quite different from personal identity. Personal identity is a self-construal in terms of idiosyncratic personality attributes that are not shared with other people (*I*), or close personal relationships that are tied entirely to the specific other person in the dyadic relationship (*me* and *you*). Personal identity has little to do with group processes, although group life often provides a context in which personal identities and interpersonal relationships are formed (e.g., friendships and enmities).

People have as many social identities and personal identities as there are groups that they feel they belong to, or personal relationships they have. Identities vary in their subjective importance and value and in how accessible they are in people's minds (chronic accessibility) or in the immediate situation (situational accessibility). However, in any given situation, only one identity is psychologically real—the salient basis of self-construal, social perception, and social conduct. Identities can change quickly in response to contextual changes; hence, social identity is context dependent not only in terms of which social identity is salient but also in terms of what form the identity may take.

Types of Selves and Identities

Traditionally, social identity research has simply distinguished between social and personal identity. However, there are some qualifications and alternative views. For example, Reid and Deaux (1996) acknowledge a basic difference between collective and individual selves. They use the terms (social) *identities* and (personal) *attributes*, rather than social identity and personal identity. They suggest that the cognitive organization of self-structure involves a significant amount of linkage between certain identities and certain attributes. Deaux, Reid, Mizrahi, and Ethier (1995) have also suggested that although social and personal identities differ qualitatively from one another, there are also important qualitative differences among types of social identity (e.g., ethnicity/religion, stigma, political).

Brewer and Gardner (1996) distinguish among three aspects of the self: *individual self* (defined by personal traits that differentiate self

from all others), *relational self* (defined by dyadic relationships that assimilate self to significant other people; see Yuki, 2003), and *collective self* (defined by group membership that differentiates *us* from *them*). Brewer (2001) goes one step further. She distinguishes four types of social identity: (a) *person-based social identities* emphasize how properties of groups are internalized by individual group members as part of the self-concept; (b) *relational social identities* define self in relation to specific other people with whom one interacts in a group context, corresponding closely to Brewer and Gardner's (1996) *relational self* and to Markus and Kitayama's (1991) *interdependent self*; (c) *group-based social identities* are equivalent to the collective self or social identity as traditionally defined; and (d) *collective identities* arise from a process whereby group members not only share self-defining attributes but also engage in social action to forge an image of what the group stands for and how it is represented and viewed by others.

Of most interest here is the status of the relational self or relational social identity; from a social identity perspective, is it a form of social identity or a form of personal identity? The social identity jury is still out, but one possibility is that sometimes, it can be one, and sometimes, the other. For example, dyadic relational identities in individualistic cultures can separate people from the group, an example being when married couples work in the same organization. In this case, relational identity is clearly personal identity, as described above. However, in collectivist cultures, group membership can be defined in terms of people's relationships to one another (Oyserman, Coon, & Kemmelmeier, 2002); one's network of relationships locates one within the group and maintains one's membership. Here, relational identity may be the way in which social identity is expressed.

Dyads, Aggregates, and Groups

What makes an aggregate of human beings a group? Most social identity researchers believe that a dyad is not a group. They believe that a group must embrace at least three people because (a) a dyad is overwhelmed by interpersonal processes and (b) you need at least three people to infer and construct common group characteristics from the behavior of others—in a dyad, there is only one other person. In addition, many group processes simply can't occur in a dyad, for example, coalition formation, majority social pressure, and deviance processes. This is consistent with the position of many other group processes researchers. For example, Forsyth (1999) believes that "dyads possess many unique characteristics simply because they include only two members. The dyad is, by definition, the only group that dissolves when one member leaves and the only group that can never be broken down into subgroups (or coalitions)" (p. 6).

Of course, two people in the same place at the same time can be a group in the sense that a shared social identity is salient, but the identity itself must rest on a larger collective. For example, two Americans meeting in Iraq may feel American and act like Americans. In this sense, they are a group, but the group they belong to is Americans, not the two of them in Iraq. To pursue this logic, from a social identity perspective, a person can quite easily act as a group member when he or she is entirely alone—in the Iraqi example, a lone American may feel and act American just on seeing the American flag.

What makes an aggregate of three or more people a group? From a social identity perspective, the critical factor is the subjective salience of social identity: People need to identify with the group as a group. This is not to say that common fate, interdependence, interaction, shared goals, group structure, and so forth do not play a role. These are all factors that raise entitativity (Campbell, 1958; Hamilton & Sherman, 1996; Lickel, Hamilton, Wieczorkowska, Lewis, & Sherman, 2000) and make a group more "groupy" and perhaps more cohesive.

In addition, groups vary in size, function, longevity, distribution, and so forth (Deaux et al.,

1995). One general distinction is between similarity-based/categorical groups and interaction-based/dynamic groups (Arrow, McGrath, & Berdahl, 2000; Wilder & Simon, 1998)—what Prentice, Miller, and Lightdale (1994) call *common-identity* groups (groups based on direct attachment to the group) and *common-bond* groups (groups based on attachment among members). This distinction has an impressive pedigree. It goes back to an important distinction in the social sciences, originally made in 1857 by Tönnies (1955) between *Gemeinschaft* (i.e., community) and *Gesellschaft* (i.e., association); that is, social organization based on close interpersonal bonds and social organization based on more formalized and impersonal associations.

Although these distinctions capture important differences in the nature of a group, social identity theorists believe that the essence of groupness is still social identification. People can be in a common-bond or a common-identity group, but if they have no sense of belonging, do not identify, and do not define and evaluate self in terms of the properties of the group, then they are unlikely to think, feel, and behave as group members.

Social Categorization, Prototypes, and Depersonalization

Prototypes

Social categorization is the cognitive heart of social identity processes (Turner et al., 1987). Quite simply, without categories of people, there can be no social groups. People cognitively represent social categories in terms of group *prototypes*. A prototype is a fuzzy set of attributes (perceptions, attitudes, feelings, and behaviors) that are related to one another in a meaningful way and that simultaneously capture similarities and structural relationships within the group and differences between the group and other groups or people who are not in the group.

Prototypes not only describe categories but also evaluate them and prescribe membership-related behavior.

Prototypes map out the representational contours of social groups; they tell us not only what characterizes a group but how that group is different from other groups. In this sense, prototypes maximize entitativity, the extent to which a category appears to be a cohesive and clearly structured entity that is distinct from other entities (e.g., Campbell, 1958; Hamilton & Sherman, 1996). Prototype formation and change are governed by the *metacontrast principle*, prototypes maximizing the ratio of perceived intergroup differences to intragroup differences, and thus, they accentuate similarity within groups and differences between groups (cf. Tajfel, 1959).

There are a number of implications of this analysis.

1. The content of a prototype rests on which human attributes best satisfy the meta-contrast principle—with the caveat that people behave more like motivated tacticians than cognitive misers (Fiske & Taylor, 1991) and therefore are motivated (see below) to try to select attributes that favor the in-group over the out-group.

2. Because intergroup differentiation is an intrinsic component of metacontrast, prototypes rarely describe average or typical in-group members; rather they are polarized away from out-group features and describe ideal, often hypothetical, in-group members.

3. Because metacontrast rests on making comparisons within and between groups, any change in the social comparative context (e.g., the specific out-group or in-group members present, or specific goals embedded in the context) affects the prototype. Prototypes are context specific and can change if the context changes. This variability may be dramatic (e.g., in relatively small and new groups), but it may

also be more modest due to the inertial anchoring effect of enduring group representations (e.g., in large ethnic groups).

4. Intra- and intergroup behaviors are inextricable: What happens between groups affects what happens within groups, and vice versa.

Categorization and Depersonalization

Social categorization transforms social perception; rather than seeing people as idiosyncratic individuals, you see them through the lens of the prototype, measuring them against the prototype and assigning prototypical attributes to them. They become *depersonalized*.

Depersonalization is not the same thing as deindividuation or dehumanization. Depersonalization means viewing a person as a category representative rather than a unique individual, and it is associated with a change in identity. Deindividuation, on the other hand, implies a loss of identity (often associated with primitive antisocial impulses; Zimbardo, 1970), and dehumanization implies the treatment of someone as less than human and therefore beneath contempt. Depersonalization can produce antisocial behavior and dehumanized treatment of others, but only if the relevant prototype prescribes such conduct (cf. Reicher et al., 1995).

Social categorization depersonalizes both in-group and out-group members. Depersonalized perception of out-group members is more commonly called stereotyping; you view "them" as being similar to one another and all having out-group attributes. When you categorize yourself, exactly the same depersonalization process applies to self: You view yourself in terms of the attributes of the in-group (self-stereotyping), and because prototypes also describe and prescribe group-appropriate ways to feel and behave, you feel and behave normatively. In this way, self-categorization also produces, within a group, conformity and patterns of in-group liking, trust, and solidarity.

A slightly different but generally compatible emphasis on depersonalization has been proposed by Wright and his associates (e.g., Wright et al., 2002). Drawing on the ideas that people can internalize the properties of other people as part of themselves (e.g., Aron, Aron, Tudor, & Nelson, 1991) and that people can include the in-group as part of the self (e.g., Smith & Henry, 1996), Wright and his colleagues propose that strength of identification is a function of the degree to which the group is included in the self.

Salience

For a social categorization to affect one's behavior, it must be psychologically real; that is, it must be psychologically salient as the basis for perception and self-conception. The principle governing social identity salience, developed and elaborated by Oakes (1987) from work by Bruner (1957), rests on the twin notions of *accessibility* and *fit*.

People draw on readily accessible social categorizations, ones that are valued, important, and frequently employed aspects of the self-concept (they are chronically accessible in memory), and/or self-evident and perceptually salient in the immediate situation (they are situationally accessible). For example, gender and race are often chronically and situationally accessible social categorizations (e.g., Mackie, Hamilton, Susskind, & Rosselli, 1996).

People use accessible categories to make sense of the social context, in terms of people's attitudes, behaviors, and so forth. They investigate the extent to which the categorization accounts for similarities and differences among people (called structural or comparative fit) and the extent to which the stereotypical properties of the categorization account for why people behave as they do (called normative fit). If the fit of the categorization to the social field is poor (e.g., similarities and differences do not correspond to people's gender

or race, and people do not behave in gender- or race-stereotypical ways), people cycle through other accessible categorizations (e.g., political orientation, religion, profession, and so forth) until an optimal level of fit is obtained. People are not passive pawns in the accessibility by fit process. In line with the motivated tactician model of social cognition, people are motivated to make categorizations that favor the in-group fit, and they may go to some lengths to do this. Salience is not only a cognitive perceptual process but also a social process in which people may compete or "negotiate" over category salience.

Optimal fit identifies and locks in the psychologically salient categorization, which now acts as the basis of depersonalization and self-categorization in that context. The salient categorization accentuates perceived similarities within groups and differences between groups, to construct in-group and out-group prototypes that maximize entitativity and intergroup separateness and clarity in that particular context.

Motivation: Self-Enhancement, Uncertainty Reduction, and Optimal Distinctiveness

Social identity processes are guided by two basic motivations: self-enhancement and uncertainty reduction. These motivations are cued by the intergroup social comparison idea: that groups strive to be both better and more distinct. A third motivation that may play a role is optimal distinctiveness.

Self-Enhancement and Positive Distinctiveness

One of the key features of group life and intergroup relations is positive distinctiveness: We are better than them. Groups struggle to protect or promote their relative status and prestige. The reason they do this is that social identity ties self-evaluation to group evaluation (self is group, and group evaluation is self-evaluation), and one of the most basic human motives is for self-enhancement and self-esteem (Sedikides & Strube, 1997). In salient group contexts, the *self* in self-enhancement and self-esteem is the collective self or social identity (Abrams & Hogg, 1988; Crocker & Luhtanen, 1990; Long & Spears, 1997; Rubin & Hewstone, 1998). Positive distinctiveness is motivated by collective-self enhancement.

Although possession of a devalued or stigmatized social identity can depress self-esteem, people have substantial capacity to buffer themselves from this consequence (e.g., Crocker, Major, & Steele, 1998). People can also, as we saw above, respond in many different ways to a devalued or negative social identity. However, having a valued social identity and belonging to a prestigious high-status group has, in salient intergroup contexts, a more generally positive effect on self-esteem. Self-esteem may be an index of successfully belonging to a positively distinctive group; it may act as a sociometer (Leary, Tambor, Terdal, & Downs, 1995).

Uncertainty Reduction

The other social identity motive is uncertainty reduction (Hogg, 2000b, 2001a). This is an epistemic motive that is tied directly to the social categorization process. People strive to reduce subjective uncertainty about their social world and about their place within it: They like to know who they are and how to behave, and who others are and how they might behave. Social categorization ties self-definition, behavior, and perception to prototypes that describe and prescribe behavior; as a result, it reduces uncertainty. Certainty, particularly self-conceptual certainty, renders others' behavior predictable and therefore allows one to avoid harm and plan effective action. It also allows one to know how one should feel and behave. The more self-conceptually

uncertain one is, the more one strives to belong to high entitativity groups that have clearly defined consensual prototypes.

Under extreme circumstances, these groups might be orthodox and extremist, possess closed ideologies and belief systems, and be rigidly structured in terms of leadership and authority (Hogg, 2004). Ideological belief systems such as belief in a just world (Furnham & Procter, 1989), the Protestant work ethic (Furnham, 1990), and right-wing authoritarianism (Altemeyer, 1998) are associated with conditions of social uncertainty and instability (e.g., Doty, Peterson, & Winter, 1991; Furnham & Procter, 1989). To the extent that such belief systems are tied to group memberships, identification perhaps mediates the link between social uncertainty and ideology. Another implication of the uncertainty reduction hypothesis is that subordinate groups may sometimes acquiesce in their subordinate status simply because challenging the status quo raises self-conceptual uncertainty to unacceptable levels (cf. Jost & Hunyadi, 2002; Jost & Kramer, 2003).

Perhaps, uncertainty depresses self-esteem, and it is self-esteem and not uncertainty that motivates social identity processes via self-enhancement. Although uncertainty can depress self-esteem, it does not necessarily have to do so, and research shows that uncertainty has a motivational effect on identification, independent of self-esteem (Hogg & Svensson, 2004). Self-enhancement and uncertainty reduction interact. Where people are self-conceptually uncertain, they are motivated by uncertainty reduction and identify equally with low- or high-status groups; where people are self-conceptually certain, they are motivated by self-enhancement to identify more with high- than low-status groups (Reid & Hogg, 2004).

Optimal Distinctiveness

A third motive that may be involved in social identity processes is optimal distinctiveness (Brewer, 1991). Brewer argues that people are driven by conflicting motives for inclusion/ sameness (satisfied by group membership) and for distinctiveness/uniqueness (satisfied by individuality) and that they try to strike a balance between these two motives to achieve optimal distinctiveness. Smaller groups more than satisfy the need for distinctiveness, so people strive for greater inclusiveness, whereas large groups more than satisfy the need for inclusiveness, so people strive for distinctiveness within the group. One implication of this idea is that people should be more satisfied with membership in midsize groups than groups that are very large or very small.

Social Attraction and Group Cohesion

In salient groups, the prototype is the basis of perception, inference, and behavior. Within groups, people are highly attuned to prototypicality. Reactions to and feelings about fellow members are underpinned by perceptions of how prototypical those others are, how closely they match the group prototype. Hence, if the prototype changes, then feelings for and perceptions of specific members will change as their prototypicality changes.

One implication of this is that as group membership becomes salient, the basis of one's evaluations of and feelings for other people (i.e., liking) is transformed from personal identity-based *personal attraction* (traditional interpersonal attraction) to prototype-based depersonalized *social attraction* (Hogg, 1992, 1993). Social attraction is a function of how much one identifies with the group and how prototypical the other person is; it is positive regard or liking for the in-group prototype as it is embodied by real in-group members. Social attraction tends to be relatively consensual and unidirectional: If membership is salient and there is agreement among group members on the prototype, then more prototypical members tend to be consensually popular and less prototypical

members tend to be consensually socially unpopular. The network of depersonalized prototype-based positive regard and liking within a salient group represents the affective aspect of group cohesiveness, the warm feeling of oneness with fellow members.

Although social and personal attraction are produced by different processes and are therefore orthogonal, the conditions of group life mean that they can co-occur in groups (e.g., Mullen & Copper, 1994); people like one another as group members, and this allows them to develop positive interpersonal relationships.

Social Comparison

Social comparison processes between salient groups follow a different logic than those that occur in interpersonal or intragroup contexts. Intergroup social comparisons are not oriented toward identifying similarities to enhance uniformity and assimilation. Instead, they are oriented toward identifying differences between self, as in-group member, and other, as out-group member, and accentuating those differences (Turner, 1975; also see Hogg, 2000a). According to Tajfel (1972), "social comparisons between groups are focused on the establishment of distinctiveness between one's own and other groups" (p. 296). Furthermore, because one's social identity not only describes but also evaluates who one is, intergroup comparisons strive toward in-group distinctiveness that is *evaluated positively*.

Intergroup Relations

Social identity is thus anchored in valence-sensitive social comparisons that strive for similarity within groups and differentiation between groups (Hogg, 2000a). This idea explains the ethnocentrism and in-group favoritism that is so characteristic of intergroup relations (Brewer & Campbell, 1976; Sumner, 1906). It explains why groups compete with each other to be both different and better—why they struggle over status, prestige, and distinctiveness.

Tajfel's (1974) analysis of intergroup behavior and social change integrates the logic of intergroup social comparisons with an analysis of social belief structures: people's beliefs about the reality of intergroup relations and their assessment of the availability and feasibility of different strategies to achieve or maintain positive intergroup distinctiveness (Tajfel & Turner, 1979; also see Hogg & Abrams, 1988; Ellemers, 1993). The most important components of people's social belief structures are beliefs about group status, the stability and legitimacy of intergroup status relations, the permeability of intergroup boundaries, and the possibility of achieving and sustaining an alternative status structure or, if one's group has high status, maintaining the status quo.

The combination of these belief variables (status, stability, legitimacy, permeability, and alternatives) generates a wide range of different intergroup behaviors (e.g., Ellemers, van Rijswijk, Roefs, & Simons, 1997; Ellemers, Wilke, & van Knippenberg, 1993). One example is lower status groups or their members who believe that the status quo is stable and legitimate and that intergroup boundaries are permeable. These people tend to dis-identify from their group and pursue an individual mobility strategy of "passing" (gaining acceptance) as members of the higher status group. They try to gain psychological entry into the higher status group. The belief that one can pass is consistent with wider beliefs that the world is a just and fair place (belief in a just world) and that if one works hard, one can improve one's lot (Protestant work ethic) (Furnham, 1990; Furnham & Procter, 1989).

However, mobility rarely works. This is not surprising. The world is not a fair place, hard work does not necessarily pay off, and subordinate groups' beliefs are ideologically structured by dominant groups to conceal the real nature of intergroup relations. After all, it is not in the dominant group's interest to permit wholesale passing. Successful wholesale passing would

contaminate the dominant group and erase the subordinate group, effectively abolishing the comparison group that makes the dominant group appear relatively superior. Nevertheless, the ideology of mobility is very common because it is convenient for the dominant group: It prevents subordinate groups from recognizing the illegitimacy of the status quo and pursuing more competitive (and sometimes politicized) group-based intergroup strategies that might eventually topple the dominant group and change the status quo. Passing leaves people with a marginal identity (Breakwell, 1986). They are not accepted by the dominant group, and they are rejected by their own group because they have betrayed their identity.

Social Influence, Conformity, and Group Norms

The social identity notion of *prototype* is the individual cognitive analogue of the social interactive and collective notion of *norm*. Prototypes can be understood as individual cognitive representations of group norms, where such norms are social regularities that are bounded by group memberships and describe behavior that defines group membership (Turner, 1991). Group prototypes are generally shared—"we agree that we are like this and they are like that"—and are thus themselves normative. From a social identity perspective, norms are the source of social influence in groups because they are prescriptive, not merely descriptive. The self-categorization and depersonalization process explains how people conform to or enact group norms (Abrams & Hogg, 1990; Turner, 1985; Turner & Oakes, 1989). Conformity is not merely surface behavioral compliance; it is a process whereby people's behavior is transformed to correspond to the appropriate self-defining group prototype.

The social identity perspective calls the social influence process associated with conformity *referent informational influence* (Turner, 1982; also see Hogg & Turner, 1987). In group contexts, people pay attention to information about the context-specific group norm. Typically, the most immediate and best source of this information is identity-consistent behavior of core or prototypical group members; however, out-groups can also provide relevant information ("whatever they are, we are not"). Once the norm has been recognized or established, it is internalized as the context-specific in-group prototype and conformed to via the self-categorization process. Contextual norms serve at least two functions: to express in-group similarities and in-group identity and also to differentiate and distance the in-group from the out-group. Because of this, in-group norms tend to be polarized away from out-group norms and thus to be more extreme than the average of in-group properties.

Developments and Extensions

The social identity approach has been extended and developed over the years to help make sense of a wide range of group and intergroup phenomena. The original focus, as described earlier, was mainly on intergroup relations between large social categories. Since the early to mid-1990s, however, this has been complemented with an increasing focus on intragroup processes and on smaller interactive groups (e.g., Hogg, 1996a, 1996b). In this section, I very briefly describe some of these developments and extensions of the social identity approach.

Roles, Subgroups, and Cross-Cutting Categories

Groups are rarely homogeneous. In almost all cases, they are internally structured in terms of roles, subgroups, nested categories, cross-cutting categories, and so forth. Most groups contain generic roles, such as newcomer, full member, and old-timer, which members move in and out of as they enter a group, become socialized, and leave a group (e.g., Levine &

Moreland, 1994). Role occupation is a matter of bilateral commitment between the group and the member, and, according to Moreland and Levine and colleagues, the dynamic of commitment rests on assessments of how prototypical the member is of the group as a whole and of the role within the group (e.g., Moreland & Levine, 2003; Moreland, Levine, & Cini, 1993; Moreland, Levine, & McMinn, 2001). From a social identity perspective, prototype-based commitment and in-role behavior and self-definition are clearly associated with social identification.

Another analysis of roles that fits well with the social identity perspective is provided by Ridgeway (e.g., 2001). Drawing on status characteristics theory (e.g., Berger, Fisek, Norman, & Zelditch, 1977), Ridgeway explains how people in small groups have more status and influence within the group if they possess specific status characteristics (attributes that are critical for the group's task) and diffuse status characteristics (attributes that classify them as belonging to a high-status group in society). From a social identity perspective, specific status characteristics are analogous to group prototypical characteristics, and diffuse status characteristics identify a high-status cross-cutting category membership. So, for example, in a small decision-making group, being a doctor and having a track record of making good decisions for the group provide more status within the group than being a janitor and having a poor record of making good decisions for the group.

In addition to roles, groups can contain wholly nested subgroups (e.g., sales and marketing in an organization, Scotland and Wales within the United Kingdom) or cross-cutting categories that have members in other groups (e.g., psychologists and physicists in a university, Basques in Spain and in France). These structural features of groups affect and are affected by social identity processes, and they influence group behavior in numerous ways (e.g., Brewer, 1996; Crisp et al., 2003; see Hogg & Hornsey, in press). One example is the phenomenon of schisms. Sani and Reicher (e.g., 2000) argue that a schism is most likely to occur and persist within a group when social identity is threatened and the superordinate group is intolerant of diverse views.

A critical feature of subgroup structure is that in almost all such situations, one group's attributes are better represented in the overarching group, and thus, one nested or cross-cutting group occupies a dominant position (e.g., Mummendey & Wenzel, 1999; Wenzel, Mummendey, Weber, & Waldzus, 2003). Subordinate subgroups can, therefore, feel that their distinct identity within the larger collective is threatened, which can cause them to fight strongly to maintain their independence (e.g., Hewstone, 1996; Hornsey & Hogg, 2000). This is precisely why many organizational mergers and takeovers fail (e.g., Terry, Carey, & Callan, 2001).

Groups that embrace diverse roles, subgroups, or nested categories often contain the seeds of subgroup conflict. However, this is not always the case, and this kind of diversity can sometimes be beneficial for the group. For example, diversity can improve the quality of group decisions (Tindale, Kameda, & Hinsz, 2003): Identity-related attitudinal diversity combats groupthink (Stasser, Stewart, & Wittenbaum, 1995); demographic diversity benefits organizations (Brewer, 1996); and group decision-making is improved by unshared information (Wittenbaum & Stasser, 1996), the presence of minority views (Nemeth & Staw, 1989), and tolerance for internal criticism (Hornsey & Imani, 2004). Going one step further, diversity that is internalized by members as part of their social identity may have a range of advantages for group functioning and group life as a whole (e.g., Niedenthal & Beike, 1997; Roccas & Brewer, 2002; Wright et al., 2002).

Leadership

A social identity analysis of leadership has recently been formulated (Hogg, 2001d; Hogg & van Knippenberg, 2003; van Knippenberg & Hogg, 2003). As group membership becomes psychologically more salient and members identify more strongly with the group, leadership endorsement and leadership effectiveness are increasingly based on how prototypical the leader is considered to be. In salient groups, prototypical members are the focus of depersonalization and conformity, and thus, they appear to exert greater influence than less prototypical members. Prototypical members are also the focus of consensual depersonalized social attraction, which provides them with status and the ability to gain compliance from others; they appear to have easy influence over members and can be innovative. Because they are figural against the background of the rest of the group, their behavior is internally attributed. This constructs in the eyes of the group a leadership persona for them that further facilitates effective leadership.

Prototypical members usually identify more strongly with the group, and they therefore quite naturally behave in a group-serving manner. This validates their membership credentials and builds trust among other members; they are trusted to be acting in the best interest of the group and are, paradoxically, given greater latitude to be innovative and nonconformist. Leaders who are not highly prototypical still need to prove their membership and therefore are less trusted. They need to behave in a conformist manner that stands in the way of innovation and effective leadership.

Marginal Membership and Deviance

Unlike prototypical members, who are positioned to be influential within the group, prototypically marginal members are not liked (social attraction) or trusted much and can therefore be relatively uninfluential and may be treated as deviants (e.g., Hogg, in press; Hogg, Fielding, & Darley, in press; Marques, Abrams, Páez, & Hogg, 2001). Marques's analysis of the "black sheep effect" shows that people who occupy the prototypical boundary between in- and out-group are disliked more and are more strongly rejected if they are in-group than out-group members (Marques & Páez, 1994).

Abrams and Marques's subjective group dynamics model (e.g., Abrams, Marques, Bown, & Henson, 2000; Marques, Abrams, & Serodio, 2001) goes further, attributing the group's reaction to deviants to the fact that deviants threaten the integrity of group norms. Hogg et al. (in press) build in a motivational component. They argue that the reaction of members to a deviant depends on (a) whether the deviant occupies a position on the boundary with the out-group or remote from the out-group, (b) whether there is a threat to the group's valence or its distinctiveness, and (c) whether the deviant publicly attributes his or her deviance to self or to the group.

Emler and Reicher (1995) focus on delinquency as deviant behavior. From a social identity perspective, they suggest that delinquency, particularly among adolescent boys, is strategic behavior designed to establish and manage a favorable reputation among groups of peers. Consistent with this view is the fact that delinquent behavior is most common among children who feel that they cannot meet exacting adult standards of academic achievement, and it is a group activity that occurs in public, thus satisfying its identity-confirming function.

Although marginal members are generally treated negatively by the group, they may also fulfill important social change functions for the group. For example, deviants can serve as in-group critics (e.g., Hornsey & Imani, 2004), or as minority groups that challenge the accepted wisdom of the majority (e.g., Nemeth & Staw, 1989). In both cases, marginal members may have to struggle to be heard, but their contribution to the group is ultimately constructive: Minorities and critics are effectively trying to change the group's identity from inside.

Organizations

Because organizations are groups, the social identity approach is perfectly suited to an analysis of organizations. Beginning with Ashforth and Mael (1989), social identity research on organizational processes has increased dramatically in recent years (e.g., Haslam, 2001; Hogg & Terry, 2000, 2001; van Knippenberg & Hogg, 2001). Some of this work has focused on the role of organizational identification and commitment in worker turnover (e.g., Abrams, Ando, & Hinkle, 1998; Moreland et al., 2001). Other work has shown that organizational mergers often do not work very well because members of the newly merged organization struggle to retain their former organizational identity (e.g., Terry et al., 2001). There is also research focusing on how organizations manage sociocultural diversity in the workplace (e.g., Brewer, 1996). Leadership (see above) and trust within organizations (e.g., Tyler & Huo, 2002) are two other foci of social identity research in organizational contexts.

Group Decision-Making

Many groups, particularly in organizational and work contexts, exist primarily to make decisions. From a social identity perspective, as a group becomes more salient and perhaps more cohesive, there is a greater tendency for members to conform to the group norm and to endorse a prototype-consistent group decision. The idea of normative decision-making in groups goes back, of course, to classic conformity research by Sherif (1936) and Asch (1955) and others. However, from a social identity perspective, the emphasis is on normative behavior rather than social pressure from other members; people conform to local group norms rather than comply with individuals (Abrams & Hogg, 1990; Turner, 1991).

One implication is that where group norms are polarized away from a salient out-group, group discussion or decision making will produce group polarization: a post-discussion group position that is more extreme than the pre-discussion position in a direction displaced away from a salient out-group (e.g., Abrams, Wetherell, Cochrane, Hogg, & Turner, 1990; Mackie, 1986). Another implication is that groupthink, which is generally attributed to excessive cohesiveness in small groups, may be more closely tied to excessive depersonalized social attraction rather than excessive interpersonal attraction (e.g., Hogg & Hains, 1998; Turner, Pratkanis, Probasco, & Leve, 1992).

Nowadays, organizations often make decisions via a process of computer-mediated communication (CMC) within virtual groups (Hollingshead, 2001). The social identity model of deindividuation phenomena (SIDE; Reicher et al., 1995) helps explain what may go on in such groups. CMC has a participation equalization effect that evens out many of the status effects that occur in face-to-face groups, and so people may feel less inhibited because they are less personally identifiable. However, disinhibition depends on how effectively identity and status markers are concealed by the electronic medium (Spears & Lea, 1994). If people feel anonymous in the presence of a highly salient social identity, they will conform strongly to identity-congruent norms and will be easily influenced by group leaders and normative group members (Postmes, Spears, & Lea, 1998; Postmes, Spears, Sakhel, & de Groot, 2001).

Individual Motivation in Groups

A robust finding in social psychology is that people working collectively in small groups exert less effort on a task than if they performed the task alone: They loaf (e.g., Karau & Williams, 1993). However, this effect can be muted under a number of circumstances, for example, when people believe strongly in the group and feel they need to compensate for others' poor performance (e.g., Williams, Karau, & Bourgeois, 1993). These are factors that might be associated with enhanced identification with the group. Indeed, if one identifies strongly with

the group and the task is identity defining, then people may work harder in a group than they do alone (e.g., Fielding & Hogg, 2000). In this way, social identification can transform loafing into industriousness.

Related to this is the robust finding from research on social dilemmas that selfishness prevails when a group accesses a limited or diminishing resource, such as a rainforest (e.g., Dawes & Messick, 2000; Kerr & Park, 2001). But, as in the social loafing example above, identification with the group that accesses the resource can transform selfishness into prosocial behavior and cause people to sacrifice short-term personal gain for the long-term collective good (e.g., Brewer & Schneider, 1990; de Cremer & van Vugt, 1999).

Mobilization and Collective Action

The idea that belonging to a group can increase one's motivation to exert effort on behalf of the group and its goals speaks to the topic of social mobilization: participation in social protest or social action groups (e.g., Reicher, 2001; Stürmer & Simon, in press; Stürmer, Simon, Loewy, & Jörger, 2003).

The study of social protest is the study of how individual discontents or grievances are transformed into collective action. How and why do sympathizers become mobilized as activists or participants? Klandermans (1997) argues that mobilization reflects the attitude-behavior relationship; sympathizers hold sympathetic attitudes toward an issue, yet these attitudes do not readily translate into behavior. Participation also resembles a social dilemma. Protest is generally *for* a social good (e.g., equality) or *against* a social ill (e.g., oppression), and as success benefits everyone irrespective of participation but failure harms participants more, it is tempting to *free ride*—to remain a sympathizer rather than become a participant. The role of leadership is critical in mobilizing a group to take action, and in particular, the leader needs to be viewed as a just person who can be trusted to be acting in the best interest of the group and its members (e.g., Tyler & Smith, 1998). Ultimately, however, it is social identification that increases the probability of social action and collective protest (e.g., Simon et al., 1998).

Culture and Social Identity

There is a burgeoning interest among social psychologists in the study of culture (e.g., Fiske, Kitayama, Markus, & Nisbett, 1998). Most research dwells on cultural differences between large-scale categories (individualist West vs. collectivist East; e.g., Hofstede, 1980) or on cultural differences in self-construal (independent vs. interdependent/relational self; e.g., Brewer & Gardner, 1996; Markus & Kitayama, 1991; Yuki, 2003; see Oyserman et al., 2002).

Culture, at the global level, certainly impacts how people interact and represent themselves and, therefore, how small groups operate (e.g., leadership processes). Culture can, however, also be analyzed at a more microsocial level: Different groups have different cultures, different ways of thinking, acting, and relating to and among one another (e.g., Moreland & Levine, 2003). This latter way of conceptualizing culture brings the concepts of culture and norm extremely close together and makes the social identity analysis of identity, group membership, and norms directly applicable to the analysis of culture.

From a social identity perspective, we might expect social identity processes in small groups to be more evident in collectivist than individualist societies (e.g., Hinkle & Brown, 1990). Collectivist norms prioritize the group over the individual and thus encourage social identity and group-oriented behavior. But is it true that social identity processes are less strong in individualistic societies? The answer is probably no. Cultural norms may regulate how people interact and conduct themselves in groups, but

groups still provide people with a strong sense of self, social location, and belonging. So, people in small groups with a strongly individualistic norm or local culture will, paradoxically, behave more individualistically as a function of increased identification (e.g., Jetten, Postmes, & McAuliffe, 2002; McAuliffe, Jetten, Hornsey, & Hogg, 2003).

Conclusion

The social identity approach is a general analysis of the relationship between the collective self-concept, group belonging, and group and intergroup phenomena. It is an approach that is intended to apply to groups of all sizes and forms and to all group and intergroup contexts. The group is defined cognitively: Three or more people who share the same social identity (i.e., evaluative self-definition). Social identity is distinguished from personal identity, which is associated with personal relationships and idiosyncratic attributes, not with group phenomena.

The social identity approach grew out of research on perception, categorization, prejudice, discrimination, intergroup relations, and social comparison by Henri Tajfel in the late 1950s and the 1960s. It has its intellectual and historical roots in the postwar reconstruction of a distinctive European social psychology. This heritage has provided the social identity approach with an explicit interactionist and nonreductionist metatheory. The social identity approach continues to develop and grow.

The main section of this chapter describes the conceptual building blocks of the social identity approach. These conceptual components deal with different aspects of social identity processes but are compatible with one another. People represent social categories as prototypes: fuzzy sets of attributes (attitudes, feelings, and behaviors) that maximize the ratio of intergroup differences to intragroup differences (metacontrast) and thus maximize entitativity. Social categorization of others and of self depersonalizes perception and behavior such that people, including self, are viewed in terms of the relevant prototype; they are matched against the prototype and imbued with the attributes of the prototype. Self-categorization has the additional effect of transforming one's own attitudes, feelings, and behaviors to conform to the prototype.

Social identity processes are motivated by positive distinctiveness. Because groups define and evaluate social identity and people strive for a positive rather than a negative self-concept, intergroup social comparisons are oriented toward differentiation, not similarity, and intergroup relations are a struggle over relative status and prestige. How the struggle is conducted rests on subjective beliefs about intergroup status relations in terms of how stable and legitimate such relations are, how permeable intergroup boundaries are, and how attainable alternative status relations are. Social identity processes are also motivated by uncertainty reduction: People strive to reduce subjective uncertainty about who they are, about who others are, and about how people relate to one another. Social categorization reduces uncertainty, and high-entitativity groups with clear prototypes reduce uncertainty most effectively. Sometimes, groups will suffer low status to avoid the self-conceptual uncertainty associated with social change.

Social identity effects only occur when group membership is psychologically salient, that is, when a social categorization is internalized in a specific context to define self and others. People try out different social categorizations to make sense of a social context; they draw on categorizations that are accessible in memory and/or in the immediate situation and assess how well they fit similarities and differences among people and the way in which people are actually behaving. The process is also motivated by concerns to self-enhance and to reduce uncertainty. Optimal fit renders a social categorization psychologically salient. This produces depersonalization; in-group, out-group, and self-stereotyping; conformity to in-group norms;

prototype-based liking (social attraction); in-group cohesion and solidarity; ethnocentrism; intergroup differentiation; and attention to in-group norms and in-group prototypicality.

Social identity principles have also been elaborated to provide a social identity analysis of roles, subgroup and cross-cutting category relations, leadership, deviance and marginal membership, organizational behaviors, group decision-making phenomena, motivation increments in groups, group-oriented behavior that resolves social dilemmas, culture, social mobilization, and collective action. This is a theory chapter. For recent coverage of empirical support for the social identity approach, see Abrams et al. (Chapter 18, this volume; see also Abrams & Hogg, 2001; Abrams et al., in press; Hogg, 2001b; Hogg & Abrams, 2003).

I will conclude this chapter by mentioning some misunderstandings about and unresolved issues in the social identity approach. First, many people still believe the social identity approach is all about intergroup relations and has little interest in or little to offer to small or interactive groups. This was probably true 20 years ago, but I hope this chapter has shown that this is certainly not the case now. The second possible misunderstanding is that the social identity approach places no conceptual value on social interaction and interdependence and therefore only speaks about abstract categories of human beings. From a social identity perspective, a group is psychologically real only if people identify with it. However, interaction, communication, and interdependence are bases for identification, outcomes of identification, and channels for learning about what the group stands for and about one's relative position in the group.

There are three conceptual issues. The first is that although the "accessibility X fit" formulation of salience makes good sense conceptually, it remains a challenge to operationalize salience reliably as an independent variable in experiments. The second issue has already been alluded to: the status of relational identity and the relational self. Is the relational self a social or a personal identity or a quite separate third kind of identity? One possibility is that the self, defined in terms of relationships, is a personal identity in individualist cultures and a social identity in collectivist cultures.

The third conceptual issue is whether identities are hydraulically related to one another so that the more one identity prevails, the less others do (e.g., Mullen, Migdal, & Rozell, 2003). Or can multiple identities be simultaneously salient? This issue points toward one significant future development in social identity research: In intergroup contexts, can people simultaneously identify with a subgroup and superordinate group, and, if so, might this be a means of defusing intergroup conflict and constructing groups and identities that celebrate diversity (Hogg & Hornsey, in press)?

References

Abrams, D. (1996). Social identity, self as structure, and self as process. In W. P. Robinson (Ed.), *Social groups and identities: Developing the legacy of Henri Tajfel* (pp. 143–167). Oxford, UK: Butterworth-Heinemann.

Abrams, D., Ando, K., & Hinkle, S. W. (1998). Psychological attachment to the group: Cross-cultural differences in organizational identification and subjective norms as predictors of workers' turnover intentions. *Personality and Social Psychology Bulletin, 24*, 1027–1039.

Abrams, D., & Hogg, M. A. (1988). Comments on the motivational status of self-esteem in social identity and intergroup discrimination. *European Journal of Social Psychology, 18*, 317–334.

Abrams, D., & Hogg, M. A. (1990). Social identification, self-categorization, and social influence. *European Review of Social Psychology, 1*, 195–228.

Abrams, D., & Hogg, M. A. (1998). Prospects for research in group processes and intergroup relations. *Group Processes and Intergroup Relations, 1*, 7–20.

Abrams, D., & Hogg, M. A. (2001). Collective identity: Group membership and self-conception. In M. A. Hogg & R. S. Tindale (Eds.), *Blackwell handbook of social psychology: Group processes* (pp. 425–460). Oxford, UK: Blackwell.

Abrams, D., & Hogg, M. A. (2004). Metatheory: Lessons from social identity research. *Personality and Social Psychology Review, 8*, 98–106.

Abrams, D., Hogg, M. A., Hinkle, S., & Otten, S. (in press). The social identity perspective on small groups. In M. S. Poole & A. B. Hollingshead (Eds.), *Theories of small groups: An interdisciplinary perspective*. Thousand Oaks, CA: Sage.

Abrams, D., Marques, J. M., Bown, N. J., & Henson, M. (2000). Pro-norm and anti-norm deviance within in-groups and out-groups. *Journal of Personality and Social Psychology, 78*, 906–912.

Abrams, D., Wetherell, M. S., Cochrane, S., Hogg, M. A., & Turner, J. C. (1990). Knowing what to think by knowing who you are: Self-categorization and the nature of norm formation, conformity, and group polarization. *British Journal of Social Psychology, 29*, 97–119.

Altemeyer, B. (1998). The other "authoritarian personality." In M. Zanna (Ed.), *Advances in experimental social psychology* (Vol. 30, pp. 47–92). Orlando, FL: Academic Press.

Aron, A., Aron, E. N., Tudor, M., & Nelson, G. (1991). Close relationships as including other in the self. *Journal of Personality and Social Psychology, 60*, 241–253.

Arrow, H., McGrath, J. E., & Berdahl, J. L. (2000). *Small groups as complex systems: Formation, coordination, development, and adaptation*. Thousand Oaks, CA: Sage.

Asch, S. E. (1955). Opinions and social pressures. *Scientific American, 193*(5), 31–35.

Ashforth, B. E., & Mael, F. A. (1989). Social identity theory and the organization. *Academy of Management Review, 14*, 20–39.

Berger, J., Fisek, M. H., Norman, R. Z., & Zelditch, M., Jr. (1977). *Status characteristics and social interaction*. New York: Elsevier.

Berger, P. L. (1966). Identity as a problem in the sociology of knowledge. *European Journal of Sociology, 7*, 105–115.

Berger, P. L., & Luckmann, T. (1971). *The social construction of reality*. Harmondsworth, UK: Penguin.

Billig, M. (1976). *Social psychology and intergroup relations*. London: Academic Press.

Breakwell, G. (1986). *Coping with threatened identities*. London: Methuen.

Brewer, M. B. (1991). The social self: On being the same and different at the same time. *Personality and Social Psychology Bulletin, 17,* 475–482.

Brewer, M. B. (1996). Managing diversity: The role of social identities. In S. Jackson & M. Ruderman (Eds.), *Diversity in work teams* (pp. 47–68). Washington, DC: American Psychological Association.

Brewer, M. B. (2001). The many faces of social identity: Implications for political psychology. *Political Psychology, 22,* 115–125.

Brewer, M. B., & Campbell, D. T. (1976). *Ethnocentrism and intergroup attitudes: East African evidence.* New York: Sage.

Brewer, M. B., & Gardner, W. (1996). Who is this 'we'? Levels of collective identity and self representations. *Journal of Personality and Social Psychology, 71,* 83–93.

Brewer, M. B., & Schneider, S. (1990). Social identity and social dilemmas: A double-edged sword. In D. Abrams & M. A. Hogg (Eds.), *Social identity theory: Constructive and critical advances* (pp. 169–184). London: Harvester Wheatsheaf.

Bruner, J. S. (1957). On perceptual readiness. *Psychological Review, 64,* 123–152.

Campbell, D. T. (1958). Common fate, similarity, and other indices of the status of aggregates of persons as social entities. *Behavioral Science, 3,* 14–25.

Crisp, R. J., Ensari, N., Hewstone, M., & Miller, N. (2003). A dual-route model of crossed categorization effects. In W. Stroebe & M. Hewstone (Eds.), *European review of social psychology* (Vol. 13, pp. 35–74). New York: Psychology Press.

Crocker, J., & Luhtanen, R. (1990). Collective self-esteem and ingroup bias. *Journal of Personality and Social Psychology, 58,* 60–67.

Crocker, J., Major, B., & Steele, C. (1998). Social stigma. In D. T. Gilbert, S. T. Fiske, & G. Lindzey (Eds.), *The handbook of social psychology* (4th ed., Vol. 2, pp. 504–553). New York: McGraw-Hill.

Dawes, R. M., & Messick, D. M. (2000). Social dilemmas. *International Journal of Psychology, 35,* 111–116.

Deaux, K., Reid, A., Mizrahi, K., & Ethier, K. A. (1995). Parameters of social identity. *Journal of Personality and Social Psychology, 68,* 280–291.

de Cremer, D., & van Vugt, M. (1999). Social identification effects in social dilemmas: A transformation of motives. *European Journal of Social Psychology, 29,* 871–893.

Doise, W. (1986). *Levels of explanation in social psychology.* Cambridge, UK: Cambridge University Press.

Doty, R. M., Peterson, B. E., & Winter, D. G. (1991). Threat and authoritarianism in the United States, 1978–1987. *Journal of Personality and Social Psychology, 61,* 629–640.

Ellemers, N. (1993). The influence of socio-structural variables on identity management strategies. *European Review of Social Psychology, 4,* 27–57.

Ellemers, N., van Rijswijk, W., Roefs, M., & Simons, C. (1997). Bias in intergroup perceptions: Balancing group identity with social reality. *Personality and Social Psychology Bulletin, 23,* 186–198.

Ellemers, N., Wilke, H., & van Knippenberg, A. (1993). Effects of the legitimacy of low group or individual status on individual and collective identity enhancement strategies. *Journal of Personality and Social Psychology, 64,* 766–778.

Emler, N., & Reicher, S. D. (1995). *Adolescence and delinquency: The collective management of reputation.* Oxford, UK: Blackwell.

Farr, R. M. (1996). *The roots of modern social psychology: 1872–1954.* Oxford, UK: Blackwell.

Fielding, K. S., & Hogg, M. A. (2000). Working hard to achieve self-defining group goals: A social identity analysis. *Zeitschrift für Sozialpsychologie, 31,* 191–203.

Fiske, A. P., Kitayama, S., Markus, H. R., & Nisbett, R. E. (1998). The cultural matrix of social psychology. In D. T. Gilbert, S. T. Fiske, & G. Lindzey (Eds.), *The handbook of social psychology* (4th ed., Vol. 2, pp. 915–981). New York: McGraw-Hill.

Fiske, S. T., & Taylor, S. E. (1991). *Social cognition* (2nd ed.). New York: McGraw-Hill.

Forsyth, D. R. (1999). *Group dynamics* (3rd ed.). Belmont, CA: Wadsworth.

Furnham, A. (1990). *The Protestant work ethic: The psychology of work-related beliefs and behaviors.* New York: Routledge.

Furnham, A., & Procter, E. (1989). Belief in a just world: Review and critique of the individual difference literature. *British Journal of Social Psychology, 28,* 365–384.

Hamilton, D. L., & Sherman, S. J. (1996). Perceiving persons and groups. *Psychological Review, 103,* 336–355.

Haslam, S. A. (2001). *Psychology in organisations: The social identity approach.* London: Sage.

Hewstone, M. (1996). Contact and categorization: Social-psychological interventions to change intergroup relations. In C. N. Macrae, C. Stangor, & M. Hewstone (Eds.), *Stereotypes and stereotyping* (pp. 323–368). New York: Guilford.

Hinkle, S. W., & Brown, R. J. (1990). Intergroup comparisons and social identity: Some links and lacunae. In D. Abrams & M. A. Hogg (Eds.), *Social identity theory: Constructive and critical advances* (pp. 48–70). Hemel Hempstead, UK: Harvester Wheatsheaf.

Hofstede, G. (1980). *Culture's consequences.* Beverly Hills, CA: Sage.

Hogg, M. A. (1992). *The social psychology of group cohesiveness: From attraction to social identity.* Hemel Hempstead, UK: Harvester Wheatsheaf.

Hogg, M. A. (1993). Group cohesiveness: A critical review and some new directions. *European Review of Social Psychology, 4,* 85–111.

Hogg, M. A. (1996a). Intragroup processes, group structure, and social identity. In W. P. Robinson (Ed.), *Social groups and identities: Developing the legacy of Henri Tajfel* (pp. 65–93). Oxford, UK: Butterworth-Heinemann.

Hogg, M. A. (1996b). Social identity, self-categorization, and the small group. In E. H. Witte & J. H. Davis (Eds.), *Understanding group behavior: Vol. 2. Small group processes and interpersonal relations* (pp. 227–253). Mahwah, NJ: Lawrence Erlbaum.

Hogg, M. A. (2000a). Social identity and social comparison. In J. Suls & L. Wheeler (Eds.), *Handbook of social comparison: Theory and research* (pp. 401–421). New York: Kluwer/Plenum.

Hogg, M. A. (2000b). Subjective uncertainty reduction through self-categorization: A motivational theory of social identity processes. *European Review of Social Psychology, 11,* 223–255.

Hogg, M. A. (2001a). Self-categorization and subjective uncertainty resolution: Cognitive and motivational facets of social identity and group membership. In J. P. Forgas, K. D. Williams, & L. Wheeler (Eds.), *The social mind: Cognitive and motivational aspects of interpersonal behavior* (pp. 323–349). New York: Cambridge University Press.

Hogg, M. A. (2001b). Social categorization, depersonalization, and group behavior. In M. A. Hogg & R. S. Tindale (Eds.), *Blackwell handbook of social psychology: Group processes* (pp. 56–85). Oxford, UK: Blackwell.

Hogg, M. A. (2001c). Social identity and the sovereignty of the group: A psychology of belonging. In C. Sedikides & M. B. Brewer (Eds.), *Individual self, relational self, collective self* (pp. 123–143). Philadelphia: Psychology Press.

Hogg, M. A. (2001d). A social identity theory of leadership. *Personality and Social Psychology Review, 5,* 184–200.

Hogg, M. A. (2003). Social identity. In M. R. Leary & J. P. Tangney (Eds.), *Handbook of self and identity* (pp. 462–479). New York: Guilford.

Hogg, M. A. (2004). Uncertainty and extremism: Identification with high entitativity groups under conditions of uncertainty. In V. Yzerbyt, C. M. Judd, & O. Corneille (Eds.), *The psychology of group perception: Perceived variability, entitativity, and essentialism* (pp. 401–418). New York: Psychology Press.

Hogg, M. A. (in press). All animals are equal but some animals are more equal than others: Social identity and marginal membership. In K. D. Williams, J. P. Forgas, & W. von Hippel (Eds.), *The social outcast: Ostracism, social exclusion, rejection, and bullying.* New York: Psychology Press.

Hogg, M. A., & Abrams, D. (1988). *Social identifications: A social psychology of intergroup relations and group processes.* London & New York: Routledge.

Hogg, M. A., & Abrams, D. (1999). Social identity and social cognition: Historical background and current trends. In D. Abrams & M. A. Hogg (Eds.), *Social identity and social cognition* (pp. 1–25). Oxford, UK: Blackwell.

Hogg, M. A., & Abrams, D. (2003). Intergroup behavior and social identity. In M. A. Hogg & J. Cooper (Eds.), *The Sage handbook of social psychology* (pp. 407–431). London: Sage.

Hogg, M. A., Abrams, D., Otten, S., & Hinkle, S. (2004). The social identity perspective: Intergroup relations, self-conception, and small groups. *Small Group Research, 35,* 246–276.

Hogg, M. A., Fielding, K. S., & Darley, J. (in press). Deviance and marginalization. In D. Abrams, J. Marques, & M. A. Hogg (Eds.), *The social psychology of inclusion and exclusion.* New York: Psychology Press.

Hogg, M. A., & Hains, S. C. (1998). Friendship and group identification: A new look at the role of cohesiveness in groupthink. *European Journal of Social Psychology, 28,* 323–341.

Hogg, M. A., & Hornsey, M. J. (in press). Self-concept threat and multiple categorization within groups.

In R. J. Crisp & M. Hewstone (Eds.), *Multiple social categorization: Processes, models, and applications*. New York: Psychology Press.

Hogg, M. A., & Svensson, A. (2004). *Uncertainty reduction, self-esteem, and group identification.* Manuscript submitted for publication, University of Queensland.

Hogg, M. A., & Terry, D. J. (2000). Social identity and self-categorization processes in organizational contexts. *Academy of Management Review, 25,* 121–140.

Hogg, M. A., & Terry, D. J. (Eds.). (2001). *Social identity processes in organizational contexts.* Philadelphia: Psychology Press.

Hogg, M. A., & Turner, J. C. (1987). Social identity and conformity: A theory of referent informational influence. In W. Doise & S. Moscovici (Eds.), *Current issues in European social psychology* (Vol. 2, pp. 139–182). Cambridge, UK: Cambridge University Press.

Hogg, M. A., & van Knippenberg, D. (2003). Social identity and leadership processes in groups. In M. P. Zanna (Ed.), *Advances in experimental social psychology* (Vol. 35, pp. 1–52). San Diego, CA: Academic Press.

Hogg, M. A., & Williams, K. D. (2000). From I to we: Social identity and the collective self. *Group Dynamics: Theory, Research, and Practice, 4,* 81–97.

Hollingshead, A. B. (2001). Communication technologies, the Internet, and group research. In M. A. Hogg & R. S. Tindale (Eds.), *Blackwell handbook of social psychology: Group processes* (pp. 557–573). Oxford, UK: Blackwell.

Hornsey, M. J., & Hogg, M. A. (2000). Assimilation and diversity: An integrative model of subgroup relations. *Personality and Social Psychology Review, 4,* 143–156.

Hornsey, M. J., & Imani, A. (2004). Criticising groups from the inside and the outside: An identity perspective on the intergroup sensitivity effect. *Personality and Social Psychology Bulletin, 30,* 365–383.

Jaspars, J. M. F. (1980). The coming of age of social psychology in Europe. *European Journal of Social Psychology, 10,* 421–428.

Jaspars, J. M. F. (1986). Forum and focus: A personal view of European social psychology. *European Journal of Social Psychology, 16,* 3–15.

Jetten, J., Postmes, T., & McAuliffe, B. J. (2002). We're all individuals: Group norms of individualism and collectivism, levels of identification, and identity threat. *European Journal of Social Psychology, 32,* 189–207.

Jost, J. T., & Hunyadi, O. (2002). The psychology of system justification and the palliative function of ideology. *European Review of Social Psychology, 13,* 111–153.

Jost, J. T., & Kramer, R. M. (2003). The system justification motive in intergroup relations. In D. M. Mackie & E. R. Smith (Eds.), *From prejudice to intergroup emotions: Differentiated reactions to social groups* (pp. 227–245). New York: Psychology Press.

Karau, S. J., & Williams, K. D. (1993). Social loafing: A meta-analytic review and theoretical integration. *Journal of Personality and Social Psychology, 65,* 681–706.

Kerr, N. L., & Park, E. S. (2001). Group performance in collaborative and social dilemma tasks: Progress and prospects. In M. A. Hogg & R. S. Tindale (Eds.), *Blackwell handbook of social psychology: Group processes* (pp. 107–138). Oxford, UK: Blackwell.

Klandermans, B. (1997). *The social psychology of protest.* Oxford, UK: Blackwell.

Leary, M. R., Tambor, E. S., Terdal, S. K., & Downs, D. L. (1995). Self-esteem as an interpersonal monitor: The sociometer hypothesis. *Journal of Personality and Social Psychology, 68,* 518–530.

Levine, J. M., & Moreland, R. L. (1994). Group socialization: Theory and research. *European Review of Social Psychology, 5,* 305–336.

Leyens, J.-P., Yzerbyt, V., & Schadron, G. (1994). *Stereotypes and social cognition.* London: Sage.

Lickel, B., Hamilton, D. L., Wieczorkowska, G., Lewis, A. C., & Sherman, S. (2000). Varieties of groups and the perception of group entitativity. *Journal of Personality and Social Psychology, 78,* 223–246.

Long, K., & Spears, R. (1997). The self-esteem hypothesis revisited: Differentiation and the disaffected. In R. Spears, P. J. Oakes, N. Ellemers, & S. A. Haslam (Eds.), *The social psychology of stereotyping and group life* (pp. 296–317). Oxford, UK: Blackwell.

Mackie, D. M. (1986). Social identification effects in group polarization. *Journal of Personality and Social Psychology, 50,* 720–728.

Mackie, D. M., Hamilton, D. L., Susskind, J., & Rosselli, F. (1996). Social psychological foundations of stereotype formation. In C. N. Macrae, C. Stangor, & M. Hewstone (Eds.), *Stereotypes and stereotyping* (pp. 41–78). New York: Guilford.

Manstead, A. S. R. (1990). Developments to be expected in European social psychology in the 1990s. In P. J. D. Drenth, J. A. Sergeant, & R. J. Takens (Eds.), *European perspectives in psychology* (Vol. 3, pp. 183–203). Chichester, UK: Wiley.

Markus, H., & Kitayama, S. (1991). Culture and the self: Implications for cognition, emotion, and motivation. *Psychological Review, 98,* 224–253.

Marques, J. M., Abrams, D., Páez, D., & Hogg, M. A. (2001). Social categorization, social identification, and rejection of deviant group members. In M. A. Hogg & R. S. Tindale (Eds.), *Blackwell handbook of social psychology: Group processes* (pp. 400–424). Oxford, UK: Blackwell.

Marques, J. M., Abrams, D., & Serodio, R. (2001). Being better by being right: Subjective group dynamics and derogation of in-group deviants when generic norms are undermined. *Journal of Personality and Social Psychology, 81,* 436–447.

Marques, J. M., & Páez, D. (1994). The black sheep effect: Social categorization, rejection of ingroup deviates, and perception of group variability. *European Review of Social Psychology, 5,* 37–68.

McAuliffe, B. J., Jetten, J., Hornsey, M. J., & Hogg, M. A. (2003). Individualist and collectivist group norms: When it's OK to go your own way. *European Journal of Social Psychology, 33,* 57–70.

Moreland, R. L., Hogg, M. A., & Hains, S. C. (1994). Back to the future: Social psychological research on groups. *Journal of Experimental Social Psychology, 30,* 527–555.

Moreland, R. L., & Levine, J. M. (2003). Group composition: Explaining similarities and differences among group members. In M. A. Hogg & J. Cooper (Eds.), *The Sage handbook of social psychology* (pp. 367–380). London: Sage.

Moreland, R. L., Levine, J. M., & Cini, M. (1993). Group socialization: The role of commitment. In M. A. Hogg & D. Abrams (Eds.), *Group motivation: Social psychological perspectives* (pp. 105–129). London: Harvester Wheatsheaf.

Moreland, R. L., Levine, J. M., & McMinn, J. G. (2001). Self-categorization and work group socialization. In M. A. Hogg & D. Terry (Eds.), *Social identity processes in organizational contexts* (pp. 87–100). Philadelphia: Psychology Press.

Moscovici, S. (1976). *Social influence and social change.* London: Academic Press.

Moscovici, S. (1980). Toward a theory of conversion behavior. In L. Berkowitz (Ed.), *Advances in experimental social psychology* (Vol. 13, pp. 202–239). New York: Academic Press.

Moscovici, S. (1988). Notes towards a description of social representations. *European Journal of Social Psychology, 18,* 211–250.

Mullen, B., & Copper, C. (1994). The relation between group cohesiveness and performance: An integration. *Psychological Bulletin, 115,* 210–227.

Mullen, B., Migdal, M. J., & Rozell, D. (2003). Self-awareness, deindividuation, and social identity: Unraveling theoretical paradoxes by filling empirical lacunae. *Personality and Social Psychology Bulletin, 29,* 1071–1081.

Mummendey, A., & Wenzel, M. (1999). Social discrimination and tolerance in intergroup relations: Reactions to intergroup difference. *Personality and Social Psychology Review, 3,* 158–174.

Nemeth, C., & Staw, B. M. (1989). The tradeoffs of social control and innovation in groups and organizations. In L. Berkowitz (Ed.), *Advances in experimental social psychology* (Vol. 22, pp. 175–210). San Diego, CA: Academic Press.

Niedenthal, P. M., & Beike, D. R. (1997). Interrelated and isolated self-concepts. *Personality and Social Psychology Review, 1,* 106–128.

Oakes, P. J. (1987). The salience of social categories. In J. C. Turner, M. A. Hogg, P. J. Oakes, S. D. Reicher, & M. S. Wetherell (Eds.), *Rediscovering the social group: A self-categorization theory* (pp. 117–141). Oxford, UK: Blackwell.

Oakes, P. J., Haslam, S. A., & Turner, J. C. (1994). *Stereotyping and social reality.* Oxford, UK: Blackwell.

Oyserman, D., Coon, H. M., & Kemmelmeier, M. (2002). Rethinking individualism and collectivism: Evaluation of theoretical assumptions and meta-analyses. *Psychological Bulletin, 128,* 3–72.

Postmes, T., Spears, R., & Lea, M. (1998). Breaching or building social boundaries? Side-effects of computer-mediated communication. *Communication Research, 25,* 689–715.

Postmes, T., Spears, R., Sakhel, K., & de Groot, D. (2001). Social influence in computer-mediated communication: The effects of anonymity on group behavior. *Personality and Social Psychology Bulletin, 27,* 1243–1254.

Prentice, D. A., Miller, D., & Lightdale, J. R. (1994). Asymmetries in attachment to groups and to their members: Distinguishing between common-identity and common-bond groups. *Personality and Social Psychology Bulletin, 20,* 484–493.

Reicher, S. D. (2001). The psychology of crowd dynamics. In M. A. Hogg & R. S. Tindale (Eds.), *Blackwell handbook of social psychology: Group processes* (pp. 182–207). Oxford, UK: Blackwell.

Reicher, S. D., Spears, R., & Postmes, T. (1995). A social identity model of deindividuation phenomena. *European Review of Social Psychology, 6,* 161–198.

Reid, A., & Deaux, K. (1996). Relationship between social and personal identities: Segregation or integration. *Journal of Personality and Social Psychology, 71,* 1084–1091.

Reid, S. A., & Hogg, M. A. (2004). *Uncertainty reduction, self-enhancement, and social identification.* Manuscript submitted for publication, University of California, Santa Barbara.

Ridgeway, C. L. (2001). Social status and group structure. In M. A. Hogg & R. S. Tindale (Eds.), *Blackwell handbook of social psychology: Group processes* (pp. 352–375). Oxford, UK: Blackwell.

Roccas, S., & Brewer, M. B. (2002). Social identity complexity. *Personality and Social Psychology Review, 6,* 88–109.

Rubin, M., & Hewstone, M. (1998). Social identity theory's self-esteem hypothesis: A review and some suggestions for clarification. *Personality and Social Psychology Review, 2,* 40–62.

Sani, F., & Reicher, S. D. (2000). Contested identities and schisms in groups: Opposing the ordination of women as priests in the Church of England. *British Journal of Social Psychology, 39,* 95–112.

Sedikides, C., & Strube, M. J. (1997). Self-evaluation: To thine own self be good, to thine own self be sure, to thine own self be true, and to thine own self be better. In M. P. Zanna (Ed.), *Advances in experimental social psychology* (Vol. 29, pp. 209–296). New York: Academic Press.

Sherif, M. (1936). *The psychology of social norms.* New York: Harper.

Simon, B., Loewy, M., Stürmer, S., Weber, U., Freytag, P., Habig, C., Kampmeier, C., & Spahlinger, P. (1998). Collective identification and social movement participation. *Journal of Personality and Social Psychology, 74,* 646–658.

Smith, E., & Henry, S. (1996). An in-group becomes part of the self: Response time evaluation. *Personality and Social Psychology Bulletin, 22,* 635–642.

Spears, R., & Lea, M. (1994). Panacea or panopticon? The hidden power in computer-mediated communication. *Communication Research, 21,* 427–459.

Stasser, G., Stewart, D. D., & Wittenbaum, G. M. (1995). Expert roles and information exchange during discussion: The importance of knowing who knows what. *Journal of Experimental Social Psychology, 31,* 244–265.

Stürmer, S., & Simon, B. (in press). Collective action: Towards a dual-pathway model. *European Review of Social Psychology.*

Stürmer, S., Simon, B., Loewy, M., & Jörger, H. (2003). The dual-pathway model of social movement participation: The case of the fat acceptance movement. *Social Psychology Quarterly, 66,* 71–82.

Sumner, W. G. (1906). *Folkways.* Boston: Ginn.

Tajfel, H. (1959). Quantitative judgement in social perception. *British Journal of Psychology, 50,* 16–29.

Tajfel, H. (1969). Cognitive aspects of prejudice. *Journal of Social Issues, 25,* 79–97.

Tajfel, H. (1972). Social categorization. English manuscript of La catégorisation sociale. In S. Moscovici (Ed.), *Introduction à la psychologie sociale* (Vol. 1, pp. 272–302). Paris: Larousse.

Tajfel, H. (1974). *Intergroup behaviour, social comparison, and social change.* Unpublished Katz-Newcomb lectures, University of Michigan, Ann Arbor.

Tajfel, H. (Ed.). (1984). *The social dimension: European developments in social psychology.* Cambridge, UK: Cambridge University Press.

Tajfel, H., Billig, M., Bundy R. P., & Flament, C. (1971). Social categorization and intergroup behaviour. *European Journal of Social Psychology, 1,* 149–177.

Tajfel, H., Jaspars, J. M. F., & Fraser, C. (1984). The social dimension in European social psychology. In H. Tajfel (Ed.), *The social dimension: European developments in social psychology* (Vol. 1, pp. 1–5). Cambridge, UK: Cambridge University Press.

Tajfel, H., & Turner, J. C. (1979). An integrative theory of intergroup conflict. In W. G. Austin & S. Worchel (Eds.), *The social psychology of intergroup relations* (pp. 33–47). Monterey, CA: Brooks/Cole.

Taylor, D. M., & Brown, R. J. (1979). Towards a more social social psychology? *British Journal of Social and Clinical Psychology, 18,* 173–179.

Terry, D. J., Carey, C. J., & Callan, V. J. (2001). Employee adjustment to an organizational merger: An intergroup perspective. *Personality and Social Psychology Bulletin, 27,* 267–280.

Terry, D. J., & Hogg, M. A. (1996). Group norms and the attitude-behavior relationship: A role for group identification. *Personality and Social Psychology Bulletin, 22,* 776–793.

Tindale, R. S., Kameda, T., & Hinsz, V. B. (2003). Group decision-making. In M. A. Hogg & J. Cooper (Eds.), *The Sage handbook of social psychology* (pp. 381–403). London: Sage.

Tönnies, F. (1955). *Community and association.* London: Routledge & Kegan Paul. (Original work published in German in 1887)

Turner, J. C. (1975). Social comparison and social identity: Some prospects for intergroup behaviour. *European Journal of Social Psychology, 5,* 5–34.

Turner, J. C. (1982). Towards a cognitive redefinition of the social group. In H. Tajfel (Ed.), *Social identity and intergroup relations* (pp. 15–40). Cambridge, UK: Cambridge University Press.

Turner, J. C. (1985). Social categorization and the self-concept: A social cognitive theory of group behavior. In E. J. Lawler (Ed.), *Advances in group processes: Theory and research* (Vol. 2, pp. 77–122). Greenwich, CT: JAI Press.

Turner, J. C. (1991). *Social influence.* Milton Keynes, UK: Open University Press.

Turner, J. C. (1996). Henri Tajfel: An introduction. In W. P. Robinson (Ed.), *Social groups and identities: Developing the legacy of Henri Tajfel* (pp. 1–23). Oxford, UK: Butterworth-Heinemann.

Turner, J. C. (1999). Some current issues in research on social identity and self-categorization theories. In N. Ellemers, R. Spears, & B. Doosje (Eds.), *Social identity* (pp. 6–34). Oxford, UK: Blackwell.

Turner, J. C., Hogg, M. A., Oakes, P. J., Reicher, S. D., & Wetherell, M. S. (1987). *Rediscovering the social group: A self-categorization theory.* Oxford, UK: Blackwell.

Turner, J. C., & Oakes, P. J. (1989). Self-categorization and social influence. In P. B. Paulus (Ed.), *The psychology of group influence* (2nd ed., pp. 233–275). Hillsdale, NJ: Lawrence Erlbaum.

Turner, M. E., Pratkanis, A. R., Probasco, P., & Leve, C. (1992). Threat, cohesion, and group effectiveness: Testing a social identity maintenance perspective on groupthink. *Journal of Personality and Social Psychology, 63,* 781–796.

Tyler, T. R., & Huo, Y. J. (2002). *Trust in the law: Encouraging public cooperation with the police and courts.* New York: Russell Sage Foundation.

Tyler, T. R., & Smith, H. J. (1998). Social justice and social movements. In D. T. Gilbert, S. T. Fiske, & G. Lindzey (Eds.), *The handbook of social psychology* (4th ed., Vol. 2, pp. 595–629). Boston: McGraw-Hill.

van Knippenberg, D., & Hogg, M. A. (Eds.). (2001). Social identity processes in organizations [Special issue]. *Group Processes and Intergroup Relations, 4.* London: Sage.

van Knippenberg, D., & Hogg, M. A. (2003). A social identity model of leadership in organizations. In R. M. Kramer & B. M. Staw (Eds.), *Research in organizational behavior* (Vol. 25, pp. 243–295). Greenwich, CT: JAI Press.

Wenzel, M., Mummendey, A., Weber, U., & Waldzus, S. (2003). The ingroup as pars pro toto: Projection from the ingroup onto the inclusive category as a precursor to social discrimination. *Personality and Social Psychology Bulletin, 29,* 461–473.

Wilder, D., & Simon, A. F. (1998). Categorical and dynamic groups: Implications for social perception and intergroup behavior. In C. Sedikides, J. Schopler, & C. A. Insko (Eds.), *Intergroup cognition and intergroup behavior* (pp. 27–44). Mahwah, NJ: Lawrence Erlbaum.

Williams, K. D., Karau, S. J., & Bourgeois, M. (1993). Working on collective tasks: Social loafing and social compensation. In M. A. Hogg & D. Abrams (Eds.), *Group motivation: Social psychological perspectives* (pp. 130–148). London: Harvester Wheatsheaf.

Wittenbaum, G. M., & Stasser, G. (1996). Management of information in small groups. In J. L. Nye & A. M. Brower (Eds.), *What's social about social cognition* (pp. 3–28). Thousand Oaks, CA: Sage.

Wright, S. C., Aron, A., & Tropp, L. R. (2002). Including others (and groups) in the self: Self-expansion and intergroup relations. In J. P. Forgas & K. D. Williams (Eds.), *The social self: Cognitive, interpersonal, and intergroup perspectives* (pp. 343–363). New York: Psychology Press.

Yuki, M. (2003). Intergroup comparison versus intragroup relationships: A cross-cultural examination of social identity theory in North American and East Asian cultural contexts. *Social Psychology Quarterly, 66,* 166–183.

Zimbardo, P. G. (1970). The human choice: Individuation, reason, and order versus deindividuation, impulse, and chaos. In W. J. Arnold & D. Levine (Eds.), *Nebraska symposium on motivation 1969* (Vol. 17, pp. 237–307). Lincoln: University of Nebraska Press.

9

The Communication Perspective on Group Life

Lawrence R. Frey

Sunwolf

T he 20th century might well be called the communication century. From philosophers articulating theories of symbol usage to social scientists speaking about the information society to biologists talking about cells "communicating," scholars from across the academic disciplines have come to recognize the importance of communication for explaining (human) behavior. Within this contextual discourse emerged the discipline of communication.

Given the significance of communication for understanding behavior, it should come as no surprise that the study of groups has been infused by a communication approach. Over the last half century, the study of communication in groups has developed into a full-fledged academic pursuit within the communication discipline, and it has

"established a [significant] presence within the general field of Group Studies" (Gouran, 1999, p. 22).[1]

The purpose of this chapter is to provide an overview of the communication approach to the study of groups, describing the contribution that knowledge about group communication makes. We start by differentiating two perspectives regarding the meaning of communication, offering a definition for the term that takes into account both perspectives, and explaining how these two perspectives view groups as an important communication site. An examination of some group communication theories and methods used to study communication in groups[2] is followed by an overview of research conducted about group communication predispositions, practices, processes, and products.

Defining Communication

Defining the term *communication* is not an easy task. Indeed, almost 30 years ago, Dance and Larson's (1976) survey of the literature revealed 126 different definitions for the term. Etymologically, the term is derived from the Latin word, *communis,* which means "to make common." Today, as Pearce (1995) explained, most definitions of communication emphasize one of two different views about making things common:

> There is a difference in the connotations of communication depending on whether the emphasis is on that which is made *common* (shared meanings, cultural symbols, traditions, common ground, understanding) or on the process of *making* things common (the transmission of messages from place to place; the languages in which things are framed; the patterns of action in which they occur; the things that people actually do and say to each other). (p. 7)

Those who focus on the process of *making* things common adopt what can be called an *information-exchange perspective,* for they are primarily concerned with understanding how communication can be used as a tool to transfer information from a source to a receiver. Those who emphasize that which is made *common* adopt what can be called a *meaning-based* or *constitutive perspective,* for they are concerned with understanding how "our experience of reality is a product of communicative activity" (Mokros & Deetz, 1996, p. 32).

The definition of communication that we use is the one advanced by Frey, Botan, and Kreps (2000), which attempts to acknowledge communication both as a tool used to exchange information and as a meaning-based, constitutive process: "*Communication* [italics added] refers to the processes by which verbal and nonverbal messages are used to create and share meaning" (p. 28). This definition, and the two perspectives it acknowledges, has important implications for

understanding groups as a site both of and for communication.

Groups as a Communication Site

The two views of communication just described are reflected in group communication scholarship. Frey and Sunwolf (2004), for instance, recently articulated a symbolic-interpretive perspective on groups that focuses on understanding

> (a) ways in which group members use symbols (words, objects, or actions that stand for or represent something else) to communicate and the effects of symbol usage on individual, relational, and collective processes and outcomes; and (b) how groups and group dynamics themselves are products of such symbolic activity. (pp. 277–278)

They called the study of the ways in which group members use symbols to communicate a *symbolic-management focus* and the study of how groups are a product of symbolic activity a *symbolic-constitutive focus* (see also Frey & Sunwolf, in press).

Understanding the ways in which group members (use symbols to) communicate and the effects of communication on group processes and products has dominated the study of group communication. Indeed, viewing communication in groups from a symbolic-management/ information-exchange perspective is typical of theories developed within the field of communication and, especially, theories from other disciplinary perspectives. For instance, systems theory, a dominant theory across the disciplines that study groups, including the communication discipline (see Mabry, 1999), views a group (and many other constructs) as a *system*—an organized set of interrelated and interacting parts that seeks to maintain a balance amid the influences of the environments in which it is embedded. According to this perspective, a group consists, among other things, of (a) *inputs*—antecedents that precede and potentially structure group interaction and outcomes (e.g., group members, the physical environment within which a group meets, and the resources available to a group); (b) *throughputs*—processes in which a group engages as members interact (e.g., member roles and decision-making procedures employed); and (c) *outputs*—products that result from group inputs and throughputs (e.g., decisions made and member satisfaction). Communication, from this perspective, is viewed as an important throughput variable that is influenced by group inputs and affects group outputs (see, e.g., Galanes & Adams, 2004; Tubbs, 2004).[3]

From a constitutive perspective, however, "communication is not just a tool that group members use; groups are best regarded as a phenomenon that emerges from communication" (Frey, 1994a, p. x). A group, after all, is a socially constructed symbol, not a reified entity that exists in some objective sense, and communication is the primary process that creates this significant symbol. The group symbol and its accompanying symbolic boundaries (e.g., between those considered to be inside and outside of it), according to Smith and Berg (1987), lead to "the possibility of relationship . . . [for] without boundary, there can be no relationship"; in that regard, symbolic boundaries, forged from interactants' communication behavior, "are at the base of everything in group life" (p. 103). Even systems theory acknowledges the constitutive role of communication. As Mabry (1999) explained, "a core assumption of systems theorizing is that *communication* is the observable phenomenon binding together constituent components of systemic entities. . . . Thus, group members (or sets of groups) are joined together as a social system through their communication" (p. 72).

These two perspectives of group communication inform the way in which communication scholars view the very definition of a group. Socha (1997) identified three qualities that differentiate groups from collections of people: three or more people who (a) think of themselves as a group, (b) are interdependent, and (c) communicate with one another. The third characteristic acknowledges the symbolic-management aspect of group life; the first and second characteristics recognize that the significant symbol of a group, describing a particular arrangement among a set of people (one characterized by interdependence), arises from the communication in which people engage.

Communication is, thus, the essential defining feature—the medium—of a group. Conquergood's (1994) statement about the making of culture also applies well to the making of a group: "Communication practices of 'real live human beings' become the crucible of culture—the generative site where culture gets made and re-made" (p. 25). This view of the centrality of communication to group life does not mean that other disciplinary approaches (such as those explored in this section of the text) do not explain group life; it merely means that communication is a primary process that makes possible many of the other phenomena that scholars study about groups (e.g., power and conflict in groups emerges from and is reflected in group communication). Most important, this view means that a complete and adequate account of groups is not possible without attention to the communicative aspects of group life. The lead author of this chapter once heard a famous trial attorney assert that by the time he picked the jury, the trial was over, regardless of the evidence presented, because he already knew how the jurors would vote based on their personal characteristics (e.g., age, gender, and race). A communication perspective argues against such a view, believing that although personal characteristics (or environmental conditions such as the political, social, economic, or cultural contexts in which groups are embedded, as well as many other factors) are important explanatory concepts for understanding group life, how people communicate in groups is consequential and affects them, including whether they even view themselves as a group.

Group Communication Theory and Methods

To understand the group communication perspective more fully, we briefly review some relevant group communication theories and methods used to study communication in groups.

Group Communication Theories

Table 9.1 presents seven general theories that inform the study of group communication. Some of these theories—the dialectical perspective, the feminist perspective, the functional perspective, and structuration theory—are adaptations of theories developed in other disciplines (i.e., philosophy, women's studies, psychology, and sociology, respectively) that now cut across many disciplines. Although certainly informed by theories from other disciplines, the other theories—the bona fide group perspective, symbolic convergence theory, and the symbolic-interpretive perspective—were articulated by group communication scholars.

All of these theories, in one way or another, focus on the symbolic-management feature of group communication. Dialectical theory, for instance, asserts that group members use communication to manage/massage the tensions of group life, and functional theory specifies particular critical task requirements (functions) that communication must serve if groups are to engage in high-quality problem solving and decision making. Some of these theories also focus on the symbolic-constitutive nature of group communication. In addition to the symbolic-interpretive perspective, symbolic convergence theory explains how communication creates a shared consciousness among people that results in members seeing themselves as a group, and structuration theory examines how communication results in the process of structuration (members' use of rules and resources) that creates a group system.

In addition to these general theories, many focused theories have been developed, either within the communication discipline or elsewhere, to explain group communication with regard to specific phenomena or contexts of interest (see Poole, 1999). As examples, persuasive arguments theory explains, among other things, how novel arguments advanced during group discussion provide the impetus for members to reconsider their initial decision choices (see Meyers & Brashers, 1999); the distillation model of collective information processing explains four phases of how a group develops a final information base from which a decision will be made, as mediated by characteristics of the information, group, and task environment (see Propp, 1999); and the function impact model explains how formal group communication procedures (e.g., brainstorming) affect four interrelated functions in task groups (structuring, creating, analyzing, and agreeing), as influenced by member, group, and task characteristics (see Sunwolf & Seibold, 1999). In addition, scholars use many theories from other disciplines that are not related to groups per se and theories from other areas of the communication discipline to explain group communication. One example is Henningsen, Henningsen, Cruz, and Morrill's (2003) use of the elaboration likelihood model of persuasion (Petty & Cacioppo, 1986), which argues that there are two routes to persuasion (the central route, characterized by a great amount of cognitive scrutiny of a persuasive message, and the peripheral route, characterized by little scrutiny). Another, relational framing theory (Dillard, Solomon, & Samp, 1996), asserts that two frames are evoked in any interaction (dominance-submission and affiliation-disaffiliation) and uses these to understand social influence communication in groups.

Methods for Studying Group Communication

Communication scholars often rely on the same methods to study group communication

Table 9.1   Group Communication Theories

Bona fide group perspective	How communication constructs and manages the permeable boundaries and shifting borders that characterize groups and how internal group communication is affected by and, in turn, affects the external environments in which groups are embedded and with which they are interdependent.	Lammers and Krikorian (1997) showed how permeable boundaries, in terms of group membership changes, and interdependence with relevant contexts, such as institutional norms of the organization, affected the internal communication of medical surgical teams.
Dialectical perspective	How communication manages the dialectical tensions between two or more seemingly contradictory elements that demand at least temporary resolution (e.g., group members wanting to be both a part of and apart from a group) experienced by individual members and by the group as a collective.	Kramer (2002, in press) showed how communication helped to manage dialectical tensions associated with multiple group roles in a community theater group.
Feminist perspective	How male and female group communication differs; how males' group communication (task oriented) has been privileged over females' (relationship oriented); two group communication values endemic to women—connection and cooperation—offer alternatives to male group communication values of influence and competition.	Wyatt (1982, 1988) showed how communication in a women's weaver's guild helped to create shared leadership, power, and decision making, suggesting that the values of connection and cooperation are particularly important to women's groups.
Functional perspective	How communication functions to satisfy critical task requirements (e.g., correctly understanding an issue and identifying a relevant and realistic set of alternatives for effective group problem solving and decision making.	Hirokawa and Rost (1992) showed how organizational decision-making group performance was directly related to the ability to analyze and understand the task and to identify the positive and negative qualities of alternative choices.

(Continued)

Table 9.1 (Continued)

Structuration theory	How communication simultaneously constitutes both the means of producing a group system and the dynamic product of such a system through structuration, the process by which systems are produced and reproduced through members' use of rules (statements about how things are to be done) and resources (e.g., materials, knowledge, and skills).	Witmer (1997) showed how structures of the global organization of Alcoholics Anonymous were reproduced in a local setting through individual and group communication practices.
Symbolic convergence theory	How communication creates a group consciousness among a set of people, primarily through the sharing of fantasies, a "creative and imaginative shared interpretation of events that fulfills a group psychological or rhetorical need" (Bormann, 1996, p. 88), which leads members to symbolically converge on a shared understanding of their group and engage in collective action.	Lesch (1994) showed how storytelling communication facilitated a shared consciousness that allowed a witches coven to negotiate changes in, stabilize, and sustain itself over time, including after the loss of one of its members.
Symbolic-interpretive perspective	How group symbolic (communication) predispositions, practices, processes, and products relate to individual, relational, and collective effects and how groups themselves are products of these symbolic activities.	Adelman and Frey (1994, 1997) showed how group symbolic (communication) practices (e.g., rituals and significant symbols) helped members of a residential facility for people with AIDS to create and sustain community.

164

that scholars in other disciplines use to investigate other group phenomena. For instance, some communication scholars conduct experiments to observe the effects of manipulating group communication or other variables to see the effects on group communication. Researchers have, for example, experimentally manipulated the medium used to engage in group communication by contrasting face-to-face group communication with computer-mediated group communication with regard to processes and products such as meeting efficiency, group communication (e.g., participation and information exchange), group performance, and member satisfaction (Scott, 1999). Other scholars manipulate various features of group communication in which members engage by providing members with different amounts or types of information relevant to group decision-making (e.g., full vs. partial information; Cruz, Henningsen, & Smith, 1999)[4] or by having confederates vary the quality of arguments presented in groups (e.g., strong vs. weak arguments; Limon & Boster, 2001). Still other scholars have manipulated and studied the effects of the type of performance feedback that group members receive (e.g., positive vs. negative; Limon & Boster, 2003).

Other communication scholars employ survey methods to study group communication. Survey questionnaires have been used, for instance, to discover what strategies adolescents employ in their peer groups to communicate rejection and exclusion to prospective members and to understand adolescents' thoughts and attributions for remaining silent when they disagree with peer-group exclusion of someone else (Sunwolf & Leets, 2003, 2004); to assess how co-workers use group communication strategies to encourage peers to voluntarily exit the organization (Cox, 1999); and to understand the relationship between church members' perceptions of communication within their church and their involvement with the church (Taylor, 1997). Group communication researchers have also used survey interview procedures, such as interviewing randomly selected members of community planning committees, to examine the use of parliamentary procedure (Weitzel & Geist, 1998) or conducting focus group interviews with gang members to develop effective anti-gang advertisements (Chapel, Peterson, & Joseph, 1999).

Most group communication scholars, however, use some form of *textual analysis*—treating the communication that unfolds in groups as a text by recording it in some form (e.g., via audiotape or videotape), usually transcribing the tape, and then analyzing it. One of the most popular textual-analytic approaches is *interaction analysis,* the observational coding of group communication for the purpose of quantitative analysis. Following Bales's (1950) interaction process analysis (IPA), an observational scheme for classifying the function (not the content) of a communicative act performed in a group into 12 categories (6 socioemotional and 6 task categories), scholars have created a number of interaction-analytic coding schemes that "classify objectively the communicative behaviors (or actions) of group members in accordance with a set of carefully defined, pre-established categories" (Hirokawa, 1988, p. 231). As Poole, Keyton, and Frey (1999) explained

In this procedure, trained observers identify segments of group interaction as codable units and then classify these units within the categories of a predetermined observational scheme. Such schemes provide information used to determine the interactive structure of a group, the distributional structure of interaction, and/or the sequential structure among the categorized units. (p. 103)

Group communication coding schemes have been created to study, among other things, argumentation (Canary, Brossman, & Seibold, 1987; Meyers & Brashers, 1998; Meyers, Seibold, & Brashers, 1991; Seibold, Poole, McPhee, Tanita, & Canary, 1981), conflict (Ellis & Fisher, 1975), group development (Fisher, 1970; Wheelan et al., 1994), idea and proposal generation

(Crowell & Scheidel, 1961; Jackson & Poole, 2003; Pavitt & Johnson, 2002), interaction structure (Gouran & Baird, 1972; Stech, 1970), relational control (Ellis, 1979), satisfaction of group functions (Hirokawa, 1983; Hirokawa, Rost, Fisher, Haire-Joshu, & Houston, 1990; Propp & Nelson, 1996), substantive contributions (Bonito, 2001, 2003), themes (Berg, 1967; Mabry, 1975), and valence of comments (degree of support for specific topics) expressed during group problem-solving discussions (Poole, McPhee, & Seibold, 1982). Most of these coding schemes, however, treat communication as a one-way act performed by an individual member rather than as an interaction that occurs between and among group members (for exceptions, see the interaction-based coding schemes for group argumentation, Alderton & Frey, 1983, and for topical coherence, Pavitt & Johnson, 1999).

Two other forms of textual analysis that are sometimes used to study group communication are conversation/discourse analysis and rhetorical analysis. *Conversation/discourse analysis* involves the close analysis of communication by audio- or videotaping, in this case, group interaction; transcribing the tape using a detailed system to indicate elements such as intonation, pauses, and punctuation (e.g., the transcription system created by Sacks, Schegloff, & Jefferson, 1974); and then engaging in a line-by-line analysis of the conversational turns (see, e.g., Tracy, 2001).[5] Tracy and her colleagues (Tracy & Ashcraft, 2001; Tracy & Dimock, 2004; Tracy & Muller, 2001; Tracy & Standerfer, 2003), for instance, have employed discourse analysis to analyze the deliberations of school board meetings. *Rhetorical analysis* is "a systematic method for describing, analyzing, interpreting, and evaluating the persuasive force of messages embedded within texts" (Frey et al., 2000, p. 229).[6] Hollihan and Riley (1987), for instance, assessed and evaluated the rhetorical impact of storytelling in a support group for parents with delinquent children, called "Toughlove." Parents were urged to use strict discipline to control their children's behavior and were not held

responsible for their children's failings. The rhetoric was highly compelling to parents but also quite risky in terms of potential effects (such as the recommendation to parents to eject from their home children who do not adhere to their rules).

A recent trend in the study of group communication has been the use of ethnographic methods, specifically, participant observation and in-depth interviewing (along with document analysis) (see Dollar & Merrigan, 2002). Dollar and Zimmers (1998), for example, used these methods to show how the language choices of street youth (such as referring to themselves as *houseless* instead of *homeless*) managed their social identity. Croft (1999) employed them to examine how storytelling in a group home for men with mental retardation created "locales" within which the men asserted their agency and individual identity and contested the constraining features of the group home. Bird's (1999) ethnographic research examined how communication practices in an e-mail fan group nurtured community. In many cases, ethnographic research results in inductively derived categorizations of group communication, providing a qualitative complement to the group communication coding schemes developed by interaction analysts. As an example, Cawyer and Smith-Dupre (1995), in their study of communication in a support group for people with AIDS and their caregivers, identified four functions served by the communication: "as a healing agent, as a preparatory mechanism for living with HIV/AIDS, as an outlet for expressing emotions, and as a means of changing society" (p. 243).

Finally, it should be noted that as group communication scholars have employed more qualitative methods, their focus has shifted from studying laboratory groups composed of a small number (typically, six or fewer) of undergraduate college students meeting once for a short period of time to solve artificial problems created by researchers to investigating groups in their natural environments (see Frey, 1994c). This shift from the laboratory to the field continues to include an interest in communication in decision-making groups (such as juries and organizational work teams) but has also led to the study of relationally oriented groups (such as children's and adolescents' groups, consciousness-raising groups, covens, cults, families, friendship groups, gangs, residential groups, and support groups). Moreover, group communication researchers have come to recognize that a group's task reality cannot be separated from the group's social reality, as relationships in groups significantly affect the tasks that groups confront, and vice versa (see Frey, 1994c, 1996, 2002; Keyton, 1999). Decision-making groups, such as juries, for instance, engage in frequent relational communication, whereas relationally oriented groups, such as families, face significant problem-solving and decision-making tasks. Although what we know about group communication is still largely informed by findings from laboratory studies about decision-making groups, there is a growing body of literature that has significantly expanded our understanding of group communication. With this understanding in mind, we turn to a review of research conducted on group communication predispositions, practices, and processes and products.

Research on Group Communication Predispositions, Practices, and Processes and Products

As a framework for reviewing the research conducted on group communication, we draw on Frey and Sunwolf's (2004, 2005) conceptual model for understanding three domains of symbolic (communication) activity in groups: (a) predispositions, (b) practices, and (c) processes and products. *Group communication predispositions* direct attention to ways in which people are inclined to communicate in groups. *Group communication practices* reference the specific forms of communication employed in groups. *Group communication processes and*

products constitute group dynamics (e.g., decision-making procedures employed, such as majority rule) and the specific group outcomes associated with those group dynamics (e.g., particular decisions made). Frey and Sunwolf (2004) suggested that linking processes and products together, rather than treating them as separate entities, usefully highlights their recursive and reflexive relationship (e.g., group culture is both a process and a product that results from and influences communication practices). They also emphasized that group communication predispositions, practices, and processes and products are not mutually exclusive and influence one another throughout the course of a group's life.

Group Communication Predispositions

The communication perspective acknowledges that individuals, the nucleus of any group, enter groups with personal characteristics (e.g., backgrounds, needs, values, motivations, abilities, perceptions, and personality traits) that influence ways in which they communicate (Haslett & Ruebush, 1999). Some of these characteristics undoubtedly are the result of previous group experiences. Some of these characteristics represent social categories that group people together on the basis of biological identities over which they may have little or no control (e.g., gender, age, and ethnicity; Hare, Blumberg, Davies, & Kent, 1994; Shaw, 1981). As an example, gender differences have received significant attention from group communication scholars. In line with the feminist perspective, the research shows, for instance, that men's group communication tends to be more task oriented and direct, whereas women's group communication tends to be more social and indirect (Baird, 1976; Kramarae, 1990). From a communication perspective, however, it is important to realize that

these characteristics constitute significant symbols whose importance is derived from a socially constructed process. This is true, in part, because these characteristics are conveyed largely through symbolic means, such as self-presentation style, with characteristics such as gender, race, and age each having their own distinct semaphore. (Frey & Sunwolf, in press)

The attention to group members' personal characteristics has inevitably led to a focus on the nature and effects of diversity in groups, with the understanding that "diversity itself is not an inherent, predetermined condition per se; it is a symbolic concept that is created and sustained through interaction" (Frey, 2000, p. 226). Although the bulk of this research has been conducted by scholars in other disciplines, the results generally show that communication is potentially more difficult in heterogeneous than homogeneous groups (see, e.g., Kirchmeyer, 1993; Kirchmeyer & Cohen, 1992). Heterogeneity may enhance task group performance, especially with regard to creative, innovative, and rapidly changing tasks (Eisenhart & Schoonhoven, 1990; Kono, 1988; Nemeth, 1986; Pelz & Andrews, 1976; Sunwolf, 2002), although negative results for both group performance and member morale have been found for heterogeneous groups (Ancona & Caldwell, 1992; Wiersema & Bird, 1993). Frey and Sunwolf (in press) speculate that the realization of the potential positive effects of group diversity may depend on the extent to which group communication successfully manages the tensions associated with diversity.

Researchers have also directed attention toward the effects of people's personality traits on their group communication behavior (Keyton & Frey, 2002). In addition to numerous psychological traits that have been studied (e.g., approach-avoidance tendencies, authoritarianism/dogmatism, cognitive style, and locus of control), communication researchers are especially interested in how *communication traits,* which "account for enduring consistencies and

differences in individual message-sending and message-receiving behaviors among individuals" (Infante, Rancer, & Womak, 2003, p. 77), affect individuals' communication in groups. This research has shown that communication traits such as aggressive communication, communication apprehension (CA; fear of communicating), communicator style (e.g., dramatic, precise, or open), and interaction involvement (willingness to become involved in interaction with others) have important effects on individuals' group communication. Indeed, based on a review of research studies conducted on the effects of CA, McCroskey and Richmond (1992) concluded that "in no communication situation is CA more important than in the small group context. It is not an exaggeration to suggest that CA may be the single most important factor in predicting communication behavior in a small group" (p. 368).

Group Communication Practices

It should come as no surprise that the vast amount of research conducted on group communication has focused on the verbal contributions that members make. Indeed, virtually all of the group interaction-analytic schemes created code verbal communication (although Bales's [1950] IPA was designed also to classify nonverbal behavior). The interaction-analytic research conducted from the functional perspective concerning the relationship among communication, the satisfaction of critical functions, and quality of group decision-making, for instance, has only coded, to our knowledge, verbal contributions (statements and questions). Survey researchers have also concentrated on verbal group communication, such as Mayer's (1998) questionnaire study of the specific types of utterances that organizational members perceived as substantially increasing and decreasing group effectiveness. Group communication studies conducted using conversation/discourse analysis, rhetorical analysis, and ethnography have also concentrated on verbal communication. Ellingson's (2003) longitudinal ethnographic study of an interdisciplinary geriatric oncology team at a cancer center focused on and provided as evidence excerpts of seven types of verbal backstage communication practices (information impression and information sharing, checking clinic progress, relationship building, space management, training students, handling interruptions, and formal reporting, although the latter included written reports as well). Even group-communication facilitation research has emphasized improvement in verbal communication. Glaser's (1994) 3-year case study of the effectiveness of a team-building intervention among a group of department leaders who supervised a fire management unit, for instance, reported an increase following the intervention in the group's ability to raise issues, manage conflict, and provide mutual praise and support.

The almost exclusive focus on verbal communication in groups is unfortunate, for as Burgoon (1980) concluded on the basis of a review of nonverbal communication research, "the overwhelming conclusion has been that the nonverbal channels carry more information and are believed more than the verbal band" (p. 184). Some researchers studied nonverbal communication in groups (Ketrow, 1999), concentrating on four types of nonverbal codes: (a) visual codes, such as kinesic behavior (e.g., gestures, facial expressions, posture, eye behavior, and nonverbal cue combinations), physical appearance (e.g., age, physical size, sex/gender, race, ethnicity, and culture), and artifacts; (b) place, contact, and time codes (e.g., group ecology, density and crowding, group size, group composition, and virtual group space and technology); (c) contact codes (e.g., touch and chronemics [time codes]); (d) auditory codes (e.g., voice features, talkativeness, and interruption behavior). These forms of nonverbal communication have been shown to serve five

primary functions in groups: "(a) structuring interaction; (b) presenting and managing identity; (c) communicating relationally, especially about negotiating dominance, power, and leadership; (d) communicating affect; and (e) managing conversation" (Ketrow, 1999, p. 254).

Although all communication is verbal and/or nonverbal, and the vast majority of communication is symbolic,[7] some communication practices combine verbal and nonverbal behavior in a highly symbolic manner that produces significant meaning for group members. These group communication practices have attracted the attention of scholars who employ ethnographic methods, in particular. They include particular forms of language, such as the use of *metaphor* (a figure of speech in which a word or phrase that denotes one object is applied to another) and other significant symbols; entire speech acts, such as humorous communication and *narratives* (stories that are used as organizing schemes; see Sunwolf & Frey, 2001); and collective practices, such as *rites* ("a relatively elaborate, dramatic set of activities that consolidates cultural expressions into one event"; Trice & Beyer, 1984, p. 655) and *rituals* ("organized symbolic practices and ceremonial activities which serve to define and represent the social and cultural significance of particular occasions, events or changes"; O'Sullivan, Hartley, Saunders, Montgomery, & Fiske, 1994, p. 267).

Such communication practices are especially important in creating and sustaining group identity and members' commitment to the group and for managing the dialectical tensions of group life (see Frey & Sunwolf, in press). Adelman and Frey's (1994, 1997) ethnographic research in a residential facility for people with AIDS, for instance, showed how the staff's use of the metaphor of family to describe relationships in the residence triggered negative reactions among residents because the word implied that staff were parents and residents were children. As a result, the family metaphor was replaced by the significant symbol of community, which referenced a very different group identity, one that suggested a more equal relationship between residents and staff. Adelman and Frey also explained how stories told to newcomers about the residence helped to socialize new members and commit them to the "rhetorical vision" of the residence as a place to live with AIDS, not a place to die. They further examined how the collective ritual of a balloon ceremony held for each resident who died became institutionalized in the residence, even for those who did not request it, because the ritual helped the remaining members not only to remember the deceased but also to "re-member" as a group after the loss of one of its members through the "purposive, significant unification" that comes from the act of recollection (Myeroff, 1982, p. 111).

Finally, for the purposes of this classificatory scheme, group communication practices include the medium through which group members communicate. Most of the extant research has concentrated on face-to-face group communication, but because of the increasingly dispersed nature of group work, many groups use technological means to communicate among members, including electronic meeting systems (e.g., videoconferencing) and various computer-supported group software (e.g., Lotus notes). Consequently, a growing body of scholarship has been directed toward understanding the nature and effects of using group communication technology, most typically by comparing it with face-to-face group communication (see, e.g., McLeod, 1996; Scott, 1999). That research has generally shown that some of these technologies can lead to increased meeting efficiency and improved group performance, especially when performance is measured quantitatively, although technology-aided group meetings typically take longer and the evidence is mixed with regard to member satisfaction (see Scott, 1999). Scott (1999) suggested that some of these group communication technologies may be superior to others, when compared with face-to-face group communication, because of the specific features of a technology (especially the way in which it

structures group communication) and not because of the technology itself.

Group Communication Processes and Products

Many group communication processes and products could be examined; indeed, any group process or product involves or is related to communication in some way. Here, we focus on five important group communication processes and products that have received significant attention from scholars: communication and group (a) development, (b) member relationships, (c) task accomplishment, (d) leadership, and (e) management of external environments.

Communication and group development. From a communication perspective, group development is characterized by changes in the communication in which members engage. Virtually every phase or stage model of group development (e.g., Tuckman's [1965] popular forming, storming, norming, and performing model) is based on identifying differences in the communication that characterizes the stages conceived (Frey & Sunwolf, in press). Even scholarship from psychological and psychodynamic perspectives focuses on developmental changes in group communication. As an example, Wheelan and colleagues (Verdi & Wheelan, 1992; Wheelan et al., 1994; Wheelan & Verdi, 1992), extending the work of Bion (1961), Stock and Thelen (1958), and Thelen (1954), have shown that groups develop with respect to changes in seven types of statements expressed during group discussion: (a) dependency (showing an inclination to conform with the dominant mood of the group); (b) counterdependency (asserting independence from and rejection of leadership acts); (c) fight (implying a struggle to overcome someone or something via argumentativeness and aggression); (d) flight (indicating avoidance of task and confrontation); (e) pairing (expressing warmth, friendship, support, and intimacy with others); (f) counterpairing (indicating an avoidance of intimacy and connection and a desire to keep the discussion distant and intellectual); and (g) work statements (demonstrating purposeful goal- and task-directed efforts).

In addition to studying group development globally over the course of a group's life span, communication scholars have focused on how communication is related to particular aspects of group development, most typically those involving group decision-making. Scheidel and Crowell (1964, 1966), for instance, offered a spiral model of how ideas develop in groups. They showed that although ideas were proposed, discussed, and then accepted or rejected, in that order, groups did not proceed from idea to idea in a linear manner but, instead, often circled back to discuss a particular idea throughout the course of their meetings. As another example, Fisher (1970) focused on the communication of decision proposals that characterized groups reaching consensus, finding four developmental phases: (a) orientation, characterized by the search for ideas; (b) conflict, featuring disagreement about proposals; (c) emergence, where only a few proposals gain support; and (d) reinforcement, where the final proposal receives support. As a different type of focus, Chesebro, Cragan, and McCullough's (1973) study of a group of people associated with the gay movement identified the central symbols that characterized four stages of the consciousness-raising process: (a) self-realization of a new identity (characterized by members engaging rhetorically in fantasy chains), (b) creation of a group identity through polarized discourse (with members rhetorically constructing external enemies), (c) establishment of new values for the group (featuring future-oriented discourse), and (d) relation to other revolutionary groups (demonstrating cooperative conversation).

Finally, rejecting the conception of group development as a linear phase and recognizing the simultaneous purposes that communication serves in groups, Poole (1981, 1983a, 1983b) and Poole and Roth (1989a, 1989b) offered a multiple sequence model of group development that views groups as working concurrently on three interlocking "activity tracks": (a) task-process activities (those used to manage the task), (b) relational activities (those used to manage interpersonal relationships), and (c) topical focus (issues of concern to a group). They also identified three types of "breakpoints" (normal breakpoints such as topic shifts and adjournments, delays, and disruptions) that "represent discontinuities in interaction and that may signal developmental transitions" (Poole & Baldwin, 1996, p. 223). Both breakpoints and activity tracks are demonstrated, of course, in group members' interactions.

Communication and group member relationships. Group researchers, including those in the communication field, have tended to focus on task group communication and, historically, have been concerned with member relationships only to the extent that they affect task processes and products, often perceiving relationships as inhibiting effective group performance (see, e.g., Collins & Guetzkow, 1964). Recently, however, scholars have recognized the importance, both for effective group task accomplishment and in its own right, of *relational communication in groups,* "the verbal and nonverbal messages that create the social fabric of a group by promoting relationships between and among group members" (Keyton, 1999, p. 192).

The importance of relational communication in traditional problem-solving and decision-making task groups has certainly been recognized. Scholars have identified a number of positive group processes and products in such groups that result from relational group communication (Keyton, 1999; Scheerhorn & Geist, 1997). These positive processes and products include the development of group norms, which result from the psychological closeness and communication linkages among members (Festinger, Schachter, & Back, 1968); the creation of a supportive group climate (Gibb, 1961); the feeling of *cohesiveness,* the degree to which members desire to remain in a group (Cartwright, 1968); member satisfaction; and the socialization of new group members (Anderson, Riddle, & Martin, 1999). Researchers have also identified the "dark side" of relational communication in groups. These negative group processes and products include *groupthink*, the tendency of highly cohesive groups to not engage in vigilant decision making and, consequently, to adopt faulty solutions (Janis, 1972, 1982; Janis & Mann, 1977); group stress (Keyton, 1999); and the creation of a defensive group climate (Gibb, 1961). Di Salvo, Nikkel, and Monroe (1989), in fact, found that group members cited interpersonal problems and poor communication most frequently as reasons why groups are ineffective. It is not surprising, therefore, that researchers have attempted to identify and categorize the communication practices that promote high-quality relationships in groups and those that do not, starting with Bales's 1950 identification of the positive socioemotional communication acts of *seems friendly, dramatizes,* and *agrees* and the negative acts of *disagrees, shows tension,* and *seems unfriendly.* More recently, humorous communication in groups was studied (Meyer, 1997). It is important to realize, however, that some relational communication can result in both negative and positive group processes and products. For instance, conflict between members (especially affective conflict that is based on emotions) often causes significant process and product problems for groups, but a substantial body of research also shows that a certain amount of conflict can be functional in groups by increasing the level of communication of individual members (Pavitt & Curtis, 1994), generating creative problem solving (Nicotera, 1997), improving group decision-making (e.g., Janis & Mann, 1977), and promoting cohesiveness (Nicotera, 1995).

Perhaps most important, branching out from task groups, scholars have started to focus on communication in groups that are primarily oriented toward meeting people's socioemotional needs, including families (Socha, 1999), children's peer groups (e.g., Sunwolf & Leets, 2003, 2004; Keyton, 1994), gangs (e.g., Conquergood,

1991, 1992, 1994; Conquergood & Siegel, 1990), residential facilities (e.g., Adelman & Frey, 1994, 1997), and social support groups (Cline, 1999). These studies reveal well the significance of communication to the relational dimension of group life.

Communication and group task accomplishment. By far, the most research on group communication processes and products has focused on the relationship between communication and group task accomplishment, especially as directed toward group decision-making. A significant portion of that research emerges from the functional perspective, which, as previously explained, argues that group members employ communication to attempt to satisfy prerequisites for effective group decision-making. Specifically, communication must fulfill four critical functions: (a) assessment of the problematic situation, (b) identification of goals and objectives, (c) identification of available choices, and (d) evaluation of the positive and negative aspects of available choices (for reviews of functional theory and research, see Gouran & Hirokawa, 1983, 1986, 1996; Gouran, Hirokawa, Julian, & Leatham, 1993; Hirokawa & Salazar, 1999; Hirokawa & Scheerhorn, 1986; Wittenbaum et al., 2004, in press). A meta-analysis of functional research by Orlitzky and Hirokawa (1997) found that the proper evaluation of available choices was most often related to high-quality group decision-making performance, although problem analysis was also highly correlated (average correlation of .55). In contrast, criteria establishment (identification of goals and objectives) demonstrated a weak correlation (average correlation of .27), and choice identification was largely unrelated to group decision-making performance (see Hirokawa & Salazar, 1999). Functional researchers have also tied the necessity of performing these functions to group task characteristics (e.g., goal clarity), the homogeneity of group members' prediscussion preferences, and group structural characteristics (e.g., the quality of members' relationships) (see Hirokawa & Salazar, 1997, 1999).

As group members communicate to fulfill these functions, they engage in collective information processing (Propp, 1999). Information is considered so central to group decision-making that scholars in other disciplines often view group discussion as "collective information-processing" interactions (Hinsz, Vollrath, Nagao, & Davis, 1988). Part of the reason why groups are often assumed to be superior to individuals in terms of making decisions is because groups potentially have more information available to them and should be able to process it better. Communication, of course, is the medium through which information in groups is shared and processed. Hence, communication scholars have focused on the nature and effects of communicating information in groups, finding that such communication can serve either as a promoting factor or as a disruptive influence in group decision-making (Gouran & Hirokawa, 1983).

A second important focus has been on the generation and communication of ideas in groups, especially creative ideas (Jarboe, 1997; Sunwolf, 2002). From a communication perspective, group creativity is viewed as an emergent phenomenon of group communication (Salazar, 2002). Consequently, one direction for such research has been on understanding the communication problems that prevent group creativity; Basadur (1994) said group creativity was adversely affected when group members were unable to communicate clearly and simply and talk about solutions before problems. Another direction has been the facilitation of group creativity through the use of formal procedures that structure group communication in particular ways (such as brainstorming and devil's advocacy; see Sunwolf, 2002; Sunwolf & Frey, Chapter 26, this volume; Sunwolf & Seibold, 1999), with research most often comparing the effectiveness of using various procedures to promote group creativity.

As group members share information and ideas, they engage in the communication activity of social influence (Meyers & Brashers, 1999). Social influence has been studied at three source

production sites—the individual member, subgroup, and group/intergroup sites—as manifested on at least two message levels—(a) valence (messages that express the degree of positive or negative sentiment for or against an idea, proposal, etc.) and (b) argument (messages that offer reasons for or against something) (Meyers & Brashers, 1999). The focus of most social-psychological research has been on valence, primarily at the individual level, such as the research on social comparison theory, which views communication simply as the means for members to reveal their valences toward decision choices so that comparisons can be made among members. In contrast, most communication research has focused on argument. Persuasive arguments theory, at the individual level, uses formal procedures (e.g., devil's advocacy and dialectical inquiry) that create and structure argument between two or more subgroups; conversational argument, at the group/intergroup level, focuses on the interactive nature of argument, such as argument-response interactions. The differences between these foci ultimately revolve around how central communication is considered to be regarding social influence in groups and whether communication is viewed as an act or as an interaction.

Communication and group leadership. As groups develop, form relationships among members, and attempt to accomplish tasks, group members engage in leadership practices. The communication approach to group leadership, however, stands in sharp contrast to some other approaches, which place the locus of leadership inside of particular people, such as their personality (the trait approach), or in the contexts within which people find themselves (the situational approach). Instead, the communication approach views leadership as the performance of communication practices that help group members to accomplish their goals. In that sense, the communication approach focuses not so much on the *leader* of a group as a noun, a person who occupies a particular role, but on *leadership* as a verb, as a process contributing communicatively that can be performed by any member (see Barge, 1996, 1997; Pavitt & Curtis, 1994). Because of this view, group communication research has focused less on groups with appointed leaders and more on leaderless groups to understand how leadership emerges communicatively.

The study of leadership from a communication perspective dates back to the late 1930s. Lewin and his students Lippitt and White (Lewin & Lippitt, 1938; Lewin, Lippitt, & White, 1939; Lippitt, 1939, 1940; Lippitt & White, 1952; White & Lippitt, 1960) studied the nature and effects of three styles of leadership—democratic, authoritarian, and laissez-faire—that differed, in large measure, with regard to the communication behavior these leaders enacted. Later researchers, using the functional approach, argued that leadership involves performing communication behavior that fulfills two important functions reflecting the classic dimensions of group life: task and maintenance (socioemotional) (see, e.g., Benne & Sheats, 1948; Blake & Mouton, 1968). Still later, Schultz (1974, 1978, 1982, 1986) showed in a series of studies that emergent leadership depended on the quality of the functional communication behavior members performed, as demonstrated, for instance, in communication that set goals, gave directions, and summarized group discussion. Weick (1978) offered a view of leadership as mediation, with leadership communication behavior helping to overcome task and relational problems encountered by a group. Barge and Hirokawa (1989) subsequently used this theory to propose a communication competency approach, arguing that an effective leader's communication mediates and organizes group interaction by, for instance, suggesting effective operating procedures, managing conversational turns, and displaying concern for members' feelings. Finally, Sharf (1978) studied group leadership from a rhetorical perspective. In a detailed study of two task groups, he showed how emergent leaders used significant symbols to create a rhetorical vision of the group that helped to

manage tensions resulting from divisions within the group, create bonds of identification within the group, and promote cooperation among members. All of these theories locate group leadership in the communication practices members perform, with the corresponding research consistently showing that leadership emergence is positively related to the performance of such communication practices.

Communication and group management of external environments. Most research on groups, including communication research, treats groups as a container by studying only intragroup practices, processes, and products. However, as the bona fide group perspective makes clear, groups are interdependent with the environments in which they are embedded (Putnam & Stohl, 1990, 1996; see also Alderfer's [1977, 1987, 1992] theory of embedded intergroup relations). Moreover, as Barge and Keyton's (1994) enactment view of context maintains, a group's relevant environments are not a given; they are created and re-created through group members' interactions. Scholars, therefore, have started to direct attention to ways in which group members construct their relevant environments and how group communication is affected by and, in turn, affects those environments.

Group members construct their relevant environments by attaching symbolic meaning to perceived environments. This is true even with regard to physical environments such as time and space, with, for instance, cultural groups symbolically constructing time in very different ways (e.g., monochromic cultures that highly structure time vs. polychromic cultures that loosely structure time; see Hall, 1983). Also, different groups sharing the same physical space create different meanings for and interpretations of that space as place (see, e.g., Agnew & Duncan, 1989; Harper, 1988; Massey, 1994), meanings that can symbolically transform place into "place attachment," the emotional bonding of people and groups to particular spaces (see Altman & Lowe, 1992).

Communication scholars are especially interested in ways in which internal group communication is influenced by relevant external environments. Employing the bona fide group perspective, Parrish-Sprowl (2003), for instance, revealed how a group of people attempting to plan the activities of a newly formed, market-driven recycling company in post-Communist Poland wanted to use democratic group communication practices and processes (see, e.g., Gastil, 1992, 1993; Sager & Gastil, 2002) but continually appropriated Communist practices and processes (e.g., noninteractive procedures, such as one person lecturing) that were part of their historical context. Yep, Reece, and Negrón (2003) also showed how the internal communication of a support group for Asian Americans living with HIV infection was primarily designed to counteract the cultural context of the societal stigma associated with HIV, a stigma that affected participants' daily life outside of the support group.

An important feature of a group's external environment is other groups, leading to a focus on intergroup communication and relationships (Abrams & Hogg, 1998; Austin & Worchel, 1979; Gudykunst, 1986; Harwood & Giles, in press; Hogg & Abrams, 1988), especially intergroup communication and conflict (see Abrams, Frings, & Randsley de Moura, Chapter 18, this volume). The problems of intergroup communication are well documented, for instance, in studies of environmental group negotiations and collaborations (e.g., Carpenter & Kennedy, 1988; Lange, 2003). In some cases, conflict between groups can be overcome because of the influence of the environment, as demonstrated in Houston's (2003) study of how competing expedition teams that were stranded on Mount Everest in the infamous disaster of May 1996, which took the lives of 12 individuals (see Krakauer, 1997), were forced to engage in collaborative intergroup communication, something they had refused to do, to save lives.

Finally, the realization that internal group communication is influenced by external environments has led to the study of how groups can

effectively manage their external environments, including their relationships with other groups. Researchers have documented how groups can, for instance, probe the environment regarding proposals they develop (Ancona, 1990; Stohl, 1986, 1987) and forge agreements with other groups to manage turf conflicts (Brett & Rognes, 1986). Ancona (1990) even argued that group members' management of external environments was a better predictor of group performance (in this case, collaborating groups) than the quality of the group's internal communication.

Conclusion

The communication approach offers a unique and valuable perspective to the study of groups. Although much remains to be known about the constitutive role and purposive use of communication in groups, communication scholarship has offered important explanatory frameworks and verified the significance of communication in group life through empirical research using a variety of methods. From such a perspective, groups are created in and sustained by members' communication, making groups, ultimately, a communication phenomenon.

Notes

1. For additional historical reviews and critiques of the field of group communication, see, in chronological order, Timmons (1941), Dickens and Heffernan (1949), Keltner (1960, 1961), Bormann (1970, 1980, 1994), Gouran (1970, 1973, 1985, 1988, 1994, 1999), Mortensen (1970), Fisher (1971), Larson (1971), Bochner (1974), Becker (1980), Cragan and Wright (1980, 1990), Hirokawa (1982), Gouran and Fisher (1984), Poole (1990, 1994), Sykes (1990), Wyatt (1993), Cragan, Shields, and Wright (1994), Frey (1994b, 1994c, 1995, 1996), Gouran, Hirokawa, McGee, and Miller (1994), Propp and Kreps (1994), Putnam (1994), and Seibold (1994).

2. A complete review of a communication approach to the study of groups would also include a focus on group communication facilitation. That

material, however, is not included here, as it is covered in detail in Chapter 26 of this text.

3. It should also be noted that, in systems theory, communication takes the forms of (a) feedback from outputs that generate new inputs and (b) interactions between a group and the environments in which it is embedded (see Keyton, 2002).

4. This line of research was actually initiated by social psychologist Stasser and his colleagues (e.g., Stasser, Taylor, & Hanna, 1989; Stasser & Titus, 1985, 1987) and continues to be a popular symbolic-management/information-exchange approach to the study of group communication in the field of psychology.

5. There are important conceptual and pragmatic differences between conversation analysis and discourse analysis (and other methodological approaches to the study of discourse, such as cognitive linguistics, critical language studies, pragmatics, semiotics, and sociolinguistics) that are being glossed over here for the sake of simplicity (for a useful overview, albeit within the context of organizational communication, not group communication, see Putnam & Fairhurst, 2001).

6. Rhetorical analysis includes many different types, such as dramatistic criticism, fantasy theme analysis, feminist criticism, genre criticism, historical criticism, metaphoric criticism, narrative criticism, and neo-Aristotelian criticism (see Frey et al., 2000).

7. Communication is symbolic when words and meaningfully interpreted nonverbal behaviors represent the objects to which they refer but bear no natural relationship to them (e.g., the word *group* stands for the object but bears no natural relationship to it), in contrast to a *sign* or *signal*, "something that stands for or represents something else and bears a natural, nonarbitrary relationship to it" (Infante et al., 2003, p. 354) (e.g., the calloused hands of a group of people who have just physically moved furniture is a natural sign/signal of the group's manual labor).

References

Abrams, D., & Hogg, M. A. (1998). Prospects for research in group processes and intergroup relations. *Group Processes and Intergroup Relations, 1,* 7–20.

Adelman, M. B., & Frey, L. R. (1994). The pilgrim must embark: Creating and sustaining community in a residential facility for people with AIDS. In L. R. Frey (Ed.), *Group communication in context: Studies of natural groups* (pp. 3–22). Hillsdale, NJ: Lawrence Erlbaum.

Adelman, M. B., & Frey, L. R. (1997). *The fragile community: Living together with AIDS.* Mahwah, NJ: Lawrence Erlbaum.

Agnew, J. A., & Duncan, J. S. (1989). *The power of place: Bringing together geographical and sociological imaginations.* Boston: Unwin Hyman.

Alderfer, C. P. (1977). Group and intergroup relations. In J. R. Hackman & J. L. Suttle (Eds.), *Improving life at work: Behavioral science approaches to organizational change* (pp. 227–296). Santa Monica, CA: Goodyear.

Alderfer, C. P. (1987). An intergroup perspective on group dynamics. In J. Lorsch (Ed.), *Handbook of organizational behavior* (pp. 190–222). Englewood Cliffs, NJ: Prentice Hall.

Alderfer, C. P. (1992). Contemporary issues in professional work with groups: Editor's introduction. *Journal of Applied Behavioral Sciences, 28,* 9–14.

Alderton, S. M., & Frey, L. R. (1983). Effects of reactions to arguments on group outcome: The case of group polarization. *Central States Speech Journal, 34,* 88–95.

Altman, I., & Lowe, S. M. (Eds.). (1992). *Place attachment.* New York: Plenum Press.

Ancona, D. G. (1990). Outward bound: Strategies for team survival in an organization. *Academy of Management Journal, 33,* 334–365.

Ancona, D. G., & Caldwell, D. F. (1992). Demography and design: Predictors of new product team performance. *Organization Science, 3,* 321–341.

Anderson, C. M., Riddle, B. L., & Martin, M. M. (1999). Socialization processes in groups. In L. R. Frey (Ed.), D. S. Gouran, & M. S. Poole (Assoc. Eds.), *The handbook of group communication theory and research* (pp. 139–163). Thousand Oaks, CA: Sage.

Austin, W. G., & Worchel, S. (Eds.). (1979). *The social psychology of intergroup relations.* Monterey, CA: Brooks/Cole.

Baird, J. E., Jr. (1976). Sex differences in group communication: A review of relevant research. *Quarterly Journal of Speech, 62,* 179–192.

Bales, R. F. (1950). *Interaction process analysis: A method for the study of small groups.* Cambridge, MA: Addison-Wesley.

Barge, J. K. (1996). Leadership skills and the dialectics of leadership in group decision making. In

R. Y. Hirokawa & M. S. Poole (Eds.), *Communication and group decision making* (2nd ed., pp. 301–342). Thousand Oaks, CA: Sage.

Barge, J. K. (1997). Leadership as communication. In L. R. Frey & J. K. Barge (Eds.), *Managing group life: Communicating in decision-making groups* (pp. 202–233). Boston: Houghton Mifflin.

Barge, J. K., & Hirokawa, R. Y. (1989). Toward a communication competency model of group leadership. *Small Group Behavior, 20,* 167–189.

Barge, J. K., & Keyton, J. (1994). Contextualizing power and social influence in groups. In L. R. Frey (Ed.), *Group communication in context: Studies of natural groups* (pp. 85–105). Hillsdale, NJ: Lawrence Erlbaum.

Basadur, M. (1994). Managing the creative process in organizations. In M. A. Runco (Ed.), *Problem finding, problem solving, and creativity* (pp. 237–268). Norwood, NJ: Ablex.

Becker, S. L. (1980). Directions of small group research for the 1980's. *Central States Speech Journal, 31,* 221–224.

Benne, K. D., & Sheats, P. (1948). Functional roles of group members. *Journal of Social Issues, 4,* 41–49.

Berg, D. M. (1967). A descriptive analysis of the distribution and duration of themes discussed by task-oriented small groups. *Speech Monographs, 34,* 172–175.

Bion, W. R. (1961). *Experiences in groups and other papers.* New York: Basic Books.

Bird, S. E. (1999). Chatting on Cynthia's porch: Creating community in an e-mail fan group. *Southern Communication Journal, 65,* 49–65.

Blake, R. R., & Mouton, J. S. (1968). *Corporate excellence through grid organization development.* Houston, TX: Gulf.

Bochner, A. P. (1974). Task and instrumentation variables as factors jeopardizing the validity of published group communication research, 1970–71. *Communication Monographs, 41,* 169–178.

Bonito, J. A. (2001). An information-processing approach to participation in small groups. *Communication Research, 28,* 275–303.

Bonito, J. A. (2003). A social relations analysis of participation in small groups. *Communication Monographs, 70,* 83–97.

Bormann, E. G. (1970). The paradox and promise of small group research. *Speech Monographs, 41,* 169–178.

Bormann, E. G. (1980). The paradox and promise of small group communication revisited. *Central States Speech Journal, 31,* 214–220.

Bormann, E. G. (1994). Response to "Revitalizing the study of small group communication." *Communication Studies, 45,* 86–91.

Bormann, E. G. (1996). Symbolic convergence theory and communication in group decision making. In R. Y. Hirokawa & M. S. Poole (Eds.), *Communication and group decision making* (2nd ed., pp. 81–113). Thousand Oaks, CA: Sage.

Brett, J. M., & Rognes, J. K. (1986). Intergroup relations in organizations: A negotiations perspective. In P. S. Goodman & Associates (Eds.), *Designing effective work groups* (pp. 202–236). San Francisco: Jossey-Bass.

Burgoon, J. K. (1980). Nonverbal communication research in the 1970s: An overview. In D. Nimmo (Ed.), *Communication yearbook* (Vol. 4, pp. 179–197). New Brunswick, NJ: Transaction Books.

Canary, D. J., Brossman, B. G., & Seibold, D. R. (1987). Argument structures in decision-making groups. *Southern Speech Communication Journal, 53,* 18–37.

Carpenter, S. L., & Kennedy, W. J. D. (1988). *Managing public disputes: A practical guide to handling conflict and reaching decisions.* San Francisco: Jossey-Bass.

Cartwright, D. (1968). The nature of group cohesiveness. In D. Cartwright & A. Zander (Eds.), *Group dynamics: Research and theory* (3rd ed., pp. 91–109). New York: Harper & Row.

Cawyer, C. S., & Smith-Dupre, A. (1995). Communicating social support: Identifying supportive episodes in an HIV/AIDS support group. *Communication Quarterly, 43,* 243–258.

Chapel, G., Peterson, K. M., & Joseph, J. (1999). Exploring anti-gang advertisements: Focus group discussions with gang members and at-risk youth. *Journal of Applied Communication Research, 27,* 237–247.

Chesebro, J. W., Cragan, J. F., & McCullough, P. (1973). The small group technique of the radical revolutionary: A synthetic study of consciousness-raising. *Speech Monographs, 40,* 136–146.

Cline, R. J. W. (1999). Communication in social support groups. In L. R. Frey (Ed.), D. S. Gouran, & M. S. Poole (Assoc. Eds.), *The handbook of group communication theory and research* (pp. 516–538). Thousand Oaks, CA: Sage.

Collins, B. E., & Guetzkow, H. (1964). *A social psychology of group processes for decision-making.* New York: John Wiley.

Conquergood, D. (1991). "For the nation!" How street gangs problematize patriotism. In R. Troester & C. Kelley (Eds.), *Peacemaking through communication* (pp. 8–21). Annandale, VA: Speech Communication Association.

Conquergood, D. (1992). Life in Big Red: Struggles and accommodations in a Chicago polyethnic tenement. In L. Lamphere (Ed.), *Structuring diversity: Ethnographic perspectives on the new immigration* (pp. 95–144). Chicago: University of Chicago Press.

Conquergood, D. (1994). Homeboys and hoods: Gangs and cultural space. In L. R. Frey (Ed.), *Group communication in context: Studies of natural groups* (pp. 23–55). Hillsdale, NJ: Lawrence Erlbaum.

Conquergood, D. (Producer), & Siegel, T. (Producer & Director). (1990). *The heart broken in half* [Motion picture]. New York: Filmmakers Library.

Cox, S. A. (1999). Group communication and employee turnover: How coworkers encourage peers to voluntarily exit. *Southern Communication Journal, 64,* 181–192.

Cragan, J. F., Shields, D. C., & Wright, D. W. (1994). Revitalizing the study of small group communication: A thematic critique. *Communication Studies, 45,* 92–96.

Cragan, J. F., & Wright, D. W. (1980). Small group communication research of the 1970s: A synthesis and critique. *Central States Speech Journal, 31,* 197–213.

Cragan, J. F., & Wright, D. W. (1990). Small group communication research of the 1980s: A synthesis and critique. *Communication Studies, 41,* 212–236.

Croft, S. E. (1999). Creating locales through storytelling: An ethnography of a group home for men with mental retardation. *Western Journal of Communication, 63,* 329–347.

Crowell, L., & Scheidel, T. M. (1961). Categories for analysis of idea-development in discussion groups. *Journal of Social Psychology, 54,* 155–168.

Cruz, M. G., Henningsen, D. D., & Smith, B. A. (1999). The impact of directive leadership on group information sampling, decisions, and perceptions of the leader. *Communication Research, 26,* 349–369.

Dance, F. E. X., & Larson, C. E. (1976). *The functions of human communication: A theoretical approach.* New York: Holt, Rinehart & Winston.

Dickens, M., & Heffernan, M. (1949). Experimental research in group discussion. *Quarterly Journal of Speech, 35,* 23–29.

Dillard, J. P., Solomon, D. H., & Samp, J. A. (1996). Framing social reality: The relevance of relational judgments. *Communication Research, 23,* 703–723.

Di Salvo, V. S., Nikkel, E., & Monroe, C. (1989). Theory and practice: A field investigation and identification of group members' perceptions of problems facing natural work groups. *Small Group Behavior, 20,* 551–567.

Dollar, N. J., & Merrigan, G. M. (2002). Ethnographic practices in group communication research. In L. R. Frey (Ed.), *New directions in group communication* (pp. 59–78). Thousand Oaks, CA: Sage.

Dollar, N. J., & Zimmers, B. G. (1998). Social identity and communicative boundaries: An analysis of youth and young adult street speakers in a U.S. American community. *Communication Research, 25,* 596–617.

Eisenhart, K., & Schoonhoven, C. (1990). Organizational growth: Linking founding team, strategy, environment and growth among U.S. semiconductor ventures, 1978–1988. *Administrative Science Quarterly, 35,* 504–529.

Ellingson, L. L. (2003). Interdisciplinary health care teamwork in the clinic backstage. *Journal of Applied Communication Research, 31,* 93–117.

Ellis, D. G. (1979). Relational control in two group systems. *Communication Monographs, 46,* 153–166.

Ellis, D. G., & Fisher, B. A. (1975). Phases of conflict in small group development: A Markov analysis. *Human Communication Research, 1,* 195–212.

Festinger, L., Schachter, S., & Back, K. (1968). Operation of group standards. In D. Cartwright & A. Zander (Eds.), *Group dynamics: Research and theory* (3rd ed., pp. 152–164). New York: Harper & Row.

Fisher, B. A. (1970). Decision emergence: Phases in group decision-making. *Speech Monographs, 37,* 53–66.

Fisher, B. A. (1971). Communication research and the task-oriented group. *Journal of Communication, 21,* 136–149.

Frey, L. R. (1994a). The call of the field: Studying communication in natural groups. In L. R. Frey (Ed.), *Group communication in context: Studies of natural groups* (pp. ix-xiv). Hillsdale, NJ: Lawrence Erlbaum.

Frey, L. R. (1994b). Introduction: Revitalizing the study of small group communication. *Communication Studies, 45,* 1–6.

Frey, L. R. (1994c). The naturalistic paradigm: Studying small groups in the postmodern era. *Small Group Research, 25,* 551–577.

Frey, L. R. (1995). Introduction: Applied communication research on group facilitation in natural settings. In L. R. Frey (Ed.), *Innovations in group facilitation: Applications in natural settings* (pp. 1–24). Cresskill, NJ: Hampton Press.

Frey, L. R. (1996). Remembering and "re-membering": A history of theory and research on communication and group decision making. In R. Y. Hirokawa & M. S. Poole (Eds.), *Communication and group decision making* (2nd ed., pp. 19–51). Thousand Oaks, CA: Sage.

Frey, L. R. (2000). Diversifying our understanding of diversity and communication in groups: Dialoguing with Clark, Anand, and Roberson (2000). *Group Dynamics: Theory, Research, and Practice, 4,* 222–229.

Frey, L. R. (2002). Introduction: New directions in group communication. In L. R. Frey (Ed.), *New directions in group communication* (pp. ix–xviii). Thousand Oaks, CA: Sage.

Frey, L. R., Botan, C. H., & Kreps, G. L. (2000). *Investigating communication: An introduction to research methods* (2nd ed.). Boston: Allyn & Bacon.

Frey, L. R., & Sunwolf. (2004). The symbolic-interpretive perspective on group dynamics. *Small Group Research, 35,* 277–306.

Frey, L. R., & Sunwolf. (2005). The symbolic-interpretive perspective of group life. In M. S. Poole & A. B. Hollingshead (Eds.), *Theories of small groups: An interdisciplinary perspective* (pp. 185–239). Thousand Oaks, CA: Sage.

Galanes, G. J., & Adams, K. (with Brilhart, J. K.). (2004). *Effective group discussion: Theory and practice* (11th ed.). Boston: McGraw-Hill.

Gastil, J. (1992). A definition of small group democracy. *Small Group Research, 23,* 278–301.

Gastil, J. (1993). *Democracy in small groups.* Philadelphia: New Society.

Gibb, J. R. (1961). Defensive communication. *Journal of Communication, 11,* 141–148.

Glaser, S. R. (1994). Teamwork and communication: A 3-year case study of change. *Management Communication Quarterly, 7,* 282–296.

Gouran, D. S. (1970). Response to "The paradox and promise of small group research." *Speech Monographs, 37,* 217–218.

Gouran, D. S. (1973). Group communication: Perspectives and priorities for future research. *Quarterly Journal of Speech, 58,* 22–29.

Gouran, D. S. (1985). The paradigm of unfulfilled promise: A critical examination of the history of research on small groups in speech communication. In T. W. Benson (Ed.), *Speech communication in the 20th century* (pp. 90–108, 386–392). Carbondale: Southern Illinois University Press.

Gouran, D. S. (1988). Group decision making: An approach to integrative research. In C. H. Tardy (Ed.), *A handbook for the study of human communication* (pp. 247–267). Norwood, NJ: Ablex.

Gouran, D. S. (1994). The future of small group communication research: Revitalization or continued good health? *Communication Studies, 45,* 29–39.

Gouran, D. S. (1999). Communication in groups: The emergence and evolution of a field of study. In L. R. Frey (Ed.), D. S. Gouran, & M. S. Poole (Assoc. Eds.), *The handbook of group communication theory and research* (pp. 3–36). Thousand Oaks, CA: Sage.

Gouran, D. S., & Baird, J. E., Jr. (1972). An analysis of distributional and sequential structure in problem-solving and informal group discussions. *Speech Monographs, 39,* 18–22.

Gouran, D. S., & Fisher, B. A. (1984). The functions of human communication in the formation, maintenance, and performance of small groups. In C. C. Arnold & J. W. Bowers (Eds.), *Handbook of rhetorical and communication theory* (pp. 622–658). Boston: Allyn & Bacon.

Gouran, D. S., & Hirokawa, R. Y. (1983). The role of communication in decision-making groups: A functional perspective. In M. S. Mander (Ed.), *Communication in transition: Issues and debate in current research* (pp. 168–185). New York: Praeger.

Gouran, D. S., & Hirokawa, R. Y. (1986). Counteractive functions in effective group decision-making. In R. Y. Hirokawa & M. S. Poole (Eds.), *Communication and group decision-making* (pp. 81–90). Beverly Hills, CA: Sage.

Gouran, D. S., & Hirokawa, R. Y. (1996). Functional theory and communication in decision-making and problem-solving groups: An expanded view. In R. Y. Hirokawa & M. S. Poole (Eds.), *Communication and group decision making* (2nd ed., pp. 55–80). Thousand Oaks, CA: Sage.

Gouran, D. S., Hirokawa, R. Y., Julian, K. M., & Leatham, G. B. (1993). The evolution and current status of the functional perspective on communication and group decision-making and problem-solving groups. In S. A. Deetz (Ed.), *Communication yearbook* (Vol. 16, pp. 583–600). Newbury Park, CA: Sage.

Gouran, D. S., Hirokawa, R. Y., McGee, M. C., & Miller, L. L. (1994). Communication in groups: Research trends and theoretical perspectives. In F. Casmir (Ed.), *Building communication theories: A socio/cultural approach* (pp. 241–268). Hillsdale, NJ: Lawrence Erlbaum.

Gudykunst, W. B. (1986). *Intergroup communication.* Baltimore, MD: Edward Arnold.

Hall, E. T. (1983). *The dance of life: The other dimension of time.* Garden City, NY: Anchor Press/Doubleday.

Hare, A. P., Blumberg, H. H., Davies, M. F., & Kent, M. V. (1994). *Small group research: A handbook.* Norwood, NJ: Ablex.

Harper, S. (1988). Rural reference groups and images of place. In D. C. D. Pocock (Ed.), *Humanistic approaches to geography* (pp. 32–49). Durham, NC: University of Durham, Department of Geography.

Harwood, J., & Giles, H. (Eds.). (in press). *Intergroup communication: Multiple perspectives.* New York: Peter Lang.

Haslett, B. B., & Ruebush, J. (1999). What differences do individual differences in groups make? The effects of individuals, culture, and group composition. In L. R. Frey (Ed.), D. S. Gouran, & M. S. Poole (Assoc. Eds.), *The handbook of group communication theory and research* (pp. 115–138). Thousand Oaks, CA: Sage.

Henningsen, M. L. M., Henningsen, D. D., Cruz, M. G., & Morrill, J. (2003). Social influence in groups: A comparative application of relational framing theory and the elaboration likelihood model of persuasion. *Communication Monographs, 70,* 175–197.

Hinsz, V. B., Vollrath, D. A., Nagao, D. H., & Davis, J. H. (1988). Comparing the structure of individual and small group perceptions. *International Journal of Small Group Research, 4,* 159–168.

Hirokawa, R. Y. (1982). Group communication and problem-solving effectiveness I: A critical review of inconsistent findings. *Communication Quarterly, 30,* 134–141.

Hirokawa, R. Y. (1983). Group communication and problem-solving effectiveness II: An investigation of procedural functions. *Western Journal of Speech Communication, 47,* 59–74.

Hirokawa, R. Y. (1988). Group communication research: Considerations for the use of interaction analysis. In C. H. Tardy (Ed.), *A handbook for the study of human communication: Methods and instruments for observing, measuring, and assessing communication processes* (pp. 229–245). Norwood, NJ: Ablex.

Hirokawa, R. Y., & Rost, K. M. (1992). Effective group decision making in organizations: Field test of the vigilant interaction theory. *Management Communication Quarterly, 5,* 267–288.

Hirokawa, R. Y., Rost, K. M., Fisher, E. B., Haire-Joshu, D., & Houston, C. (1990, November). *Going from the aquarium to the big ocean: A field test of the functional theory of group decision-making effectiveness.* Paper presented at the meeting of the Speech Communication Association, Chicago.

Hirokawa, R. Y., & Salazar, A. J. (1997). An integrated approach to communication and group decision making. In L. R. Frey & J. K. Barge (Eds.), *Managing group life: Communicating in decision-making groups* (pp. 156–181). Boston: Houghton Mifflin.

Hirokawa, R. Y., & Salazar, A. J. (1999). Task-group communication and decision-making performance. In L. R. Frey (Ed.), D. S. Gouran, & M. S. Poole (Assoc. Eds.), *The handbook of group communication theory and research* (pp. 167–191). Thousand Oaks, CA: Sage.

Hirokawa, R. Y., & Scheerhorn, D. R. (1986). Communication in faulty group decision-making. In R. Y. Hirokawa & M. S. Poole (Eds.), *Communication and group decision-making* (pp. 63–80). Beverly Hills, CA: Sage.

Hogg, M. A., & Abrams, D. (1988). *Social identifications: A social psychology of intergroup relations and group processes.* New York: Routledge.

Hollihan, T. A., & Riley, P. (1987). The rhetorical power of a compelling story: A critique of a "Toughlove" parental support group. *Communication Quarterly, 35*, 13–25.

Houston, R. (2003). In the mask of thin air: Intragroup and intergroup communication during the Mt. Everest disaster. In L. R. Frey (Ed.), *Group communication in context: Studies of bona fide groups* (2nd ed., pp. 137–156). Mahwah, NJ: Lawrence Erlbaum.

Infante, D. A., Rancer, A. S., & Womak, D. F. (2003). *Building communication theory* (3rd ed.). Prospect Heights, IL: Waveland Press.

Jackson, M. H., & Poole, M. S. (2003). Idea-generation in naturally occurring contexts: Complex appropriation of a simple group procedure. *Human Communication Research, 29*, 560–591.

Janis, I. L. (1972). *Victims of groupthink: A psychological study of foreign-policy decisions and fiascoes.* Boston: Houghton Mifflin.

Janis, I. L. (1982). *Groupthink: Psychological studies of policy decisions and fiascoes* (2nd ed.). Boston: Houghton Mifflin.

Janis, I. L., & Mann, I. (1977). *Decision-making: A psychological analysis of conflict, choice, and commitment.* New York: Free Press.

Jarboe, S. (1997). Group communication and creativity processes. In L. R. Frey (Ed.), D. S. Gouran, & M. S. Poole (Assoc. Eds.), *The handbook of group communication theory and research* (pp. 335–368). Thousand Oaks, CA: Sage.

Keltner, J. W. (1960). Communication in discussion and group processes: Some research trends of the decade 1950–1959. Part I. *Journal of Communication, 10*, 195–204.

Keltner, J. W. (1961). Communication in discussion and group processes: Some research trends of the decade 1950–1959. Part II. *Journal of Communication, 11*, 27–33.

Ketrow, S. M. (1999). Nonverbal aspects of group communication. In L. R. Frey (Ed.), D. S. Gouran, & M. S. Poole (Assoc. Eds.), *The handbook of group communication theory and research* (pp. 251–287). Thousand Oaks, CA: Sage.

Keyton, J. (1994). Going forward in group communication research may mean going back: Studying the groups of children. *Communication Studies, 45*, 40–51.

Keyton, J. (1999). Relational communication in groups. In L. R. Frey (Ed.), D. S. Gouran, & M. S. Poole (Assoc. Eds.), *The handbook of group*

communication theory and research (pp. 192–222). Thousand Oaks, CA: Sage.

Keyton, J. (2002). *Communicating in groups: Building relationships for effective decision making* (2nd ed.). New York: McGraw-Hill.

Keyton, J., & Frey, L. R. (2002). The state of traits: Predispositions and group communication. In L. R. Frey (Ed.), *New directions in group communication* (pp. 99–120). Thousand Oaks, CA: Sage.

Kirchmeyer, C. (1993). Multicultural task groups: An account of the low contribution levels of minorities. *Small Group Research, 24*, 127–148.

Kirchmeyer, C., & Cohen, A. (1992). Multicultural groups: Their performance and reactions with constructive conflict. *Group & Organizational Management, 17*, 153–170.

Kono, T. (1988). Factors affecting the creativity of organizations: An approach from the analysis of new product development. In K. Urabe, J. Child, & T. Kagano (Eds.), *Innovation and management: International comparisons* (pp. 105–144). New York: Walter de Gruyter.

Krakauer, J. (1997). *Into thin air: A personal account of the Mount Everest tragedy.* New York: Villard Books.

Kramarae, C. (1990). Changing the complexion of gender in language research. In H. Giles & W. P. Robinson (Eds.), *Handbook of language and social psychology* (pp. 345–361). New York: John Wiley.

Kramer, M. W. (2002). Communication in a community theater group: Managing multiple group roles. *Communication Studies, 53*, 151–170.

Kramer, M. W. (in press). Toward a theory of dialectics in group communication: An ethnographic study of a community theatre group. *Communication Monographs.*

Lammers, J. C., & Krikorian, D. H. (1997). Theoretical extension and operationalization of the bona fide group construct with an application to surgical teams. *Journal of Applied Communication Research, 25*, 17–38.

Lange, J. I. (2003). Environmental collaboration and constituency communication. In L. R. Frey (Ed.), *Group communication in context: Studies of bona fide groups* (2nd ed., pp. 209–234). Mahwah, NJ: Lawrence Erlbaum.

Larson, C. E. (1971). Speech communication research on small groups. *Speech Teacher, 20*, 89–107.

Lesch, C. L. (1994). Observing theory in practice: Sustaining consciousness in a coven. In L. R. Frey

(Ed.), *Group communication in context: Studies of natural groups* (pp. 57–82). Hillsdale, NJ: Lawrence Erlbaum.

Lewin, K., & Lippitt, R. (1938). An experimental approach to the study of autocracy and democracy: A preliminary note. *Sociometry, 1,* 292–300.

Lewin, K., Lippitt, R., & White, R. K. (1939). Patterns of aggressive behavior in experimentally created "social climates." *Journal of Social Psychology, 10,* 271–299.

Limon, M. S., & Boster, F. J. (2001). The impact of varying argument quality and minority size on influencing the majority and perceptions of the minority. *Communication Quarterly, 49,* 350–365.

Limon, M. S., & Boster, F. J. (2003). The effects of performance feedback on group members' perceptions of prestige, task competencies, group belonging, and loafing. *Communication Research Reports, 20,* 13–23.

Lippitt, R. (1939). Field theory and experiment in social psychology: Autocratic and democratic group atmospheres. *American Journal of Sociology, 45,* 26–49.

Lippitt, R. (1940). An experimental study of the effect of democratic and authoritarian group atmospheres. *University of Iowa Studies in Child Welfare, 16,* 43–195.

Lippitt, R., & White, R. K. (1952). An experimental study of leadership and group life. In G. E. Swanson, T. M. Newcomb, & E. L. Hartley (Eds.), *Readings in social psychology* (pp. 340–355). New York: Holt.

Mabry, E. A. (1975). An instrument for assessing content themes in group interaction. *Communication Monographs, 42,* 291–297.

Mabry, E. A. (1999). The systems metaphor in group communication. In L. R. Frey, D. S. Gouran, & M. S. Poole (Eds.), *The handbook of group communication theory and research* (pp. 71–91). Thousand Oaks, CA: Sage.

Massey, D. (1994). *Space, place, and gender.* Minneapolis: University of Minnesota Press.

Mayer, M. E. (1998). Behaviors leading to more effective decisions in small groups embedded in organizations. *Communication Reports, 11,* 123–132.

McCroskey, J. C., & Richmond, V. P. (1992). Communication apprehension and small group communication. In R. S. Cathcart & L. A. Samovar (Eds.), *Small group communication: A reader* (6th ed., pp. 361–374). Dubuque, IA: William C. Brown.

McLeod, P. L. (1996). New communication technologies for group decision making: Toward an integrative framework. In R. Y. Hirokawa & M. S. Poole (Eds.), *Communication and group decision making* (2nd ed., pp. 426–461). Thousand Oaks, CA: Sage.

Meyer, J. C. (1997). Humor in member narratives: Uniting and dividing at work. *Western Journal of Communication, 61,* 188–208.

Meyers, R. A., & Brashers, D. E. (1998). Argument in group decision making: Explicating a process model and investigating the argument-outcome link. *Communication Monographs, 65,* 261–281.

Meyers, R. A., & Brashers, D. E. (1999). Influence processes in group interaction. In L. R. Frey (Ed.), D. S. Gouran, & M. S. Poole (Assoc. Eds.), *The handbook of group communication theory and research* (pp. 288–312). Thousand Oaks, CA: Sage.

Meyers, R. A., Seibold, D. R., & Brashers, D. (1991). Argument in initial group decision-making discussions: Refinement of a coding scheme and a descriptive quantitative analysis. *Western Journal of Speech Communication, 55,* 47–68.

Mokros, H. B., & Deetz, S. (1996). What counts as real? A constitutive view of communication and the disenfranchised in the context of health. In E. B. Ray (Ed.), *Communication and disenfranchisement: Social health issues and implications* (pp. 29–44). Mahwah, NJ: Lawrence Erlbaum.

Mortensen, C. D. (1970). The state of small group research. *Quarterly Journal of Speech, 56,* 304–309.

Myeroff, B. G. (1982). Life history among the elderly: Performance, visibility, and remembering. In J. Ruby (Ed.), *A crack in the mirror: Reflexive perspectives in anthropology* (pp. 99–117). Philadelphia: University of Pennsylvania Press.

Nemeth, C. (1986). Differential contributions of majority vs. minority influence. *Psychological Review, 93,* 23–32.

Nicotera, A. M. (1995). *Communication and conflict: Communicative processes.* Albany: State University of New York Press.

Nicotera, A. M. (1997). Managing conflict communication in groups. In L. R. Frey & J. K. Barge (Eds.), *Managing group life: Communicating in decision-making groups* (pp. 104–130). Boston: Houghton Mifflin.

Orlitzky, M. O., & Hirokawa, R. Y. (1997, November). *To err is human, to correct for is divine: A meta-analysis of research testing the functional theory of group decision-making effectiveness.* Paper presented at the meeting of the National Communication Association, Chicago.

O'Sullivan, T., Hartley, J., Saunders, D., Montgomery, M., & Fiske, J. (1994). *Key concepts in communication and cultural studies* (2nd ed.). London: Routledge.

Parrish-Sprowl, J. (2003). Indexing the Polish transformation: The case of Eco-S from a bona fide group perspective. In L. R. Frey (Ed.), *Group communication in context: Studies of bona fide groups* (2nd ed., pp. 291–305). Mahwah, NJ: Lawrence Erlbaum.

Pavitt, C., & Curtis, E. (1994). *Small group discussion: A theoretical approach* (2nd ed.). Scottsdale, AZ: Gorsuch Scarisbrick.

Pavitt, C., & Johnson, K. K. (1999). An examination of the coherence of group discussions. *Communication Research, 26,* 303–321.

Pavitt, C., & Johnson, K. K. (2002). Scheidel and Crowell revisited: A descriptive study of group proposal sequencing. *Communication Monographs, 69,* 19–32.

Pearce, W. B. (1995). *Public dialogue and democracy: A guide for the discussion leader.* Chicago: Loyola University Chicago.

Pelz, D. C., & Andrews, F. M. (1976). *Scientists in organizations: Productive climates for research and development* (Rev. ed.). Ann Arbor: University of Michigan, Institute for Social Research.

Petty, R. E., & Cacioppo, J. T. (1986). *Communication and persuasion: Central and peripheral routes to attitude change.* New York: Springer-Verlag.

Poole, M. S. (1981). Decision development in small groups I: A comparison of two models. *Communication Monographs, 48,* 1–24.

Poole, M. S. (1983a). Decision development in small groups II: A study of multiple sequences in decision making. *Communication Monographs, 50,* 206–232.

Poole, M. S. (1983b). Decision development in small groups, III: A multiple sequence model of group decision development. *Communication Monographs, 50,* 321–341.

Poole, M. S. (1990). Do we have any theories of group communication? *Communication Studies, 41,* 237–247.

Poole, M. S. (1994). Breaking the isolation of small group communication studies. *Communication Studies, 45,* 20–28.

Poole, M. S. (1999). Group communication theory. In L. R. Frey (Ed.), D. S. Gouran, & M. S. Poole (Assoc. Eds.), *The handbook of group communication theory and research* (pp. 37–70). Thousand Oaks, CA: Sage.

Poole, M. S., & Baldwin, C. L. (1996). Developmental processes in group decision making. In R. Y. Hirokawa & M. S. Poole (Eds.), *Communication and group decision making* (2nd ed., pp. 215–241). Thousand Oaks, CA: Sage.

Poole, M. S., Keyton, J., & Frey, L. R. (1999). Group communication methodology: Issues and considerations. In L. R. Frey (Ed.), D. S. Gouran, & M. S. Poole (Assoc. Eds.), *The handbook of group communication theory and research* (pp. 92–112). Thousand Oaks, CA: Sage.

Poole, M. S., McPhee, R. D., & Seibold, D. R. (1982). A comparison of normative and interactional explanations of group decision-making: Social decision schemes versus valence distributions. *Communication Monographs, 49,* 1–19.

Poole, M. S., & Roth, J. (1989a). Decision development in small groups IV: A typology of group decision paths. *Human Communication Research, 15,* 323–356.

Poole, M. S., & Roth, J. (1989b). Decision development in small groups V: Test of a contingency model. *Human Communication Research, 15,* 549–589.

Propp, K. M. (1999). Collective information processing in groups. In L. R. Frey (Ed.), D. S. Gouran, & M. S. Poole (Assoc. Eds.), *The handbook of group communication theory and research* (pp. 225–250). Thousand Oaks, CA: Sage.

Propp, K. M., & Kreps, G. L. (1994). A rose by any other name: The vitality of group communication research. *Communication Studies, 45,* 7–19.

Propp, K. M., & Nelson, D. (1996). Problem-solving performance in naturalistic groups: A test of the ecological validity of the functional perspective. *Communication Studies, 47,* 35–45.

Putnam, L. L. (1994). Revitalizing small group communication: Lessons learned from a bona fide group perspective. *Communication Studies, 45,* 97–102.

Putnam, L. L., & Fairhurst, G. T. (2001). Discourse analysis in organizations: Issues and concerns. In F. M. Jablin & L. L. Putnam (Eds.), *The new handbook of organizational communication: Advances in theory, research, and methods* (pp. 78–136). Thousand Oaks, CA: Sage.

Putnam, L. L., & Stohl, C. (1990). Bona fide groups: A reconceptualization of groups in context. *Communication Studies, 41,* 248–265.

Putnam, L. L., & Stohl, C. (1996). Bona fide groups: An alternative perspective for communication and small group decision making. In R. Y. Hirokawa & M. S. Poole (Eds.), *Communication and group decision making* (2nd ed., pp. 179–214). Thousand Oaks, CA: Sage.

Sacks, H., Schegloff, E. A., & Jefferson, G. (1974). A simplest systematics for the organization of turn-taking for conversation. *Language, 50,* 696–735.

Sager, K. L., & Gastil, J. (2002). Exploring the psychological foundations of democratic group deliberation: Personality factors, confirming interaction, and democratic decision making. *Communication Research Reports, 19,* 54–65.

Salazar, A. J. (2002). Self-organizing and complexity perspectives of group creativity: Implications for group communication. In L. R. Frey (Ed.), *New directions in group communication* (pp. 179–199). Thousand Oaks, CA: Sage.

Scheerhorn, D., & Geist, P. (1997). Social dynamics in groups. In L. R. Frey & J. K. Barge (Eds.), *Managing group life: Communicating in decision-making groups* (pp. 81–103). Boston: Houghton Mifflin.

Scheidel, T. M., & Crowell, L. (1964). Idea development in small discussion groups. *Quarterly Journal of Speech, 50,* 140–145.

Scheidel, T. M., & Crowell, L. (1966). Feedback in small group communication. *Quarterly Journal of Speech, 52,* 273–278.

Schultz, B. (1974). Characteristics of emergent leaders: An exploratory study of the salience of communication functions. *Small Group Behavior, 9,* 9–14.

Schultz, B. (1978). Predicting emergent leaders: An exploratory study of the salience of communicative functions. *Small Group Behavior, 9,* 9–14.

Schultz, B. (1982). Argumentativeness: Its effect in group decision-making and its role in leadership perceptions. *Communication Quarterly, 30,* 368–375.

Schultz, B. (1986). Communication correlates of perceived leaders in the small group. *Small Group Behavior, 17,* 51–65.

Scott, C. R. (1999). Group communication technology and group communication. In L. R. Frey (Ed.), D. S. Gouran, & M. S. Poole (Assoc. Eds.), *The handbook of group communication theory and research* (pp. 432–472). Thousand Oaks, CA: Sage.

Seibold, D. R. (1994). More reflection or more research? To (re)vitalize small group communication research, let's "just do it." *Communication Studies, 45,* 103–110.

Seibold, D. R., Poole, M. S., McPhee, R. D., Tanita, N. E., & Canary, D. J. (1981). Argument, group influence, and decision outcomes. In C. Ziegelmueller & J. Rhodes (Eds.), *Dimensions of argument: Proceedings of the second SCA/AFA summer conference on argumentation* (pp. 663–692). Annandale, VA: Speech Communication Association.

Sharf, B. F. (1978). A rhetorical analysis of leadership in small groups. *Communication Monographs, 45,* 156–172.

Shaw, M. E. (1981). *Group dynamics: The psychology of small group behavior* (3rd ed.). New York: McGraw-Hill.

Smith, K. K., & Berg, D. N. (1987). *Paradoxes of group life: Understanding conflict, paralysis, and movement in group dynamics.* San Francisco: Jossey-Bass.

Socha, T. J. (1997). Group communication across the life span. In L. R. Frey & J. K. Barge (Eds.), *Managing group life: Communicating in decision-making groups* (pp. 3–28). Boston: Houghton Mifflin.

Socha, T. J. (1999). Communication in family units: Studying the first "group." In L. R. Frey (Ed.), D. S. Gouran, & M. S. Poole (Assoc. Eds.), *The handbook of group communication theory and research* (pp. 475–492). Thousand Oaks, CA: Sage.

Stasser, G., Taylor, L. A., & Hanna, C. (1989). Information sampling in structured and unstructured discussions of three- and six-person groups. *Journal of Personality and Social Psychology, 57,* 67–78.

Stasser, G., & Titus, W. (1985). Pooling of unshared information in group decision making: Biased information sampling during discussion. *Journal of Personality and Social Psychology, 48,* 1467–1478.

Stasser, G., & Titus, W. (1987). Effects of information load and percentage of shared information on the dissemination of unshared information during group discussion. *Journal of Personality and Social Psychology, 69,* 619–628.

Stech, E. (1970). An analysis of interaction structure in the discussion of a ranking task. *Speech Monographs, 37,* 249–256.

Stock, D., & Thelen, H. A. (1958). *Emotional dynamics and group culture: Experimental studies of individual and group behavior.* Washington, DC: National Training Laboratories.

Stohl, C. (1986). The role of memorable messages in the process of organizational socialization. *Communication Quarterly, 34,* 231–249.

Stohl, C. (1987). Bridging the parallel organization: A study of quality circle effectiveness. In M. L. McLaughlin (Ed.), *Communication yearbook* (Vol. 10, pp. 416–429). Beverly Hills, CA: Sage.

Sunwolf (2002). Getting to "GroupAha!": Provoking creative processes in task groups. In L. R. Frey (Ed.), *New directions in group communication* (pp. 203–217). Thousand Oaks, CA: Sage.

Sunwolf & Frey, L. R. (2001). Storytelling: The power of narrative communication and interpretation. In W. P. Robinson & H. Giles (Eds.), *The new handbook of language and social psychology* (pp. 119–135). New York: John Wiley.

Sunwolf & Leets, L. (2003). Communication paralysis during peer group exclusion: Social dynamics that prevent children and adolescents from expressing disagreement. *Journal of Language and Social Psychology, 22,* 355–384.

Sunwolf & Leets, L. (2004). Being left out: Rejecting outsiders and communicating group boundaries in childhood and adolescent peer groups. *Journal of Applied Communication Research, 32,* 197–227.

Sunwolf & Seibold, D. R. (1999). The impact of formal procedures on group processes, members, and task outcomes. In L. R. Frey (Ed.), D. S. Gouran, & M. S. Poole (Assoc. Eds.), *The handbook of group communication theory and research* (pp. 395–431). Thousand Oaks, CA: Sage.

Sykes, R. E. (1990). Imagining what we might study if we really studied small groups from a speech perspective. *Communication Studies, 41,* 200–211.

Taylor, C. B. (1997). Communication satisfaction: Its role in church membership satisfaction and involvement among Southern Baptist churches. *Southern Communication Journal, 62,* 293–304.

Thelen, H. A. (1954). *Dynamics of groups at work.* Chicago: University of Chicago Press.

Timmons, W. M. (1941). Discussion, debating, and research. *Quarterly Journal of Speech, 27,* 415–421.

Tracy, K. (2001). Discourse analysis in communication. In D. Schiffrin, D. Tannen, & H. Hamilton (Eds.), *Handbook of discourse analysis* (pp. 725–749). Malden, MA: Blackwell.

Tracy, K., & Ashcraft, C. (2001). Crafting policies about controversial values: How wording disputes manage a group dilemma. *Journal of Applied Communication Research, 29,* 297–316.

Tracy, K., & Dimock, A. (2004). Meetings: Discursive sites for building and fragmenting community. In P. J. Kalbfleisch (Ed.), *Communication yearbook* (Vol. 28, pp. 127–165). Mahwah, NJ: Lawrence Erlbaum.

Tracy, K., & Muller, H. (2001). Diagnosing a school board's interactional trouble: Theorizing problem formulation. *Communication Theory, 11,* 84–104.

Tracy, K., & Standerfer, C. (2003). Selecting a school superintendent: Interactional sensitivities in the deliberative process. In L. R. Frey (Ed.), *Group communication in context: Studies of bona fide groups* (2nd ed., pp. 109–134). Mahwah, NJ: Lawrence Erlbaum.

Trice, H. M., & Beyer, J. M. (1984). Studying organizational cultures through rites and ceremonials. *Academy of Management Review, 9,* 653–669.

Tubbs, S. L. (2004). *A systems approach to small group interaction* (8th ed.). Boston: McGraw-Hill.

Tuckman, B. W. (1965). Developmental sequences in small groups. *Psychological Bulletin, 63,* 384–399.

Verdi, A. F., & Wheelan, S. (1992). Developmental patterns in same-sex and mixed-sex groups. *Small Group Research, 23,* 356–378.

Weick, K. E. (1978). The spines of leaders. In M. McCall & M. Lombardo (Eds.), *Leadership: Where else can we go?* (pp. 37–61). Durham, NC: Duke University Press.

Weitzel, A., & Geist, P. (1998). Parliamentary procedure in a community group: Communication and vigilant decision making. *Communication Monographs, 65,* 244–259.

Wheelan, S. A., McKeage, R. L., Verdi, A. F., Abraham, M., Krasick, C., & Johnston, F. (1994). Communication and developmental patterns in a system of interacting groups. In L. R. Frey (Ed.), *Group communication in context: Studies of natural groups* (pp. 153–180). Hillsdale, NJ: Lawrence Erlbaum.

Wheelan, S., & Verdi, A. F. (1992). Differences in male and female patterns of communication in groups: A methodological artifact? *Sex Roles, 27,* 1–15.

White, R. K., & Lippitt, R. (1960). *Autocracy and democracy: An experimental inquiry.* New York: Harper.

Wiersema, M. F., & Bird, A. (1993). Organizational demography in Japanese firms: Group heterogeneity, individual dissimilarity, and top management team turnover. *Academy of Management Journal, 36,* 996–1025.

Witmer, D. F. (1997). Communication and recovery: Structuration as an ontological approach to organizational culture. *Communication Monographs, 64,* 324–349.

Wittenbaum, G. M., Hollingshead, A. B., Paulus, P. B., Hirokawa, R. Y., Ancona, D. C., Peterson, R. S., Jehn, K. A., & Yoon, K. (2004). The functional perspective as a lens for understanding groups. *Small Group Research, 35,* 17–43.

Wittenbaum, G. M., Hollingshead, A. B., Paulus, P. B., Hirokawa, R. Y., Ancona, D. C., Peterson, R. S., Jehn, K. A., & Yoon, K. (in press). The functional perspective. In M. S. Poole & A. B. Hollingshead (Eds.), *Theories of small groups: An interdisciplinary perspective.* Thousand Oaks, CA: Sage.

Wyatt, N. (1982). Power and decision making. In G. M. Phillips & J. T. Wood (Eds.), *Emergent issues in human decision-making* (pp. 50–60). Carbondale: Southern Illinois University Press.

Wyatt, N. (1988). Shared leadership in the Weaver's Guild. In B. Bate & A. Taylor (Eds.), *Women communicating: Studies of women's talk* (pp. 147–176). Norwood, NJ: Ablex.

Wyatt, N. (1993). Organizing and relating: Feminist critique of small group communication. In S. P. Brown & N. Wyatt (Eds.), *Transforming visions: Feminist critiques in communication studies* (pp. 51–86). Cresskill, NJ: Hampton Press.

Yep, G. A., Reece, S. T., & Negrón, E. L. (2003). Culture and stigma in a bona fide group: Boundaries and context in a "closed" support group for "Asian Americans" living with HIV infection. In L. R. Frey (Ed.), *Group communication in context: Studies of bona fide groups* (2nd ed., pp. 157–180). Mahwah, NJ: Lawrence Erlbaum.

10

The Systems Perspective

Yvonne Agazarian

Susan Gantt

The introduction of systems theory into the study of groups and group practice provides a metatheory for understanding groups and group dynamics. Systems theory can be used to look at the functioning of any group, regardless of the theoretical orientation of the group practitioner or leader, or of the group goal. This applies to all groups, whether a therapy or work group, an organization, or a political body. Systems theory offers an orientation for thinking about how groups form, develop and change, and manage the vicissitudes of group dynamics.

Systems thinking emerged from the shift of scientific assumptions that occurred in the early 20th century as theories of relativity and quantum mechanics upended the security of Newtonian reductionist explanations (Agazarian & Janoff, 1993; Boer & Moore, 1994; H. E. Durkin, 1981). This shift in the Zeitgeist influenced the work of Lewin (1951) and Bion (1959), neither of whom actually labeled

themselves systems thinkers but who both contributed significantly to systems thinking.

Lewin (1935, 1951) stated that the whole is different from the sum of its parts and formulated a field theory that postulates individual behavior as an output of the person's perception of his or her environment. Agazarian (1986) translated Lewin's *person* into *system* and formulated system behavior as an output of system function.

Bion (1959) postulated three basic assumptions about the dynamics of groups (flight/fight, dependency, and pairing). These basic assumptions laid the foundation for the important work on the reciprocal influence of the group and the individual in both small groups and organizations; it also laid the foundation for the open systems theorists (Miller & Rice, 1967). Bennis and Shepard (1956) developed Bion's basic assumptions into a theory of group development. Agazarian (1981, 1994), building on Bennis and Shepard's work, reconceptualized these phases as subsystems within the developmental process of all living human systems.

The shift from implicit to explicit systems thinking originated in the social and biological sciences. One of the most important systems thinkers was von Bertalanffy (1969), who developed a general systems theory that focused on the dynamic interactions among living systems. He introduced the concepts of isomorphy, hierarchy, boundary permeability, autopoesis, energy, and goals. Miller (1978) stressed the importance of information and energy flow in open systems. Most important, Miller equated energy and information in systems and noted that information provides energy to a human system. Miller (1978) credited Shannon for recognizing that "the statistical measure for negative entropy is the same as that for information, which Schroedinger has called negentropy" (p. 13). Later, Agazarian and Gantt (2000) translated entropic and negentropic communications into the driving and restraining forces that determine the quasi-stationary equilibrium of the system. Wiener (1948/1968) focused on system feedback through self-regulation of system boundaries and introduced the term *cybernetics*. Bateson (1972; Bateson, Jackson, & Haley, 1956) applied the cybernetic concepts of equilibrium and feedback to family therapy.

Helen Durkin (1972a, 1972b) was the first to apply von Bertalanffy's general systems theory to group psychotherapy and initiated the American Group Psychotherapy Association's General System Theory Committee to explore the application of systems theory to group therapy. This think tank provided an important environment and influence for a number of theorists and practitioners who were beginning to apply systems theories to their group practice and research (Agazarian, 1986, 1989; Beck, 1981; J. Durkin, 1981, 1989; Fidler, 1987; Vassiliou, 1973).

Subsequently, other practitioners and theorists have applied the principles of general systems theory to groups (Astrachan, 1970; Barber, 1988; Beeber, 1988, 1991; Borriello, 1992; Brabender, 1997; Burck, Hildebrand, & Mann, 1996; Donigian & Malnati, 1997; Hildebrand, 1988; Hildebrand & Forbes, 1987; Hills, 1994; Lapponi, 1996; MacKenzie, 1990; Mathews, 1992; O'Neill & Stockwell, 1991; Wilson & Hutton, 1992), child and adolescent day treatment programs (Kiser & Pruitt, 1991), training trainees (Bor, 1989; Nicholas, 1989), and ecosystemic group therapy (Boer & Moore, 1994; O'Connor, 1999).

Agazarian's (1997) theory of living human systems, with its systems-centered approach to group practice, represents the most fully developed and comprehensive systems theory applied to groups thus far. The theory of living human systems has defined theoretical constructs and operational definitions that function as hypotheses to test both the validity of the theory and the reliability of its practice. In this chapter, we define *group* using her theory of living human systems and its systems-centered practice as the orientation to group theory and practice.

Applying the Constructs of a Theory of Living Human Systems to Understanding Groups

The theory of living human systems defines a hierarchy of isomorphic systems that are energy organizing, self-correcting, and goal directed (Agazarian, 1989, 1992, 1997). Defining all groups as living human systems makes it possible to view them from the perspectives of hierarchy and isomorphy. In the hierarchy, every system exists in the environment of the system above it and is the environment for the system below it. Both conceptually and practically, this is the core system in a hierarchy. Thus, hierarchy is defined by a series of core systems, each core system existing in the environment of the core system above it and existing as the environment for the system below it. The member system exists in a group system, the group system exists in organizations of groups, and organizations exist in nations, and so on. Because all systems in a defined hierarchy are isomorphic (similar in structure and function), the core system is governed by the same principle as all systems in the hierarchy.

Hierarchy

Operationally, the core system is defined for group practice as the group-as-a-whole system, the subgroup systems of the group-as-a-whole, and the member systems that make up the subgroups. The subgroup exists in the environment of the system above it and is the environment of the system below it. As the midlevel system, the subgroup shares its boundaries with both the group-as-a-whole system and the member system. Thus, the most efficient way of influencing the core system is through the subgroup because its boundaries are contiguous to the group-as-a-whole and to its members.

Testing this assumption began with observing how subgroups within groups respond to group conflicts. This, in turn, led to actively intervening to move the group away from stereotypical responses to conflict and toward functional responses. Thus the systems-centered therapy (SCT) technique of functional subgrouping was developed as a conflict resolution method, which influenced both the group-as-a-whole and its members.

Functional subgroups differ from stereotypical subgroups in that members address the information that is relevant to the task by joining only those who have the same point of view. Only when the one side is thoroughly discussed is the other side addressed by the contending or different subgroup. Functional subgrouping precludes the *we/they* and *yes, but* . . . pattern of communication that generates stereotypical subgrouping. For example, rather than condoning a *yes, but* . . . fight, all the members who are for the issue (the *yes* subgroup) explore how their agreement relates to furthering the understanding of what is involved in their *yes*. When

this *yes* subgroup peters out, the *but* subgroup explores the contribution that their caveats contain. Predictably, as both subgroups hear the work of the other subgroup, not only does a greater understanding of each develop, but also each subgroup notices the similarities between them and how those similarities relate to the task at hand.

Practically, introducing functional subgrouping into groups has had a predictable impact on the development of the task and process dimensions in groups, as well as the developmental phases. Transforming redundant stereotypical subgroups into task-related functional subgroups changes both the task and process dimensions, reducing the restraining forces that lie on the path to the goal.

For example, in hierarchical organizations, typical subgrouping is often redundant and stereotypical, based on status (structure) rather than on function. In stereotypical subgrouping, high-status members speak to high-status members, and low-status members talk to high-status members. Thus, the high-status subgroup can process information, whereas the low-status subgroup cannot. Thus, information that would arise from low-status subgrouping is unavailable to the system as a whole. Transforming the subgrouping pattern from stereotype (structure) to function (process) enables members to subgroup around the information that is relevant to the task, independent of status.

Isomorphy

Applying the construct of isomorphy also had important implications for understanding group system dynamics. Isomorphy is defined as similarity of structure and function within a defined hierarchy. In other words, all system dynamics are equivalent.

Structure is defined by boundaries. Boundaries are potentially permeable to transactions of energy. Energy is defined as information in living human systems (Miller, 1978). The permeability of boundaries determines what information/energy crosses into the system. Boundaries open to clear information and close to noise. For example, just as static on a telephone line makes it hard to hear what a caller is saying, a significant amount of noise in communication makes it less likely the information will get across. Shannon and Weaver (1964) identified noise in communication as ambiguities, redundancies, and contradictions. Vague memos, for example, are frequently either misinterpreted or reinterpreted in terms of wishes and fears, and the intent of the memo is lost; when the same information is reiterated in different words at a meeting, members are easily lost to boredom; and the fastest way to create a climate of suspicion is to say one thing and mean another. Reducing noise is a function of filtering out the noise from the information. The more efficiently the system develops a process to filter out the noise, the more energy is available for work.

Function is defined as the ability to discriminate and integrate differences. The system's function, then, is to organize energy (information) through discriminating and integrating differences—both differences in the apparently similar and similarities in the apparently different. This is the process by which living human systems survive, develop, and transform. The method of functional subgrouping discriminates and contains differences in separate subgroups, where each viewpoint is explored until the similarities in the differences are recognized and the differences are integrated in the system-as-whole.

Thus, with isomorphy, whatever one learns about the way one system functions (by discriminating and integrating similarities and differences) also applies to every other system in the hierarchy. Whatever one learns about the principles by which groups manage the permeability of their boundaries will apply to all core systems within that system hierarchy: all member systems, all subgroup systems, and all system-as-a-whole systems.

Groups as Systems

In the systems-centered approach, a group is a core system. Like all living human systems, the group also exists within a hierarchy of core systems. The core system exists at every level of the hierarchy and is defined as a hierarchy of three. Each system in the core system exists in the environment of the system above it and is the environment for the system below it. Whereas a group-as-a-whole is the containing system for the subgroup (and the subgroup for its members), from a different perspective, the group-as-a-whole in its turn can be viewed as a subsystem of a larger system. For example, an employee is a member of a department, which is in turn a subgroup of an organization, which in turn is a subgroup of a nation, and so on.

Applying the idea of the core system to group is especially significant for change agents in that every change strategy always has a three-point impact. Thus, in all SCT interventions, the subsystem that is the target of the intervention is chosen with this three-point impact in mind. Interventions involving a subgroup will influence both the group-as-a-whole and its members. Interventions involving a department are made with the knowledge that they will have an impact not only on the department but also on the work groups within it and the division in which the department is located.

Individuals as Systems

The concept of the core system also applies to individuals. Individuals as living human systems are described as a system-as-a-whole with subsystems. In earlier work, Agazarian (1981) suggested that *role* was a bridge construct between the individual and the group. From the systems-centered perspective, role is a midlevel subsystem in the person, just as the subgroup is a midlevel subsystem in the group. Like subgroups, roles can be functional or nonfunctional. A good example of a nonfunctional role is a stereotypical role with boundaries impermeable to information. Every subsystem has a role in every context, and every role is a subsystem. Thus, these two words are interchangeable, and which one is used depends on which fits best with the context. For example, influencing the role system in the individual is equivalent to influencing the subgroups in the group-as-a-whole.

When a person moves into a stereotypical role, it is the role that determines his or her perceptions and behavior. Role boundaries are closed to any information that contradicts the role system and open to information that reinforces it. For example, someone in a stereotypical "victim" role is oriented predominantly to all the ways he or she has been mistreated. Similarly, the boundaries of a stereotype subgroup are closed to differences that do not support the stereotypes. An all-too-familiar example of stereotypical subgroups in group is when all the women complain about the men not understanding them, and all the men complain about the women always criticizing them. Roles have the potential for being adaptive or maladaptive depending on the group context in which they manifest. For example, the scapegoat in one group may be the innovator in another.

The scapegoat is also a good example of how stereotypical roles function, for both the group and the individual. For example, the group creates a scapegoat role to contain the differences that the group system is not yet ready to integrate. By keeping an impermeable boundary between the scapegoat system and the group, the group system maintains its equilibrium. Similarly, taking on the scapegoat role sets up impermeable boundaries between the person system and the differences in the group, thus maintaining the equilibrium of the person system. When (and if) the boundaries between the group and the scapegoat become permeable (which they do, either through an intervention or through group development), both the person and the group can gain access to information that can then be integrated.

An individual relates to many subsystems and plays many roles in life. For example, every individual has a role at home and a different role at work. The many roles people play represent membership not only in outside subgroups but also in internal subgroups. There is an internal change when one shifts from home to work. Different internal resources are relevant in each of the two contexts. How efficiently people take up their roles influences both their internal and their external environments.

Goals

The theory of living human systems defines two levels of goals. The primary goals of systems are to survive, develop, and transform from simpler to more complex (Agazarian, 1997). In practice, the primary goals relate to the system development and transformation in each of the phases of system development, which are authority, collaboration, and work (Agazarian, 1994, 1999). The secondary goals of systems are the explicit goals, which are represented by the tasks that a group has come together to accomplish. For systems to function, information (energy) must be organized in such a way that the system can move along the path to its goals.

Applied to group processes, this formulation is translated into a force field of driving and restraining forces. This force field represents the position of a system on its path to its goal (Lewin, 1951). Lewin demonstrated that it is simpler and more efficient in energy expenditure to reduce the restraining forces along the path to a goal than it is to attempt to increase the driving forces. Each phase of system development can then be defined in terms of a force field of driving and restraining forces. This makes it possible to map change strategies that target the restraining forces for the relevant system phase (Agazarian & Gantt, 2003).

For example, a work group was having difficulty with the task of clarifying work roles. The group was largely silent, and members were not participating. Rather than trying to push the group to work (the Sisyphus approach!), the facilitator suggested the group identify what was making it hard to work (the restraining forces). After identifying and reality-testing the group's concerns that the work of identifying roles would be too controversial (a restraining force of negative predictions characteristic of the flight subphase in the authority phase), the group energy was released, and members were able to do the work.

Reducing the Restraining Forces of Noise and Reactions to Difference

From a systems perspective, achieving primary goals is dependent on the system's ability to appropriately open and close its boundaries to the energy/information transactions within the system hierarchy. How permeable system boundaries are to information depends on two major factors: the ratio of noise to information in the communication transaction and the degree of difference in the communication relative to the existing system. Systems close their boundary to noise. Noise is entropic to information. There is an inverse relationship between noise and information in a communication channel: the greater the noise, the lower the probability that the information contained within the channel will be transferred (Shannon & Weaver, 1964). Therefore, systems-centered leaders deliberately reduce the restraining force of noise (the ambiguities, redundancies, and contradictions in communication) to increase the permeability of group, subgroup, and individual boundaries to information (Agazarian & Philibossian, 1998).

The systems-centered filtering methods reduce entropy by systematically reducing the entropic contaminants of contradictions (*yes, but*... rebuttals), ambiguity (vagueness), and redundancy (repetitive talk and storytelling). Filtering methods also reduce the restraining forces of cognitive distortions, restrictive tensions, avoidance of frustrations, misdirections of the retaliatory impulse, role-locks, and resistance to autonomy and collaboration.

The second factor that affects boundary permeability is *difference,* which is the compatibility between the information that is crossing the boundary and the organization of the information within the system. When information is too different, it acts as entropic noise to the system. A system responds in several ways to information that is too different. A system closes its boundaries to prevent the information from entering the system. If the information has already entered the system (or if the difference is generated from within the system), the system encapsulates the difference in a subsystem behind impermeable boundaries. This subsystem is either contained as a closed system or extruded. These are the system dynamics that explain the phenomenon of scapegoating, institutionalizing, or boycotting individuals, groups, and organizations (Agazarian, 1983).

However, if the system continues to develop its ability to discriminate and integrate differences, the encapsulated information has the potential for being integrated within the system at a later time. If a later integration does not occur, then the potential resources in the information contained within the encapsulated system remain unavailable to the system, and the system's potential for development is permanently reduced.

The systems-centered method of functional subgrouping is a conflict resolution technique that directly addresses the issue of integrating differences so that the primary goals can be worked on rather than disrupted by reactions to differences. Differences can then be explored as potential resources toward goal achievement.

Asch's (1953) well-known experiments on the effect of social pressure illustrated the enormous challenge that groups face in addressing differences. In his research, two lines were presented: Line A was long, and Line B was short. When the group was asked which the longer line was, all but one person said B. This left one naive subject to struggle with group pressure. Asch found that more than one third of the naive subjects yielded to group pressure, with one of three predictable responses: (1) deciding their perceptions were inaccurate and the strong majority viewpoint was accurate, (2) deciding to go along with the majority in order not to appear different, or (3) literally misperceiving in a way that put them in line with the majority viewpoint. Those who remained independent in their judgment ranged from confident to withdrawn and anxious.

What is particularly important for us is Asch's (1953) follow-up study. He found that if just one other person validated Line A as the longest, the naive individuals had no difficulty standing by their own perception: They did not need to rationalize, they did not need to comply, they did not need to misperceive, and they were not anxious. This highlights an added dimension of the importance of exploring reality in functional subgrouping, where no individual ever stands alone without another member subgrouping with them to explore a perception or a viewpoint. This is particularly significant for organizational work groups in that functional subgrouping maximizes the likelihood that information can be introduced as a potential resource important to the issues under discussion, rather than withheld because of social pressure.

Functional subgrouping is one of two major methods for reducing the entropic effect of difference. Functional subgrouping influences the way systems discriminate and integrate differences in the organization of information inside the system. The second method, filtering, titrates the permeability at the boundaries of the system by filtering out noise, on the one hand, and attuning to the internal capacity of the system to manage differences, on the other. Both of these methods influence the ability of a group to achieve its primary and secondary goals.

Group Formation

Human beings are social animals and have, from the beginning of time, come together in groups around common interests and goals. Also from the beginning of time, humans have split away as a result of differences and come together around similarities. Humans always have closed the boundaries around their own groups and attacked groups on the other side of their boundaries. In short, we humans tolerate similarities and have great difficulty integrating differences.

In the 21st century, many million years since the beginning of human existence, human beings still operate with the same predispositions: to come together around similarities and to split away as a result of differences. Whether this is built into human nature or constitutes a failure of humans to develop past the conflict phase of human development remains a question. Applying systems thinking has allowed us to explicitly develop groups whose norms are to explore these apparent human predispositions rather than acting them out. The group culture that results has enabled individuals in these training groups to do much of the work that is usually attempted in therapy groups. A systems-centered assumption is that who one is at any one time has more to do with the group culture that one is in than it does with one's individual potential.

Typically, the systems approach assumes that systems (like groups) come together around secondary or task goals. Once formed, their dynamics are governed by the inherent drive to come together around similarities and split as a result of differences. Stereotypical groups form as a function of coming together around similarities and separating (splitting away) as a result of differences. Functional groups form as a result of coming together around similarities and discriminating and integrating differences.

Joining around similarities inevitably leads to stereotyping. In our culture, it manifests as male and female, high status and low status, white and nonwhite, old and young, in-group and out-group, and the like. Joining such groups tends to serve group survival. Stereotypical subgrouping is predictable and stabilizing but also fixating and expensive in terms of group development. Stereotypical groups are closed systems.

Stereotypical groups are excellent arenas for understanding the individual dynamics that are elicited in response to stereotypical norms.

Given these predispositions, the challenge for the systems-centered approach was to develop a nonstereotypical, functional group culture that supported both primary and secondary system goals. In systems-centered groups, the goal of the member is to join a subgroup by function rather than stereotype; the goal of the subgroup is to discriminate, contain, explore, and integrate differences. The goal of the group-as-a-whole is to use its resources to solve the problems that lie along the path to the goal.

Systems-centered groups form by deliberately developing appropriately permeable boundaries, discriminating and integrating differences, and developing familiarity with the issues inherent in each phase of development. We assume that restraining forces never disappear and that whenever there is a return to an earlier phase, those same restraining forces reappear (at deeper and deeper levels of meaning). However, as the group becomes increasingly able to recognize and undo these forces, the group increases its ability to work and move toward the goals.

The Individual and the Group

The theory of living human systems was developed to create a common language for talking about groups and their members. It also was developed to make it possible to research the dynamics that occur with individuals and groups (and groups of groups) using a common set of definitions (Agazarian, 1981, 1997; Agazarian & Gantt, 2000). What made this possible was the systems concept of isomorphy.

When individuals and groups (and subgroups) are conceptualized as isomorphic systems in the same hierarchy, their structure and dynamic function are equivalent. This means that whatever one learns about the dynamics of the individual as a system will apply to the group

system, and whatever one learns about the dynamics of the group system will apply to the individual. This solves the problem created when using the language of psychodynamics to understand the individual and the language of group dynamics to understand the group. It also renders unimportant the controversy in the field as to whether a group is simply a collection of individuals or whether a group is different from a collection of individuals.

To make systems concepts useful, one not only has to learn the language, but also has to see individuals and groups as systems, not as people. Systems do not exist in the real world. They exist only as ideas in the mind. The test as to whether thinking systemically is useful or not is whether or not we as people can understand things and do things in groups that are more useful to us than before we applied the principles of systems thinking.

A group member and the group are interdependent systems. The member influences the group, and the group influences the member. Unfortunately, once the group norms are established, it is no longer so easy (and sometimes impossible) for the member to influence the group and all too easy for the group to influence the member, as we know from incidents such as the mass suicides at Jonestown.

This is due to an important fact of human life: reactions to difference. Groups require conformity to their norms and are powerfully influential in maintaining them. Therefore, the initial norms that are set have long-lasting impact. If boundary permeability is not titrated against the stereotypical norms of the outside culture, it is all too easy for members to import these norms and for the group to replicate and maintain stereotypical cultural norms. However, it can equally be said that group norms themselves can easily become stereotypical if the group becomes fixated in its development.

The systems-centered method of functional subgrouping builds a functional relationship between the individual and the group and specifically addresses the issue of splitting and stereotyping for the individual and the group. Introducing functional subgrouping into a group redirects the stereotyping tendency to split in order to avoid differences by substituting functional splitting.

Functional splitting requires subgrouping around each difference that the system cannot integrate. Coming together in the relative comfort of similarity, each subgroup explores the issues around which its members have come together. In so doing, each subgroup discovers the "just noticeable" differences in their apparent similarity.

Functional subgroups work alternately. When one subgroup's energy diminishes, the next subgroup takes over the work of exploring its side of an issue. For example, one subgroup may be exploring the impulse to take care of a member of a group, while the other subgroup may be exploring the impulse to vicariously take care of others rather than to take care of themselves. Thus, rather than acting out, both the individuals and the group contain and explore the dynamics of the "identified patient."

Through the subgrouping process, differences are recognized and integrated within each subgroup. Thus, each subgroup develops from simpler to more complex. As complexity of awareness develops, not only do issues become clearer, but also a culture develops within each subgroup (and within each member) that supports tolerating and exploring differences rather than splitting.

Then, at some unpredictable point in time, it is as if the system-as-a-whole has developed a critical mass. The different subgroups come to recognize the similarities between them, which they were unable to see when the issues they contained had seemed too different. This is the moment of integration of the group-as-a-whole, which also is a transformation of the group-as-a-whole from simpler to more complex. Isomorphically, as the group-as-a-whole develops and transforms through integrating its subgroups, so do the individuals. System dynamics are the larger system context, the character of

which is determined by how functional the subgroups are, which in turn is determined by how functionally members can work within subgroup norms. Similarly, how functionally members work to create functional subgroups determines subgroup functionality. Subgroup functionality determines how successfully the group-as-a-whole is able to move toward its primary and secondary goals. Thus, influencing the subgroups so that they are functional in the service of the group's development provides a way of intervening on both the individual and the group-as-a-whole level.

Group Culture and Structure

The norms of a group tend to reflect the norms of the larger context unless there is a structural intervention that permits a different group culture to develop. From the systems perspective, therefore, leaders of systems-centered groups cannot afford to allow maladaptive norms to be imported, in that norms, once set, are very difficult to change. What is more, the norms that are set stereotypically also will reflect the repetition of individual role conflicts at the individual level, and they will develop stereotypical role conflicts within the group. Worse, the communications between the group-as-a-whole and the larger environment will also reflect stereotypical conflicts of role.

A systems-centered group with its unique culture and structure is developed through applying the methods and technique that are the operational definitions of the theory. Systems-centered groups do not just happen; they are deliberately developed to create functional norms and to weaken the cultural stereotypes and maladaptive roles that impede group development. Thus, developing a systems-centered group requires using systems-centered methods from the very beginning so that the culture of the larger environment is not imported into the group.

The systems-centered leader works actively from the first moments of the group to influence the group toward a systems-centered culture and norms. The hypothesis is that developing a systems-centered culture will make it possible for the group and its members to work in ways they could not work, were a stereotypical culture to develop.

The four major methods (and the techniques that implement the methods) used to build the systems-centered culture are described below: functional subgrouping, vectoring and the fork-in-the-road technique, filtering, and contextualizing. These methods operationally define the theoretical constructs discussed earlier.

Functional Subgrouping

The leader introduces functional subgrouping right from the beginning. As soon as one member responds, the leader begins actively training group members to follow their contribution with the question, "Anybody else?" This makes it possible to train a group in a relatively short time (less than 30 minutes) to subgroup functionally around the similarities that are emerging in the group. Members learn to build on similarities and hold differences until the actively working subgroup pauses; then, those who have been holding the difference are encouraged to start the other subgroup around the difference.

Functional subgrouping is an essential method in building a systems-centered culture, as it implements the principle of discrimination and integration described earlier. It makes it possible for a group to explore its differences and conflicts without enacting the culturally stereotyped roles in relation to differences, institutionalizing the differences in an identified patient role, or targeting them in a scapegoat role.

Fork in the Road

The fork-in-the-road technique operationally defines the method of vectoring. The fork-in-the-road technique of choice also develops the systems-centered culture. Members

learn to choose one or the other side of their conflict to explore in a subgroup with others. Typically, the first fork in the road introduced in a therapy group is between *explaining,* which takes one to what one knows already, or *exploring* the experience one does not yet know, an option that becomes available as one shifts away from the explanations. The fork-in-the-road technique implements the construct of vectoring as members learn to choose and then vector their energy in relation to their goals.

In an organizational work group, establishing the culture of choice with the fork-in-the-road technique helps build autonomous work groups and reduces nonfunctional dependency. For example, giving a free choice to a work group about which aspect of a problem to explore first reduces the typical power struggles characteristic of much organizational work.

Filtering in the Phases of Group Development

Once a working climate of functional subgrouping is established, the systems-centered leader introduces filtering techniques, which implement structure (Agazarian, 1997). Filtering out noise at the boundary into the group increases the permeability of the boundary so that more clear information and less noise comes into the group and information is available for work.

For instance, in systems-centered groups in the flight phase, members learn to undo the anxiety that comes from cognitive distortions such as negative predictions about the future and to reduce the tensions that constrict access to the emotional knowledge centered in the body. These methods make it more likely that members and groups in organizations can develop emotional intelligence (Damasio, 1994; Goleman, 1995), which is one of the variables that help groups to work with common sense (Gantt & Agazarian, 2004). Each of the systems-centered protocols implements systems-centered structure and develops the culture by reducing the restraining forces that link to the specific phase of the group's development.

Contextualizing

The other important method that develops the systems-centered culture is contextualizing. From the beginning, members are trained to see themselves not only as a voice for themselves as a person but also as a voice for a subgroup (as members learn to ask, "Anyone else?"). Similarly, group members begin to see the two sides of whatever issue is being explored contained in the two different subgroups and, later, to see their personal experience as a by-product of the conflict the group is managing as contained in the subgroup voices. This training makes it possible for group members to reduce the human tendency to personalize (and to reduce the anguish that comes from personalizing). Instead, members learn through contextualizing to develop an array of perspectives from which to view their experience and discover how their relationship to their experience changes as they change perspectives.

The Culture in a Developed Group

Establishing a systems-centered group requires training the group actively until the systems-centered norms are established and the group has learned the skills it needs to work. Thus, an established systems-centered group subgroups functionally, explores rather than explains, and supports the norm that no member works alone. Members learn to attune to each other and to explore the inevitable "misattunements" among them. Group members learn to reduce defenses as they surface and to explore their undefended experience or alternately to explore their defenses. Furthermore, members learn the alternatives to personalizing as they begin to see their experience in the context of the group work and the group's phase of development. This makes it possible for systems-centered groups to develop a culture of curiosity about their experience and its relevance for the context.

Group Productivity

From a systems perspective, a productive and successful group has developed itself as a system that is able to solve the problems along the path to its primary and secondary goals. Two major factors are prerequisites for both primary and secondary goal achievement. One factor is managing the structure that contains a group's existence. This is put into practice by developing boundaries with appropriate permeability to the information/energy exchanges, both within the group's core system (member system, subgroup system, group-as-a-whole system) and between its core system and the other systems in its hierarchy. The other factor is managing the way the group's functions to organize the energy within the system. How successfully the system can move toward its goals depends on how efficiently the information is discriminated and integrated and vectored toward the goals.

Meeting the primary goals (survival, development, and transformation as a living human system) is necessary but not sufficient for secondary goal achievement. The amount of energy available in a group is determined by how much energy is available after the primary goals are met. The amount of work that a group can do at any one time is governed by the boundaries of its phase of group development. Therefore, how successful and productive a group can be at any time is governed by how much energy is bound up in the vicissitudes of the developmental phase and how much energy is free to be directed toward the task.

Groups change and adapt to accomplish goals by weakening the restraining forces so that the drive toward the system's primary and secondary goals is released. All group movement toward the goal can be conceptualized as systems moving along a goal line. As problems occur along the path to a goal, the system can approach the problems, avoid the problems, or freeze at the problems (Howard & Scott, 1965). These three different reactions pose three different system challenges, each one of which has a characteristic primary and secondary field of driving and restraining forces.

Conclusion

The theory of living human systems is an umbrella theory in that its definitions apply to all systems in a defined hierarchy. As an umbrella theory, it neither contradicts nor detracts from any other theories of how groups work. The methods and techniques that guide the systems-centered approach to change can be applied to all living human systems, as small as an individual or a group and as large as an organization or a nation. This enables change agents, working in small or large systems, to use a systematic series of interventions that are directly related to the context in which they are attempting to influence change.

Formal research on this new theory of living human systems is just beginning. Preliminary studies suggest that a systems-centered approach to group therapy has positive effects on individuals diagnosed with generalized anxiety disorder and depression (Ladden, Gantt, & Agazarian, 2004). Also, members of task groups who had been trained to use functional subgrouping reported greater satisfaction in their task and evidenced greater efficiency in decision making than those in the control or icebreaker group (Parks, 2003).

In addition to these early investigations, an action research component is built into this model. This enables practitioners to track the effectiveness of their interventions in that every intervention is understood as a hypothesis that tests the reliability of the practice and the validity of the methods. For example, the technique used for crossing the boundary and decreasing noise in the communications into the group is called *undoing distractions*. This technique is implemented at the beginning of a group with the goal of the distracted member becoming more present and ready to work. Built into the technique is the group leader asking this research question: Do you feel more present in the group, less present in the group, or the same? This kind of action research is built into all clinical applications.

We have also collected survey data from practitioners and trainees who are members of training groups learning to apply the SCT methods. Of those completing the survey, 21% were consultants to organizations, 19% workshop leaders or trainers, 40% therapists, and 12% members of a group. In effect, the questionnaire presented the major hypotheses operationally defined by the SCT methods and asked the participants about whether or not these hypotheses were confirmed based on their experience in SCT groups. Overall, participants' responses strongly supported the systems-centered hypotheses.

Research on systems-centered theory and practice has just begun. However, both system-centered theory and practice draw strength from research in other theoretical perspectives. The social identity perspective's investigations of stereotyping and studies of group development are particularly relevant. Important research remains to be done. We hope that this theoretical explication will generate questions for future research.

References

Agazarian, Y. M. (1981). *The visible and invisible group*. London: Karnac.

Agazarian, Y. M. (1983). Theory of invisible group applied to individual and group-as-a-whole interpretations. *Group: The Journal of the Eastern Group Psychotherapy Society, 7*(2), 27–37.

Agazarian, Y. M. (1986). Application of Lewin's life space concept to the individual and group-as-a-whole systems in group psychotherapy. In E. Stivers & S. Wheelan (Eds.), *The Lewin legacy* (pp. 101–112). New York: Springer-Verlag.

Agazarian, Y. M. (1989). Group-as-a-whole systems theory and practice. *Group, 13*(3–4), 131–155.

Agazarian, Y. M. (1992). A systems approach to the group-as-a-whole. *International Journal of Group Psychotherapy, 42*(3), 177–203.

Agazarian, Y. M. (1994). The phases of development and the systems-centered group. In M. Pines & V. Schermer (Eds.), *Ring of fire: Primitive object relations and affect in group psychotherapy* (pp. 36–85). London: Routledge, Chapman & Hall.

Agazarian, Y. M. (1997). *Systems-centered therapy for groups.* New York: Guilford.

Agazarian, Y. (1999). Phases of development in the systems-centered group. *Small Group Research, 30*(1), 82–107.

Agazarian, Y. M., & Gantt, S. P. (2000). *Autobiography of a theory.* London: Jessica Kingsley.

Agazarian, Y. M., & Gantt, S. P. (2003). Phases of group development: Systems-centered hypotheses and their implications for research and practice. *Group Dynamics, 7*(3), 238–252.

Agazarian, Y. M., & Janoff, S. (1993). Systems theory and small groups. In I. Kaplan & B. Sadock (Eds.), *Comprehensive textbook of group psychotherapy* (3rd ed., pp. 33–44). Baltimore, MD: Williams & Wilkins, Division of Waverly.

Agazarian, Y. M., & Philibossian, B. (1998). A theory of living human systems as an approach to leadership of the future with examples of how it works. In E. Klein, F. Gabelnick, & P. Herr (Eds.), *The psychodynamics of leadership* (pp. 127–160). Madison, CT: Psychosocial Press.

Asch, S. E. (1953). Effects of group pressure upon the modification and distortion of judgments. In D. Cartwright & A. Zander (Eds.), *Group dynamics: Research and theory* (pp. 151–162). Evanston, IL: Row, Peterson and Co.

Astrachan, B. M. (1970). Towards a social systems model of therapeutic groups. *Social Psychiatry, 5*(2), 110–119.

Barber, W. H. (1988). Inpatient adolescent group therapy as a social system. *Group, 12*(4), 233–240.

Bateson, G. (1972). *Steps to an ecology of mind.* New York: Ballantine Books.

Bateson, G., Jackson, D. D., & Haley, J. (1956). Toward a theory of schizophrenia. *Behavioral Science, 1,* 251–264.

Beck, A. (1981). Developmental characteristics of the system forming process. In J. Durkin (Ed.), *Living groups: Group psychotherapy and general systems theory* (pp. 316–332). New York: Brunner/Mazel.

Beeber, A. R. (1988). A systems model of short-term, open-ended group therapy. *Hospital & Community Psychiatry, 39*(5), 537–542.

Beeber, A. R. (1991). Psychotherapy with schizophrenics in team groups: A systems model. *American Journal of Psychotherapy, 45*(1), 78–83.

Bennis, W. G., & Shepard, H. A. (1956). A theory of group development. *Human Relations, 9*(4), 415–437.

Bertalanffy, L. von (1969). *General systems* (Rev. ed.). New York: George Braziller.

Bion, W. R. (1959). *Experiences in groups.* London: Tavistock.

Boer, C., & Moore, C. (1994). Ecosystemic thinking in group therapy. *Group Analysis, 27*(1), 105–117.

Bor, R. (1989). Introducing trainees to systems concepts in a clinical setting. *The Clinical Supervisor, 7*(2–3), 117–137.

Borriello, J. F. (1992). The clinical application of social systems theory. In R. H. Klein, H. S. Bernard, & D. L. Singer (Eds.), *Handbook of contemporary group psychotherapy: Contributions from object relations, self psychology, and social systems theories* (pp. 209–225). Madison, CT: International Universities Press.

Brabender, V. (1997). Chaos and order in the psychotherapy group. In F. Masterpasqua & P. A. Perna (Eds.), *The psychological meaning of chaos: Translating theory into practice* (pp. 225–252). Washington, DC: American Psychological Association.

Burck, C., Hildebrand, J., & Mann, J. (1996). Women's tales: Systemic groupwork with mothers post-separation. *Journal of Family Therapy, 18*(2), 163–182.

Damasio, A. (1994). *Descartes error.* New York: Gosset/Putnam.

Donigian, J., & Malnati, R. (1997). *Systemic group therapy: A triadic model.* Belmont, CA: Brooks-Cole.

Durkin, H. E. (1972a). Analytic group therapy and general systems theory. In C. J. Sager & H. S. Kaplan (Eds.), *Progress in group and family therapy* (pp. 9–17). New York: Brunner/Mazel.

Durkin, H. E. (1972b). General systems theory and group therapy: An introduction. *International Journal of Group Psychotherapy, 22*(2b), 159–166.

Durkin, H. E. (1981). General systems theory and group psychotherapy. In J. E. Durkin (Ed.), *Living groups: Group psychotherapy and general systems theory.* New York: Brunner/Mazel.

Durkin, J. (1981). *Living groups: Group psycho-therapy and general systems theory.* New York: Brunner/Mazel.

Durkin, J. (1989). Mothergroup as a whole formation and systemic boundarying events. *Group, 13*(3–4), 198–211.

Fidler, J. W. (1987). Group therapy and society. *American Journal of Social Psychiatry, 7*(1), 24–26.

Gantt, S. P., & Agazarian, Y. M. (2004). *Systems-centered emotional intelligence: Beyond individual systems to organizational systems.* Manuscript submitted for publication.

Goleman, D. (1995). *Emotional intelligence.* New York: Bantam.

Hildebrand, J. (1988). The use of group work in treating child sexual abuse. In A. Bentovim, A. Elton, J. Hildebrand, M. Teamer, & E. Vizard (Eds.), *Child sexual abuse within the family* (pp. 205–237). London: Wright.

Hildebrand, J., & Forbes, C. (1987). Group work with mothers whose children have been sexually abused. *British Journal of Social Work, 17*(3), 285–303.

Hills, J. (1994). A systemic approach to group therapy. *Context, 18,* 9–13.

Howard, A., & Scott, R. A. (1965). A proposed framework for the analysis of stress in the human organism. *Journal of Applied Behavioral Science, 10*(2), 141–160.

Kiser, L. J., & Pruitt, D. B. (1991). Child and adolescent day treatment: A general systems theory perspective. In S. G. Zimet & G. K. Farley (Eds.), *Day treatment for children with emotional disorders* (pp. 85–96). New York: Plenum.

Ladden, L. J., Gantt, S. P., & Agazarian, Y. M. (2004). *Systems-centered therapy: A pilot for treating generalized anxiety disorder with a 10-session protocol.* Unpublished manuscript.

Lapponi, E. (1996). Psychodynamic and systemic paradigms: An attempted integration in the light of personal experience with groups. *American Journal of Psychoanalysis, 56*(2), 177–185.

Lewin, K. (1935). *A dynamic theory of personality: Selected papers* (D. K. Adams & K. E. Zener, Trans.). New York: McGraw-Hill.

Lewin, K. (1951). *Field theory in social science.* New York: Harper & Row.

MacKenzie, K. R. (1990). The changing role of emotion in group psychotherapy. In R. Plutchik & H. Kellerman (Eds.), *Emotion, psychopathology, and psychotherapy* (Emotion, theory, research, and experience, Vol. 5, pp. 147–173). San Diego: Academic Press.

Mathews, C. O. (1992). An application of general system theory (GST) to group therapy. *The Journal for Specialists in Group Work, 17*(3), 161–169.

Miller, E. J., & Rice, A. K. (1967). *Systems of organization.* London: Tavistock.

Miller, J. G. (1978). *Living systems.* New York: McGraw-Hill.

Nicholas, M. W. (1989). A systemic perspective of group therapy supervision: Use of energy in the supervision-therapist-group system. *Journal of Independent Social Work, 3*(4), 27–39.

O'Connor, K. (1999). Child, protector, confidant: Structured group ecosystemic play therapy. In D. S. Sweeney & L. E. Homeyer (Eds.), *The handbook of group play therapy: How to do it, how it works, whom it's best for* (pp. 105–138). San Francisco: Jossey-Bass.

O'Neill, M., & Stockwell, G. (1991). Worthy of discussion: Collaborative group therapy. *Australian & New Zealand Journal of Group Therapy, 12*(4), 201–206.

Parks, E. (2003). *Subgrouping and conflict management: A research update.* Paper presented at the Systems-Centered Training Conference, Philadelphia.

Shannon, C. E., & Weaver, W. (1964). *The mathematical theory of communication.* Urbana: University of Illinois Press.

Vassiliou, G. (1973). What general systems theory offers to the group therapist. *International Mental Health Research Newsletter, 15*(4), 8–9.

Wiener, N. (1968). Cybernetics, or control and communications in the animal and the machine (2nd ed.). Cambridge: MIT Press. (Original work published 1948)

Wilson, A., & Hutton, J. (1992). Groups for incest survivors: A new context. *Australian & New Zealand Journal of Family Therapy, 13*(3), 129–134.

11

Chaos, Complexity, and Catastrophe

The Nonlinear Dynamics Perspective

Holly Arrow

Life is inherently open . . .

—Stuart Kauffman (2002), p. 140

The nonlinear dynamics perspective is not indigenous to the small groups field. Instead, scholars who were (for the most part) originally trained in one or more of the other perspectives represented in this handbook have enriched or transformed their thinking about groups by adopting, adapting, grafting, and integrating dynamic systems concepts from catastrophe, chaos, and complexity theories.

Scholars have talked about small groups as dynamic systems since the middle of the last century (e.g., Lewin, 1947a, 1947b), and this perspective has survived in lines of research such as group development. So the compatibility of groups research with a perspective that emphasizes dynamics and change seems logical (see Meara, 1999; Smith & Gemmill, 1991; Stacey, 2001; Wheelan, 1996, for introductory articles). What I refer to here as the nonlinear dynamics perspective, however, refers to the application of more recent models and methods that emerged and developed in other disciplines.

Author's Note: Thanks to Bob Weiss and Sara Hodges for support and encouragement and to Susan Wheelan for her patience. I am grateful to the Society for Chaos Theory in Psychology & Life Sciences and The Santa Fe Institute for educating me in the basics of nonlinear dynamics in the early 1990s when I was first puzzling out how to apply this perspective to groups, and to Joe McGrath and Jennifer Berdahl for sharing my enthusiasm in this quest.

Catastrophe theory, which models discontinuous change, emerged in the 1960s and 1970s (e.g., Poston & Stewart, 1978), and a modest trickle of articles applying catastrophe ideas to groups and dyads began in the 1980s (e.g., Guastello, 1988; Tesser, 1980). Chaos theory, which studies how the iterated application of simple deterministic rules generates chaotic behavior, was brought to the attention of the general public in the late 1980s (e.g., Gleick, 1987), and complexity theory, which focuses on the spontaneous emergence of organization and the interface between order and chaos, flowered in the 1980s and 1990s (e.g., Lewin, 1992; Prigogine & Stengers, 1984). Articles and books applying chaos and complexity ideas to small groups began to appear with some regularity only in the past decade (e.g., Arrow, McGrath, & Berdahl, 2000; Guastello, 1995; McClure, 1998; Stacey, 2001, 2003).

Thus, although work in this perspective resonates with some long-standing ideas in group theory, it is nevertheless in an early stage of development. Nonlinear dynamics constitutes a "second language" for many first-wave scholars, and fluency in this second tongue—which uses terms such as *self-organization, attractor,* and *bifurcation* to describe dynamic processes and the structures that emerge from them—varies widely. Although some scholars have received systematic training in the concepts and methods of this perspective, many of us are largely self-taught. Hence, the ways in which we have interpreted and applied concepts that developed originally in physics or mathematics or biochemistry or meteorology are quite idiosyncratic.

Theory and research that takes a nonlinear dynamics perspective on small groups is hence both diverse and unstable. It ranges from purely metaphorical interpretations of dynamic systems concepts to mathematically challenging applications of techniques unfamiliar to most groups scholars. This chapter presents a snapshot of a dynamic array of work in progress, rather than explicating a settled body of ideas. We are, in the terminology of the field, working far from equilibrium at the edge of chaos, a state in which creativity and disorganization are both readily available.

Despite this fluid state of affairs, some common themes and convictions tie the work together: an emphasis on how processes in groups unfold at multiple levels, an interest in instability and discontinuous change, and an appreciation for the paradox of coherent patterns arising out of group behavior that remains unpredictable in its particulars and always holds the potential for novelty and surprise. My approach in this chapter will be to highlight common themes while also noting the variety of ways in which scholars from a variety of disciplines—including psychology, sociology, political science, and communications—have interpreted or applied them. In the last section, I identify some pitfalls common to this perspective and identify the approaches I believe are most likely to take root and flourish in small groups theory and practice.

Overview

Machine, Organism, Network, Process: How to Define a Group?

Kant, credited as the first to use the term *self-organization,* characterized the difference between a machine (or mechanism) and an organism as follows. In a machine, the idea of a functional whole precedes the creation of parts, which are designed and fit together to make a whole. In an organism, the whole emerges as the parts arise together (and by means of one another) in interaction. They unfold and "self-organize" (Kant, 1790/1987, summarized in Stacey, 2003, pp. 264–265). This organismic idea of a self-organizing whole has been adopted in characterizing both small groups and larger organizations (e.g., Arrow et al., 2000; Contractor & Seibold, 1993; Goldstein, 1994; Guastello & Philippe, 1997; McClure, 1998; Stacey, 1996). Arrow and colleagues (2000) define groups as "self-organizing systems in which global patterns emerge from local action and structure subsequent local action" (p. 38). The cross-level *circular causality* embedded in this definition is an idea imported from systems theory.

Theorists who emphasize the multilevel conception of groups refer to at least three levels—members, groups, and embedding context—and often acknowledge that other levels (such as dyads and subgroups within groups or competing groups in the embedding context) contribute as well to the unfolding group dynamics (Arrow et al., 2000; McPherson & Rotolo, 1996; von Cranach, 1996).

In some work, the idea of a self-organizing whole is combined with a network conception of groups as a dynamic set of connections among members (e.g., Zeggelink, 1995) and other components of the group such as tasks, tools, or information (Arrow et al., 2000; Carley, 1991; Stacey, 1996). The intragroup network is an organized cluster embedded within a larger network of connections that extends beyond the group boundaries.

All work in this perspective views the patterning of interaction as central to the definition of a group. Stacey (2003) has lately taken this to an extreme, defining groups as complex responsive processes and rejecting the systems concept of an organized whole. This departs from his earlier work, in which Stacey (1996, p. 169) defines a group as a nonlinear feedback network. Von Cranach (1996) also takes the position that groups only exist by virtue of acting but retains the systems idea of a self-organizing whole. The nonlinear dynamics perspective both builds on and departs from general systems theory (GST). Like GST, it focuses on the interaction between individuals rather than on the attributes of individuals. Unlike GST, which emphasizes the movement of systems toward a single stable equilibrium, the nonlinear perspective treats the group as a system that is both *open* (resources flow into and out of the group) and *far from equilibrium*—in other words, it requires the constant input and transformation of energy to maintain itself as a system. If the input of energy ceases, the system dissolves.

Integrating these elements, a core definition of a group from the nonlinear dynamics perspective might take the following form:

A group is a self-organizing, open system of dynamic connections among interacting members, embedded within and interacting with its context.

This suggests that in studying groups, we should focus on the nature of connections and interactions among members both within and across group boundaries to gain insight into processes, structures, and other outcomes of interest.

What Kinds of Groups?

The nonlinear dynamics perspective applies to any set of people who are engaged in interaction. Although theorists who fit in this perspective clearly differ on whether a group continues to "exist" in some sense, even when its members are not interacting, all would likely agree that social groups defined by categories—such as Polish Americans or lawyers—would not qualify as groups in the nonlinear dynamics sense.

The range of collectives to which the perspective applies is otherwise extremely broad. It covers the full temporal range, from ephemeral groups of people in conversation (e.g., Newtson, 1994) to very long term groups such as families (e.g., Pincus, 2001) and to groups that range in size from dyads (e.g., Tesser, 1980) to large organizations (e.g., Goldstein, 1994). It applies to electronic groups (e.g., Arrow, 1997; Contractor & Seibold, 1993), which lack access to many nonverbal channels available face-to-face, to co-located groups whose members coordinate their actions without talking to one another (e.g., Guastello & Guastello, 1998), and also to the behavior of individuals interacting with simulated group members in an experimental setting (e.g., Tesser & Achee, 1994).

As long as individuals are connected and communicating in some way and information is flowing across this connected network, the nonlinear dynamics perspective applies. The breadth of application across a variety of kinds of groups and settings is not surprising for a perspective that has been usefully applied to understand the collective behavior of aggregates as different as slime molds (Keller & Segel, 1970), ant colonies (Cole, 1991), and flocks of birds (Reynolds, 1987). This breadth is something that the nonlinear dynamics perspective has in common with evolutionary psychology as a perspective on human behavior. Both presume that scholars can usefully study and understand human behavior and interaction in many of the same ways that scholars have studied behavior and interaction in other species.

How and Why Do Groups Form?

The nonlinear dynamics perspective provides several ways to think about the group formation process. It is stronger on the "how" question than on the "why" question. The general answer to the how question is that groups form as people interact, adjust their behavior in response to one another, and become coordinated in a new collective in which they play a role as members (Arrow et al., 2000). At the most basic level of nonverbal behavior, interpersonal coordination appears to emerge spontaneously, via *shadowing,* for example, in which people mimic the gestures of conversational partners (crossing legs, for example) after a short time lag (Newtson, 1994). The coordination of attitudes, which facilitates collective action, also emerges as an outcome of social influence processes experienced in group interaction (Latané & L'Herrou, 1996).

A typology of group formation proposed by Arrow and colleagues differentiates four prototypical group formation routes based on the relative importance of forces internal and external to the group and of planning versus emergent process.

In *concocted* groups, agents external to the group deliberately assign people to groups and typically designate the group's purpose as well. Many work groups and therapy groups, and the vast majority of groups in social psychology experiments, fall into this quadrant. In such groups, the processes of adjustment and coordination occur once members begin interacting. (Of course, external agents may also select people for the group based on expectations of complementarity among members.) In *circumstantial* groups, events throw people together and give them a reason to interact, but this outcome is not planned or intended. An example would be people sharing a lifeboat after a cruise ship sinks. Circumstantial groups often include members who would otherwise be highly unlikely to find themselves undertaking the challenges of collective action together.

In *founded* groups, people collect around (or are collected by) a founder or founders who have a purpose in mind for the group—such as making music or money or promoting a new ideology. In these groups, self-selection will ensure that members are coordinated and aligned with the founder in some way, but they may not be coordinated with one another. In *self-organized* groups, a new collective arises out of interaction among a subset of people in a larger social setting. These people are not actively trying to form a group—it just happens. Many friendship groups arise in this manner, and such groups are likely to show high levels of intermember coordination from the start because the selection process is operating among all member pairs—not just between members and founders—and because interpersonal interaction prior to group formation is also tuning the coordination among members.

Applying the term *self-organized* only to the latter category is somewhat misleading because some degree of self-organization is required for any set of people to become a functional collective. However, groups that fall into this quadrant (with internal, emergent group formation processes predominating) provide the clearest analogue to group formation across a broad range of species whose members interact. Birds or fish are not assigned to a flock or school, nor individually recruited to join a new collective by a founder bird or fish. Instead, birds and fish spontaneously display flocking or schooling behavior whenever a collection of them are moving together in close proximity.

Computer simulations, in which individual agents follow preset rules for interaction, demonstrate how groups can emerge when agents use the behavior or opinions of others as an input to their own behavior or opinions. One of the simpler approaches uses a *cellular automata* model, in which the state of each node in a lattice of agents is determined by the states of nearby nodes. Nowak, Szamrej, and Latané (1990) used a cellular automaton to demonstrate that a set of individuals whose opinions are initially randomly assigned can, when they all respond to the influence of others around them, become organized into coherent clusters of agents who share the same opinion. The rules that determined whether an agent changed its opinion or not (its state) were an implementation of social impact theory (Latané, 1981), in which the degree of influence is based on strength and immediacy of influence by others. Although it often takes many iterations of agents checking the opinions of others and adjusting their own opinions accordingly, the simulation typically settles into a relatively stable set of clustered subgroups. This dynamic has been replicated in experiments with people communicating via a computer network (Latané & L'Herrou, 1996).

This program of research illustrates one effective strategy for conducting studies using the nonlinear dynamics perspective. The first step is to articulate a theory that is explicitly dynamic. In this case, it meant extending the static social impact theory (Latané, 1981) to incorporate dynamics. The second step is to build a computer simulation that explores the implications of the theory for collective behavior. Implementing the theory in a computer program allows one to discover what the outcome of the nonlinear process specified by the theory will be. In this case, the process is nonlinear because multiple agents simultaneously determine their own future states based on observing the current states of others. The third step is to see whether observed patterns of human behavior conform to the patterns generated by the simulation. Results from Steps 2 and 3 helped inform the elaboration of dynamic social impact theory (Latané, 1996).

Another set of empirical studies investigated how the pattern of rewards available to groups and individuals affects the size and stability of emergent groups in which members pool their resources to obtain a collective reward (Arrow & Burns, 2003; Arrow & Crosson, 2003). These groups were formed deliberately by their members, placing them in the founded quadrant of the Arrow et al. (2000) group formation typology. Both the size and stability of the groups were affected by the differential rewards available to group members versus isolated individuals. When multiple individuals attempt to simultaneously found groups, the outcome depends not only on individual preferences for different alternative group members but also on the way in which individual choices and behavior are constrained, facilitated, and adjusted in response to the choices and behaviors of others. Actual groups with a defined set of members emerge as the large array of potential groups collapses into a smaller and smaller set of plausible groups as individuals make commitments to one another.

In this approach to studying group formation, the focus is not on predicting which particular individuals will end up with one another. Instead, the goals are to (1) characterize the dynamics by which a set of initially unconnected individuals form groups, (2) identify contextual factors that affect the stability of the process and the outcomes, and (3) infer the rules that actors within the system are likely to be following. Plausible rules can then be tested in computer simulations to see if they would, indeed, result in outcomes similar to the observed patterns.

The Individual, the Member, and the Group

Three approaches to characterizing the relationship between the individual member and the group can be discerned within the nonlinear dynamics perspective. The first follows the approach of methodological individualism, in which collective behavior arises out of the behavior of autonomous individuals (agents) who are interacting with other individuals following rules. This presumption is sometimes explicit (e.g., Zeggelink, 1995) and is often implicit within agent-based models of collective interaction. Although the collective structures that emerge are understood as constraining individual behavior, the individual has ontological priority.

Adaptive structuration theory, which draws on the ideas of Giddens (1984), exemplifies this approach. The group is viewed as a *system* that gives rise to observable patterns of relations. The causal engine that generates this observable system, however, is *structures*—the rules and resources that actors use to generate and sustain the system. "The observable system is of interest and can influence structures, but the structure is what does the real work" (Poole & DeSanctis, 1990, p. 179).

The second approach rejects the notion of autonomous individuals, focusing instead on the simultaneous emergence of the individual and the social world. Drawing on the ideas of Hegel and Mead (and rejecting Kantian systems thinking), Stacey (2001) asserts that "the individual and the social are at one level of analysis, not two" and that "individuals are forming and being formed by the group at the same time" (pp. 460, 461). This epitomizes relational thinking. Both group and individual are viewed as abstractions from the foundational patterning activity that Stacey calls complex responsive processes.

A third approach to this conundrum redirects attention away from *individuals* as autonomous agents and toward interconnected *members* and their interactions (Arrow & McGrath, 1995; Arrow et al., 2000). From this perspective, groups are composed not of individuals but of members, and members emerge as the dynamic group coordination network is enacted, maintained, and modified. This conception fits the Kantian notion of an organism, in which the parts arise out of interactions through which they become differentiated into heart, lungs, and brain or into stem, leaf, and

flower. If we think of groups as composed of individuals, the parts clearly precede the whole, which is more like a mechanism. If we think of groups as composed of members, however, members emerge and differentiate into roles as the group develops.

This organismic view of groups also has its limitations, of course. Groups lose and develop new members with an ease that individual humans do not, and concocted groups in particular (those formed deliberately by forces external to the group) may be assembled of more or less prefabricated members who have been trained to quickly enact particular predefined sets of connections and interactions. McGrath and colleagues (Arrow et al., 2000; McGrath, Berdahl, & Arrow, 1995) call this type of group a *crew,* and like a mechanism, the members of such groups have been designed with the whole in mind. Even in such groups, however, some adjustment and elaboration—adaptive structuration—must occur before the collective is a fully functional unit.

All three approaches share an emphasis on the generation of structure and pattern as the core activity that either occurs at the interface of individual and group or creates the primordial unity of the two. This process of morphogenesis is the focus of the next section.

Group Culture and Structure

How do groups develop a unique culture and structure? Work in the nonlinear dynamics perspective has explored this process using computational modeling, mathematical modeling, observational data, and experimental paradigms. The common conceptual themes are a search for multiple attractors generated through a process of self-organization in which the dynamic interaction among group members creates and stabilizes structure. *Attractors* are constrained regions in the *state space* of all theoretically possible states into which a dynamical system settles over time. *Self-organization* is the emergence of higher level order out of the initially disorganized or *chaotic* activity of lower level components. *Chaos* is distinguished from randomness (a more complete form of disorder) because it also orders the behavior of the system and constrains it to a defined region of state space, in ways that are difficult for an observer to detect. Higher level order, which is clearly detectable to an observer, emerges as the components come into local coordination, as the coordination spreads throughout the interacting system, and as this global pattern then influences the subsequent behavior of the components.

If we think of group culture as the personality of a group, then it makes sense to apply dynamical models of personality to gain insight into how a collective can also come to exhibit distinctive recurrent patterns. Shoda, LeeTiernan, and Mischel (2002) use a connectionist network model to show how a small number of stable *attractor states* can arise as characteristic output behaviors (the personality system) in simulated individuals.

In the simulation, cognitive-affective processing involves detecting features of a situation as input, transferring information among processing units, and then adjusting behavioral output. Functionally equivalent situations (starting sets of stimuli) resulted in a simulated individual settling into the same attractor. The researchers then coupled the simulated individuals into dyads, so that each partner's behavior became an input into the other partner's personality system, and ran the simulation with the same array of starting situations used for the uncoupled individuals. Distinctive attractor states emerged for the members of the dyad that did not match the array of attractor states exhibited by the uncoupled individuals. This illustrates the nonadditive nature of collectives, which is generated by the nonlinearity of the interactions that create and structure them.

In contrast to this computational modeling approach, Gottman and colleagues use coupled nonlinear difference equations to create a mathematical model of marriage (Gottman, Murray, Swanson, Tyson, & Swanson, 2002), an approach

they have also extended to modeling the behavior of individuals in groups (Gottman, Guralnick, Wilson, Swanson, & Murray, 1997). The model formalizes marital interaction using two influence functions, one for each partner, plus terms for dynamic corrections such as repair of negative affect and damping of positive affect. The parameters for the model can be estimated for each marriage based on a time series of observed behavior for the couple, and the equations can then be solved to discover what the emotional/behavioral attractors are for that particular couple. The set of equations is meant to apply to all marriages (not just to a hypothetical average marriage) and can also characterize the idiosyncratic dynamic signatures of a particular marriage, once the parameters for that marriage have been estimated from observational data.

A modified version of the model was used to examine data from children's play groups (Gottman et al., 1997). The equations were adjusted to represent mutual influence between an individual and a group, with the group represented by whomever the focal individual was interacting with at a given point. This approach holds promise as a way to formalize Moreland and Levine's (1982) group socialization model, which Baron, Amazeen, and Beek (1994) interpret in dynamic system terms as representing the movement of members among qualitatively different attractor states such as new member, full member, or marginal member based on the coordination between member commitment to the group and group commitment to the member. The simplifying assumption of Gottman et al. (1997)—that the influence of each member represents the group as a whole—fails, however, to distinguish between dyadic interactions and member-group interactions.

The interplay of intrapersonal, dyadic, and group-level interactions in stabilizing and destabilizing structure is evident in a study by Arrow and Burns (2003) of the emergence and evolution of allocation norms. Sets of eight people repeatedly played a group formation game in which groups of three to five people formed, earned a group payoff, and then decided how to divide the payoff among members. Even when the membership of the groups was not completely stable from round to round, initial confusion about how to proceed (the disorganized initial condition) typically resolved quickly into a consistent pattern of allocation procedures and outcomes (self-organization).

Members were not necessarily happy about the norms, however, as indicated by their private evaluation of the fairness of the procedures and the outcomes on questionnaires completed after each round. In one case, widespread intrapersonal unhappiness did not lead to system-level change. In another case, similar instability at the intrapersonal level found expression when two people shared their dissatisfaction with one another, and this dyadic meeting of minds resulted in a shake-up of both group membership and the adoption of two new norms (both different from the initial norm) within the two groups formed by the eight interacting players. In dynamic terms, the two groups in the system were both on the same attractor for a while, passed through a period of dynamic instability, and then diverged onto two new attractors after a *bifurcation* in which the initial attractor disappeared. A *bifurcation* is a change in the array of attractors available to a system; it occurs when an existing attractor vanishes, new ones are created, or both.

In their version of self-organizing systems theory (SOST), Contractor and Seibold (1993) identify four requirements for self-organization to occur and three qualitatively different outcomes. They apply these to a study of how groups appropriate new technology. The four requirements are *mutual causation* (in which two components both influence one another), *autocatalysis* (at least one component influences another in a way that increases itself—a positive feedback loop), *far-from-equilibrium* conditions (the system imports energy from outside), and *external random variations*. The three qualitatively different outcomes are a *point attractor* (a single steady state, also called a fixed-point attractor),

a *periodic attractor* (in which the group reliably cycles among two or more different states), or a *chaotic (strange) attractor*, in which the group fails to self-organize and behaves unpredictably.

After formalizing the expected relations among member expertise, communication levels, and member perception of norms, Contractor and Seibold (1993) ran computer simulations, which suggested that changing the amount of training in the new technology would lead to qualitatively different results, with the group shifting from a steady state to a cycle. This result identifies training as a *control parameter* in the system and illustrates two important objectives of dynamic systems analyses: (1) discover which (and how many) attractors are available and (2) determine which control parameters (a) affect the likely trajectory of a system toward one attractor or another and/or (b) change the nature or number of available attractors via one or more bifurcations.

Group Success

Work in the nonlinear dynamics perspective has considered a variety of outcomes in groups, including group performance in problem solving and other group coordination tasks (e.g., Guastello & Guastello, 1998; Tschan, Semmer, Nägele, & Gurtner, 2000), levels of cooperation in social dilemmas (e.g., Axelrod, 1997; Huberman & Glance, 1993), creativity (e.g., Guastello, 1998; Stacey, 1996), the therapeutic quality of member interactions in a therapy group (e.g., Burlingame, Fuhriman, & Barnum, 1995; Tschacher, Scheier, & Grawe, 1998), and accident rates in an industrial setting (Guastello, 1988).

Task Performance

Three basic themes are evident in theories of group performance informed by this perspective. The first is adaptation: the idea that good performance results when a group adapts its activity (and sometimes, its tools) to match the task and contextual demands (Poole & DeSanctis, 1990). A second, logically related theme is *equifinality:* the idea that groups can and do take many paths that can lead to equally good outcomes. Studies of decision development (Poole & Roth, 1989a, 1989b) have demonstrated both a wide variety of decision paths and the ways in which groups adjust to contingencies. Evidence that multiple paths can lead to good performance has been supplied by a study originally conducted in hopes of finding the "one correct" path (Hirokawa, 1983).

The third theme is that task activity involves iterated cycles that entrain and regulate collective action (e.g., complex action systems theory; McGrath & Tschan, 2004), rather than a simpler, idealized progression of problem analysis, solution choice, and implementation. Although the content of group action and interaction will depend on the specific features of the group and task, consistent recurrent cycles of orienting, enacting, and monitoring (and, if necessary, modifying) have been associated with better task performance on a problem-solving motor task (Tschan, 1995). Task-adaptive cycles also predicted performance on an air traffic control task, above and beyond general process variables such as amount of communication (Tschan et al., 2000).

Cooperation

In groups, members often are faced with a choice between actions that would benefit them individually at the expense of the group and actions that will benefit the group as a whole. In this case, better group outcomes result when members select the more cooperative, group-benefiting choice. Social dilemmas such as these have been extensively investigated using games such as the Prisoner's Dilemma game and the resource trap (Allison & Messick, 1985).

Computer simulations of players making choices in many iterations of such games have provided insight into how variations of rules

and other parameters such as group size affect group outcomes. The outcome of interest is the proportion of cooperation (% C) that determines the overall earnings of the collective. Although many such studies simulate a large population in which agents play dyadic Prisoner's Dilemma games, either with every other agent in the population or with randomly selected others, some have investigated outcomes for populations of small-group size. Results indicate that for populations of size 9, stable and diametrically opposite results (0% and 100% C, which correspond to universal selfishness versus universal group-benefiting choices) can result from the iterative application of different rules, yet these opposite results can also be generated by the application of an identical rule (Messick & Liebrand, 1995). In nonlinear dynamics language, such groups converge on one of two fixed-point attractors.

The three rules investigated in this study were tit-for-tat (TFT), in which an agent reciprocates cooperation (C) with cooperation, and defection (D) with defection; win-stay, lose-change (WSLC), in which an agent sticks with the same choice if a game has a good outcome and switches to the other choice if the outcome is bad; and win-cooperate, lose-defect (WCLD), in which an agent cooperates on the next turn if there is a good outcome, regardless of whether this outcome was obtained through cooperation or defection. For the first round, agents selected C or D randomly, with 50% probability for each.

In nine-person groups, WSLC led reliably to 0% cooperation (all-D), and it took an average 65 rounds of play for groups to settle on this attractor. WCLD led reliably to 100% cooperation (all-C), and it took an average of only 15 rounds to reach this attractor. These results indicate how the choice of a different rule for interaction can both lead to different results and alter the dynamics (i.e., slower or faster process of stabilizing collective behavior). Groups playing TFT converged in only five to six rounds, on average, but groups had an equal chance of settling on either attractor, all-C or all-D. This illustrates the counterintuitive effect of *ulti-stability,* common in situations governed by nonlinear dynamics, in which a system can arrive at qualitatively different stable states (even diametrically opposed states) by exactly the same process.

The results differed substantially for larger groups of size 16 or 25. Both groups converged on attractors for TFT, but the number of rounds it took to converge increased proportional to group size. For WCLD, the number of rounds increased nonlinearly by almost a full order of magnitude for each step, with 16-agent groups taking an average of 102 rounds and 25-agent groups taking an average of 614 rounds to converge. For WSLC, 16-agent groups took an average of 1,645 rounds to converge, and most 25-agent groups did not converge even after 30,000 rounds of play.

Huberman and Glance (1993) also varied group size in an iterated social dilemma and demonstrated critical sizes below which the group would converge to all-C and above which the group would converge to all-D. Within the middle range, more variety was possible. Huberman and Glance also investigated the impact of imperfect translation of intentions into actions, plus differences in the values group members placed on different outcomes. They found that both "noise" in the system (errors in executing intended behaviors) and greater diversity in member preferences for cooperation increased the likelihood of a group converging on one of the two attractors.

The difference in the findings of Messick and Liebrand (1995; with smaller groups operating in a bi-stable two-attractor landscape) and Huberman and Glance (1993; with smaller groups converging to a single attractor) likely result from two differences between the simulations. The former was based on dyadic games among the members of a small population, whereas the latter was based on N-person games in which the collective outcome was determined by the choices of all group members. The second difference was in the temporal influences on behavior. In dyadic TFT, an actor's behavior is determined entirely by the partner's choice in the preceding round. It operates completely on short-term memory. In the N-person game devised by Huberman and Glance, an actor's behavior is determined by the proportion of members expected to cooperate in the current round plus the expected impact of one's own choice on the future choices of members, and this expectation is adjusted based on the length of anticipated future interaction with the group.

Viewing the results of the latter study from the perspective of catastrophe theory, Guastello (1995, Chapter 9) proposed that the dynamics could be represented in a cusp catastrophe model, with group size as the *asymmetry parameter* (moving groups from all-C through mixed outcomes to all-D) and diversity as the *bifurcation parameter* (which collapses this continuum into an all-or-nothing two-attractor regime, with smaller groups on one attractor and larger groups on the other). The asymmetry and bifurcation parameters are the two *control variables* of a system exhibiting cusp catastrophe properties of both continuous and discontinuous change in a single outcome variable.

Guastello (1988) also used a catastrophe model to make sense of accident rates in organizational subgroups at a steel factory, discussed here because it seems likely that accident rates reflect, among other things, the quality of teamwork, that is, intragroup cooperation. Larger groups had accident rates typical of the industry average, whereas smaller groups (fewer than 17) had rates either near average (like the large groups) or close to zero. In this case, group size was the bifurcation parameter (determining whether there was one attractor or two), while the asymmetry parameter was level of hazard (which increased accident rates in a more continuous manner for the large groups). The cusp catastrophe model resolves the apparent paradox of a small reduction in hazard rates leading to a (proportionately) small reduction of accidents in large groups, while it virtually eliminates accidents in small groups.

Quality of Therapeutic Outcomes

Both theoretical and empirical work has considered outcome in therapy groups or dyads from a nonlinear dynamics perspective, usually looking either at coherence (level of coordination), chaos, or complexity levels as predictors of success (see Pincus, 2001, for an overview). Theorists typically propose that beneficial groups should display complex dynamics, exhibiting patterns that are neither fixed (i.e., fixed-point attractor) nor rigidly repetitive (i.e., periodic attractor) nor chaotic but exist at the "edge of chaos," exhibiting both stability and instability at the same time (Stacey, 2001). New meaning is created, and members transition from illness to health as the complex responsive process of group interaction moves members from the "stuck pattern of stability" to more complex variable patterns (Stacey, 2003, p. 145). Group therapy is envisioned as a process of coevolution in which the members "co-create" one another in an "adaptive, evolving ecosystem" (Rubenfeld, 2001, pp. 454–455).

Consistent with this reasoning, Burlingame et al. (1995; see also Fuhriman & Burlingame, 1994) found that the complexity of group conversation in therapy groups (as indicated by the *fractal dimension* of the conversation time series; see Guastello, Chapter 14, this volume, for technical details) both increased over time and was positively associated with the therapeutic quality of the conversation.

In a dyadic setting (individual therapy), Tschacher and colleagues (1998) found that dimensionality in a battery of self-report measures by the clients and the therapists (indicated by the number of principal components extracted from interaction measures) *decreased* over time, which they interpreted as evidence for beneficial self-organization. The decrease in dimensionality was, as predicted, positively related to therapeutic outcomes. Following the principle of *internal causation* (Vallacher & Nowak, 1998), therapeutic benefits are viewed as emerging from the self-organizing process by which new

order emerges out of the "unorganized initial state of the therapeutic alliance" as it enters a more synchronized phase (Tschacher et al., 1998, p. 197).

Although the latter characterization echoes the claims of complex action systems theory about the importance of emergent coordination and entrainment, the two studies also illustrate the sometimes confusing nature of work in the nonlinear dynamics perspective. In the first, higher dimensionality indicates greater complexity, which is good; in the second, lower dimensionality indicates improved coherence and order, which is also good. One source of confusion is the different meanings and measures of dimension: fractal dimension versus number of principal components. More profoundly, the paradox reflects the somewhat counterintuitive process by which both order (self-organization, increasing coherence) and complexity increase simultaneously.

Readers may also be wondering what sort of attractor, if any, is associated with supposedly beneficial "complex dynamics" in which behavior is neither fixed, periodic, or chaotic. These were the three attractor types identified by Contractor and Seibold (1993) and are the most thoroughly investigated types of dynamic structures. However, a fourth regime of complex behavior was identified by Wolfram (2002; see especially Chapter 6), which is characterized by a mixture of order and randomness at many different scales. A system in this regime never settles permanently on a single attractor, although its behavior is nonetheless characterized by persistent structures. These differences are illustrated by the visual patterns created by the unfolding of such systems in cellular automata, a variety of computer simulation (see Figure 11.1).

Figure 11.1 shows the temporal evolution of a string of nodes (reading across the pictures from right to left) that can be either black or white, with time unfolding from the top of each image down and with the state of each node depending (according to some rule) on the state

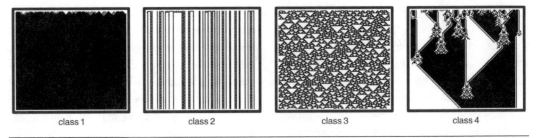

class 1   class 2   class 3   class 4

Figure 11.1   Four Classes of Behavior in the Evolution of Cellular Automata From Random Initial Conditions: Fixed Point (Class 1), Periodic (Class 2), Chaotic (Class 3), and Complex (Class 4)

SOURCE: Reprinted with permission from Wolfram, 2002, p. 231. © 2002, Stephen Wolfram LLC.

of its nearby neighbors in the previous time step. For small groups, each node might represent a member who is either behaving cooperatively (white) or defecting (black). The images for Classes 1 to 3 show evolution to fixed, periodic, and chaotic attractors; Class 4 is complex behavior. Class 1 behavior is simple: After a few iterations, all nodes are the same: black, the fixed-point attractor (complete defection, perhaps). Class 2 behavior is periodic (cyclic), with some of the nodes switching back and forth from white to black in a regular pattern as we read down the image from top to bottom. The chaotic behavior of a Class 3 system looks much less regular and more random—especially when considering the pattern of change from white to black and back for individual nodes. Some structure and pattern is evident when viewing the time evolution as a whole, yet the behavior of each individual node (member) is erratic rather than patterned.

When the attractor landscape for a system is adjusted by systematically varying a control parameter, the complex patterns at multiple scales, which characterize Class 4 behavior, typically appear in the parameter space between periodic (Class 2) and chaotic (Class 3) regimes—hence the designation "edge of chaos" (Langton, 1991). The combination of persistence and change marks this state as the most creative regime, capable of generating novel patterns of behavior

with no change in the rules governing the system. Applying this to group behavior, at different times, two or more subgroups of similarly behaving members might emerge, with those subgroups growing or shrinking over time. Although coherence over time is evident, the group doesn't settle into a single predictable pattern.

Creativity

One of the hallmarks of nonlinear dynamics is, indeed, surprise and novelty; as Casti (1994) notes, "systems that display surprising (i.e., unpredictable) behavior are more or less synonymous with those we regard as being in some way 'complex'" (p. xi). How does this novelty occur? Stacey (2003) draws on the work of Prigogine and Stengers (1984) to propose that novel behavior in groups emerges when small variations are amplified through *resonance,* which is the coupling of frequencies between individuals. The variation that drives divergence might be a difference between members or a momentary fluctuation in member behavior that is taken up and communicated throughout the system (Stacey, 2003, pp. 46–49). As Contractor and Seibold (1993) noted, random variations can also be supplied by the group's external environment.

The impact of small variations can be small, medium, or large, depending on how the nonlinear feedback loops that make up the group as a dynamic system handle the input.

Negative feedback corrects any deviation in group behavior from what is planned (in the case of deliberate goal-oriented action) or from what is simply preferred based on existing group norms. Hence, negative feedback damps down change and secures stability (Stacey, 1996). Positive feedback, in contrast, amplifies and destabilizes the normative behavior of a group. As Stacey (1996) notes, "Much of politics and most rumors are a form of positive feedback, but so is the spreading of revolutionary new ideas to challenge activities in beneficial ways" (p. 35). The power of positive feedback to capitalize on chance and magnify a small deviation into a new global pattern provides a dynamic account of how novelty emerges. Whether or not the result is deemed creative will likely depend on whether it solves a meaningful problem in an effective way.

Change and Group Learning

How do groups change and adapt? General systems theory, one of the intellectual sources that inform nonlinear dynamics, has trouble handling the problem of second-order, qualitative change, because of its emphasis on homeostasis and stable equilibria. Nonlinear dynamics, however, pays equal attention to instability and the associated process of bifurcation in which attractors may appear or vanish. Applying this to family systems, Koopmans (1998) notes how fluctuations in interaction patterns between two family members (for example, a father and adolescent son) can reverberate throughout the system and create change. This result is unexpected when the system has settled into a stable attractor, but when a prior attractor has lost its stability, the resulting turbulence facilitates this sort of upward cascade from a subsystem to the whole system. This is the now familiar story of self-organization, but in this case it is a *restructuring* force rather than the engine of initial structuration.

If a group has a sufficiently complex process, chaos is a state that is relatively easy to access by tuning a control parameter that temporarily moves the system from Class 4 (complex) to Class 3 (chaotic) behavior. This facilitates adaptation through reorganization whenever the group perceives a poor match between its own behavior and the demands of the environment. A straightforward strategy is simply to heighten attention to the naturally variable input from both the internal (member behavior) and external (contextual) environment. In her study of punctuated equilibrium patterns of abrupt change in task groups, Gersick (1988) noted that at the midpoint transition period, groups suddenly noticed or sought out external input that had previously been completely ignored. The value of short bursts of chaotic activity is suggested by the prevalence of "disorganized behavior" among all the groups studied by Poole and Roth (1989b); otherwise, the groups behaved quite rationally in adapting their decision paths to task and structure contingencies.

McGrath and Tschan (2004) describe both the group perception of a problem and appropriate corrective action as emerging from the bottom-up process of *modify* embedded within the ongoing cycles of orient-enact-monitor-modify. If modifying the low-level action does not solve the problem, modification is directed toward the next level up in the hierarchy of work activity— the operational structure for completing the task. If this doesn't work, the upward cascade continues, and the group considers a change in strategy. This account suggests a very rational sequence, presumably followed by orderly deliberation by the group. However, a short excursion into chaos may be usefully included to clear the way to reorganization.

Groups in Context

Why might a group require chaotic disruption in order to adapt? One theory (Arrow et al., 2000) draws on the concept of a fitness landscape, adapted from evolutionary theory, which models the relationship between a group and its embedding contexts. In a fitness landscape, some positions are better than others because they yield better performance, higher rewards, and fewer costs. Other positions have lower fitness—they are less productive and rewarding.

If group members know which set of behaviors corresponds to which set of rewards and costs, one might expect them to move quickly toward the more rewarding positions. However, this may be difficult because the layout of attractors—the map of group dynamics—does not match the fitness landscape. In other words, group states that are stable and easy to maintain (attractors) may also be characterized by poor performance and rewards (bad position in the fitness landscape). Even if it is obvious to group members that a move to a better position is in order, change is difficult because it is an uphill battle, as opposed to the easy downhill slide into an attractor. If the group can shift into chaos, this can spur a reorganization and the emergence of a new attractor, ideally one positioned more favorably in the fitness landscape.

The process of adaptation can be directed or undirected. Directed adaptation is a deliberate change process by which a group attempts to move to a more favorable position in the fitness landscape. It is driven by what Poole and colleagues (Poole, Van de Ven, Dooley, & Holmes, 2000) call a teleological motor of goal-oriented action. Undirected adaptation corresponds to an evolutionary motor of variation, selection, and retention. Applied to a single group, undirected adaptation describes the behavioral shaping that results from rewards and punishments: Choosing among its expressed repertoire of collective behaviors, groups will tend to repeat behaviors that have good results and avoid those that have bad results. The cumulative change in characteristic behaviors constitutes a gradual move toward a peak of fitness. This may or may not correspond to the highest peak in the landscape, as undirected adaptation can only work by moving the group up whatever slope it finds

itself on, based on a gradient of differential rewards. In a rugged landscape of many peaks (Kauffman, 1993), undirected adaptation is myopic: It is more likely to move a system toward the top of a foothill or mesa than toward the summit of a lofty peak.

At the next level of analysis, a variety of groups arrayed on the same fitness landscape may all be competing for a more favorable position. Teams within a sports league, for example, are more or less successful depending on how well they do in games. The fitness landscape is dynamic because as each team adjusts its behavior to improve its chances against the other teams, previously winning strategies can become losing strategies. As the teams continue to adjust to one another, they coevolve, exploring and altering the fitness landscape. In this case, the relationship between teams is strongly competitive. Talented members on poorly performing teams may defect to better teams, and unsuccessful teams may lose their funding and go extinct. In other settings—for example, different functional groups within an organization or different departments in a college—the interactions may be more of a mixture of cooperation and competition.

When we consider an array of groups on a fitness landscape, our reasoning about adaptation is more congruent with evolutionary thinking, which normally applies to variation among a population and selection of fitter individuals in that population. However, the unit of selection is the group, in line with multilevel selection theory (see Sober & Wilson, 1998, for an explanation and historical overview). According to this theory, the resolution of the group versus individual social dilemma in favor of the group is more likely in a context of between-group competition. In this setting, higher levels of cooperative behavior will enhance group performance compared with groups in which members act in a more egotistical fashion.

McPherson and Rotolo (1996) take a group selection approach in building a dynamic model of voluntary group composition and stability.

In their model, society is the context in which voluntary groups compete for member time and resources. Groups specialize to fill different sociodemographic niches within society, with the result that some groups are in direct competition for the time and resources of the same target population, and some are not. In line with this theory, Popielarz and McPherson (1995) show that the greater the density of voluntary groups within a niche, the higher the attrition rate of their members; data presented by McPherson and Rotolo (1996) also confirm model predictions that the diversity of groups will increase or decrease depending on the density and location of other groups competing for members.

This model exemplifies three features characteristic of the nonlinear dynamics perspective on groups. First, it embraces a multilevel view of groups as embedded within a hierarchy of levels from individuals to groups to populations to communities (p. 198). Second, it moves from a static conception of voluntary group membership to model the dynamics of change in groups over time. Third, it attends to fluctuations in carrying capacity as drivers of change in group composition, rather than viewing fluctuations as meaningless variation to be averaged away by aggregating across time.

Conclusion

Despite the diversity of work reviewed in this chapter, some common themes should be apparent. One is an emphasis on studying how unfolding processes in groups create and alter structure, coordinate member activity, accomplish work, generate novelty, and transform people. Through the process of self-organization, order and pattern arise from internal processes, rather than being designed or imposed from outside the group.

The logic of analysis in studying the dynamics of self-organization necessarily differs from approaches that focus on measuring relations among variables at a single point in time. Instead, the goal is to describe the emergence and evolution of a global variable of interest, such as cooperation, conflict, or coordinated task behavior; to identify control parameters that determine the number, nature, and stability of any attractors; and to determine the rules that govern the interactions of group members.

Another theme common to the nonlinear dynamics perspective is a departure from the traditional focus on efficient cause. In building theories of efficient (also called mechanical) cause, causes and effects are strictly differentiated, causes are required to precede effects, and causal forces are understood (sometimes jointly with other causes) to determine the type of effect that will be observed. In contrast, those working in the nonlinear dynamics perspective emphasize formal (also called formative) cause, in which the dynamics of a process constrain what is being created without directly determining the outcome. A recurrent lesson that emerges from this perspective is the limits of prediction when nonlinear interactions play out over time.

In the introduction, I characterized work in this perspective as both diverse and unstable. Among the many approaches that fall under this perspective, some will take root and flourish in the small groups field while others will wither. The strongest contender for the former category, in my view, is computational modeling, exemplified in this chapter by the work of Messick and Liebrand (1995), Nowak et al. (1990), Huberman and Glance (1993), and Shoda et al. (2002). Collecting and analyzing data on interacting groups is exceedingly time and labor intensive, and studying groups over time makes the problem worse (Arrow, Henry, Wheelan, Poole, & Moreland, 2004). Computer simulations allow us to explore the space of possibilities and test out the implications of theories relatively cheaply. Empirical studies can then be targeted to investigate the most robust and interesting findings of the computer simulations, to see if they hold up in real groups.

Work that steers a middle way between the Scylla of pure metaphor and the Charybdis of indigestible findings is also more likely to attract and retain the attention of small groups scholars. The danger of the pure metaphor approach is that scholars can become captivated by a new set of terms without actually changing how they conceptualize and study groups. This turns the distinctive concepts of nonlinear dynamics into rhetorical ornaments, a new set of catchphrases that one can sprinkle about in introduction and discussion sections, with no real change in perspective or approach. Readers of too many such exemplars will soon conclude that the approach has little or nothing to contribute.

The indigestible findings pitfall is characterized by lengthy discussions of obscure quantities that go up or down in some pattern while the significance of this finding for understanding groups remains largely mysterious. Because most groups scholars are relatively unfamiliar with the arcana of nonlinear dynamics—such as the many flavors of entropy and colors of noise—the requirement for careful explanations and interpretation of results is much greater than is the case when using more familiar methods. Answering the "so what" question is critical. Work in the indigestible findings vein may prove interesting to other devoted initiates, but it will have little impact on the trajectory of small groups research if no one can divine what has been learned about what and why we should care.

Some examples of middle-way work include the theorizing of Stacey (1996, 2003), which integrates complexity concepts with organizational theory and psychoanalysis in a way that illuminates all three, and McPherson and Rotolo's (1996) dynamic model of voluntary group composition, which builds on long-standing findings in the literature and is tested using a longitudinal data set. In the group development area, Arrow (1997) examined whether face-to-face and computer-mediated groups had different trajectories of influence patterns, using data from a 15-week study; in the related field of decision development, Poole and Roth's (1989a,

1989b) work is also accessible to groups scholars with no background in nonlinear dynamics.

The mathematical modeling of Gottman and Murray and colleagues (Gottman et al., 2002) qualifies as another promising middle-way strategy, although the model has not yet been fully generalized to model more than two actors at once. Although some readers may judge the work to fall in the "very-hard-to-digest" category, it is fully integrated with the substantive concerns of marital research, and its contribution to understanding fundamental processes and addressing important questions is clear.

Because this first wave of work in the nonlinear dynamics perspective relies on adapting and translating concepts and methods borrowed from very different fields, it is perhaps inevitable that some of us will misrepresent concepts, confuse ourselves and others by applying methods inappropriate to our data, and (in some cases) retreat to a more established approach after the initial flush of enthusiasm has worn off. This chapter was written primarily for the benefit of the next wave of scholars, most of them graduate students now, who will (I hope) build on our efforts, learn from our mistakes, and firmly integrate the nonlinear dynamics perspective within the mainstream of small groups research.

References

Allison, S. T., & Messick, D. M. (1985). Effects of experience on performance in a replenishable resource trap. *Journal of Personality and Social Psychology, 49*, 943–948.

Arrow, H. (1997). Stability, bistability, and instability in small group influence patterns. *Journal of Personality and Social Psychology, 72*, 75–85.

Arrow, H., & Burns, K. L. (2003). Self-organizing culture: How norms emerge in small groups. In M. Schaller & C. Crandall (Eds.), *The psychological foundations of culture* (pp. 171–199). Mahwah, NJ: Lawrence Erlbaum.

Arrow, H., & Crosson, S. B. (2003). Musical chairs: Membership dynamics in self-organized group formation. *Small Group Research, 5*, 523–556.

Arrow, H., Henry, K. B., Wheelan, S. A., Poole, M. S., & Moreland, R. L. (2004). Time, change, and development: The temporal perspective on groups. *Small Group Research, 35*(1), 73–105.

Arrow, H., & McGrath, J. E. (1995). Membership dynamics in groups at work: A theoretical framework. In B. M. Staw & L. L. Cummings (Eds.), *Research in organizational behavior* (Vol. 17, pp. 373–411). Greenwich, CT: JAI Press.

Arrow, H., McGrath, J. E., & Berdahl, J. L. (2000). *Small groups as complex systems: Formation, coordination, development, and adaptation.* Thousand Oaks, CA: Sage.

Axelrod, R. (1997). *The complexity of cooperation: Agent-based models of competition and collaboration.* Princeton, NJ: Princeton University Press.

Baron, R. M., Amazeen, P. G., & Beek, P. J. (1994). Local and global dynamics in social relations. In R. R. Vallacher & A. Nowak (Eds.), *Dynamical systems in social psychology* (pp. 111–138). New York: Academic Press.

Burlingame, G. M., Fuhriman, A., & Barnum, K. R. (1995). Group therapy as a nonlinear dynamical system: Analysis of therapeutic communication for chaotic patterns. In A. Gilgen & F. Abraham (Eds.), *Chaos theory in psychology* (pp. 87–105). Westport, CT: Greenwood.

Carley, K. M. (1991). A theory of group stability. *American Sociological Review, 56,* 331–354.

Casti, J. L. (1994). *Complexification: Explaining a paradoxical world through the science of surprise.* New York: Harper Collins.

Cole, B. J. (1991). Is animal behavior chaotic? Evidence from the activity of ants. *Proceedings of the Royal Society, London, Series B, 244,* 253–259.

Contractor, H., & Seibold, D. R. (1993). Theoretical frameworks for the study of structuring processes in group decision support systems: Adaptive structuration theory and self-organizing systems theory. *Human Communication Research, 19,* 528–563.

Fuhriman, A., & Burlingame, G. M. (1994). Measuring small group process: A methodological application of chaos theory. *Small Group Research, 25,* 502–519.

Gersick, C. J. G. (1988). Time and transition in work teams: Toward a new model of group development. *Academy of Management Journal, 31,* 9–41.

Giddens, A. (1984). *The constitution of society: Outline of the theory of structuration.* Berkeley: University of California Press.

Gleick, J. (1987). *Chaos: Making a new science.* New York: Viking Penguin.

Goldstein, J. (1994). *The unshackled organization.* Portland, OR: Productivity Press.

Gottman, J. M., Guralnick, M. J., Wilson, B., Swanson, C. C., & Murray, J. D. (1997). What should be the focus of emotion regulation in children? A nonlinear dynamic mathematical model of children's peer interaction in groups. *Development and Psychopathology, 9,* 421–452.

Gottman, J. M., Murray, J. D., Swanson, C., Tyson, R., & Swanson, K. R. (2002). *The mathematics of marriage: Dynamic nonlinear models.* Cambridge: MIT Press.

Guastello, S. J. (1988). Catastrophe modeling of the accident process: Organizational subunit size. *Psychological Bulletin, 103*(2), 246–255.

Guastello, S. J. (1995). *Chaos, catastrophe, and human affairs: Applications of nonlinear dynamics to work, organizations, and social evolution.* Mahwah, NJ: Lawrence Erlbaum.

Guastello, S. J. (1998). Creative problem solving groups at the edge of chaos. *Journal of Creative Behavior, 32,* 38–57.

Guastello, S. J., & Guastello, D. D. (1998). Origins of coordination and team effectiveness: A perspective from game theory and nonlinear dynamics. *Journal of Applied Psychology, 83*(3), 423–437.

Guastello, S. J., & Philippe, P. (1997). Dynamics in the development of large information exchange groups and virtual communities. *Nonlinear Dynamics, Psychology, and Life Sciences, 1,* 123–149.

Hirokawa, R. Y. (1983). Group communication and problem solving effectiveness: An investigation of group phases. *Human Communication Research, 12,* 203–224.

Huberman, B. A., & Glance, N. S. (1993). Diversity and collective action. In H. Haken & A. Mikhailov (Eds.), *Interdisciplinary approaches to nonlinear systems* (pp. 44–64). New York: Springer-Verlag.

Kant, I. (1987). *Critique of judgement* (W. S. Pluhar, Trans.). Indianapolis, IN: Hackett. (Original work published 1790)

Kauffman, S. A. (1993). *The origins of order: Self-organization and selection in evolution.* New York: Oxford University Press.

Kauffman, S. (2002). What is life? In J. Brockman (Ed.), *The next fifty years: Science in the first half of the twenty-first century* (pp. 126–141). New York: Vintage Books.

Keller, E. F., & Segel, L. A. (1970, September 26). Conflict between positive and negative feedback as an explanation for the initiation of aggregation in slime mold amoebae. *Nature, 227,* 1365–1366.

Koopmans, M. (1998). Chaos theory and the problem of change in family systems. *Nonlinear Dynamics, Psychology, and Life Sciences, 2*(2), 133–148.

Langton, C. G. (1991). Life at the edge of chaos. In C. G. Langton, C. Taylor, J. D. Farmer, & S. Rasmussen (Eds.), *Santa Fe Institute studies in the sciences of complexity: Vol. 10. Artificial life II* (pp. 41–91). Reading, MA: Addison-Wesley.

Latané, B. (1981). The psychology of social impact. *American Psychologist, 36*(4), 343–356.

Latané, B. (1996). Dynamic social impact: The creation of culture by communication. *Journal of Communication, 46,* 13–25.

Latané, B., & L'Herrou, T. L. (1996). Spatial clustering in the conformity game: Dynamic social impact in electronic groups. *Journal of Personality and Social Psychology, 70,* 1218–1230.

Lewin, K. (1947a). Frontiers in group dynamics: Channels of group life: Social planning and action research. *Human Relations, 1,* 143–153.

Lewin, K. (1947b). Frontiers in group dynamics: Concept, method, and reality in social science: Social equilibria and social change. *Human Relations, 1,* 5–41.

Lewin, R. (1992). *Complexity: Life at the edge of chaos.* New York: Macmillan.

McClure, B. A. (1998). *Putting a new spin on groups: The science of chaos.* Mahwah, NJ: Lawrence Erlbaum.

McGrath, J. E., Berdahl, J. L., & Arrow, H. (1995). Traits, expectations, culture, and clout: The dynamics of diversity in work groups. In S. E. Jackson & M. N. Ruderman (Eds.), *Diversity in work teams: Research paradigms for a changing workplace* (pp. 17–45). Washington, DC: American Psychological Association.

McGrath, J. E., & Tschan, F. (2004). *Temporal matters in social psychology: Examining the role of time in the lives of groups and individuals.* Washington, DC: American Psychological Association.

McPherson, J. M., & Rotolo, T. (1996). Testing a dynamic model of social composition: Diversity and change in voluntary groups. *American Sociological Review, 61,* 179–202.

Meara, A. (1999). The butterfly effect in therapy: Not every flap of a butterfly's wing . . . *Gestalt Review, 3*(3), 205–225.

Messick, D. M., & Liebrand, W. B. G. (1995). Individual heuristics and the dynamics of cooperation in large groups. *Psychological Review, 102*(1), 131–145.

Moreland, R. L., & Levine, J. M. (1982). Socialization in small groups: Temporal changes in individual-group relations. In L. Berkowitz (Ed.), *Advances in experimental social psychology* (Vol. 15, pp. 137–192). New York: Academic Press.

Newtson, D. (1994). The perception and coupling of behavior waves. In R. R. Vallacher & A. Nowak (Eds.), *Dynamical systems in social psychology* (pp. 139–167). San Diego, CA: Academic Press.

Nowak, A., Szamrej, J., & Latané, B. (1990). From private attitude to public opinion: A dynamic theory of social impact. *Psychological Review, 97,* 367–376.

Pincus, D. (2001). A framework and methodology for the study of nonlinear self-organizing family dynamics. *Nonlinear Dynamics, Psychology, and Life Sciences, 5,* 139–173.

Poole, M. S., & DeSanctis, G. (1990). Understanding the use of decision support systems: The theory of adaptive structuration. In J. Fulk & C. Steinfield (Eds.), *Organizations and communication technology* (pp. 173–193). Newbury Park, CA: Sage.

Poole, M. S., & Roth, J. (1989a). Decision development in small groups IV: A typology of group decision paths. *Human Communication Research, 15,* 323–356.

Poole, M. S., & Roth, J. (1989b). Decision development in small groups V: Test of a contingency model. *Human Communication Research, 15,* 549–589.

Poole, M. S., Van de Ven, A. H., Dooley, K., & Holmes, M. E. (2000). *Organizational change and innovation processes: Theory and methods for research.* New York: Oxford University Press.

Popielarz, P. A., & McPherson, J. M. (1995). On the edge or in between: Niche position, niche overlap, and the duration of voluntary association memberships. *American Journal of Sociology, 101*(3), 698–720.

Poston, T., & Stewart, I. (1978). *Catastrophe theory and its applications.* Mineola, NY: Dover.

Prigogine, I., & Stengers, I. (1984). *Order out of chaos.* New York: Bantam.

Reynolds, C. W. (1987). Flocks, herds, and schools: A distributed behavioral model. *Computer Graphics, 21*(4)(SIGGRAPH '87 Conference Proceedings), 25–34.

Rubenfeld, S. (2001). Group therapy and complexity theory. *International Journal of Group Psychotherapy, 51*(4), 449–471.

Shoda, Y., LeeTiernan, S., & Mischel, W. (2002). Personality as a dynamical system: Emergence of stability and distinctiveness from intra- and interpersonal interactions. *Personality and Social Psychology Review, 6* (4), 316–325.

Smith, C., & Gemmill, G. (1991). Change in the small group: A dissipative structure perspective. *Human Relations, 44*(7), 697–716.

Sober, E., & Wilson, D. S. (1998). *Unto others: The evolution and psychology of unselfish behavior.* Cambridge, MA: Harvard University Press.

Stacey, R. D. (1996). *Complexity and creativity in organizations.* San Francisco: Berrett-Koehler.

Stacey, R. D. (2001). Complexity and the group matrix. *Group Analysis, 34*(2), 201–239.

Stacey, R. D. (2003). *Complexity and group processes: A radically social understanding of individuals.* New York: Brunner-Routledge.

Tesser, A. (1980). When individual dispositions and social pressure conflict: A catastrophe. *Human Relations, 33,* 393–407.

Tesser, A., & Achee, J. (1994). Aggression, love, conformity, and other social psychological catastrophes. In R. R. Vallacher & A. Nowak (Eds.), *Dynamical systems in social psychology* (pp. 95–109). New York: Academic Press.

Tschacher, W., Scheier, C., & Grawe, K. (1998). Order and pattern formation in psychotherapy. *Nonlinear Dynamics, Psychology, and Life Sciences, 2,* 195–216.

Tschan, F. (1995). Communication enhances small group performance if it conforms to task requirements: The concept of ideal communication cycles. *Basic and Applied Social Psychology, 17,* 371–393.

Tschan, F., Semmer, N. K., Nägele, C., & Gurtner, A. (2000). Task adaptive behavior and performance in groups. *Group Processes & Interpersonal Relations, 3*(4), 367–386.

Vallacher, R. R., & Nowak, A. (1998). *Dynamical social psychology.* New York: Guilford Press.

von Cranach, M. (1996). Toward a theory of the acting group. In E. Witte & J. H. Davis (Eds.), *Understanding group behavior: Small group processes and interpersonal relations* (pp. 147–187). Hillsdale, NJ: Lawrence Erlbaum.

Wheelan, S. (1996). An initial exploration of the relevance of complexity theory to group research and practice. *Systems Practice, 9*(1), 49–70.

Wolfram, S. (2002). *A new kind of science.* Champaign, IL: Wolfram Media.

Zeggelink, E. (1995). Evolving friendship networks: An individual-oriented approach implementing similarity. *Social Networks, 17,* 83–110.

PART III

Methods in Group Research and Practice

12

Design and Analysis of Experimental Research on Groups

Rick H. Hoyle

When the goal of research on groups is to establish a causal relation between individual or group outcomes and one or more characteristics of groups, group members, interacting groups, or the settings within which groups function, the preferred method is the experiment. An experiment is any study in which at least one variable (the putative cause) is manipulated, the units of observation (individuals, groups, or interacting groups) are randomly assigned to levels of the manipulated variable, and there is at least one control condition. Experiments can be contrasted with quasi-experiments, in which the putative cause is manipulated, but there either is no randomization or no control condition, and non-experiments, in which there is neither

manipulation, randomization, nor a control condition. Although quasi- and nonexperimental designs are useful, and sometimes necessary strategies for studying the behavior of groups, the information they provide is of limited value when the goal is to establish causal relations. Experimental designs, by virtue of manipulation, randomization, and control conditions, address the principal shortcomings of quasi- and non-experiments for making causal inferences.

In this chapter, I focus specifically on the use of experimental designs for studying intragroup and intergroup phenomena. Although I contrast experiments with quasi- and nonexperiments, these families of research designs are best viewed as complementary. Each can contribute to the understanding of intragroup and intergroup

Author's Note: During the writing of this chapter, the author was supported by grants R01-DA12371 and P20-DA017589 from the National Institute on Drug Abuse.

phenomena in ways that the others cannot. In this first section of the chapter, I describe characteristics that are unique and essential to experimental designs; then, I describe a set of characteristics that, although not essential, are typically seen in uses of experimental designs. I conclude the section by formally comparing experimental designs with quasi- and nonexperimental designs.

Essential Elements

The defining features of the experimental method are control and isolation. These features are realized through manipulation of the putative cause, randomization of groups or group members to levels of the manipulated variable, and the inclusion of a control group. The control and isolation provided by manipulation, randomization, and a control group provide a firm logical basis for inferences of causality.

Before I elaborate on the concepts of control and isolation and describe how randomization, manipulation, and control groups contribute to them, I specify the conditions that must be satisfied before a causal inference is warranted. First, it is necessary to document an *association* between the presumed cause and effect. Causality is a special case of association; hence, in the absence of association, there can be no causality. Second, it is necessary to establish that the association between the presumed cause and effect is *directional*. That is, change in the putative cause produces change in the effect, but not the converse. Finally, it is necessary to demonstrate that changes in the effect associated with changes in the presumed cause are indeed attributable to the presumed cause and not to other variables that occur with it or with both the presumed cause and the effect (Cook & Campbell, 1979). In other words, the presumed cause has been *isolated* from extraneous variables that might account for its association with the effect.

The design-related issues associated with these criteria are illustrated in path diagram form in Figure 12.1. For illustrative purposes,

consider the association between group cohesion and the performance by the group on a task. The path diagram in the top panel of the figure illustrates a simple association between these two variables; r_{12} denotes a correlation coefficient or some other index of effect size. The curved, two-headed arrow indicates a nondirectional association between the two. The strength of the association would be reflected by the magnitude of r_{12}. Although this model satisfies a necessary condition for a causal inference, it does not provide sufficient information to warrant such an inference.

In the lower left panel of Figure 12.1 are three elaborations on the simple association model. Moving from top to bottom, the first model specifies a causal effect of cohesion on performance. The strength of the direct effect is reflected in b_{12}, and e_2 corresponds to variance in performance not attributable to cohesion. The next model reverses the direction of influence, and the final model indicates bidirectional influence. Typically, the key concern is distinguishing the first model from the second. (The bidirectional model cannot be evaluated using an experimental design and would require multiple observations of each variable over time.) It is important to see that the two unidirectional models are statistically equivalent to each other and to the nondirectional model in the top panel of the figure. That is, these models cannot be distinguished on statistical grounds. The only effective strategy for distinguishing one from the other is research design.

In the lower right panel of Figure 12.1 are two additional models of the association between group cohesion and performance. The first indicates that the effect on each variable is caused by a third variable and the extent of contact among group members, and the apparent association between the two is fully attributable to this common cause. The broken line indicates that the correlation (now a partial correlation) between them is no longer significant when contact is partialled from each. The second model is one in which a presumed causal influence of cohesion on performance is in reality attributable

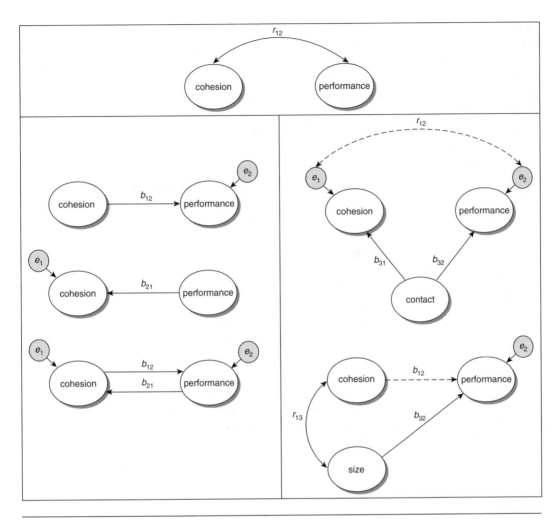

Figure 12.1   Path Diagrams Illustrating the Criteria for Inferring a Causal Effect of Group Cohesion on Group Performance

to group size. That is, group cohesion and group size are correlated (as reflected in r_{13}), and when group size is partialled from group cohesion, the effect of cohesion on performance is no longer significant (as indicated by a broken line).

With this example before us, I return to the issues of control and isolation. Control concerns the presumed causal variable in a cause-effect relation. Assuming that a simple association has been documented to make a convincing case for directionality, variability in the presumed cause should be under the control of the experimenter. Such control rules out the possibility that any causal influence runs from the presumed effect

to the presumed cause. Moreover, the context within which the putative cause varies must be controlled. Control in this sense involves attending to other variables that might either covary with the presumed cause or be present in the research context (e.g., experimenter demand). These potential confounds are ruled out by isolating the presumed cause from other variables that might produce change in the effect. Isolation concerns the potential co-occurrence of a putative cause and other variables. To the extent that the putative cause is confounded with other variables, inferences about its influence will be ambiguous or even incorrect. Control over variability in the presumed cause and isolation of it from other potential causes are necessary for unequivocal inferences of causal influence.

How do experimental designs produce the control and isolation necessary for causal inferences? Let us first consider manipulation. When the researcher produces variability in the putative cause, the only logical direction of association is from it to the presumed effect. Alternatively, when the putative cause is outside the control of the researcher, it is possible that it varies because of influence from the presumed effect or any number of other variables (such as contact or size in the example described earlier and illustrated in Figure 12.1).

Although randomization also figures into control over the putative cause, its primary contribution to the activity of causal inference is isolation. As an illustration, return to the example presented earlier and consider the manipulation of group cohesion. Imagine that a researcher organizes previously unacquainted students into three-person groups. About half the groups are assigned to participate in a set of experiences designed to foster cohesion, and the remaining groups are not. If the groups are assigned randomly to a condition, then apart from the manipulation, they are presumed to be probabilistically equivalent (Trochim, 2000). I describe them as *probabilistically* equivalent because there is some probability that, apart from the manipulation, the groups differ. This probability is accounted for in the construction of statistical tests such that any apparent difference between groups can be attributed either to the manipulation or chance (Haslam & McGarty, 2000). This caveat aside, I can with considerable confidence assume that any differences between the two groups on performance are attributable to variability in the manipulated variable.

Although randomization goes a long way toward isolating the presumed cause from other causal influences, it does not rule out all alternative explanations for differences on an outcome variable. For instance, a skeptic might argue that our manipulation of cohesion did nothing more than provide group members an opportunity to learn each other's names and potential contributions to the upcoming group task. As such, superior performance should be attributed to these more mundane factors rather than to group cohesion per se. A strategically chosen control group could rule out this alternative explanation. For instance, groups in a control condition might be given the same amount of time together as their counterparts in the experimental condition but not participate in the exercises designed specifically to foster cohesion. In such a design, if the experimental and control groups differ on performance, the difference cannot be attributed to comfort level among group members or knowledge of group members' talents or skills relevant to the task.

An alternative perspective on the contributions of manipulation, randomization, and control conditions to inference is *internal validity;* that is, the degree to which a causal inference is justified given the design of the study and the conditions under which it was done. Campbell and Stanley (1963) identified nine potential threats to the internal validity of a study; a subset is relevant to inferences from experimental designs. *Selection* involves characteristics that group members or groups bring with them to the experiment. If randomization is successful, these characteristics are evenly distributed across conditions and unlikely to account for variability in outcomes. When the number of groups or group members per condition is small, randomization failure is possible, setting the stage for selection threats to validity. Both *history* and *maturation* involve the passage of time between manipulation of the presumed cause and measurement of the effect. Both are addressed by the inclusion of an appropriately designed control condition.

By including a control group and ensuring that, with the exception of the manipulation, its experience is identical to that of the experimental group, the researcher rules out the alternative explanation that something in the environment other than the manipulation or naturally occurring changes in groups, group members, or interacting groups produced change in the outcome. A control group also provides a means for avoiding the interpretation of *statistical regression* as causal influence. Statistical regression is likely when the groups or group members are chosen for a study because they are extreme on some characteristic that is related to the outcome variable. When the outcome is measured, for purely artifactual reasons, their scores will be less extreme. Because any regression to the mean will be evident for the control group as well, the concern that statistical regression will be interpreted as causal influence is eliminated. A final threat to the internal validity of experiments is *experimental mortality*. Mortality in this instance means dropping out of the study after randomization. Losing even one group or group member that has been randomized to condition lowers the probabilistic equivalence of the groups to be compared and, in so doing, raises the probability of an incorrect inference. Although this threat to internal validity is not overcome by experimental designs, it can negate the important contribution of randomization to causal inferences and, therefore, must be kept in mind.

Typical Elements

Although manipulation, randomization, and control groups are the only essential elements of experimental research, a number of additional elements are typically found in experimental studies. Two of these concern distinctions among variables expected to be influenced by the presumed cause, or independent variable. All experimental and quasi-experimental research includes dependent variables. These are the outcome variables of primary interest: the effects in the presumed cause-effect relation. Experiments also may include manipulation checks and mediating variables.

The primary aim of manipulation checks is to demonstrate that the manipulation produced the desired effect. There are three types of manipulation checks. The most useful are those designed to gauge the impact of the manipulation on the theoretical variable of interest. For example, if a researcher designs a manipulation to produce group cohesion in newly formed groups, the manipulation check might be a suitable measure of group cohesion. If the experimental group scores higher on a measure of group cohesion than the control group, then the researcher can infer that any differences on the dependent variables are due, at least in part, to group cohesion. A second type of manipulation check focuses on theoretical variables that the manipulation was not designed to vary, theoretical variables that represent plausible alternative explanations for differences on dependent variables. For instance, a by-product of the manipulation of group cohesion might be to engender confidence among group members in their abilities, and this, not group cohesion, explains the performance advantage of groups in the control condition. Including measures of such potential confounds and finding no difference between experimental and control groups strengthens the researcher's inference that performance differences are uniquely attributable to group cohesion. On the more mundane side, a researcher might wish to secure evidence that research participants actually perceived the manipulation. For instance, if they were given normative information about performance on a test and their own score, it is important to document that they correctly processed the normative information, which would be critical to correctly interpreting their own score. One would hope for 100% accuracy on manipulation checks of this sort. On manipulation checks of the first sort, one would hope for a very large effect size accompanying the statistical test.

As a research program matures, the focus shifts from simply establishing a causal relation between two variables to searching for the causal mechanisms that produce the relation. Such mechanisms are captured by mediating or intervening variables (Hoyle & Robinson, 2003). For example, in our running example, we might conjecture that group cohesion contributes to superior performance on a group task because the more attached members feel to their group, the more trusting they are of fellow group members. Mediating variables are a type of dependent variable with reference to the presumed cause. That is, the mediating variable is assumed to be caused by the independent variable. In addition, however, the mediating variable functions as a type of independent variable with reference to the dependent variable. Hence, mediating variables are intermediary in a causal change that runs from cause to causal mechanism to effect. In our example, cohesion causes trust, which causes performance. Mediating variables enrich the account of causal relations documented by experimental research.

It is not uncommon for experimental studies to be conducted in the laboratory, an artificial setting in which the researcher has a high degree of control over what participants experience. Indeed, one review of social psychological research on groups suggested that about 75% of such studies are experiments conducted in a laboratory setting (Moreland, Hogg, & Hains, 1994). A significant advantage of the laboratory setting is that the researcher, through careful structuring of the social and physical environment, is able to achieve a high level of internal validity. This advantage is offset by several disadvantages (Levine & Moreland, 1998; McGrath, Arrow, & Berdahl, 2000). Foremost among these is the fact that group research conducted in the laboratory setting tends to involve ad hoc groups; that is, groups that did not exist before and will not exist after the experiment. These groups typically are small and include college students who are strangers. They are brought together to engage in what often are trivial tasks for a brief period of time in an artificial, often sterile setting. The proliferation of this sort of group study has led some to conclude that, at least with reference to social psychological research on groups, the literature is primarily relevant to how people behave in hypothetical groups (e.g., Månson, 1993). Moreover, the constraints involved with laboratory research involving young adults limits the range of group phenomena that can be studied (Levine & Moreland, 1998). There is reason to believe that, for at least some group phenomena, the generalizability of findings from laboratory experiments is good. For instance, a meta-analysis of the literature on group cohesiveness and performance found similar effects for laboratory and field-based studies (Mullen & Copper, 1994). Interestingly, although the effect was apparent across all settings and designs, the effect was strongest for studies conducted in real-world settings, whether experimental or nonexperimental. This analysis raises an important point: Experiments do not have to be conducted in artificial settings. Although field experiments pose challenges not associated with laboratory experiments, they are a compelling strategy for producing findings high in internal validity and generalizability to real-world settings.

Comparison With Other Designs

As noted earlier, two alternatives to experimental designs are quasi-experimental and nonexperimental designs. Recall that quasi-experimental designs include at least one manipulated variable, but either people or groups are not randomly assigned to levels of the manipulated variable(s) or there is no control group. Nonexperimental designs involve neither manipulation, randomization, nor a control group. These distinctions are illustrated in Figure 12.2.

Although at first blush, experimental designs would appear to be superior in every respect to quasi- and nonexperimental designs, such is not the case. Experimental designs are uniquely suited to the task of demonstrating causal relations. However, research on groups might be motivated by other goals (Brewer, 2000). For

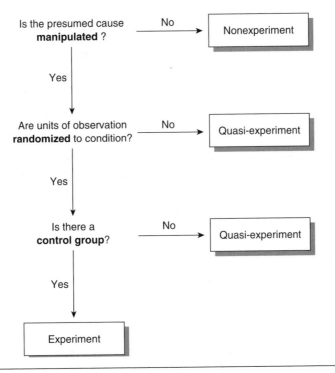

Figure 12.2   The Distinction Between Experiments, Quasi-experiments, and Nonexperiments

instance, the goal of a study of the amount of time group members spend together and group cohesion might simply be to demonstrate an association between the two. Satisfaction of this goal requires neither isolation of the variables nor determination of directionality in their association. In such cases, neither manipulation nor randomization (and the various complications they bring to a study) are necessary. Indeed, a manipulation of time spent together might not yield the same association as time that group members *voluntarily* spend with each other. Alternatively, it might be impossible to produce varying levels of cohesion that approximate variability of cohesion in naturally occurring groups. In some instances, the presumed cause is a relatively stable characteristic of group members that is not subject to manipulation. For instance, personality and demographic characteristics of group members are qualities that cannot be manipulated. When manipulation is

either undesirable or not feasible, experimental designs cannot be used.

In some instances, manipulation of a putative cause is feasible but randomization to condition is not possible. For instance, a researcher might be interested in the relative satisfaction of students assigned to classroom work groups that are homogeneous or heterogeneous with respect to gender. The school research director might not approve of randomization to group, meaning the researcher must compare the satisfaction of students who self-select to groups of a particular composition. Although the causal factor has, in effect, been manipulated, students have not been randomized to levels of it. As a result, students at different levels of the causal factor are not equivalent with respect to a host of variables other than gender composition that might affect satisfaction. Nonetheless, useful information has been generated regarding the association between work-group composition and satisfaction.

Even when it is feasible to manipulate a presumed cause and randomize groups or group members to condition, it might not be ethical to do so. For instance, a researcher might be interested in conflict resolution between groups. Although finding and studying groups with varying degrees of naturally occurring conflict might be an option, creating conflict for the purpose of research likely would not. In some instances, it might be acceptable on ethical grounds to manipulate a presumed cause, but ethically unacceptable to randomize groups or group members to levels of the variable. This is particularly true when the causal factor is an intervention likely to produce positive outcomes. Because individuals or groups randomized to the control condition would not receive the intervention, they would, in effect, be denied a benefit extended to individuals or groups randomized to the intervention condition. The only option available to the researcher is to allow self-selection to condition and, in a quasi-experimental design, attempt to identify potential confounds, measure them, and statistically control for them.

A final concern when considering the relative merits of experimental, quasi-experimental, and nonexperimental designs is *external validity,* which concerns the degree to which the findings would generalize to other people, places, and times. Research on groups that uses college students in a laboratory setting is particularly vulnerable to criticisms of low external validity. One means of raising the external validity of a study such as this would be to design a study high in *mundane realism,* which refers to the extent to which the experimental conditions reflect natural conditions. Such a focus stands in contrast to the typical focus of laboratory experiments, *experimental realism,* which is the degree to which the experimental setting produces the desired impact on research participants. Another strategy for increasing external validity would be to move from the laboratory to the field, a move that often requires a move from experimental to quasi- or nonexperimental designs. Similarly, external validity is enhanced

when the research participants are randomly sampled from the population for which inferences are intended. Finally, confidence in the external validity of findings from a study is increased when the study is replicated, whether the findings were produced by an experimental, a quasi-experimental, or a nonexperimental design.

In short, internal and external validity are difficult to achieve using a single design. Whereas internal validity is optimized in experimental designs, external validity tends to be strongest in quasi- or nonexperimental designs. The strongest research programs strike a balance between these two considerations, using various designs that, collectively, form the basis of a causal inference of relevance to a broad range of individuals behaving in real-world settings.

In the next section of the chapter, I describe and illustrate research questions appropriate for study using experimental designs.

Research Questions

Experimental designs are well suited for research on groups motivated by the goal of establishing a causal relation between variables. Key concerns are that the presumed cause can and should be manipulated; the research participants can be randomized to condition; and the causal agent can be withheld from a subset of the participants so as to create a control group. Assuming these conditions can be met, a wide array of research questions relevant to groups researchers can be addressed using experimental designs.

Research questions on groups amenable to study using experimental designs can be organized under three headings: individual, intragroup, and intergroup. The primary distinction between these types of group research is the presumed impact of the causal factor. That is, the presumed cause might exert its influence at the individual level and, thereby, affect the group through effects on individual group members. Alternatively, the presumed cause might influence group-level outcomes or behavior with little or no individual-level variability. Finally, the presumed cause might be relevant to interaction between groups, affecting only outcomes or behaviors that emerge as a result of the interdependence between two or more groups. Although intragroup and intergroup research are most clearly relevant to the study of phenomena unique to the group experience, a surprisingly large proportion of research on groups focuses on the experience or behavior of individual group members (Levine & Moreland, 1998). To some degree, this focus on the individual is attributable to researchers' comfort with research designs and statistical methods that require individual-level data (Hoyle & Crawford, 1994). It also reflects the reductionistic approach to behavior that is characteristic of an era during which explanatory models tend to focus on cognitive more than social processes (Levine & Moreland, 1998). There is some evidence that the pendulum has begun to swing back toward a focus on emergent properties of groups that cannot be understood by focusing on individuals (e.g., Bond & Kenny, 2002). Nonetheless, as I now illustrate, there is a place for experimental research on groups of all three types.

In an example of experimental groups research focused on the individual, Wenzel (2001; Study 2) investigated the influence of identification with one's group on the allocation of resources to self and a fellow group member whose performance contributes most strongly to a positive group outcome. Although the focus of the research was the implications of resource allocation strategies for the group as a whole, the focus was the behavior of individual group members. Specifically, university students were assigned at random to one of four conditions produced by crossing the manipulated independent variables, identification (low or high), and in-group strength (one aspect of performance vs. another). Research participants played a computer game, knowing that their group would receive a bonus as a result. They then rated the degree to which

each in-group member, including themselves, deserved the bonus. The author predicted that regardless of the particular strength of the in-group, individuals who strongly identified with the in-group would be more likely than their counterparts to rate the best performing member of the group as more deserving of the bonus than themselves. The prediction was confirmed by a significant effect for identification. That is, group values trumped self-interest when group identification was high.

Experimental groups research focused on the group is illustrated in a study by Henningsen, Henningsen, Jakobsen, and Borton (2004). These researchers randomly assigned 188 university students to one of 47 four-person groups, then randomly assigned groups to one of four experimental conditions. Group leaders were appointed either at random or ostensibly according to leadership potential, and assigned leaders received either full or partial information relevant to a decision their group had to make. Focal outcomes were whether the group chose the optimal alternative and the degree of group cohesion reported by group members. The authors predicted and found that groups make better decisions and evince greater group cohesion when the leader is appointed according to potential and possesses full information relevant to the group decision.

An example of experimental research on intergroup processes is a study of the difference between interindividual and intergroup interactions by Insko, Schopler, Hoyle, Dardis, and Graetz (1990; Study 2). Six research participants were present at each laboratory session. Sessions were randomized such that in some sessions, the participants interacted as 2 three-person groups (intergroup condition), and in some sessions, the participants interacted as three pairs of individuals (interindividual condition). The focus of the research was the difference in competitiveness evinced across a set of Prisoner's Dilemma choice trials. In the intergroup condition, before each trial, the members of each group met to reach consensus on a choice for the group. One member of each group then made the decision for his or her group. Because the payout from each choice was determined by the combination of the two groups' or individuals' choices, there was a single outcome for each interaction. Thus, for the intergroup condition, the unit of analysis was the interacting groups. That is, each data point for this condition represented an interaction involving six individuals. For the interindividual condition, the unit of analysis was the interacting dyad, yielding one data point for each pair of individuals. Although 252 university students participated in the study, the analyses were based on 70 observations (28 across the intergroup conditions and 42 across the interindividual conditions).

As noted earlier in the chapter, experimental designs are not well suited for addressing all research questions on groups. Generally speaking, if, as illustrated in Figure 12.2, the presumed cause cannot be manipulated, the participants cannot be randomized to condition, or a control condition cannot be justified, then the question cannot be addressed using an experimental design. Even if all these conditions could be met, an experimental design might not be justified. If, for example, the research is motivated by the goal of documenting an association among two or more qualities of groups, then nonexperimental designs typically will suffice and usually come at lower cost. If the research is motivated by the goal of developing a predictive model of a group-level outcome (e.g., productivity, efficiency), then nonexperimental or, perhaps, quasi-experimental designs will suffice. In general, such studies are characterized by a focus on measurement (rather than manipulation) and a general lack of control (desired or undesired) over the variables of interest. In many cases, a critical concern is external validity, and therefore, the research is undertaken in a natural setting and involves research participants responding as they naturally would to features of that setting. Such research is of value in its own right and, moreover, is an important complement to research using experimental designs.

In the final major section of the chapter, I detail formal aspects of experimental design and take up the complex issue of analyzing data from intra- and intergroup studies.

Research Designs and Data Analysis

Experimental Designs

The primary distinction in experimental designs is between between-subjects and within-subjects manipulations of presumed causes. When a presumed cause is operationally defined as a between-subjects factor, each group member or group is subjected to one and only one level of the factor. The most rudimentary design of this sort, the posttest-only equivalent groups design, is illustrated in Figure 12.3. The Rs indicate that the focal entity—individuals, groups, or interacting groups—are randomized to one of two levels of the experimental factor, or treatment condition. The Xs indicate receipt of one level of the treatment condition. (If the control group experiences no treatment at all, the X in the second line could be eliminated.) The Os indicate that the focal entities are observed; that is, the dependent variable is, in some manner, assessed. Because of randomization, the two groups are probabilistically equivalent when the manipulation is delivered, and therefore, any differences on O can, with an acceptable degree of probability, be attributed to the presumed cause.

Also illustrated in Figure 12.3 is the pretest-posttest equivalent groups design. As is evident, this design differs from the posttest-only design in that the dependent variable is observed prior to the manipulation as well as after it. The pretest-posttest design is particularly useful when naturally occurring variability in the dependent variable is high. In such cases, some portion of variability at the second observation might be attributable to the causal factor; however, this effect might be difficult to detect in the presence

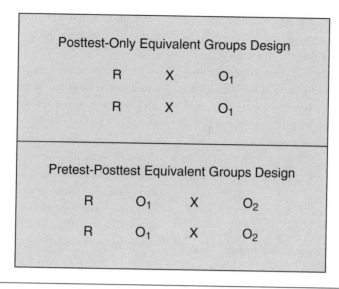

Figure 12.3   Basic Between-Subjects Experimental Designs (R = Randomized,
O = Observation, X = Manipulation)

of variability attributable to other sources. By including an assessment of the dependent variable prior to the introduction of the causal factor, it is possible to statistically partition pre-existing variability from variability attributable to the causal factor.

A feature of the pretest-posttest design worth noting is that it includes a within-subjects as well as a between-subjects factor. In this case, the within-subjects factor might be labeled *time,* and any effect for this factor, particularly for the control group, would indicate naturally occurring change in the dependent variable. More generally, within-subjects factors are those for which all group members, groups, or interacting groups are exposed to all levels of the factor. Randomization is not a concern for within-subjects factors because equivalence is achieved by observing the same people or groups at each level of the variables. In some instances, equivalence can be compromised by the effects of having been exposed to prior levels of the within-subjects variable; however, this can be managed by systematically varying the order in which the focal entities are exposed to levels of the within-subjects factor.

It is rare for an experimental study of groups to include only a single independent variable. Moreover, it is possible, even likely, that each independent variable would have more than two levels. When two or more independent variables, between- or within-subjects, are included in a single experimental design, the variables typically are fully crossed, yielding a factorial design. In a factorial design, every combination of every level of each independent variable is represented. For instance, in the study of group values versus self-interest described earlier, both group identification and in-group strength were manipulated (Wenzel, 2001). Each variable had two levels. A virtue of manipulating both variables in a single experiment is the opportunity to consider the interactive effects of the two variables. In that particular study, the author predicted only a main effect of group identification. That is, he expected the effect of group identification to be unqualified. Nonetheless, in-group strength is a plausible qualifier, and the demonstration that it did not qualify the group identification effect strengthened the inference. More typically, multiple factors are included because one expects to find interactive effects of the factors. Although such effects are impressive when predicted in advance, interactive effects involving more than three factors, particularly when one or more factors has more than two levels, can be confusing as well as difficult to describe and explain. As such, factorial designs tend to include three or fewer factors with no more than three levels of the factors.

Data Analysis

A principle concern in the analysis of data generated by experiments on groups is the proper unit of analysis (Hoyle, Georgesen, & Webster, 2001). To illustrate the issue, consider these three examples of randomization in a study involving college students who belong to a fraternity or sorority:

1. Obtain a sample of 500 college students who belong to a Greek organization at a large public university. Randomize 250 to a treatment condition and 250 to a control condition.

2. Draw a random sample of 20 Greek organizations and obtain a sample of 25 students from each organization. Randomize 10 organizations to a treatment condition and 10 organizations to a control condition.

3. Draw a random sample of 10 universities. From each university, draw a random sample of two Greek organizations and obtain a sample of 25 students from each organization. Randomly assign five universities to the treatment condition and five universities to the control condition.

In each case, the total number of individuals participating in the study is 500, and half are assigned to each condition. The key distinction is the level of randomization. In the first instance, randomization is at the individual level; in the second instance, randomization is at the fraternity/sorority level; and in the third instance, randomization is at the university level.

The issue is further complicated when we consider the fact that the unit of observation can vary without regard for the unit of randomization. For instance, in all three cases, the unit of observation could be the individual. Alternatively, the unit of observation could correspond to the unit of randomization. That is, the dependent variable would refer to individuals in the first case, organizations in the second case, and universities in the third. Complications arise when the unit of observation, which presumably is the level at which inferences are drawn, does not match the unit of randomization, which, in the strict sense, is the level at which inferences can appropriately be drawn (Murray, 1998).

The crux of the problem is the statistical nonindependence of data when the unit of observation is at a lower level than the unit of randomization. For instance, assume we have randomized according to the second scenario described earlier: We sample 25 students from each of 20 Greek organizations, 10 of which we randomize to either a treatment or control condition. Our interest is cohesiveness of the organization. We assess cohesiveness by gathering data on perceived cohesion from each of the 500 individuals. In this case, the unit of randomization is the organization, and the unit of observation is the individual. The unit of observation is nested within the unit of randomization, and therefore, there is potential nonindependence of observations.

Nonindependence refers to the fact that when observations are nested within a family, group, or organization, or share an experience they do not share with all observations, there is a measure of redundancy in the information they provide on the dependent variable. As such, although each observation is allocated a full degree of freedom in the analysis, its contribution to variability on the dependent variable probably does not warrant it. Thus, any analysis that allocates each observation a full degree of freedom will be in error. The magnitude of the error will be commensurate with the degree of redundancy in information provided by members of the same nesting group.

What forces contribute to redundancy in the information provided by units of observation that are nested? In the example provided earlier, in which individuals were nested in organization, it is relatively easy to see that the common experience of belonging to a fraternity or sorority with a person pervades the assessment of any variable relevant to that experience. More formally, Kenny and Judd (1986) describe three potential sources of nonindependence among nested observations. *Compositional effects* result when individuals are nonrandomly sorted into groups. For instance, we might expect that individuals who join a particular sorority share characteristics reflective of their common interest in the particular sorority they have chosen to join. *Common fate* arises when members of a group share a context or environment. For instance, members of a sorority often live together. Sometimes, individuals share a common fate without ever encountering each other. For instance, in a study of psychotherapy outcomes, 100 individuals might receive care from one of 10 therapists. Individuals who see the same therapist share a potential causal influence they do not share with other individuals in the sample. Finally, nonindependence might arise in the presence of *mutual influence.* In the simplest case, mutual influence occurs when nested individuals interact directly with each other, as they might if they belong to the same sorority (but not if they are receiving individual psychotherapy from the same therapist). These sources of nonindependence are illustrated in Figure 12.4. The three diagrams refer to the relation between any two observations, *i* and *j,* in a nested design. In the top panel, the association is assumed to be not causal, but rather a by-product of the individuals' (self-)selection to the group. In the middle and bottom panels, the relation is causal. In the common fate situation, information about the individuals covaries because they are exposed to a common causal agent, *C,* that

affects all members of the group; e_i and e_j refer to variability not attributable to the common cause. In the mutual influence situation, group members *i* and *j* have direct interaction with each other, interaction they do not have with individuals in other groups, which gives rise to nonindependence of the information each contributes to the analysis.

The extent of nonindependence among nested observations can be estimated using the intraclass correlation coefficient. If the coefficient is, in effect, 0 (as indicated by a nonsignificant value using a criterion of $p > .25$), then analyses can proceed using standard statistical procedures even when units of observation are nested within units of randomization. When the coefficient differs from 0, standard statistical procedures will not provide valid tests of hypotheses. In such cases, researchers must choose a data-analytic strategy that deals explicitly with statistical nonindependence.

Perhaps the simplest approach is to aggregate the data at the level of observation to produce independent scores on the dependent variable at the level of randomization. For instance, in the Henningsen et al. (2004) study of group leadership and group decision making described earlier, the sample comprised 188 individuals but consistent with the unit of randomization, the analysis of variance was based on 47 data points (one per group) for each dependent variable. In the Insko et al. (1990) example of intergroup research, the 168 students who were randomized to the 3-on-3 intergroup conditions yielded only 28 data points for analyses. This aggregation strategy worked in these situations because there were sufficient numbers of groups or interacting groups to yield adequate power for hypothesis tests. Sometimes, the number of units of randomization is too small to provide adequate power, as in our example of 10 Greek organizations per condition in a two-group experiment.

Even when statistical power is not a concern, the aggregation strategy has the drawback of glossing over variability at the level of observation that might be of interest. For instance, individuals

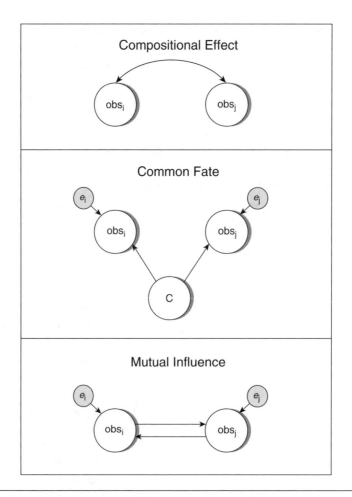

Figure 12.4   Potential Sources of Nonindependence in Nested Data

in the four-person groups in the Henningsen et al. (2004) study provided ratings of perceived cohesion, which were combined to produce a composite score on cohesion for the group. It seems unlikely that all group members evinced the same degree of perceived cohesion, and it is possible that individual characteristics in combination with the manipulated variables could explain this variability. Thus, an analytic strategy that avoids aggregating within-group and makes between-individual as well as between-group variability available for analysis would be advantageous.

Random coefficient models allow for simultaneous tests of effects at multiple levels in hierarchical data (Bryk & Raudenbush, 1992; Kreft & de Leeuw, 1998). A detailed description of these models is beyond the scope of this chapter; however, a number of informative treatments have been published and are accessible to most groups researchers (e.g., Kenny, Mannetti, Pierro, Livi, & Kashy, 2002; Nezlek & Zyzniewski, 1998). In the simplest random coefficient model for data generated by an experimental design in which the unit of observation is the individual and the unit of randomization is the group, the first step is the fitting of the individual-level data in each group to a model that includes only an intercept term and a residual. The intercepts are random coefficients (i.e., they have a variance) that correspond to the means for the groups. These coefficients are then regressed on one or more variables representing the conditions to which groups were randomized (i.e., the causal factors). It is important to note that information about nonindependence is estimated in the course of the analysis and is factored into the computation of test statistics.

Summary and Conclusions

The experimental method is the strategy of choice when the goal of research on groups is to document causal relations. The unique strengths of experimental designs are the control they afford over variability in presumed causes and the isolation they provide of presumed causes from extraneous factors that might otherwise be considered alternative explanations for the cause-effect relation. These features, control and isolation, are realized through the three essential elements of experimental designs: manipulation, randomization, and one or more control conditions. These elements allow the researcher to fulfill the three criteria for drawing a causal inference: (a) the cause and effect are associated, (b) the direction of influence runs from the cause to the effect, and (c) the cause has been isolated from plausible alternative explanations for the association. Manipulation of the putative cause ensures that it is not influenced by the effect and, when experimental realism is high, increases the likelihood that an association will be observed. Randomization isolates the putative cause from characteristics that group members, groups, or interacting groups bring to the study. And strategically designed control conditions isolate the putative cause from potential confounds in the manipulation of extraneous factors in the experimental setting.

Key concerns in experimental research on groups are the units of randomization and analysis. In research on groups, randomization, data analysis, and inference can be done at one of three levels: the individual, the group, or interacting groups. In the simplest case, randomization,

analysis, and inference occur at the same level. Realistically, that is often not the case in research on groups. For instance, individuals might be randomly assigned to groups, which are then randomized to condition in a study that focuses on individuals' perceptions of out-group members, given the condition to which their group was assigned. In this case, the unit of randomization, the group, is not the same as the unit of analysis and inference, the individual. Moreover, the data provided by individuals in a given group are likely to be influenced by their interaction with fellow group members, introducing nonindependence at the individual level. Random coefficient models offer a statistically sound approach to addressing this complex set of concerns.

The experimental method is not the strategy of choice for all research on groups. For some research questions, quasi- and nonexperiments are sufficient, and because they often are less costly and raise fewer ethical concerns, they may be preferred. In some instances, although the experimental method best matches the goals of the research, an experimental design cannot be justified because it would be unethical or impractical to manipulate the putative cause, to randomize groups or group members to condition, or to withhold treatment from some participants to produce a control condition. In such cases, quasi-experimental designs that include explicit measurement of extraneous factors are a viable choice. Finally, explicit in some research questions is an interest in the behavior of individuals in natural settings under the influence of naturally occurring stimuli. When this is the case, external validity trumps internal validity, and nonexperimental designs are appropriate and recommended.

Although the basic experimental designs—posttest only and pretest-posttest—are efficient and effective for documenting simple causal relations, as typically implemented, they are not suitable for capturing the rich and dynamic aspects of group life. McGrath et al. (2000) offer two general recommendations regarding research on groups that can be incorporated into these basic experimental designs. The first concerns the nature of the association between the cause and effect. Implicit in analyses of data generated in experimental designs is the assumption of linear effects of the causal factor. This, of course, need not be the case and likely is not the case for many group processes. The classic experimental design includes only two levels of the causal factors, often a control and treatment group. This design does not allow for tests of nonlinearity. When the causal factor can be quantified, additional levels can be added and, with additional levels, increasingly complex nonlinear relations can be considered. A notable example is research inspired by Latané's (1981) theory of social impact, which explicitly predicts nonlinear effects for variables such as group size and immediacy of fellow group members.

Experimental research on groups might also be enriched by adding the element of time to the assessment of dependent variables (McGrath et al., 2000). Although the basic pretest-posttest design includes time in a rudimentary sense, this feature of the design is more for control than for conceptual interest. Most applications of experimental design to the study of groups measure the dependent variable one time, almost immediately after delivery of the manipulation. Such research misses the opportunity to observe patterns of responding that may vary across individuals and groups. By tracking standing on dependent variables that are amenable to repeated assessment, researchers can model patterns of change as they unfold over time. These patterns can be explicitly modeled in random coefficient models such as those described earlier. In these applications, a level corresponding to time is added below the individual level. Thus, one might have a multilevel design in which time is nested with individual and individual is nested within group. With four or more assessments, precise predictions regarding the pattern of change on the dependent variable can be tested.

In conclusion, experimental designs are uniquely suited to research on groups when the objective is to document a causal relation between individual or group outcomes and one or more characteristics of groups, group members, interacting groups, or the settings within which groups function. Experimental designs afford high internal validity and, when conducted in natural settings, can evince reasonable external validity as well. The increasing accessibility of statistical methods such as random coefficient growth curve models has increased the appeal of the experimental method for groups researchers, particularly when the research involves individuals interacting in intact groups. As groups researchers become more familiar and comfortable with these methods, experimental research on groups will become more sophisticated, persuasive, and appealing.

References

Bond, C. F., Jr., & Kenny, D. A. (2002). The triangle of interpersonal models. *Journal of Personality and Social Psychology, 83,* 355–366.

Brewer, M. B. (2000). Research design and issues of validity. In H. T. Reis & C. M. Judd (Eds.), *Handbook of research methods in social and personality psychology* (pp. 3–16). New York: Cambridge University Press.

Bryk, A. S., & Raudenbush, S. W. (1992). *Hierarchical linear models: Applications and data analysis methods.* Thousand Oaks, CA: Sage.

Campbell, D. T., & Stanley, J. C. (1963). *Experimental and quasi-experimental designs for research.* Chicago: Rand McNally.

Cook, T. D., & Campbell, D. T. (1979). *Quasi-experimentation: Design and analysis for field settings.* Chicago: Rand McNally.

Haslam, S. A., & McGarty, C. (2000). Experimental design and causality in social psychological research. In C. Sansone, C. C. Morf, & A. T. Panter (Eds.), *Handbook of methods in social psychology* (pp. 237–264). Thousand Oaks, CA: Sage.

Henningsen, D. D., Henningsen, M. L. M., Jakobsen, L., & Borton, I. (2004). It's good to be a leader: The influence of randomly and systematically selected leaders on decision-making groups. *Group Dynamics: Theory, Research, and Practice, 8,* 62–76.

Hoyle, R. H., & Crawford, A. M. (1994). Use of individual-level data to study group phenomena: Issues and strategies. *Small Group Research, 25,* 464–485.

Hoyle, R. H., Georgesen, J. C., & Webster, J. M. (2001). Analyzing data from individuals in groups: The past, the present, and the future. *Group Dynamics: Theory, Research, and Practice, 5,* 41–47.

Hoyle, R. H., & Robinson, J. I. (2003). Mediated and moderated effects in social psychological research: Measurement, design, and analysis issues. In C. Sansone, C. Morf, & A. T. Panter (Eds.), *Sage handbook of methods in social psychology* (pp. 213–233). Thousand Oaks, CA: Sage.

Insko, C. A., Schopler, J., Hoyle, R. H., Dardis, G. J., & Graetz, K. A. (1990). Individual-group discontinuity as a function of fear and greed. *Journal of Personality and Social Psychology, 58,* 68–79.

Kenny, D. A., & Judd, C. M. (1986). Consequences of violating the independence assumption in analysis of variance. *Psychological Bulletin, 99,* 422–431.

Kenny, D. A., Mannetti, L., Pierro, A., Livi, S., & Kashy, D. A. (2002). The statistical analysis of data from small groups. *Journal of Personality and Social Psychology, 83*(1), 126–137.

Kreft, I. G. G., & de Leeuw, J. (1998). *Introducing multilevel modeling.* Thousand Oaks, CA: Sage.

Latané, B. (1981). The psychology of social impact. *American Psychologist, 36,* 343–356.

Levine, J. M., & Moreland, R. L. (1998). Small groups. In D. Gilbert, S. Fiske, & G. Lindzey (Eds.), *The handbook of social psychology* (Vol. 2, pp. 415–469). New York: McGraw-Hill.

Månson, P. (1993). What is a group? A multilevel analysis. In E. J. Lawler & B. Markousky (Eds.), *Advances in group process* (Vol. 10, pp. 253–281). Greenwich, CT: JAI Press.

McGrath, J. E., Arrow, H., & Berdahl, J. L. (2000). The study of groups: Past, present, and future. *Personality and Social Psychology Review, 4,* 95–105.

Moreland, R. L., Hogg, M. A., & Hains, S. C. (1994). Back to the future: Social psychological research on groups. *Journal of Experimental Social Psychology, 30,* 527–555.

Mullen, B., & Copper, C. (1994). The relation between group cohesiveness and performance: An integration. *Psychological Bulletin, 115,* 210–227.

Murray, D. M. (1998). *Design and analysis of group-randomized trials.* New York: Oxford University Press.

Nezlek, J. B., & Zyzniewski, L. E. (1998). Using hierarchical linear modeling to analyze grouped data. *Group Dynamics: Theory, Research, and Practice, 2,* 313–320.

Trochim, W. M. (2000). *The research methods knowledge base* (2nd ed.). Retrieved May 6, 2004, from Research Methods Knowledge Base Web site: http://trochim.human.cornell.edu/kb/index.htm

Wenzel, M. (2001). What is social about justice? Inclusive identity and group values as the basis of the justice motive. *Journal of Experimental Social Psychology, 38,* 205–218.

13

Field Studies

A Focus on Group Research

Maria T. Riva

Maximillian Wachtel

This chapter will focus on methodological and functional considerations of conducting group research in field settings. It will primarily concentrate on research that investigates small groups and small group phenomena rather than discussing research on large group interactions. The emphasis also will be broad based and multidisciplinary, including group field studies that cut across several different but related disciplines, such as social psychology, social work, business, human communication, and counseling.

In many ways, this chapter can be seen as a logical extension of the material presented in Chapter 12 that discusses experimental group research (Hoyle, this volume). In experimental designs, control of the independent, dependent, and extraneous variables is expected and generally more easily attainable because the laboratory environment where these experiments are typically conducted is more predictable. The naturalistic environment as a setting for research poses myriad problems compared with research designs conducted in the laboratory, yet it also has its advantages. Field studies can use what is known from these well-controlled experimental designs and test them out in more naturalistic settings to determine if the group processes and positive findings are applicable to real-world groups.

This chapter will review studies that investigate group phenomena in field settings where some control is possible, yet many other variables are left to operate as they typically do. Field studies encompass a variety of different research methodologies, although the common denominator relates to the *field*, defined as the environment where the behavior naturally occurs (e.g., in neighborhoods, work sites, schools, psychotherapy clinics).

Because various research methodologies are used to conduct group field studies, a somewhat arbitrary categorization system is used to organize this chapter. The chapter subdivides designs that predominately use the following methods: (a) observation, (b) survey and interview, and (c) intervention. Each of these three sections will include a definition, strengths, and limitations. Throughout the chapter, examples of group field studies will be used to underscore the presented material. This chapter then concludes with recommendations for conducting field studies on group processes.

In Search of a Definition

Field studies have been defined in various ways by both qualitative and quantitative researchers. Speaking specifically about qualitative field research, Neuman and Kreuger (2003) stated that "it is difficult to pin down a specific definition of field research because it is more of an orientation toward research than a fixed set of techniques to apply" (p. 361). Cherry (2000) defined a field study as "the process of collecting and analyzing detailed and descriptive observations of individuals and groups in a given setting" (p. 333). Cherry underscores the astute observations required for some types of field studies, particularly those that observe groups of people often without their knowledge that they are being observed. These studies usually are conducted in public places such as playgrounds, parks, grocery stores, and city streets.

Kantowitz, Roediger, and Elmes (1997) said,

Rather than attempting to bring some phenomenon into the laboratory for study in a controlled setting, the researcher instead attempts to introduce enough control into a setting (in "the field") to allow inferences to be made about how variations in the independent variable affect a dependent variable. (p. 410)

This definition points to field studies where some intervention is introduced by the experimenter. The most typical research design fitting this description is a quasi-experimental one when random assignment is not possible due to the study of already existing groups (e.g., students in a classroom, already assigned business teams). Data collection may be obtained through such means as observation, standardized assessment measures and surveys, reports from other people in the participants' environment (e.g., supervisor, family member, teacher), or physiological measures.

Other views of field research include interactions between the researcher and participants, typically using one or more interviews. Interview methods often are used to learn more about situations that may not be location-specific, such as studies of people's reactions to working for a female CEO or social interaction networks for children who are homeschooled. Given the time requirements of interviews for both researcher and interviewee, these studies are often qualitative. They study group phenomena in considerable depth with a few participants. All of these methods can be considered group field research as long as they are conducted in a naturalistic setting or attempt to gather information about group behavior that occurs in a naturalistic setting.

Observational Methods

Neuman and Kreuger (2003) suggested that "field research is appropriate when the research question involves learning about, understanding, or describing a group of interacting people" (p. 357). They believe it is best used when investigating how people accomplish a specific behavior in the social world, or what life is like for a person or a group of people. These authors and many others see the interactive life of people as one of the primary emphases of field research. The study of group interactions and interpersonal relationships is a pivotal feature across many different disciplines that are curious about group attitudes and behaviors (e.g., human communications, social psychology, group psychology, social work, etc.). Observing people as they go about their daily lives has been an important avenue in obtaining information about how groups of people function.

Many studies on bystander interventions, for example, were spurred by the 1964 New York stabbing and rape of Kitty Genovese. Ms. Genovese managed to scare off the attacker by her screams for help, yet the attacker returned when no one came to her aid. She was raped and stabbed repeatedly, and none of the more than 38 witnesses called police until the attacker fled the scene. This is one area where observations in the naturalistic environment were then tested out in the laboratory (Latané & Darley, 1970). Results of later studies (e.g., Darley & Latané, 1968) have shown that it may not be the personality characteristics of the people witnessing the incident that make the difference in whether they choose to intervene but rather the number of observers present. The larger the number of witnesses, the less likely it is that individuals will respond.

Harkins and Latané (1998) found a similar result when social impact analysis was used to study voter responsibility. One finding of this study was that voting in local political elections decreased as the size of the town increased. These findings have implications for many types of groups, as size seems to be one potent variable in how and if group members will respond.

Field studies that rely on observation have been conducted in many settings to illuminate the interactions and reactions of the people who inhabit them. Neuman and Kreuger (2003) identified numerous group field studies. These authors state that studies have been conducted in a wide array of settings (laundromats, retirement communities, waiting rooms, women's shelters, etc.), whereas many other studies have looked at such areas as children's social behavior, different occupations, and deviant behavior.

Limitations of Observational Field Studies

Field studies in naturalistic settings are by definition fraught with challenges, which often play out in the inability to control (or even predict) the environment. In experimental studies, participants are typically selected for certain characteristics, interventions are carefully designed and implemented, multiple assessment measures are used to gain information, and a laboratory or insulated setting is used to decrease distractions. In field studies where observation is the primary method, none of these types of controls are possible or even desired. The goal is to gather information about how groups respond in these settings when there is *no* intervention or intrusion by the researcher.

There are several complexities in conducting observational studies of groups. Field researchers need to be careful observers of phenomena. This necessitates that the observer captures as closely as possible the true phenomenon under study. Without this careful attention to detail, the researcher may observe some anomaly in the group process. This could happen if the observations are stopped before the group process is sufficiently developed or if something obstructs the researchers' view of an important interaction. The investigator also needs to be flexible during the observation process because there is no way to know what will happen as phenomena unfold in the natural environment. Researchers also will need to be aware of the biases they bring to their observations, which unchecked can distort what the observer perceives.

Another potential limitation is whether it is ethical to study people when they are unaware that they are being observed. Often, it is impossible or impractical to obtain consent from participants. For example, in studies of behavior in crowded facilities, there are often large groups of people who would need to give permission. Obtaining consent from all of them would be prohibitively difficult if not impossible. Thus, consent is often waived when "public behavior" is being observed, individual people are not identifiable from the data, and people are not placed at any risk from being observed. Ethical decisions about what constitutes "public" settings may become more blurred in the future as technology has now made it possible to observe and take pictures of people in restrooms and other private places.

Strengths of Observational Field Studies

Studying people unobtrusively in their natural environment captures a more accurate picture of how people actually interact and behave. It has long been known that people behave differently when they know that someone is watching. Therefore, carefully documenting behavior under realistic situations can provide firsthand information, which does not need to be inferred from using less direct methods such as self-report instruments. For example, observing customers' responses to a new store opening where special prizes are given to the first 25 customers is very different than asking respondents to think about how they would act in this situation.

Not needing to ask research participants to consent to be in a study can also be an advantage. Besides the difficulties of obtaining consent in naturalistic settings, a problem with obtaining consent is that members then know that they are in a study or are being observed. If research participants are aware that they are being observed, they may act differently than they would otherwise. Participants may tend to act in ways that are thought to be socially desirable rather than demonstrate the way they would actually behave if unobserved.

Observational field studies are important mechanisms for obtaining information about group interactions and individual responses to groups. Field research has provided substantial contributions about how groups of people and cultures function in their everyday lives and how they respond to circumstances that occur to them and to people in their environment. Most

studies are qualitative, and several journals and excellent books are available on field studies that observe group dynamics.

Group Field Studies Using Surveys

Many investigations do not include an intervention or manipulate some variable but rather study the relationship between variables that occur within the group environment or consider how certain variables operate at different times during the process of the group. There are many examples of field studies that have used surveys to learn about particular group dynamics. They are generally self-report and allow researchers to compare members based on demographic (e.g., gender, age, culture) or group variables (e.g., group status, group cohesion). Many of these field studies look at work groups in large and small business organizations. Using a survey instrument is an effective way to gain information from a large sample, and respondents can discuss their perceptions of their own and other members' group behavior.

In a recent study where data were collected from a manager rather than by self-report, Liden, Wayne, Jaworski, and Bennett (2004) examined the concept of social loafing in groups. These researchers looked at 23 different work groups with a total of 168 participants from two different organizations. In each of the work groups, all members worked in the same physical location and interacted with each other daily to complete their job requirements. Managers of the work groups completed a series of measures for each individual and for the group. The researchers examined what factors, both at the individual and group levels, would increase the likelihood that social loafing would occur. Of the group factors, increased group size and decreased levels of cohesion were related to increases in social loafing.

In another example using both interviews and questionnaires to obtain information, Sarin and McDermott (2003) investigated the effect of team leader characteristics on various measures of performance for new product development teams. The study looked at a multitude of team leader variables and measures of performance for the product development teams. In the first phase of the two-phase investigation, the researchers conducted qualitative interviews of 26 team leaders from nine different organizations. These interviews lasted from 45 to 60 minutes. In Phase 2, surveys were given to 246 participants from a total of 64 different teams. These teams ranged in size from 3 to 22 teammates. Samples were gathered over a 2-year period from six different organizations. Findings suggested that team learning had a positive effect on new product development, and initiation of structured goals by the team leader helped to encourage democratic leadership.

Limitations of Survey Data

Information obtained via survey is only as good as the survey questions. Item development is complicated, and many iterations may be needed to eliminate confusing questions. If possible, a pilot study is always recommended. One disadvantage is related to missing data, which often cannot be restored, particularly if the surveys are anonymous or the event that is being studied has been completed. Another limitation is that the data are more indirect than observations, and they are based on self-report, which can differ depending on when the survey is given (e.g., the length of time after the end of the group phenomenon being studied). Another possibility, for example, is that the work group is in progress during the collection of data. Many studies rely on only one data point to capture the complexities of group behavior. The decision then is to decide at what period of the group's progress information should be obtained.

Strengths of Using Surveys

Using surveys as the primary source of data in the field has several advantages. Surveys can be anonymous, and therefore, information about private, illegal, or embarrassing behavior can be obtained more easily than in studies where the participants can be identified by the researcher. Large samples are often possible, and the length of participation time is often short.

This is not to suggest that surveys or questionnaires are easy to administer and do not need considerable planning and organization, an error made by many graduate students. For example, Myers, Feltz, and Short (2004) examined the relationship between collective efficacy and team performance for 10 different universities competing in Division III football. Participants included 197 intercollegiate offensive football players, who were asked to complete questionnaires prior to eight consecutive games, usually completing the questionnaire at the final practice before the game. In this study, the head coaches explained the study to the teams, requiring interactions between researchers and head coaches so that information was given accurately and the players would be motivated to give consent and to participate. On each team, a trainer administered the questionnaires, again requiring considerable collaboration and organization, especially because the questionnaires had to be completed in a time-specific manner.

Group Field Studies Using an Intervention

This section describes research in the field when there is some type of intervention or manipulation by the researcher. One question regularly asked is whether methods that are applied in a controlled setting have the same effect on participants when the controls are less stringent. Many times, this type of research applies models, theories, and techniques to field settings that were tested first in laboratory studies. For example, using an example from group psychotherapy, one might ask whether manualized group psychotherapy (sequenced outline of therapeutic processes and procedures of a specific length) is as effective when conducted in mental health centers as it is in laboratory studies.

Seligman (1996) pointed to two methods that are used to study psychotherapy outcomes. One method, "the *efficacy* method," tests manualized treatments that include specific types of clients, for a specific number of sessions. The advantages of this method are related to controlling extraneous variables, although the type of therapy that is studied only minimally resembles psychotherapy as it is delivered in the field, resulting in serious problems with generalizability to actual practice. The other method, "the *effectiveness* method," investigates the effectiveness of psychotherapy as it is actually practiced. These studies have less control over extraneous variables and are harder to conduct, yet they are much more consistent with the manner in which psychotherapy is actually delivered. Both types of research are important, although Seligman stated that "the efficacy study is the wrong method for empirically validating psychotherapy as it is actually done, because it omits too many crucial elements of what is done in the field" (p. 1075).

In one effectiveness study, Ogrodniczuk and Piper (2003) examined how group climate affected the outcome of two different types of short-term group psychotherapy in a research study of groups conducted at a public treatment clinic affiliated with a university hospital. They recruited participants for 16 groups with participants receiving either interpretive or supportive brief group therapy. Group climate was measured with a standardized self-report questionnaire, and outcome was measured using self-report assessment instruments specific to the field of grief therapy—the common individual stressor among the 107 research participants. Using a variety of statistical procedures, the researchers found that engagement in the group was related to positive group outcome.

Numerous disciplines and settings use a wide variety of groups to disseminate information, improve decision making, obtain information about effective leadership, and help people change their behaviors and thoughts. Although it is extremely important to determine whether a treatment or group method is internally valid by testing it in a controlled situation, research is also needed in real-world settings. Shaw (1976) stated that "the field approach represents the best compromise between the need to control significant variables and the desire to extend findings to everyday events and situations" (p. 39). An example is a study conducted by North, Tarrant, and Hargreaves (2004). The study examined the effects of music on helping behavior in 646 users of a university gym. During their workout, participants listened to either uplifting or annoying music and then were asked to participate in either a low-cost task (signing a petition) or a high-cost task (distributing leaflets).

Limitations of Intervention Studies

By continuing the example of comparing group psychotherapy laboratory (efficacy) studies with those in the field (effectiveness), the differences between the two become apparent, along with the potential sources of error variance in applied research. Studies in applied settings have group leaders with widely different levels of experience and training, who see clients of various ages, who come from diverse cultural and lifestyle backgrounds and have wide variability in levels of severity, motivation, psychological mindedness, expectations about group psychotherapy, and ability to interact with and tolerate others.

Group leaders rarely use only one theoretical orientation. They have clients who often do not meet a specific diagnostic category in the *Diagnostic and Statistical Manual of Mental Disorders* (*DSM-IV;* American Psychiatric Association, 1994), or who meet more than one. Group facilitators have clients who drop out of treatment, who do not come to all sessions, and who may not be exclusively in group psychotherapy. Clients may also attend individual sessions, see their minister, or attend a support group. From a methodological perspective, group leaders may not have enough clients in the research groups with adequate membership, and random assignment to group treatment may be unethical due to the severity of the client's problem. Of course, many of these situations can be controlled, yet the more control that is instituted, the less likely that the group's membership resembles the population of clients in treatment.

Another obstacle is that the current training in conducting research often emphasizes the superiority of experimental design, random assignment, careful group member selection, and reduction of error variance by eliminating or controlling extraneous variables. Many researchers are better equipped to conduct efficacy studies than effectiveness studies, and funding agencies typically prefer well-controlled studies. It is important to stress here that this chapter does not espouse any method or research design over all others but rather argues that the questions being studied should drive the research design and the data collection methods used. In fact, Forsyth (1993) and several others stress the importance of both basic and applied research.

Another hurdle relates to collaborating with a field site or multiple field sites and coordinating the data collection. An example may help to illuminate the intricacies of conducting field research. Layne et al. (2001) evaluated a manualized trauma/grief-focused psychotherapy group for 55 war-traumatized adolescents from 10 Bosnian schools. This is an excellent example of the collaboration required to conduct field research. Staff from UNICEF, universities in several countries, and secondary school personnel in Bosnia worked together to make this field study possible.

Strengths of Intervention Studies

Some of the advantages of research in the field are obvious. "The focus of small group research is moving in a direction that considers not only the results found in the lab but also the growing amount of literature studying groups in real and dynamic settings" (Stasson, Markus, & Hart, 1999, p. 315). Numerous group studies have been conducted in applied settings with people who live and work in that environment rather than with undergraduate students. As an example, in a meta-analysis of group psychotherapy research with children and adolescents, Hoag and Burlingame (1997) found that almost 74% of the 56 studies included were conducted in school settings, while another 14% were located in outpatient and inpatient clinics. Schools are common sites for group research on social skills, disruptive behavior, and adjustment to divorce (Riva & Haub, 2004). School systems and school personnel have also been the subject of studies concerning their responses to bullying, student suicide, and incidents of prejudice.

Increased generalizability is one positive aspect of intervention studies. Discussing group psychotherapy, for example, Garcia and Weisz (2002) stated that "clinical practice contexts may lack some of the methodological precision that is possible in research clinics, but it offers superior external validity" (p. 442). Ultimately, practitioners are looking for what works with their clients, employees, or students and not what is effective with a specially chosen group of people who do not represent the variability of the people working in or coming to their site. One caveat, however, is that making generalizations to sites that are not similar to those studied is problematic in much the same way as assuming that laboratory studies can be generalized to the field. Weisz, Donenberg, Han, and Weiss (1995), distinguishing between laboratory studies and research conducted in clinics with children and adolescents, suggested that laboratory clients are recruited, have less severe problems, and receive quicker treatment compared with the longer term treatment used in psychotherapy clinics. These same considerations are true for school field settings versus clinic field settings. School group members are typically recruited or recommended by teachers and have less severe behavior problems, and group treatment tends to be more often cognitive behavioral, highly structured, and brief. These characteristics suggest that generalizing from school to clinic settings is unwarranted.

Applied settings where group research is conducted vary widely. Some examples include health clubs (North et al., 2004), psychiatric treatment clinics (e.g., Piper, Ogrodniczuk, McCallum, Joyce, & Rosie, 2003), rugby teams (Beauchamp, Bray, Eys, & Carron, 2002), support groups for cancer patients (Lieberman & Golant, 2002), and corporate and government work groups (Bliese, 1998; Kuhn & Poole, 2000). Conducting research in applied settings provides both opportunities and challenges. One of the opportunities involves increased collaboration. Done well, studies in the field should result in increased collaboration among the many agencies, personnel, and disciplines that make up or interact with the groups to be studied.

In a special issue of the *Journal for Specialists in Group Work* titled "Group Research: Encouraging a Collaboration Between Practitioners and Researchers," Riva and Smith (1997) discussed the need for additional collaboration and communication between researchers and practitioners when conducting group studies in field settings. They stated, "One obstacle is that much of the expertise of group practitioners goes unrecognized and is not incorporated into research questions" (p. 266). In a separate article, Riva and Kalodner (1997) stated, "Practitioners have astute ideas about what works in groups. Often these ideas come directly from group leaders' observations of group phenomena—ideas that are ripe for research attention" (p. 226). Collaboration between researchers and practitioners would be especially helpful for those researchers who study groups but may have little experience leading them.

Collaboration can come in different forms, both on a small and large scale. Some major group research projects have included multiple field sites across the United States. Another area where collaboration needs to increase is across disciplines. There are several disciplines—social psychology, counseling, sociology, social work, business, anthropology, and family systems—that look at different (and at times similar) aspects of group dynamics.

> Important findings in one field are often unknown to another, and few multidisciplinary research projects are conducted. Future research will benefit not only from collaboration between research and practice, but from an association with other related fields, so that salient findings do not occur in a vacuum. (Riva & Smith, 1997, p. 267)

Recommendations for Conducting Group Research in the Field

1. Start with a theory. Applied research questions will be much more valuable to the field if they have a theoretical foundation.

2. Appreciate that group researchers come from many disciplines; incorporating theories and findings from other areas will strengthen the research base.

3. If you are going into a field site where you have no affiliation, be careful to collaborate with those who work in that site. Often, site personnel see researchers as people who use field sites for their own research endeavors without the site seeing any benefits.

4. Although the chapter discussed qualitative and quantitative methods as if they are mutually exclusive, consider mixed designs that combine intervention, observation, and interview methods.

5. Although the complexities of conducting group research in the field can be considered "noise" or error variance, they can also be seen as the dynamic and richness of conducting group research.

6. Few studies have focused on cultural diversity and its effect on group dynamics. Many

groups are composed of people who come from vastly different cultures, who speak various languages, and who see the benefits of groups from alternate perspectives. This seems to be an important area for future research.

7. Group field studies, like all other types of research, should be self-correcting. Therefore, one cannot rely on a single study to provide a definitive answer. Replication is also necessary in group field studies.

Conclusion

Field research and research in the field are two essential methods of obtaining information about how groups function. Some studies of group phenomena have been conducted with undergraduate psychology majors; yet, an increasing number of studies have investigated group dynamics in the field. Group research, even in laboratory settings, is complex and more difficult than studying individual behavior. Added to these complications are the logistics of studying groups in naturalistic environments. Without these types of studies, much of the richness of group phenomena may be lost or diluted. Discussing the study of groups, Worchel (1994) stated, "careful descriptions of events provide valuable data for understanding human behavior and developing new hypotheses and predictions" (p. 218). Worchel also suggested that groups are complex and dynamic and that group research should not represent just a snapshot. Instead, it should be more like a feature film that captures the life of the group as it unfolds. Although research in the field can present numerous challenges, understanding the vitality of groups as they actually unfold and are experienced by group members is an essential goal for group researchers.

References

American Psychiatric Association. (1994). *Diagnostic and statistical manual of mental disorders* (4th ed.). Washington, DC: Author.

Beauchamp, M. R., Bray, S. R., Eys, M. A., & Carron, A. V. (2002). Role ambiguity, role efficacy, and role performance: Multidimensional and mediational relationships within interdependent sports teams. *Group Dynamics: Theory, Research and Practice, 6,* 229–242.

Bliese, P. D. (1998). Group consensus and psychological well-being: A large field study. *Journal of Applied Social Psychology, 28,* 563–580.

Cherry, A. L. (2000). *A research primer for the helping profession.* Belmont, CA: Wadsworth/Thomson Learning.

Darley, J. M., & Latané, B. (1968). Bystander intervention in emergencies: Diffusion of responsibility. *Journal of Personality and Social Psychology, 8,* 377–383.

Forsyth, D. R. (1993). Building a bridge between basic social psychology and the study of mental health. *Contemporary Psychology, 38,* 931–932.

Garcia, J. A., & Weisz, J. R. (2002). When youth mental health care stops: Therapeutic relationship problems and other reasons for ending youth outpatient treatment. *Journal of Consulting and Clinical Psychology, 70,* 439–443.

Harkins, S., & Latané, B. (1998). Population and political participation: A social impact analysis of voter responsibility. *Group Dynamics: Theory, Research, and Practice, 2,* 192–207.

Hoag, M. M., & Burlingame, G. M. (1997). Evaluating the effectiveness of child and adolescent group treatment: A meta-analytic review. *Journal of Clinical Child Psychology, 26,* 234–246.

Kantowitz, B. H., Roediger, H. L., III, & Elmes, D. G. (1997). *Experimental psychology* (6th ed.). St. Paul, MN: West.

Kuhn, T., & Poole, M. S. (2000). Do conflict management styles affect group decision making? Evidence from a longitudinal field study. *Human Communication Research, 26,* 558–590.

Latané, B., & Darley, J. M. (1970). *The unresponsive bystander: Why doesn't he help?* New York: Appleton-Century-Crofts.

Layne, C. M., Pynoos, R. S., Saltzman, W. R., Arslanagic, B., Black, M., Savjak, N., et al. (2001). Trauma/grief-focused group psychotherapy: School-based postwar intervention with traumatized Bosnian adolescents. *Group Dynamics: Theory, Research, and Practice, 5,* 277–290.

Liden, R. C., Wayne, S. J., Jaworski, R. A., & Bennett, N. (2004). Social loafing: A field investigation. *Journal of Management, 30,* 285–304.

Lieberman, M. A., & Golant, M. (2002). Leader behaviors as perceived by cancer patients in professionally directed support groups and outcomes. *Group Dynamics: Theory, Research, and Practice, 6,* 267–276.

Myers, N. D., Feltz, D. L., & Short, S. E. (2004). Collective efficacy and team performance: A longitudinal study of collegiate football teams. *Group Dynamics: Theory, Research, and Practice, 8,* 126–138.

Neuman, L. W., & Kreuger, L. W. (2003). *Social work research methods: Qualitative and quantitative approaches.* Boston: Allyn & Bacon.

North, A. C., Tarrant, M., & Hargreaves, J. J. (2004). The effects of music on helping behavior: A field study. *Environment & Behavior, 36,* 266–275.

Ogrodniczuk, J. S., & Piper, W. E. (2003). The effect of group climate on outcome in two forms of short-term therapy. *Group Dynamics: Theory, Research and Practice, 7,* 64–76.

Piper, W. E., Ogrodniczuk, J. S., McCallum, M., Joyce, A. S., & Rosie, J. S. (2003). Expression of affect as a mediator of the relationship between quality of object relations and group therapy outcome for patients with complicated grief. *Journal of Consulting and Clinical Psychology, 71,* 664–771.

Riva, M. T., & Haub, A. (2004). Group counseling in the schools. In J. DeLucia-Waack, D. Gerrity, C. Kalodner, & M. T. Riva (Eds.), *Handbook of group counseling and psychotherapy* (pp. 309). Thousand Oaks, CA: Sage.

Riva, M. T., & Kalodner, C. R. (1997). Group research: Encouraging a collaboration between practitioners and researchers. *Journal for Specialists in Group Work, 22,* 226–227.

Riva, M. T., & Smith, R. D. (1997). Looking into the future of group research: Where do we go from here? *Journal for Specialists of Group Work, 22,* 266–276.

Sarin, S., & McDermott, C. (2003). The effect of team leader characteristics on learning, knowledge application, and performance of cross-functional new product development teams. *Decision Sciences, 34,* 707–739.

Seligman, M. E. P. (1996). Science as an ally of practice. *American Psychologist, 51,* 1074–1079.

Shaw, M. E. (1976). *Group dynamics: The psychology of small group behavior.* New York: McGraw-Hill.

Stasson, M. F., Markus, M. J., & Hart, J. W. (1999). Theory and research on small groups [Book review]. *Group Dynamics: Theory, Research, and Practice, 3,* 313–316.

Weisz, J., Donenberg, G., Han, S., & Weiss, B. (1995). Bridging the gap between lab and clinic in child and adolescent psychotherapy. *Journal of Consulting and Clinical Psychology, 63,* 688–701.

Worchel, S. (1994). You can go home again: Returning group research to the group context with an eye on developmental issues. *Small Group Research, 25,* 205–223.

14

Nonlinear Methods
for the Social Sciences

Stephen J. Guastello

Theories concerning attractors, bifurcations, chaos, fractals, and self-organization need to be tested eventually. Although the literature on nonlinear methods is vast, most of it has been written for applications that do not share the concerns or intellectual traditions of the social sciences, especially when short time series are concerned. This chapter is thus written for researchers who have a basic understanding of dynamical concepts and who want to test hypotheses concerning them in social psychological research, particularly for problems in group dynamics.

Fortunately, knowledge has evolved to a point where some important connections between fractal dimensions, Lyapunov exponents, chaos and other dynamics, Shannon information and entropy, catastrophes, and self-organization are now understood. These relationships can be exploited to produce a concise set of analytic tools that can be used with available software and

with sufficient flexibility. Sprott (2003), Heath (2000), and Puu (2000) nonetheless serve as valuable supplementary resources on dynamics and time series analysis.

The following section of this chapter describes commonly used graphic techniques for nonlinear analysis. Next, I present some important relationships among dynamical constructs that give rise to useful statistical analysis. The statistical theory encompasses hypothesis construction, measurement theory, and two series of structural models that have wide flexibility; they involve continuously valued variables. The last section of this chapter describes analyses for nominally coded system states that are also changing in a time series.

Because the concentration of this chapter is on the analysis of real data, simulation techniques are not included here. Conceptual issues and relevant techniques for nonlinear analysis can be found in Elliott and Kiel (2004), Epstein and Axtell (1996), and Wolfram (2002). Chapter 16 of this volume, by Nielsen, Sundstrom, & Halfhill is devoted to simulation techniques for group research.

Graphic Techniques

Phase Portraits

The graphic of the control points' paths in the neighborhood of one or more attractors is called its *phase portrait*. Phase portraits can be drawn by plotting a behavior value at time *t* on the Y-axis against the value of the same behavior at time *t* − 1 on the X-axis. For more complex dynamics, the *change* in behavior from time *t* − 1 to *t* can be plotted on the Y-axis against the value of behavior differences at a previous pair of time frames (*t* − 2, *t* − 1) on the X-axis. A phase portrait of a fixed-point attractor would show trajectories moving into the center. A limit cycle would be round or elliptic.

Phase portraits need not be restricted to the one-variable case. One might then plot Y_t versus X_t, or ΔY versus ΔX. Often, however, researchers have a time series that should be projected into more than two dimensions, but exactly how many of these *embedding dimensions* are appropriate is unknown. Some work in progress uses methods based on principal components analysis for finding the most appropriate embedding dimension (Abarbanel, 1996; Abraham, 1997; Guastello & Bock, 2001). Until then, however, a convenient theorem to rely on states that all information about the dimensional complexity of a time series is contained in the time series itself. *Information* would include the embedding dimension and lag structures (Packard, Crutchfield, Farmer, & Shaw, 1980).

In the early days of applied chaos theory, some attempts were made to interpret dynamics of a real system (as opposed to a mathematically defined system) directly from an inspection of the phase portraits themselves (Kiel, 1994; Priesmeyer, 1992). The technique was quietly

abandoned when it became clear that many of the time series were far too short, as in the case of Priesmeyer's (1992) examples, to determine whether chaos or anything else was taking place. In the case of sufficiently longer time series (e.g., those in Kiel, 1994), some examples showed visual differences that could be traced to real events, but most did not. The pretty attractors such as the one shown in Figure 14.1 were seldom obtained; the phase portraits tended to look like junk. Again, noise and embedding dimension were the top two reasons for this repeated outcome. Currently, the thinking is that analytic techniques should be applied first, and phase portraits should be drawn and compared afterward, if desired. This is similar to the thinking in conventional statistical analysis, where graphs do not substitute for statistical analysis; they just amplify the findings.

Poincaré Sections

A Poincaré section is a transverse slice of an attractor. It allows the viewer to inspect the interior of an attractor that is projected in three dimensions. A Poincaré section of the Henon-Heiles attractor appears in Figure 14.1. Once again, the interpretive meaning of a Poincaré section has not evolved for the same reasons associated with phase portraits.

Recurrence Plots

A recurrence plot is a graphic that shows the amount of patterning in a numeric time series for one variable. An example appears in Figure 14.2. The matrix of points is square, with *t*, the number of observations over time, occupying the two axes of the graph. The variate *X* is shown on the diagonal. Then, for each possible value of *X*, a point is plotted showing first and second time that particular value of *X* appears. If the same value appears again, another point is plotted showing the second and third time a particular value of *X* appears, and so on.

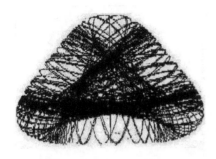 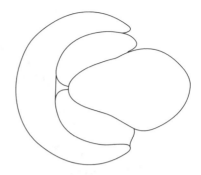

Figure 14.1   Henon-Heiles Attractor: (Left) Phase Portrait and (Right) Corresponding PoincarJ Section

The amount of patterning in a finished recurrence plot reflects the *correlation dimension* inherent in the time series. A correlation dimension is the degree of patterning in the data and is not directly related to the Pearson product-moment correlation or related statistics. The calculation and use of the correlation dimension are discussed in the next section of this chapter. For present purposes, we continue by saying that the "same" value of X is actually an arbitrarily small difference in value. Visual differences in plots can be obtained by simply increasing or decreasing the arbitrary definition of sameness.

Researchers who find value in recurrence plots or correlation dimensions in other ways compare the results of their analysis of a real time series with the results obtained from surrogate data. Surrogate data are usually produced by randomly shuffling the observations. This procedure will disrupt patterns that are detectable as a correlation dimension but preserve the autocorrelation among observations (Heath, 2000). A shuffled data set will produce a gray mass, as shown in Figure 14.2 in the case of extreme randomness, and a gray mass that is dense with diagonals in the case of autocorrelation, plus a great deal of noise.

The test of a hypothesis is again visual, but there are at least two targets to compare. Better grounding for any conclusions would require a more deliberate analysis of dynamical properties and a statistical analysis thereof.

Dimensions and Dynamical Footprints

It is now known that the basins of chaotic attractors are fractal in shape (Farmer, Ott, & Yorke, 1983; Mandelbrot, 1977, 1983). The dimensionality of an attractor is now regarded as a measure of the attractor's complexity and the complexity of the process that generated it. The exact relationship between dimensionality and the number of real variables that affect a process is not exact.

Fractal Dimensions

The calculation of fractal dimension is thus important for assessing the complexity of an attractor or other phenomena that are expressed in a spatial series or a time series. The concept of fractal dimension dates back to Hausdorff (1919) and was later modified by Mandelbrot (1983):

$$D_f = \lim_{1 \to 0} \frac{\log[1/M(1)]}{\log 1}. \tag{1}$$

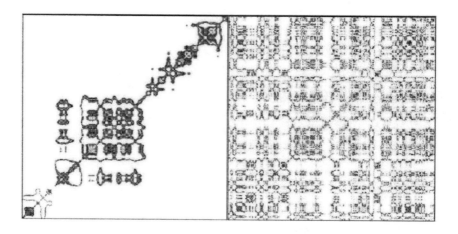

Figure 14.2   Recurrence Plot for Heartbeat Data: Actual Data (Left), Shuffled Data (Right)

SOURCE: Reprinted with permission from Sabelli, 2001, p. 95.

Imagine that a fractal image is covered with cubes with sides of length 1. M(1) is a function of the *embedding dimension*, ε. A true line will require $\varepsilon = 1$, a surface $\varepsilon = 2$, and volume $\varepsilon = 3$ and so forth. The number of squares required to cover a point is proportional to M(1), where

$$M(1) = 1/1^{-\varepsilon}. \qquad (2)$$

The *correlation dimension* has led to an often used algorithm for calculating attractor dimension. They defined dimension as:

$$D_c = \lim_{1 \to 0} \frac{log \, \|u_i\|_y}{log \, 1} \qquad (3)$$

where 1 represents the diameter of a circle rather than the side of a square, and $\|u_i\|_y$ denotes the average value of $1/M(1)$ over all points in a time or spatial series of points. Although D_c was meant to approximate D_f, it is now known that $D_c < D_f$ (Girault, 1991; Kugiumtzis, Lillekjendlie, & Christophersen, 1994).

When applied to a time series, however, Equation 3 produces unreliable results depending on the amount of noise present in the data and whether the data are oversampled or undersampled (Theiler & Eubank, 1993). Because smooth mapping exists in the near neighborhood of an attractor (Wiggins, 1988), overly short time intervals would lead to a bias toward the conclusion that favored a linear interpretation of the data. Choice of time interval can seriously affect the definitions of attractors that one might extract from an analysis (Yee, Sweby, & Griffiths, 1991). When studying real systems (as we are in this chapter), Theiler and Eubank (1993) recommended that the rate of sampling be set relative to the physical properties of the system that is generating the data. For instance, if the system produces values every 2 seconds, a 2-second interval is appropriate. Similarly, if a particular type of economic data is generated every quarter of the year, then four observations per year would be appropriate.

Inverse Power Law

Another way to reach the correlation dimension is to rely on the principle of scale: If we take a frequency distribution of events and order the events by size, we would notice that the large examples of the event are relatively infrequent. The small examples would be more frequent. Next, let the size of the event be X in Equation 4, which is the *inverse power law:*

$$\text{Freq}(X) = a\, X^{-b} \tag{4}$$

The parameters a and b can be estimated by nonlinear regression. The value of b that we obtain from that procedure is the fractal dimension. The examples of the inverse power law are widespread and varied according to Bak (1996) and West and Deering (1995).

The inverse power law function can also be obtained by transforming Equation 4 into Equation 5:

$$\log (\text{Freq}\, [X]) = -\, b \log [X] + a \tag{5}$$

Although the two forms are mathematically equivalent, they are only statistically equivalent in the asymptotic case where there is no noise.

Lyapunov Exponents and Dimensions

Although chaotic attractors may exhibit fractional dimensionality, the presence of a fractional D_f is not a sufficient test of chaos. The property of sensitivity to initial conditions is still missing. The *Lyapunov exponent* is based on a concept of entropy; the exponent reflects the rate at which information that allows a forecast of a variable y is lost. It is calculated (Kaplan & Glass, 1995, p. 334–335; Puu, 2000, p. 157) by taking pairs of initial conditions y_1 and y_2 and their iterates one step ahead in time, which would be y_2 and y_3. If the ratio of absolute values of differences

$$L \approx |y_3 - y_2|\, /\, |y_2 - y_1| \tag{6}$$

is less than 1.0, then the series is contracting. If the value of the function is greater than 1.0, then the function is expanding and sensitive

dependence is present. The Lyapunov exponent, λ, is thus

$$\lambda = \ln [L]. \tag{7}$$

For an ensemble of trajectories in a dynamical field, Lyapunov exponents, λ_i, are computed for all values of y. If the largest value of λ is positive, and the sum of λ_i is negative, then the series is chaotic.

The calculation of Equation 7 is made on the entire time series and averaged by taking the geometric mean of N values where N is the last entry in the time series. It is also possible to rearrange the terms:

$$\lambda = (1/N) \sum_{N=1}^{N} \ln (L) \tag{8}$$

The foregoing calculations generalize as

$$y = e^{\lambda t}, \tag{9}$$

which is actually insensitive to initial conditions. A positive value of λ indicates an expanding function, which is an indicator of chaos. A negative λ indicates a contracting process, which could be a fixed point or limit cycle attractor. Dimension, D_L becomes a function of the largest value of λ in the series (Frederickson, Kaplan, Yorke, & Yorke, 1983; Kugiumtzis et al., 1994; Wiggins, 1988):

$$D_L = e^{\lambda} \tag{10}$$

The statistical approach for determining 1 is presented subsequently in this chapter. The statistical approach is a variant of Equation 9, and restores sensitivity to initial conditions.

The Lyapunov exponent is an indicator of turbulence (Ruelle, 1991), such as the turbulence that occurs in air and fluid flows. The relationships among entropy and information as defined by Shannon (1948), topological entropy, and the Lyapunov exponent are considered later in this chapter in the context of nominally coded system states.

Self-Organizing Dynamics

The mathematical elements of self-organizing dynamics fall into a few different categories depending on whether one is working from the vantage point of sandpile dynamics (Bak, 1996), rugged landscapes (Kauffman, 1993, 1995), synergetics (Haken, 1984, 2002), agent-based models (Epstein & Axtell, 1996; Holland, 1995), or cellular automata (Wolfram, 2002). All forms of self-organization depict the origins of order in a system as arising from the local interaction of system elements. All local interactions, furthermore, can be characterized by the flow of information between system elements.

Sandpiles

The sandpile dynamic (Bak, 1996) characterizes a system as one that changes from a small and formless entity to more complex distribution of entities as interacting elements are added. At a critical point in time, the single sandpile incurs an avalanche that results in a $1/f^b$ distribution of large and small piles. The analysis of a $1/f^b$ distribution and the relationship between the fractal dimension and chaos were elaborated above. It is noteworthy to add at this point that a $1/f^b$ distribution is, in essence, an exponential distribution. Exponential distributions are fundamental to several forms of nonlinear dynamical statistical analysis, as elaborated below.

Rugged Landscapes

The rugged landscape model of self-organization (Kauffman, 1993, 1995) originated with the spin-glass simulation. In essence, if we take a sample of molecules that are heterogeneous for their electron configurations, put them in a suitable container, and introduce energy to spin

the container around, we eventually obtain a separation of molecular variations such that similar forms cluster together. In the evolutionary counterpart to this metaphor, a heterogeneous species or organism on a mountaintop encounters an environmental force that requires the colony of organisms to separate and find new ecological niches on the new landscape. The erstwhile heterogeneous species now clusters into smaller and more homogeneous groups.

The distribution of new homogeneous groups is characterized by the NK distribution, where a large number of new groups (N) share a small number of common characteristics (K), whereas a smaller number of new groups share larger numbers of common characteristics. The NK distribution is a member of the exponential family, but unlike a simple exponential distribution, it is actually multimodal (Guastello, 1998a). Fortunately, catastrophe theory (Guastello, 1995; Thom, 1975; Zeeman, 1977) has produced not only a series of interesting mathematical models that are applicable to self-organizing dynamics, but also a series of statistical models for multimodal distributions within the exponential family. Catastrophe models might express the differentiation of a heterogeneous system state into multiple homogeneous states. They can also model the discontinuous movement of an entity from one ecological niche to another.

Phase Shifts

The synergetic approach to self-organization describes phase shifts and coupled dynamics (Haken, 1984, 2002). A phase shift, such as the transition of a liquid to a gas, generalizes as a qualitative change in the nature of the interaction among molecules or interaction among people in a social system (Galam, 1996). The relationship between phase shifts and catastrophes was known long ago (Gilmore, 1981). The master equation for a phase shift is generally written as

$$f(y) = y^4/4 - ky^2/2 - ay, \qquad (11)$$

where y is the behavior and a is a control parameter that governs how close a person or object is to the critical point of behavioral transition. In many applications to self-organizing systems, k is a constant that depicts the size or suddenness of the behavioral transition. If k were a variable denoting that some people make bigger changes than others, then we obtain a full-fledged cusp catastrophe model instead of just a single slice of it. Note that no one really cares about the constants 4 and 2 in Equation 11 for reasons that should be clear before the conclusion of this chapter.

A cusp catastrophe model is shown in Figure 14.3, where a is the asymmetry parameter and k is the bifurcation parameter (which is henceforward denoted as the variable b). The model for the changes of behavior in the system forms the response surface that is shown in Figure 14.3. The response surface depicts two stable states of behavior that are separated by a bifurcation manifold that has critical points of instability lined up on its outer edges. The equation of the response surface is the derivative of Equation 11:

$$df(y)/dy = y^3 - by - a \qquad (12)$$

However, the implicit derivative as a function of time is perhaps more intuitively appealing (Guastello, 1995):

$$dy/dt = y^3 - by - a \qquad (13)$$

Coupled Dynamics

Coupled dynamics are situations where y is a nonlinear function of itself and x, and x also displays nonlinear dynamical properties. In Haken's (1984) terminology, x would be a *driver* variable, and y would be a *slave*. A driver is a dynamical subsystem that produces output that greatly affects the dynamics of another subsystem. The latter subsystem is the slave, which, although it contributes dynamics of its own,

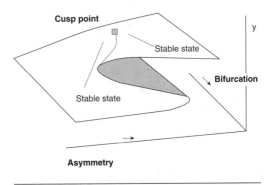

Figure 14.3   Cusp Catastrophe Model

produces dynamics that are greatly influenced by the driver. Driver-slave dynamics form the basis of the hierarchical dynamical system. I will return to coupled dynamics after simpler dynamical systems are explained.

Edge of Chaos

The basic concept (Waldrop, 1992) is that systems poised on the edge of chaos could self-organize at any moment in response to a critical stimulus of some sort. A critical stimulus would be one that could not be assimilated by the existing structure of the system, and thus a new structure would be necessary for an effective response. The effective response may involve unraveling the existing subsystems. Repeated unraveling and reorganization of a system would be expected occasionally from a functional complex adaptive system.

It is noteworthy that the earliest studies of chaotic behavior in physiological systems relied on computations of the fractal dimension, which is a relative of the Lyapunov exponent; a comparison of the relative assets and limitations of the two indicators is beyond the scope of this chapter. Some qualitative trends in those studies are relevant nonetheless: Studies of cell tissue, electroencephalograms (EEGs), and electrocardiograms (EKGs) indicate that greater irregularity (turbulence, complexity) appears in the output (or cell morphology) from healthy systems. Unhealthy systems gravitate toward periodic and simplistic output (Goldberger, Peng, Mietus, Havlin, & Stanley, 1996; Hornero, Alonso, Jimeno, Jimeno, & Lopez, 1999; Meyer et al., 1998; Sabelli & Kauffman, 1999). This trend has been extended to organizational behavior (Dooley, 1997) and communication dynamics within families (Pincus, 2001).

For analytic purposes, the point here is that a system that is in the process of self-organizing can exhibit a chaotic dynamic and a self-organizing dynamic at the same time. The case of a dual function in a group learning situation will be considered later in this chapter. Therein, we see the dynamics of both chaos and learning.

The Structural Equations Technique

The structural equations technique begins by defining a model in the form of an equation, then testing it statistically with real (as opposed to simulated) data. The analysis separates the deterministic portion of the data from noise. *Noise* here denotes that portion of the data variance that is not explained by the deterministic equation. Social scientists will recognize this model-versus-noise approach as "business as usual." This technique contrasts with a prevailing habit in the physical sciences, which works in the opposite fashion: Separate the noise first, then make calculations on what remains (e.g., Kanz & Schreiber, 1997). Although social scientists have adopted a filter-first approach to data analysis (e.g., Heath, 2000), filtering is clearly not recommended for the techniques described below.

Two series of hierarchical models are considered here. The first is the catastrophe models for discontinuous change (Guastello, 1992a, 1995, 2002) based on Thom (1975). The second set involves exponential models for continuous change and includes a test for the Lyapunov exponent, which distinguishes between chaos and nonchaotic dynamics. The latter set was introduced by Guastello (1995) and built on

previous work by May and Oster (1976), Wiggins (1988), and numerous other contributors to the field of nonlinear dynamical systems.

Each model in a hierarchy subsumes properties of the simpler models. Each progressively complex model adds a new dynamical feature. This chapter covers models involving only one order parameter (dependent measure). Two-parameter models can be tested as well, but the reader is directed to Guastello (1995) to see how those extrapolations can be accomplished.

The following sections of this chapter address the type of data and amounts that are required; probability functions, location, and scale; the structure of behavioral measurements; the catastrophe model group, which can be tested through power polynomial regression; the exponential series of models, which can be tested through nonlinear regression; and catastrophe models that are testable as static probability functions through nonlinear regression.

Types and Amount of Data

The procedures that follow require dependent measures (order parameters) that are taken at a minimum of two points in time. One may have many entities that are measured at two points in time, or one long time series of observations from one entity. Alternatively, one may have an ensemble of shorter time series taken from several entities.

In general, it is better to have a smaller number of observations that cover the full dynamical character of a phenomenon than to have a large number of observations that cover the underlying topology poorly. Because these are statistical procedures, all the usual rules and caveats pertaining to statistical power apply. The simplest models can be tested with 50 data points and sometimes fewer, if there are (a) good models of the phenomenon in question, (b) reliable measurements, and (c) only one or two regression parameters to estimate. In all cases, more data is better than less data so long as the data are actually covering all the nonlinear dynamics that are thought to exist in the system.

Statistical Power

The calculation of statistical power for ordinary multiple regression depends on the intended effect size, overall sample R^2, population R^2, the number of independent variables, the degree of correlation among the independent variables, and occasionally the assumption that all independent variables are equally weighted. Not surprisingly there are different rubrics for determining proper sample size.

According to Cohen (1988), to detect a medium effect size of .15 for one of the independent variables with a power of .80, the appropriate sample size is 52 plus the number of estimated parameters (Maxwell, 2000). Thus, the required sample size would be 58 observations for a six-parameter model. According to a similar rubric by Green (1991), a sample size of 110 should detect an effect size of .075 for one of six independent variables with a power of .80; A sample size of 200 would thus detect effect size of .04, with a power of .80. However, neither rubric takes into account that the odds of finding a smaller partial correlation increase to the extent that the overall R^2 is large. According to Maxwell (2000), the odds of detecting one of the effects within a multiple regression model drop sharply as the correlations among independent variables increase.

One should bear in mind that the calculation of statistical power for nonlinear regression is still generally uncharted territory. It is thus necessary to rely on the rubrics for linear models. If there is sufficient statistical power for the linear comparison models, which in the past have been generally weaker in overall effect size than nonlinear models when the nonlinear model was held true, there should not be much concern with the statistical power of the nonlinear models. On the other hand, the power for specific effects within a nonlinear model probably depends on whether the regression parameter is associated with an additive, exponential, multiplicative, or other type of mathematical operator.

Optimal Time Lag

Put simply, the time lag between observations is optimal if it reflects the real time frame in which data points are generated. For instance, catastrophe models are usually lagged "before" and "after" a discrete event. Macroeconomic variables such as inflation and unemployment rates are studied best at lags equal to an economic quarter of the year (e.g., Guastello, 1999b). Economic policies are usually implemented on a quarterly basis, even if some of the important indicators are posted monthly.

Probability Density Functions

It is convenient that any differential function can be transformed into a probability density function (pdf) using the Wright-Ito transformation. The variable y in Equation 15 is a dependent measure that exhibits the dynamical character under study; y is then transformed into z with respect to *location* (λ) and *scale* (σ_s, Equation 15):

$$\text{pdf}(y) = \xi \exp[-\int f(z)] \qquad (14)$$

$$z = (y - \lambda) / \sigma_s \qquad (15)$$

Location. In most discussions of probability functions, *location* refers to the mean of the function. In dynamics, the pdf is a member of an exponential family of distributions and is asymmetrical, unlike the so-called normal distribution. Thus, the location parameter for Equation 14 is the lower limit of the distribution, which is the lowest observed value in the series. The transformation in Equation 15 has the added advantage of fixing a zero point and thus transforming measurements with interval scales (common in the social sciences) to ratio scales. A fixed location point defines where the nonlinear function is going to start.

Scale. The scale parameter in common discussions of pdfs is the standard deviation of the distribution. The standard deviation is also used here. The use of the scale parameter later on while testing structural equations serves the purpose of eliminating bias between two or more variables that are multiplied together. Although the results of linear regression are not affected by values of location and scale, nonlinear models are clearly affected by the transformation.

Occasionally, one may obtain a better fit using the alternative definition of scale in Equation 16, which measures variability around statistical modes rather than around a mean:

$$\sigma_s = \sqrt{\left[\sum_{y=1} \sum_{m=1} (y_{m-}^{m+} - mi)^2 \right] / N - M} \quad (16)$$

To use it, the distribution must be broken into sections, each section containing a mode or an antimode. The values of the variable around a mode will range from $m-$ to $m+$ as depicted in Equation 16.

Corrections for location and scale should be made on control variables as well as dependent measures. The ordinary standard deviation is a suitable measure of scale for control variables.

Structure of Behavioral Measurements

In the classic definition, a measurement consists of true scores (T) plus error (e). The variance structure for a population of scores is thus

$$\sigma^2(X) = \sigma^2(T) + \sigma^2(e). \quad (17)$$

The classical assumption is that all errors are independent of true scores and all other errors.

In nonlinear dynamics, our true score is the result of a linear (L) and nonlinear deterministic process (NL), dependent error (DE), and independent error (IIDE):

$$\sigma^2(X) = \sigma^2(L) + \sigma^2(NL - L) + \sigma^2(DE) + \sigma^2(IIDE) \quad (18)$$

"Independent error" in conventional psychometrics is known as independently and identically distributed (IID) error in the nonlinear dynamical systems literature. Dependent error is commonly observed in time series applications where the amount of error is dependent on the value of X. In dynamical systems, a modicum of error that occurs at one point in time becomes part of X on the next iteration and is thus amplified or computed by the system along with the true score component of X. It is significant that the non-IID (DE) error is a result of the nonlinear deterministic process (Brock, Hseih, & LeBaron, 1991).

Catastrophe Models

The analysis that follows requires the polynomial form of multiple linear regression. The analysis can be performed with most any standard statistical software package. Several concepts for hypothesis testing carry through to subsequent analyses of other dynamics.

The set of catastrophe models was the result of the classification theorem by Thom (1975): Given certain constraints, all discontinuous changes in events can be described by one of seven elementary models. Four of the models contain one order parameter; this is the cuspoid series: fold model (one control parameter), cusp model (two control parameters), swallowtail model (three control parameters), and butterfly model (four control parameters). The remaining three models, known as the umbilic group, contain two order parameters. The descriptions that follow pertain to the cusp but generalize readily to the cuspoid group.

The process of hypothesis testing begins with choosing a model that appears to be closest to

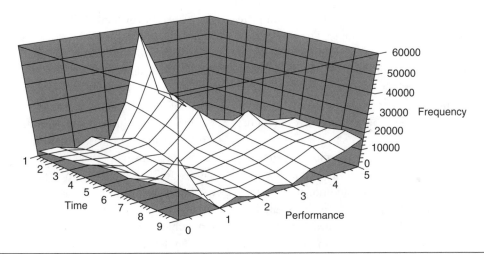

Figure 14.4   Cusp pdf From a Multistage Personnel Selection Application

SOURCE: Reprinted with permission from Guastello, 2002, p.136.

the phenomenon under investigation. Because the cusp is the most often used model, the following remarks are framed in terms of the cusp model, which is described in Figure 14.3. Note that two or more experimental variables may be hypothesized for each control parameter without changing the basic model or analytic procedure. Examples of analyses using the polynomial regression method for catastrophes date back to Guastello (1982). Recent examples, however, can be found in Guastello (1995, 2002), Guastello, Gershon, and Murphy (1999), Clair (1998), Lange (1999), and Byrne, Mazanov, and Gregson (2001).

Nonlinear statistical model. The deterministic equation for the cusp is shown in Equation 12 and followed by its pdf using the Wright-Ito transformation in Equation 19:

$$\text{pdf}(z) = \xi \exp\left[-z^4/4 + bz^2/2 + az\right] \quad (19)$$

Figure 14.4 depicts a cusp pdf that was produced from real data (Guastello, 2002, p. 136).

Next, we take the deterministic equation for the cusp response surface and insert regression weights and a quadratic term:

$$\Delta z = \beta_0 + \beta_1 z_1^3 + \beta_2 z_1^2 + \beta_3 b z_1 + \beta_4 a \quad (20)$$

The quadratic term is an additional correction for location. The dependent measure Δz denotes a change in behavior over two subsequent points in time.

Several hypotheses are being tested in the power polynomial equation (Equation 20). The F test is used for the model overall; the R^2 coefficient can be retained and saved for later use. There are t tests on the beta weights; they denote which parts of the model account for unique portions of variance.

Some model elements are more important than other elements. The cubic term expresses whether the model is consistent with cusp structure; the correct level of complexity for a catastrophe model is captured by the leading power term. If there is a cusp structure, then one must identify a bifurcation variable as represented by the βbz_1 term. A cusp hypothesis is not complete without a bifurcation term; shabby results may be expected otherwise. The asymmetry term βa is important in the model, but failing to find one does not negate the cusp structure if the cubic and bifurcation elements are present. The lack of an asymmetry term only means that the model is not complete.

The quadratic term is the most expendable. It is not part of the formal deterministic cusp structure. Rather, it is an additional correction for location (Cobb, 1981a). In the event that unique weights are not obtained for all model components, the quadratic term can be deleted and the remaining elements tested again.

Note the procedural contrast with linear regression analysis: In common linear regression, when a variable does not attain a significant weight, we simply delete that variable. In nonlinear dynamical systems, we delete variables based on their relative importance to the structural model. In linear analyses, only a linear structure is under consideration, so particular variables are then kept or discarded. In nonlinear analyses, different variables may be playing different structural roles.

Linear comparison models. In Equations 21 and 22, we compare the R^2 coefficients against the R^2 that was obtained for the cusp:

$$y_2 = B_0 + B_1 y_1 + B_2 a + B_3 b \tag{21}$$

$$\Delta y = B_0 + B_1 a + B_2 b \tag{22}$$

Next, the elements of the cusp model are evaluated. If all the necessary parts of the cusp are significant, and the R^2 coefficients compare favorably, then a clear case of the cusp has been obtained.

Exponential Model Series

This section describes a series of models that exhibit continuous but nevertheless interesting change. The model structures are functions of

the Naperian constant e. They produce, among other things, the Lyapunov exponent, which is a test for chaos and a value comparable to the fractal dimension.

Nonlinear regression is required to test this series of models. Nonlinear regression may be familiar to biologists, but it is probably much less familiar to social scientists at the present time. This schism in uptake of nonlinear regression is probably related to the dearth of explicit nonlinear models in the social sciences prior to the advent of nonlinear dynamical systems. The hierarchical series of models ranges from simple to complex as follows: (a) simple Lyapunov exponent, (b) Lyapunov with additional fitting constants, (c) May-Oster model with the bifurcation parameter unknown, (d) model with an explicitly hypothesized bifurcation model, and (e) models with two or more order parameters.

Examples of analyses using the nonlinear regression method for chaos and related exponential models date back to Guastello (1992b). More recent examples can be found in Guastello (1995, 1998b, 1999a, 1999b, 2001, 2002), Guastello and Philippe (1997), Guastello and Guastello (1998), Guastello and Johnson (1999), Guastello, Johnson, and Rieke (1999), Guastello and Bock (2001), Rosser, Rosser, Guastello, and Bond (2001), and Guastello and Bond (2004). For examples that compare dimensionality estimates made through nonlinear regression with values obtained by other means, see Johnson and Dooley (1996) and Guastello and Philippe (1997).

Lyapunov models. The simplest model predicts behavior z_2 from a function of z_1. Note that the corrections for location and scale apply here as well:

$$z_2 = e^{(\theta_1 z_1)} \tag{23}$$

The nonlinear regression weight θ_1 located in the exponent is also the Lyapunov exponent. It is a measure of turbulence in the time series. If θ_1 is positive, then chaos is occurring. If θ_1 is negative, then a fixed point or periodic dynamic is occurring. D_L is an approximation of the fractal dimension (Ott, Sauer, & Yorke, 1994):

$$D_L = e^{\theta_1} \tag{24}$$

The second model in the series (Equation 25) is the same as the first except that two constants have been introduced to absorb unaccounted variance. The Lyapunov exponent is now designated as θ_2:

$$z_2 = \theta_1 e^{(\theta_2 z_1)} + \theta_3 \tag{25}$$

In nonlinear regression, it is necessary to specify the placement of constants in a model. Unlike the case in the general linear model, constants in nonlinear models can appear anywhere at all. Hence θ_1 and θ_3 are introduced in Equation 25.

The suggested strategy here is to start with the second model (Equation 25). If statistical significance is not obtained for all three weights, delete θ_1 and try again. If that result is not good enough, drop the additive constant θ_3 and return to the simplest model of the series (Equation 23).

Bifurcation models. The third level of model is shown in Equation 26. Note the introduction of z_1 between θ_1 and e:

$$z_2 = \theta_1 z_1 e^{\theta_2 z_1} + \theta_3 \tag{26}$$

Equation 26 tests for the presence of a variable that is possibly changing the dynamics of a model. For instance, some learning curves may be sharper than others. A positive test for the model indicates that a variable is present, but its identity is not yet known.

The computation of dimension is similar to that of previous exponential models, except that a value of 1 must be added to account for the presence of a bifurcation variable:

$$D_L = e^{\theta_2} + 1 \tag{27}$$

At the fourth level of complexity, the researcher has a specific hypothesis for the bifurcation variable, which is designated as c in Equation 28:

$$z_2 = \theta_1 c z_1 e^{\theta_2 z_1} + \theta_3 \tag{28}$$

Linear contrasts. As in the case of the catastrophes, we test the R^2 for the nonlinear regression model against that of the linear alternatives, such as

$$y_2 = B_0 + B_1 y_1 \tag{29}$$

or

$$y_2 = B_0 + B_1 t, \tag{30}$$

where t is time.

Tips for using nonlinear regression. On the model parameter command line (or comparable command in statistical packages), the names of the regression weights are specified with initial values. Researchers either use the initial values of 0.5 or pick their own. When in doubt, initial weights can be given equal value. Often, it does not matter whether the iterative computational procedure starts off with equal weights or not. If the model results are not affected by the initial values, then the resulting model is more robust than otherwise would be the case.

In cases where there is an option to choose constrained versus unconstrained nonlinear regression, the unconstrained option is typically the default. Constraints indicate that the researcher expects the values of parameters to remain within numerical boundaries that have been predetermined. Occasionally, there may be a good rationale for containing parameters, but they are generally specific to the problem.

If there is an option to choose least squares or maximum likelihood error term specification, be forewarned: Maximum likelihood is more likely to capitalize on chance aspects of the pdf and is thus more likely to return a significant result. It may be better to use least squares for this reason.

If the results of a nonlinear regression analysis are so poor that they produce a negative R^2, researchers need not be alarmed. The negative R^2 can be treated as if it were .00.

When testing for significance, the tests on the weights are very important. Some researchers value them more than the overall R^2. Tests for weights are made using the principle of confidence intervals. An alpha level of $p < .05$ is regarded as unilaterally sufficient. A nonsignificant weight with a high overall R^2 could be the result of a high correlation among the parameter estimates; this condition is akin to multicollinearity in ordinary linear models.

Testing Catastrophes Through Nonlinear Regression

The two strategies previously delineated can now be combined for some special circumstances. Sometimes, one might obtain a pdf that bears a strong resemblance to that of an elementary catastrophe, and it is logical to frame a hypothesis as to whether that association is true or false. In another situation, a catastrophe process may be occurring, but all the time–1 measurements are the same value of 0.00. In both types of situations, it would be good to test a hypothesis concerning the catastrophe distribution. Examples of analyses using the nonlinear regression method for testing catastrophe pdfs are sparse, although the method was proposed by Cobb some time ago (1981a, 1981b). More recent examples can be found in Hanges, Braverman, and Rentch (1991), Guastello (1998a, 2002), and Zaror and Guastello (2000).

Dual Functions

Three interesting cases are known where two dynamical functions were operating concurrently in a system. One such example was identified in a creative problem-solving study that involved a periodic driver and a chaotic slave

(Guastello, 1998b). The resulting model took the form

$$z_2 = f(z_1) + \beta_1 a + \beta_2 b + \beta_3 c, \qquad (31)$$

where $f(z)$ was an exponential function from the model series above; a, b, and c were control parameters; and β_i were regression weights that held the model together. The primary function $f(z)$ displayed a positive Lyapunov exponent. Control variables a and b were categorical variables that contributed additive explanatory variance. Variable c, however, was itself a different exponential function over time with a negative exponent.

The interpretation of driver and slave had to be made in the context of the problem. The important result from the study, however, was that two dynamics were involved and that it was possible to state the effects produced by each variable. A procedural annoyance, however, was that the linear comparison model contained four additive elements, of which one was still nonlinear. The R^2 for the linear comparison model was relatively high, but not greater than the R^2 for the nonlinear model. Nonetheless, the linear model "cheated" a bit.

A second interesting example was identified in a group coordination learning experiment (Guastello & Guastello, 1998). The group readily learned the coordination task for two of the experimental conditions. Exponential models with the bifurcation effect characterized their behavior over time. Figure 14.5 depicts the relationship between learning curves and a cusp bifurcation manifold. The exponential model characterizes only a slice of the full surface that pertains to the behavior of the groups in the study.

One experimental condition in the coordination study was very difficult for the participants. The first function to be extracted was a chaotic function, which indicated in this context that the adaptive self-organizing response had not kicked in for some of the groups. When that variance was removed from the behavioral

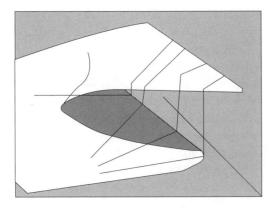

Figure 14.5   Learning Curves Represented as Slices From a Cusp Catastrophe Manifold

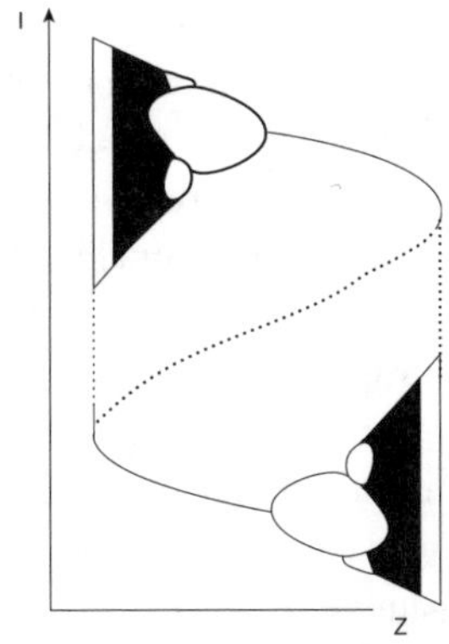

Figure 14.6   Compound Dynamic for Hysteresis Between Two Chaotic Attractors

variable, however, the analysis of the residual showed a second function that contained a negative exponent. Thus, an incomplete self-organized response may contain two kinds of functions, and an analysis of residuals would be required to find them both.

The third interesting case involved a combination of a cusp catastrophe model and chaotic attractors (Rosser et al., 2001). The stable states, or attractors, in a catastrophe model are fixed point attractors, although the presence of limit cycles would not usually impair the analysis. The theory that Rosser et al. were working with indicated a cusp manifold for hysteresis, but the attractors were chaotic. A graphic representation of this combination of dynamics appears in Figure 14.6.

They did not know what the control variables could be, so they simply analyzed the dynamics of their two economic indicators (annual infrastructure investment by the Soviet government and the annual investment in construction by the Soviet government) using the exponential series. One variable displayed a bifurcation effect and a negative exponent. The other displayed no bifurcation and a positive exponent. Although the dynamics that were obtained did not show a clear illustration of what was hypothesized in simpler terms, the dynamics did display portions of the intended dynamics. Ideally, they would have found a chaotic function, a bifurcation effect, and a dimensionality in the neighborhood of 3.0.

Perhaps, longer data sets with control variables would have produced different results; one variable consisted of 53 annual numbers, and the other consisted of 27 annual numbers. The epoch of Soviet history that they were studying ended, however, and they were compelled to extract meaning out of what data actually existed.

Symbolic Dynamics and the Method of Orbital Decomposition

Symbolic dynamics is an area of mathematics that finds patterns in series of qualitative data. Furthermore, the elementary patterns can be treated like qualitative states themselves and subjected to pattern detection for higher order patterns. This is the basic concept behind Turing's Universal Computational Machine. The approach is ideally suited to analyzing chaotic and related complex nonlinear dynamics (Robinson, 1999), particularly when self-organizing phenomena are likely to emerge (Crutchfield, 1994). The process is usually applied to continuously valued time series. Events such as spikes and small or large uptrends and downtrends are coded nominally (e.g., with letter codes A, B, C, D, etc.) and then analyzed. Several computational procedures have been advanced; some include computations of Shannon's entropy or other dynamical indicators.

Numerous biomedical applications of symbolic dynamics techniques have been reported recently (Yamada et al., 2000; Yeragani, Nadella, Hinze, Yeragani, & Jampala, 2000). In principle, symbolic dynamics might be applied to any situation where nonlinear behavior or living systems are involved (Arecchi, 2001). Within psychology, symbolic dynamics have been recommended for the study of firing patterns of individual neurons within a network (Lewis & Glass, 1992), activation of neural circuits involved in memory processes (Guastello, Nielson, & Ross, 2002), linguistics problems (Sulis, 1998), and the analysis of conversations between a psychotherapist and a client (Rapp & Korslund, 2000). Actual applications have been published on topics concerning artificial grammars (Bollt & Jones, 2000), creative problem-solving groups (Guastello, 2000; Guastello, Hyde, & Odak, 1998), and family systems dynamics (Pincus, 2001).

The foregoing techniques vary in their method for determining symbol sequences and the length of those sequences. They also vary in the extent to which they produce results that interface with other dynamical concepts such as topological entropy and the Lyapunov exponent. The latter three studies involve the method of orbital decomposition, which is assisted by a statistical analysis, unlike the other current offerings. The method of orbital decomposition is decribed next.

The method of orbital decomposition (Guastello et al., 1998) is based on the principle that a minimum of three coupled oscillators are required to produce chaos (Newhouse, Ruelle, & Takens, 1978). The procedure does not require the presence of chaos; it merely accommodates systems of sufficient complexity to qualify as chaos. The procedure requires three calculations

in parallel: Shannon entropy (H_S), topological entropy (H_T), and a likelihood χ^2 test for strings of responses of varying length C. The calculations provide measures of dimensional complexity, the determination of an optimum behavior string length, a set of behavior strings with associated probabilities, and a chi-square test that provides a measure of fitness for the string structures.

Shannon (1948; Ott et al., 1994) entropy (H_S) is defined in Equation 32, where p_i is the probability associated with one categorical outcome in a set of r categories:

$$H_S = \sum_{i=1}^{r} p_i \ln (1/p_i). \qquad (32)$$

The second calculation, topological entropy (H_T), is based on strings, or hypothetical orbits, of length C. C takes on a small range of integer values beginning with 1. For $C = 1$, a transition matrix, M^C, is created, which is square, and $r \times r$ in size. Each cell entry is binary and indicates whether a particular behavior category is followed in time by any other behavior category. Its diagonal entries indicate whether an outcome is followed by itself in a consecutive period of time. Topological entropy is a function of the trace of M^C (Lathrop & Kostelich, 1989, p. 4030):

$$H_T = \lim_{c \to 4} (1/C) \log_2 \mathrm{tr}(M^C) \qquad (33)$$

As the string length goes to infinity, H_T approaches the base -2 logarithm of the trace of M^C, and is in turn equal to the maximum Lyapunov exponent, which is also the largest eigenvalue of M^C. Dimensionality is, therefore,

$$D_L = e^{HT}. \qquad (34)$$

The construction of M^C is repeated for all $C > 1$, and Equations 32 to 34 are calculated for each. For $C = 2$, one axis of M^C represents all possible pairs of categories, although some possible combinations might not actually appear in the data if their combinatorial probability is too low.

The third calculation is the χ^2 for goodness of fit, and it is also carried out for each value of C used. The essential question posed by the test is whether the behavior strings observed in the data occur at rates different from chance, where chance is simply the combinatorial probability of each categorical element in the string. The likelihood χ^2 is preferred over the Pearson variety because the expected (F_{Ex}) and observed (F_{Ob}) frequencies for many elementary categories and strings are small:

$$\chi^2 = 2 \, \Sigma \, F_{Ob} \ln(F_{Ob}/F_{Ex}). \qquad (35)$$

Given N strings of length C in a set, the expected frequency of string X-Y-Z is

$$F_{Ex} = P_X P_Y P_Z N. \qquad (36)$$

Finally, ϕ^2 coefficients are calculated for all χ^2 tests to provide a measure of variance accounted for by the observed strings for all lengths C:

$$\phi^2 = \chi^2/N. \qquad (37)$$

Optimal C is determined as the length of a string one step before the step at which H_T drops to 0.00. Having determined the optimal string length, it is possible to describe the contents and distribution of strings with that length; these were used as a basis of comparison with other conversations, along with the associated values of C, H_T, and H_S. The array of strings identified at this stage could be analyzed for hierarchical dynamics using a repetition of the process just outlined (cf. Crutchfield, 1994).

H_T is in indicator of the amount of information produced by the underlying (neuronal) process. H_T decreases as C increases; it is the primary indicator of the asymptotic limit of C. A comparison of the asymptotic H_T and C values across experimental conditions would indicate which neuronal processes are more complicated than others and how.

To date, the available applications of the orbital decomposition technique have pertained to the analysis of creative problem-solving conversation (Guastello, 2000; Guastello et al., 1998) and conflict resolution conversations among members of dysfunctional families (Pincus, 2001). Guastello et al. (1998) analyzed a string of more than 500 responses in one real-time problem-solving session used in the study just described. Responses were coded in one of nine possible types of input: requesting information, giving information, tension reduction, clarifying responses and ideas, gate keeping, initiating, following, harmonizing, and unclassified responses. Guastello et al. found that sequences of four responses emerged and that the sequences could not be reduced to the simple effects of combinatorial probabilities. In a subsequent study (Guastello, 2000), the elementary conversational units were themselves combinations of conversation contribution types. Table 14.1 (from Guastello, 2000) illustrates the array of data that led to the conclusion that, for a particular coding scheme that was applied to a creative problem-solving conversation, the optimal string length consisted of sequences of 3. Thereupon, the trace of the pattern matrix was 4, and other relevant computations appear in the same row. The ϕ_2 value indicated that 95% of the variance in states within the original data set was accounted for by the strings produced at $C = 3$.

Once the correct length of C has been determined, it is then possible to interpret the strings themselves; each string, which corresponds to an orbit, contains three qualitative states in the example above. A frequency distribution of string frequencies will inevitably show that some strings occur very often whereas others occur less frequently. We speculate that the frequency distribution of string frequencies will correspond to a $1/f^a$ distribution, which is typically indicative of a fractal or self-organizing process (Bak, 1996; West & Deering, 1995). It is noteworthy that some strings that are possible do not actually appear. It is currently recommended

Table 14.1 Trace of Binary M^c, Topological Entropy, Dimensionality, χ^2, ϕ^2, and Shannon Entropy for Strings of Length 1 through 4; Analysis of a Group Problem-Solving Conversation

C	$Tr(M^c)$	H_T	D_L	χ^2	df	N	ϕ^2	H_S
1	5	2.322	10.196	46.92	8	81	.58	2.239
2	4	1.000	2.718	34.84	36	80	.44	3.478
3	4	0.667	1.948	74.87	64	79	.95	5.031
4	0	undef	undef	16.99	60	78	.22	4.439

NOTE: C = String length; H_T = Topological entropy; D_L = Lyapunov dimensionality; H_S = Shannon entropy.

SOURCE: Guastello (2000). Reprinted with permission.

that strings that appear at least twice should be inspected for interpretive value.

All three applications produced sets of orbits that had diagnostic value for interpreting the behaviors of the groups. The complexities of the final sets of sequences were dependent on the particular scoring protocols that were used. Guastello (2000) applied two different scoring schemes to the same conversation and found that different string lengths, entropy levels, and so forth resulted from the two coding schemes. Rapp and Korslund (2000) also observed that the results of a symbolic dynamics analysis would be predicated on the particular scoring protocols that were used. It would appear, furthermore, that complex results would be improbable if the behavior coding systems were overly simplistic.

Conclusion

This chapter summarized three perspectives on nonlinear data analysis. Graphic techniques emanated from mathematical problems in which it was not possible to observe all the critical features of a function by simply inspecting a descriptive equation. They are potentially valuable in social science research as descriptive tools, but at present, they have little relevance to model building or hypothesis testing except, perhaps, in the crudest sense.

The mathematical concepts concerning dimensions are of primary importance for determining the nature of a dynamical process. If we know the dynamical process, then a great deal of variance over time can be explained. On the other hand, specific values of dimension are of lesser importance except in a comparative sense, such as healthy versus unhealthy systems.

The analytic habits of the natural sciences and social sciences vary sharply on the matter of filtering data before analysis, and it has been acknowledged that filtering distorts results. Analyses for the social sciences are now rooted in a relevant statistical theory that appears to make the filtering issue both a nonproblem and a nonrecommended procedure.

Nonlinear regression techniques are very versatile, and they can accommodate virtually any structural equation. Perhaps, the asset of versatility has become the limitation of the daunting number of possible models that a researcher might select for a hypothesis. The method of structural equations presented here limits the possibilities to hierarchical sets and should facilitate hypothesis formulation as it has done already.

The nonlinear regression approach can be expanded to encompass sinusoidal functions for the decomposition of limit cycles. Such problems are more frequently encountered in the biological sciences (Koyama, Yoneyama, Sawada,

& Ohtomo, 1994) and economics (Puu, 1993) than they are in psychological problems. Symbolic dynamics techniques, such as the method of orbital decomposition, are also highly versatile for this purpose, especially where system states are observed rather than continuous numerical measurements.

References

Abarbanel, H. D. I. (1996). *Analysis of chaotic data.* New York: Springer-Verlag.

Abraham, F. D. (1997). Nonlinear coherence in multivariate research: Invariants and the reconstruction of attractors. *Nonlinear Dynamics, Psychology, and Life Sciences, 1,* 7–34.

Arecchi, F. T. (2001). Complexity versus complex systems: A new approach to scientific discovery. *Nonlinear Dynamics, Psychology, and Life Sciences, 5,* 21–36.

Bak, P. (1996). *How nature works.* New York: Springer-Verlag.

Bollt, E. M., & Jones, M. A. (2000). The complexity of artificial grammars. *Nonlinear Dynamics, Psychology, and Life Sciences, 4,* 153–168.

Brock, W. A., Hseih, D. A., & LeBaron, B. (1991). *Nonlinear dynamics, chaos, and instability: Statistical theory and economic evidence.* Cambridge: MIT Press.

Byrne, D. G., Mazanov, J., & Gregson, R. A. M. (2001). A cusp catastrophe analysis of changes to adolescent smoking behavior in response to smoking prevention programs. *Nonlinear Dynamics, Psychology, and Life Sciences, 5,* 115–138.

Clair, S. (1998). A cusp catastrophe model for adolescent alcohol use: An empirical test. *Nonlinear Dynamics, Psychology, and Life Sciences, 2,* 217–241.

Cobb, L. (1981a). Multimodal exponential families of statistical catastrophe theory. In C. Taillie, G. P. Patel, & B. Baldessari (Eds.), *Statistical distributions in scientific work* (Vol. 6, pp. 67–90). Hingham, MA: Reidel.

Cobb, L. (1981b). Parameter estimation for the cusp catastrophe model. *Behavioral Science, 26,* 75–78.

Cohen, J. (1988). *Statistical power analysis for the behavioral sciences.* Hillsdale, NJ: Lawrence Erlbaum.

Crutchfield, J. P. (1994). The calculi of emergence: Computation, dynamics, and induction. *Physica D, 75,* 11–54.

Dooley, K. J. (1997). A complex adaptive systems model of organization change. *Nonlinear Dynamics, Psychology, and Life Sciences, 1,* 69–97.

Elliott, E., & Kiel, L. D. (Eds.). (2004). Agent-based models [Special issue]. *Nonlinear Dynamics, Psychology, and Life Sciences, 8,* 121–302.

Epstein, J. M., & Axtell, R. (1996). *Growing artificial societies: Social science from the bottom up.* Cambridge: MIT Press.

Farmer, J. D., Ott, E., & Yorke, J. A. (1983). The dimension of chaotic attractors. *Physica D, 7,* 153–180.

Frederickson, P., Kaplan, J. L., Yorke, E. D., & Yorke, J. A. (1983). The Lyapunov dimension of strange attractors. *Journal of Differential Equations, 49,* 185–207.

Galam, S. (1996). When humans interact like atoms. In E. Witte & J. H. Davis (Eds.), *Understanding group behavior* (Vol. 1, pp. 293–312). Mahwah, NJ: Lawrence Erlbaum.

Gilmore, R. (1981). *Catastrophe theory for scientists and engineers.* New York: John Wiley.

Girault, P. (1991). Attractors and dimensions. In C. Cherbit (Ed.), *Non-integral dimensions and applications* (pp. 60–82). West Sussex, UK: Wiley.

Goldberger, A. L., Peng, C. K., Mietus, J., Havlin, S., & Stanley, H. E. (1996). Fractals and the heart. In P. M. Iannaconne & M. Khokha (Eds.), *Fractal geometry in biological systems: An analytic approach* (pp. 249–266). Boca Raton, FL: CRC Press.

Green, B. F. (1991). How many subjects does it take to do a regression analysis? *Multivariate Behavioral Research, 12,* 263–288.

Guastello, S. J. (1982). Color matching and shift work: An industrial application of the cusp-difference equation. *Behavioral Science, 27,* 131–137.

Guastello, S. J. (1992a). Clash of the paradigms: A critique of an examination of the polynomial regression technique for evaluating catastrophe theory hypotheses. *Psychological Bulletin, 111,* 375–379.

Guastello, S. J. (1992b). Population dynamics and workforce productivity. In M. Michaels (Ed.), *Proceedings of the annual conference of the Chaos Network: The second iteration* (pp. 120–127). Urbana, IL: People Technologies.

Guastello, S. J. (1995). *Chaos, catastrophe, and human affairs: Applications of nonlinear dynamics to work, organizations, and social evolution.* Mahwah, NJ: Lawrence Erlbaum.

Guastello, S. J. (1998a). Creative problem solving groups at the edge of chaos. *Journal of Creative Behavior, 32,* 38–57.

Guastello, S. J. (1998b). Self-organization and leadership emergence. *Nonlinear Dynamics, Psychology, and Life Sciences, 2,* 303–316.

Guastello, S. J. (1999a). Hierarchical dynamics affecting work performance in organizations. In W. Tschacher & J.-P. Dauwaulder (Eds.), *Dynamics, synergetics, and autonomous agents* (pp. 277–302). Singapore: World Scientific.

Guastello, S. J. (1999b). Hysteresis, bifurcation, and the natural rate of unemployment. In E. Elliott & L. D. Kiel (Eds.), *Nonlinear dynamics, complexity, and public policy* (pp. 31–46). Commack, NY: Nova Science.

Guastello, S. J. (2000). Symbolic dynamic patterns of written exchange: Hierarchical structures in an electronic problem-solving group. *Nonlinear Dynamics, Psychology, and Life Sciences, 4,* 169–188.

Guastello, S. J. (2001). Attractor stability in unemployment and inflation rates. In Y. Aruka (Ed.), *Evolutionary controversies in economics: A new transdiscipinary approach* (pp. 89–99). Tokyo: Springer-Verlag.

Guastello, S. J. (2002). *Managing emergent phenomena: Nonlinear dynamics in work organizations.* Mahwah, NJ: Lawrence Erlbaum.

Guastello, S. J., & Bock, B. R. (2001). Attractor reconstruction with principal components analysis: Application to work flows in hierarchical organizations. *Nonlinear Dynamics, Psychology, and Life Sciences, 5,* 175–192.

Guastello, S. J., & Bond, R. W., Jr. (2004). Coordination in stag hunt games with application to emergency management. *Nonlinear Dynamics, Psychology, and Life Sciences, 8,* 345–374.

Guastello, S. J., Gershon, R. M., & Murphy, L. R. (1999). Catastrophe model for the exposure to blood-borne pathogens and other accidents in health care settings. *Accident Analysis and Prevention, 31,* 739–750.

Guastello, S. J., & Guastello, D. D. (1998). Origins of coordination and team effectiveness: A perspective from game theory and nonlinear dynamics. *Journal of Applied Psychology, 83,* 423–437.

Guastello, S. J., Hyde, T., & Odak, M. (1998). Symbolic dynamic patterns of verbal exchange in a creative

problem-solving group. *Nonlinear Dynamics, Psychology, and Life Sciences, 2,* 35–58. Erratum: *NDPLS, 1999, 3,* 127–128.

Guastello, S. J., & Johnson, E. A. (1999). The effect of downsizing on hierarchical work flow dynamics in organizations. *Nonlinear Dynamics, Psychology, and Life Sciences, 3,* 347–378.

Guastello, S. J., Johnson, E. A., & Rieke, M. L. (1999). Nonlinear dynamics of motivational flow. *Nonlinear Dynamics, Psychology, and Life Sciences, 3,* 259–273.

Guastello, S. J., Nielson, K. A., & Ross, T. J. (2002). Temporal dynamics of brain activity in human memory processes. *Nonlinear Dynamics, Psychology, and Life Sciences, 6,* 323–334.

Guastello, S. J., & Philippe, P. (1997). Dynamics in the development of large information exchange groups and virtual communities. *Nonlinear Dynamics, Psychology, and Life Sciences, 1,* 123–149.

Haken, H. (1984). *The science of structure: Synergetics.* New York: Van Nostrand Reinhold.

Haken, H. (2002). *Information and self-organization: A macroscopic approach to complex systems* (2nd ed.). New York: Springer-Verlag.

Hanges, P. J., Braverman, E. P., & Rentch, J. R. (1991). Changes in raters' perception of subordinates: A catastrophe model. *Journal of Applied Psychology, 76,* 878–888.

Hausdorff, F. (1919). Dimension und ausseres mass. *Mathematical Annalen, 79,* 157–179.

Heath, R. (2000). *Nonlinear dynamics: Techniques and applications in psychology.* Mahwah, NJ: Lawrence Erlbaum.

Holland, J. (1995). *Hidden order.* Reading, MA: Addison-Wesley.

Hornero, R., Alonso, A., Jimeno, N., Jimeno, A., & Lopez, M. (1999). Estimation of correlation dimension to evaluate cognitive performance in schizophrenic patients using a new computer technique. *Nonlinear Dynamics, Psychology, and Life Sciences, 3,* 49–64.

Johnson, T. L., & Dooley, K. J. (1996). Looking for chaos in time series data. In W. Sulis & A. Combs (Eds.), *Nonlinear dynamics in human behavior* (pp. 44–76). Singapore: World Scientific.

Kanz, H., & Schreiber, T. (1997). *Nonlinear time series analysis.* New York: Cambridge University Press.

Kauffman, S. A. (1993). *The origins of orders: Self-organization and selection in evolution.* New York: Oxford University Press.

Kauffman, S. A. (1995). *At home in the universe: The search for laws of self-organization and complexity.* New York: Oxford University Press.

Kiel, L. D. (1994). *Managing chaos and complexity in government.* San Francisco: Jossey-Bass.

Koyama, A., Yoneyama, K., Sawada, Y., & Ohtomo, N. (Eds.). (1994). *A recent advance in time series analysis by maximum entropy method: Applications to medical and biological sciences.* Hokkaido, Japan: Hokkaido University Press.

Kugiumtzis, D., Lillekjendlie, B., & Christophersen, N. (1994). *Chaotic time series, Part I: Estimation of invariant properties in state space* (Technical Report). Oslo: University of Oslo, Department of Informatics.

Lange, R. (1999). A cusp catastrophe approach to the prediction of temporal patterns in the kill dates of individual serial murderers. *Nonlinear Dynamics, Psychology, and Life Sciences, 3,* 143–159.

Lathrop, D. P., & Kostelich, E. J. (1989). Characterization of an experimental strange attractor by periodic orbits. *Physics Review A, 40,* 4028–4031.

Lewis, J. E., & Glass, L. (1992). Nonlinear dynamics and symbolic dynamics of neural networks. *Neural Computation, 4,* 621–642.

Mandelbrot, B. B. (1977). Fractals and turbulence: Attractors and dispersion. In P. Bernard & T. Raiu (Eds.), *Turbulence Seminar Berkeley 1976/1977* (pp. 83–93). New York: Springer-Verlag.

Mandelbrot, B. B. (1983). *The fractal geometry of nature.* New York: Freeman.

Maxwell, S. E. (2000). Sample size and multiple regression analysis. *Psychological Methods, 5,* 343–458.

May, R. M., & Oster, G. F. (1976). Bifurcations and dynamic complexity in simple ecological models. *American Naturalist, 110,* 573–599.

Meyer, M., Marconi, C., Rahmel, B., Grassi, G., Ferretti, G., Skinner, J. E., & Cerretelli, N. (1998). Fractal dynamics of heartbeat interval fluctuations in health and disease. In F. Orsucci (Ed.), *The complex matters of the mind* (pp. 105–128). Singapore: World Scientific.

Newhouse, R., Ruelle, D., & Takens, F. (1978). Occurence of strange attractors: An axiom near quasi-periodic flows on T^m, *m* > 3. *Communications in Mathematical Physics, 64,* 35–41.

Ott, E., Sauer, T., & Yorke, J. A. (Eds.). (1994). *Coping with chaos.* New York: John Wiley.

Packard, N. H., Crutchfield, J. P., Farmer, J. D., & Shaw, R. S. (1980). Geometry from a time series. *Physics Review Letters, 45,* 712–716.

Pincus, D. (2001). A framework and methodology for the study of nonlinear, self-organizing family dynamics. *Nonlinear Dynamics, Psychology, and Life Sciences, 5,* 139–174.

Priesmeyer, R. (1992). *Organizations and chaos.* Westport, CT: Quorum.

Puu, T. (1993). *Nonlinear economic dynamics* (3rd ed.). New York: Springer-Verlag.

Puu, T. (2000). *Attractors, bifurcations, and chaos: Nonlinear phenomena in economics.* New York: Springer-Verlag.

Rapp, P., & Korslund, K. E. (2000, July). *Quantitative characterization of patient-therapist communication in dialectical behavior therapy.* Paper presented at the annual conference of the Society for Chaos Theory in Psychology & Life Sciences, Philadelphia.

Robinson, C. (1999). *Dynamical systems: Stability, symbolic dynamics, and chaos* (2nd ed.). Boca Raton, FL: C R C Press.

Rosser, J. B., Rosser, M. V., Guastello, S. J., & Bond, R. W., Jr. (2001). Chaotic hysteresis and systemic economic transformation: Soviet investment patterns. *Nonlinear Dynamics, Psychology, and Life Sciences, 5,* 345–368.

Ruelle, D. (1991). *Chance and chaos.* Princeton, NJ: Princeton University Press.

Sabelli, H., & Kauffman, L. (1999). The process equation: Formulating and testing the process theory of systems. *Cybernetics and Systems, 20,* 261–294.

Shannon, C. E. (1948). A mathematical theory of communication. *The Bell System Technical Journal, 27,* 379–423.

Sprott, J. C. (2003). *Chaos and time-series analysis.* New York: Oxford University Press.

Sulis, W. (1998). Dynamical systems in psychology: Linguistic approaches. In F. Orsucci (Ed.), *The complex matters of the mind* (pp. 33–57). Singapore: World Scientific.

Theiler, J., & Eubank, S. (1993). Don't bleach chaotic data. *Chaos, 3,* 771–782.

Thom, R. (1975). *Structural stability and morphegenesis.* New York: Benjamin-Addison-Wesley.

Waldrop, M. M. (1992). *Complexity: The emerging science at the edge of chaos.* New York: Simon & Schuster.

West, B. J., & Deering, B. (1995). *The lure of modern science: Fractal thinking.* Singapore: World Scientific.

Wiggins, S. (1988). *Global bifurcations and chaos.* New York: Springer-Verlag.

Wolfram, S. (2002). *A new kind of science.* Champaign, IL: Wolfram Media.

Yamada, A., Hayano, J., Sakata, S., Okata, A., Mukai, S., Ohte, N., & Kimura, G. (2000). Reduced ventricular irregularity is associated with increased mortality in patients with chronic atrial fibrillation. *Circulation, 102,* 300–306.

Yee, H. C., Sweby, P. K., & Griffiths, D. F. (1991). Dynamical approach study of spurious steady-state numerical solutions on nonlinear differential equations I: The dynamics of time discretization and its implications for algorithm development in computational fluid dynamics. *Journal of Computational Physics, 97,* 249–310.

Yeragani, K., Nadella, R., Hinze, B., Yeragani, S., & Jampala, V. C. (2000). Nonlinear measures of heart period variability: Decreased measures of symbolic dynamics in patients with panic disorder. *Depression & Anxiety, 12,* 67–77.

Zaror, G., & Guastello, S. J. (2000). Self-organization and leadership emergence: A cross-cultural replication. *Nonlinear Dynamics, Psychology, and Life Sciences, 4,* 113–119.

Zeeman, E. C. (1977). *Catastrophe theory: Selected papers (1972–1977).* Reading, MA: Addison-Wesley.

15

Social Life *in Silico*

The Science of Artificial Societies

Damon M. Centola

Michael W. Macy

Computational modeling has become well established as an essential methodology in the biological and physical sciences (Strogatz, 1994) and has recently begun a migration into the social sciences (Axelrod, 1997; Axtell, 2000; Epstein & Axtell, 1996; Gilbert & Troitzsch, 1999). Interest in modeling the microfoundations of macrosocial patterns has led to advances in evolutionary and cognitive game theory (Axelrod, 1984, 1997; Roth & Erev, 1995), organizational ecology (Lomi & Larsen, 1998), social networks (Carley, 2003), artificial societies (Epstein & Axtell, 1996), cultural differentiation and diffusion (Mark, 1998), and collective action (Chwe, 1999; Macy, 1991; Marwell & Oliver, 1993).

The growing interest in this tool for theoretical research can be attributed in part to the lowering of technological barriers. Most social scientists now have access to machines capable of running very complex and computationally intensive modeling programs. Moreover, graphical interfaces facilitate highly intuitive representations of the results.

The power of inexpensive desktop computers explains the widening access to computational modeling but not the lure. In the physical and life sciences, the attraction centers on the ability to use numerical integration to solve problems that would otherwise be mathematically intractable. In physics, systems with nonlinear dynamics and sensitive dependence on initial conditions

Authors' Note: The research on which this study is based was supported by a National Science Foundation IGERT Fellowship for the study of nonlinear dynamics to the first author and a National Science Foundation grant (SES0241657) to the second author. We also thank Arnout Van de Rijt for helpful comments on an earlier draft.

(so-called complex systems) have motivated the use of a wide variety of computational techniques (Strogatz, 1994). And in biology, large systems that exhibit stochasticity and periodic dynamics have motivated the adoption of many of the computational techniques developed by physicists (May, 1974, 1976; Strogatz, 2003).

Similarly, social scientists have begun to appreciate that the complexity of social systems cannot be understood using traditional analytical techniques. In particular, contrary to traditional intuitions, the emergence of macrosocial patterns out of microsocial interactions exhibits a high degree of nonlinearity. Thus, it should not be surprising that interest in computational modeling has migrated from "artificial life" to "artificial societies" (Epstein & Axtell, 1996), in which investigators attempt to grow complex macrosocial patterns from the bottom up.

Increasingly, these bottom-up computational techniques use agents embedded in a network to study how local interactions can generate system-level dynamics. The agent-based model (hereafter ABM) allows researchers to study how local decision heuristics and network topology interact to produce highly complex and often surprising global patterns.

Why Not Just Use Game Theory Instead?

Agent-based computational modeling extends the traditional microsocial approach of classical game theory. Game theory is not a computational technique but a formal mathematical tool that allows the behavior of a population of two or more players to be analytically derived from the utility-maximizing behavior of every member, based on the solution concept proposed by John Nash (1950). Nash proved that every general-sum noncooperative game has at least one Nash equilibrium in mixed strategies. A Nash equilibrium is a configuration of strategies in which no player has an incentive to deviate unilaterally. Hence, Nash equilibria are self-enforcing; no contract is necessary to guarantee compliance. This allows for the possibility that social order can self-organize, even in the absence of the Leviathan.

Although this result is clearly of enormous significance across all the social sciences, important limitations to the classical analytical approach have spurred the development of evolutionary and learning-theoretic extensions. Nash equilibrium analysis tells us if any strategic configurations are stable, and if so, how they are characterized. Knowing that a configuration is an equilibrium means that if this state should obtain, the system will remain there forever. However, this does not imply that this state will ever be reached. Where multiple equilibria exist, the normal-form Nash solution[1] cannot tell us which equilibria will be selected or with what relative probability. Nor does it tell us how such states might be achieved or what will happen if an equilibrium should be perturbed. In short, the static focus on the identification of equilibrium fails to capture the out-of-equilibrium dynamics that guide a population of players from some initial condition to a stable social arrangement or from one equilibrium (when perturbed) to another.

Moreover, Nash equilibria cannot explain social stability among interacting agents who are themselves dynamically changing their strategies. Put differently, a strong limitation of the Nash equilibrium concept is the assumption that population stability is predicated on the stability of the individual members: the unwillingness of anyone to change strategies unilaterally. ABMs extend equilibrium analysis to cases in which social stability arises even though individual strategies are constantly changing.[2] A dynamic equilibrium obtains when the forces pushing the system in one direction are precisely balanced by countervailing forces, as happens in a market when changes in consumer behavior prompt changes in the distribution of production strategies, which in turn drive the consumer behavior back into balance. Empirical studies of market behavior (Kirman, 1989, 1992) show that ABMs with dynamic agents yield better approximations of market equilibria than traditional game theoretic models with all players in Nash equilibrium.

The Nash-solution concept has another important limitation: the mathematical intractability of heterogeneity of preferences among the actors. It is difficult to derive equilibria for a population of players with different preferences and incomplete information about the preferences of other players. ABMs show how agents with different preferences can interact dynamically to produce macrosocial outcomes.

The tractability of classical game theoretic solutions also requires that players have unlimited cognitive capacity, complete and perfect information, and common knowledge.[3] However, the analytical power is purchased at a very high price. Game theory becomes the theory of games played by game theorists (Macy & Flache, 2002).

ABMs allow us to relax the cognitive and informational demands of the classical approach and to explore the behavior of a lay population. In place of the standard *homo economicus* of classical game theory, ABMs allow investigators to explore how different cognitive and behavioral mechanisms affect aggregate dynamics. These mechanisms include imitation, heuristic decision, stochastic learning, Bayesian updating, best reply with finite memory, and local optimization.

We conclude this litany of limitations by pointing to what we regard as the most important of all: the assumption that the players interact in a fully connected (or complete) network or in randomized subsets. Although game theoretic analysis has been applied to network interactions (Buskens, 2002), mathematically, tractability imposes severe constraints on the exploration of structural parameters. Yet, social scientists increasingly appreciate the importance of social structure in the study of population dynamics. The assumption of random or fully connected ties among players in a population is an abstraction that ignores a crucial vector of explanation in the social sciences, the structure of social ties. ABMs facilitate exploration of the effects of network topology on aggregate dynamics.

These extensions of traditional game theory can be stated very succinctly: ABMs allow researchers to systematically explore (independently and in combination) the effects of heterogeneity, bounded rationality, and network structure on the dynamics and stability of social systems (Axtell, 2000). This short summary implies an indefinitely long research agenda, with unexpected branches and turns that remain to be pursued.

A simple but highly illuminating example comes from recent efforts to model social cooperation in a game called the Prisoner's Dilemma, which formalizes the paradox in which individually rational players produce a collectively irrational outcome. In the Prisoner's Dilemma, defection (or cheating) is the dominant strategy; that is, each player is better off defecting, no matter what the partner chooses. Yet, the payoff for mutual defection is less than that for mutual cooperation.

An early computational refinement of this result, called the *replicator dynamics,* looked at changes over time in the distribution of *cooperate* and *defect* strategies in a population of players. Whereas the Nash solution for the Prisoner's Dilemma is static, the replicator dynamics assumes a heterogeneous population of agents and evaluates differential reproduction rates based on their local success in the game by using numerical integration to iterate over many generations. Interestingly, the replicator dynamic solution is identical to the Nash solution: global defection. Indeed, Nash noted the convergence between the static equilibrium that bears his name and what he called the *mass action* equilibrium based on reasoning that anticipated the replicator dynamics.

The replicator dynamics are not agent based, however. An early contribution of agent-based modeling to the study of the Prisoner's Dilemma was presented by Nowak and May (1993). They used a spatial lattice to show that local clusters of cooperation could be sustained indefinitely in a heterogeneous population constrained by nonrandom interactions. The success of cooperation in the Nowak and May model is due to the topology of interaction. Agents interacting in a spatial lattice have more contact with neighbors who are similar to them than to those who differ; thus, cooperators will fare better (on average) than defectors and be able to reproduce at competitive rates. This result shows how bottom-up aggregation, from microinteraction to population behavior, can be very different when the system is studied as an ABM than when studied under either the replicator dynamics or the Nash formalization.

What Are We Modeling, Anyway?

Despite the advantages of ABMs over traditional game theoretic methods, skepticism remains about the validity and robustness of results obtained from computer simulations. The criticisms are similar to those directed at laboratory research in social psychology: How can experiments under artificial conditions be used to make predictions about behavior outside the lab?

These criticisms reflect a misunderstanding of experimental methodology that applies to both laboratory and computational research. Experiments are used to test predictions about outcomes under controlled conditions, not in natural settings where predictions are likely to be confounded by unmeasured effects. Should the predictions be supported in the lab, it may be useful to apply the theory to real-world conditions that violate its scope, so as to generate intuitions about how the theory might be extended or elaborated.

With agent-based modeling, the misunderstanding may also reflect confusion created by the widely misused term *simulation,* whose meaning was shaped by earlier generations of computational techniques. Classical simulation models (e.g., Cyert & March, 1963) used computers to simulate dynamical systems, such as control and feedback processes in organizations, industries, cities, and even global populations. The value of these models depends entirely on predictive accuracy and realism.

In contrast, artificial societies are highly abstract thought experiments.[4] Contrary to the critics, making these models more realistic would add complexity that is likely to undermine their usefulness. The priority in building ABMs is to keep them as simple and abstract as possible. From this perspective, the artificiality of ABMs is a virtue, not a vice. When simulation is used to make predictions or for training personnel (e.g., flight simulators), the assumptions need to be highly realistic, which usually means they will also be highly complicated (Axelrod, 1997). "But if the goal is to deepen our understanding of some fundamental process," Axelrod (1997) continues, "then simplicity of the assumptions is important and realistic representation of all the details of a particular setting is not" (p. 5).

This principle extends to the behavioral assumptions about the cognitive complexity of the agents. The principle of emergence suggests that the complexity of social life need not be reducible to the cognitive complexity of individuals. Although agents may follow simple rules, the interactions can produce global patterns that may not be at all obvious and are very difficult to understand. Modeling artificial worlds allows us to explore the complexity of the social environment by removing the cognitive complexity (and idiosyncrasy) of constituent individuals. The intent behind these models is to understand the minimal conditions, the simplest set of assumptions about human behavior, required for a given social phenomenon to emerge at a higher level of organization.

Don't the Results Simply Depend on the Assumptions?

Another concern is that the global patterns generated by ABMs are artifacts of arbitrary assumptions about local behavior or interaction. In one important sense, this should always be the case because the explanatory strategy in agent-based modeling, as in mathematical proofs, is to demonstrate that the *explanandum* follows from the *explanans*. Nevertheless, it can also happen that two similar but nonidentical models generate similar but nonidentical results. Which is to be believed?

The answer can be found through a modeling technique called *alignment* (Axtell, Axelrod, Epstein, & Cohen, 1996). Alignment is a way of integrating two models so that each becomes a special case of a more general model, and thus to formalize the logical implications of the different model specifications. A recent example of alignment involved two prominent and very similar models of social dilemma[5] games played by adaptive agents, the Bush-Mosteller stochastic learning model (Bush & Mosteller, 1955) and the Roth-Erev payoff-matching model (Roth & Erev, 1995). The two models share three behavioral assumptions that relax the cognitive demands of the Nash approach: experiential induction (vs. logical deduction), reward and punishment (vs. utility), and melioration (vs. optimization). Both models identify two new solution concepts for the problem of cooperation in social dilemmas. One solution is a socially deficient self-correcting equilibrium (or social trap), and the other is a self-reinforcing equilibrium that is usually (but not always) socially efficient. The models also identify the mechanism by which players can escape the social trap: stochastic collusion, based on a random walk in which both players wander far enough out of equilibrium that they escape its gravitational pull. Random walk, in turn, implies that a principal obstacle to escape is the coordination complexity of stochastic collusion. Thus, these learning models direct attention to conditions that reduce coordination complexity, including small-world networks (Watts, 1999), which minimize the average number of partners for each player yet still permit locally successful strategies to propagate. Temporal Schelling points are another potential solution, such as the holidays that coordinated locally self-organizing truces in the trenches of World War I.

Coordination complexity can also be reduced by high learning rates, which reduce the number of steps that must be coordinated in the random walk.

It is here—in the effect of learning rates on stochastic collusion—that the two learning models diverge. The divergence might easily go unnoticed, given the theoretical isomorphism of two learning theoretic models based on the same three fundamental behavioral principles. Yet, each model implements these principles in different ways and with different results.

To identify the differences, Flache and Macy (2002) aligned and then integrated the two models as special cases of a general reinforcement learning model. The integration uncovered a key hidden assumption, the *power law of learning*. This is the curious but plausible tendency for learning to diminish with success and intensify with failure, which the authors labeled *fixation*. Fixation, in turn, affects the effective learning rate and, through that, the probability of stochastic collusion. This exercise showed how the integration of alternative models can uncover underlying principles and lead to a more general theory.

Is "Computational Experiment" an Oxymoron?

Social psychologists interested in the subtleties of motivation may find ABMs too abstract and coarse-grained to be useful for studying highly idiosyncratic individual behavior. However, we believe it is just the opposite. ABMs are ideally suited for experimental social psychology precisely because of their abstractness. Computational experiments using ABMs can provide a propaedeutic that lays the groundwork for laboratory experiments. ABMs serve a proto-experimental function by testing the internal validity of proposed explanatory mechanisms. By assigning agents simple rules that isolate a mechanism, an experimental researcher can use the agent model as a test run to see whether the proposed mechanism can, in principle, account for the aggregate patterns of behavior that are of interest. Computational results can help to focus and refine directions of empirical research and also assist in framing the design of experimental tests. Computational experiments may even show that the behavioral mechanism being studied can produce unanticipated consequences, thus leading to new experimental hypotheses.

For example, suppose we want to know whether residential segregation can be diminished by promoting multiculturalism. One of the earliest ABMs, implemented by Thomas Schelling (1971) on a large checkerboard, suggests that a better strategy might be to promote ethnic color blindness rather than appreciation of diversity. His "tipping" model revealed a surprisingly strong tendency toward neighborhood segregation, so long as individuals take into account ethnic composition even when they have a preference for diversity.

ABMs can also identify social psychological mechanisms that might account for enigmatic behaviors. These mechanisms can then be tested under controlled conditions in the laboratory to see if the predicted outcomes obtain. For example, a recent application (Centola, Willer, & Macy, in press) addressed the curious tendency for people to pretend to believe something they know not to be true and to disparage those who disagree, a behavioral pattern that is mocked in Hans Christian Andersen's story "The Emperor's New Clothes." Everyday examples include college students who celebrate and encourage intoxication through drinking games, yet who privately express discomfort with excessive consumption (Prentice & Miller, 1993). The foible is not limited to students. We all know "naked" scholars whose incomprehensible writings are applauded by those who pretend to understand and appreciate every word and who disparage critics for being intellectually shallow. The pattern extends to social snobbery by posturing elitists who are privately bored by Bavarian opera and to citizens in totalitarian

regimes who denounce their neighbors so as to affirm their loyalty to the regime (Kuran, 1995).

Centola, Willer, and Macy (in press) wanted to know if the fear of exposure as an imposter was sufficient to sustain a cascade that might then trap a population into thinking a norm was highly popular when in fact almost everyone shared their strong (but private) wish that the norm would go away. More precisely, they wanted to see if this could happen even in the absence of any explicit pressure to enforce the norm. In addition, they wanted to identify the conditions that might make a population highly vulnerable to such a cascade.

To find out, they modeled a population of agents who are willing to comply with a norm they privately dislike in order to win social approval or avoid disapprobation, but only if the pressure to comply is sufficiently strong. Having complied with the norm, they may also enforce compliance by others for a similar reason: out of fear of exposure as an opportunistic imposter who does not really believe in the norm. The motivating question was whether popular enforcement of an unpopular norm could spread without any explicit social pressure to enforce the norm.

The Emperor's Dilemma is a cascade model in which agents are assigned thresholds for compliance and enforcement that reflect the strength of the agent's antipathy toward the norm. The enforcement threshold is always higher than the compliance threshold, reflecting the additional costs of sanctioning others, over and above the costs of compliance. Agents comply and enforce when the social pressure for and against the norm exceeds the compliance and enforcement thresholds, respectively. This pressure comes not from seeing one's neighbors comply (as in a model of herd behavior), but only from seeing them enforce compliance (as in a model of norm enforcement).

The model is initialized with a population that contains only a tiny fraction of vigilant "true believers" (1 percent), who truly support the norm and will always apply pressure if they spot any deviance at all. The rest of the population opposes the norm, and in the absence of enforcement, the skeptics refuse to comply. The model assumes that agents live in a clustered network, but with nontrivial overlap between the clusters, such that nonneighbors who have one neighbor in common are likely to have more than one.

The model demonstrated that it is indeed possible for widespread enforcement of an unpopular norm to emerge even in the absence of any pressure to enforce the norm, so long as the fear of exposure as an imposter is sufficient to motivate enforcement as a way to signal the sincerity of compliance. This suggests the need to test whether this fear of exposure can lead to enforcement behavior under controlled conditions in the laboratory.

A skeptic might counter that one could have arrived at the computational result by mere intuition and then gone directly to the lab. Not so. The computational model also identifies some surprising conditions that are necessary for these cascades to emerge. For example, it turns out that cascades are not possible if there are too many true believers. For another, the authors discovered that unpopular norms tend to collapse if agents eventually change their private beliefs to conform to their public behavior, thereby making the norm *less* unpopular over time. Allowing agents with weak convictions to eventually switch sides caused a reverse cascade that undermined support for the unpopular norm. The norm collapses not when a child laughs at the naked emperor, but when the adults begin to believe they can actually see the beautiful new clothes!

Having observed this unexpected result, the authors dug deeper to find out how this had happened and found a straightforward explanation that might easily have been missed had they relied solely on intuition to predict the macrosocial consequences of the microsocial postulates. An agent who comes actually to believe the norm no longer worries about exposure as an imposter and is thus no longer compelled to falsely enforce. Thus, converted agents conform to the norm, but they no longer enforce, given

the weakness of their convictions. When these converts stop enforcing, there is insufficient social pressure to induce compliance by those of their neighbors with strong private convictions. They, in turn, stop complying and pressuring others to do so, which further reduces local pressure in the neighborhood. The social stability of an unpopular norm is thus undermined by increased popularity of the norm!

We also found that changing the network structure dramatically changed the results. In particular, adding *bridge ties* between otherwise distant clusters tends to inhibit the cascades. Why this sensitivity to network topology? These shortcuts across the network tend to dissipate social pressure below the local critical mass needed to fuel the cascade. Contrary to an extensive literature on small worlds and the strength of weak ties, bridge ties across clusters actually reduce the propagation of unpopular norms.

These results deepened our understanding of the dynamics of a puzzling social phenomenon that has perplexed social scientists for years. Furthermore, the results helped to elaborate the experimental design in a laboratory study of the effects of social structure and changing preferences on the enforcement decisions of individuals.

Conclusion

We conclude with a brief set of principles of agent-based modeling. First, the researcher must specify the rules that govern the agent's behavior and whether they are deterministic or probabilistic. These rules define the agents as instrumental (agents respond to payoffs relative to aspiration levels), emotional (agents respond to behavior by others), or normative (agents act on internalized obligations). These agent specifications need not be fixed. On the contrary, by manipulating agent knowledge and ability, the researcher can explore the macrosocial consequences of changes in individual behavior. Agents' rules can also change endogenously over time through processes of learning or evolution.

Second, the researcher must specify a network structure in which the agents will interact. The network structure is the environment or social space in which the agents are located and constrains who may interact with whom. Note that this specification does not preclude the possibility that agents decide with whom to interact, creating a dynamic network. Network structure can also be a complete graph in which all agents interact with everyone. Because it is exterior to the agent, the network specification is the purely structural component of the model. Agents can interact in social networks, with spatial constraints, with random pairing, or in specified or dynamic group structures.

With these simple specifications, we can study the emergent (and often surprising) macrosocial consequences of psychological mechanisms and local interactions. These results can then inform experimental designs for testing the theories in the laboratory.

The process can also go the other way. Laboratory experiments can also inform elaboration of agent models. This feedback between agent modeling and laboratory experimentation can lead to a fecund bottom-up exploration of the self-organization of social life.

Notes

1. The problems with equilibrium selection and out-of-equilibrium dynamics apply mainly to normal-form games (those in which players must choose simultaneously). The Nash solution for extensive-form games with complete information allows for subgame perfect-equilibrium selection and for identification of the path to that equilibrium via backward induction.

2. Young (1993, 1998) has proposed an analytical solution concept, *stochastic stability*, that overcomes this limitation of the Nash solution concept. Other recent extensions to classical game theory also provide analytical tools for exploring boundedly rational agents, heterogeneity, and simple network structures. However, ABMs have the advantage that model parameters can be much more easily explored, allowing researchers to understand a system's behavior under a

wider range of parameter settings than would be possible (or mathematically tractable) using an analytical apparatus.

3. Perfect information means that each player knows the entire history of moves and outcomes; complete information means there is no private information; and common knowledge means that all players know that all of the other players know what they know, know that they know it, and so on.

4. For a more detailed overview of the history of social simulation, see Gilbert and Troitzsch, 1999.

5. A social dilemma is a noncooperative game with at least one Pareto-deficient Nash equilibrium, such as Prisoner's Dilemma or Stag Hunt (in which mutual defection is deficient), or Chicken (probabilistic cooperation is deficient).

References

Axelrod, R. (1984). *The evolution of cooperation.* New York: Basic Books.

Axelrod, R. (1997). *The complexity of cooperation: Agent-based models of competition and collaboration.* Princeton, NJ: Princeton University Press.

Axtell, R. (2000). *Why agents: On the varied motivations for agent computing in the social sciences* (CSED Working Paper No. 17). Washington, DC: The Brookings Institution.

Axtell, R., Axelrod, R., Epstein, J. M., & Cohen, M. D. (1996). Aligning simulation models: A case study and results. *Computational and Mathematical Organization Theory, 1*(2), 123–141.

Bush, R. R., & Mosteller, F. (1955). *Stochastic models for learning.* New York: John Wiley.

Buskens, V. (2002). *Social networks and trust.* New York: Kluwer Academic.

Carley, K. M. (2003). Dynamic network analysis. In R. Breiger, K. Carley, & P. Pattison (Eds.), *Dynamic social network modeling and analysis: Workshop summary and papers* (pp. 133–145). Washington, DC: The National Academies Press.

Centola, D., Willer, R., & Macy, M. (in press). The emperor's dilemma: A computational model of self-enforcing norms. *American Journal of Sociology.*

Chwe, M. S. Y., (1999). Structure and strategy in collective action. *American Journal of Sociology, 105*(1), 128–156.

Cyert, R., & March, J. G. (1963). *A behavioral theory of the firm.* Englewood Cliffs, NJ: Prentice Hall.

Epstein, J., & Axtell, R. (1996). *Growing artificial societies: Social science from the bottom up.* Boston: MIT Press.

Flache, A., & Macy, M. (2002). Stochastic collusion and the power law of learning. *Journal of Conflict Resolution, 46,* 629–653.

Gilbert, N., & Troitzsch, K. (1999). *Simulation for the social scientist.* Buckingham, UK: Open University Press.

Kirman, A. (1989). The intrinsic limits of modern economic theory: The emperor has no clothes. *Economic Journal, 99*(395), 126–139.

Kirman, A. (1992). Whom or what does the representative individual represent? *Journal of Economic Perspectives, 6*(2), 117–136.

Kuran, T. (1995). *Private truths, public lies: The social consequences of preference falsification.* Cambridge, MA: Harvard University Press.

Lomi, A., & Larsen, E. R. (1998). Density delay and organizational survival: Computational models and empirical comparisons. *Computational and Mathematical Organization Theory, 3*(4), 219–247.

Macy, M. (1991). Chains of cooperation: Threshold effects in collective action. *American Sociological Review, 56,* 730–747.

Macy, M., & Flache, A. (2002). Learning dynamics in social dilemmas. *Proceedings of the National Academy of Sciences, 99,* 7229–7236.

Mark, N. (1998). Social differentiation from first principles. *American Sociological Review, 63,* 309–330.

Marwell, G., & Oliver, P. (1993). *The critical mass in collective action: A micro-social theory.* New York: Cambridge University Press.

May, R. M. (1974). *Stability and complexity in model ecosystems.* Princeton, NJ: Princeton University Press.

May, R. M. (1976). Simple mathematical model with very complicated dynamics. *Nature, 26,* 457.

Nash, J. (1950). Equilibrium points in N-person games. *Proceedings of the National Academy of Sciences, 36,* 48–49.

Nowak, M., & May, R. (1993). Evolutionary games and spatial chaos. *Nature, 359,* 826–929.

Prentice, D. A., & Miller, D. T. (1993). Pluralistic ignorance and alcohol use on campus: Some consequences of misperceiving the social norm. *Journal of Personality and Social Psychology, 64*(2), 243–256.

Roth, A. E., & Erev, I. (1995). Learning in extensive-form games: Experimental data and simple dynamic models in the intermediate term. *Games and Economic Behavior, 8,* 164–212.

Schelling, T. (1971). Dynamic models of segregation. *Journal of Mathematical Sociology, 1,* 143–186.

Strogatz, S. H. (1994). *Nonlinear dynamics and chaos: With applications to physics, biology, chemistry, and engineering.* Reading, MA: Perseus Books.

Strogatz, S. H. (2003). *Sync: The emerging science of spontaneous order.* New York: Hyperion.

Watts, D. J. (1999). Networks, dynamics, and the small-world phenomenon. *American Journal of Sociology, 105,* 493–527.

Young, H. P. (1993). The evolution of conventions. *Econometrica, 61,* 57–84.

Young, H. P. (1998). *Individual strategy and social structure: An evolutionary theory of institutions.* Princeton, NJ: Princeton University Press.

PART IV

Applied Group Research

16

Group Dynamics and Effectiveness

Five Years of Applied Research

Tjai M. Nielsen

Eric D. Sundstrom

Terry R. Halfhill

Work groups have received increasing scientific attention (Cohen & Bailey, 1997; Kozlowski & Bell, 2003; Sundstrom, McIntyre, Halfhill, & Richards, 2000) and coverage in the management press (Edwards & Wilson, 2004; Nielsen, Sundstrom, Soulen, Halfhill, & Huff, 2003; Sundstrom, 1999). Attention to teams has coincided with their increasing application in organizations. In 1996, by one estimate, as many as 78% of *Fortune 1000* companies used self-managing work teams (Lawler, Mohrman, & Ledford, 1998, p. 44), in a sharp upward trend from previous years that apparently continues today. Yet, although organizations embrace work groups, many questions remain unanswered.

This chapter offers a field-based perspective on applied group research. We begin by defining the research area; then we discuss its history, examine key theoretical perspectives and types of work groups, and selectively review field studies of work group effectiveness conducted from mid-1999 to mid-2004. We conclude by offering ideas for future research and practice.

We define *work group* and *work team* as interdependent collections of individuals who share responsibility for specific outcomes for their organizations (Sundstrom, DeMeuse, & Futrell, 1990). Although some authors (Katzenbach & Smith, 1993) have argued for distinguishing work groups from work teams, we use the terms interchangeably. A distinction has yet to be widely accepted among researchers or practitioners (Guzzo & Shea, 1992; Kozlowski & Bell, 2003; Sundstrom et al., 2000).

History of Applied Group Research

Applied group research involves the study of work groups in naturally occurring settings. People have organized themselves and worked in groups for centuries, but the empirical study of work groups is a more recent phenomenon. One of the earliest examples of empirically studying the world of work was published before World War I.

Group Research and Application Before 1980

Along with the classic work of Frederick Taylor (1911) regarding the theory of scientific management, Hugo Münsterberg contributed significantly to the study of work and work groups. A German scientist who chaired Harvard's psychology department, Münsterberg wrote more than a dozen books during his career, of which his best-known include *On the Witness Stand* (1908), *Psychology, General and Applied* (1914), and *Psychology and Industrial Efficiency* (1913). Many scholars have not heard of Münsterberg, although he earned his MD and PhD degrees by the age of 22, studied with Wilhelm Wundt, was asked by William James to work at Harvard, and was a primary factor in establishing psychology as a science in the United States (Nielsen, 1999). He often gets credit for establishing applied psychology and initiating the study of individual differences (Landy, 1992). While Münsterberg's work refers to work groups, they were not his primary focus. One of the first empirical examinations of work groups was a series of studies conducted at Western Electric's Hawthorne Works in Chicago.

The Hawthorne studies (Roethlisberger & Dickson, 1939) encompassed a series of projects conducted in the late 1920s and early 1930s. These projects sought to identify factors in productivity. Initially, the effect of lighting (Sundstrom, 1986) was examined, but this produced unexpected results. After learning that variables other than lighting intensity were at work, researchers shifted their focus to the interpersonal dimension. They began to focus on relationships among employees and management.

Many of the important findings from the Hawthorne studies related to work groups came out of the Bank Wiring Observation Room (Homans, 1950). A group of employees was selected and split into three teams. Each team, consisting of three wiremen and a solderer, was responsible for wiring banks of switching terminals, and the work was inspected by one of two inspectors. Over time, two informal groups developed, the "group in front" and the "group in back." The "group in front" developed norms involving consistently high levels of performance, whereas the "group in back" developed norms resulting in low levels of performance (Homans, 1950). The Hawthorne studies have had a lasting impact on the study of work groups. Sundstrom and colleagues (2000) observed,

> Among legacies for later research and application concerning work groups were: detailed illustration of methods for studying groups in work settings; evidence of development of informal groups among workers; evidence of mutual relevance of formal and informal social structure; demonstration of informal production norms in work groups; and perhaps most interesting, a clear example of a work group enforcing a production norm. (p. 45)

The Hawthorne studies contributed significantly to the subsequent study *and* use of work groups.

Although the impact of the Hawthorne studies was significant, there was a delay in the subsequent study and use of work groups like those at the Hawthorne Works. Many organizations followed the theory espoused by Frederick Taylor (1911) in *The Principles of Scientific Management*. Taylor's theory focused on (a) developing a science for every job as opposed to following the classic rule-of-thumb method; (b) using scientific selection, training, and development of workers; (c) creating effective cooperation between workers and management based on processes devised scientifically; and (d) dividing work between management and employees based on who would be most effective in completing the job, as opposed to assigning the majority of work to employees. Taylor's theory highlighted a narrowly defined approach to specialized individual jobs. Although many organizations adopted Taylor's ideas, work groups still existed in a variety of settings. Some examples include cockpit and tank crews in the military and informal assembly groups in manufacturing organizations. Examples such as these often involved close supervision and limited independence to make decisions and pursue new directions. Work groups were often implemented with the goal of increasing flexibility and efficiency, as fewer employees handled greater and more fluctuating amounts of work (Kelly, 1982). Between 1950 and 1980, interest in work groups was evidenced more by researchers than managers (Sundstrom et al., 2000).

After the Hawthorne studies of the 1920s and 1930s and even more after World War II, analysis and research on work groups increased (e.g., Bass, 1954; Homans, 1950; Lundberg, 1940; McGrath & Altman, 1966; Seashore, 1954). Psychologists conducted much of the early research on work groups (e.g., Homans, 1950; Seashore, 1954; Torrence, 1954). Walker and Guest (1952) examined automobile factory workers who were deployed in 10-person work groups. Torrence (1954) found that rank was related to influence among members of B-26

flight crews. Perhaps one of the most significant early contributions to work group research was made by Stanley E. Seashore (1954). He examined the relationship between group cohesion and performance among 228 work groups. He found that group norms can have both positive and negative relationships with performance depending on the nature of a group's norms. Groups with positive, productive norms will outperform those with deleterious, less productive norms.

These studies and others represented a dramatic increase in the study of work groups, which occurred primarily in the 1950s. In a review study, McGrath and Altman (1966) identified more than 2,100 studies on small groups conducted from 1950 to 1959. The majority of this work was done in laboratory settings, with about 5% taking place in the field. While the study of groups declined in coming decades, researchers gradually started shifting their focus by examining more work groups in field or organizational settings (Bettenhausen, 1991; Guzzo & Shea, 1992; Sanna & Parks, 1997).

Industrial/organizational (I/O) psychologists joined their colleagues in studying work groups (Cummings & Molloy, 1977; Pasmore, Francis, Haldeman, & Shani, 1982; Pasmore & Sherwood, 1977). A significant amount of research by I/O psychologists was prompted by the work of Trist and Bamforth (1951), who analyzed a British coal mine from a sociotechnical perspective (Pasmore & Sherwood, 1977). A large proportion of the experiments conducted in the sociotechnical arena examined work groups (Pasmore et al., 1982). Other researchers analyzed industrial applications of work groups (Cummings & Molloy, 1977). Cummings and Molloy found that about 82% of experiments involving the application of work groups resulted in productivity improvements. Research on work groups declined in the 1960s and 1970s, but the success of some practical applications (Wagel, 1987) and research demonstrating the benefits of work groups produced greater levels of interest by researchers and organizations in the 1980s and 1990s (Hoerr, 1989; Lawler et al., 1998; Sanna & Parks, 1997).

Group Research and Application in the 1980s

The implementation of work groups expanded in the 1980s. This expansion can be traced to the advent of *total quality management* (TQM; Hackman & Wageman, 1995). Many organizations pursued improvement in quality with the expectation that this would result in better and more sustainable business results. Organizations such as Ford (Banas, 1988), Martin Marietta (Thompson, 1982), and Lockheed Martin's missile division (Ledford, Lawler, & Mohrman, 1988) experimented with quality circles—groups of employees tasked with identifying solutions to specific business issues. Some organizations, such as Ford, Motorola, General Electric, and Boeing, grouped employees together to form production, project, and service teams (Hoerr, 1989; Wagel, 1987). An increase in research on work groups coincided with the increased use of teams in organizations (Bettenhausen, 1991; Guzzo & Shea, 1992; Sanna & Parks, 1997).

Sanna and Parks (1997) conducted a review of 445 work group studies published in three organizational psychology journals (*Journal of Applied Psychology, Organizational Behavior and Human Decision Processes,* and *Academy of Management Journal*) from 1975 through 1994. The authors found that the frequency of group research began increasing in the mid-1980s; 64% of the articles examined group performance, and 28% were conducted in the field. A review by Moreland, Hogg, and Hains (1994) of 707 group research articles found in three social psychology journals (*Journal of Experimental Social Psychology, Personality and Social Psychology,* and *Social Psychology Bulletin*) found the same frequency trend; however, in those journals, 23% of the articles analyzed group performance, and 4% were conducted in the field.

Bettenhausen (1991) also conducted a review of 250 studies published between January 1986 and October 1989. Bettenhausen categorized the reviewed studies into four categories: (a) studies examining how groups develop and change over time; (b) projects exploring how groups' interaction context affects processes and outcomes; (c) studies pertaining to group polarization, social influence, social loafing, group cohesion, commitment, conflict, and goal setting; and (d) projects addressing group effectiveness, self-managed teams, quality circles, and team building interventions. Unfortunately, Bettenhausen (1991) did not distinguish studies based on whether they were conducted in the field or laboratory. The crescendo of group research and application in the 1980s only increased in the 1990s (Sundstrom et al., 2000).

Group Research and Application in the 1990s

The use of work groups by organizations became common in the 1990s (Attaran & Nguyen, 2000; Lawler et al., 1998; Liebowitz & Holden, 1996). Chevron established interfunctional work teams in an effort to maximize the use of human resources in a key profit center (Attaran & Nguyen, 2000). Miller Brewing Company implemented cross-functional teams to complete a variety of tasks (Wellins, Byham, & Dixon, 1994). Liebowitz and Holden (1996) compared and contrasted the successful application of self-managed work teams in a unionized environment (Dow Corning) and in a non-unionized environment (Motorola). Wellins and colleagues (1994) explored the implementation of teams at the Kodak Customer Assistance Center. Support for using teams seemed to be ubiquitous. *Fortune* magazine referred to self-managed teams as the productivity breakthrough of the 1990s, while management guru Tom Peters (1988, p. 210) identified teams as an organizational building block. In 1987, Richard Hackman correctly predicted, "Organizations in the future will rely heavily on member self-management" (p. 90). Sheridan (1993) profiled the use and maintenance of work teams at one of Exxon Chemical Company's most honored plants. Reflecting the emergence of and belief in teams, Reich (1987) wrote, "If we are to compete in today's world, we must begin to celebrate . . . endeavors in which the whole of the effort is greater than the sum of individual contributions. We need to honor our teams more" (p. 78). The increased attention given to and the more widespread application of work groups coincided with greater attention by researchers (Cohen & Bailey, 1997; Halfhill, Sundstrom, Lehner, Calderone, & Nielsen, in press; Nielsen et al., 2003; Sundstrom et al., 2000).

Several review articles (Cohen & Bailey, 1997; Guzzo & Dickson, 1996; Sundstrom et al., 2000) identified an increasingly large amount of research geared toward work groups. More important, these authors identified an increase in the number of studies conducted in the field. Cohen and Bailey (1997) reviewed 54 articles published between January 1990 and April 1996 that focused on work teams found in organizational settings and included measures of effectiveness. They said the importance of conducting group research in the field is due to greater levels of generalizability, the importance of organizational features external to the team as determinants of effectiveness, and the utility of focusing on a coherent body of work that will improve opportunities to provide guidance to managers. Similarly, Sundstrom and his colleagues (2000) reviewed 90 research articles conducted in work organizations between 1980 and 1999. They echoed the importance of conducting research on work groups in work environments.

We focus on research in actual work settings for two reasons. First, operating within an organization is arguably one of the defining features of a work group (Argote & McGrath, 1993; Guzzo & Shea, 1992; Hackman, 1990). Second, although generic laboratory groups and simulations provide a valuable arena for studying group dynamics (Driskell & Salas, 1992; Forsyth, 1999), groups in these settings differ in important ways from intact work groups.

Sundstrom and colleagues (2000) selected studies in which researchers (a) examined work groups, (b) collected data in work settings, (c) measured some facet of group effectiveness, (d) treated groups as the unit of analysis, (e) reported results at the group level, and (f) included more than one work group or time of measurement. Several trends emerged from this review. First, service teams had attracted increasing attention and application. Second, more studies examined multiple types of groups than in earlier research, which tended to look at just one type of work group. Third, a few consistent differences emerged among types of work groups in correlates of effectiveness. Sundstrom and colleagues identified this as an important area for future research. Fourth, multiple studies identified criterion-specific predictors, that is, predictors that correlated with only one facet of effectiveness. Finally, the review uncovered no consistent pattern regarding relationships between groups of predictive factors (i.e., organizational context, group composition and size, group work design, intragroup processes, and external group processes) and effectiveness.

Types of Work Groups

One important issue for the study and application of work groups involves the wide range of work groups in organizations today. How do we differentiate one type of work group from another? Do different factors across varying types of teams have differential effects on team effectiveness? Researchers have addressed these questions by suggesting different theories and typologies (Bell & Kozlowski, 2002; Cohen & Bailey, 1997; Devine, 2002; Sundstrom et al., 1990).

The classification of different types of work groups aids in understanding team effectiveness in various contexts. Ideally, a taxonomy of work groups uses mutually exclusive and exhaustive categories while maximizing between-category variance and minimizing within-category variance (Devine, 2002). Some of the first attempts at classification involved differentiating task-oriented groups based on interpersonal relationships (Lundberg, 1940); primary task type (Carter, Haythorn, & Howell, 1950); different variable categories (Roby & Lanzetta, 1958); and group member behavior, required group member behavior, group member ability, and group task characteristics (McGrath & Altman, 1966).

Steiner (1972) distinguished four types of group tasks based on the relationship between individual member performance and the group's performance. Shaw (1973) identified six factors underlying all group tasks: cooperation requirements, solution multiplicity, population familiarity, intrinsic interest, task difficulty, and manipulative versus physical requirements. In his seminal work on small groups, McGrath (1984) integrated previous typologies and identified eight group tasks organized under three broader dimensions: the conflict-cooperation dimension, the conceptual-behavioral dimension, and the choice-execution dimension. Similar to Shaw's (1973) six categories of group tasks, Driskell, Hogan, and Salas (1987) grouped team tasks into six areas based on their behavioral requirements. More recent attempts at organizing team types have been widely cited (Hackman, 1990; Sundstrom et al., 1990).

Sundstrom and colleagues used an ecological approach to create a team taxonomy of four types of teams (Sundstrom & Altman, 1989; Sundstrom et al., 1990) based on their degree of internal differentiation (member heterogeneity) and external integration (link to the organization). The four types of teams were (1) advice/involvement teams, (2) production/service teams, (3) project/development teams, and (4) action/negotiation teams.

Hackman (1990) used a six-category typology: top management groups, task forces, professional support groups, performing groups, human service teams, and customer service teams. The management literature has also provided different examples of team classifications, usually containing fewer than seven types of teams (Devine, 2002).

Sundstrom et al. (2000), building on earlier typologies, identified six types of work groups: (a) production groups (which consist of front-line employees who repeatedly produce tangible output, such as automobile assembly groups or paper mill work crews), (b) service groups (which consist of employees who cooperate to conduct repeated transactions with customers, as in airline attendant teams, maintenance groups, and telecommunications sales groups), (c) management teams (which consist of an executive or senior manager and the managers or supervisors who report directly to him or her, such as corporate executive teams or regional steering committees), (d) project groups (which consist of members who tend to come from different departments or units, such as product development groups or strategy teams), (e) action and performing groups (which consist of individual experts and support staff who conduct complex, time-limited performance events involving audiences, adversaries, or challenging environments, such as surgery teams or search and rescue teams), and (f) advisory groups (which consist of different employees, sometimes from multiple levels within the organization, who solve problems and recommend solutions, such as task forces and quality circles). In some settings, these groups work outside of and in parallel with production processes and are "parallel groups." A more recent effort at integrating previous typologies was suggested by Dennis Devine (2002).

Devine's (2002) typology centers on seven underlying contextual dimensions (i.e., fundamental work cycle, physical ability requirements, temporal duration, task structure, active resistance, hardware dependence, and health risk). Devine suggests 14 different types of teams divided into an intellectual work teams cluster (i.e., executive, command, negotiation, commission, design, and advisory) and physical work teams cluster (i.e., service, production, performance, medical, response, military, transportation, and sports). Each team type has specific functions: (a) Executive teams plan and direct (e.g., board of directors, senior management team); (b) command teams integrate and coordinate (e.g., control tower, combat center teams; (c) negotiation teams deal and persuade (e.g., labor-management, international treaty); (d) commission teams choose and investigate (e.g., search committee, jury); (e) design teams create and develop (e.g., research and development, marketing); (f) advisory teams diagnose and suggest (e.g., quality circle, steering committee); (g) service teams provide and repair (e.g., fast food, auto service); (h) production teams build and assemble (e.g., home construction, automobile assembly); (i) performance teams enact and display (e.g., movie cast, orchestra); (j) medical teams treat and heal (e.g., surgery, emergency room); (k) response teams protect and rescue (e.g., fire station, paramedic); (l) military teams neutralize and protect (e.g., tank crew, infantry squad); (m) transportation teams convey and haul (e.g., airline cockpit, train crew); and (n) sports teams compete and win (e.g., baseball, soccer).

For present purposes, we distinguish six types of work teams: (a) production groups (e.g., assembly groups, paper mill work crews), (b) service groups (e.g., airline attendant teams, maintenance groups, and telecommunications sales groups), (c) management teams (e.g., corporate executive teams, regional steering committees), (d) project groups (e.g., product development groups, strategy teams), (e) action and performing groups (e.g., surgery teams, search and rescue teams), and (f) advisory groups (e.g., task forces, quality circles).

Theories of Work Group Effectiveness

Theories of group effectiveness address the definition of group effectiveness, seek to identify factors that predict it, and explain how those factors operate. Examples include early models of group performance offered by McGrath (1964) as well as later ones focused on effectiveness, such as those offered by Cohen and Bailey (1997) and Sundstrom et al. (1990).

McGrath (1964) pioneered the widely cited input-process-output (IPO) model of group performance. Although the idea is more than 40 years old, most models of work group effectiveness still rely on it to some extent. McGrath suggested that inputs are the key cause of processes, which then mediate the effect of inputs on outcomes. Inputs can be defined as things people bring to the group (expertise, status, personality, and experience); processes can be defined as the interaction among group members (social exchange of information, influence attempts, and leadership); and outputs can be defined as products yielded by the group (Guzzo & Shea, 1992). Researchers have suggested a variety of other group effectiveness models that have subsequently motivated other researchers to address them empirically (e.g., Cummings, 1978; Hackman & Morris, 1975).

In a model that focused on control over social and task-related processes and group self-regulation, Cummings (1978) offered a model based on sociotechnical theory. Another model based on sociotechnical theory included one suggested by Kolodny and Kiggundu (1980), which concentrated on leadership and supervision. Hackman and Oldham (1980) put forth a model based on the IPO sequence that designated as key factors: organizational context, interpersonal processes, design features (group task, composition, and norms), technology, and intermediate criteria of effectiveness (application of effort, knowledge and skill, and strategies). Building on the work of McGrath (1964), Gladstein (1984) offered a model containing six factors: group structure, resources, group process, task, organizational structure, and group composition. Sundstrom et al. (1990) and Hackman (1987) added group design, synergy, autonomy, physical environment, and a factor for group boundaries as additional variables important in a model of group effectiveness. Additional models were suggested in subsequent work (e.g., Campion, Medsker, & Higgs, 1993;

Cohen & Bailey, 1997), and increased emphasis was placed on the utility of using five categories of factors related to work group effectiveness. These categories generally include (a) organizational context (e.g., training, reward, measurement, and information systems), (b) group composition (e.g., number of members and the mixture of individual traits like personality and ability), (c) group work design (e.g., task interdependence, task predictability, task complexity, task significance, level of group autonomy, and degree of self-management), (d) intragroup processes (e.g., conflict, communication, collaboration, cohesion, and team norms), and (e) external group processes (e.g., external member interactions with peers, managers, suppliers, and customers) (Sundstrom et al., 2000). These models suggest that a number of factors contribute to work team effectiveness.

Key Research Findings: Five-Year, Selective Review, 1999–2004

Identifying appropriate studies for inclusion in the review portion of this chapter involved an extensive literature search of major journals in industrial/organizational psychology, management, social psychology, marketing, and related fields. The most frequently cited was the *Journal of Organizational Behavior* (e.g., Cannon & Edmondson, 2001; Langfred, 2000a), providing 29% of the included studies. Following that journal came the *Journal of Applied Psychology* (e.g., Austin, 2003; Tesluk & Mathieu, 1999), which provided 18% of the included studies; and the *Academy of Management Journal* (e.g., Kirkman, Rosen, Tesluk, & Gibson, 2004; Stewart & Barrick, 2000) and *Small Group Research* (e.g., Bain, Mann, & Pirola-Merlo, 2001; Naumann & Bennett, 2002), both providing 10% of the included studies.

Studies were included when researchers (a) assessed work teams or groups in their natural performance settings; (b) assessed some criteria

of group effectiveness such as supervisor ratings (e.g., Man & Lam, 2003; Tjosvold, Hui, Ding, & Hu, 2003), customer ratings (e.g., Pearce & Sims, 2002), and/or objective criteria such as financial performance (e.g., Barsade, Ward, Turner, & Sonnenfeld, 2000; Naumann & Bennett, 2002); (c) treated teams or groups as the unit of analysis; (d) reported results at the group level of analysis; and (e) examined at least two groups or included two times of measurement. Studies were not included when researchers: (a) studied student groups (e.g., Au, 2004; Mohammed, Mathieu, & Bartlett, 2002); (b) examined sports teams (e.g., Chen et al., 2002; Watson, Chemers, & Preiser, 2001); (c) focused on other variables as the unit(s) of analysis (e.g., Thamhain, 2004); (d) studied work groups put together for research purposes or training (e.g., Bown & Abrams, 2003; Jordan, Field, & Armenakis, 2002); (e) did not gather data from at least some group members under study (Devine, Clayton, Philips, Dunford, & Melner, 1999); (f) did not gather some measure of group effectiveness (Totterdell, Kellett, Teuchmann, & Briner, 1998); or (g) reported results at the individual level (Ang, Van Dyne, & Begley, 2003; Knouse & Dansby, 1999).

Of 119 studies initially identified for possible inclusion, 50 satisfied the selection criteria and are included in this review. The number of studies we identified seems to extend a finding by Sundstrom and his colleagues (2000) that the study of work groups increased during the 1980s and through the 1990s. Sundstrom et al. (2000) identified 90 studies for their review spanning 20 years. We identified 50 studies spanning a quarter of that time, using very similar inclusion criteria. The studies included in our review span five years, with the first being published in 1999 (Tesluk & Mathieu, 1999) and the most recent in 2004 (Kirkman, Tesluk, & Rosen, 2004). In total, the studies include more than 24,000 participants ($M = 490$) and more than 3,500 work teams ($M = 71$). More specific information including author(s), number of groups, average size, organizational setting, and a brief description is provided in Table 16.1.

(*Text continues on page 296*)

Table 16.1 Selective Applied Group Research From 1999 to 2004

Authors and Date	Number of Groups	Number of Size	Organizational Setting	Work Group Description
Action and Performing Teams (n = 2)				
Edmondson (2003)	16	~10	Hospital	Cardiac surgery teams
Langfred (2000a)	61	~7	Military regiment	Danish army infantry companies
Management Teams (n = 4)				
Barsade et al. (2000)	62	~5	Multiple organizations	CEOs and their senior management teams
Ensley & Pearce (2001)	70	~2	Fortune 500 (1995) firms	Top management teams
	88	~2	Fortune 500 (1994) firms	Top management teams
Peterson et al. (2003)	17	~5	Multiple organizations	CEOs and their senior management teams
Production Teams (n = 3)				
Bunderson (2003)	35	~6	High-technology firm	Manufacturing facility production teams
Stewart & Barrick (2000)	45	~14	Manufacturing	Manufacturing plant production teams
Tesluk & Mathieu (1999)	88	~5	Construction company	Road construction crews
Project Teams (n = 9)				
Bain et al. (2001)	38	~5	Australian R&D organizations	R&D project teams
Cady & Valentine (1999)	50	~6	High-technology firm	Cross-functional problem-solving project teams
Cramton & Webber (in press)	39	~6	International consulting firm	Software development teams
Cummings & Cross (2003)	182	~8	Telecommunications	Project teams working on different tasks
Hoegl et al. (2004)	39	~9	Automotive industry	New product development teams
Lemieux-Charles et al. (2002)	97	~5	Hospitals	Quality training teams in acute care hospitals
Pearce & Sims (2002)	71	~7	Automotive manufacturing	Change-management teams
Sarin & McDermott (2003)	52	~7	High-technology firm	New-product development teams
Tjosvold et al. (2003)	106	~8	Chinese state enterprises	Functional project teams

(Continued)

Table 16.1 (Continued)

Authors and Date	Number of Groups	Number of Size	Organizational Setting	Work Group Description
Service Teams (n = 18)				
Ahearn et al. (2004)	100	~5	State welfare agency	Caseworker teams
Austin (2003)	27	~10	Apparel and sporting goods	Product service teams
Carless & De Paola (2000)	59	~2	Australian retail industry	Retail outlet service teams
De Dreu & West (2001)	21	~5	Dutch postal service	Postal distribution teams
De Jong et al. (2004)	61	~15	Dutch bank	Branch routine and nonroutine service teams
Deeter-Schmelz & Kennedy (2003)	68	~10	Regional medical center	Patient care teams
Drach-Zahavy & Somech (2001)	48	~6	Schools	School teams enrolled in training programs
Early & Mosakowski (2000)	5	~7	Multinational clothing company	Service teams responsible for product development, sales, and marketing
Gibson (2001)	91	~3	Hospitals	Ward nursing teams
Glisson & James (2002)	33	~10	Child welfare and juvenile justice organization	Case management teams
Hoegl et al. (2003)	145	~6	German software development laboratories	Software development teams
Langfred (2000a)	67	~9	Department of child and family services	Regional teams in child and family services
Man & Lam (2003)	381	~5	Financial industry	Teller and retail customer service teams
Naumann & Bennett (2002)	34	~6	Banking industry	Bank tellers
Sawyer et al. (1999)	5	~17	Military	Maintenance, materials storage, and distribution units
Van Der Vegt (2002)	25	~8	Dutch elementary schools	Elementary school teaching teams

Authors and Date	Number of Groups	Number of Size	Organizational Setting	Work Group Description
Wagner et al. (2003)	204	~13	Retail industry	Retail service teams
Weldon & Yun (2000)	31	~4	State Department of Health	Inspection teams of nurses
Multiple Types of Teams (n = 14)				
Bommer et al. (2003)	56	~9	Manufacturing company	Management, service, and production teams
Cannon & Edmondson (2001)	51	~8	Manufacturing company	Project, production, and service teams
Colquitt et al. (2002)	88	~20	Automotive manufacturing	Service and production teams
De Dreu & Van Vianen (2001)	27	~7	Multiple organizations	Management and cross-functional project teams
De Dreu & West (2001)	28	~7	Multiple organizations	Management and project teams
Kirkman, Rosen, et al. (2004)	35	~8	Travel industry (high-tech)	Multiple types of teams operating virtually
Kirkman, Tesluk, et al. (2004)	111	~10	Multiple organizations	Production and service teams
Mason & Griffin (2003)	97	~15	Australian state government organization	Management and service teams
Langfred (2000b)	25	~10	Computer company	Service, production, and management teams
Liden et al. (2004)	23	~7	Multiple organizations	Production and service teams
Pearce & Ensley (2004)	69	~7	Automotive manufacturing	Product/process innovation teams
Schippers et al. (2003)	54	~8	Multiple organizations from the Netherlands	Management, production, and service teams
Van Der Vegt et al. (2003)	20	~3	Dutch telecommunications	Software development and project management teams
Xie & Johns (2000)	63	~13	Chinese manufacturing organization	Management and production teams

Types of Teams

More than a third (36) of the included studies focused on service teams (e.g., Man & Lam, 2003; Naumann & Bennett, 2002); similarly, the review by Sundstrom and colleagues (2000) found that 33% of 90 studies focused on service teams. Studies examining multiple types of teams (e.g., Mason & Griffin, 2003; Schippers, Den Hartog, Koopman, & Wienk, 2003) and project teams (e.g., Hoegl, Weinkauf, & Gemuenden, 2004; Pearce & Sims, 2002) were the next most common (29% and 18%, respectively). This finding indicates an increase in studies examining multiple types of teams. Studies examining two or more types of teams made up only 10% of those included in the review by Sundstrom and colleagues (2000), compared with 29% in our review. Percentages of studies examining project teams in our review matched those in the review by Sundstrom and colleagues (18% and 17%, respectively). Management (e.g., Barsade et al., 2000), production (e.g., Bunderson, 2003), and action teams (e.g., Edmondson, 2003) each made up less than 10% of the included studies (8%, 6%, and 4%, respectively). Similar to findings by Sundstrom and his colleagues (2000) that suggested that advisory teams were the least studied, no studies included in our review focused on advisory teams. Different types of teams were examined in a wide variety of organizational contexts.

Organizational Context

Organizational contexts varied widely across the included studies. Groups were examined from industries such as telecommunications (e.g., Cummings & Cross, 2003), high tech (Cady & Valentine, 1999), military (Langfred, 2000a), health care (e.g., Edmondson, 2003; Lemieux-Charles et al., 2002), finance (e.g., Man & Lam, 2003; Naumann & Bennett, 2002), manufacturing (e.g., Pearce & Sims, 2002; Stewart & Barrick, 2000), and construction (e.g., Tesluk & Mathieu, 1999). Interestingly, a large percentage of studies (22%) examined teams working in locations outside of the United States (e.g., De Jong, De Ruyter, & Lemmink, 2004; Hoegl, Parboteeah, & Gemuenden, 2003; Van Der Vegt, Van De Vliert, & Oosterhof, 2003).

Operational Definitions of Work Groups

One of our initial questions dealt with the operational definition of work groups. There have been different approaches to defining work teams and groups (e.g., Hackman, 1990; Katzenbach & Smith, 1993; Sundstrom et al., 1990). However, there seem to be some basic features necessary for a collection of individuals to be identified as a work group. First, they are composed of two or more people. Second, their most basic function is to perform some type of job for an organization. Third, group members interact (as suggested by Kozlowski & Bell, 2003) and rely on one another to complete the work of the group (i.e., exhibit a form of interdependence). For the review, we included groups in which members interacted virtually—via electronic communication—as well as face-to-face.

Some studies cited few specific criteria for defining the work groups included in their studies (e.g., Austin, 2003; Sarin & McDermott, 2003; Stewart & Barrick, 2000), whereas others used an extensive list of criteria (e.g., Bunderson, 2003; De Dreu & West, 2001; Tesluk & Mathieu, 1999). Austin (2003) focused on groups existing within an organization, stating, "The data gathered in this project were drawn from the 27 continuing groups" (p. 869). Similarly, Stewart and Barrick (2000) defined teams included in their study by stating, "Our research sample consisted of employees working in teams at three different manufacturing plants" (p. 140). Some researchers focused more on the defining characteristics of the organizations within which the included teams operated (Sarin & McDermott, 2003). Others discussed a series of specific criteria:

These crews display many of the important characteristics of intact, ongoing work groups (Guzzo & Shea, 1992; Sundstrom et al., 1990) in that they view themselves and are seen by others as groups, and they interact and share resources to accomplish group tasks, responsibilities, and goals. In addition to shared resources and responsibilities, work is often sequentially interdependent. (Tesluk & Mathieu, 1999, p. 205)

Bunderson (2003) took another approach by observing and interviewing team members involved in his study to capture "what they did, how they did it, and in what ways they interacted with other team members in doing their work" (p. 567). De Dreu and West (2001) were more specific in selecting groups that fit a predetermined set of criteria, "part of organizational groups that fitted the definition of teams as ongoing, semiautonomous groups in which members had joint responsibility for accomplishing a set of tasks" (Guzzo & Shea, 1992, p. 1196). Similarly, Naumann and Bennett (2002) defined participating groups with multiple criteria: "In each bank, branches were conceptualized as formally defined work groups of interdependent individuals at the same level of the organizational hierarchy who performed similar tasks, worked together, and shared a supervisor" (p. 367). Although researchers differed in how they defined and operationalized work groups, the majority identified a minimum of one of the following features in describing or screening participating groups: (a) existing work groups (e.g., De Dreu & Van Vianen, 2001; Deeter-Schmelz & Kennedy, 2003; Gibson, 2001; Man & Lam, 2003); (b) opportunities to interact and work together (e.g., Early & Mosakowski, 2000; Liden, Wayne, Jaworski, & Bennett, 2004; Naumann & Bennett, 2002); (c) interdependence (Colquitt, Noe, & Jackson, 2002; Drach-Zahavy & Somech, 2001; Pearce & Sims, 2002; Schippers et al., 2003); (d) reporting to the same team leader (e.g., Hoegl et al., 2003; Langfred, 2000a; Van Der Vegt et al., 2003);

(e) minimum percentage of group members participating (e.g., Ahearn, Ferris, Hochwarter, Douglas, & Ammeter, 2004; Glisson & James, 2002; Kirkman, Rosen, et al., 2004; Kirkman, Tesluk, et al., 2004; Schippers et al., 2003); and (f) shared physical work location (e.g., Liden et al., 2004).

Approaches to Studying Groups in the Field

Researchers whose studies were included in Table 16.1 generally used two approaches in their examination of work groups. The vast majority of these studies sought to discover the correlates of work group effectiveness in field studies of ongoing work groups. For example, Cummings and Cross (2003) explored the possible relationship between group structure and the performance of 182 project teams from a telecommunications company. Service teams working in retail outlets were studied by Carless and De Paola (2000) in an effort to uncover relationships between group cohesion and group performance. Other researchers explored different facets of group effectiveness such as innovation in research and development teams (Bain et al., 2001), turnover in child welfare case management teams (Glisson & James, 2002), social integration in elementary school service teams (Van Der Vegt, 2002), and customer satisfaction of multiple types of teams working virtually (Kirkman, Rosen, et al., 2004). Several studies examined work groups operating outside of the United States (e.g., Hoegl et al., 2004; Van Der Vegt et al., 2003; Xie & Johns, 2000). The approach to studying management teams seems to be different in that archival data are frequently used (e.g., Ensley & Pearce, 2001; Peterson, Smith, Martorana, & Owens, 2003). The use of archival data in the study of management teams may be due to the difficulty of gaining access to these types of teams and the very limited amount of time senior management teams have available. Some field studies included in Table 16.1 examined teams from multiple organizations (e.g., De Dreu & Van Vianen, 2001; Kirkman, Tesluk, et al., 2004; Schippers et al., 2003), whereas others examined teams from a single organization (e.g., Austin, 2003; Cannon & Edmondson, 2001; Langfred, 2000a). Another, much smaller group of studies used different quasi-experimental approaches to study work groups in the field (e.g., Gibson, 2001; Weldon & Yun, 2000).

In a study of 31 nursing inspection teams, Weldon and Yun (2000) randomly assigned each team to one of two goal-setting conditions in an effort to assess the impact of different approaches to goal setting on group performance. Gibson (2001) used a quasi-experimental design to study the effects of training on individual nurses and nursing teams working in hospitals. Two thirds of the nursing teams were randomly assigned to the training condition and one third to the control condition to explore the impact of training on effectiveness and efficacy at the individual and group levels of analysis.

Factors Contributing to Work Group Success

Studies included in Table 16.1 considered a broad array of variables producing an equally large number of findings. It is beyond the scope of this chapter to fully review all of these findings. We concentrate on selected studies and categorize them based on a general model of work group effectiveness highlighting five factor categories: (a) organizational context (e.g., training, reward, measurement, and information systems); (b) group composition (e.g., number of members and the mixture of individual traits like personality and ability); (c) group work design (e.g., task interdependence, task predictability, task complexity, task significance, level of group autonomy, and degree of self-management); (d) intragroup processes (e.g., conflict, communication, collaboration, cohesion, organizational citizenship behavior, and team norms); and (e) external group processes (e.g., external member interactions with peers,

managers, suppliers, and customers) (Sundstrom et al., 2000). It should be mentioned that intragroup process variables such as cohesion and organizational citizenship behavior can often represent outcomes (e.g., Nielsen et al., 2003). Variables such as cohesion have been identified as contributing to group viability—the ability of a team to work together in the future (Sundstrom et al., 1990)—and that has been included in definitions of group effectiveness (Hackman, 1990; Sundstrom et al., 1990).

Organizational context. This category includes variables representing systems or processes of the host organization that involve multiple stakeholders, such as performance management systems, reward processes, training, information technology and systems, competitors, and market dynamics. The primary organizational context variable considered was training. Deeter-Schmelz and Kennedy (2003), for example, examined patient care teams in a regional medical center to assess the impact of team cohesiveness training on the quality of patient care. Results indicated a positive relationship between cohesiveness training and the quality of patient care as well as patient satisfaction. One variable considered by Cannon and Edmondson (2001) in a study of project, production, and service teams was the supportiveness of the organizational context. Their findings pointed to a positive relationship between supportiveness and manager-rated group performance. In another study on the effects of training, Gibson (2001) found a positive relationship between training and effectiveness at the individual level but not at the group level for teams of nurses.

Group composition. Studies looked at the mix of team member traits (e.g., personality, demographics, ability) as well as variables such as collective expertise, diversity, and heterogeneity. Group size was routinely examined as a control variable (e.g., Austin, 2003; De Dreu & West, 2001; Pearce & Sims, 2002). In the past, many researchers focused on group members' average cognitive ability (e.g., Barrick, Stewart, Neubert, & Mount, 1998; Neuman & Wright, 1999) and average levels of conscientiousness (Barrick et al., 1998; Neuman & Wright, 1999) in an effort to predict group performance. However, it seems that this trend did not continue after 1999. None of the studies included in this review examined group levels of cognitive ability or conscientiousness. Researchers after 1999 seemed more focused on various forms of diversity. Cady and Valentine (1999) focused on project teams from a high-tech organization while examining the relationships among racial, gender, age, and functional diversity and group performance. Racial diversity was found to be positively correlated with the quantity and quality of ideas generated, whereas gender diversity was positively related to quality only. Drach-Zahavy and Somech (2001) considered functional heterogeneity among several other variables in their study of school service teams. Team innovation, the criterion in this study, was found to be positively related to team functional heterogeneity. In a study of service teams in an apparel and sporting goods company, Austin (2003) found no relationship between group task knowledge and group goal attainment and performance. Kirkman, Tesluk, et al. (2004) explored relationships between demographic heterogeneity (i.e., race, gender, age, organizational tenure, team tenure) of team members and team leaders, on the one hand, and team empowerment and effectiveness. Findings revealed that team empowerment and effectiveness were positively related to specific facets of demographic fit between team members and leaders.

Group work design. This category includes features of groups' work such as task characteristics, reporting relationships (e.g., group autonomy, degree of self-management, and decision-making authority), performance feedback, and goal setting. A relatively large number of studies included in Table 16.1 examined some facet of group work design. Interdependence,

autonomy, and decision making were the most often studied variables concerning group work design (e.g., Langfred, 2000b; Lemieux-Charles et al., 2002; Man & Lam, 2003; Schippers et al., 2003). Results were inconsistent across different studies with no discernable trends. Lemieux-Charles and colleagues (2002) examined, among others, the relationship between decision making and group effectiveness in project teams conducting quality training. Their findings indicated a positive relationship between decision making and group effectiveness, as rated by both team members and leaders. De Dreu and West (2001) found decision-making participation to be positively correlated with manager-rated team innovation in self-managed service teams. Goal interdependence was not related to team helping behavior in a study of service teams from a telecommunications company in the Netherlands (Van Der Vegt et al., 2003). Schippers et al. (2003) examined teams from an Australian state government organization. Results indicated that outcome interdependence was not related to team performance and satisfaction. Langfred (2000b) studied multiple types of teams from a large computer company and found a positive relationship between group autonomy and performance when teams were highly task interdependent. Similar findings occurred in studies of military and service teams (Langfred, 2000a).

Intragroup process. This category is represented primarily by relationships and interactions among team members (i.e., communication, coordination, conflict, collaboration, cohesion, social integration, collective efficacy, group norms). Cohesion has traditionally been one of the most studied predictors of team performance (Sundstrom et al., 2000). Although some of the included studies examined cohesion as an intragroup process variable (e.g., Carless & De Paola, 2000; Man & Lam, 2003; Xie & Johns, 2000), researchers focused on conflict with greater vigor (e.g., De Dreu & Van Vianen, 2001; Ensley & Pearce, 2001; Stewart & Barrick, 2000;

Tjosvold et al., 2003). Stewart and Barrick (2000) found a negative relationship between team conflict and performance in production teams. Results from a study by Ensley and Pearce (2001) indicated a positive relationship between cognitive conflict and sales volume for top management teams. However, in a similar study, they found no relationship between conflict and performance (Ensley & Pearce, 2001). Tjosvold and colleagues (2003) found a positive relationship between attitudes toward conflict and effectiveness in Chinese project teams. In a study involving management and cross-functional project teams, De Dreu and Van Vianen (2001) found no relationship between relationship conflict and group effectiveness.

Results from Xie and Johns's (2000) study of teams from a Chinese manufacturing enterprise indicated a negative correlation between group cohesiveness and absenteeism. Carless and De Paola (2000) examined task and social cohesion in service teams working in retail outlets. They found positive correlations between both types of cohesion and team job satisfaction and effectiveness.

External group processes. Relationships and interactions of work group members directed outside of the group (e.g., external integration, coordination, communication) define this category. Consistent with past reviews (Sundstrom et al., 2000), the majority of studies in this review that focused on external processes involved project teams (e.g., Hoegl et al., 2004; Lemieux-Charles et al., 2002). However, other studies (e.g., Tesluk & Mathieu, 1999) focused on external processes by examining groups other than project teams. Hoegl and colleagues (2004) chose project teams working in the European automotive industry to assess the relationship between interteam coordination and group effectiveness. Results indicated a positive relationship between interteam coordination at Times 1 and 2 with overall team performance and adherence to schedule at Time 3. Results from another study of project teams indicated a

positive relationship between external support and group effectiveness (Lemieux-Charles et al., 2002). In a study of production teams, Tesluk and Mathieu (1999) found external performance barriers correlated negatively with adherence to schedule, use of experience, and cohesion. De Jong and colleagues (2004) studied service teams from a bank in the Netherlands. Their findings indicated a positive relationship between interteam support and what they called *share of the customer.* De Jong and colleagues defined this as the "average number of different service categories used by the customers of a specific team" (p. 25) and used it as one of their criterion measures. Studies included in this review used a plethora of different criteria to assess group effectiveness.

Criteria of Work Group Effectiveness

The studies included in Table 16.1 employed a wide variety of different criteria. More studies examined subjective performance criteria (66%) than objective criteria (14%), with a relatively large proportion including both (20%). This pattern is similar to one found in a review of studies examining the link between prosocial behavior and performance at multiple levels of analysis (Nielsen, Halfhill, & Nielsen, in press). Nielsen and colleagues (in press) reviewed 28 studies published between 1966 and 1999, of which 68% examined subjective criteria, 18% used objective criteria, and 14% analyzed both types. Studies in this review collected performance ratings from customers in 14% ($n = 7$) of the included studies (e.g., Gibson, 2001; Kirkman, Rosen, et al., 2004; Pearce & Ensley, 2004). Table 16.2 organizes the included studies by criteria type and lists author(s), group type, criteria source, and criteria type.

Subjective criteria. The majority of studies included in this review used subjective criteria to assess group effectiveness. Of those studies including only subjective criteria, 39% collected ratings from managers (e.g., Bunderson, 2003;

Table 16.2   Criteria in Applied Group Research From 1999 to 2004

Authors and Date	Group Type	Criteria Source	Criteria Description
Subjective Criteria (n = 33)			
Austin (2003)	Service	Team members and manager	Ratings of group goal attainment and performance
Bain et al. (2001)	Project	Manager	Ratings of multiple dimensions of performance
Bommer et al. (2003)	Multiple	Team members and manager	Ratings of individual and group OCB
Bunderson (2003)	Production	Manager	Ratings of group performance
Cannon & Edmondson (2001)	Multiple	Manager	Ratings of group performance
Carless & De Paola (2000)	Service	Team members and manager	Ratings of group performance and satisfaction
Cramton & Webber (in press)	Project	Team members	Ratings of group effectiveness
Cummings & Cross (2003)	Project	Team members and manager	Ratings of team performance
Deeter-Schmelz & Kennedy (2003)	Service	Team members and patients	Quality of patient care and patient satisfaction
Van Der Vegt (2002)	Service	Team members	Ratings of social integration
Drach-Zahavy et al. (2001) reference is for Drach-Zahavy & Somech	Service	Team members and manager	Ratings of team innovation
De Dreu & Van Vianen (2001)	Multiple	Manager	Ratings of group functioning and effectiveness
De Dreu & West (2001)	Multiple	Manager	Ratings of team innovation
De Dreu & West (2001)	Service	Manager	Ratings of team innovation
Early & Mosakowski (2000)	Service	Observer and manager	Ratings of team effectiveness
Gibson (2001)	Service	Customer	Ratings of nursing care quality
Hoegl et al. (2004)	Project	Manager	Ratings of quality, adherence to budget and schedule, and overall performance
Hoegl et al. (2003)	Service	Team members, manager, and customers	Ratings of effectiveness and efficiency
Kirkman, Tesluk, et al. (2004)	Multiple	Team members and leader	Team empowerment and effectiveness
Langfred (2000b)	Multiple	Manager	Ratings of team performance
Langfred (2000a)	Service	Team members and manager	Ratings of group cohesiveness and performance
Langfred (2000a)	Action	Team members and manager	Ratings of group cohesiveness and performance
Lemiux-Charles et al. (2002)	Project	Team members and manager	Ratings of group effectiveness
Liden et al. (2004)	Multiple	Manager	Ratings of social loafing
Man & Lam (2003)	Service	Manager	Ratings of group performance

(Continued)

Table 16.2 (Continued)

Authors and Date	Group Type	Criteria Source	Criteria Description
Pearce & Ensley (2004)	Multiple	Manager and customers	Ratings of innovation effectiveness
Pearce & Sims (2002)	Project	Team members, customers, and manager	Ratings of team effectiveness
Schippers et al. (2003)	Multiple	Team members	Ratings of team performance and satisfaction
Stewart & Barrick (2000)	Production	Manager	Ratings of group performance
Tesluk & Mathieu (1999)	Production	Manager	Ratings of multiple dimensions of performance
Tjosvold et al. (2003)	Project	Manager	Ratings of effectiveness and OCB
Van Der Vegt et al. (2003)	Multiple	Team members	Ratings of team identification, OCB, and loyalty
Weldon & Yun (2000)	Service	Quality reviewers	Ratings of documentation accuracy

Objective Criteria (n = 7)

Authors and Date	Group Type	Criteria Source	Criteria Description
Ahearn et al. (2004)	Service	Company records	Number of placements and average placements
Edmondson (2003)	Action	Company records	Volume, frequency, and trend of implementation
Ensley & Pearce (2001)	Management	Company records	Sales growth, profitability, and sales volume
Ensley & Pearce (2001)	Management	Company records	Sales growth, profitability, and sales volume
Mason & Griffin (2003)	Multiple	Company records	Employee absence over one year
Peterson et al. (2003)	Management	Company records	Organizational income growth
Sawyer et al. (1999)	Service	Company records	Multiple indices of team effectiveness

Subjective and Objective Criteria (n = 10)

Authors and Date	Group Type	Criteria Source	Criteria Description
Barsade et al. (2000)	Management	Team members and company records	Conflict, cooperation, and financial performance
Cady & Valentine (1999)	Project	Records, expert panel, team members	Quantity and quality of ideas
Colquitt et al. (2002)	Multiple	Managers and company records	Team performance and absenteeism
De Jong et al. (2004)	Service	Customer and company records	Customer-perceived service quality, sales productivity, share of customer
Glisson & James (2002)	Service	Team members and company records	Service quality and turnover
Kirkman, Rosen, et al. (2004)	Multiple	Company records and customers	Process improvement and customer satisfaction
Naumann & Bennett (2002)	Service	Manager and company records	Group and financial performance
Sarin & McDermott (2003)	Project	Manager and company records	Speed to market and level of innovation
Wagner et al. (2003)	Service	Team members and company records	Attitudes and financial performance
Xie & Johns (2000)	Multiple	Team members and company records	Group absence norm and absenteeism

De Dreu & Van Vianen, 2001; Stewart & Barrick, 2000) while 33% collected ratings from both team members and managers (e.g., Cummings & Cross, 2003; Langfred, 2000a). General ratings of *effectiveness* and *performance* were the most common (e.g., Cannon & Edmondson, 2001; De Dreu & Van Vianen, 2001; Lemieux-Charles et al., 2002). Cannon and Edmondson (2001), in a study of project, production, and service teams, assessed group effectiveness using manager ratings of group performance. Several studies assessed group performance and satisfaction of members (e.g., Carless & De Paola, 2000; Schippers et al., 2003). Often, researchers combined ratings of group performance or effectiveness with an additional variable such as organizational citizenship behavior, empowerment, cohesiveness, or innovation. Kirkman, Rosen, and colleagues (2004) assessed the effectiveness of multiple types of teams working virtually by gathering ratings of team empowerment and effectiveness from team leaders and members. In a study of production teams, Tesluk and Mathieu (1999) collected manager ratings on a number of dimensions including cohesion, effort, customer service, problem management, quality, and adherence to schedule. Criteria used in studies using only objective data were less varied.

Objective criteria. A much smaller number of studies analyzed only objective criteria (14%). Financial performance was a frequent criterion used in those studies that included objective criteria (e.g., Barsade et al., 2000; Ensley & Pearce, 2001; Naumann & Bennett, 2002; Peterson et al., 2003). Studies using only objective criteria collected the majority of criterion data from various types of company records. These ranged from the frequency with which cardiac surgery teams used a new procedure (Edmondson, 2003) to employee absenteeism over the course of a year (Mason & Griffin, 2003). In two studies of top management teams, Ensley and Pearce (2001) analyzed sales growth, profitability, and sales volume as indicators of effectiveness. Interestingly, each study focusing on management teams used

objective criteria (Barsade et al., 2000; Ensley & Pearce, 2001; Peterson et al., 2003). Like the study by Barsade and colleagues (2000), several studies included both objective and subjective data.

Subjective and objective criteria. Of the studies included in Table 16.1, 20% (*n* = 10) assessed both subjective and objective data (e.g., Cady & Valentine, 1999; Colquitt et al., 2002). Of these, 40% included financial data while 30% included absenteeism or turnover (e.g., De Jong et al., 2004; Naumann & Bennett, 2002; Xie & Johns, 2000). In a study of project teams, Cady and Valentine (1999) assessed the quantity and quality of ideas generated by teams. An expert panel was convened to assess the quality of ideas generated (Cady & Valentine, 1999). Glisson and James (2002) examined turnover rates and team member ratings of service quality in assessing the effectiveness of service teams in a child welfare and juvenile justice organization.

Conclusion

The selected findings we have reported represent only a portion of those published. However, findings from the last 5 years of applied group research have yielded answers to some of our initial questions and point us to trends and directions for future research.

Current Trends in Applied Group Research

Increased teams research. Our review seems to support a trend that has been highlighted by past reviews (Cohen & Bailey, 1997; Sundstrom et al., 2000). The number of studies we identified seems to echo a conclusion by Sundstrom and colleagues (2000) that the study of work groups increased during the 1980s and through the 1990s. Sundstrom and colleagues (2000) reviewed 20 years of applied group research and identified 90 studies for inclusion in their study. Using very similar inclusion criteria, we identified 50 studies spanning only a quarter of that time. About the same number of studies appeared each year from 1999 to 2002 ($M = 7.5$), with a substantial increase in 2003 ($M = 15$). We identified eight studies in the first half of 2004, so that trend seems likely to continue. The studies included in our review span 5 years, with the first being published in 1999 (Tesluk & Mathieu, 1999) and the most recent in 2004 (Kirkman, Tesluk, et al., 2004).

More teams. Augmenting the trend of additional research on teams is the ability of researchers to recruit more teams to study. Research on work teams has consistently suffered from low sample sizes. Sundstrom and colleagues (2000) found the average number of groups per study was 55, whereas the average number of groups across the studies we reviewed was 71. This trend may be linked to increases in the application of work teams (e.g., Kirkman, Rosen, Gibson, Tesluk, & McPherson, 2002).

Utility. Another significant trend was an increased focus on contextual or design features that promote performance, as opposed to understanding the interpersonal dynamics related to effectiveness. Design features such as hierarchical group structure (Cummings & Cross, 2003), group autonomy (Langfred, 2000a, 2000b), formalization of group structure (Glisson & James, 2002), and job complexity (Man & Lam, 2003) were design variables examined as frequently as group process variables such as cohesion. There were no significant trends regarding the relationship between design variables and group effectiveness.

The trend toward utility may also be represented by researchers spending less time focusing on intragroup process variables such as cohesion. Cohesion has traditionally been one of the most studied predictors of team performance (Sundstrom et al., 2000), but researchers paid significantly more attention to conflict as a correlate of team effectiveness (e.g., De Dreu & Van Vianen, 2001; Ensley & Pearce, 2001; Stewart & Barrick, 2000; Tjosvold et al., 2003).

Again, there were mixed results regarding the relationship between conflict and group effectiveness.

Diversity. The research we reviewed represents a significant increase in diversity. There are two levels of diversity to which we refer. First, the included studies incorporate a diversity of teams (types, designs, tasks, membership, and contexts), variables studied, and criteria of success. This may represent an increase in the number of ways teams are used in organizations today as well as an expansion of thought about what teams can and should do. Organizations are expanding the roles and responsibilities of teams while simultaneously increasing accountability.

Second, more researchers examined different types of within-team diversity. Of the studies in Table 16.1, 15% examined some form of within-team diversity (e.g., Austin, 2003; Barsade et al., 2000; Cady & Valentine, 1999; Drach-Zahavy & Somech, 2001; Kirkman, Tesluk, et al., 2004; Van Der Vegt, 2002; Van Der Vegt et al., 2003). Functional diversity and demographic diversity were the most common. Results were mixed regarding the relationship between diversity and performance. As our workforce becomes more diverse and teams are held accountable for a larger variety of tasks, there is little doubt the trend toward increased diversity will continue. Although there were no significant trends regarding the link between diversity and effectiveness, the level of similarity between team leaders and members across different factors was consistently and positively related to team effectiveness. The impact of leader-team homogeneity on effectiveness may be limited if teams rarely work face-to-face. The increased deployment of teams working as a unit in separate locations marks another trend, the virtual team (Kirkman, Rosen, et al., 2004).

Virtual teams. Virtual teams have been defined as "groups of employees with unique skills, situated in distant locations, whose members must collaborate using technology across space and time to accomplish important organizational tasks" (Kirkman, Rosen, et al., 2004, p. 175). The study of various types of teams working virtually has received increased attention by researchers (e.g., Halfhill & Nielsen, 2002; Kirkman, Rosen, et al., 2004; Nielsen & Halfhill, 2003) and the management press (Gibson & Cohen, 2003). However, most of our understanding of virtual teams has come from books, practitioner articles, and case studies (Kirkman, Rosen, et al., 2004). Organizations are using virtual teams more frequently, but there is a paucity of empirical evidence demonstrating what variables are related to more effective virtual teams. Only one article out of 50 included in our review examined teams working virtually (Kirkman, Rosen, et al., 2004). The focus on different types of teams working virtually seems logical, as does the consideration of teams' degree of virtual-ness (Webster & Wong, 2003). Many management teams spend the majority of their time working in separate locations. Do management teams that spend more time together perform better? This may be one possible direction for future research.

Agenda for Future Research

After considering a sample of applied group research from the last 5 years, we have identified a significant number of issues requiring greater attention by researchers. However, it is beyond the scope of this chapter to cover each of these areas in detail. Instead, we focus on several broad issues we deem important for future research.

Team leadership. A significant amount of research has been done on leadership, producing what may be one of the largest literatures in existence. However, a noticeable gap in this literature relates to the leadership of teams. Relatively little attention has been given to specific leadership factors that promote team effectiveness. Moreover, research exploring specific

leadership behaviors that contribute to the success of different types of teams is also lacking. What can a CEO do to contribute to the performance of her or his management team? How does this change if members of the management team spend 90% of their time in separate locations? These are just some examples of the types of questions future research should begin to address.

Mature teams. Relatively little research has explored factors related to team effectiveness across significant periods of time. We know less about correlates of team effectiveness after teams have been together for long periods of time. Are there interventions during a team's life cycle that promote performance? What is the role of team viability regarding the long-term existence and effectiveness of teams? Is it a good thing for teams to stay together for long periods of time? These are some possible future directions for researchers and practitioners.

Team type. Work groups in organizations come in many shapes and sizes and serve a plethora of important functions for their organizations. The increasingly diverse nature of team tasks makes specifying correlates of effectiveness more difficult. There seems to be a research gap regarding different types of teams and the different factors that contribute to their success. Future research should explicitly identify the fundamental characteristics differentiating types of teams and related factors promoting their effectiveness. This would contribute to theory development and help identify specific interventions to improve team effectiveness.

Group composition. Early research on group composition primarily focused on size and demographics. Later research has concentrated on latent constructs such as ability (e.g., Barrick et al., 1998) and personality (e.g., Halfhill et al., in press). However, there have been fewer efforts made at combining these areas. As stated by Kozlowski and Bell (2003), "demographic composition has demonstrated effects, but it is difficult to imagine that such effects occur without mediation by psychological characteristics" (p. 365). Future research would add value by examining these factors simultaneously and exploring the potential moderating and mediating effects of each.

This chapter provided a field-based perspective on applied group research by briefly discussing its history, examining issues around group typology and effectiveness, and reviewing applied group research conducted in the past 5 years. Our review captured 50 studies including more than 24,000 participants and more than 3,500 work teams. Researchers examined teams using both quasi-experimental and field study designs and focused on organizational context, group composition, work design, intragroup process, and external process variables as factors related to effectiveness. Researchers employed a wide array of subjective and objective criteria from team members, managers, customers, outside observers, and company and public records. The majority of studies used subjective criteria to assess team effectiveness.

The increase in competition for organizations continues to increase. Companies today are challenged not only to improve efficiency but also to optimize their innovation and creativity. Work teams provide a method of structure and organization that, implemented and supported effectively, allows organizations to continually develop their competitive position.

References

Ahearn, K. K., Ferris, G. R., Hochwarter, W. A., Douglas, C., & Ammeter, A. P. (2004). Leaders' political skills and team performance. *Journal of Management, 30*(3), 309–327.

Ang, S., Van Dyne, L., & Begley, T. M. (2003). The employment relationships of foreign workers versus local employees: A field study of organizational justice, job satisfaction, performance, and OCB. *Journal of Organizational Behavior, 24,* 561–583.

Argote, L., & McGrath, J. E. (1993). Group processes in organizations: Continuity and change. In C. L. Cooper & I. T. Robertson (Eds.), *International review of industrial and organizational psychology* (Vol. 8, pp. 333–389). West Sussex, UK: Wiley.

Attaran, M., & Nguyen, T. T. (2000). Creating the right structural fit for self-directed teams. *Team Performance Management, 6,* 25–33.

Au, W. (2004). Criticality and environmental uncertainty in step-level public goods dilemmas. *Group Dynamics, 8*(1), 40–61.

Austin, J. R. (2003). Transactive memory in organizational groups: The effects of content, consensus, specialization, and accuracy on group performance. *Journal of Applied Psychology, 88*(5), 866–878.

Bain, P. G., Mann, L., & Pirola-Merlo, A. (2001). The innovative imperative: The relationships between team climate, innovation, and performance in research and development teams. *Small Group Research, 32*(1), 55–73.

Banas, P. (1988). Employee involvement: A sustained labor/management initiative at Ford Motor Company. In J. P. Campbell & R. J. Campbell (Eds.), *Productivity in organizations* (pp. 388–416). San Francisco: Jossey-Bass.

Barrick, M. R., Stewart, G. L., Neubert, J. M., & Mount, M. K. (1998). Relating member ability and personality to work-team processes and team effectiveness. *Journal of Applied Psychology, 83,* 377–391.

Barsade, S. G., Ward, A. J., Turner, J. D. F., & Sonnenfeld, J. A. (2000). To your heart's content: A model of affective diversity in top management teams. *Administrative Science Quarterly, 45*(4), 802–836.

Bass, B. M. (1954). The leaderless group discussion as a leadership evaluation instrument. *Personnel Psychology, 7,* 470–477.

Bell, B. S., & Kozlowski, S. J. (2002). A typology of virtual teams: Implications for effective leadership. *Group and Organization Management, 27*(1), 14–49.

Bettenhausen, K. L. (1991). Five years of group research: What we have learned and what needs to be addressed. *Journal of Management, 17,* 345–381.

Bown, N. J., & Abrams, D. (2003). Despicability in the workplace: Effects of behavioral deviance and unlikeability on the evaluation of in-group and out-group members. *Journal of Applied Social Psychology, 33*(11), 2413–2426.

Bunderson, J. S. (2003). Recognizing and utilizing expertise in work groups: A status characteristics perspective. *Administrative Science Quarterly, 48*(4), 557–591.

Cady, S. H., & Valentine, J. (1999). Team innovation and perceptions of consideration: What difference does diversity make? *Small Group Research, 30*(6), 730–750.

Campion, M. A., Medsker, G. J., & Higgs, A. C. (1993). Relations between work group characteristics and effectiveness: Implications for designing effective work groups. *Personnel Psychology, 46*, 823–850.

Cannon, M. D., & Edmondson, A. C. (2001). Confronting failure: Antecedents and consequences of shared beliefs about failure in organizational work groups. *Journal of Organizational Behavior, 22*(2), 161–177.

Carless, S. A., & De Paola, C. (2000). The measurement of cohesion in work teams. *Small Group Research, 31*(1), 71–88.

Carter, L., Haythorn, W., & Howell, M. (1950). A further investigation of the criteria of leadership. *Journal of Abnormal and Social Psychology, 45*, 350–358.

Chen, G., Webber, S. S., Bliese, P. D., Mathieu, J. E., Payne, S. C., Born, D. H., & Zaccaro, S. J. (2002). Simultaneous examination of the antecedents and consequences of efficacy beliefs at multiple levels of analysis. *Human Performance, 15*(4), 381–410.

Cohen, S. G., & Bailey, D. (1997). What makes teams work: Group effectiveness research from the shop floor to the executive suite. *Journal of Management, 23*, 239–290.

Colquitt, J. A., Noe, R. A., & Jackson, C. L. (2002). Justice in teams: Antecedents and consequences of procedural justice climate. *Personnel Psychology, 55*, 83–109.

Cramton, C. D. & Webber, S. S. (In Press). Relationships among geographic dispersion, team processes, and effectiveness in software development teams. *Journal of Business Research.*

Cummings, J. N., & Cross, R. (2003). Structural properties of work groups and their consequences for performance. *Social Networks, 25*(3), 197–210.

Cummings, T. G. (1978). Self-regulating work groups: A socio-technical synthesis. *Academy of Management Review, 3*, 625–634.

Cummings, T. G., & Molloy, E. S. (1977). *Improving productivity and the quality of work life.* New York: Praeger.

De Dreu, C. K. W., & Van Vianen, A. E. M. (2001). Managing relationship conflict and the effectiveness of organizational teams. *Journal of Organizational Behavior, 22*(3), 309–328.

De Dreu, C. K. W., & West, M. A. (2001). Minority dissent and team innovation: The importance of participation in decision making. *Journal of Applied Psychology, 86*(6), 1191–1201.

Deeter-Schmelz, D. R., & Kennedy, K. N. (2003). Patient care teams and customer satisfaction: The role of team cohesion. *Journal of Services Marketing, 17*(7), 666–684.

De Jong, A., De Ruyter, K., & Lemmink, J. (2004). Antecedents and consequences of the service climate in boundary-spanning self-managing service teams. *Journal of Marketing, 68*, 18–35.

Devine, D. J. (2002). A review and integration of classification systems relevant to teams in organizations. *Group Dynamics, 6*(4), 291–310.

Devine, D. J., Clayton, L. D., Philips, J. L., Dunford, B. B., & Melner, S. B. (1999). Teams in organizations: Prevalence, characteristics, and effectiveness. *Small Group Research, 30*(6), 678–711.

Drach-Zahavy, A., & Somech, A. (2001). Understanding team innovation: The role of team processes and structures. *Group Dynamics, 5*(2), 111–123.

Driskell, J. E., Hogan, R., & Salas, E. (1987). Personality and group performance. *Review of Personality and Social Psychology: Group Processes and Intergroup Relations, 14*, 91–112.

Driskell, J. E., & Salas, E. (1992). Can you study real teams in contrived settings? The value of small group research to understanding teams. In R. W. Swezey & E. Salas (Eds.), *Teams: Their training and performance* (pp. 101–122). Norwood, NJ: Ablex.

Early, P. C., & Mosakowski, E. (2000). Creating hybrid team cultures: An empirical test of transformational team functioning. *Academy of Management Journal, 43*(1), 26–49.

Edmondson, A. C. (2003). Speaking up in the operating room: How team leaders promote learning in interdisciplinary action teams. *Journal of Management Studies, 40*(6), 1419–1452.

Edwards, A., & Wilson, J. R. (2004). *Implementing virtual teams: A guide to organizational and human factors.* Hampshire, UK: Gower.

Ensley, M. D., & Pearce, C. L. (2001). Shared cognition in top management teams: Implications for new venture performance. *Journal of Organizational Behavior, 22*(2), 145–160.

Forsyth, D. R. (1999). *Group dynamics* (3rd ed.). Belmont, CA: Wadsworth.

Gibson, C. B. (2001). Me and us: Differential relationships among goal-setting training, efficacy, and effectiveness at the individual and team level. *Journal of Organizational Behavior, 22*(7), 789–808.

Gibson, C. B., & Cohen, S. G. (Eds.). (2003). *Virtual teams that work: Creating conditions for virtual team effectiveness.* San Francisco: Jossey-Bass.

Gladstein, D. L. (1984). Groups in context: A model of task group effectiveness. *Administrative Science Quarterly, 29*, 499–517.

Glisson, C., & James, L. R. (2002). The cross-level effects of culture and climate in human service teams. *Journal of Organizational Behavior, 23*(6), 767–794.

Guzzo, R. A., & Dickson, M. A. (1996). Teams in organizations: Recent research on performance and effectiveness. *Annual Review of Psychology, 47*, 307–338.

Guzzo, R. A., & Shea, G. P. (1992). Group performance and intergroup relations in organizations. In M. D. Dunnette & L. M. Hough (Eds.), *Handbook of industrial and organizational psychology* (2nd ed., Vol. 3, pp. 269–313). Palo Alto, CA: Consulting Psychologists Press.

Hackman, J. R. (1987). The design of work teams. In J. Lorsch (Ed.), *Handbook of organizational behavior* (pp. 315–342). New York: Prentice Hall.

Hackman, J. R. (1990). *Groups that work (and those that don't): Creating conditions for effective teamwork.* San Francisco: Jossey-Bass.

Hackman, J. R., & Morris, C. G. (1975). Group tasks, group interaction process, and group performance effectiveness: A review and proposed integration. In L. Berkowitz (Ed.), *Advances in experimental psychology* (Vol. 8, pp. 45–49). New York: Academic Press.

Hackman, J. R., & Oldham, G. R. (1980). *Work redesign.* Reading, MA: Addison-Wesley.

Hackman, J. R., & Wageman, R. (1995). Total Quality Management: Empirical, conceptual, and practical issues. *Administrative Science Quarterly, 40*, 309–342.

Halfhill, T., & Nielsen, T. M. (2002). *Virtual teams: Exploring the role of communication and trust.* Symposium conducted at the 2002 Society for Industrial and Organizational Psychology Conference, Toronto, Ontario, Canada.

Halfhill, T., Sundstrom, E., Lehner, J., Calderone, W., & Nielsen, T. M. (in press). Group personality composition and group effectiveness: An integrative review of empirical research. *Small Group Research.*

Hoegl, M., Parboteeah, K. P., & Gemuenden, H. G. (2003). When teamwork really matters: Task innovativeness as a moderator of the teamwork-performance relationship in software development projects. *Journal of Engineering and Technology Management, 20*, 281–302.

Hoegl, M., Weinkauf, K., & Gemuenden, H. G. (2004). Interteam coordination, project commitment, and teamwork in multiteam R&D projects: A longitudinal study. *Organizational Science, 15*(1), 38–55.

Hoerr, J. (1989, July 10). The payoff from teamwork. *BusinessWeek*, pp. 56–62.

Homans, G. C. (1950). *The human group.* New York: Harcourt, Brace & World.

Jordan, M. H., Field, H. S., & Armenakis, A. A. (2002). The relationship of group process variables and team performance: A team-level analysis in a field setting. *Small Group Research, 33*, 121–150.

Katzenbach, J. R., & Smith, D. K. (1993). *The wisdom of teams: Creating the high-performance organization.* Boston: Harvard Business School Press.

Kelly, J. (1982). *Scientific management, job redesign, and work performance.* London: Academic Press.

Kirkman, B. L., Rosen, B., Tesluk, P. E., & Gibson, C. B. (2004). The impact of team empowerment on virtual team performance: The moderating role of face-to-face interaction. *Academy of Management Journal, 47*(2), 175–192.

Kirkman, B. L., Tesluk, P. E., & Rosen, B. (2004). The impact of demographic heterogeneity and team leader-team member demographic fit on team empowerment and effectiveness. *Group & Organization Management, 29*(3), 334–368.

Knouse, S. B., & Dansby, M. R. (1999). Percentage of work-group diversity and work-group effectiveness. *Journal of Psychology, 133*(5), 486–494.

Kolodny, H. F., & Kiggundu, M. N. (1980). Towards the development of a systems model in woodlands mechanical harvesting. *Human Relations, 33*, 623–645.

Kozlowski, S. W. J., & Bell, B. S. (2003). Work groups and teams in organizations. In W. C. Borman, D.

R. Ilgen, & R. Klimoski (Eds.), *Handbook of psychology: Industrial and organizational psychology* (Vol. 12, pp. 333–375). New York: John Wiley.

Landy, F. J. (1992). Hugo Munsterberg: Victim or visionary. *Journal of Applied Psychology, 77,* 787–802.

Langfred, C. W. (2000a). The paradox of self-management: Individual and group autonomy in work groups. *Journal of Organizational Behavior, 21,* 563–585.

Langfred, C. W. (2000b). Work group design and autonomy: A field study of the interaction between task interdependence and group autonomy. *Small Group Research, 31*(1), 54–70.

Lawler, E. E., Mohrman, S. A., & Ledford, G. E. (1998). *Strategies for high performance organizations: Employee involvement, TQM, and reengineering programs in Fortune 1,000 corporations.* San Francisco: Jossey-Bass.

Ledford, G. E., Lawler, E. E., & Mohrman, S. A. (1988). The quality circle and its variations. In J. P. Campbell & R. J. Campbell (Eds.), *Productivity in organizations* (pp. 255–294). San Francisco: Jossey-Bass.

Lemieux-Charles, L., Murray, M., Baker, G. R., Barnsley, J., Tasa, K., & Ibrahim, S. A. (2002). The effects of quality improvement practices on team effectiveness: A mediational model. *Journal of Organizational Behavior, 23*(5), 533–553.

Liden, R. C., Wayne, S. J., Jaworski, R. A., & Bennett, N. (2004). Social loafing: A field investigation. *Journal of Management, 30*(2), 285–304.

Liebowitz, S. J., & Holden, K. T. (1996). Are self-managing teams worthwhile? A tale of two companies. *The Journal of Product Innovation Management, 13,* 461–462.

Lundberg, G. A. (1940). Some problems of group classification and measurement. *American Sociological Review, 5,* 351–360.

Man, D. C., & Lam, S. S. K. (2003). The effects of job complexity and autonomy on cohesiveness in collectivistic and individualistic work groups: A cross-cultural analysis. *Journal of Organizational Behavior, 24*(8), 979–1001.

Mason, C. M., & Griffin, M. A. (2003). Group absenteeism and positive affective tone: A longitudinal study. *Journal of Organizational Behavior, 24*(6), 667–687.

McGrath, J. E. (1964). *Social psychology: A brief introduction.* New York: Holt, Rinehart & Winston.

McGrath, J. E. (1984). *Groups: Interaction and performance.* Englewood Cliffs, NJ: Prentice Hall.

McGrath, J. E., & Altman, I. (1966). *Small group research: A synthesis and critique of the field.* New York: Holt, Rinehart & Winston.

Mohammed, S., Mathieu, J. E., & Bartlett, A. L. (2002). Technical-administrative task performance, leadership task performance, and contextual performance: Considering the influence of team- and task-related composition variables. *Journal of Organizational Behavior, 23,* 795–814.

Moreland, R. L., Hogg, M., & Hains, S. C. (1994). Back to the future: Social psychological research on groups. *Journal of Experimental Social Psychology, 30,* 527–555.

Münsterberg, H. (1908). *On the witness stand: Essays on psychology and crime.* Garden City, NY: Doubleday.

Münsterberg, H. (1913). *Psychology and industrial efficiency.* New York: Houghton Mifflin.

Münsterberg, H. (1914). *Psychology: General and applied.* New York: D. Appleton.

Naumann, S. E., & Bennett, N. (2002). The effects of procedural justice climate on work group performance. *Small Group Research, 33*(3), 361–377.

Neuman, G. A., & Wright, J. (1999). Team effectiveness: Beyond skills and cognitive ability. *Journal of Applied Psychology, 84,* 376–389.

Nielsen, T. M. (1999). *Hugo Munsterburg: A brief history.* Unpublished manuscript, University of Tennessee, Knoxville.

Nielsen, T. M., & Halfhill, T. (2003). *Virtual teams: Exploring new frontiers in research and practice.* Symposium conducted at the 2003 Society for Industrial and Organizational Psychology Conference, Orlando, FL.

Nielsen, T. M., Halfhill, T., & Nielsen, S. K. (in press). Prosocial behavior and performance at three levels of analysis: An integrative model. In D. Turnipseed (Ed.), *Handbook of organizational citizenship behavior: A review of "good soldier" activity in organizations.* Hauppauge, NY: Nova Science Publishers.

Nielsen, T. M., Sundstrom, E., Soulen, S. K., Halfhill, T., & Huff, J. (2003). Corporate citizenship in team-based organizations: An essential ingredient for sustained success. In M. Beyerlein, D. Johnson, & S. Beyerlein (Eds.), *Advances in interdisciplinary studies of work teams* (pp. 169–187). Greenwich, CT: JAI Press.

Pasmore, W., Francis, C., Haldeman, J., & Shani, A. (1982). Sociotechnical systems: A North American reflection on empirical studies of the seventies. *Human Relations, 35,* 1179–1204.

Pasmore, W. A., & Sherwood, J. J. (Eds.). (1977). *Sociotechnical systems: A sourcebook.* San Diego, CA: University Associates.

Pearce, C. L., & Ensley, M. D. (2004). A reciprocal and longitudinal investigation of the innovation process: The central role of shared vision in product and process innovation teams (PPITs). *Journal of Organizational Behavior, 25,* 259–278.

Pearce, C. L., & Sims, H. P. (2002). Vertical versus shared leadership as predictors of the effectiveness of change management teams: An examination of aversive, directive, transactional, transformational, and empowering leadership behaviors. *Group Dynamics, 6*(2), 172–197.

Peters, T. (1988). *Thriving on chaos: Handbook for a management revolution.* New York: HarperCollins.

Peterson, R. S., Smith, D. B., Martorana, P. V., & Owens, P. D. (2003). The impact of chief executive officer personality on top management team dynamics: One mechanism by which leadership affects organizational performance. *Journal of Applied Psychology, 88*(5), 795–808.

Reich, R. B. (1987). *Tales of a new America: The anxious liberal's guide to the future.* New York: Random House.

Roby, T. B., & Lanzetta, J. T. (1958). Considerations in the analysis of group tasks. *Psychological Bulletin, 55,* 88–101.

Roethlisberger, F. J., & Dickson, W. J. (1939). *Management and the worker.* Cambridge, MA: Harvard University Press.

Sanna, L. J., & Parks, C. D. (1997). Group research trends in social and organizational psychology. *Psychological Science, 8,* 261–267.

Sarin, S., & McDermott, C. (2003). The effect of team leader characteristics on learning, knowledge application, and performance of cross-functional new product development teams. *Decision Sciences, 34*(4), 707–739.

Sawyer, J. E., Latham, W. R., Pritchard, B. D., & Bennett, W. R. (1999). Analysis of work group productivity in an applied setting: Application of a time series panel design. *Personnel Psychology, 52,* 927–967.

Schippers, M. C., Den Hartog, D. N., Koopman, P. L., & Wienk, J. A. (2003). Diversity and team outcomes: The moderating effects of outcome interdependence and group longevity and the mediating effect of reflexivity. *Journal of Organizational Behavior, 24*(6), 779–802.

Seashore, S. E. (1954). *Group cohesiveness in the industrial work group.* Ann Arbor, MI: Institute for Social Research.

Shaw, M. E. (1973). Scaling group tasks: A method for dimensional analysis. *JSAS Catalog of Selected Documents in Psychology, 3,* 8.

Sheridan, J. H. (1993). Exxon Chemical Co. *Industry Week, 242*(20), 42–44.

Steiner, I. (1972). *Group process and productivity.* New York: Academic Press.

Stewart, G. L., & Barrick, M. R. (2000). Team structure and performance: Assessing the mediating role of intrateam process and the moderating role of task type. *Academy of Management Journal, 43*(2), 135–148.

Sundstrom, E. (1986). *Workplaces.* Cambridge, UK: Cambridge University Press.

Sundstrom, E. (1999). Challenges of supporting work team effectiveness. In E. Sundstrom & Associates (Eds.), *Supporting work team effectiveness: Best management practices for fostering high performance* (pp. 3–23). San Francicso: Jossey-Bass.

Sundstrom, E., & Altman, I. (1989). Physical environments and work-group effectiveness. In L. L. Cummings & B. Staw (Eds.), *Research in organizational behavior* (Vol. 11, pp. 175–209). Greenwich, CT: JAI Press.

Sundstrom, E., DeMeuse, K. P., & Futrell, D. (1990). Work teams: Applications and effectiveness. *American Psychologist, 45,* 120–133.

Sundstrom, E., McIntyre, M., Halfhill, T. R., & Richards, H. (2000). Work groups: From the Hawthorne studies to work teams of the 1990s and beyond. *Group Dynamics, 4,* 44–67.

Taylor, F. W. (1911). *Principles of scientific management.* New York: Harper.

Tesluk, P. E., & Mathieu, J. E. (1999). Overcoming roadblocks to effectiveness: Incorporating management of performance barriers into models of work group effectiveness. *Journal of Applied Psychology, 84*(2), 200–217.

Thamhain, H. J. (2004). Leading technology-based project teams. *Engineering Management Journal, 16*(2), 35–42.

Thompson, P. C. (1982). Quality circles at Martin Marietta Corporation, Denver Aerospace/Michoud Division. In R. Zager & M. Rosow (Eds.), *The innovative organization* (pp. 3–20). New York: Pergamon.

Tjosvold, D., Hui, C., Ding, D. Z., & Hu, J. (2003). Conflict values and team relationships: Conflict's contributions to team effectiveness and citizenship in China. *Journal of Organizational Behavior, 24*(1), 69–85.

Torrence, E. P. (1954). *Some consequences of power differences on decisions in B-26 crews* (Research Bulletin #AFPTRC-TR-54-128). San Antonio, TX: Lackland Air Force Base, Air Force Personnel and Training Research Center.

Totterdell, P., Kellett, S., Teuchmann, K., & Briner, R. B. (1998). Evidence of mood linkage in work groups. *Journal of Personality and Social Psychology, 74*(6), 1504–1515.

Trist, E. L., & Bamforth, K. W. (1951). Some social and psychological consequences of the longwall method of coal getting. *Human Relations, 4,* 3–38.

Van Der Vegt, G. S. (2002). Effects of attitude dissimilarity and time on social integration: A longitudinal panel study. *Journal of Occupational and Organizational Psychology, 75,* 439–452.

Van Der Vegt, G. S., Van De Vliert, E., & Oosterhof, A. (2003). Informational dissimilarity and organizational citizenship behavior: The role of intrateam interdependence and team identification. *Academy of Management Journal, 46*(6), 715–727.

Wagel, W. H. (1987, September). Working (and managing) without supervisors. *Personnel, 64,* 8–11.

Walker, C. R., & Guest, R. H. (1952). *The man on the assembly line.* Cambridge, MA: Harvard University Press.

Watson, C. B., Chemers, M. M., & Preiser, N. (2001). Collective efficacy: A multi-level analysis. *Personality and Social Psychology Bulletin, 27*(8), 1057–1068.

Webster, J., & Wong, W. K. P. (2003). Group identity, trust, and communication in naturally-occurring project teams. In T. M. Nielsen & T. Halfhill (Chairs), *Virtual teams: Exploring new frontiers in research and practice.* Symposium presented at the 2003 Society for Industrial and Organizational Psychology Conference, Orlando, FL.

Weldon, E., & Yun, S. (2000). The effects of proximal and distal goals on goal level, strategy development, and group performance. *Journal of Applied Behavioral Science, 36*(3), 336–344.

Wellins, R. S., Byham, W. C., & Dixon, G. (1994). *Inside teams: How twenty world-class organizations are winning through teamwork.* San Francisco: Jossey-Bass.

Xie, J. L., & Johns, G. (2000). Interactive effects of absence culture salience and group cohesiveness: A multi-level analysis of work absenteeism in the Chinese context. *Journal of Occupational and Organizational Psychology, 73*(1), 31–52.

17

Conflict Within and Between Groups

R. Scott Tindale

Amanda Dykema-Engblade

Erin Wittkowski

Humans are by nature social creatures. Thus, we have tended to live throughout our evolutionary history in social aggregates or groups of various sizes and types (Caporael, 1997). Group living provides many benefits to the individual members (potentially the most important of which is survival), but it also comes with costs. A fair number of these costs revolve around the notion of conflict—both between and within groups. Both intra- and intergroup conflict can inflict extraordinary damage on group members: Family conflict can lead to interpersonal violence, poverty, and criminal behavior, while intergroup conflict can lead to genocide and war. Much of the work on conflict resolution in the social sciences has focused on avoiding such costs. Areas such as negotiation, mediation, arbitration, and family therapy are oriented toward resolving conflicts within and between groups in ways that prevent the destruction of groups and their members.

More recent research endeavors have begun to focus not only on the potential costs but also on the possible benefits of conflicts between and within groups. A complete lack of conflict (i.e., complete agreement early on) can lead groups to ignore potentially relevant information and decision alternatives (Stasser & Birchmeier,

Author's Note: The authors would like to acknowledge the support of the National Science Foundation (# SES 0136332, R. Scott Tindale, PI) during the preparation of this chapter. Reprint requests should be sent to R. Scott Tindale, Department of Psychology, Loyola University Chicago, 6525 N. Sheridan Rd., Chicago, IL 60626, rtindal@luc.edu.

2003). Recent investigations of creativity and problem solving in groups have tended to show that diversity of opinion relates positively to group performance (Hollenbeck, Colquit, Ilgen, LePine, & Hedlund, 1998; Laughlin, Zander, Knievel, & Tan, 2003; Paulus & Nijstad, 2003; Schulz-Hardt, Jochims, & Frey, 2002). Thus, some degree of conflict among group members seems useful for group performance. At the intergroup level, recent research has shown that cooperation within groups is enhanced in the presence of intergroup competition (Gorum & Bornstein, 2000). In addition, Tauer and Harackiewicz (2004) found that intragroup cooperation in conjunction with intergroup competition increased both intrinsic task motivation and performance in groups. So it would seem that costs as well as benefits accrue to groups as a function of conflict.

The current chapter provides a targeted review of the literature on intra- and intergroup conflict. Rather than attempting to be comprehensive (which would require a book-length endeavor), we highlight the major theories and findings in both areas in an attempt to describe the current knowledge base on the role of conflict in and between groups. Evidence for the costs and benefits, as well as the dynamic and dialectic nature of conflict, will be presented. We will close with recent ideas on how best to use conflict in groups and with a discussion of issues yet unsolved in the field.

Intragroup Conflict

Some of the earliest experimental work on groups (e.g., Bales, 1950; Lewin, 1947) argued that task-performing groups have two major functions: group locomotion (task performance or reaching group goals) and group maintenance (conflict management or keeping the group together). Bales's famous Interaction Process Analysis framework for studying groups divided all group behaviors into these two overarching categories (task/instrumental and social-emotional/expressive). Bales argued that as groups

move toward task goals, conflicts develop among the members as they resolve differences of opinion. To prevent groups from dissolving as a function of such conflicts, certain behaviors are necessary to resolve tension. He theorized and found that member behavior would flow back and forth between these two functions, with more social emotional behaviors becoming prevalent after bouts of task performance behavior. He argued that groups would reach equilibrium between both types of behaviors as a function of the degree of conflict involved in the task. He also discovered that different members of the group emerged to lead the group in these two domains, with the "first" leader being mainly task oriented and a second leader being mainly group maintenance oriented.

More recent work has attempted to classify conflicts of different types. One early distinction that emerged differentiated between *cognitive conflicts* and *conflicts of interest* (Brehmer, 1976; McGrath, 1984). Cognitive conflicts involve tasks where group members share the same goals but disagree on how best to get there. Brehmer (1976) argued that many group conflicts could be avoided if members could see or understand the cognitive processes that underlie each member's decision. He designed the Social Judgment Technique to help alleviate cognitive conflicts in multi-cue decision situations. The technique uses multiple regressions to model each individual member's decision process (i.e., how they weight the decision cues). Then, all members review the cue or information weights obtained for themselves and other group members, and the subsequent discussion focuses on how best to weight the cues as a group rather than on which alternative each member prefers. By modeling and sharing the member cognitions, the reasons behind different member preferences become clear, and the conflicts become easier to resolve. Rohrbaugh (1979) found that groups both performed well and preferred using the social judgment technique over other less transparent group-decision strategies.

Conflicts of interest arise in situations where resources are limited and each group member prefers more to less. Thus, a meeting among department chairpersons deciding how to allocate new faculty hires is a clear example of a conflict of interest task. Most of the early work on conflict in groups tended to focus on conflicts of interest and used a game theoretic paradigm (Kahn & Rappoport, 1984; von Neumann & Morgenstern, 1947). Although some interest conflicts are of a pure variety (i.e., zero sum games), most research on conflicts of interest used mixed motive games—those situations where both cooperation and competition/defection are possible and defensible.

Probably the most heavily studied mixed-motive game is the Prisoner's Dilemma game (Axelrod, 1984; Axelrod, Riolo, & Cohen, 2002). The Prisoner's Dilemma is a two-person game with two options, cooperation and defection. When both players cooperate, they both receive a modest payoff, which is better than the payoff for mutual defection. However, if one player defects and the other cooperates, the defecting player receives the best possible payoff, and the cooperating player receives the worst possible payoff. This sets up a situation where mutual cooperation is best for the group, yet each individual is better off defecting regardless of what the other player does. Axelrod (1984) and others have shown that without communication among the players, mutual defection is the most likely outcome. Games of similar structure have been used to show how easily conflicts escalate when communication is lacking or incomplete. Communication prior to making individual choices, however, tends to dramatically increase cooperation. Axelrod (1984) also showed that a strategy called "tit-for-tat" or reciprocity was by far the most successful strategy for inducing cooperation in an opponent. The strategy rests on cooperating on the first play of the game and then responding from then on exactly as your opponent responded on the last play. Cooperation is rewarded by cooperation, and defection is penalized with defection. More recent work has shown that more benign versions of reciprocity—those that are more forgiving of opponent defections—can be more effective than pure reciprocity in

situations where it is difficult to directly infer an opponent's intentions (Kramer, 2001). Kramer has argued that the more benign versions of reciprocity allow for trust to develop in noisy environments.

Another form of mixed motive situation that recently has received a large amount of research attention is the social dilemma or public goods problem (Dawes, 1980; Foddy, Smithson, Schneider, & Hogg, 1999). Social dilemmas are multiperson extensions of the Prisoner's Dilemma. In a social dilemma, cooperating with the group increases the total group outcome, but each party shares the group outcome regardless of whether he or she cooperates. Thus, each person is always better off defecting (often referred to as *free riding*); yet, the group outcome is worse as each person decides to do so. An example of a public goods dilemma is public television. All people who have televisions can watch the public stations, whether they donate money to them or not. However, if no one donates, the public good cannot be provided. Thus, once again, individually rational behavior leads to collective disaster. Free riding has been characterized as one of the key issues of social living (Kameda, Takezawa, & Hastie, 2003). How such issues are best dealt with, however, depends heavily on the context of the dilemma (Messick, 1999).

In cases where free-riding behavior is easily identifiable, sanctions or punishments for such behaviors may work well. Recent research has shown that social exclusion is a particularly useful sanction when group membership is important (Kerr, 1999). Helping group members to feel important in terms of providing the public good or preserving the common resource pool has also been found to be effective (Kerr & Kaufman-Gilliland, 1994). In smaller groups, simply allowing members to discuss the dilemma drastically increases cooperation (Dawes, Orbell, Simmons, & van de Kragt, 1986). Although how communication achieves this goal is not completely understood, both creating a common group identity and leading members to cooperate seem to be involved (De Cremer & Van Vugt, 1999; Kerr & Kaufman-Gilliland, 1994).

Starting in the 1980s, researchers studying conflicts of interest began to frame them partially in cognitive terms (Bazerman, Curhan, Moore, & Valley, 2000; Bazerman & Neale, 1983; Thompson, 1990). In an attempt to understand why even trained negotiators could often not reach optimal solutions, researchers began to study how people thought about conflict situations and discovered a number of common misperceptions. For example, perceptions of outcome fairness tend to be biased in an egocentric fashion, such that each party sees outcomes that favor their side as fair (Thompson & Loewenstein, 1992). Another common misperception is the "fixed pie" bias (Bazerman & Neale, 1983). Parties tend to see negotiation situations as fixed pie or zero sum games, even when their interests are compatible with their opponents on some issues. This perception prevents parties from finding common ground and trading off issues based on issue importance (log rolling). Thus, the parties often perceive conflicts of interest as more difficult to resolve than they are in reality.

Negotiation can also be seen in terms of the motivations of the participating parties (De Dreu & Carnevale, 2004). Early conceptions of human behavior tended to view the main (and often only) motivation as self-interest (Smith, 1872). However, more recent ideas have incorporated a number of different social motives: motives that define the preferred relationship between one's own and one's opponent's outcomes (McClintock, 1977). *Social value orientations* (McClintock, 1977; Van Lange, 1999) are seen as individual proclivities toward one or another social motive and are often divided into three types: prosocials (who prefer equality and good outcomes for both themselves and others), individualists (who prefer good outcomes for themselves with little concern for others), and competitives (who prefer better outcomes for themselves relative to others). All three orientations exist in most or all cultures, but collectivist cultures tend to encompass greater numbers of prosocials (although their prosocial tendencies

often only apply to other members of their culture) (Carnevale & Leung, 2001).

Differences in motivation can also be seen as related to the likelihood of different types of negotiation behavior or strategies. Negotiation behavior can be classified into three types or strategies: concession making (reducing one's goals, demands, or offers), contenting (trying to induce concessions from the other party while not making any of your own), and problem solving (trying to locate and adopt options that satisfy both parties' goals) (Carnevale & Leung, 2001). The fixed-pie bias mentioned above often leads to concession making or contenting because parties see the situation as a zero sum game. Such strategies lead to either compromise or stalemate, but opportunities to maximize both parties' outcomes are often missed. Thus, taking a problem-solving orientation is seen as the most useful negotiation strategy in most conflict situations. Problem solving is thought the best for reaching "win-win" or mutually beneficial outcomes leaving no resources unused (Thompson, 1998).

Recently, De Dreu and Carnevale (2004) have proposed a slightly different two-motive system for understanding conflict resolution. They discuss social motivation as moving from selfish to prosocial (both purely individualistic and competitive motivations would be seen as selfish). In addition, they argue that *epistemic motivation,* or the motive to develop and hold accurate and well-informed conclusions about the world (Kruglanski & Webster, 1996), interacts with social motivation to guide negotiation behavior. They argue that both high epistemic motivation and prosocial orientation are needed to lead to truly integrative and mutually optimal bargaining outcomes. Recent empirical work (De Dreu, Koole, & Oldersma, 1999; De Dreu, Koole, & Steinel, 2000) has tended to support the contentions of the model.

Research on teams in organizations has tended to identify three different types of conflicts that correspond only loosely to the cognitive versus interest distinction mentioned above

(Jehn, 1995; Jehn & Mannix, 2001). According to Jehn (1995), teams can experience task, relationship, and process conflict. Task conflict is similar to Brehmer's (1976) notion of cognitive conflict in that the conflict stems from member differences in their perceptions of how the task should be done. Relationship conflict stems from personal or social disagreements within a team that are non-work related. Process conflict involves disagreements concerning who should be doing what within the team. Each of the conflict types relates differently to performance. The least attention has been paid to process conflict, potentially because job titles, roles, leadership, and so on could quite easily resolve process conflict issues. However, process conflict could be useful for pointing out ambiguities in role assignments and important tasks that have remained unassigned. Process conflict may also indicate free-rider problems within the group, and a lack of clear task assignments may actually exacerbate free-rider behavior.

Relationship conflict is generally considered detrimental to both group maintenance and performance. Group cohesiveness suffers as members' liking for one another diminishes, and resolving conflicts can deplete cognitive resources and can cause teams to move their focus away from the task at hand (Carnevale & Probst, 1998). A fair amount of research evidence shows that relationship conflict relates negatively to team productivity and performance (De Dreu & Weingart, 2003; Saavedra, Earley, & Van Dyne, 1993). However, a number of researchers (Jehn, 1995; Levine, Resnick, & Higgins, 1993; Schulz-Hardt et al., 2002) have argued that moderate levels of task conflict are good for groups. Recent work in the area of group creativity (Paulus & Nijstad, 2003) and group problem solving (Laughlin et al., 2003) has tended to show that diversity of opinions and ideas within groups leads to better as opposed to worse performance. Schulz-Hardt et al. (2002) have found evidence that groups make better decisions and use more information when the members initially disagree with one another.

Interestingly, a recent meta-analysis by De Dreu and Weingart (2003) found that both task and relationship conflict show significant and negative correlations with both task performance and member satisfaction. Thus, at the present time, data and theory in relation to task conflict do not always match. One issue that may be at play in the discrepancy is that relationship conflict and task conflict are often correlated, and task conflict may lead to relationship conflict if not handled well within the group. At least some of the research demonstrating positive aspects of task conflict has defined task conflict as member preference or knowledge differences. The work showing negative effects of task conflict often used member reports of conflict. It may be that differences of opinion in groups are not always perceived as conflict. In addition, other factors may be involved as well. For example, task conflict may show positive effects only when relationship conflict is low (Jehn & Chatman, 2000). Trust has also been found to be important in conflict situations, and future research may find that task conflict is beneficial in groups or teams with high member trust, but negative in groups where trust is low or nonexistent.

Another area of research where conflict has also been found to be beneficial is minority influence (De Dreu & West, 2001; Moscovici, 1976; Nemeth, 1986). Like conflict in the early theories, minorities within groups were often considered a nuisance to be converted or rejected by the majority (Festinger, 1954; Levine, 1980). However, Moscovici (1976) argued that almost all truly innovative social influence starts with minorities. In addition, he argued that the conflict minorities initially engender in groups is what eventually leads to innovation. Nemeth (1986) later argued that compared with majorities, minorities create different cognitive processes in groups. She argued and demonstrated that minority influence led to *divergent thinking* (more cognitive effort or thought and more diverse thought), whereas majorities led to convergent thinking—narrowed focus on the majority position and fewer thoughts overall. Thus, the conflict in groups created by minority positions leads to more thorough and creative thought processes and, sometimes, to better performance (De Dreu & West, 2001; Nemeth & Kwan, 1987).

There is not a lot of research attempting to distinguish between conflicts due to minority presence versus task conflict in general, but what little there is tends to suggest something special about conflict due to minorities. De Dreu and West (2001) looked at both minority influence and task conflict as separate predictors of group performance in organizational settings. They found that minority influence was positively related to performance, whereas task conflict showed a negative relation. Recent research by Smith (2003) also indicates that conflict in and of itself does not lead to divergent thinking. However, if the conflict involves a minority position, divergent thinking does occur. Thus, it is possible that only task conflict representing a minority versus a majority opinion leads to the performance increases found in the past.

Intergroup Conflict

Like intragroup conflict, intergroup conflict has a long and rich research tradition in the social sciences (Allport, 1954; Campbell, 1956; see Brown & Gaertner, 2001, for a recent review). However, two research programs that began in the 1960s set the stage for much of the theory and research that has followed. The first encompassed a series of studies known as the Robber's Cave Experiments (Sherif, 1966; Sherif, Harvey, White, Hood, & Sherif, 1961). These now classic studies each involved groups of young boys (about 12 years of age) at summer camp. When they arrived at camp, they were divided into two groups (Eagles and Rattlers) and given identifying T-shirts and so on. The two groups were then placed in a series of competitive settings not at all uncommon for summer camp activities. The activities always were associated with prizes that only one of the groups could obtain.

After 4 days of these activities, the tension and conflict between the two groups was severe enough that occasional fights broke out, and the camp counselors (researchers) had to separate the boys at times. Although the boys had not known each other before the beginning of the experiment, most at this point chose their friends from the group to which they were assigned and rated their group as superior to the other group, regardless of the outcomes of the competitions. Following the creation of intergroup conflict, Sherif and colleagues attempted to ameliorate the conflict by creating a superordinate group with shared goals and outcome interdependence among the members. By creating tasks where neither group could reach the goal without the other group, Sherif et al. were able to drastically reduce the tension and dislike across group boundaries.

This research provided the groundwork for Sherif's (1966) *realistic conflict theory*. According to Sherif, intergroup conflicts revolve around real conflicts over resources. In other words, Sherif argues that group members' intergroup attitudes and behavior will reflect the actual interests of the group relative to other groups (Brown & Gaertner, 2001). When groups vie for the same set of resources, the actions of one group tend to thwart the goal attainment of the other, which causes resentment and dislike. Taking a competitive stance to such other groups and derogating their members makes sense in terms of furthering the groups' goals. In addition, cohesive bonds within a group, or intragroup liking, also makes sense in that group members will work hard for the benefit of the other members as well as themselves. However, intergroup conflict is not a foregone conclusion. If the goals of the two groups and the related outcomes correspond with one another, cooperation with the other group will tend to occur. Again, this makes sense in terms of maximizing one's own and one's group's outcomes. In addition, if the goals are only obtainable with the help of the other group, this interdependence furthers the positive orientation to the other group and favors cooperation. Such ideas are consistent with general notions of exchange and rationality at the individual and group level (Homans, 1961; Thibaut & Kelley, 1959).

The second set of studies that defined the area of intergroup conflict took a minimalist approach to the issue of group membership (Tajfel, Flament, Billig, & Bundy, 1971); the paradigm used now is referred to as the *minimal group paradigm* (Tajfel, 1970). Tajfel et al. (1971) assigned schoolboys to one of two groups based on their alleged preferences for one of two artists, Paul Klee or Vassilij Kandinsky. This categorization (which was really random) was the only basis on which the study participants were members of one group or the other. They never met or knew which classmates were members of their group. Following the initial categorization phase, the children were asked to fill out decision matrices, which asked participants to choose a particular monetary allocation between an unknown member of their group and an unknown member of the other group. The matrices presented 12 to 13 payoff options that awarded points (worth money) to each designated person. Each matrix differed in terms of the types of payoffs available, but some offered even splits, some offered much more to the in-group or same-group person, and others offered more to the out-group person. The children could not allocate money to themselves and did not know who would receive their allocations. One might assume that under such minimal group conditions, allocators would choose even splits or payoffs that maximized joint gains (two options that were frequently available). However, on average, members tended to choose allocations that favored the in-group member. Such results were surprising because they appeared to involve no (individual) self-interest and no real conflict between groups (see Gaertner & Insko, 2000, for some recent data questioning the complete lack of self-interest in this paradigm).

Based on these preliminary findings, Tajfel (1981; Tajfel & Turner, 1979) presented a theory of intergroup behavior that attempted to explain the now well replicated minimal group paradigm findings. Social identity theory (Tajfel & Turner, 1979; see also Hogg & Abrams, 1988) starts with the assumption that a person's identity is partly determined by the social categories or groups in which he or she is a member. The theory defines a dimension from individual identity to group or social identity along which a particular individual's self-concept can vary at any particular time. At the individual or personal level, a person's identity distinguishes him or her from other individuals based on the perceived characteristics that make him or her distinctive. However, if a person's group membership is made salient, the theory argues that the attributes of the group are used to form the person's social identity. Thus, the things that differentiate that group from other groups become the salient features of identity.

The theory argues that categorization is the basic process that underlies identity (Hogg, 2001; Hogg & Abrams, 1988; Turner, Hogg, Oakes, Reicher, & Wetherell, 1987). People categorize themselves and others through group membership and social category labels (e.g., female, professor, soccer team member, etc.). One role that categorization serves is to reduce the cognitive load associated with trying to remember information about each specific stimulus that one comes across. By placing a person in a category, one can then use the category definition to infer characteristics of the person. For example, if I know a person is a member of a skydiving club, I can infer that he or she is not afraid of risks—without having to remember any specific information about him or her. Although categorization is efficient, it is not always accurate. A large literature on the use of stereotypes has shown that people overgeneralize, using stereotypic information as if it applied equally to all group members (Fiske, 1998).

The second major tenet of the theory is that group members tend to perceive the groups they are in as being different from the groups they are not in (Hogg & Abrams, 1988). Tajfel (1981) argued that people want to feel good about themselves and to have positive self-images. This is true for both personal and social aspects of identity. In fact, if one can focus on the positive aspects of groups one is in, one can use those to bolster self-esteem. For this process to work, people generally must feel that their in-groups (groups to which they belong) are at least slightly more positive or worthwhile than their out-groups (groups to which they do not belong). This is how Tajfel (1981) explained his minimal-group experimental findings. Even in the case of minimal categorization, members tend to favor and regard as more positive members of their category or group. Thus, they are biased toward rewarding in-group members over out-group members.

Later work by Turner et al. (1987) showed that categorization processes tend to work toward maximal distinctiveness by differentiating between the in-group and the out-group. The stronger the differentiation, the better the in-group can be defined. This tends to lead to more extreme in-group favoritism and out-group derogation as social identity increases. These tendencies also increase either when self-esteem is threatened (Abrams & Hogg, 1988) or when uncertainty is high (Hogg & Mullins, 1999). The key aspect of this approach to inter-group conflict is that it both occurs and is fostered by very natural processes associated with group membership. Whereas Sherif's (1966) real-istic conflict theory argued that intergroup conflict stemmed from competition over resources, Tajfel's (1981) social identity theory posits that simple categorization and basic needs for self-regard lead to conflict even in the absence of resource competition.

Recent research has shown that intergroup conflicts occur and persist even in situations where interindividual conflicts are rather easily resolved. This is interesting because groups are often better than individuals at solving problems and finding ways to maximize outcome (Laughlin, 1980; Morgan & Tindale, 2002; Thompson, Peterson, & Brodt, 1996). For

example, when individuals play the Prisoner's Dilemma game without communication, mutual defection is a common occurrence, which leads to poor collective and individual outcomes (Carnevale & Pruitt, 1992). However, when players are allowed to communicate and discuss the dilemma prior to making individual choices, mutual cooperation is quite likely, often close to 90% of the time (Dawes, van de Kragt, & Orbell, 1988; Insko & Schopler, 1987). If multiple plays of the game are expected, it is quite easy for players to realize that some degree of trust and cooperation is necessary for either player to gain in the long run. One would also expect that teams of players negotiating a Prisoner's Dilemma would reach this same conclusion and thus act accordingly. However, Insko, Schopler, and colleagues have now shown across numerous replications that groups do not play the game in the same way individuals do (Insko & Schopler, 1987; Insko et al., 1988, 1992, 1993; Wildschut, Pinter, Vevea, Insko, & Schopler, 2003). Whereas individuals tend to cooperate, groups are much more likely to defect under the same circumstances. Insko and Schopler have referred to this phenomenon as the *individual-group discontinuity effect,* following from LeBon's (1896) descriptions of the discontinuity between individual and mob behavior. The discontinuity effect has been demonstrated using different numbers of Prisoner's Dilemma trials (Insko & Schopler, 1987; Pinkley, Griffith, & Northcraft, 1995), different payoff schedules (Schopler et al., 1993), different communication and consensus conditions (Insko et al., 1993; Schopler & Insko, 1992), and different levels of identifiability of group members (Schopler et al., 1995). Thus, the discontinuity effect appears extremely robust over a number of situations and contexts.

Schopler and Insko (1992) have argued, and empirically demonstrated, that both fear and greed play a role in the greater competitiveness of groups in the Prisoner's Dilemma. First, groups are generally seen as more competitive than individuals, and even the anticipation of interacting with another group seems to arouse fear and expectations of deceit and competitive behavior (Hoyle, Pinkley, & Insko, 1989; Pemberton, Insko, & Schopler, 1996). In addition, Schopler et al. (1993) demonstrated that both fear and greed can lead to the group discontinuity effect by adding a withdraw option to the Prisoner's Dilemma. The withdraw option allows one to not compete but also to not lose. Schopler et al. found that groups were more likely than individuals to use the withdraw option, thus supporting the idea that groups showed more fear. However, groups still chose the competitive response more than individuals. Given that the withdraw option should be chosen due to fear, the greater competitiveness of groups in this game was attributed to greed. In an additional study, Schopler et al. showed that greed, as a motive for competition, required social support. By adding confederates to the groups and manipulating feedback about the other groups' choices, they found that group members would compete when the other group cooperated only if the confederate suggested it.

A recent study by Morgan and Tindale (2002) found that groups are more competitive than individuals even when they are playing against individuals. However, there appeared to be a shift in motivation when the opponent changed from being another group to a single individual. When groups were playing against groups, their rationale for defecting revolved around fear or lack of trust concerning the other group. In contrast, when playing against individuals, groups tended to use greed as the main reason for defection. Thus, in an intergroup situation, in-group protection tended to be weighted most heavily, whereas in-group enhancement seemed more salient when the opponent was simply an individual. Morgan and Tindale also found that the move toward defection by groups was at least partly a function of in-group discussions. Even a single member of a three-person group arguing for defection was often enough to lead the group to defect. This is consistent with a general in-group favoritism norm, as proposed

by Wildschut et al. (2003) and Gaertner and Insko (2000).

Although often leading to negative (or less than optimal) outcomes, intergroup conflict can sometimes produce benefits. Tauer and Harackiewicz (2004) showed that both satisfaction and performance were enhanced on a team when interteam competition was present as opposed to absent. It appears that intragroup cooperation and intergroup competition provided the highest levels of interpersonal enthusiasm (team spirit), whereas competition generally increases goal pursuit and perceptions of challenge. Recent work on intergroup social dilemmas (Bornstein, 1992; Bornstein & Rappoport, 1988) has shown that free riding is drastically reduced within a group when the group's payout becomes embedded in a competitive intergroup situation. People expend more effort and resources on behalf of their own groups in the presence of a competing group, which can lead to positive outcomes for the groups involved. However, the same processes can lead to less than optimal outcomes for both groups in situations where intergroup cooperation is more collectively rational (Rappoport & Amaldoss, 1999).

Resolving Intra- and Intergroup Conflicts

Research on resolving intra- and intergroup conflicts has tended to focus on similar issues, although sometimes with somewhat inconsistent results. In general, trust seems to be a key aspect in resolving conflicts of both types. Kramer (1999) has argued that one of the biggest problems in organizations revolves around *collective paranoia*. Groups often distrust the motives of other groups and, as such, find it difficult to interact with them in an open and productive fashion. Distrust among members of a group is often one of the key factors that lead groups to break up or disband (Levine & Thompson, 1996; Moreland & Levine, 1982). In her book on negotiation, Thompson (2001) devotes an entire chapter to building trust. In a group, two members who do not trust each other can sometimes be brought back together by other members who are trusted by both parties. In intergroup situations, mediation (bringing in a third party to help resolve the dispute) is a common technique used to resolve difficult conflicts or stalled negotiations (Ury, Brett, & Goldberg, 1988). However, mediation only works when both parties trust the mediator. Burt (1999) also demonstrates how tight-knit or "dense" groups in organizations tend to perform less well because they interact with other groups less and thus trust them less than more open or loose-knit groups.

Communication appears to be one of the best ways of both establishing and repairing trust in intragroup conflicts (Dawes et al., 1988; Deutsch, 1973). Individuals playing multiple Prisoner's Dilemma games rarely end up in the mutual defection cell if they are allowed to communicate with one another. Open communication allows group members not only to get a better understanding of both the needs and priorities of the other members but also to see what other options might be available. Promises and commitments also are possible when open communication is present, and group members tend to honor their in-group commitments (Dawes et al., 1988; Kerr & Kaufman-Gilliland, 1994). Communication also allows people to state why they feel or think as they do, rather than simply asserting what they feel, think, or prefer (Brehmer, 1976). Such process or justification feedback can often point to new ways of resolving the conflict—the key to the problem-solving approach to negotiation. However, communication must be structured to be productive rather than destructive. Simply issuing demands and threats associated with their not being met can actually impede conflict resolution and lead to worse overall outcomes (Deutsch, 1973).

Although trust is equally important for intergroup conflicts, it appears that trust between groups is much harder to obtain. Schopler and Insko's (1992) work on the discontinuity effect shows quite clearly that communication, commitments, promises, and so on—which work well for producing cooperation between individuals—fail miserably when the players are groups. Two major theoretical orientations have dominated much of the literature on resolving intergroup conflicts: the contact hypothesis approach (Allport, 1954; Pettigrew, 1998), and the common in-group identity model (Brewer & Miller, 1984; Gaertner & Dovidio, 2000). Both have grown to be rather similar over the years, but they stem from slightly different theoretical perspectives. The contact hypothesis is more in line with Sherif's (1966) realistic conflict theory, whereas the common in-group identity model's theoretical ancestor is social identity theory.

The contact model basically argues that real or perceived conflict between groups tends to isolate the members from each other. Thus, the negative stereotypes of the out-group, which form as a function of the conflict, are never tested. Allport (1954) argued that contact, under the appropriate circumstances, can aid in the falsification of the stereotypes and thus attenuate intergroup prejudices. In its most recent rendition (Pettigrew, 1998), contact between the members of the two groups must occur under the conditions of equal status within the situation, common goals, intergroup cooperation, support of the authorities (the original four), and friendship potential. It should be noted that all five of these conditions were present in the second half of the Robber's Cave Experiments (Sherif, 1966). Pettigrew also argued that changes in identity over time are necessary for the contact to produce the desired effects. Early contacts must lead to decategorization, so that members no longer immediately think of out-group members as different. Once the members of different groups have begun to trust and interact with one another, intergroup categories must be made salient again so that they can be overridden by "recategorization" into one larger, superordinate category. Once the recategorization has taken place, the situation is no longer one of intergroup conflict but of common group identity, which should lead to cooperation (Eller & Abrams, 2004). It is interesting to note that sometimes, the superordinate category and common goals stem from a threat from an out-group at the superordinate level (e.g., both whites and blacks in New York felt more like Americans after the September 11, 2001, attacks).

Gaertner and Dovidio (2000) argue that social or group identity is the key factor in inter-group relations, and the level of categorization acts as a mediator between intergroup contact and the attitudes, beliefs, and behaviors that follow. For instance, positive contact with members of the out-group should lead to super-ordinate categorization of the group (i.e., we all belong to a larger group). This categorization then leads to favorable attitudes and behaviors toward the group. Gaertner and Dovidio also add a fourth level of categorization, referred to as *dual identity*. Dual identity is a recategoriza-tion that acknowledges both the initial group identity and the new superordinate identity. In situations where the superordinate category is large or the original identity is particularly strong, dual identity may actually be better for improving intergroup relations (Gonzalez & Brown, 2003). If neither level of identity changes, contact or new information about the out-group will have little effect on attitudes and behaviors.

Both of these approaches have received sup-port in the literature (see Eller & Abrams, 2004), but there is also a fair amount of evidence that change, even under the best of conditions, is difficult if social identities are strong and the con-flict is severe and has endured over long periods (Bar-Tal, 1990). However, consistent use of the principles laid out by the aforementioned models can have a positive impact, even in situations of extreme intergroup conflict. Kelman (1997) has spent much of the past two decades using social psychological and communication principles to aid in the resolution of the Israeli-Palestinian

conflict. His workshops bring between 8 and 16 Israelis and Palestinians together for discussions and collective problem-solving endeavors. Social science facilitators are present and help to guide both the discussions and interactions that occur. Through open discussions about beliefs and feelings, about both their own groups and the others' groups, they learn that they are more similar than different. By framing issues in terms of problems to be solved collaboratively, and keeping the notion of peace as the overarching goal of both peoples, Kelman has successfully trained a number of members of both groups to be effective negotiators and activists for peace in the region. Kelman's work in this regard illumi-nates both the achievements of theoretically and empirically based approaches to intergroup con-flict and the difficulties that yet remain beyond our reach.

Future Research Directions

Although both intra- an intergroup conflict have rich research traditions, we still have much to learn about how conflict operates and how and when it becomes a problem. Probably one of the key issues in intragroup conflict is to dis-cover exactly when conflict serves to improve group performance rather than impede it. Jehn (1997) has laid out an interesting framework from which to work, but the research evidence has yet to truly differentiate the types of conflict at an empirical level (De Dreu & Weingart, 2003). Good work is already under way on this important topic (Schulz-Hardt et al., 2002; West, 2003), but more subtle distinctions or bet-ter descriptions of the situational factors that enhance or constrain the positive and negative aspects of conflict are needed.

One topic that may contribute to making progress in this area is minority influence research (De Dreu & West, 2001; Smith, 2003). Most theoretical orientations on minority influ-ence hypothesize a positive effect on groups, even if only indirectly. By carefully contrasting conflict in general with conflict created by minority factions, the key issues surrounding the positive effects of conflict on both the social and cognitive processes inherent in group interaction may emerge.

Probably the most important topic for future research in intergroup conflict is how to engender trust between groups. Trust has been shown to be a key factor in resolving conflicts within groups and organizations, and a number of strategies are available for engendering trust among group members (Korsgaard, Schweiger, & Sapienza, 1995; Thompson, 2001). However, many of these strategies work either less well or not at all when dealing with intergroup conflicts (Morgan & Tindale, 2002; Schopler & Insko, 1999). Schopler and Insko (1999) have shown that focusing groups on the long-term consequences of their behavior can reduce intergroup conflict in the laboratory, and there is at least anecdotal evidence that this can work in real-world applications as well. More research is warranted on how and when such time frame shifting is effective at easing intergroup tensions. Also, a greater understanding of how in-group processes affect intergroup conflict is needed as well. Generally, there seems to be an inverse relationship between in-group identity or cohesiveness and out-group distrust and derogation (Burt, 1999). When intergroup tensions have been severe, finding ways to create meaningful dual identities that lead to "loose" social networks might be a promising area to explore. It might also be interesting to focus on how new technology might aid in the reduction or productive use of conflict (Hobman, Bordia, Irmer, & Chang, 2002; McGrath & Hollingshead, 1994). Communication from afar may be a good way to begin building trust before face-to-face communication is possible. Given that many of the world's most pressing problems revolve around intergroup conflict, this area of research should remain vibrant for many years to come.

References

Abrams, D., & Hogg, M. A. (1988). Comments on the motivational status of self-esteem in social identity and intergroup discrimination. *European Journal of Social Psychology, 18,* 317–334.

Allport, G. W. (1954). *The nature of prejudice.* Reading, MA: Addison-Wesley.

Axelrod, R. (1984). *Evolution of cooperation.* New York: Basic Books.

Axelrod, R., Riolo, R., & Cohen, M. (2002). Beyond geography: Cooperation with persistent links in the absence of clustered neighborhoods. *Personality and Social Psychology Review, 4,* 341–346.

Bales, R. F. (1950). *Interaction process analysis: A method for the study of small groups.* Cambridge, MA: Addison-Wesley.

Bar-Tal, D. (1990). *Group beliefs: A conception for analyzing group structure, processes, and behavior.* New York: Springer-Verlag.

Bazerman, M. H., Curhan, J. R., Moore, D. A., & Valley, K. L. (2000). Negotiation. *Annual Review of Psychology, 51,* 279–314.

Bazerman, M. H., & Neale, M. (1983). Heuristics in negotiation: Limitations to effective dispute resolution. In M. H. Bazerman & R. J. Lewicki (Eds.), *Negotiation in organizations* (pp. 51–67). Beverly Hills, CA: Sage.

Bornstein, G. (1992). The free rider problem in intergroup conflicts over step-level and continuous public goods. *Journal of Personality and Social Psychology, 62,* 597–602.

Bornstein, G., & Rappoport, A. (1988). Intergroup competition for the provision of step-level public goods: Effects of pre-play communication. *European Journal of Social Psychology, 18,* 125–142.

Brehmer, B. (1976). Social judgment theory and the analysis of interpersonal conflict. *Psychological Bulletin, 83,* 985–1003.

Brewer, M. B., & Miller, N. (1984). Beyond the contact hypothesis: Theoretical perspectives on desegregation. In N. Miller & M. B. Brewer (Eds.), *Groups in contact: The psychology of desegregation* (pp. 281–302). Orlando, FL: Academic Press.

Brown, R., & Gaertner, S. (Eds.). (2001). *Blackwell handbook of social psychology: Intergroup processes.* Oxford, UK: Blackwell.

Burt, R. S. (1999). Entrepreneurs, distrust, and third parties: A strategic look at the dark side of dense networks. In L. Thompson, J. M. Levine, & D. M. Messick (Eds.), *Shared cognitions in organizations: The management of knowledge* (pp. 213–244). Mahwah, NJ: Lawrence Erlbaum.

Campbell, D. T. (1956). Enhancement of contrast as a composite habit. *Journal of Abnormal and Social Psychology, 53,* 350–355.

Caporael, L. R. (1997). The evolution of truly social cognition: The core configurations model. *Personality and Social Psychology Review, 1,* 276–298.

Carnevale, P. J., & Leung, K. (2001). Cultural dimensions of negotiations. In M. A. Hogg & R. S. Tindale (Eds.), *Blackwell handbook of social psychology: Group processes* (pp. 482–496). Oxford, UK: Blackwell.

Carnevale, P. J., & Probst, T. M. (1998). Social values and social conflict in creative problem solving and categorization. *Journal of Personality and Social Psychology, 74,* 1300–1309.

Carnevale, P. J., & Pruitt, D. G. (1992). Negotiation and mediation. In M. R. Rosenzweig & L. W. Porter (Eds.), *Annual review of psychology* (Vol. 43, pp. 531–582). Palo Alto, CA: Annual Reviews.

Dawes, R. M. (1980). Social dilemmas. *Annual Review of Psychology, 31,* 169–193.

Dawes, R., Orbell, J., Simmons, R., & van de Kragt, A. (1986). Organizing groups for collective action. *American Political Science Review, 80,* 1171–1185.

Dawes, R. M., van deKragt, A. J. C., & Orbell, J. M. (1988). Not me or thee but we: The importance of group identity in eliciting cooperation in dilemma situations: Experimental manipulations. *Acta Psychologica, 68,* 83–97.

De Cremer, D., & Van Vugt, M. (1999). Social identification effects in social dilemmas: A transformation of motives. *European Journal of Social Psychology, 29,* 871–893.

De Dreu, C. K. W., & Carnevale, P. J. (2004). Motivational bases of information processing and strategy in conflict and negotiation. *Advances in Experimental Social Psychology, 35,* 235–291.

De Dreu, C. K. W., Koole, S., & Oldersma, F. L. (1999). On the seizing and freezing of negotiator inferences: Need for cognitive closure moderates the use of heuristics in negotiation. *Personality and Social Psychology Bulletin, 25,* 348–362.

De Dreu, C. K. W., Koole, S., & Steinel, W. (2000). Unfixing the fixed pie: A motivated information processing of integrative negotiation. *Journal of Personality and Social Psychology, 79,* 975–987.

De Dreu, C. K. W., & Weingart, L. R. (2003). Task versus relationship conflict, team performance, and team member satisfaction: A meta-analysis. *Journal of Applied Psychology, 88,* 741–749.

De Dreu, C. K. W., & West, M. A. (2001). Minority dissent and team innovation: The importance of participation in decision making. *Journal of Applied Psychology, 86,* 1191–1201.

Deutsch, M. (1973). *The resolution of conflict.* New Haven, CT: Yale University Press.

Eller, A., & Abrams, D. (2004). Come together: Longitudinal comparisons of Pettigrew's reformulated intergroup contact model and the common ingroup identity model in Anglo-French and Mexican American contexts. *European Journal of Social Psychology, 34,* 229–256.

Festinger, L. (1954). A theory of social comparison processes. *Human Relations, 7,* 117–140.

Fiske, S. T. (1998). Stereotyping, prejudice, and discrimination. In D. T. Gilbert, S. T. Fiske, & G. Lindzey (Eds.), *The handbook of social psychology* (4th ed., Vol. 2, pp. 357–414). New York: Oxford University Press.

Foddy, M., Smithson, M., Schneider, S., & Hogg, M. (Eds.). (1999). *Resolving social dilemmas: Dynamic, structural, and intergroup aspects.* Philadelphia: Psychology Press.

Gaertner, S. L., & Dovidio, J. F. (2000). The aversive form of racism. In J. F. Dovidio & S. L. Gaertner (Eds.), *Prejudice, discrimination, and racism* (pp. 61–89). Orlando, FL: Academic Press.

Gaertner, L., & Insko, C. A. (2000). Intergroup discrimination in the minimal group paradigm: Categorization, reciprocation, or fear? *Journal of Personality and Social Psychology, 79,* 787–794.

Gonzalez, R., & Brown, R. J. (2003). Generalization of positive attitude as a function of subgroup and superordinate group identification in intergroup contact. *European Journal of Social Psychology, 33,* 195–214.

Gorum, H., & Bornstein, G. (2000). The effects of intragroup communication on intergroup cooperation in the repeated intergroup prisoner's dilemma (IPD) game. *Journal of Conflict Resolution, 44,* 700–719.

Hobman, E., Bordia, P., Irmer, B., & Chang, A. (2002). The expression of conflict in computer-mediated and face-to-face groups. *Small Group Research, 33,* 439–465.

Hogg, M. A. (2001). Social categorization and group behavior. In M. A. Hogg & R. S. Tindale (Eds.), *Blackwell handbook of social psychology: Group processes* (pp. 56–85). Oxford, UK: Blackwell.

Hogg, M. A., & Abrams, D. (1988). *Social identifications: A social psychology of intergroup relations and group processes.* London & New York: Routledge.

Hogg, M. A., & Mullins, B. A. (1999). Joining groups to reduce uncertainty: Subjective uncertainty reduction and group identification. In D. Abrams & M. Hogg (Eds.), *Social identity and social cognition* (pp. 249–279). Oxford, UK: Blackwell.

Hollenbeck, J. R., Colquit, J. A., Ilgen, D. R., LePine, J. A., & Hedlund, J. (1998). Accuracy decomposition and team decision making: Testing theoretical boundary conditions. *Journal of Applied Psychology, 83,* 494–500.

Homans, G. C. (1961). *Social behavior: Its elementary forms.* New York: Harcourt, Brace/Random House.

Hoyle, R. H., Pinkley, R. L., & Insko, C. A. (1989). Perceptions of social behavior: Evidence of differing expectations for interpersonal and intergroup interaction. *Personality and Social Psychology Bulletin, 15,* 365–376.

Insko, C. A., Hoyle, R. H., Pinkley, R. L., Hong, G., Slim, R. M., Dalton, B., Lin, Y. W., Ruffin, P. P., Dardis, G. J., Bernthal, P. R., & Schopler, J. (1988). Individual-group discontinuity: The role of a consensus rule. *Journal of Experimental Social Psychology, 24,* 505–519.

Insko, C. A., & Schopler, J. (1987). Categorization, competition, and collectivity. In C. Hendrick (Ed.), *Review of personality and social psychology* (pp. 213–251). New York: Sage.

Insko, C. A., Schopler, J., Drigotas, S. M., Graetz, K. A., Kennedy, J., Cox, C., & Bornstein, G. (1993). The role of communication in interindividual-intergroup discontinuity. *Journal of Conflict Resolution, 37,* 108–138.

Insko, C. A., Schopler, J., Kennedy, J. F., Dahl, K. R., Graetz, K. A., & Drigotas, S. M. (1992). Individual-group discontinuity from the differing perspectives of Campbell's realistic group conflict theory and Tajfel and Turner's social identity theory. *Social Psychology Quarterly, 55,* 272–291.

Jehn, K. (1995). A multimethod examination of the benefits and detriments of intragroup conflict. *Administrative Science Quarterly, 40,* 256–282.

Jehn, K. (1997). Affective and cognitive conflict in work groups: Increasing performance through value-based intragroup conflict. In C. K. De Dreu & E. Van de Vliert (Eds.), *Using conflict in organizations.* (pp. 87–100). Thousand Oaks, CA: Sage.

Jehn, K., & Chatman, J. A. (2000). Reconceptualizing conflict: Proportional and relational conflict. *International Journal of Conflict Management, 11,* 51–69.

Jehn, K., & Mannix, E. (2001). The dynamic nature of conflict: A longitudinal study of intragroup conflict and group performance. *Academy of Management Journal, 44,* 238–251.

Kahn, J. P., & Rappoport, A. (1984). *Theories of coalition formation.* Hillsdale, NJ: Lawrence Erlbaum.

Kameda, T., Takezawa, M., & Hastie, R. (2003). The logic of social sharing: An evolutionary game analysis of adaptive norm development. *Personality and Social Psychology Review, 7,* 2–19.

Kelman, H. C. (1997). Group processes in the resolution of international conflicts: Experiences from the Israeli-Palestinian peace. *American Psychologist, 52,* 212–220.

Kerr, N. L. (1999). Anonymity and social control in social dilemmas. In M. Foddy, M. Smithson, S. Schneider, & M. Hogg (Eds.), *Resolving social dilemmas: Dynamic, structural, and intergroup aspects* (pp. 103–120). Philadelphia: Psychology Press.

Kerr, N. L., & Kaufman-Gilliland, C. M. (1994). Communication, commitment, and cooperation in social dilemmas. *Journal of Personality and Social Psychology, 66,* 513–529.

Korsgaard, M. A., Schweiger, D. M., & Sapienza, H. J. (1995). Building commitment, attachment, and trust in strategic decision-making teams: The role of procedural justice. *Academy of Management Journal, 38,* 60–84.

Kramer, R. M. (1999). Trust and distrust in organizations: Emerging perspectives, enduring questions. *Annual Review of Psychology, 50,* 569–598.

Kramer, R. M. (2001). Golden rules and leaden worlds: Exploring the limitations of Tit-for-Tat as a social decision rule. In J. Darley, D. M. Messick, & T. Tyler (Eds.), *Ethics and social influence* (pp. 177–199). Mahwah, NJ: Lawrence Erlbaum.

Kruglanski, A. W., & Webster, D. M. (1996). Motivated closing of the mind: "Seizing" and "freezing." *Psychological Review, 103,* 263–283.

Laughlin, P. R. (1980). Social combination processes of cooperative, problem-solving groups on verbal intellective tasks. In M. Fishbein (Ed.), *Progress in social psychology* (Vol. 1, pp. 127–155). Hillsdale, NJ: Lawrence Erlbaum.

Laughlin, P. R., Zander, M. L., Knievel, E. M., & Tan, T. K. (2003). Groups perform better than the best individuals on letter-to-numbers problems: Informative equations and effective strategies. *Journal of Personality and Social Psychology, 85,* 684–694.

LeBon, G. (1896). *The crowd: A study of the popular mind.* London: Unwin.

Levine, J. M. (1980). Reactions to opinion deviance in small groups. In P. Paulus (Ed.), *Psychology of group influence* (pp. 375–430). Hillsdale, NJ: Lawrence Erlbaum.

Levine, J. M., Resnick, L., & Higgins, E. T. (1993). Social foundations of cognition. *Annual Review of Psychology, 44,* 585–612.

Levine, J., & Thompson, L. (1996). Conflict in groups. In E. Tory Higgins & A. Kruglanski (Eds.), *Social psychology: Handbook of basic principles* (pp. 745–776). New York: Guilford.

Lewin, K. (1947). Frontiers in group dynamics: Concept, method, and reality in social science. *Human Relations, 1,* 5–42.

McClintock, C. (1977). Social motives in settings of outcome interdependence. In D. Druckman (Ed.), *Negotiations: Social psychology perspective* (pp. 49–77). Beverly Hills, CA: Sage.

McGrath, J. E. (1984). *Groups: Interaction and performance.* Englewood Cliffs, NJ: Prentice Hall.

McGrath, J. E., & Hollingshead, A. B. (1994). *Groups interacting with technology.* Thousand Oaks, CA: Sage.

Messick, D. M. (1999). Models of decision making in social dilemmas. In M. Foddy, M. Smithson, S. Schneider, & M. Hogg (Eds.), *Resolving social dilemmas: Dynamic, structural, and intergroup aspects* (pp. 209–218). Philadelphia: Psychology Press.

Moreland, R. L., & Levine, J. M. (1982). Group socialization: Temporal changes in individual-group relations. In L. Berkowitz (Ed.), *Advances in experimental social psychology* (Vol. 15, pp. 137–192). New York: Academic Press.

Morgan, P. M., & Tindale, R. S. (2002). Group vs. individual performance in mixed-motive situations: Exploring an inconsistency. *Organizational Behavior and Human Decision Processes, 87,* 44–65.

Moscovici, S. (1976). *Social influence and social change.* London: Academic Press.

Nemeth, C. (1986). Differential contributions of majority and minority influence. *Psychological Review, 93,* 23–32.

Nemeth, C., & Kwan, J. (1987). Originality of word associations as a function of majority vs. minority influence processes. *Social Psychology Quarterly, 48,* 277–282.

Paulus, P. B., & Nijstad, B. A. (2003). *Group creativity: Innovation through collaboration.* Oxford, UK: Oxford University Press.

Pemberton, M. R., Insko, C. A., & Schopler, J. (1996). Memory for and experience of differential competitive behavior of individuals and groups. *Journal of Personality and Social Psychology, 71,* 1–14.

Pettigrew, T. F. (1998). Intergroup contact theory. *Annual Review of Psychology, 49,* 65–85.

Pinkley, R. L., Griffith, T., & Northcraft, G. B. (1995). "Fixed pie" a la mode: Information availability, information processing, and the negotiation of suboptimal agreements. *Organizational Behavior & Human Decision Processes, 62,* 101–112.

Rappoport, A., & Amaldoss, W. (1999). Social dilemmas embedded in between-group competitions: Effects of contest and distribution rules. In M. Foddy, M. Smithson, S. Schneider, & M. Hogg (Eds.), *Resolving social dilemmas: Dynamic, structural, and intergroup aspects* (pp. 67–86). Philadelphia: Psychology Press.

Rohrbaugh, J. (1979). Improving the quality of group judgment: Social judgment analysis and the Delphi technique. *Organizational Behavior and Human Performance, 24,* 73–92.

Saavedra, R., Earley, P. C., & Van Dyne, L. (1993). Complex interdependence in task-performing groups. *Journal of Applied Psychology, 78,* 61–72.

Schopler, J., & Insko, C. A. (1992). The discontinuity effect in interpersonal and intergroup relations: Generality and mediation. In W. Stroebe & M. Hewstone (Eds.), *European review of social psychology* (Vol. 3, pp. 122–151). New York: John Wiley.

Schopler, J., & Insko, C. A. (1999). The reduction of the interindividual-intergroup discontinuity effect: The role of future consequences. In M. Foddy, M. Smithson, S. Schneider, & M. Hogg (Eds.), *Resolving social dilemmas: Dynamic, structural, and intergroup aspects* (pp. 281–294). Philadelphia: Psychology Press.

Schopler, J., Insko, C. A., Drigotas, S. M., Wieselquist, J., Pemberton, M. B., & Cox, C. (1995). The role of identifiability in the reduction of interindividual-intergroup discontinuity. *Journal of Experimental Social Psychology, 31*, 553–574.

Schopler, J., Insko, C. A., Graetz, K. A., Drigotas, S. M., Smith, V. A, & Dhal, K. (1993). Individual-group discontinuity: Further evidence for mediation by fear and greed. *Personality and Social Psychological Bulletin, 19*, 419–431.

Schulz-Hardt, S., Jochims, M., & Frey, D. (2002). Productive conflict in group decision making: Genuine and contrived dissent as strategies to counteract biased information seeking. *Organizational Behavior and Human Decision Processes, 88*, 563–586.

Sherif, M. (1966). *Group conflict and cooperation.* London: Routledge & Kegan Paul.

Sherif, M., Harvey, O. J., White, B. J., Hood, W. R., & Sherif, C. W. (1961). *Intergroup conflict and cooperation: The Robber's Cave experiments.* Norman: University of Oklahoma Press.

Smith, A. (1872). *The wealth of nations.* London: Penguin.

Smith, C. M. (2003). *Linking minority status to divergent thinking: Disentangling exposure to minority influence and exposure to conflict.* Paper presented at the Small Group Meeting on Minority Influence Processes, New College, Oxford, UK.

Stasser, G., & Birchmeier, A. (2003). Group creativity and collective choice. In P. B. Paulus & B. A. Nijstad (Eds.), *Group creativity* (pp. 85–109). New York: Oxford University Press.

Tajfel, H. (1970). Experiments in intergroup discrimination. *Scientific American, 223*, 96–102.

Tajfel, H. (1981). *Human groups and social categories: Studies in social psychology.* Cambridge, UK: Cambridge University Press.

Tajfel, H., Flament, C., Billig, M. G., & Bundy, R. F. (1971). Social categorization and intergroup behavior. *European Journal of Social Psychology, 1*, 149–177.

Tajfel, H., & Turner, J. C. (1979). An integrative theory of intergroup conflict. In W. G. Austin & S. Worchel (Eds.), *The social psychology of intergroup relations* (pp. 33–47). Monterey, CA: Brooks/Cole.

Tauer, J. M., & Harackiewicz, J. M. (2004). The effects of cooperation and competition on intrinsic

motivation and performance. *Journal of Personality and Social Psychology, 86*, 849–861.

Thibaut, J. W., & Kelley, H. H. (1959). *The social psychology of groups.* New York: John Wiley.

Thompson, L. (1990). Negotiation behavior and outcomes: Empirical evidence and theoretical issues. *Psychological Bulletin, 108*, 315–332.

Thompson, L. (1998). *The mind and heart of the negotiator.* Upper Saddle River, NJ: Prentice Hall.

Thompson, L. L. (2001). *Making the team: A guide for managers* (2nd ed.). Upper Saddle River, NJ: Pearson Education.

Thompson, L. L., & Loewenstein, G. (1992). Egocentric interpretation of fairness in interpersonal conflict. *Organizational Behavior and Human Decision Processes, 51*, 176–197.

Thompson, L. L., Peterson, E., & Brodt, S. E. (1996). Team negotiation: An examination of integrative and distributive bargaining. *Journal of Personality and Social Personality, 70*, 66–78.

Turner, J. C., Hogg, M. A., Oakes, P. J., Reicher, S. D., & Wetherell, M. S. (1987). *Rediscovering the social group: A self-categorization theory.* Oxford, UK: Blackwell.

Ury, W. L., Brett, J. M., & Goldberg, S. B. (1988). *Getting disputes resolved: Designing systems to cut the cost of conflict.* San Francisco: Jossey-Bass.

Van Lange, P. A. M. (1999). The pursuit of joint outcomes and equality of outcomes: An integrative model of social value orientation. *Journal of Personality and Social Psychology, 77*, 337–349.

von Neumann, J., & Morgenstern, O. (1947). *Theory of games and economic behavior* (2nd ed.). Princeton, NJ: Princeton University Press.

West, M. (2003). Innovative implementation in work teams. In P. Paulus & B. Nijstad (Eds.), *Group creativity* (pp. 245–276). Oxford, UK: Oxford University Press.

Wildschut, R., Pinter, B., Vevea, J. L., Insko, C. A., & Schopler, J. (2003). Beyond the group mind: A quantitative review of the interindividual-intergroup discontinuity effect. *Psychological Bulletin, 129*, 698–722.

18

Group Identity and Self-Definition

Dominic Abrams

Daniel Frings

Georgina Randsley de Moura

This chapter outlines some key concepts and evidence in research on group identity and self-definition. We place particular emphasis on the social identity perspective and explain how it relates to alternative approaches. Various topics, such as stereotypes and intergroup prejudice, are beyond the scope of this chapter. Therefore, we have limited our discussion to evidence about the relationship between group identity and self-definition as it relates to the regulation of group behavior, organizational identity, ways people deal with social dilemmas as group members, collective action, deviance within groups, and leadership.

What Is Group Identity?

There are many possible perspectives on group identity, including political, historical, and economic. However, at the core of psychological theory and research, there has been continuing debate as to what group identity is and the extent to which the self is implicated. The research area covered in this chapter reflects this debate—the question of the relationship between group and individual in terms of self-definition, motivation, and action. The underlying theoretical questions pervade most areas of research into groups, especially intergroup activity. The research literature is certainly too vast to encompass, and therefore, we focus on selected topics, generally with an eye on the applied implications.

Much of the framework for research is provided by the social identity perspective on intergroup relations (see Hogg & Abrams, 1988; Tajfel & Turner, 1979), and there have been many developments of this approach to embrace areas such as social influence, group cohesiveness, leadership, deviance, and identity management. The fundamental assumption of this approach is that people experience identity as members of social groups just as vividly as they experience identity as an individual person. In short, the self is not restricted to the individual being but embraces collective being. The group is not separate from the self but is part of the self. Such an assumption is far from controversial, and the metatheory behind it (Abrams & Hogg, 2004) has provided the basis for four decades of research and numerous refinements and developments. We therefore draw on the social identity perspective to frame many of the questions in this chapter.

Central Questions in Group Identity Research

The central questions surrounding group identity and the self are these:

- What are the necessary and sufficient psychological determinants of whether people behave as individuals or as members of groups?
- Under what circumstances will people prioritize their groups over themselves personally?
- What is the psychological basis of social influence within groups? How is group behavior possible?
- How can intergroup prejudice and discrimination be explained (and reduced)?
- What changes occur in the self-concept when social identity is salient?

- What is the relationship between intergroup and intragroup behavior?
- What are the primary motivations for group behavior?

These questions have been addressed in both laboratory/experimental settings and very frequently in practical, applied situations in which the self may be firmly embedded in the group. For example, researchers have investigated the role of group identity in collective action and protest; organizational behavior, including reactions to deviant group members; turnover intentions; leadership and mergers; cooperation in social dilemmas; and reduced intergroup conflict through changes in self-other linkages.

The History of Research on Group Identity

It is often tempting to explain extreme actions by members of different groups in terms of the personal or individual characteristics of their members. For example, there is continuing media investigation and speculation about the "mind of the suicide bomber," as writers try to pinpoint the type of person who becomes a terrorist/religious fanatic/great leader/despot, and so on. This is not surprising. For the greater part of the 19th and 20th centuries, the self has been conceptualized in Western cultures as a unique, individual entity, determined by a particular history, genetic makeup, and set of relationships. The idea that the individual self could be achieved or perfected is inherent in Freudian theory, in which the role of groups was largely restricted to either primitive instinct or parental superego. Similarly, Le Bon's (1896/1906) conception of the crowd was that of a primitive mob reduced to base instincts and characterized by the abandonment of individual control. The self, therefore, is cast as a deep and mysterious entity to which people have little direct access and which must be analyzed by experts. The conceptual gauntlet was thrown down most dramatically by Floyd Allport (1924), who felt sufficiently confident to proclaim, "There is no psychology of groups which is not essentially and entirely a psychology of individuals" (p. 4).

Appealing as such accounts may be, they are seriously deficient as explanations for mass behavior (Billig, 1976). Can we really accept that Hitler was able to mobilize Germany against the rest of Europe simply because he and others had particular types of personality? How or why do people such as Saddam Hussein or Slobodan Milosovic attain such power and control? Huge energy was invested in pursuing such questions in Adorno, Frenkel, Levinson, and Sanford's (1950) exploration of the authoritarian personality. Although the psychodynamic perspective they adopted is largely out of favor for explaining political extremism these days, there is plenty of energy expended on understanding how other individual differences may play a role in prejudice toward minority groups (e.g., Sidanius & Pratto's [1999] social dominance theory). Yet, arguably, accounting for mass action by analyzing characteristics of individuals leaves obvious gulfs in our explanations and tends to focus only on some individuals involved in group behavior, while regarding others as irrelevant. There may also be a risk of explaining intergroup conflicts in terms of the personality of people who represent the out-group side of the relationship (Milosovic, Bin Laden, Saddam Hussein, etc.), while regarding the personalities of in-group members as noncausal or unproblematic (Bush, Blair). This tendency to focus on pathology among out-groups is well documented. For example, Pettigrew (1979) identified the ultimate attribution error, whereby people tend to attribute negative acts more to dispositional causes when they are conducted by out-group rather than by in-group members.

By the 1960s, the predominant social psychological explanations for intergroup behavior rested on aggregation of processes that affect individuals, such as the link between frustration and aggression. However, Sherif's (1966) work on realistic group conflict did much to highlight that the structure of relationships between groups (not just individuals) could itself be a cause of intergroup attitudes. Their studies in boys' summer camps showed that when the boys were assigned to groups that had competitive and incompatible goals, they developed strongly negative attitudes and behavior toward members of opposing groups, along with more positive attitudes toward their own teams. Moreover, the imposition of common superordinate goals seemed to be sufficient to reverse this pattern and to generate more harmonious intergroup relations.

Dissatisfaction with explanations for intergroup conflict that rested either on aggregation of individual responses or on material conflicts of interest fueled the development of a different metatheoretical perspective, primarily within European social psychology. With roots more in the ideas of sociologists Marx (1844/1963) and Durkheim (1893/1933), this work emphasized a more social view of collective behavior. It embraced the idea that people's perceptions, choices, and actions are associated with a socially shared construction of the world. Henri Tajfel, Serge Moscovici, Willem Doise, Hilde Himmelweit, and other European scholars emphasized that social psychological processes are not fundamentally individual processes (e.g., Moscovici, 1982), but concern the relationship between individuals within a shared social structure (Doise, 1982; Jaspars, 1980, 1986; Tajfel, 1972). Focusing on that relationship would yield more insight into collective and group behavior, they believed. Their aim was to develop a less reductionist social psychology, that is, one that did not explain societal phenomena purely on the basis of individual psychology. The task was to explain the way individuals embrace the social reality defined by collectives or groups and thus to explain why group concerns become the individual's concern, and vice versa. Throughout the 1970s and 1980s, there were vigorous debates about the validity and usefulness of the European perspective (see Tajfel, 1978; Tajfel, Jaspars, & Fraser, 1984; Turner & Giles, 1981).

The social identity perspective on group and intergroup behavior is part of that European contribution to social psychology, and it is represented in numerous collections of social identity research (Abrams & Hogg, 1990b, 1999; Capozza & Brown, 2000; Ellemers, Spears, & Doosje, 1999; Hogg & Abrams, 1988; Robinson, 1996; Worchel, Morales, Paez, & Deschamps, 1998).

Theoretical Perspectives on Group Identity and Self-Definition

Social Identity Theory

Social identity theory (Tajfel & Turner, 1979) holds that identity can be characterized and experienced on a continuum from very personal to very social. Personal identity as an individual may be based on unique traits or attributes, whereas social identity is based on attributes shared among members of social groups and categories to which people belong. More formally, social identity was defined as "that *part* of the individual's self-concept which derives from his knowledge of his membership of a social group (or groups) together with the value and emotional significance attached to that membership" (Tajfel, 1978, p. 63). A central aspect of the approach is that different personal and social identities become salient depending on variations in the social context. People categorize themselves and others according to salient differences between themselves and others in a social comparative context. Social comparisons between one's own and other categories provide both the basis and evaluative outcomes for the self.

Group behavior happens when people share a social category and act in terms of a common social identity as members of that category. This coordination of perceptions and actions through a shared identity marks the social identity perspective as different from other approaches to group behavior. In particular, compared with other perspectives on group behavior, the social identity perspective attaches relatively less importance to the role of physical and "objective" qualities of a group, such as its size, amount of interaction, degree of interdependence, and proximity and contact among members. All of these may affect the group, but these effects should be mediated largely by the extent to which members identify with the group as a whole.

A method that has been used to underpin the social identity approach is the minimal group paradigm (see Bourhis, Sachdev, & Gagnon, 1994). Research participants are assigned randomly to different categories (e.g., red vs. blue, X vs. Y). They remain unaware of others in each category and are asked to assign money or points to anonymous pairs of in-group and out-group members, but not to themselves personally. This paradigm is intended to rule out the possibility that allocation of resources reflects direct self-interest, or that it can be influenced by any personal relationships among group members. The typical finding is that people display in-group bias, often to the extent of ensuring that in-group members gain more than out-group members rather than ensuring that in-group members maximize their total gains. These findings posed a direct challenge and alternative to previous theorizing by showing how social categorization alone could be sufficient to generate intergroup bias.

Social identity theory also concerns the macrosocial relationships among groups, such as the different status of in-groups and out-groups, the legitimacy and stability of status differences, and the ways groups respond to such differences. The theory identifies conditions and belief structures that should lead group members to engage in social change, social creativity, or social mobility strategies. These strategies correspond, respectively, to directly opposing the status quo, enhancing group status by finding new ways to define it, and moving out of the group, perhaps by assimilating with the other group. An important motivation was identified as the desire for positive in-group distinctiveness from the out-group, which in turn served a need for positive self-esteem as a group member (Abrams & Hogg, 1988, 2001; Rubin & Hewstone, 1998).

Self-Categorization Theory

Social identity theory was supplemented by a more sociocognitive theory of self-categorization, which provided a set of general principles governing the link between self and group (Turner, Hogg, Oakes, Reicher, & Wetherell, 1987). According to self-categorization theory, identities are self-categorizations that operate at different hierarchical levels of inclusion. Thus, categorization of people at one particular level includes numerous potential subcategories within subsequent levels. The categorization *American* may embody successive subcategorizations as African American, New Yorker, working at New York University or as a psychologist, in social psychology, on the topic of groups, in a particular office, and so on. Moreover, quite different bases of categorization may be relevant (gender, age, etc.). At the most and least abstract extremes, the categorizations are self as a human being and self as a unique individual. The level of self-categorization that is salient, and dimensions that are relevant for defining it at a particular time, provide identity and a basis for action. According to self-categorization theory, the salience of a particular categorization is dependent on the social comparative context, together with one's readiness to use a particular self-category (e.g., its chronic availability). Categorization is highly flexible and adapts to fit the particular situation at hand.

Thus, categorization implies shared membership at a particular level of inclusiveness, and it is applied flexibly to maximize the comparative and normative fit of individuals to their categories. The level of inclusiveness that we use to categorize people can range from the relatively particular to the relatively general, depending on what best fits the situation or task at hand. At a supermarket checkout, people wearing shop uniforms may be assumed to be *staff,* and they can easily be distinguished from *shoppers* (high comparative fit). However, imagine that half of the uniformed people have finished their shifts and are now doing their personal shopping. In this case, normative fit would be low (there is a poor correspondence between the categorization and expected behavior), and we might try to find an alternative basis for categorization (e.g., those in front vs. behind the checkout). In this example, the categorization (shopper/staff) remains in place, but the membership of the categories becomes defined using revised criteria. Suppose that a fire alarm sounds, and all people must leave the store. Immediately, a different categorization gains relevance (e.g., firefighters vs. civilians) and provides the basis for action.

Other Approaches to the Structure and Processes of Self and Group Identity

Other approaches to group identity regard it as more stable and less situationally determined than self-categorization theory does. For example, Stryker's (1987) identity theory builds on symbolic interactionism and role theory. Identity theory holds that people have multiple identities that reflect their involvement in various intersecting and overlapping role relationships. Identities are thought to be located in a hierarchical framework, wherein some identities are more likely to be salient than others, given particular situational cues. Those roles to which people have the greatest commitment, and which are embedded in the largest number of important relationships, are most likely to provide the basis for salient identities. Moreover, people are motivated to sustain and support those identities that are most central, although they must also operate within the constraints of reality. This approach fully acknowledges the social construction of identity, but it does not assign a particular role to the concept of group. Therefore, although it emphasizes that identity must be located in a subjective conception of social structure and relationships, it does not readily lend itself to an explanation of the social coordination of behavior through the medium of group membership.

Other approaches within social psychology that accept the concept of social identity hold that the self-concept is represented as a stable, predictable structure (e.g., as self-schemas) and that group identities provide very meaningful and long-term bases for the self (e.g., Breakwell, 1992; Deaux, 1996).

Brewer's (1991) optimal distinctiveness theory considers that people may identify with groups as a result of a motivated process. Brewer proposes that people seek optimal levels of inclusion and differentiation from social groups to provide an acceptable balance between the two. Groups that are too large, that leave no room for distinctions among people, and so on will be less attractive, as will situations in which the person feels isolated, exposed, or unconnected to others (Pickett & Brewer, 2005).

Researchers have made several types of distinction between levels and aspects of identity. For example, Greenwald and Pratkanis (1984) proposed that the self could be distinguished in terms of the private, public, and collective elements. Trafimow, Triandis, and Goto (1991) showed that self-descriptions using the Twenty Statements Test revealed that elements of private and collective selves were in distinct clusters, suggesting that they are represented discretely in memory. Brewer and Gardner (1996) distinguished between the individual self (based on personal traits that make individuals distinctive from one another), the relational self (defined by dyadic relationships that create bonds with significant other individuals), and the collective self (definitions of self in terms of *us* and *them*). Moreover, Brewer (2001) suggested that social identity itself could take different forms, ranging from personal acceptance/adoption of group memberships in the self, to relational social

identities that are specific to particular group contexts, and to the more general levels of identification proposed by self-categorization theory and social identity theory. With related ideas, Henry, Arrow, and Carini (1999) show that group identification may be based on distinct elements associated with self-categorization, interpersonal attraction, and interdependence.

Jackson and Smith (1999) conceptualize social identity as having distinctive cognitive, emotional, and connotative components, echoing Tajfel's original ideas and evidence from Hinkle, Taylor, Fox-Cardamone, and Crook (1989). There may be good reason to make distinctions between elements or components of social identity. For example, intergroup emotions theory (Mackie, Devos, & Smith, 2000; Smith, 1993) has been used to explore how different emotions are associated with threats to social identity and how these emotions produce different action tendencies (e.g., fight or flight).

Despite the general acceptance that collective identity can be a basis for behavior of group members, there remains a lively debate over the central question of whether the collective or individual self has primacy. This debate is played out in several ways. For example, there is the question of whether social categorization causes people to apply in-group stereotypes to themselves or whether they simply assume greater similarity between themselves and group members without changing their self-image (Cadinu & Rothbart, 1996; Clement & Krueger, 2000). Otten's research using a minimal groups paradigm (see Otten, 2002) reveals stronger evidence that people generalize attributes from themselves to their in-groups than vice versa. Sedikides and Gaertner (2001) argue strongly for the primacy of the individual self. They argue that the individual self is "relatively stable . . . resistant to external influences and self preserving" (Sedikides & Gaertner, 2001, p. 19). Far from being subsidiary to social identities, individual selves are more precious to us and essentially separate from group selves. Indeed, some might argue that the individual self has a deeper essence than collective selves, as the individual self is contained within one's physical body and genetic makeup (cf. Medin & Ortony, 1989).

In support of the idea that the individual self has primacy, Gaertner, Sedikides, and Graetz (1999) gave participants feedback about either themselves or their group. It was reasoned that if the individual self was more important than the group self, criticism aimed at the individual should have more impact than criticism aimed at the group, a finding that was confirmed for both negative and positive feedback. In a second experiment, this effect was not moderated by the strength with which participants identified with their group. In addition, whereas negative feedback aimed at the individual resulted in raised identification with the group, participants did not increase their individual identification when negative criticism had been directed at the group, illustrating a greater need to find ways to bolster the self when the individual level is threatened than when the group level is threatened.

Gaertner and Insko (2001) also challenged the interpretation of minimal group experiments that seemed to show people will sacrifice total in-group gain to attain relative in-group superiority over the out-group. Using a modified version of the minimal group paradigm, Gaertner and Insko found that male (but not female) participants only allocated more resources to the in-group when they were dependent on other in-group members.

Contrary to Gaertner et al. (1999), Spears, Doosje, and Ellemers (1997) observed different reactions among participants who identified more or less with their group when the group was under threat. Whereas low identifiers distanced themselves from the group (psychologically protecting the individual self), high identifiers closed ranks and emphasized their collective self. Such evidence suggests that the question of whether the individual or collective self is primary may be of only limited importance. The more critical questions are when and why one or the other level of self takes primacy (cf. Sedikides & Brewer, 2001; Simon, 2004).

Evolution

A further perspective on the relationship between group identity and the self is offered by evolutionary approaches. One of the most effective ways of meeting needs for food, safety, security, and perpetuation of one's genes is to be part of a group. Caporael (2001) presents a typology of benefits that accrue from group membership. A work/family group of five people allows for more efficient hunting or gathering and the ability to bring several minds to bear on a problem. The *deme* (or band) of 30 people provides the ability to process resources, move safely from place to place, and effectively coordinate family groups. In addition, shared knowledge and a social construction of reality become a possibility. Hunter-gatherer groups would often meet, and the bands would become microbands for the duration of the meeting. These allowed the exchange of goods, ideas, and information as well as genetic code to prevent species stagnation.

It is reasoned that, because being in a group confers such massive benefits, individuals who have evolved to operate efficiently in groups will prosper, and their genetic code will gradually become more prevalent over generations. However, individuals within species that operate in an environment dominated by groups need to ensure that they are accepted, are liked, and achieve a sufficiently high place in the hierarchy to attract acceptable mates and resources. Therefore, it can be argued, we have evolved functions of the self that foster these outcomes.

Leary, Tambor, Terdal, and Downs (1995) reconceptualized self-esteem as a *sociometer*, or gauge, that provides feedback on how a person is doing in the social sphere. Kirkpatrick and Ellis (2001) further propose that this gauge helps people to monitor how well they are accepted by the groups that make up their social environment, their level of social inclusion or exclusion. Indeed, Kirkpatrick and Ellis hold that the self did not really emerge until evolutionary pressures made it adaptive. They adopt the domain-specificity view (Tooby & Cosmides, 1992) that certain psychological mechanisms evolved to cope with certain adaptive challenges. Kirkpatrick and Ellis argue that the sociometer measures various specific aspects of our social existence and guides subsequent behavior, for instance, in the negotiation of hierarchies and challenges toward the status quo within a group. Animals that exist in groups rarely fight, and when a confrontation arises, the weaker of the animals typically defers. Among more sophisticated animals, such as chimpanzees, individuals within the group display different kinds of behavior (i.e., deferential/assertive) depending on the relative status of the animal with which they are dealing. A parallel effect is found in self-presentational strategies of people with differing levels of self-esteem. Baumeister, Tice, and Hutton (1989) found that people with higher self-esteem presented themselves in a very outgoing fashion whereas those with lower self-esteem tried to stay out of sight and mind and to lower others' expectations of them. Kirkpatrick and Ellis argue that in this situation, the sociometer uses self-esteem as a measure of hierarchical position, and they interpret the strategies observed by Baumeister et al. (1989) as being broadly dominant or deferential and as highlighting one way the self is intertwined with the group. Evaluations of the self and resultant self-esteem are viewed as being individual-based cognitions and emotions that are guided by the group context. In this evolutionary perspective, the self (or the sociometer of self-esteem) provides a linkage between the individual and the group, but it does not become transformed by different levels of categorization as is assumed by self-categorization theory.

Cultural Differences

The distinction between individualism and collectivism seems naturally connected to the idea that group identity might be more important in particular cultures (Triandis, 1995). For example, it appears that people in collectivist cultures such as Japan and China display more conformity to group norms (Bond & Smith, 1996),

less social loafing (Earley, 1993), and greater orientation to the values and norms of groups such as one's organization (Abrams, Ando, & Hinkle, 1998; Morris, Podolny, & Ariel, 2001). However, it would be vastly oversimplifying to argue that collectivist cultures are inherently more group oriented. Instead, it seems that such cultures foster more commitment to specific types of group and interdependencies (Markus & Kitayama, 1994). Indeed, in Western cultures, the expression of individualism can itself be viewed as a type of group norm (Jetten, Postmes, & McAuliffe, 2002), and it may be that people choose their groups rather than being chosen by groups. Therefore, it seems possible that it is the forms of group identity, rather than the extent or underlying processes, that may differ cross-culturally.

Consequences of Group Identity: Evidence From Research

What are the consequences of the categorization process for the way groups and their members perceive themselves? According to self-categorization theory, a meta-contrast principle operates such that differences between categories are maximized relative to those within categories. An important outcome is that the prototypical position that best represents each category becomes polarized (i.e., more extreme than the actual average position), and group members are judged in terms of their closeness to these polarized prototypes of each group. Perceptions of group members and of the self become depersonalized because, instead of viewing each group member as a unique individual, we focus on those attributes that are relevant for judging all group members in comparison to the group prototype. The more salient and meaningful a social categorization becomes, the more group members and the self will be depersonalized.

Depersonalization is the key to the coordination of group behavior. The more depersonalized the situation is, the more people use their in-group prototype as a norm, their in-group stereotype as a reflection of themselves, their in-group's outcomes as outcomes that matter to themselves, and threats to their in-group as threats to themselves (see Turner, 1999; Turner et al., 1987).

Deindividuation

An example of how the idea of depersonalization can change the explanation of group behavior comes from research on deindividuation. Diener (1980) reviewed evidence and concluded that anonymity and lack of accountability within a crowd resulted in a loss of self-regulation. When immersed in groups, people succumbed to influences, many of which were irrational or chaotic, that as individuals they would normally resist. This conclusion was consistent with previous theorizing dating back to Le Bon (1896/1906), Zimbardo (1969), and perhaps Milgram (1965): that individuals cede control to the group, rendering the group capable of greater extremity than individuals acting alone would countenance.

In contrast, the social identity deindividuation (SIDE) model (Reicher, Spears, & Postmes, 1995) holds that the extremity of crowd behavior stems from the fact that members quickly establish a common social identity and common norms in relation to other groups, and this explains why crowd violence is usually restricted in both space and time and focused on particular targets such as the police (Reicher, 1984). Postmes and Spears's (1998) meta-analysis of deindividuation research concluded that behavior could more readily be accounted for in terms of conformity to situation-specific group norms, when social identity is salient, than to lack of self-regulation.

The social self-regulation model (Abrams, 1990, 1992) proposes that personal and social identity salience is orthogonal to self-regulatory processes. Deindividuation exists when neither form of identity is salient and self-regulation is low. As self-regulatory processes begin to operate at higher levels of control, behavior will conform more closely either to personal or to group standards, depending on which aspect of identity is most salient.

The SIDE model is also relevant to less dramatic phenomena such as computer-mediated communications. The visual anonymity of computer-based communication can increase group-based self-categorization, as well as stereotyping and attraction to the group (Lea, Spears, & de Groot, 2001). Sassenberg and Boos (2003) examined group polarization in face-to-face versus computer-mediated groups (which were anonymous). Participants had to deal with a moral dilemma in which they decided what chance of their partner's recovery would warrant breaking into a pharmacy to steal medication. Either social or personal identity was made salient prior to the interaction. In line with the SIDE model, polarization was greatest in the computer-mediated condition when social identity was salient and when there was a clear group norm. However, in the absence of a clear group norm, there was less attitude change in the computer-mediated condition.

Group Identity in the Workplace

In experimental situations, it is relatively easy to manipulate group memberships so that different groups may be salient at different times. In organizations, the situation may be different. Organizations may be highly structured so that people are located within specific buildings, teams, sectors, and so on. Moreover, moves between these categories may be far from flexible in reality. This makes it interesting to examine how organizations might deal with the relationships between different subgroups, and between groups and their leaders, as well as the relationships between subgroups and the organization as a whole.

There is evidence that organizational identity affects intergroup attitudes in the same way as other aspects of group identity—for example, in the form of intergroup bias against other work groups within an organization (Hennessy & West, 1999)—even when it is also related to positive overall commitment to the organization. This finding reflects a general dilemma for social identity researchers, namely, how to promote positive relationships *within* groups without jeopardizing relationships *between* groups. A particularly important element for maintaining positive identity with organizations appears to be the application of accepted procedural justice in decision making, as outlined in Tyler and Blader's (2003) group engagement model.

Mergers present special challenges to social identity. For example, the emergent group is quite likely to compromise the identities of members of both originating organizations without substituting an equivalently valued new identity (e.g., Terry, Carey, & Callan, 2001). For groups that experience continuity of identity into the merged organization, the new superordinate identity may be strengthened rather than reduced (van Leeuwen, van Knippenberg, & Ellemers, 2003). For example, a larger, more powerful group is likely to feel enhanced by merging with a smaller one because its own identity remains at the forefront of the new group.

For simple hierarchically structured group situations, research testing the common in-group identity model (Gaertner & Dovidio, 2000) shows that relations between subgroups become more harmonious when the members perceive that they share a common superordinate category. However, there are differing views about the impact of superordinate categories on subgroup identity. For example, Hornsey and Hogg (2000) have suggested that identification with both the subgroup and superordinate levels might prove an effective solution to such situations. Research is increasingly directed toward the dynamics of social identity when groups are internally structured into nested subgroups (Brewer, 1996; Hogg & Hornsey, in press), such as sales and marketing in an organization, or are intersected by wider cross-cutting categories (e.g., psychologists and physicists in a university; see Crisp, Ensari, Hewstone, & Miller, 2003). Currently, it seems that the mere salience of a superordinate category is not always

sufficient to generate positive relations among subgroups.

An additional complexity is that subgroups are likely to differ in their power and status, so that the superordinate level offers different opportunities for each. Mummendey and Wenzel's in-group projection model (e.g., Mummendey & Wenzel, 1999; Wenzel, Mummendey, Weber, & Waldzus, 2003) holds that it is almost invariably the case that one group's attributes are more fully represented in the overarching group, and thus, one nested group appears to occupy a dominant position. As a result, the lower status subgroups may experience identity threat and choose to fight strongly for their independence within the wider collective. In addition, needs for distinctiveness as well as inclusiveness (Brewer, 1991), along with situations in which the overarching group is unwilling to accommodate a subgroup's views, may result in schisms (Sani & Reicher, 2000). For example, Waldzus and Mummendey (2004) observed that an out-group to Germans (Polish people) was evaluated more negatively when presented in terms of prototypical membership of a superordinate category for Germans (Europe). The more that German participants viewed Germany as prototypical of Europe, the less positively they evaluated Poland.

Haslam, Eggins, and Reynolds (2003) have proposed a procedure for creating a successful group structure within organizations. Their actualizing social and personal identity resources (ASPIRe) model aims to take into account the multiple social identities to encourage creative problem solving. Haslam et al. suggest that successful group integration will lead to higher trust, better communication, and improved cooperation. In an ideal situation, the process has four stages that should occur in the following sequence: airing, subcasing, supercasing, and organizing. In the *airing* stage, members generate ideas about what group divisions exist within the company and how they define themselves. Once the organization can map how its employees locate themselves in different groups, a period of *subcasing* occurs. This second stage defines the goals and needs of each subgroup through discussion within the group. Barriers to achieving these goals are also identified. Haslam et al. assume that subcasing will foster a sense of group identity. At the third stage, *supercasing,* the groups (or their representatives) meet and attempt to create a shared organizational identity based on shared goals, while discussing problems and tensions that may exist between the subgroups. This allows the creation of a superordinate identity that acknowledges the uniqueness of the subgroups. The shared goals and identified problems are then used by the organization's management in the final stage, *organic goal setting,* to create specific goals based on the goals suggested and revealed through the previous three stages.

Haslam et al. (2003) argue that the advantages of this procedure stem primarily from the bottom-up nature of the social identities that are created. The use of both subgroups and superordinate groups is thought to avoid the sense that the superordinate group is monolithic and does not represent members. This is encouraged by the self-referential categorization in the airing stage, which should encourage both self-categorization and a positive social identity. Nonetheless, the ASPIRe process may have several potential pitfalls. For example, if the initial subgroup identification is very strong, and superordinate categorization is weak or unsuccessful, relationships between subgroups are likely to be characterized by intergroup biases. It remains to be seen how well, and across what types of organizational structures, the ASPIRe sequence is most effective. Beyond its relevance to organizations, the model provides a useful illustration of how social identity processes may operate when different levels of self-categorization vary in salience over a time period within a context.

Social Dilemmas and Group Decisions

The relationship between group and individual is a focus of research on social dilemmas. These are situations in which it pays the individual personally to avoid investing in a common resource such as a neighborhood watch program or other community initiatives, as they receive the benefit regardless of their level of input. If too few people invest, then the scheme/resource pool will fail altogether. In resource dilemmas, a resource pool gradually grows, and participants are given the opportunity to take from it at set intervals. The more people take from the pool, the more slowly it will grow. If too much is taken from the pool, it will shrink and eventually be extinguished. Participants have to decide whether to consume in a managed way along with the group (conserving and maximizing the overall output) or adopt an individual "take take take" strategy that will be more beneficial for themselves, but detrimental if everyone adopts it. A common metaphor for this type of dilemma is fishing stocks. If beds are overfished, all will suffer, but some fishermen will try to benefit by fishing over their quota. Clearly, in both of these dilemmas, cooperation is the key to ensuring the continuation of the benefits on offer. An optimal balance between using the resource and exercising restraint for the common good is typically required.

Sharing a social identity with the rest of the group increases the amount of cooperation participants display in social dilemmas (Brewer & Schneider, 1990). De Cremer and Van Vugt (1999) argue that social identity may play a role in two possible ways. High social identity may decrease the perceived difference between individual welfare and the welfare of the group. Thus, in line with self-categorization theory, self-interest is simply transformed from a personal level to a collective level, that is, a "transformation of motivation," according to De Cremer and van Vugt. Second, social identity may improve cooperation by increasing trust and confidence that fellow group members will make an equal contribution. De Cremer and van Vugt found evidence for the former explanation rather than the latter. One implication is that groups that can secure high levels of identification will also benefit from greater cooperation and long-term benefits. In addition, De Cremer and Van Dijk (2002) observed that in repeated dilemmas, when failure feedback was provided, contributions were higher in group identity conditions compared with personal identity conditions. Failure, when collective self is high, actually *increases* subsequent attempts to make the optimal solution work. Evidence that motivation to be part of the group is key comes from De Cremer and Leonardelli's (2003) study, which showed participants in large groups cooperated more if they had a higher need to belong.

Wit and Kerr (2002) induced three levels of categorization, *us all* (the whole group), *just us* (a subgroup categorization within the main group), or *me* (individual). They found that cooperation was highest in the whole group condition and lowest in the subgroup condition. Participants tried to serve the interests of the level of categorization (and presumably the self) that was presented to them. Wit and Kerr suggest that a further way to bolster cooperation in groups is to individuate out-group members (therefore removing the intergroup context) or to create shared fate between subgroup members.

Although raising group identification can promote cooperation, it may not always be practical, and the attractions of personal gain may be so salient that group identity has little impact. In these circumstances, groups may need to impose additional sanctions or rewards to constrain their members (see Foddy, Smithson, Schneider, & Hogg, 1999). One means by which members may be motivated to serve the group rather than themselves is through the presence of a trusted and prototypical group leader (e.g., Van Vugt & de Cremer, 1999).

There may be reasons for group cooperation other than social identity, in particular the possibility that group members simply recognize the nature of the contingencies in the situation. For example, following research by Bouas and Komorita (1996), Hopthrow and Hulbert (in press) showed that the *demonstrability* of a correct solution rather than group identification predicted levels of cooperation in group decisions. The role

of group identity in group decision seems likely to be complex but important for future research. Groups seem to be disposed toward focusing on shared rather than unshared knowledge (Stasser & Titus, 1985), and group members who hold information that overlaps more with others are perceived to be more central to the group (Kameda, Ohtsubo, & Takezawa, 1997). These findings suggest that, at least initially, group members may seek consensus by focusing on prototypical opinions and members. However, the extent to which group members have a shared representation of the nature of the task (Tindale & Kameda, 2000) may itself be affected by whether they have a common social identity.

The social identity perspective would certainly expect that small group processes, including group decision processes, are likely to be framed either explicitly or implicitly by intergroup contexts (Abrams, Hulbert, & Davis, 1996; Hogg, 1996; Marques, Abrams, Paez, & Martinez-Taboada, 1998). In principle, group members who express opinions reflecting prototypical differences that distinguish their group from out-groups should be especially influential. The important theoretical point is that a group's decision and course of action will not reflect some mathematical aggregation of members' preexisting opinions. The intergroup context will affect the focus for the decision and, therefore, the selection of opinions relevant to that decision. That is, the context has a qualitative effect: It determines the issues that are important to the group. Moreover, there is a quantitative effect because group norms should be extremitized in contrast to the norms that the out-group is believed to adopt. Equally important is that this identity-based displacement of the norm may arise prior to any interaction within the group (see Abrams & Hogg, 1990a; Turner, 1991).

Collective Action

For many years, social psychological explanations of collective political protest rested solely on individual-level processes (e.g., Rotter, Seeman, & Liverant, 1962). Kelly and Breinlinger (1996) provided a comprehensive review of individual-level theories of collective action and concluded that the evidence was limited in scope and much of the research was correlational.

Klandermans's expectancy-value model (e.g., 1984, 1986) proposes that two processes are necessary if individuals are to decide to participate in union-based protest. These are consensus mobilization and action mobilization. Consensus mobilization refers to unions' attempts to familiarize members with the industrial aims and objectives for industrial action, whereas action mobilization refers to the persuasion processes to motivate union members. Klandermans (e.g., 1997) claims that individuals make a rational choice to participate or not based on an expectancy-value calculation. The calculation involves the extent to which three motives can be satisfied: goal motives, social motives (how important others, such as family and friends, will react to the participation), and reward motives (the nonsocial costs such as job security, loss of earnings). Despite clear support, the model was limited in scope, for example, by not addressing the role of the wider social and historical context. Collective political protest often involves conflicts between groups regarding perceived injustice or unfair inequality, and this intergroup dimension was not part of Klandermans's original model.

Both relative deprivation theory (e.g., Crosby, 1976; Runciman, 1966) and social identity theory have been used to explain collective protest. Runciman (1966) distinguished between *egoistic* and *fraternal* deprivation, the former involving inequalities between individuals and the latter between groups. This distinction has proven very useful. For example, egoistic relative deprivation is related to individual-level outcomes such as psychological stress (e.g., Walker & Mann, 1987) and personal protest behavior (e.g., Hafer & Olson, 1993). Fraternal relative deprivation has been shown to be related to support for programs that enhance an in-group's standing

(e.g., Beaton & Tougas, 1997) and to collective protest (e.g., Grant & Brown, 1995; Guimond & Dubé-Simard, 1983).

A missing element from relative deprivation theory is why people would be motivated to protest about group disadvantage. This missing link is provided by group identity. Petta and Walker (1992) argued that "cognitive identification with an in-group must precede cognitive recognition of in-group deprivation relative to some out-group" (p. 292). The point highlights a major problem for relative deprivation theory. The concept of perceived fraternal relative deprivation assumes that individuals consider a specific in-group and out-group to be relevant for the purposes of comparison. This, in turn, means that the individual must find the in-group important and valuable and in a relationship with a specific out-group. For this reason, understanding the intergroup context and group identification helps to account for the nature and target of collective action (Kawakami & Dion, 1995).

As mentioned earlier, the stability and legitimacy of status relations between groups are theorized to be a basis for different types of action within social identity theory. The permeability of intergroup boundaries (the ease with which a person may move from one group to another) is a third factor that will affect people's response to intergroup injustice (e.g., Ellemers, van Knippenberg, & Wilke, 1990; Kelly & Breinlinger, 1996; Wright, Taylor, & Moghaddam, 1990). The predominant finding appears to be that individual strategies are generally preferred, and collective action does not appear to be an easy or usual option for most individuals (e.g., Ellemers et al., 1990; Lalonde & Silverman, 1994). For example, Wright et al. (1990) experimentally manipulated the perceived degree of openness of an out-group whose higher status was illegitimate. Only when there was no prospect that participants could join the high-status group did they opt for nonnormative collective action (i.e., protest). When there was even a token amount of access (to 2% of participants), they opted for individual courses of action. This situation is probably representative of many real intergroup relationships and illustrates one reason why intergroup inequalities so often remain unchallenged.

The combination of social identity and relative deprivation theories offers a powerful framework for analyzing collective action (e.g., Abrams & Randsley de Moura, 2001). There is also evidence that identity and rational choice may have additive and independent effects (Simon et al., 1998). The theoretical perspectives and research outlined above demonstrate that both the individual- and collective-level self can influence political behavior. However, it appears that when relating specifically to collective protest, the collective self is strongly implicated. Simon and Klandermans (2001) proposed a model of politicized collective identity, which proposes that political mobilization involves a sequence from construing shared grievances to attributing blame to political opponents and then seeking to make connections between one's own group and society as a whole (e.g., by making a right-wing extremist cause one that appears to concern the national interest).

Deviance

The major part of the social identity perspective dwells on intergroup behavior, but there is growing interest in the role of social identity in intragroup judgments and behavior. Research in the small groups tradition has shown that groups react to deviance by attempting to control or remove deviant members (Schachter, 1959; Shaw, 1976). However, social identity affects perceptions of variation within groups and the way that conforming and deviant group members are judged and treated. Reactions to deviants appear to depend on whether people are judging in-group or out-group deviants and on variations in intergroup context. There is substantial evidence for a "black sheep" effect, in which unlikable in-group members are derogated more than equally unlikable out-group

members (Marques & Paez, 1994). Marques et al.'s (1998) model of subjective group dynamics holds that group members are more concerned with their group's validity and cohesiveness than they are with the objective nature of a deviant's behavior. Group members seize on evidence that subjectively establishes the validity of their own group's norms. Consequently, it is not the amount by which a group member differs from the rest of the group that determines how that member is evaluated, but the direction in which that member differs.

In-group loyalty is a valued attribute among group members (Zdaniuk & Levine, 2001), but people appear to tolerate deviants unless they adopt attitudes that move in the direction of salient out-groups (Abrams, Marques, Bown, & Henson, 2000). Conversely, people may be quite positive toward out-group members whose deviance implies support for in-group norms (Abrams, Marques, Bown, & Dougill, 2002). These effects are larger when group members identify more highly with the group, and in children, they become more strongly associated with global in-group bias with age (Abrams, Rutland, & Cameron, 2003).

Bown and Abrams (2003) examined reactions to deviance among workers in a commercial bank. Consistent with the distinction made by Hogg (1992) between interpersonal attraction and social (group-based) attraction, evaluations of a fellow worker's personal traits were affected by their levels of personal likability (relevant to personal identity and interpersonal evaluations), but evaluations of them as workers were affected distinctly by their compliance with norms of in-group loyalty. Moreover, in line with the idea that social identity is particularly concerned with evaluation of the in-group, these differences were also larger when the targets were in-group rather than out-group members.

When intergroup situations become more competitive, people are likely to become more concerned with the cohesiveness of their own group. For example, Marques, Abrams, and

Serodio (2001) found that deviant in-group members are judged more extremely as the heterogeneity of the group increases and as its status becomes less secure. Hogg, Fielding, and Darley (2005) propose that specific reactions to deviants also will be affected by whether there is a threat to the group's valence or its entitativity and whether the deviant publicly attributes his or her deviance to self or to the group.

Other perspectives on deviance focus on deviants as in-group critics (e.g., Hornsey & Imami, in press) or as minority groups that challenge the accepted wisdom of the majority (e.g., Nemeth & Staw, 1989). For example, delinquency has been theorized as a form of deviance that appears to provide actors with a reputation and social identity as being against "the system" (Emler & Reicher, 1995, 2005). In these theoretical perspectives, deviance is sometimes viewed as a dynamic feature of group life—minorities and critics are effectively trying to change the majority's hold over the status quo.

Leadership

Group identity is now recognized as a significant factor in leadership (e.g., Hogg, Hains, & Mason, 1998; Morris, Hulbert, & Abrams, 2000). The social identity analysis of leadership (see Hogg & van Knippenberg, 2003) holds that when group membership salience increases, members judge one another increasingly in terms of prototypicality. The most prototypical members are distinctive compared with the rest of the group, and this confers status and ability to gain compliance from others. Their behavior is likely to be attributed internally, and they are likely to be accorded leadership status. De Cremer and Van Vugt (1999) found that leaders in social dilemma situations are preferred more by highly identified group members if the leader shares the group's values. Moreover, leaders that are more prototypical are likely to have higher influence and attract more confidence among group members.

Conclusions and Future Directions

Research on group identity has burgeoned in the last 20 years, and any of the sections of this chapter could fill a substantial review article. Although research is consistent with the idea that the self is, in many situations, inextricably linked to the groups to which we belong, the relative importance of social identity in group behavior is still under debate. Current questions include the relative stability and flexibility of the self-concept generally and the extent to which it is useful to distinguish between different types of self.

Related to these issues is debate over the range of motives and emotions that characterize group identity (Hogg & Abrams, 1993; Smith, 1999). It is not at all clear that these can be extrapolated from individual-level emotions and motives. In addition to motives for group behavior, such as self-esteem and uncertainty reduction, greater attention needs to be paid to transitory and proximal motivations and emotions that exist within specific groups (e.g., loyalty, social exchange/dependency, fear, greed, etc.).

Further interesting work remains to be conducted to understand how intergroup and intragroup relationships affect one another. There is also a need to develop a more detailed account of the way intergroup, intragroup, and interpersonal processes are interrelated and coordinated. For example, an important question is how group identity relates to processes of social inclusion and exclusion within and between groups (Abrams, Hogg, & Marques, 2005). Economic models are beginning to recognize the value of social relationships and networks as providers of social capital. However, there has been rather little investigation of the impact of people's psychological relationship to the many alternative groups (sources of capital) that might exist in their social environment.

Another emerging research priority is the question of how and why the relationship between self and group changes over time. This is of interest both as a question of life span development (e.g., Bennett & Sani, 2004) and in terms of transitions that might occur because new intergroup relationships arise and dissolve.

Finally, much remains to be discovered about cultural differences in the way individuals and groups are represented in identity and the way these identities relate to different sociocultural contexts. Understanding more about cultural differences will tell us more about the generality of identity processes and also the social and contextual variables that affect the manifestations of these processes.

References

Abrams, D. (1990). How do group members regulate their behavior? An integration of social identity and self-awareness theories. In D. Abrams & M. A. Hogg (Eds.), *Social identity theory: Constructive and critical advances* (pp. 89–112). London and New York: Harvester Wheatsheaf and Springer-Verlag.

Abrams, D. (1992). Processes of social identification. In G. Breakwell (Ed.), *Social psychology of identity and the self-concept* (pp. 57–99). San Diego, CA: Academic Press.

Abrams, D., Ando, K., & Hinkle, S. W. (1998). Psychological attachment to the group: Cross-cultural differences in organizational identification and subjective norms as predictors of workers' turnover intentions. *Personality and Social Psychology Bulletin, 24,* 1027–1039.

Abrams, D., & Hogg, M. A. (1988). Comments on the motivational status of self-esteem in social identity and intergroup discrimination. *British Journal of Social Psychology, 18,* 317–334.

Abrams, D., & Hogg, M. A. (1990a). Social identification, self-categorization, and social influence. *European Review of Social Psychology, 1,* 195–228.

Abrams, D., & Hogg, M. A. (Eds.). (1990b). *Social identity theory: Constructive and critical advances.* London: Harvester Wheatsheaf.

Abrams, D., & Hogg, M. A. (Eds.). (1999). *Social identity and social cognition.* Oxford, UK: Blackwell.

Abrams, D., & Hogg, M. A. (2001). Collective self. In M. A. Hogg & S. Tindale (Eds.), *Blackwell handbook of social psychology: Vol 3. Group processes* (pp. 425–461). Oxford, UK: Blackwell.

Abrams, D., & Hogg, M. A. (2004). Metatheory: Lessons from social identity research. *Personality and Social Psychology Review, 8*(2), 98–107.

Abrams, D., Hogg, M. A., & Marques, J. M. (Eds.). (2005). *The social psychology of inclusion and exclusion.* New York: Psychology Press.

Abrams, D., Hulbert, L. G., & Davis, J. H. (1996, October 16). *Social context and group decisions.* Paper presented at the Society of Experimental Social Psychology Annual Conference, Sturbridge, MA.

Abrams, D., Marques, J. M., Bown, N. J., & Dougill, M. (2002). Anti-norm and pro-norm deviance in the bank and on the campus: Two experiments on subjective group dynamics. *Group Processes and Intergroup Relations, 5,* 163–182.

Abrams, D., Marques, J. M., Bown, N. J., & Henson, M. (2000). Pro-norm and anti-norm deviance within in-groups and out-groups. *Journal of Personality and Social Psychology, 78,* 906–912.

Abrams, D., & Randsley de Moura, G. (2001). Organizational identification: Psychological anchorage and turnover. In M. A. Hogg & D. Terry (Eds.), *Social identity processes in organizational contexts* (pp. 131–148). Philadelphia: Psychology Press.

Abrams, D., Rutland, A., & Cameron, L. (2003). The development of subjective group dynamics: Children's judgments of normative and deviant in-group and out-group individuals. *Child Development, 74,* 1840–1856.

Adorno, T. W., Frenkel, B. E., Levinson, D. J., & Sanford, R. N. (1950). *The authoritarian personality.* Oxford, UK: Harpers.

Allport, F. H. (1924). *Social psychology.* Boston: Houghton Mifflin.

Baumeister, R. F., Tice, D. M., & Hutton, D. G. (1989). Self-presentational motivations and personality differences in self-esteem. *Journal of Personality, 57,* 547–579.

Beaton, A. M., & Tougas, F. (1997). The representation of women in management: The more, the merrier? *Personality and Social Psychology Bulletin, 23*(7), 773–782.

Bennett, M., & Sani, F. (Eds.). (2004). *The development of the social self.* Philadelphia: Psychology Press.

Billig, M. (1976). *Social psychology and intergroup relations.* London: Academic Press.

Bond, R., & Smith, P. B. (1996). Culture and conformity: A meta-analysis of studies using Asch's 1952b, 1956 line judgment task. *Psychological Bulletin, 119,* 111–137.

Bouas, K. S., & Komorita, S. S. (1996). Group discussion and cooperation in social dilemmas. *Personality and Social Psychology Bulletin, 22,* 1144–1150.

Bourhis, R. Y., Sachdev, I., & Gagnon, A. (1994). Intergroup research with the Tajfel matrices: Methodological notes. In M. Zanna & J. Olson (Eds.), *The psychology of prejudice: The Ontario symposium* (Vol. 7, pp. 209–222). Hillsdale, NJ: Lawrence Erlbaum.

Bown, N. J., & Abrams, D. (2003). Despicability in the workplace: Effects of behavioral deviance and unlikability on the evaluation of in-group and out-group members. *Journal of Applied Social Psychology, 33,* 2413–2426.

Breakwell, G. (1992). *Social psychology of identity and the self-concept.* San Diego, CA: Academic Press.

Brewer, M. B. (1991). The social self: On being the same and different at the same time. *Personality and Social Psychology Bulletin, 17,* 475–482.

Brewer, M. B. (1996). Managing diversity: The role of social identities. In S. Jackson & M. Ruderman (Eds.), *Diversity in work teams* (pp. 47–68). Washington, DC: American Psychological Association.

Brewer, M. B. (2001). The many faces of social identity: Implications for political psychology. *Political Psychology, 22,* 115–125.

Brewer, M. B., & Gardner, W. (1996). Who is this "we"? Levels of collective identity and self-representations. *Journal of Personality and Social Psychology, 71,* 83–93.

Brewer, M. B., & Schneider, S. K. (1990). Social identity and social dilemmas: A double edged sword. In D. Abrams & M.A. Hogg (Eds.), *Social identity theory: Constructive and critical advances* (pp. 169–184). London: Harvester Wheatsheaf.

Cadinu, M. R., & Rothbart, M. (1996). Self-anchoring and differentiation processes in the minimal group setting. *Journal of Personality and Social Psychology, 70,* 661–677.

Caporael, L. R. (2001). Parts and wholes: The evolutionary importance of groups. In C. Sedikides & M. B. Brewer (Eds.), *Individual self, relational self, collective self* (pp. 241–258). Philadelphia: Psychology Press.

Capozza, D., & Brown, R. J. (Eds.). (2000). *Social identity processes.* London: Sage.

Clement, R. W., & Krueger, J. (2000). The primacy of self-referent information in perceptions of social consensus. *British Journal of Social Psychology, 39,* 279–299.

Crisp, R., Ensari, N., Hewstone, M., & Miller, N. (2003). A dual-route model of crossed categorization effects. In W. Stroebe & M. Hewstone (Eds.), *European review of social psychology,* (Vol. 13, pp. 35–74). New York: Psychology Press.

Crosby, F. (1976). A model of egoistic relative deprivation. *Psychological Review, 83,* 85–113.

Deaux, K. (1996). Social identification. In E. T. Higgins & A. W. Kruglanski (Eds.), *Social psychology: Handbook of basic principles* (pp. 777–798). New York: Guilford.

De Cremer, D., & Leonardelli, G. J. (2003). Cooperation in social dilemmas and the need to belong: The moderating effect of group size. *Group Dynamics: Theory, Research, and Practice, 7,* 168–174.

De Cremer, D., & Van Dijk, E. (2002). Reactions to group success and failure as a function of identification level: A test of the goal-transformation hypothesis in social dilemmas. *Journal of Experimental Social Psychology, 38,* 435–442.

De Cremer, D., & Van Vugt, M. (1999). Social identification effects in social dilemmas: A transformation of motives. *European Journal of Social Psychology, 29,* 871–893.

Diener, E. (1980). Deindividuation: The absence of self-awareness and self-regulation in group members. In P. B. Paulus (Ed.), *Psychology of group influence* (pp. 209–242). Hillsdale, NJ: Lawrence Erlbaum.

Doise, W. (1982). Report on the European Association of Experimental Social Psychology. *European Journal of Social Psychology, 12,* 105–111.

Durkheim, E. (1933). *The division of labour in society* (G. Simpson, Trans.). New York: Macmillan. (Original work published 1893)

Earley, P. C. (1993). East meets West meets Mideast: Further explorations of collectivistic and individualistic work groups. *Academy of Management Journal, 36,* 319–348.

Ellemers, N., Spears, R., & Doosje, B. (Eds.). (1999). *Social identity.* Oxford, UK: Blackwell.

Ellemers, N., van Knippenberg, A., & Wilke, H. (1990). The influence of permeability of group boundaries and stability of group status on strategies of individual mobility and social change. *British Journal of Social Psychology, 29,* 233–246.

Emler, N., & Reicher, S. D. (1995). *Adolescence and delinquency: The collective management of reputation.* Oxford, UK: Blackwell.

Emler, N., & Reicher, S. D. (2005). Delinquency: Causes or consequences of social exclusion? In D. Abrams, M. A. Hogg, & J. M. Marques (Eds.), *The social psychology of inclusion and exclusion* (pp. 211–242). New York: Psychology Press.

Foddy, M., Smithson, M., Schneider, S., & Hogg, M. A. (Eds.). (1999). *Resolving social dilemmas: Dynamic, structural, and intergroup aspects.* Philadelphia: Psychology Press.

Gaertner, S. L., & Dovidio, J. F. (2000). *Reducing intergroup bias.* Philadelphia: Psychology Press.

Gaertner, L., & Insko, C. A. (2001). On the measurement of social orientations in the minimal group paradigm: Norms as moderators of the expression of intergroup bias. *European Journal of Social Psychology, 31,* 143–154.

Gaertner, L., Sedikides, C., & Graetz, K. (1999). In search of self-definition: Motivational primacy of the individual self, motivational primacy of the collective self, or contextual primacy? *Journal of Personality and Social Psychology, 76,* 5–18.

Grant, P. R., & Brown, R. (1995). From ethnocentrism to collective protest: Responses to relative deprivation and threats to social identity. *Social Psychology Quarterly, 58,* 195–211.

Greenwald, A. G., & Pratkanis, A. R. (1984). The self. In R. S. Wyer & T. K. Srull (Eds.), *Handbook of social cognition* (Vol. 3, pp. 129–178). Hillsdale, NJ: Lawrence Erlbaum.

Guimond, S., & Dubé-Simard, L. (1983). Relative deprivation theory and the Quebec Nationalist Movement: The cognition-emotion and the personal-group deprivation issue. *Journal of Personality and Social Psychology, 44,* 526–535.

Hafer, C., & Olson, J. (1993). Discontent, beliefs in a just world, and assertive actions by working women. *Personality and Social Psychology Bulletin, 19,* 30–38.

Haslam, A., Eggins, R. A., & Reynolds, K. J. (2003). The ASPIRe model: Actualizing social and personal identity resources to enhance organizational outcomes. *Journal of Occupational and Organizational Psychology, 76,* 83–113.

Hennessy, J., & West, M. (1999). Intergroup behavior in organizations: A field test of social identity theory. *Small Group Research, 30,* 361–382.

Henry, K. B., Arrow, H., & Carini, B. (1999). A tripartite model of group identification: Theory and measurement. *Small Group Research, 30,* 558–581.

Hinkle, S., Taylor, L. A., Fox-Cardamone, D. L., & Crook, K. F. (1989). Intragroup identification and intergroup differentiation: A multi-component approach. *British Journal of Social Psychology, 28,* 305–317.

Hogg, M. A. (1992). *The social psychology of group cohesiveness: From attraction to social identity.* Hemel Hempstead, UK: Harvester Wheatsheaf.

Hogg, M. A. (1996). Social identity, self-categorization, and the small group. In E. H. Witte & J. H. Davis (Eds.), *Understanding group behavior: Vol. 2. Small group processes and interpersonal relations* (pp. 227–253). Mahwah, NJ: Lawrence Erlbaum.

Hogg, M. A., & Abrams, D. (1988). *Social identifications: A social psychology of intergroup relations and group processes.* London: Routledge.

Hogg, M. A., & Abrams, D. (1993). Towards a single-process uncertainty-reduction model of social motivation in groups. In M. A. Hogg & D. Abrams (Eds.), *Group motivation: Social psychological perspectives* (pp. 173–190). London: Harvester Wheatsheaf.

Hogg, M. A., Fielding, K. S., & Darley, J. (2005). Fringe dwellers: Processes of deviance and marginalization in groups. In D. Abrams, M. A. Hogg, & J. M. Marques (Eds.), *The social psychology of inclusion and exclusion* (pp. 191–210). New York: Psychology Press.

Hogg, M. A., Hains, S. C., & Mason, I. (1998). Identification and leadership in small groups: Salience, frame of reference, and leader stereotypicality effects on leader evaluations. *Journal of Personality and Social Psychology, 75,* 1248–1263.

Hogg, M. A., & Hornsey, M. J. (in press). Self-concept threat and multiple categorization within groups. In R. J. Crisp & M. Hewstone (Eds.), *Multiple social categorization: Processes, models, and applications.* New York: Psychology Press.

Hogg, M. A., & van Knippenberg, D. (2003). Social identity and leadership processes in groups. In M. P. Zanna (Ed.), *Advances in experimental social psychology* (Vol. 35, pp. 1–52). San Diego, CA: Academic Press.

Hopthrow, T., & Hulbert, L. G. (in press). Social dilemmas and group decision making. *Group Processes and Intergroup Relations.*

Hornsey, M., & Hogg, M. A. (2000). Subgroup relations: Two experiments comparing subgroup differentiation and common ingroup identity models of prejudice reduction. *Personality and Social Psychology Bulletin, 28*, 242–256.

Hornsey, M. J., & Imami, A. (in press). Criticising groups from the inside and the outside: An identity perspective on the intergroup sensitivity effect. *Personality and Social Psychology Bulletin, 30*, 365–383.

Jackson, J. W., & Smith, E. R. (1999). Conceptualizing social identity: A new framework and evidence for the impact of different dimensions. *Personality and Social Psychology Bulletin, 25*, 120–135.

Jaspars, J. M. F. (1980). The coming of age of social psychology in Europe. *European Journal of Social Psychology, 10*, 421–428.

Jaspars, J. M. F. (1986). Forum and focus: A personal view of European social psychology. *European Journal of Social Psychology, 16*, 3–15.

Jetten, J., Postmes, T., & McAuliffe, B. J. (2002). We're all individuals: Group norms of individualism and collectivism, levels of identification, and identity threat. *European Journal of Social Psychology, 32*, 189–207.

Kameda, T., Ohtsubo, Y., & Takezawa, M. (1997). Centrality in socio-cognitive network and social influence: An illustration in a group decision making context. *Journal of Personality and Social Psychology, 73*, 296–309.

Kawakami, K., & Dion, K. L. (1995). Social identity and affect as determinants of collective action: Towards an integration of relative deprivation and social identity theories. *Theory and Psychology, 5*, 551–577.

Kelly, C., & Breinlinger, S. (1996). *The social psychology of collective action: Identity, injustice, and gender.* London: Taylor & Francis.

Kirkpatrick, L. A., & Ellis, B. J. (2001). Evolution and self-esteem. In G. J. O. Fletcher & M. S. Clark (Eds.), *Blackwell handbook of social psychology: Interpersonal processes* (pp. 411–436). Oxford, UK: Blackwell.

Klandermans, B. (1984). Mobilization and participation in trade union action: An expectancy-value approach. *Journal of Occupational Psychology, 57*, 107–120.

Klandermans, B. (1986). Psychology of trade union participation: Joining, acting, and quitting. *Journal of Occupational Psychology, 59*, 189–204.

Klandermans, B. (1997). *The social psychology of protest.* Oxford, UK: Blackwell.

Lalonde, R. N., & Silverman, R. A. (1994). Behavioral preferences in response to social injustice: The effects of group permeability and social identity salience. *Journal of Personality and Social Psychology, 66*, 78–85.

Lea, M., Spears, R., & de Groot, D. (2001). Knowing me knowing you: Anonymity effects on social identity processes within groups. *Personality and Social Psychology Bulletin, 27*, 526–537.

Leary, M. R., Tambor, E. S., Terdal, S. K., & Downs, D. L. (1995). Self-esteem as an interpersonal monitor: The sociometer hypothesis. *Journal of Personality and Social Psychology, 68*, 518–530.

Le Bon, G. (1906). *The crowd: A study of the popular mind.* London: Unwin. (Original work published 1896)

Mackie, D. M., Devos, T., & Smith, E. R. (2000). Intergroup emotions: Explaining offensive action tendencies in an intergroup context. *Journal of Personality and Social Psychology, 79*, 602–616.

Markus, H. R., & Kitayama, S. (1994). A collective fear of the collective: Implications for selves and theories of selves. *Personality and Social Psychology Bulletin, 20*, 568–579.

Marques, J., Abrams, D., Paez, D., & Martinez-Taboada, C. (1998). The role of categorization and in-group norms in judgments of groups and their members. *Journal of Personality and Social Psychology, 75*, 976–988.

Marques, J. M., Abrams, D., & Serodio, R. (2001). Being better by being right: Subjective group dynamics and derogation of in-group deviants when generic norms are undermined. *Journal of Personality and Social Psychology, 81*, 436–447.

Marques, J. M., & Paez, D. (1994). The black sheep effect: Social categorization, rejection of ingroup deviates, and perception of group variability. In W. Stroebe & M. Hewstone (Eds.), *European review of social psychology* (Vol. 5, pp. 37–68). Chichester, UK: Wiley.

Marx, K. (1963). *Early writings* (T. B. Bottomore, Ed. & Trans.). New York: McGraw-Hill. (Original work published in German 1844)

Medin, D. L., & Ortony, A. (1989). Psychological essentialism. In S. Vosniadou & A. Ortony (Eds.), *Similarity and analogical reasoning* (pp. 179–195). Cambridge, UK: Cambridge University Press.

Milgram, S. (1965). Some conditions of obedience and disobedience to authority. *Human Relations, 18,* 57–76.

Morris, L., Hulbert, L., & Abrams, D. (2000). An experimental investigation of group members' perceived influence over leader decisions. *Group Dynamics: Theory and Research, 4,* 157–167.

Morris, M. W., Podolny, J. M., & Ariel, S. (2001). Culture, norms, and obligations: Cross-national differences in patterns of interpersonal norms and felt obligations toward coworkers. In W. Wosinska & R. B. Cialdini (Eds.), *The practice of social influence in multiple cultures: Applied social research* (pp. 97–123). Mahwah, NJ: Lawrence Erlbaum.

Moscovici, S. (1982). The coming era of representations. In J. P. Codol & J. P. Leyens (Eds.), *Cognitive analysis of social behavior* (pp. 115–150). The Hague, The Netherlands: Martinus Nijhoff.

Mummendey, A., & Wenzel, M. (1999). Social discrimination and tolerance in intergroup relations: Reactions to intergroup difference. *Personality and Social Psychology Review, 3,* 158–174.

Nemeth, C., & Staw, B. M. (1989). The tradeoffs of social control and innovation in groups and organizations. In L. Berkowitz (Ed.), *Advances in experimental social psychology* (Vol. 22, pp. 175–210). San Diego, CA: Academic Press.

Otten, S. (2002). "Me" and "us" or "us" and "them"? The self as heuristic for defining novel in-groups. In W. Stroebe & M. Hewstone (Eds.), *European review of social psychology* (Vol. 13, pp. 1–33). New York: Psychology Press.

Petta, G., & Walker, I. (1992). Relative deprivation and ethnic identity. *British Journal of Social Psychology, 31,* 285–293.

Pettigrew, T. F. (1979). The ultimate attribution error: Extending Allport's cognitive analysis of prejudice. *Personality and Social Psychology Bulletin, 5,* 461–476.

Pickett, C. L., & Brewer, M. B. (2005). The role of exclusion in maintaining in-group inclusion. In D. Abrams, M. A. Hogg, & J. Marques (Eds.), *The social psycholny of inclusion and exclusion* (pp. 89–112). New York: Psychology Press.

Postmes, T., & Spears, R. (1998). Deindividuation and antinormative behavior: A meta-analysis. *Psychological Bulletin, 123,* 238–259.

Reicher, S. D. (1984). Social influence in the crowd: Attitudinal and behavioral effects of deindividuation in conditions of high and low group salience. *British Journal of Social Psychology, 23,* 341–350.

Reicher, S. D., Spears, R., & Postmes, T. (1995). A social identity model of deinidividuation phenomena. *European Journal of Social Psychology, 6,* 161–198.

Robinson, W. P. (Ed.). (1996). *Social groups and identities: Developing the legacy of Henri Tajfel.* Oxford, UK: Butterworth-Heinemann.

Rotter, J. B., Seeman, M. R., & Liverant, S. (1962). Internal versus external control of reinforcements: A major variable in behavior theory. In W. F. Washburn (Ed.), *Decisions, values, and groups* (Vol. 2, pp. 473–516). New York: Pergamon.

Rubin, M., & Hewstone, M. (1998). Social identity theory's self-esteem hypothesis: A review and some suggestions for clarification. *Personality and Social Psychology Review, 2,* 40–62.

Runciman, W. G. (1966). *Relative deprivation and social justice.* London: Routledge.

Sani, F., & Reicher, S. D. (2000). Contested identities and schisms in groups: Opposing the ordination of women as priests in the Church of England. *British Journal of Social Psychology, 39,* 95–112.

Sassenberg, K., & Boos, M. (2003). Attitude change in computer-mediated communication: Effects of anonymity and category norms. *Group Processes & Intergroup Relations, 6,* 405–422.

Schachter, S. (1959). *The psychology of affiliation.* Stanford, CA: Stanford University Press.

Sedikides, C., & Brewer, M. B. (2001). Individual self, relational self, and collective self: Partners, opponents, or strangers? In C. Sedikides & M. B. Brewer (Eds.), *Individual self, relational self, collective self* (pp. 1–6). Philadelphia: Psychology Press.

Sedikides, C., & Gaertner, L. (2001). A homecoming to the individual self: Emotional and motivational primacy. In C. Sedikides & M. B. Brewer (Eds.), *Individual self, relational self, collective self* (pp. 7–25). Philadelphia: Psychology Press.

Shaw, M. E. (1976). *Group dynamics* (2nd ed.). New York: McGraw-Hill.

Sherif, M. (1966). *In common predicament: Social psychology of intergroup conflict and cooperation.* Boston: Houghton-Mifflin.

Sidanius, J., & Pratto, F. (1999). *Social dominance.* Cambridge, UK: Cambridge University Press.

Simon, B. (2004). *Identity in a modern society: A social psychological perspective.* Oxford, UK: Blackwell.

Simon, B., & Klandermans, B. (2001). Politicized collective identity: A social psychological analysis. *American Psychologist, 56,* 319–331.

Simon, B., Loewy, M., Sturmer, S., Weber, U., Freytag, P., Habig, C., Kampmeier, C., & Spahlinger, P. (1998). Collective identification and social movement participation. *Journal of Personality and Social Psychology, 74*(3), 646–658.

Smith, E. R. (1993). Social identity and social emotions: Toward new conceptualizations of prejudice. In D. M. Mackie & D. L. Hamilton (Eds.), *Affect, cognition, and stereotyping: Interactive processes in group perception* (pp. 297–315). San Diego: Academic Press.

Smith, E. R. (1999). Affective and cognitive implications of a group becoming part of the self: New models of prejudice and of the self-concept. In D. Abrams & M. A. Hogg (Eds.), *Social identity and social cognition* (pp. 183–196). Malden, MA: Blackwell.

Spears, R., Doosje, B., & Ellemers, N. (1997). Self-stereotyping in the face of threats to group status and distinctiveness: The role of group identification. *Personality and Social Psychology Bulletin, 23,* 538–553.

Stasser, G., & Titus, W. (1985). Pooling of unshared information in group decision making: Biased information sampling during discussion. *Journal of Personality and Social Psychology, 48,* 1467–1478.

Stryker, S. (1987). Identity theory: Developments and extensions. In K. Yardley & T. Honess (Eds.), *Self and identity: Psychosocial perspectives* (pp. 89–103). Chichester, UK: Wiley.

Tajfel, H. (1972). Some developments in European social psychology. *European Journal of Social Psychology, 2,* 307–322.

Tajfel, H. (Ed.). (1978). *Differentiation between social groups: Studies in the social psychology of intergroup relations.* London: Academic Press

Tajfel, H., Jaspars, J. M. F., & Fraser, C. (1984). The social dimension in European social psychology. In H. Tajfel (Ed.), *The social dimension: European developments in social psychology* (Vol. 1, pp. 1–5). Cambridge, UK: Cambridge University Press.

Tajfel, H., & Turner, J. C. (1979). An integrative theory of intergroup conflict. In W. G. Austin & S. Worchel (Eds.), *The social psychology of intergroup relations* (pp. 33–47). Monterey, CA: Brooks/Cole.

Terry, D. J., Carey, C. J., & Callan, V. J. (2001). Employee adjustment to an organizational merger: An intergroup perspective. *Personality and Social Psychology Bulletin, 27,* 267–280.

Tindale, R. S., & Kameda, T. (2000). Social sharedness as a unifying theme for information processing in groups. *Group Processes and Intergroup Relations, 3,* 123–140.

Tooby, J., & Cosmides, L. (1992). The adapted mind: Evolutionary psychology and the generation of culture. In L. Cosmides & J. H. Barkow (Eds.), *The adapted mind: Evolutionary psychology and the generation of culture* (pp. 19–136). London: Oxford University Press.

Trafimow, D., Triandis, H. C., & Goto, S. G. (1991). Some tests of the distinction between the private self and the collective self. *Journal of Personality and Social Psychology, 60,* 649–655.

Triandis, H. C. (1995). *Individualism and collectivism.* Boulder, CO: Westview Press.

Turner, J. C. (1991). *Social influence.* Milton Keynes, UK: Open University Press.

Turner, J. C. (1999). Some current issues in research on social identity and self-categorization theories. In N. Ellemers, R. Spears, & B. Doosje (Eds.), *Social identity* (pp. 6–34). Oxford, UK: Blackwell.

Turner, J. C., & Giles, H. (Eds.). (1981). *Intergroup behavior.* Oxford, UK: Blackwell.

Turner, J. C., Hogg, M. A., Oakes, P. J., Reicher, S. D., & Wetherell, M. S. (1987). *Rediscovering the social group: A self-categorisation theory.* London: Blackwell.

Tyler, T. R., & Blader, S. L. (2003). The Group Engagement Model: Procedural justice social identity and cooperative behavior. *Personality and Social Psychology Review, 7,* 349–361.

van Leeuwen, E., van Knippenberg, D., & Ellemers, N. (2003). Continuing and changing group identities: The effects of merging on social identification and ingroup bias. *Personality and Social Psychology Bulletin, 29,* 679–690.

Van Vugt, M., & De Cremer, D. (1999). Leadership in social dilemmas: The effects of group identification on collective actions to provide public goods. *Journal of Personality and Social Psychology, 76,* 587–599.

Waldzus, S., & Mummendey, A. (2004). Inclusion in a superordinate category, in-group prototypicality, and attitudes towards out-groups. *Journal of Experimental Social Psychology, 40*(4), 466–477.

Walker, I., & Mann, L. (1987). Unemployment, relative deprivation, and social protest. *Personality and Social Psychology Bulletin, 13*(2), 275–283.

Wenzel, M., Mummendey, A., Weber, U., & Waldzus, S. (2003). The ingroup as pars pro toto: Projection from the ingroup onto the inclusive category as a precursor to social discrimination. *Personality and Social Psychology Bulletin, 29,* 461–473.

Wit, A. P., & Kerr, N. L. (2002). "Me versus just us versus us all": Categorization and cooperation in nested social dilemmas. *Journal of Personality and Social Psychology, 83,* 616–637.

Worchel, S., Morales, J. F., Paez, D., & Deschamps, J. C. (Eds.). (1998). *Social identity: International perspectives* (pp. 166–179). London: Sage.

Wright, S. C., Taylor, D. M., & Moghaddam, F. M. (1990). Responding to membership in a disadvantaged group: From acceptance to collective protest. *Journal of Personality and Social Psychology, 58,* 994–1003.

Zdaniuk, B., & Levine, J. M. (2001). Group loyalty: Impact of members' identification and contributions. *Journal of Experimental Social Psychology, 37,* 502–509.

Zimbardo, P. G. (1969). The human choice: Individuation, reason, and order vs. deindividuation, impulse, and chaos. In W. J. Arnold & D. Levine (Eds.), *Nebraska symposium on motivation, 1969* (Vol. 17, pp. 237–307). Lincoln: University of Nebraska Press.

19

Groups and Individual Change

Randy H. Magen

Eugene Mangiardi

It is indisputable that groups can produce individual change, but what are the mechanisms by which groups help people? What is it that groups "do" to people? What are the group process variables, independent of any specific theory or method of treatment, that help people change? For example, psychoanalytic theory postulates that the mind is an open system that is continually being modified, while also modifying the mind(s) of others, in an ongoing process of projection and introjection. Cognitive behavioral theory asserts that the individual can change by testing and practicing new ways to think about self and others. In cognitive behavioral group treatment, what is it in the group that influences change independent of cognitive behavioral techniques? How does group process contribute to the psychoanalytic treatment in groups? What is the same in the cognitive behavioral group and the psychoanalytic group?

In this chapter, we examine the relationship between groups and individual change. The focus will be on groups as the context, medium, or method to help achieve change in individuals. These types of groups are traditionally referred to as psychotherapy groups or skills training groups. Three characteristics differentiate this type of group from individual treatment and from other types of groups. First, in psychotherapy or skills groups, help for the individual comes from both the professional leading the group and the other individuals in the group; this is the primary difference between individual treatment and group treatment. In groups, the individual has a responsibility to help others in the group. In individual treatment, the client is not responsible for helping the professional. Second, in these groups, successful outcome is defined in terms of members' individual goals. Although this may be similar to individual treatment, it is different from support groups or social action groups. Third, in psychotherapy groups as opposed to self-help groups, a professional who does not share the clients' difficulties provides leadership.

If a practitioner or a researcher were to search an electronic database on groups, the results would be voluminous; Bednar and Kaul's (1994) search of an 8-year period in PsychLit produced 3,826 articles, and a recent 5-year review of four journals identified 326 small group research articles (Brower, Arndt, & Ketterhagen, 2004). The articles identified by both groups of authors were typically investigations into the links between a theory or method and a diagnosis or behavioral problem, using the group as the context for treatment. Although group psychotherapy was the medium in which the independent and dependent variables met, the effect of group was rarely the focus of investigation. In fact, the group has often been ignored in applied research. Frequently, the research question has asked whether an intervention for a problem previously found to be effective in individual treatment is as effective when offered in group sessions. As a result, it is difficult for both researchers and practitioners to identify specifically how the group contributes to individual treatment.

In his seminal book on group psychotherapy, Yalom (1970) grappled with the myriad group modalities and associated theoretical approaches by teasing out *curative factors* he believed to be common to all helping groups. He stated that his first strategy was simplification to induce order by

separating "front" from "core" in each of the group therapies. The "front" consist[s] of the trappings, the form, the techniques, the specialized language, and the aura surrounding each of the schools of therapy; the "core" consist[s] of those processes— that is, the bare-boned mechanisms of change. (p. vii)

Thirty-five years later, the landscape of group therapy is more complex. In spite of an ever-growing clinical and research literature, the bare bones have added very little flesh, and the specific mechanisms by which groups help people to change remain elusive. The literature is replete with new theories of helping while older approaches have either waned or have developed in unexpected directions. The nomenclature of many clinical disorders has changed with the ongoing development of the *Diagnostic and Statistical Manual of Mental Disorders* (including entirely new diagnoses), and entirely new social problems have moved to the forefront. This changing context has made it very difficult to follow the threads of research and practice over time.

This chapter is organized to focus on one central question: What knowledge and skills are essential to leading groups in the service of individual change? In an effort to find a balance between oversimplification and the need to meaningfully explore the literature, each section seeks to identify the principles that appear to be "taken for granted" as essential for group practitioners.

The History of Groups for Individual Change

History of Research Related to Groups for Individual Change

The beginning of group therapy has been traced to Joseph Pratt's psychoeducational groups for patients with tuberculosis (Ettin, 1988). Group dynamics, as a distinct area of social science research, began near the end of the 1930s (Cartwright & Zander, 1960). The two likely came together in the 1940s when the U.S. Army advocated the use of brief group treatment for soldiers (Ettin, 1989). The first published experimental or quasi-experimental studies of group psychotherapy appeared in the 1950s. After reviewing the first 50 years of group psychotherapy outcome research, Bednar and Kaul (1994) restated the conclusion they had reached 16 years earlier: "Accumulated evidence indicates that group treatments have been more effective than no treatment, than placebo or nonspecific treatments, or than other recognized psychological treatments, at least under some circumstances" (p. 632).

The key phrase, for clients, practitioners, and researchers is "under some circumstances." In its examination of individual change in psychotherapy, group research has identified key variables likely involved in producing positive outcomes, but it has not discovered cause-effect linkages. The state of the field, at this point, is better described as a consensus of practice wisdom and exploratory research. To put this another way, groups are the proverbial black box: Clients enter the box in one state and exit in a changed state. What occurs inside the black box remains a bit of a mystery. To explain what occurs inside the black box, theories about groups have been developed. To understand how an individual changes in groups, theories of groups have been melded with theories of individual change. However, theories of group psychotherapy are not theories of personality and are not theories about individual change per se, but are theories about the means by which the group supports an individual's growth. These theories of intervention and group dynamics interact to offer theoretical explanations for how groups produce change in individuals.

For example, Rose (1998) has written extensively about the application of cognitive behavioral theory in the context of group therapy. He notes advantages to delivering cognitive behavioral therapy in the group context: limiting clients' sense of isolation; providing a source of feedback, opportunities for mutual reinforcement, and the experience of dealing with individual differences; offering a more efficient modality to deliver a wide range of therapeutic procedures; and using group norms to build a therapeutic community. Rose also notes potential disadvantages: the possibility of an antitherapeutic culture within the group; group contagion; challenges to individualize each client's needs; and the maintenance of confidentiality. On either side of the equation, group leaders would be hard-pressed to maximize the positive while also addressing the challenges without knowledge of cognitive behavioral theory, group dynamics, and group leadership.

Key Findings

There is consensus in the literature about the basic prerequisites for training and supervision in group treatment (Association for the Advancement of Social Work With Groups, 1999; Association for Specialists in Group Work, 1998, 2000). Textbooks on groups are also consistent in identifying the core elements of group practice: group purpose, group composition, group cohesiveness, group development, and group communication. These core elements can be found in any group, formed or natural, psychotherapy or self-help, task or treatment. What distinguishes groups is how the various elements are interwoven with the ultimate goal of individual change inherent in psychotherapy groups.

Group Purpose

Purpose has been defined as "the end which the group will pursue. It defines where the group will go—the group's aims and the ultimate destination" (Kurland & Salmon, 1998, p. 6). Group failures are frequently linked to the inability of group leaders to carefully craft a statement of purpose that reflects the needs and wishes of group participants (Conyne, 1999). Kurland and Salmon (1998) identify a series of common errors related to group purpose. First, leaders may confuse group process and content with group purpose. A group leader might address a new anger management group with the statement "We're here to practice ways to manage anger" rather than a clear statement of purpose such as "By the end of this series of 10 sessions, we expect that you will be able to control your anger better than you did at the beginning." The clear statement of purpose, in addition to clarifying expectations, also provides a standard from which to evaluate the group. In some settings, group participants may not share the group leader's initial statement of purpose. In the anger management group, one participant might, in all sincerity, assert that the purpose of attending is to avoid jail, while another may say that he's in the group to save his marriage. Such individual discrepancies are inevitable; however, failure to discuss and negotiate individual expectations will render it impossible to develop group cohesion around a shared purpose.

A second error identified by Kurland and Salmon (1998) is the failure of group leaders to carefully anchor group purpose to specific, clearly understood goals. Global statements such as "coping better with depression" do not describe how clients would be different if the depression lessened. Clear statements of clients' goals provide an individual measure of outcome, in addition to the group outcome measure provided by a clear statement of the group's purpose.

Third, the stated purpose of the group may be different from the intended purpose of the group. For example, group leaders of an activity group for children might stress enjoyable activities to lure children into the group but hide that the goal is to improve the children's social behavior. Ethical treatment demands that clients give informed consent. A clear statement of the purpose of the group is part of that consent process. In addition, the group purpose helps to clarify the roles and responsibilities of the clients and the group leaders. It is interesting to note that group leaders often state that they are "running" a group, while the same workers shun saying that they "run" individuals or families in treatment. A central question relevant to group (perhaps more than individual or family) treatment is, Whose group is this? Who decides if this will be a dictatorial or a democratic process? What happens when group leaders and participants differ about important group issues? The statement of group purpose is a first step in answering these questions.

Last, groups sometimes fail to flower because group leaders do not recognize group purpose to be dynamic and evolving over time in response to the changing needs of the members. In some groups, participants may grow beyond the original formulation of purpose and move to a different sense of the group's work.

A therapeutic relationship demands that the group leader and client share a congruent understanding about the nature of their work together. Similar assumptions about the clarity of purpose underlie all treatment contracts. However, it is more important in the group setting because the first steps in group development are founded on the degree to which the group members—including the group leader(s)—can establish a consensus about the reason why they are together and where they intend to go. Unlike individuals or families, groups must address the fundamental question of whether the group will exist or not. Frequently, the first test of the group leader's ability is around the basic questions about who should participate in the group.

Group Composition

Anecdotal evidence suggests that social service agencies, for reasons of efficiency and economics, are increasingly using group psychotherapy. As a result, more and more clients find themselves in groups. Group leaders are faced with decisions about how to blend the demographic and diagnostic characteristics of clients into a group with a high potential for achieving success. This, of course, assumes that the composition of the group is under the control of the group leader. Shulman (1994) argues that composing groups according to scientific principles is a myth; the reality is that we "take what we can get." In many agencies, waiting for the optimal mix of clients is impossible because of productivity demands, client needs, and client characteristics. However valid this reality may be, there are sound principles—although they are not empirically validated—that can guide group leaders. Also, a number of laboratory studies offer suggestions on the composition of psychotherapy groups.

Group composition, like all other decisions about the group, does not take place in a vacuum. Decisions about group composition are affected by group structure. In an open-ended group, composition decisions may be made at periodic intervals; these changes in composition in turn affect group development (Galinsky & Schopler, 1989). A closed-membership, time-limited group is affected by the initial decisions of the practitioner when forming the group.

On one hand, it is logical to compose groups that are heterogeneous. Heterogeneity is a reflection of the world in which we live. Heterogeneous groups meet agency needs by allowing clients to be quickly placed in groups without waiting for other clients who meet some predetermined entry criteria. Finally, heterogeneous groups are more democratic and empowering of the members. There is no force outside of the group itself that is controlling the membership. The literature contains reports of groups in which members have had similar presenting problems, yet have been quite dissimilar demographically (e.g., Erickson, 2003; Meyer, 2000; Scapillato & Manassis, 2002).

On the other hand, heterogeneity can be a problem if there is no common ground among the members. To develop cohesion and to relate to each other, members require some commonalities. Research on interpersonal attraction has demonstrated that people have positive views of others who are similar to them whereas people who are dissimilar are viewed positively if they supplement personal traits (Toseland, Jones, & Gelles, 2004).

Two principles regarding group composition that have won widespread acceptance are Redel's law and Yalom's Noah's ark principle. Fritz Redel (1951) crafted what is referred to as the law of optimum distance: "Groups should be homogeneous in enough ways to insure their stability and heterogeneous in enough ways to insure their vitality" (Northen, 1969, p. 95). An operational definition of Redel's law is that extremes are a problem; clients can be neither too similar nor too different. Imagine the lack of conversation in a group of individuals diagnosed with major depression. This group would not have enough heterogeneity to "insure . . . vitality."

Yalom (1970) used the analogy of Noah's ark to recommend that groups be composed so that no one member is isolated. For each characteristic that is important to consider in group composition, at least two members should share that quality.

Complicating these principles is research by Davis (1979) indicating that clients from dominant groups prefer settings where the racial and gender composition mirrors that of the larger society. African Americans, however, indicate a preference for groups that are composed of equal numbers of African Americans and Caucasians. Further compounding this is additional research that points to lower levels of expressiveness among women who are in mixed gender groups (Davis & Proctor, 1989). Obviously, this research presents a dilemma for practitioners attempting to compose a group that adheres to Redel's law and the Noah's ark principle while following the recommendations from empirical research.

Another issue related to group composition is the size of the group. An examination of the literature finds reports of groups ranging in size, on average, from 5 to 10 members. Like the 50-minute therapeutic hour, this is likely a practical convention. Group size is dependent on many factors, including the number of group leaders, the purpose of the group, and the level of disturbance of the clients. Finally, some group leaders compose groups anticipating that some clients will drop out.

In several studies, the number of clients who drop out of group psychotherapy has been reduced by preparing clients for group membership (e.g., Meadow, 1988; Piper & Perrault, 1989). In addition to reducing the number of dropouts, pregroup participation also leads to better attendance, reduced anxiety, and increased initial motivation. A variety of written, verbal, role-play, and audiovisual techniques have been used to provide the pregroup preparation.

Group Cohesiveness

Yalom (1970) identified group cohesiveness as one of the most important curative factors that enable groups to help individual members. He stated, "Several hundred research articles exploring cohesiveness have been written, many with widely varying definitions. In general, however, there is agreement that groups differ from one another in the amount of 'groupness' present" (p. 37). High levels of cohesiveness have been linked to individual change, whereas low cohesiveness has been shown to correlate highly with members dropping out of groups (Dies & Teleska, 1985; Lieberman, Yalom, & Miles, 1973).

Group cohesion is a necessary condition for a group's existence over time but, by itself, is not sufficient to ensure the group experience will be of help to the members. For example, a group in a day treatment program for delinquent adolescents might develop a great deal of cohesiveness, but in direct antipathy to the therapeutic goals of the organization. In order for a group to organize itself in the service of individual change, cohesion must develop as a binding factor that assists the group to develop further.

Group Development

In a review of the literature about group development, Magen (2002) concluded,

Although the concept of group development is of heuristic value, there are multiple problems identified in the group development literature including the failure to validate stages of group development empirically, the arbitrary division of the group into phases, the failure to realize that development is not one predetermined sequence, and the attribution of stages as group phenomena when in fact what is actually being described may be the development of an individual member. (p. 219)

Group development is a metaphor that conceives of the growth (or regression) of groups over time *as if* a group were a living organism with an identifiable life span. It is also important to note that while models of group development presume a closed-ended group, the concepts remain useful in all group therapy endeavors.

Taken from the point of view of a practitioner, the validity of the concept of group development is less important than its usefulness to organize attention to the dynamics of group and to adapt to those dynamics as they change over time. A sense of group development helps the clinician to develop a sense of empathy for "where the group is at," to find a realistic starting point, and to speak to the shared concerns of group members session by session. For example, in a twice-weekly group on an admission unit of an involuntary psychiatric hospital, the practitioner can expect membership to shift daily as new patients are admitted and others discharged or transferred to other units; a few group members may be angry about attending, some may be acutely psychotic, and others may be veterans of a few weeks of meetings. In models of group development, each day's group will be focused on tasks related to the first stage of development. Members struggle with the basic questions: Why am I here? Who are these people? What can I expect of them? Who is this group leader? What will she or he do to me? It is important for the group leader to carefully address those themes every session and to help group members appreciate that they are not alone with their concerns. A simple but universal theme should be selected that can be addressed in some meaningful way in a single group session. For example, the group might focus on the questions of what happened that resulted in hospitalization and what supports will be needed for discharge home. In this sense, the group experience becomes a microcosm of the ward, and it supports patients' efforts to connect with each other about common fears and common goals.

Like the literature on group composition, the literature on group development displays a consensus opinion. This consensus was identified by Toseland and Rivas (2005), who reviewed 10 authors' contributions over 40 years. They concluded that while there were differences in the number and naming of stages, there were common themes about the tasks of groups in the beginning, middle, and end phases.

For example, in the first stages of group development, group members tend to be leader dependent and to direct questions—and eye contact—to the group leader rather than to other group members. There is likely to be an undercurrent of ambivalence about joining the group and about the intentions of the group leader and other group members. At this stage, group leaders need to be active, to avoid long periods of silence, and to support the creation of an atmosphere of safety and curiosity.

Each successive stage places unique demands on the group leader and offers differing opportunities for the group at large. A second stage might be described as a struggle to settle questions of leadership and limits, a time of conflict during which group members reach a final decision to continue with the group or not. Group leaders need to be sensitive to the themes of this stage and to realize that it is a poor time to introduce new members.

A third stage consists of an evolved sense of cohesion and purpose. Group members tend to be less reliant on group leaders for direction. The group begins to develop and act on a culture of its own; members frequently use the pronouns *we* and *us* and communicate a sense of belonging. At this point, the group is better able to absorb and acculturate new members into the group.

A subsequent stage has been described by different authors as performing, problem solving, or working (e.g., Garland, Jones, & Kolodny, 1976; Northen, 1969; Tuckman, 1963). At this point, the group functions as a mutual aid system in which group members have achieved sufficient trust to approach each other for help and support. Group roles are more flexible than at earlier stages. The group develops a sense of its own history and can apply shared past experience as a frame of reference to solve problems in the present. Members identify with the group, are self-directed, and depend less on the group leader.

The final stage, often neglected in the literature, is termination. There are many scenarios in which termination may occur in a group: for example, the purposeful dissolution of a closed-ended group; successful graduation of a group member from an ongoing group; early leaving, dropping out, or expulsion of a group member; forced termination due to external factors such as denial of insurance or loss of agency funding; and change in leadership.

All terminations, whether in individual, family, or group treatment, offer unique opportunities for therapy gains. Yalom (1970) noted, "Termination is more than the end of therapy; it is an integral part of the process of therapy and, if properly understood and managed, may be an important force in the instigation of change" (p. 274). Yalom added that termination is "a jolting reminder of the inbuilt cruelty of the psychotherapeutic process" (p. 373).

Authors have identified two central themes in termination: the importance of time and adaptation. Mann (1973), in discussing 12-session brief psychotherapy, recommended that the therapist and client begin to consider termination in the first session and continue the discussion through the last meeting. Mackenzie (1995) applied a similar approach to time-limited group therapy and noted several important topics: group members' belief that there has not been enough time and associated feelings of deprivation, resentment, and anger; feelings of rejection; grief; and a heightened sense of the need to take care of oneself.

Other authors, although they are also aware of the impact of time and loss, have stressed the adaptive potential for clients in the termination phase of therapy. Fieldsteel (1995) linked the process of termination to the tasks of separation/individuation and the development of autonomy. Walsh (2003) identified the group leader's tasks during the termination phase: encourage members to practice newly learned skills outside of the group, discuss strategies for possible setbacks, reinforce awareness of gains made, identify areas that will require continued work, and assist with referrals. Toseland and Rivas (2005) added reducing group attraction and promoting the independent functioning of individual members; planning for the future; and evaluating the work of the group.

However, terminating group treatment is qualitatively different than ending individual and family treatment. In the latter, the relationship between the therapist and the individual or family comes to an end, but the therapist, patient, and family continue to exist, and the possibility remains that the therapeutic relationship will resume in the future. The end of a group is literally that: The group ceases to exist. Group leader and members go their separate ways, and reunion is extremely unlikely. Walsh (2003) notes that groups are small communities, and their endings merit different consideration than other treatment modalities. The dissolution of the group is truly the end of something that cannot be reclaimed. The dissolution of groups engenders powerful feelings in all participants, including the group leader (Schermer & Klein, 1996). The group leader's tasks at termination are to support group members to accept the ending of the group and to help members use the experience in service of separation/individuation and autonomous functioning.

The successful termination of a group member from an ongoing group offers the group-as-a-whole the opportunity to review the experience of the group and to reaffirm the ability of group members to effect change in one another. Rice (1996) also notes that premature termination and dropouts threaten the group's cohesion. He suggests that it is possible to make such premature endings effective for the individual and for the group by focusing on understanding the group member's wish to leave. The same can be said for all terminations from the group, whether they are judged to be successful terminations or not.

Less has been written about the purposeful expulsion of a group member in response to behavior toxic to the group. A second kind of forced termination, an ending dictated by forces external to the group, has received even less attention in the literature. This issue is especially pressing for two reasons: Managed care looms as a major determinant in client's length of participation in treatment, and programs may close suddenly and unexpectedly in response to lack of funding. Although the clinical issues about ending therapy are identical to those above, there is an additional burden. Group leaders and members may feel—perhaps justifiably—that the end of the group, or the inability of a group member to continue, is unfair and unreasonable. In each of the above cases, group leaders must identify the events for what they are: inevitable vicissitudes of life that must be managed. Schaffer and Pollak (1984) documented the mirroring of feelings and behavior between staff and children, which offered the children subtle support for regressive behavior. The task for the group can be to discuss and practice means of coping with those events. Although group leaders may feel angry with the insurance company or the community's lack of support for programs, it is essential that clients not become entangled in the process.

Group Communication

Viewed from the perspective of systems theory, a group can be conceived as an entity that is more than the sum of its individual members.

In a seminal paper about group function, Stanton and Swartz (1949) described the social organization of a psychiatric ward as "a group of interlocking whirlpools where, if one whirlpool is altered . . . the whole pattern, and each part of it, will be altered to a greater or lesser extent" (p. 13). Thus, as in the case of what was later deemed the Stanton/Swartz effect, a patient's symptoms worsened (or improved) in response to the degree to which staff resolved conflicts between each other. Murray Bowen (1978) described a similar process of triangulation in family functioning in which one family member is called on to stabilize the relationship between two other members. Other family theorists understood the symptoms of individual family members to be an expression of family conflict; thus, the "identified patient" was perceived to be an expression of family dynamics rather than the problems of a single individual.

The meaning of group communication and behavior is often complex and difficult to read. As when viewing an iceberg, which is only partly revealed above the sea, the informed observer realizes that a great deal of communication remains below the surface and must be inferred. Communication within the group must be understood on both levels; experienced group leaders learn to listen with a "third ear" for subtle but frequently vital messages that reveal the meaning of communication as it relates to the individual and to the group as a whole. Obviously, there is no prescriptive format for group leaders to follow. However, it is essential for group leaders to listen to each member while also listening and responding to the group. Doing so enhances the likelihood that important communications will be discussed in the group.

Group leaders need also to pay attention to the details of patterns of interaction that evolve between the group leader and the group and between group members and subgroups, developing skills to bring the group's attention to those patterns. In the course of that effort, group leaders model skills to question, to seek clarification, to offer feedback, and to invite discussion.

Conclusion

If group leaders follow the principles identified in this chapter related to the key elements of group psychotherapy—clear statements of group purpose, attention to group composition, development of group cohesion, awareness of group developmental stage, and interest in communication within the group—will the group be successful? To put this another way, given what we know, is group psychotherapy efficacious? Miller (2000) suggests that question is similar to asking whether surgery is efficacious; the question is too broad, and any answer will be so general that it is not useful. There are specific studies, largely in the laboratory, but some in less highly controlled practice settings, which have answered specific questions about the key elements of group psychotherapy. For example, across settings, group members identify cohesion as central to their group experience (e.g., Bednar & Kaul, 1994; Heil, 1992; Lieberman & Borman, 1979; Magen & Glajchen; 1999; Weinberg, Uken, Schmale, & Adamek, 1995). But the relationship between these findings about cohesion and group composition or group development or group communication or group purpose is unexplored. We have empirical knowledge about some of the small pieces related to the group psychotherapy, but not the general enterprise (Miller, 2000). At best, practitioners can evaluate what they do and subscribe to the common principles laid out in this chapter.

References

Association for Specialists in Group Work. (1998). ASGW best practice guidelines. *Journal for Specialists in Group Work, 23,* 237–244.

Association for Specialists in Group Work. (2000). Professional standards for the training of group workers. *Journal for Specialists in Group Work, 25*(4), 327–343.

Association for the Advancement of Social Work With Groups. (1999). *Standards for social work practice with groups.* Akron, OH: Author.

Bednar, R. L., & Kaul, T. J. (1994). Experiential group research: Can the canon fire? In A. E. Bergin & S. L. Garfield (Eds.), *Handbook of psychotherapy and behavior change* (4th ed., pp. 631–663). New York: John Wiley.

Bowen, M. (1978). *Family therapy in clinical practice.* New York: Jason Aronson.

Brower, A. M., Arndt, R. G., & Ketterhagen, A. (2004). Very good solutions really do exist for group work research design problems. In C. D. Garvin, L. M. Gutiérrez, & M. J. Galinsky (Eds.), *Handbook of social work with groups* (pp. 435–446). New York: Guilford Press.

Cartwright, D., & Zander, A. (1960). *Group dynamics: Research and theory* (2nd ed.). Evanston, IL: Row, Peterson & Company.

Conyne, R. K. (1999). *Failures in group work: How we can learn form our mistakes.* Thousand Oaks, CA: Sage.

Davis, L. (1979). Racial composition in groups. *Social Work, 24,* 208–213.

Davis, L. E., & Proctor, E. K. (1989). *Race, gender, & class: Guidelines for practice with individuals, families, and groups.* Englewood Cliffs, NJ: Prentice Hall.

Dies, R. R., & Teleska, P. A. (1985). Negative outcome in group psychotherapy. In D. T. Mays & C. M. Franks (Eds.), *Negative outcome in psychotherapy and what to do about it* (pp. 141–181). New York: Springer.

Erickson, D. H. (2003). Group cognitive behavioral therapy for heterogeneous anxiety disorders. *Cognitive Behavior Therapy, 32*(4), 179–186.

Ettin, M. F. (1988). "By the crowd they have been broken, by the crowd they shall be healed": The advent of group psychotherapy. *International Journal of Group Psychotherapy, 38*(2), 139–167.

Ettin, M. F. (1989). "Come on, Jack, tell us about yourself": The growth spurt of group psychotherapy. *International Journal of Group Psychotherapy, 39*(1), 35–57.

Fieldsteel, N. (1995). The process of termination in long-term psychoanalytic group psychotherapy. *International Journal of Group Psychotherapy, 46*(1), 25–39.

Galinsky, M. J., & Schopler, J. H. (1989). Developmental patterns in open-ended groups. *Social Work With Groups, 12*(2), 99–114.

Garland, J., Jones, H., & Kolodny, R. (1976). A model of stages of group development in social work groups. In S. Bernstein (Ed.), *Explorations in group work* (pp. 17–71). Boston: Charles River Press.

Heil, R. A. (1992). A comparative analysis of therapeutic factors in self-help groups (Alcoholics Anonymous, Overeaters Anonymous). *Dissertation Abstracts International, 53*(08), 4373B.

Kurland, R., & Salmon, R. (1998). Purpose: A misunderstood and misused keystone of group work practice. *Social Work With Groups, 21*(3), 5–17.

Lieberman, M. A., & Borman, L. D. (1979). *Self-help groups for coping with crisis: Origins, members, processes, and impact.* San Francisco: Jossey-Bass.

Lieberman, M. A., Yalom, I. D., & Miles, M. B. (1973). *Encounter groups: First facts.* New York: Basic Books.

Mackenzie, R. (1995). Time limited group psychotherapy. *International Journal of Group Psychotherapy, 46*(1), 41–59.

Magen, R. H. (2002). Practice with groups. In M. A. Mattaini, C. T. Lowrey, & C. H. Meyer (Eds.), *Foundations for social work practice: A graduate text* (3rd ed., pp. 208–229). Silver Springs, MD: NASW Press.

Magen, R. H., & Glajchen, M. (1999). Cancer support groups: Client outcome and the context of group process. *Research on Social Work Practice, 9*(5), 541–554.

Mann, J. (1973). *Time limited psychotherapy.* Cambridge, MA: Harvard University Press.

Meadow, D. (1988). Preparation of individuals for participation in a treatment group: Development and empirical testing of a model. *International Journal of Group Psychotherapy, 37*(3), 367–385.

Meyer, P. A. (2000). Variety is the spice: Survivor groups of mixed sexual orientation. In J. Cassese (Ed.), *Gay men and childhood sexual trauma: Integrating the shattered self* (pp. 91–106). Binghamton, NY: Haworth Press.

Miller, R. R. (2000). Perspectives on the efficacy of psychotherapy. *Smith College Studies in Social Work, 70*(2), 207–216.

Northen, H. (1969). *Social work with groups.* New York: Columbia University Press.

Piper, W. E., & Perrault, E. L. (1989). Pretherapy preparation for group members. *International Journal of Group Psychotherapy, 3,* 17–34.

Redel, F. (1951). The art of group composition. In S. Schulze (Ed.), *Creative group living in a children's institution.* New York: Association Press.

Rice, C. A. (1996). Premature termination of group therapy: A clinical perspective. *International Journal of Group Psychotherapy, 46*(1), 5–23.

Rose, S. D. (1998). *Group therapy with troubled youth: A cognitive-behavioral interactive approach.* Thousand Oaks, CA: Sage.

Scapillato, D., & Manassis, K. (2002). Cognitive-behavioral/interpersonal group treatment for anxious adolescents. *Journal of the American Academy of Child & Adolescent Psychiatry, 41*(6), 739–741.

Schaffer, S., & Pollak, J. (1984). Parallel process and the forced termination of a milieu group. *Clinical Social Work Journal, 12*(2), 118–128.

Schermer, V. L., & Klein, R. H. (1996). Termination in group psychotherapy from the perspectives of contemporary object relations theory and self psychology. *International Journal of Group Psychotherapy, 46*(1), 99–115.

Shulman, L. (1994). Group work method. In A. Gitterman & L. Shulman (Eds.), *Mutual aid groups, vulnerable populations, and the life cycle* (2nd ed., pp. 29–58). New York: Columbia University Press.

Stanton, A., & Swartz, M. (1949). The management of a type of institutional participation in mental illness. *Psychiatry, 12,* 13–26.

Toseland, R. W., Jones, L. V., & Gelles, Z. D. (2004). Group dynamics. In C. D. Garvin, L. M. Gutiérrez, & M. J. Galinsky (Eds.), *Handbook of social work with groups* (pp. 13–31). New York: Guilford Press.

Toseland, R. W., & Rivas, R. F. (2005). *An introduction to group work practice* (5th ed.). Boston: Allyn & Bacon.

Tuckman, B. (1963). Developmental sequence in small groups. *Psychological Bulletin, 63,* 384–399.

Walsh, J. (2003). *Endings in clinical practice.* Chicago: Lyceum Books.

Weinberg, N., Uken, J. S., Schmale, J., & Adamek, M. (1995). Therapeutic factors: Their presence in a computer-mediated support group. *Social Work With Groups, 18*(4), 57–69.

Yalom, I. (1970). *The theory and practice of group psychotherapy.* New York: Basic Books.

20

Virtual Teams

Marshall Scott Poole

Huiyan Zhang

Virtual teams, once a novelty, are increasingly common. Articles about virtual teams frequently appear in the popular management literature. How-to books on effective virtual teams can be found in bookstores. It is not uncommon today to belong to—or know someone who belongs to—a virtual team. In 2001, Ahuja and Galvin (2001) estimated that as many as 8.4 million U.S. employees participated in one or more virtual teams or groups, and that number has certainly grown since.

There are several drivers behind the growth of virtual teams. The first is the march of technology, including the growth of internetworking, developments in information and communication technologies (ICTs) such as videoconferencing and collaboration technologies, and the increasing bandwidth available for connection. A second driver is economic transformation fed by the increasing globalization of societies and economies and the transition to a knowledge-based economy. A change in the nature of organizations is the third driver, as exhibited in trends toward increasing geographical dispersion of organizations; growth in partnerships and alliances among private, public, and nonprofit organizations; and spread of the network organizational form. A final driver operates at the individual level, as many valuable workers, especially knowledge workers, desire and are demanding greater flexibility in work arrangements, which results in telework arrangements.

Virtual teams can take a wide variety of forms. The archetypal—and most commonly studied—virtual team is one developing a design or system that incorporates several members in the United States, Europe, and Asia. But the corporate sales team, its personnel scattered over the Eastern seaboard of the United States, is also a virtual team, as is a quality improvement group whose members are drawn from three different government offices in a large midwestern city and a group of geography teachers in several middle schools located in different parts of a rural county. Although much less studied, virtual teams exist in gaming communities like Everquest and even among bloggers working hard to keep their site full of fresh content. What these teams have in common is that most of their work and interaction is done via ICTs such as e-mail, telephone, videoconference, and integrated collaborative tools.

The emergence of the virtual team has interested both academics and practitioners who attempt to map out what makes virtual teams work and how to make them effective. From 1990 to 2000, the number of publications on virtual teams remained modest although there was an increase. From 2000 to 2002, the rate of growth accelerated, and in the past 2 years, there has been a great jump in the number of books and articles on virtual teams. Our knowledge about virtual teams is still fairly thin, but it grows increasingly sophisticated. This chapter attempts to organize what we know about virtual teams in terms of the factors that influence how they work, their effectiveness, and key processes in virtual teams.

What Is a Virtual Team?

A wide range of definitions of virtual teams have been advanced in both the research (e.g., Bell & Kozlowski, 2002; Gibson & Cohen, 2003; Knoll & Jarvenpaa, 1998; Windsor, 2001) and practitioner literatures (e.g., Lipnack & Stamps, 1997; O'Hara-Devereaux & Johansen, 1994). The key defining features of virtual teams are these: (a) Their members are dispersed and do not conduct much work face-to-face, and (b) most interaction between members is mediated by ICTs (Knoll & Jarvenpaa, 1998). While some definitions of virtual teams also specify characteristics such as geographical and temporal dispersion or cultural and organizational diversity, these are better viewed as variables that make virtual teamwork more complex, rather than a

defining feature (Dube & Pare, 2004). While many virtual teams are dispersed over time and space and draw their members from different cultures and organizations, there also are cases in which team members are located in the same city or even the same building. What makes a virtual team virtual is that its members interact and work primarily via ICTs and do not have a common physical space that they meet in with any frequency.

There are varying degrees of "virtuality" in virtual teams. In some, members never physically meet and interact entirely via media whereas in others, members meet face-to-face from time to time. There are also virtual teams in which subsets of members are co-located and the subsets communicate via media. For example, Ngwenyama (1998) studied a virtual team composed of four subgroups of co-located members, one in Europe, two in the United States, and one in Asia. Members of these subgroups communicated with each other via media but conducted much of the communication with others in their subgroup face-to-face. Many of the effects discussed in subsequent sections are stronger the more virtual the team, that is, the less face-to-face communication there is among members.

Virtual teams are, of course, also teams. Teams are a particular type of group in which members share common goals, are chosen so that their knowledge and skills complement one another and contribute to goal attainment, and manage their activities and interactions so that they work as effectively and efficiently as possible (Katzenbach & Smith, 1993). Members of teams regard their team as an entity that binds them together and hold themselves mutually accountable for their goals.

Organization of This Review

We have adopted an input-process-output framework to organize the literature on virtual teams. Much of the research and practitioner literature is focused on factors and practices that influence their effectiveness. Hence, we start with a definition of team outcomes and then summarize thinking and evidence on key inputs that influence virtual teams and then on team processes themselves. In discussing inputs and processes, we will often touch on outcomes, because the literature on virtual teams is strongly outcome oriented. At this point, it seems premature to offer an integrative framework on virtual teams, because thinking in this area is still forming itself. Hence, we will focus on organizing streams of findings, with the hope that this can serve as a preface to a more substantive theory of virtual teams.

Outcomes

Following McGrath (1984), we can distinguish three meaningful sets of outcomes for virtual teams: (a) productivity, the degree to which the group effectively and efficiently meets its goals and succeeds in its projects and activities; (b) group well-being, the degree to which the group's activities build it as a cohesive unit and increase its ability to function effectively in the future; and (c) member support, the degree to which the group is able to satisfy or meet its individual members' needs and thereby keep them committed to the group. McGrath originally advanced these as meaningful groupings of outcomes for traditional teams, but they also apply to virtual teams, although with somewhat different requirements for that context. For example, group well-being for a virtual team would include improving its ability to coordinate over a distance.

As subsequent sections show, studies of virtual teams have been concerned with all three of these goals. They have particularly focused, however, on group well-being. This is largely, we believe, because virtual teams present formidable challenges in terms of creating a sense of the group as a unit and building capacities for teamwork.

Inputs

Inputs include the raw materials that are used to constitute a virtual team—its members and technologies—the tasks the team carries out, and the structures that are imposed on or developed by the team, including group structures, external linkages, and reward structures. All of these can be viewed as "set," so that they represent conditions under which the virtual team operates as it pursues its work through various group processes. Of course, these inputs themselves are likely to change over time through the action of group processes, and this is sometimes an object of study (e.g., Majchrzak, Rice, Malhotra, King, & Ba, 2000; Ngwenyama, 1998), but for purposes of organization and analysis, we will regard them as factors prior to group processes and outcomes.

Members

Most practitioner-oriented books and articles on virtual teams emphasize the importance of team members (e.g., Duarte & Snyder, 1999; Lipnack & Stamps, 1997). In addition to the issues that confront all types of teams, such as selecting members with the proper mix of skills, knowledge, and experience and with high levels of motivation, these sources suggest that it is important to select members who are able to work independently and have high tolerance for uncertainty (Kirkman, Rosen, Gibson, Tesluk, & McPherson, 2002). Working in virtual teams often requires independence and initiative and is sufficiently different from typical teamwork that high levels of uncertainty are likely. Murphy (2004) argues that people with "social" or "procedural" personalities will tend to be uncomfortable in virtual teams and that the members best suited for virtual teams are those with "a high capacity for self-steering" (p. 340). McDonald (1999) echoes this reasoning in his claim that members who function best on virtual teams are individualists. However, Kirkman et al. (2002) also found that interpersonal skills were regarded as critically important to the success of virtual teams in one large corporation that employs them.

Research also suggests that members with a stronger disposition to trust others are more effective in virtual teams than those with lower levels of dispositional trust (Jarvenpaa, Knoll, & Leidner, 1998; Jarvenpaa & Shaw, in press). Jarvenpaa and Shaw (in press) found that predisposition to trust influenced the development of trust early in the development of virtual teams. If early trust emerged in the teams, this in turn fostered communication and group cohesiveness that subsequently influenced longer term cohesiveness, satisfaction with the group, and members' perceptions of quality. Poole et al. (2004) found that personality types that expected to trust others were more likely to participate willingly in virtual collaborative work than those that did not.

The cultural background of members exerts a strong effect on virtual teams that include members from different cultures. Culturally diverse teams must deal with differences in cultural values, communication, and conflict management styles, as well as differences in understanding leadership roles and members' roles and responsibilities. Bhappu, Zellmer-Bruhn, and Anand (2001) argue that cultural (and also demographic) diversity has a negative effect on knowledge acquisition and sharing and that in virtual teams, this effect increases due to the lack of face-to-face contact. Kayworth and Leidner (2001/2002) found that U.S. and European members of virtual teams were frustrated by the slow response of Mexican members and attributed it to lack of commitment. It seems more likely, however, that the difference in response time and the resulting interpretations stemmed from cultural differences in time orientation. In a study of 22 virtual team leaders, Connaughton and Daly (2004) found that learning and taking into account different cultural norms was regarded as an important contributor to team effectiveness. Zolin, Hinds, Fruchter, and Levitt (2004) found that cultural diversity in virtual teams composed of engineering students reduced the perceived trustworthiness of other members and posed a barrier to effective team functioning.

The virtual environment may also mitigate cultural differences. Computer-mediated communication eliminates many nonverbal cues that may signal culture, such as accent or appearance, and so it may focus members more on contributions to the team rather than cultural stereotypes (Bhappu, Griffith, & Northcraft, 1997). Ngwenyama (1998) reports a case in which Asian members of a large international virtual team who were originally slotted into a support role by U.S. counterparts evolved to take a much more prominent role in the team. This was attributed in part to the use of e-mail, which elided differences in command of spoken English and enabled Asian members to actively contribute. Despite the challenges it poses for virtual teams, cultural diversity also brings a good mix of resources to the table. If the problems and difficulties cultural diversity poses can be surmounted, a virtual team can harness these resources to enhance its creativity and effectiveness.

Group Structure

Group structure refers to the basic configuration of the team in terms of the locations and roles of the members and in how the team fits into larger organizational structures. One important structural feature is group size. Virtual teams are often larger than traditional work groups. Their use of ICTs enables more members to participate more actively than members of face-to-face groups can, so a larger number of members can be accommodated. Windsor (2001) notes that ICTs enable managers to have a much larger span of control, which enables larger groups to form. Field studies of actual virtual teams provide some evidence for this. Although the teams in some studies ranged from 5 to 8 members (Kirkman et al., 2002; Leonard, Brand, Edmondson, & Fenwick, 1998; Staples, Wong, & Cameron, 2004), others reported teams with 10 or more members (Fernandez, 2004; Kirkman, Rosen, Tesluk, & Gibson, 2004) including teams of 25 (Panteli, 2004) and 79 members (Ngwenyama, 1998).

Degree of dispersion across space and time is another structural feature of virtual teams. As Dube and Pare (2004) note, the more dispersed the team, the more complex virtual teamwork is. Knoll and Jarvenpaa (1998) concluded that their student virtual teams were "burdened, rather than liberated, by the time zones" (p. 9). Time zone differences delayed the response time and became a barrier in coordinating synchronous interaction among all team members. Dispersion also creates feelings of isolation among members (Connaughton & Daly, 2004) and doubts concerning why members do not respond to messages.

Stability of membership is another key structural variable for virtual teams. In teams with dedicated, full-time members, it is possible to work out roles that give the group clear expectations and standard operating procedures. Teams whose membership is more fluid or whose members are assigned part-time are more problematic because the team must devote a good deal of time and energy to orienting new members and determining how they will fit in and because new members may question and wish to rework existing arrangements. Loyalties of dedicated, full-time members will also differ from those of temporary or part-time members, who are less likely to develop commitment to the virtual team.

Virtual teams may have different types of authority structures. In some teams, lines of authority are clearly defined, and there is a definite leadership structure. For example, in Ngwenyama's (1998) study of an international virtual team engaged in system development, coordination of the effort was planned by a strategy team, and the development was managed by U.S. components of the team. In other cases, virtual teams are largely self-organizing and may not have formally defined authority structures.

External authority lines affect the structure of teams because they complicate responsibilities and commitments of members. In cross-functional or cross-departmental virtual teams, members typically are responsible to a supervisor outside the team as well as to the team and its leadership. If not handled properly, this can cause role conflicts and introduce uncertainty. In general, the more external lines of authority extend into the group, the more complex teamwork becomes. This effect interacts with dispersion, because if a member is physically contiguous to his or her external supervisor, the supervisor may be able to exert more influence on the member than the virtual supervisor can. It is important for the team and its leaders to coordinate demands on its members with external authorities.

Many of the effects discussed in this section hold for co-located as well as virtual teams. However, as Dube and Pare (2004) note, because virtual teams interact through the use of ICTs, the effects may be stronger and more complex than those occurring in co-located teams.

External Team Linkages

The larger organizational structure in which virtual teams operate can also influence processes and outcomes. Some teams, such as the cross-functional teams in Sabre, Inc., operate relatively independently (Kirkman et al., 2002). Others are tightly coupled with other teams or embedded in networks and organizational alliances (Windsor, 2001). Fernandez (2004) describes a meta-team composed of several individual teams from different organizations that undertook a major information technology project in the telecommunication industry. The teams in this loose assemblage were linked by

ICTs. The meta-team had to operate in the context of different and sometimes conflicting goals of the organizations the teams represented, organizational fragmentation that made it difficult to control and plan the project, barriers to interteam communication, and complex interdependencies among teams that operated according to different norms and standards. This posed a formidable challenge for team leaders and members alike.

In some cases, the virtual team is linked to its environment in the sense that changes in its environment have the potential to affect the team. For example, a change in priorities by a parent organization may have important implications. Hornett (2004) makes the case that in such instances, virtual teams may be slower to respond than traditional teams, because their members are dispersed and do not interact as much as those in co-located teams. Hence, virtual teams may be relatively slow to process and grasp the significance of information about their environments.

Tasks and Goals

Most of the virtual teams in the literature perform knowledge-based work such as the development of new products, customer service, and process improvement. Kirkman et al. (2004) go so far as to state that this is the most typical task for virtual teams. Although the increasing use of wireless devices and pervasive computing may well increase the number of virtual teams involved in physical tasks such as managing a supply chain, information-intensive tasks are the easiest to manage in virtual teams.

Key dimensions of tasks in virtual teams include whether the team's task is ongoing or a single-time project, the degree of interdependence required by the task, and task complexity. Riopelle et al. (2003) define task complexity in terms of four dimensions: work flow interdependence, dynamism of task environment, degree of coupling of the team to its environment,

and degree to which members of the team are interdependent. A high-complexity task would have high work-flow interdependence among members; a rapidly changing environment; tight coupling of team members with external individuals, groups, and organizations; and highly coupled members. An example of this type of virtual team would be the software development team working for an alliance of organizations described by Fernandez (2004). A low-complexity task would have few interdependencies in the work flow, a fairly stable environment, few connections to outside groups or individuals, and members who were not particularly dependent on one another. The Texaron sales team, described by Riopelle et al. (2003), is an example of this type of virtual team; its members work independently as they make sales, and their primary linkage is to support personnel in their team.

The nature of the virtual team's task should affect its media use. Media richness theory (Rice & Gattiker, 2001) suggests a general ordering of media from rich to poor as follows: face-to-face interaction, videoconferencing, audioconferencing and phone, e-mail, written documents, and numerical information. It also predicts that more complex tasks require richer media. In line with this prediction, Riopelle et al. (2003) found that the Texaron virtual team, which had low to moderate task complexity, relied primarily on asynchronous media such as e-mail and occasional face-to-face meetings, whereas five other teams with higher levels of complexity used a mix of media that included synchronous media, such as audio- and videoconferencing, application sharing, and more frequent face-to-face meetings. Other studies suggesting that complex tasks are better handled through richer media include Connaughton and Daly (2004), Majchrzak et al. (2000), and Kirkman et al. (2002).

Tasks should also influence virtual team dynamics, although there is little evidence on how they do. Virtual teams with a limited term, single-time task, such as task forces, are likely to emphasize their task in communicating and spend less time developing relationships than will virtual teams with long-term tasks (Dube & Pare, 2004). This may inhibit team development and could cause problems for limited-term virtual teams, so it is important for limited-term teams to get to know each other quickly and work to develop relationships. Swift trust (Jarvenpaa & Leidner, 1999), described below, is also likely to help this type of virtual team.

Technological Support

Virtual teams typically have access to a variety of ICTs. These technologies may provide one or more of the following functions: (a) real-time communication, such as that provided by phone, instant messaging, teleconferencing, and videoconferencing; (b) electronic information sharing, such as e-mail and file sharing; (c) repositories recording the process of the group, including minutes and records of discussions and decisions; (d) meta-information on entries into the repository; and (e) decision and process support. Virtual teams vary in terms of the number of functions provided and the degree to which they are integrated into a seamless system or kept separate. ICTs also vary in their degree of sophistication and the degree to which they structure the team's work. Some teams prefer relatively simple technological support, such as phone and e-mail, whereas others employ complex integrated collaboration technologies (Majchrzak et al., 2000).

The face-to-face medium is also used by most virtual teams. The frequency of these meetings and their importance determines the level of reliance on ICTs in the team. As noted below, a common recommendation is that virtual teams have a face-to-face meeting near their initiation and one or more meetings per year. Also, as noted previously, members of virtual teams may differ in the degree of face-to-face access they have to other members. When a subset of a virtual team is co-located, its members may interact face-to-face quite often while communicating with other virtual team members primarily via media.

Virtual teams vary in the mix of ICTs they use and how they shift between media or use media in combinations. Interestingly, shifts between or combinations of media are not particularly well understood because there is surprisingly little research on them. The impact of integrated systems such as Lotus Notes (Montoya-Weiss, Massey, & Song, 2001) and distributed group support systems (Dufner, Hiltz, & Turoff, 1994) on virtual teams has received more research attention. Some of these will be discussed below in the section on processes.

Reward Structure

Many scholars and practitioners assume that reward structures must be specially designed for virtual teams. The rationale for this is that members of virtual teams must work under quite different circumstances than members of regular teams. Kirkman et al. (2004) argue that extrinsic motivation is weaker in virtual teams than in co-located teams due to the lack of a physically present leader to monitor and motivate and the lack of physically present members to motivate via peer pressure and norms. A counterweight to this effect is the benefit of having a more independent schedule and ability to balance work and family, which virtual work may provide to some members. There is also the intrinsic motivation inherent in many knowledge-intensive jobs.

In his study of a meta-team, Fernandez (2004) found that incentives to encourage collaboration, such as team rather than individually based rewards, will foster better teamwork. Lawler (2003) argues that reward systems for virtual teams should include a mix of individual and team-based incentives. Because many members of virtual teams are likely to be knowledge workers with unique skills and experiences, skill-based reward systems that focus on the individual's skill-knowledge mix will work better to motivate and retain members than will position-based systems. Team-based rewards should vary depending on the nature of the work. For virtual teams in which members are not highly interdependent, there should be a balance of individual and team rewards. For virtual teams in which members are highly interdependent, incentives should be skewed toward team-based rewards. Lawler also recommends incentives for cross-training in virtual teams because this can improve problem solving and team integration.

Virtual Team Processes

We will consider a number of virtual team processes, starting with communication. Then we will consider both relational and work processes and conclude with a discussion of leadership and power in virtual teams.

Communication

Communication, the glue that holds teams together, is a fundamental challenge for virtual teams. In an influential study, Cramton (2001) argued that a primary problem in geographically dispersed virtual teams is achieving the grounding necessary to use communication to create shared understandings and commitments (see also Hinds & Weisband, 2003). Cramton identified five problems connected to failures to create the mutual knowledge necessary for team effectiveness: "failure to communicate and retain contextual information, unevenly distributed information, difficulty communicating and understanding the salience of information, differences in speed of access to information, and difficulty interpreting the meaning of silence" (p. 346). These problems are enhanced by the use of media such as e-mail or conferencing, which reduce social cues significantly. Although there is a good deal of evidence that members of virtual teams can eventually learn to communicate with

one another effectively in "poorer" media such as e-mail, it takes time, and lack of cues continues to constitute a barrier to communication (Walther, 1995; Walther & Burgoon, 1992). We will trace the impacts of communication, beneficial and harmful, in several subsequent sections on group processes.

Several studies have noted that virtual teams often lack norms and protocols for electronically mediated team interaction (Lea & Spears, 1991; Leonard et al., 1998; Zigurs, 2003). As Zigurs put it,

> Traditional teams typically operate within a shared culture that includes deeply buried assumptions about basic communication practices. Virtual teams, however, have to take explicit steps, during the early stage of team formation in order to surface those assumptions. (p. 341)

When virtual team interaction crosses multiple boundaries (cultural, organizational, functional expertise), members transfer their individual, often conflicting expectations into the team interaction process (Zigurs, 2003), which makes it even more difficult at the outset for members to agree about norms regarding how to use electronic media. For a virtual team to be effective, it is important to articulate and negotiate those rules during the early stage of team formation. Others (Armstrong & Cole, 1995; Leonard et al., 1998) have suggested that leaders play an important role as norm setters and facilitate norm development and routine practices early on. An important norm related to communication is language choice: Knoll and Jarvenpaa (1998) recommend that multilingual groups develop an agreement about which language to use when collaborating. Switching between languages leads to misunderstandings and less effective virtual teams.

Choice of communication medium can make a difference in communication and effectiveness. Maznevski and Chudoba (2000) observed that both task and group characteristics influenced virtual team members' media choice decisions. For example, they found that boundary spanning (organizational, cultural, and location boundaries) increased message complexity, which necessitated the use of richer media. Similarly, Pauleen (2003b) reported that both organizational and cultural factors influenced media choice. The author also indicated that various factors, including geographical proximity, cultural preferences, technological availability, and relational needs, influenced media usage in team interaction. Postmes, Spears, Sakhl, and de Groot (2001) reported group variance in content and style of media usage as a result of social influence. The study asserted that normative influence emerged within virtual groups in use of technology and that conformity to group norms increased over time.

Culture also seems to affect media choice. Leonard et al. (1998), for example, found contrasting preferences regarding media choice between Americans and Europeans. American members "live and die" by voice mail and e-mail, whereas Europeans "live and die" by fax. Another instance of cultural differences in media choice was reported in Pierson and Jaeger's (1995) study, in which they found that American managers preferred face-to-face communication and Singaporeans preferred e-mail messages. Last, Pauleen (2003a) concluded, "the full use of communication channels appeared to have much to do with cultural (including organizational) preferences for particular channels, and to a lesser degree with familiarity and skill in using certain channels" (p. 251). The indigenous (Maori) members of the group Pauleen studied had strong preferences for traditional channels such as face-to-face meetings and formal letters, which influenced the group's media usage.

Are face-to-face meetings essential for effective virtual teams? Most practitioner-oriented sources stress the importance of a kick-off meeting to initiate the team and at least one yearly face-to-face meeting (Duarte & Snyder, 1999; Lipnack & Stamps, 1997). An important function of these meetings is to develop social connections

among members (see below). Kirkman et al. (2002) reported that teams at Sabre began work with a 3-day team-building workshop and met once per year face-to-face thereafter. Other researchers suggest that the nature of the task should be taken into account (DeSanctis & Monge, 1999; Maznevski & Chudoba, 2000). Maznevski and Chudoba, for instance, speculated that face-to-face meetings are essential only when there is high degree of interdependence among team members in task completion and when boundary spanning is involved in team interaction. In their study of 22 leaders of virtual teams, Connaughton and Daly (2004) found that the leaders believed face-to-face meetings were superior for establishing vision whereas telephone was best for feedback and e-mail for information and updates. Leonard et al. (1998), in line with media richness scholars, reported that face-to-face media were best for complex tasks such as negotiations. They also reported a negative relationship between telephone and videoconferencing and team effectiveness.

Other studies, however, suggest that face-to-face meetings may not be necessary. Malhotra, Majchrzak, Carman, and Lott (2001) studied a technology innovation team whose task was highly interdependent and required "convergent thinking, conflict resolution, and consensus development" (p. 246), as well as boundary-spanning activities. The team managed to collaborate successfully without using face-to-face meetings. In explaining this result, the authors cited DeSanctis and Monge (1999), who pointed out that most existing studies used teams that relied on either e-mail or computer conferencing systems. Instead, the team that Malhotra et al. studied used what they call "knowledge portal technology" (p. 246) and multiple media for team interaction. Their findings seemed to echo the experiences of one of the teams Lipnack and Stamps (1997) described. In that study, the virtual team used what they regarded as the most advanced technology, a WORM hole with a high-speed, full bandwidth, and continuously available audio-video data link, to interact and to create a sense of "being there." As a result, the team asserted that the greatly enhanced communication tool made face-to-face meetings unnecessary. Montoya-Weiss et al. (2001) found that student virtual teams could be effective without face-to-face meetings; Panteli (2004) had a similar outcome for an engineering team. Clearly, the case is not closed on this issue, one way or the other.

Several studies focus specifically on communication strategies used by effective virtual teams. One is to schedule regular communication among members (Connaughton & Daly, 2004; Kayworth & Leidner, 2001/2002; Knoll & Jarvenpaa, 1998; Yoo & Alavi, 2004). This becomes something members can count on, reduces uncertainty, and promotes more effective information exchange. Panteli (2004) found that effective virtual team members negotiated availability and sent "do not disturb" messages to each other when they wanted to work privately. Sharing of contextual information, such as information on other demands on one's time and general descriptions of surroundings and current events, also seems to help members appreciate others' situations better (Lipnack & Stamps, 1997). Maznevski and Chudoba (2000) identified two general patterns in their study of effective global virtual teams, namely, "appropriate interaction incidents and the structuring of those incidents into a temporal rhythm" (p. 489). They found the level of decision process and the complexity of the message influenced medium choice and the duration of communication incidents. Malhotra et al. (2001) studied a virtual team that used a virtual collaboration tool, the Internet notebook. The team created coordination protocols in advance and constantly modified its norms of technology use over the team's life span. For instance, to guarantee that all information would be equally shared among all team members, the team enforced a rule that prohibited face-to-face interaction. Over time, however, they adapted a norm "allowing for one-to-one discussions when need arises but documenting results for everyone" (p. 244). The adaptation and restructuring of the work process was crucial for the unexpected success of the team.

Social Cognition

Cramton (2001) found that members of virtual teams tended to make relatively negative attributions regarding others' behavior. A member who did not answer e-mails, for example, was assumed to be uncommitted to the team, and the possibility that there was a technical problem or the member was out of town was not considered. Other studies suggest that behavior that increases uncertainty, such as not answering e-mails or not meeting deadlines, fosters negative perceptions (Fernandez, 2004; Kayworth & Leidner, 2001/2002; Panteli, 2004). In an extended analysis of attributions in virtual teams, Cramton (2002) reasons that members of virtual teams are more likely to attribute other team members' behavior to personal traits (i.e., to make dispositional attributions) than are members of traditional teams. Furthermore, she argues that in teams with some distant and some co-located members, co-located members are likely to make more favorable attributions about each other than about distant members. This implies that negative dynamics and conflict are much more likely to occur in virtual teams than in co-located teams.

Walther (1995; Walther & Burgoon, 1992) found that students communicating via computer conferencing initially formed more negative impressions of each other compared with students communicating face-to-face. However, with continued communication over time, these differences disappeared, and in some cases, attitudes toward "virtual others" were ultimately more positive than those toward face-to-face others. The differences between Walther's results and those of the other studies may be due to different degrees of time pressure. Walther's subjects were engaged in a relatively pressure-free project whereas those in other studies had tight deadlines for task completion. However, Ngwenyama (1998) reported results similar to Walther's for a virtual team with strict deadlines.

Research on social identity processes in computer-mediated communication (Abrams, Hogg, Hinkle, & Otten, 2004; Lea & Spears, 1991) suggests that under some conditions, computer-mediated communication may accentuate tendencies to form attitudes and act toward others based on the social groups they belong to rather than considering them as individuals. This may result in stereotyping and other reactions that polarize the team. However, some studies of international virtual teams (Bhappu et al., 1997; Jarvenpaa & Leidner, 1999) suggest that the lack of nonverbal cues, fewer language errors in written messages, and the absence of accents in e-mail and other leaner communication media may foster perceptions of increased similarity among virtual team members. Cultural differences that might provoke social identity processes may be rendered less salient. This is consistent with an analysis by Pratt, Fuller, and Northcraft (2000), who posit that richness of media will have complex effects on social identity. They argue that two types of social identity are relevant in virtual teams, *goal group identity* via identification with the virtual team (which is desirable from the group's point of view) and *fault line identities* due to identification of different members with competing social groups (which is not desirable from the group's point of view). Pratt et al. argue that low-richness media such as e-mail and online chat, which make it difficult to transmit extraneous cues about social group membership but easily transmit task-oriented cues that emphasize the group's goals, will accentuate goal group identity and minimize fault line identity. Videoconferencing, on the other hand, is likely to accentuate social cues, thereby accentuating both fault line identity and goal group identity. Which social identity prevails depends on other factors, such as whether norms of politeness are strong.

Relational Processes

Task-related interaction tends to be emphasized in virtual teams because the absence of face-to-face contact reduces the social dimension (Blackburn, Furst, & Rosen, 2003). Several studies, however, found that developing social bonds among members through joking and social interactions contributed to team development and effectiveness (Knoll & Jarvenpaa, 1998; Mansour-Cole, 2001; Panteli, 2004). Hart and McLeod (2003) found that social relationships were built through work on the task, not only through personal messages. Pauleen (2003a) comments that "the selection and use of communication channels in virtual teams for the purpose of relationship building are likely to be critical factors" (p. 252). Face-to-face meetings of virtual teams are advocated as a means of building social relationships (Armstrong & Cole, 1995; Kirkman et al., 2002; Lipnack & Stamps, 1997; Maznevski & Chudoba, 2000). However, relationships can also be built through other media, such as e-mail or phone conversations. Lipnak and Stamps (1997) advocate using videoconferencing to build relationships, although other studies have found videoconferencing to be more problematic (Leonard et al., 1998).

Walther (1996) proposed a stronger claim regarding the issue of relational communication in virtual teams. In his study, he found that long-term virtual teams stressing members' social identity as part of the team achieved higher levels of productivity and greater member satisfaction than virtual teams that did not. Therefore, according to Walther, conditions for virtual teams should be managed to strengthen relational interaction among members and identification with the team. Presumably, an important condition to investigate would be the anticipation of future interaction with one's teammates (most of the studies on the topic used ad hoc student groups, whose members did not anticipate any opportunities for task-oriented future interaction). For instance,

Jarvenpaa and Leidner (1999) defined global virtual teams as groups that share "no common past or future" (p. 809), which might imply relatively fleeting commitment to the virtual team.

Trust is the substrate of effective virtual teams. It substitutes for direct physical contact and the expectation that others will deliver, and it encourages members to meet their own commitments in order to maintain the trust that others have in them. Trust builds or decays in a cyclical process (Fernandez, 2004; Zand, 1972). If a member fulfills his or her obligations, this increases the trust of other members, who fulfill their obligations, which increases the member's trust and encourages further contributions, which builds others' trust and so on; the decay of trust follows a similar cycle. Findings on the development of trust in virtual teams and its role in team effectiveness are inconsistent, however. Consistent with media richness theory, some scholars have argued that due to the absence of social context as well as nonverbal cues, the virtual environment presents unprecedented challenges to relational communication and trust building (e.g., Gibson & Manuel, 2003). A study by Aubert and Kelsey (2003), for instance, found that trust was higher among local teammates than among the remote partners in virtual teams (Aubert & Kelsey, 2003). Cramton's study (2001) provided partial explanations for the challenges in building trust in virtual groups. She suggested that "human and technical errors in information distribution" permeate the entire process of mediated interaction, which, when understood as "failures of personal reliability," hinders trust building in geographically dispersed teams (Cramton, 2001, p. 365). Gibson and Manuel (2003) compared three virtual teams and found that cultural differences among members also inhibited the formation and expression of trust.

Other studies (Jarvenpaa et al., 1998; Jarvenpaa & Leidner, 1999), however, indicate that "swift trust" can form in virtual teams faced with pressure to complete their tasks in a relatively short time. According to Jarvenpaa and Leidner (1999), trust took the form of "swift, depersonalized, action-based trust" (p. 810) in some of the global virtual teams they studied. Swift trust, however, appeared to be very fragile and could be broken if remote partners did not follow through on their assignments. Moreover, Connaughton and Daly (2004) warned that swift trust, based as it is on attributions, may be granted or withheld based on cultural and other types of stereotypes that do not accurately apply to the members involved.

Communication behaviors conducive to trust building included predictable and continuous interaction, prompt response and substantive feedback, and the presence of social communication (Jarvenpaa & Leidner, 1999). Jarvenpaa et al. (1998) suggested that structure and normative consensus may reinforce trust in mediated situations. In addition, several studies (see the section on leadership) suggest that virtual team leaders can play a critical role in building personal relationships with team members before proceeding to team task.

A few studies have considered substitutes for trust, such as contracts or formal control systems, including financial accounting systems or task tracking systems built into collaboration technologies (Fernandez, 2004; Gallivan, 2001). Fernandez (2004) observed that swift trust did not form in the interlinked system development virtual teams he studied. Instead, members had to build trust by showing their competence and submitting high-quality deliverables on schedule. Trust was initially fostered by contractual arrangements among the teams and a manager who monitored work performed. Murphy (2004) argued that "trust between strangers" is best generated not through developing personal relationships but through allowing the virtual team to self-organize and to develop processes that enable the team to do high-quality work and monitor what is going on in a common space. The development of this shared "commons" gives members of virtual teams something to cultivate together, a common superordinate goal to work for that creates a different type of trust, which Murphy calls "stoic trust."

Regarding the relationship between trust and team performance, interestingly, Aubert and Kelsey (2003) found effective team performance was independent of the formation of trust in virtual teams, although the authors concurred that due to process loss, low-trust teams may have "expended significantly more effort" (p. 605) to deliver a high-quality result. On the other hand, others (e.g., Pauleen, 2003a, 2003b; Walther & Burgoon, 1992) claimed that relational links are associated with team effectiveness in various ways including task performance, increased morale, and better decisions.

Fernandez (2004) noted that too much trust can lower virtual team performance. If team members develop a high level of trust, they often cease monitoring one another. This can result in loss of coordination, and, worse, if one member does not deliver a critical deliverable on time, the team is left without recourse. Paradoxically, if there was somewhat less trust in the virtual team, members would have been monitoring each other more closely, and the problem would have been detected and addressed much earlier.

Group Development

A great deal of writing on virtual teams centers on the issues of how to develop them and build stronger teams. Much less has been written on how such teams actually develop. Most cases (e.g., Gluesing et al., 2003) describe development as progressing from a basically unformed state at the outset to higher levels of "maturity," with the possibility of regressions and setbacks along the way. A mature virtual team is one that has "a common task that team members believe in and are committed to, collaborative interactions with one another and with important groups outside the team, and the ability to sustain a common task focus and collaboration across multiple contexts" (Gluesing et al., 2003, p. 59). Walther's (1995, 1996) research on long-term relational development in virtual teams suggests that relationships among members

develop continuously over time. Similarly, Armstrong and Cole (1995) observed that "similarities of shared goals, norms, and expectations were built over time among group members, evidenced by a more frequent spontaneous use of 'we,' 'us,' and 'our way'" (Armstrong & Cole, 1995, p. 200).

As virtual teams grow more mature, they become more integrated. Following Moreland (1985), Mansour-Cole (2001) distinguishes four aspects of social integration: (a) environmental integration, which depends on proximity; (b) behavioral integration, which depends on interdependence and mutual satisfaction of needs by members; (c) affective integration, which leads to group cohesion and arises from shared affect; and (d) cognitive integration, which depends on developing a common social identity as group members. As virtual teams develop, behavioral, affective, and cognitive integration increase, and members' identification with the group increases as well.

Furst, Reeves, Rosen, and Blackburn (2004) applied Tuckman's classic model of group development to virtual teams. They analyzed several cases, showing how the virtual team proceeds through forming, storming, norming, and performing stages. The problems and issues the teams face in each stage parallel those described by Tuckman, but these interact with the communication, social identity, and relational processes discussed in previous sections.

Structuring Virtual Team Work and Interaction

To counteract problems of working at a distance, virtual teams develop procedures and structures to help coordinate and control member activities. These may be developed informally by members, or they may be tools built into the ICTs that the virtual team uses. One common type of procedural structure is designed to help the virtual team manage and coordinate member interaction and activities over time. These include agendas, project management tools, timelines, deadlines, and reminders. Massey, Montoya-Weiss, and Hung (2003), Maznevski and Chudoba (2000), and Montoya-Weiss et al. (2001) linked the presence of temporal coordination mechanisms to team performance. Maznevski and Chudoba (2000), for instance, argued that effective teams were distinguished by "a strong, repeating temporal pattern" (p. 486). The authors found that effective virtual teams used periodic face-to-face interaction to set the rhythm for team interaction, and once the rhythm was set, it "drove the action rather than the other way around" (p. 488). Similarly, Montoya-Weiss et al. (2001) observed that temporal coordination "enables synchronization of effort, makes response times more predictable, and helps in decision-making by allowing more time for critical discussion" (p. 1260), which in turn improves performance. Massey et al. (2003) found that the conflict management styles of avoidance and compromise had negative effects on performance for virtual teams without temporal coordination procedures, but that teams with temporal coordination did not suffer these negative effects.

A second type of structure is designed to provide members with awareness of other team members' activities in electronic space. Awareness tools serve a function in virtual teams analogous to eyes and ears in co-located teams. They enable members to know who is available to interact at a given time and also help members keep track of what others have been doing. Awareness of who is online is built into many conferencing tools. Steinfield, Jang, and Pfaff (1999) describe a more elaborate awareness system, TeamSCOPE.

A third type of procedural structure pulls together and organizes documents, meeting records, and discussion. These structures may be as simple as categorized e-mail messages (Ngwenyama, 1998), but they may also include shared directories and more elaborate team spaces in which threaded discussions and libraries of documents and designs are stored

(e.g., Majchrzak et al., 2000). Knoll and Jarvenpaa (1998) observed that shared documents and records of activities were important coordination mechanisms for their virtual teams. These structures provide members with a sense of the virtual team's history, clarify rationales behind previous decisions, keep records of actions taken and planned, and provide resources for future actions.

A fourth type of procedural structure is designed to ensure participation of virtual team members. Knoll and Jarvenpaa (1998) note a paradox of participation: the fewer members who participate, the easier it is to coordinate the group. However, participation by as many members as possible is most desirable because it enables the team to capitalize on the diverse knowledge, experience, skills, and perspectives of its members. Procedures to enhance participation include polling tools and asynchronous conferences. As we will note below, the virtual team leader or facilitator is instrumental in eliciting broad participation from virtual team members.

Finally, there are procedural structures that provide meeting and decision support for the virtual team. These can be informal, as when a leader sends a message to the virtual team members suggesting how a decision ought to be made. There are also formal tools for meeting support. Dufner et al. (1994), for example, studied virtual teams using a distributed group decision support system (DGDSS) that enabled members to brainstorm ideas, discuss them, and rate or vote on them. They found that teams using the DGDSS were more effective than groups using a more unstructured computer conferencing system. It is ironic, however, that the members of the virtual teams did not like the DGDSS very well because they perceived that it constrained and slowed their work.

Studies of groups using ICTs to manage their work indicate constant adjustment of the technology, group, and group processes as the group works. Ngwenyama (1998) and Majchrzak et al. (2000) document how virtual teams continually adjust their work practices and how they appropriate ICTs in their work.

Leadership

Although virtual team leaders are expected to possess skills and perform roles that are similar to those required of leaders of traditional teams, they face special challenges (Dubs & Hayne, 1992). When communication routinely crosses geographical, organizational, and cultural boundaries, both relationship building and task coordination become more difficult. Hymowitz (1999; described in Connaughton & Daly, 2004) surveyed 500 virtual managers; 90% reported that it was more difficult to manage virtual teams than face-to-face teams, and 40% reported that members were less productive in virtual teams.

First, it appears that in comparison to traditional teams, virtual team leaders play a more important role in scheduling and structuring the communication practices as well as the work process. Kayworth and Leidner (2001/2002), for instance, found that the leaders' role in coordinating communication "may take on added importance in distributed groups" (p. 27). According to the authors, effective leaders are "extremely effective at providing regular, detailed, and prompt communication with their peers and in articulating role relationships (responsibilities among the virtual team members)" (p. 7). Connaughton and Daly (2004) conducted in-depth interviews with 22 leaders, who reported that one of their main challenges was combating members' feelings of isolation, which they do by scheduling interactions. Phone calls in which there is "small talk" as well as task discussions help to build leader-follower relationships.

Bell and Kozlowski (2002) pointed out that virtual team leaders needed to be "more proactive and structuring" (p. 26); "developing appropriated habitual routines early on in the team's lifecycle" (p. 26) can help leaders to accomplish that goal. Zigurs (2003) also stressed that one important function of virtual team leaders is to structure the work process with appropriate tools, which allows both predictability and flexibility. Kayworth and Leidner (2001/2002) speculate that a leader's ability to manipulate ICTs (e.g., creating Web pages) is an important aspect of virtual leadership.

Several studies (e.g., Cascio & Shurygailo, 2003; Kayworth & Leidner, 2000; Pauleen, 2003a, 2003b; Zigurs, 2003) suggest the crucial role that leaders can play in facilitating social exchanges and relational interaction among virtual team members. For example, Kayworth and Leidner (2000) stress that certain leadership roles are particularly important in virtual teams and that "leaders must be able to build and maintain a social climate necessary for ensuring adequate levels of team unity and cohesiveness" (p. 190). In addition, according to Pauleen's (2003b) three-stage model of leader-initiated relationship building, virtual team leaders can build personal relationships with their members through purposeful selection of communication channels. According to Pauleen, face-to-face meetings were the most preferable channel that leaders chose in getting to know virtual team members, followed by the telephone, which "can pick up paralinguistic clues, such as tension or uncertainty in a team member's voice" (p. 157). In contrast, the leaders studied believed that "e-mail was more suitable for communicating information and coordinating projects than for building relationships" (p. 159). Zigurs (2003) emphasized the concept of *telepresence*—creating a sense of "being there" through effective use of media.

Yoo and Alavi (2004) conducted a groundbreaking study of leadership emergence in virtual teams. They studied seven experimental groups of 8 to 10 members who worked virtually for 10 weeks. They found that members who emerged as leaders sent more messages and that those messages primarily focused on the task and on procedures such as scheduling the group's work. Leader messages were longer, sent earlier in the sessions, and integrated and summarized the group's work. Some leaders also became experts in the technologies the virtual teams used. What emergent leaders did not do is to shape or overly influence the content of the virtual team's work. They left this to followers who were experts in the subject matter involved in the group's work. This finding is inconsistent with the work of Kayworth and Leidner (2001/2002), who found that leaders did provide "task mentorship," shaping the content of the group's work.

Conflict Management

By definition, virtual teams are geographically dispersed, and often, virtual teams are composed of several co-located subgroups with different interests, work practices, and cultural backgrounds. Consequently, virtual teams are likely to experience conflicts. Several scholars have argued that virtual teams experience higher degrees of conflict than traditional teams (Griffith, Mannix, & Neale, 2003; Hinds & Bailey, 2003), and several empirical studies have shown that this is the case (Armstrong & Cole, 1995; Cramton, 2001; Hinds & Mortensen, 2004).

Cramton (2001) explained the emergence of conflict in virtual teams as a function of mutual knowledge problems. Unlike co-located teams, members in virtual teams do not share local contexts, and this gives rise to misunderstandings, misinterpretations, and subsequent misattributions. In addition, Cramton found that human errors in using technology as well as technological problems caused unevenly distributed communication and lags in feedback, which in turn resulted in tension among remote partners because members tended to attribute those problems to personal instead of situational factors. Armstrong and Cole (1995) found that team members labeled other members *them* versus *us* based on their different geographical locations. They commented that "site cultures seemed comparable to national cultures

as sources of misunderstandings and conflicts" (p. 198).

In addition, computer-mediated communication may not be as conducive to consensus building and conflict resolution as face-to-face communication. As DeSanctis and Monge (1999) concluded, "About the only consistent finding in the empirical literature with regard to task and media is that [the tasks of] thinking convergently, resolving conflict, or reaching consensus [are] better done face-to-face than electronically" (p. 697, as cited in Malhotra et al., 2001).

Conflicts in virtual contexts may not surface as quickly and easily as in face-to-face situations, which has a negative impact on the process of conflict management. Procedures may help conflict surface in virtual teams. Montoya-Weiss et al. (2001), for instance, found that the presence of a temporal coordination mechanism "significantly weakened the negative effect of avoidance behavior on virtual team performance" (p. 1257). The existence of such a mechanism compelled members to state their individual opinions up front and also set time limits for specific tasks, which was believed to counteract tendencies to "watch and wait."

With regard to conflict styles, Paul, Seetharaman, Samarah, and Mykytyn (2004) reported a weak link between group heterogeneity (in terms of cultural backgrounds, functional expertise, experience levels, etc.) and the use of collaborative conflict management style within the team, which was found to be positively related to the performance of virtual teams. Montoya-Weiss et al. (2001) found that competitive and collaborative conflict styles had positive effects on virtual team performance, whereas avoidance and compromise had negative effects. They posit that competition will not elicit negative reactions from other members of virtual teams because it is perceived to be an attempt to actively participate and shape the discussion. An accommodative conflict style was not related to performance.

In an insightful study that compared virtual teams and traditional co-located teams, Hinds and Mortensen (2004) found that overall conflict was higher in virtual teams than in traditional teams. However, those virtual teams that had higher levels of spontaneous, informal communication and in which it was easy to coordinate work had a level of conflict no greater than traditional teams. This suggests that as virtual teams develop relationships and work out procedures over time, they will improve their conflict management capabilities.

Power

Power has not been studied much in the context of virtual teams. One exception is Ngwenyama (1998), who noted the difference in power between U.S. and Asian subgroups in a system development virtual team. As communication between subgroups continued and U.S. members increasingly came to respect the Asian members, power differences decreased. However, they were never entirely mitigated and influenced the development of the virtual team in significant ways.

Status, an important basis of power, has been the focus of several studies of distributed groups and computer-mediated communication (Owens, Neale, & Sutton, 2000). Weisband, Schneider, and Connolly (1995) found that status differences emerged in text-based computer-mediated communication, despite expectations that the relatively poor textual medium would equalize status differences. Owens et al. (2000) developed a model of status dynamics and the various moves members of distributed groups might use to manage status in virtual teams.

Kirkman et al. (2004) studied the role of team empowerment in virtual teams. They found that team empowerment (in which virtual teams were given the ability to organize their own work) led to significant process improvement in virtual teams that had few face-to-face meetings, but in teams with many face-to-face meetings, empowerment led to lower levels of process improvement.

Discussion: The Future of Virtual Teams and Virtual Team Research

As this review suggests, there are a considerable number of interrelationships among the inputs and processes discussed in this chapter. However, at this point, advancing an integrative model that ties up the virtual team is premature. Current research and practice provide us with a clear view of certain aspects of virtual teams, but only a glimpse at many others. A number of books have advanced frameworks and formulas for effective virtual teams, but with all due respect, at this point in time, they are at best partial and tentative, based on a fairly small research base.

To further develop our understanding of virtual teams, we need a broader and deeper research base. The upsurge of virtual team research since 2000 is heartening in this respect (see Robey & Jin, 2004, for a review of research methods for the study of virtual teams and work). As research continues, there is a need for studies with larger samples of virtual teams. The majority of studies in this review report on fewer than 10 teams. While the in-depth analysis of these cases is quite useful, rigorous comparative analysis requires larger sample sizes. In the past few years, more studies have appeared that are based on 30 or more virtual teams (not particularly large samples in the absolute sense, but large for group research), and many of these have tested conclusions drawn in small-sample case studies. More such studies will greatly increase our confidence in generalizations about virtual teams.

A second useful development would be a better balance between laboratory and field studies. The majority of studies in our review are studies of virtual teams in the field. There are considerably fewer lab studies, although several of these have had a good deal of influence on other research, both lab and field based. Although studies of virtual teams in the field are valuable because of their realism and contextualization, it is difficult to draw strong conclusions from them without complementary backing from lab studies. Much of what we know with confidence about traditional teams comes from the combination of lab studies—which show what, in principle, holds—and field studies that echo these findings in realistic contexts. The lack of lab studies is certainly due in part to the logistical difficulties involved in creating virtual teams, but several studies in this review, such as the work by Jarvenpaa, Leidner, and their colleagues, offer excellent models.

Our knowledge of some phenomena, including the impacts of group structure communication in virtual teams, communication media effects, social cognition, relationship dynamics, trust, process structures, and leadership, is fairly extensive and seems to be growing apace. Some other phenomena, such as the impact of tasks, reward structures, and conflict, seem to be gaining increasing attention from researchers and practitioners. However, there are gaps in our knowledge: Aspects of virtual teams such as power, media switching and combination, the effect of external linkages, and group development have received much less attention. Furthermore, our knowledge in almost all these areas is limited by the fact that most research is focused on business and educational teams, and other possible types of teams are for the most part unexamined.

We also know less about the phenomenological experience of virtuality than would be desirable. Authors have commented in passing on the fact that the passage of time seems different in virtual teams than in face-to-face interaction (e.g., Knoll & Jarvenpaa, 1998). An intriguing analysis by Saunders, Van Slyke, and Vogel (2004) suggests that members of virtual teams may have very different perceptions of time and that this can complicate the work of multicultural and international virtual teams. Shockley-Zalabak (2002) advances the metaphor of *protean places* in an attempt to capture some of the ways in which virtual work may change time-space perceptions of virtual teams.

It seems likely that virtual teams will continue to become ever more common. As they do, increasing attention is likely to be paid to networks of teams and the meta-teams studied by Fernandez (2004) and Ngwenyama (1998). It also seems likely that more complex ICTs, such as collaboration technologies, enhanced video, three-dimensional animation via avatars, and even tele-immersive environments, will demand the attention of researchers and practitioners alike. These richer technologies may well make virtual work "the next best thing to being there."

Finally, it is important to note that in a few years, much of what is summarized in this review may be interesting but quaint history. It takes people time to become used to media contexts, and the virtual team is no exception. Once people become accustomed to working in virtual contexts—as they rapidly are—many of the findings reported above will cease to be relevant because they are based on the fact that the virtual team context is unusual and somewhat foreign to most. When the telephone was first introduced, people used it awkwardly. Today, it is an extension of interpersonal communication for most people in the developed and developing worlds—literally "the next best thing to being there." It is likely that as people get used to working via e-mail, conferencing, video connections, and even tele-immersive media, they will work out natural, widely shared routines for these media. This will transform the virtual team from an unusual to an everyday context, and working in virtual teams will no longer pose a special challenge but will be a taken-for-granted skill. In such a world, much of what we have so far written will no longer apply.

References

Abrams, D., Hogg, M., Hinkle, S., & Otten, S. (2004). The social identity perspective on groups. In M. S. Poole & A. Hollingshead (Eds.), *Theories of small groups: Interdisciplinary perspectives* (pp. 99–138). Thousand Oaks, CA: Sage.

Ahuja, M. K., & Galvin, J. E. (2001). Socialization in virtual groups. *Journal of Management, 29,* 1–25.

Armstrong, D. J., & Cole, P. (1995). Managing distances and differences in geographically distributed work groups. In S. E. Jackson & M. N. Ruderman (Eds.), *Diversity in work teams* (pp. 187–215). Washington, DC: American Psychological Association.

Aubert, B. A., & Kelsey, B. L. (2003). Further understanding of trust and performance in virtual teams. *Small Group Research, 34,* 574–618.

Bell, B. S., & Kozlowski, S. W. J. (2002). A typology of virtual teams: Implications for effective leadership. *Group & Organization Management, 27,* 14–50.

Bhappu, A. D., Griffith, T. L., & Northcraft, G. B. (1997). Media effects and communication bias in diverse groups. *Organizational Behavior and Human Decision in Processes, 70,* 199–205.

Bhappu, A. D., Zellmer-Bruhn, M., & Anand, V. (2001). The effects of demographic diversity and virtual work environments on knowledge processing in teams. In M. M. Beyerlein, D. A. Johnson, & S. T. Beyerlein (Eds.), *Advances in interdisciplinary studies of work teams: Virtual teams* (Vol. 8, pp. 149–165). Amsterdam: Elsevier.

Blackburn, R., Furst, S., & Rosen, B. (2003). Building a winning virtual team: KSAs, selection, training, and evaluation. In C. B. Gibson & S. G. Cohen (Eds.), *Virtual teams that work* (pp. 95–120). San Francisco: Jossey-Bass.

Cascio, W., & Shurygailo, S. (2003). E-Leadership and virtual teams. *Organizational Dynamics, 31,* 362–376.

Connaughton, S. L., & Daly, J. A. (2004). Long distance leadership: Communicative strategies for leading virtual teams. In D. J. Pauleen (Ed.), *Virtual teams: Projects, protocols, and processes* (pp. 116–144). Hershey, PA: Idea Group.

Cramton, C. (2001). The mutual knowledge problem and its consequences for dispersed collaboration. *Organization Science, 12,* 346–371.

Cramton, C. (2002). Attribution in distributed work groups. In P. J. Hinds & S. Kiesler (Eds.), *Distributed work* (pp. 191–212). Cambridge: MIT Press.

DeSanctis, G., & Monge, P. (1999). Communication processes for virtual organizations. *Organization Science, 10,* 693–703.

Duarte, D. L., & Snyder, N. T. (1999). *Mastering virtual teams.* San Francisco: Jossey-Bass.

Dube, L., & Pare, G. (2004). The multifaceted nature of virtual teams. In D. J. Pauleen (Ed.), *Virtual teams: Projects, protocols, and processes* (pp. 1–39). Hershey, PA: Idea Group.

Dubs, S., & Hayne, S. C. (1992). Distributed facilitation: A concept whose time has come? In *Computer Supported Cooperative Work 92 Proceedings* (pp. 314–321). New York: ACM Press.

Dufner, D., Hiltz, S. R., & Turoff, M. (1994). Distributed group support: A preliminary analysis of the effects of the use of voting tools and sequential procedures. In R. Sprague (Ed.), *Proceedings of the Hawaii International Conference on System Sciences.* New York: ACM Press.

Fernandez, W. D. (2004). Trust and the trust placement process in metateam projects. In D. J. Pauleen (Ed.), *Virtual teams: Projects, protocols, and processes* (pp. 40–69). Hershey, PA: Idea Group.

Furst, S. A., Reeves, M., Rosen, B., & Blackburn, R. S. (2004). Managing the life cycle of virtual teams. *Academy of Management Executive, 18,* 6–20.

Gallivan, M. J. (2001). Striking a balance between trust and control in a virtual organization: A content analysis of open source software case studies. *Information Systems Journal, 11,* 277–304.

Gibson, C. B., & Cohen, S. G. (Eds.). (2003). *Virtual teams that work: Creating conditions for virtual team effectiveness.* San Francisco: Jossey-Bass.

Gibson, C. B., & Manuel, J. A. (2003). Building trust: Effective multicultural communication processes in virtual teams. In C. B. Gibson & S. G. Cohen (Eds.), *Virtual teams that work: Creating conditions for virtual team effectiveness* (pp. 59–86). San Francisco: Jossey-Bass.

Gluesing, J. C., Alcordo, T. C., Baba, M. J., Britt, D., Wagner, K. H., McKether, W., Monplaisir, L., Ratner, H. H., & Riopelle, K. (2003). The development of global virtual teams. In C. B. Gibson & S. G. Cohen (Eds.), *Virtual teams that work:*

Creating conditions for virtual team effectiveness (pp. 59–86). San Francisco: Jossey-Bass.

Griffith, T. L., Mannix, E. A., & Neale, M. A. (2003). Conflict and virtual teams. In C. B. Gibson & S. G. Cohen (Eds.), *Virtual teams that work: Creating conditions for virtual team effectiveness* (pp. 335–352). San Francisco: Jossey-Bass.

Hart, R. K., & McLeod, P. L. (2003). Rethinking team building in geographically dispersed teams: One message at a time. *Organizational Dynamics, 3,* 352–361.

Hinds, P. J., & Bailey, D. E. (2003). Out of sight, out of synch: Understanding conflict in distributed teams. *Organization Science, 14,* 615–632.

Hinds, P. J., & Mortensen, M. (2004, August). *Understanding conflict in geographically distributed teams: An empirical investigation.* Presented at the Academy of Management Conference, New Orleans, LA.

Hinds, P. J., & Weisband, S. P. (2003). Knowledge sharing and shared understanding in virtual teams. In C. B. Gibson & S. G. Cohen (Eds.), *Virtual teams that work: Creating conditions for virtual team effectiveness* (pp. 21–36). San Francisco: Jossey-Bass.

Hornett, A. (2004). The impact of external factors on virtual teams: Comparative cases. In D. J. Pauleen (Ed.), *Virtual teams: Projects, protocols, and processes* (pp. 70–90). Hershey, PA: Idea Group.

Hymowitz, C. (1999, April 6). Remote managers find ways to narrow the distance gap. *Wall Street Journal,* p. B1.

Jarvenpaa, S. L., Knoll, K., & Leidner, D. (1998). Is anybody out there? Antecedents of trust in global virtual teams. *Journal of Management Information Systems, 14,* 29–64.

Jarvenpaa, S. L., & Leidner, D. E. (1999). Communication and trust in global virtual teams. *Organization Science, 10,* 791–815.

Jarvenpaa, S. L., & Shaw, M. (in press). Toward contextualized theories of trust: The role of trust in global virtual teams. *Information Systems Research.*

Katzenbach, J. R., & Smith, D. K. (1993, March/April). The discipline of teams. *Harvard Business Review,* pp. 111–120.

Kayworth, T. R., & Leidner, D. E. (2000). The global virtual manager. *European Management Journal, 18*(2), 183–194.

Kayworth, T. R., & Leidner, D. E. (2001/2002). Leadership effectiveness in global virtual teams.

Journal of Management Information Systems, 18, 7–40.

Kirkman, B. L., Rosen, B., Gibson, C. B., Tesluk, P. E., & McPherson, S. O. (2002). Five challenges to virtual team success: Lessons from Sabre, Inc. *Academy of Management Executive, 16,* 67–79.

Kirkman, B. L., Rosen, B., Tesluk, P. E., & Gibson, C. B. (2004). The impact of team empowerment on virtual team performance: The moderating role of face-to-face interaction. *Academy of Management Journal, 47,* 175–192.

Knoll, K., & Jarvenpaa, S. L. (1998). Working together in global virtual teams. In M. Igbaria & M. Tan (Eds.), *The virtual workplace* (pp. 2–23). Hershey, PA: Idea Group.

Lawler, E. E. (2003). Pay systems for virtual teams. In C. B. Gibson & S. G. Cohen (Eds.), *Virtual teams that work: Creating conditions for virtual team effectiveness* (pp. 121–144). San Francisco: Jossey-Bass.

Lea, M., & Spears, R. (1991). Computer-mediated communication, de-individuation, and group decision-making. *International Journal of Man-Machine Studies, 34,* 283–301.

Leonard, D. A., Brand, P. A., Edmondson, A., & Fenwick, J. (1998). Virtual teams: Using communications technology to manage geographically dispersed development groups. In S. P. Bradley & R. L. Nolan (Eds.), *Sense & respond: Capturing value in the network era* (pp. 285–298). Boston: Harvard Business School Press.

Lipnack, J., & Stamps, J. (1997). *Virtual teams: Reaching across space, time, and organizations with technology.* New York: John Wiley.

Majchrzak, A., Rice, R. E., Malhotra, A., King, N., & Ba, S. (2000). Technology adaptation: The case of a computer-supported inter-organizational virtual team. *MIS Quarterly, 24,* 569–600.

Malhotra, A., Majchrzak, A., Carman, R., & Lott, V. (2001). Radical innovation without collocation: A case study at Boeing-Rocketdyne. *MIS Quarterly, 25,* 229–248.

Mansour-Cole, D. (2001). Team identity formation in virtual teams. In M. M. Beyerlein, D. A. Johnson, & S. T. Beyerlein (Eds.), *Advances in interdisciplinary studies of work teams* (Vol. 8, pp. 41–58). Amsterdam: Elsevier.

Massey, A. P., Montoya-Weiss, M. M., & Hung, Y. (2003). Because time matters: Temporal coordination in global virtual project teams. *Journal of Management Information Systems, 19,* 129–155.

Maznevski, M. L., & Chudoba, K. M. (2000). Bridging space over time: Global virtual team dynamics and effectiveness. *Organization Science, 11,* 473–492.

McDonald, T. (1999). A whole new ball game. *Successful Meetings, 48,* 19.

McGrath, J. E. (1984). *Groups: Interaction and performance.* Upper Saddle River, NJ: Prentice Hall.

Montoya-Weiss, M. M., Massey, A. P., & Song, M. (2001). Getting it together: Temporal coordination and conflict management in global virtual teams. *Academy of Management Journal, 44,* 1251–1262.

Moreland, R. L. (1985). Social categorizations and the assimilation of "new" group members. *Journal of Personality and Social Psychology, 48,* 1173–1190.

Murphy, P. (2004). Trust, rationality, and the virtual team. In D. J. Pauleen (Ed.), *Virtual teams: Projects, protocols, and processes* (pp. 317–343). Hershey, PA: Idea Group.

Ngwenyama, O. K. (1998). Groupware, social action, and organizational emergence: On the process dynamics of computer mediated distributed work. *Accounting, Management, and Information Technologies, 8,* 127–146.

O'Hara-Devereaux, M., & Johansen, R. (1994). *GlobalWork: Bridging distance, cultural, and time.* San Francisco: Jossey-Bass.

Owens, D. A., Neale, M. A., & Sutton, R. I. (2000). Technologies of status management: Status dynamics in e-mail communications. In T. L. Griffith (Ed.), *Research on managing groups and teams: Technology* (Vol. 3, pp. 205–230). Stamford, CT: JAI Press.

Panteli, N. (2004). Discursive articulation of presence in virtual organizing. *Information and Organization, 14,* 59–81.

Paul, S., Seetharaman, P., Samarah, I., & Mykytyn, P. P. (2004). Impact of heterogeneity and collaborative conflict management style on the performance of synchronous global virtual teams. *Information & Management, 41,* 303–321.

Pauleen, D. J. (2003a). An inductively derived model of leader-initiated relationship building with virtual team members. *Journal of Management Information Systems, 20,* 227–256.

Pauleen, D. J. (2003b). Leadership in a global virtual team: An action learning approach. *Leadership & Organization Development, 24,* 153–162.

Pierson, J. K., & Jaeger, D. (1995). *Communication in the multinational team: Coordinating culture and distance through information technology.* Poster session presented at the annual meeting of the Speech Communication Association, San Antonio, TX.

Poole, M. S., Brown, H. G., Forducey, P., Deng, L., Moorad, A., & Smeltzer, S. (2004). Trust, trait theory, and collaboration in telemedicine: An empirical test. In R. Sprague (Ed.), *Proceedings of the Hawaii International Conference on System Science* [CD-ROM]. New York: ACM Press.

Postmes, T., Spears, R., Sakhl, K., & de Groot, D. (2001). Social influence in computer mediated communication: The effects of anonymity on group behavior. *Personality and Social Psychology Bulletin, 27,* 1243–1254.

Pratt, M. G., Fuller, M. A., & Northcraft, G. B. (2000). Media selection and identification in distributed groups: The potential costs of "rich" media. In T. L. Griffith (Ed.), *Research on managing groups and teams: Technology* (Vol. 3, pp. 205–230). Stamford, CT: JAI Press.

Rice, R. E., & Gattiker, U. E. (2001). New media and organizational structuring. In F. M. Jablin & L. L. Putnam (Eds.), *The new handbook of organizational communication* (pp. 544–581). Thousand Oaks, CA: Sage.

Riopelle, K., Gluesing, J. C., Alcordo, T. C., Baba, M. L., Britt, D., McKether, W., Monplaisir, L., Ratner, H. H., & Wagner, K. H. (2003). Context, task, and the evolution of technology use in global virtual teams. In C. B. Gibson & S. G. Cohen (Eds.), *Virtual teams that work: Creating conditions for virtual team effectiveness* (pp. 239–264). San Francisco: Jossey-Bass.

Robey, D., & Jin, L. (2004). Studying virtual work in teams, organizations, and communities. In M. E. Whitman & A. B. Woszczynski (Eds.), *The handbook of information systems research* (pp. 150–163). Hershey, PA: Idea Group.

Saunders, C., Van Slyke, C., & Vogel, D. R. (2004). My time or yours? Managing time visions in global virtual teams. *Academy of Management Executive, 18,* 19–31.

Shockley-Zalabak, P. (2002). Protean places: Teams across time and space. *Journal of Applied Communication Research, 30,* 231–250.

Staples, D. S., Wong, I. K., & Cameron, A. F. (2004). Best practices for virtual team effectiveness. In D. J. Pauleen (Ed.), *Virtual teams: Projects, protocols, and processes* (pp. 160–185). Hershey, PA: Idea Group.

Steinfield, C., Jang, C. Y., & Pfaff, B. (1999). Supporting virtual team collaboration: The TeamSCOPE system. In S. Hayne (Ed.), *Group '99: Proceedings of the international ACM SIGGROUP conference on supporting group work* (pp. 81–90). New York: ACM Press.

Walther, J. B. (1995). Relational aspects of computer-mediated communication: Experimental observations over time. *Organization Science, 6,* 186–203.

Walther, J. B. (1996). Group and interpersonal effects in international computer mediated collaboration. *Human Communication Research, 23,* 342–369.

Walther, J. B., & Burgoon, J. K. (1992). Relational communication in computer-mediated interaction. *Human Communication Research, 18,* 50–88.

Weisband, S. P., Schneider, S. K., & Connolly, T. (1995). Computer mediated communication and social information: Status salience and status awareness. *Academy of Management Journal, 38,* 1124–1151.

Windsor, D. (2001). International virtual teams: Opportunities and issues. In M. M. Beyerlein, D. A. Johnson, & S. T. Beyerlein (Eds.), *Advances in interdisciplinary studies of work teams: Virtual teams* (Vol. 8, pp. 1–30). Amsterdam: Elsevier.

Yoo, Y., & Alavi, M. (2004). Emergent leadership in virtual teams: What do emergent leaders do? *Information and Organization, 14,* 27–58.

Zand, D. (1972). Trust and managerial problem solving. *Administrative Science Quarterly, 17,* 229–239.

Zigurs, I. (2003). Leadership in virtual teams: Oxymoron or opportunity? *Organizational Dynamics, 31*(4), 339–351.

Zolin, R., Hinds, P. J., Fruchter, R., & Levitt, R. E. (2004). Interpersonal trust in cross-functional, geographically distributed work: A longitudinal study. *Information and Organization, 14,* 1–26.

PART V

Group Practice: Methods and Outcomes

21

Group Psychotherapy

Gary M. Burlingame

Suad Kapetanovic

Steven Ross

A consensually accepted definition of group psychotherapy is simply not available in the extant literature. This lack of uniformity is readily understandable when one considers the striking differences that result when one varies a few basic group characteristics. We consider three dimensions that may assist in explaining conceptual and clinical differences found between contemporary psychotherapy groups. The first dimension is *the formal change theory* that guides treatment. We define formal change theory to include the principal change mechanisms being used by the group leader. This includes not only the formal theoretical orientation of the therapist (e.g., psychodynamic or behavioral) but also change mechanisms and goals (e.g., psycho-education or support). To illustrate, let's follow the case of Mary, a 25-year-old accountant who has been recently diagnosed

with major depressive disorder (MDD) and subsequently experienced a variety of groups to treat the same set of symptoms.

Mary was initially admitted to an acute inpatient psychiatric unit following a suicide attempt. The goal of her inpatient *supportive* group treatment was not to "cure" her depression but to let her meet with patients suffering from similar problems in a supportive, unstructured interactive environment. Prior to discharge, Mary was placed in a *psycho-educational* (PE) group that focused on the goal of gaining empowering knowledge about the etiology of major depressive disorder, different treatment options, medication side effects, treatment resources in her community, and basic suicide-prevention strategies that would enable her to continue her treatment in a less restrictive environment. After stabilization, Mary was discharged, and her case manager enrolled her in a time-limited outpatient *cognitive-behavioral therapy* (CBT) group for treatment of major depressive disorder. Here, she worked on the more ambitious goal of cognitive restructuring and behavioral change over 12 weeks. Finally, as Mary became more in control of her symptoms, her case manager suggested an open-ended, *process-oriented interpersonal* group with a heterogeneous membership. The goal of this group was increased self-awareness and personal growth, a process that typically assumes a corrective emotional experience that can take years. Clearly, Mary's goal of treating her depression took on very different forms depending on the formal change theory guiding the groups that she attended. Interestingly, Mary reported benefit from each group experience.

A second dimension that determines the form and substance of a group is who attends. Prior to the 1970s, most psychotherapy groups were composed of patients with heterogeneous psychiatric disorders (Fuhriman & Burlingame, 1994). However, when certain treatment models were found to be particularly effective for specific psychiatric disorders (e.g., exposure and response prevention for obsessive compulsive disorder; cf. Burlingame, MacKenzie, & Strauss, in press), the emergence and study of homogeneous groups composed of particular patient populations increased exponentially. This development adds a second layer of complexity in defining group psychotherapy—disorder-specific group protocols—and also introduces our second dimension for classifying group treatments—*patient/member population*.

Finally, we have described a host of *structural features* that can affect the form and substance of group treatments (Burlingame, MacKenzie, & Strauss, 2004, in press). For instance, factors that have substantive influence on group functioning include setting (e.g., outpatient vs. inpatient); duration, frequency, and number of group sessions (e.g., daily, weekly, 90-minute sessions, 2-hour sessions, etc.), the degree to which the

group is open to new members (open, slow-open, closed), leadership (co- vs. single) and leader training (cf. Burlingame et al., 2002), size, the degree to which membership is voluntary or mandatory, and prior or concurrent treatment. The interested reader is directed to Burlingame et al. (in press) for a more complete treatment of how these factors affect group treatment.

The intersection of formal change theory, patient population, and structural features is depicted in Figure 21.1, which graphically reflects the fact that group psychotherapy has evolved into a multifaceted field of practice. This historic reality explains the diversity of definitions that are reflected in both the research and practice of group psychotherapy. Today, not only can we use the group medium to provide a therapeutic experience for a specific patient population with reliance on a specific formal change theory, but also we can meet additional needs such as psycho-education or support. The possible permutations of dimensions and cells found in Figure 21.1 lead to a nearly endless number of group experiences. However, we believe that the reader of the group literature will better disentangle the myriad of potential group goals by paying attention to its formal theory of change, patient population, and structural factors.

The model depicted in Figure 21.1 is offered as one way to classify the plethora of groups found in today's practice. In this chapter, we use the first dimension—formal change theories—to introduce and briefly describe the key group models. However, its inclusive nature creates a serious obstacle when one attempts to summarize research findings on small group treatments. As noted above, the diversity of available group treatments challenges efforts at developing meaningful interpretive conclusions. Thus, we've adopted a more restricted definition of group psychotherapy to guide our review of the empirical literature. Specifically, we defined group psychotherapy as "the treatment of emotional or psychological disorders or problems of

Structural Features

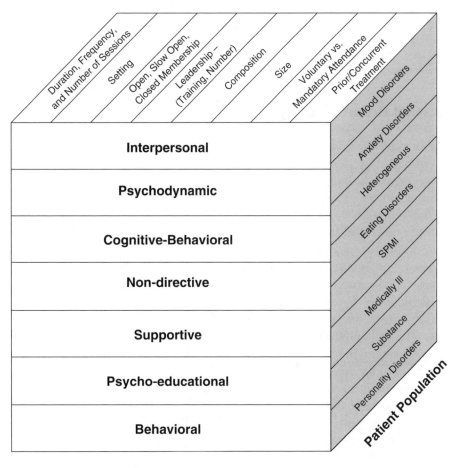

Interpersonal

Psychodynamic

Cognitive-Behavioral

Non-directive

Supportive

Psycho-educational

Behavioral

Formal Theory of Change

Figure 21.1   Classifying Small Group Treatments in a Multidimensional Space

adjustment through the medium of a group setting, the focal point being the interpersonal (social), intrapersonal (psychological), or behavioral change of the participating clients or group members" (Fuhriman & Burlingame, 2000, p. 31). For the purposes of this chapter, we will use this definition to review the research evidence that is organized by the second dimension of the cube—patient population. Finally, we conclude the chapter with thoughts regarding future research.

The Most Commonly Used Group Methods

A common practice is to classify methods of group psychotherapy from the standpoint of theoretical orientation (e.g., Alonso, 2000; Brabender, 2002). In this section, we briefly describe six approaches reflecting historical and contemporary clinical practice. Although some models have undergone significant modifications to address the needs of specific patient populations and treatment settings, we will introduce the traditional or "pure" forms of these models. Our description relies heavily on Brabender's (2002) text, and the interested reader is advised to review this material for more complete coverage.

Interpersonal Group Therapy

Also known as process-oriented therapy, this model was pioneered by Harry Stack Sullivan and was popularized by Irvin Yalom's (1970/ 1995) classic book, *The Theory and Practice of Group Psychotherapy*. Originally designed for long-term, open-ended outpatient groups with diagnostically heterogeneous membership, interpersonal group therapy has also been applied to time-limited groups, as well as in inpatient and diagnostically homogeneous groups (Brabender, 2002). The interpersonal model is based on the belief that a person's psychopathology is inevitably reflected in his or her interpersonal relationships. Therefore, an emphasis is given to interpersonal interactions that occur in the "here and now" of the group. Immediate events in the session take precedence over events both in the current outside life and in the distant past of the members (Yalom, 1970/1995). Moreover, the group process or here-and-now member interaction is seen as the primary vehicle of change (Fuhriman & Burlingame, 1990). For instance, Yalom argues that a process focus is not just one of many possible procedural orientations, but rather an indispensable and a common denominator to all effective interactional groups, "the power cell of the group" (p. 137). Thus, by emphasizing and exploring interpersonal interactions, therapists facilitate feedback, catharsis, meaningful self-disclosure, and acquisition of socializing techniques.

Psychodynamic Group Therapy

Various psychodynamic theories of change have found their applications in group psychotherapy

(e.g., classical analytic, object-relations, ego psychology, self psychology, etc.; Alonso, 2000). Rutan and Stone (2001) provide a step-by-step tutorial in conducting these types of groups. Brabender (2002) contends that the object-relations approach has provided particularly important contributions, with its goal to create "healthy intrapsychic change and help the individual mature internally" (p. 355; also see Ganzarain, 1989; Klein, Bernhard, & Singer, 1992). A basic assumption is that group members project their infantile representations at different levels of the group: group-as-a-whole, other members, subgroups, or the therapist, and so on. Over time, the safe, "holding environment" of the group enables members to integrate more realistic and functional representations. Therapists facilitate this goal by combining empathic statements, which help patients reflect on their negative emotional experiences, with insight-oriented dynamic interpretations, which help patients integrate these negative experiences (Brabender, 2002).

Like interpersonal groups, psychodynamic groups were originally designed for a long-term time frame. However, William Piper and his team have been instrumental in developing and empirically testing brief applications for outpatient, day treatment, and inpatient settings (e.g., Piper, Joyce, McCallum, Azim, & Ogrodniczuk, 2002; Piper, McCallum, & Azim, 1992; Piper, Rosie, Joyce, & Azim, 1996).

Nondirective Group Therapy

The nondirective approach originates from Carl Rogers's approach to individual therapy, also known as the client-centered or Rogerian approach.[1] It is based on the belief that every person has an innate tendency to grow (i.e., a self-actualizing tendency; e.g., Rogers, 1951), once the obstacles to growth are removed. Applied to psychotherapy, this means that personal growth will occur once clients are able to let their defenses go. According to Rogers, this is more likely to occur in a nonthreatening, nonjudgmental therapeutic climate. Ensuring such a growth-promoting therapeutic climate is the main goal of nondirective therapy, while the alteration of specific behaviors or symptoms is considered to be a by-product of this climate. The nondirective group leader works on achieving this goal by consistently conveying genuineness, empathy, unconditional positive regard toward the members, and a minimum of direction. Group members determine the content and set the pace of the therapy according to their own level of comfort. As a result of free member-to-member and member-to-leader interactions and feedback, they begin to change their perceptions and move in the direction of increased self-understanding and genuineness (e.g., Patterson, 1974).

Historically, nondirective groups have presented with a wide range of structural features (e.g., from large intensive weekend encounter groups to weekly open-ended small groups; from inpatient settings to private homes, and so on), with both heterogeneous and homogeneous membership structure.

Cognitive Behavioral Therapy (CBT) Groups

Originally designed for individual psychotherapy, the CBT model has been successfully adapted for group psychotherapy and has become highly prevalent in both group clinical practice and group research (Barlow, Burlingame, & Fuhriman, 2000). CBT groups are typically structured, often manualized, short-term, problem focused (e.g., depression, eating disorders, etc.), and therefore diagnostically homogeneous; symptom relief and skill acquisition are the main goals. Group members work on meeting these goals by learning how to recognize their cognitive distortions and restructuring their dysfunctional cognitive schemas through a variety of structured exercises, including role playing, homework assignments, bibliotherapy, and the like. The unique

properties of the group (i.e., group processes) often are marginally used in these groups (Burlingame et al., 2004), although empirical evidence suggests that these properties might make CBT groups more effective (Fuhriman & Burlingame, 1994).

Support Groups

These groups gather members who struggle with a common problem such as breast cancer or divorce. They are based on the assumption that "emphasizing common struggles is effective therapy for many people" (Vinogradov & Yalom, 1989, p. 147). They may be without a formal leader (i.e., lay self-help groups) or professionally led (Burlingame & Davies, 2002), and improvement in both types of groups is often equivalent (Barlow, Burlingame, Nebeker, & Anderson, 2000). Members join these groups to feel less isolated and to learn coping skills. Therapists facilitate therapeutic factors of cohesion and universality, actively encouraging group members not only to support each other and give advice but also to confront each other about their maladaptive ways of coping with the problem in question. There seems to be an inherent therapeutic power in this type of feedback when it comes from one group member to another, as opposed to feedback that comes from the group leader, who is viewed as an outsider who cannot fully understand the problem because she or he has not experienced it (Vinogradov & Yalom, 1989).

Behavioral Groups

The behavioral therapy model focuses on modifying observable, measurable behaviors associated with a disorder (Gelder, 1997). Initially applied in individual therapy, the behavioral model began to rely on the group format in the 1970s as a cost-effective or time-limited treatment (Burlingame et al., 2004;

Sundel & Sundel, 1985). The group medium provides behavioral therapists with an opportunity to address problems within a testable conceptual framework. The social learning that occurs in groups has a crucial role in modifying maladaptive responses by the use of modeling and reinforcement of approximations to new behaviors.

Different behavioral techniques (e.g., exposure and response prevention, problem solving, assertiveness training, and so on) are differentially applied to specific clinical indications (e.g., agoraphobia, obsessive-compulsive disorder, children, Type A behavioral pattern, elderly; cf. Gelder, 1997; Upper & Ross, 1985) using time-limited models, although long-term approaches also have been proposed (Belfer & Levendusky, 1985).

Psycho-education (PE) Model

The PE model focuses on providing information about an illness or problem and teaching coping strategies (Burlingame & Ridge, in press). Typical PE groups are diagnostically homogeneous (e.g., schizophrenia, multiple sclerosis, etc.), time-limited groups with very structured classroom-type agendas (e.g., 12 lectures delivered in 12 weekly sessions). They take place in a variety of settings, including inpatient psychiatric units, day treatment programs, and medical specialty clinics. In traditional mental health settings, these groups often are led by psychiatric nurses, social workers, and counselors. PE group models for families or partners of mentally ill individuals also are in use (e.g., Dyck, Hendryx, Short, Voss, & McFarlane, 2002). The goal of PE groups is to increase members' knowledge about the etiology of their illness, treatment options, available resources in their community, and ways that certain behaviors (e.g., medication adherence) can affect the course of their illness. These groups also help decrease the stigma attached to mental illness. PE groups are typically used to enhance a primary treatment component (e.g., psychotropic medication in treatment of schizophrenia,

hemodialysis in end-stage renal disease, etc.). The group literature indicates that PE is most effective when it responds to client-specific concerns (e.g., Payson, Wheeler, & Wellington, 1998).

Evidence for Effectiveness

The current health care climate of accountability necessitates clinicians' ability to identify effective treatments for patients suffering from specific disorders (Burlingame, Lambert, Reisinger, Neff, & Mosier, 1995). Consequently, the past few decades of empirical group research have predominantly focused on the effectiveness of group protocols that target specific patient diagnoses or problems. In this section, we will evaluate this evidence, relying heavily on recent reviews and meta-analyses rather than focusing on individual studies. More specifically, we focus on mood, eating, anxiety, substance-related, and personality disorders as well as a few special populations. For a more complete summary, the reader is invited to consult the original sources (e.g., Burlingame, Fuhriman, & Mosier, 2003; Burlingame et al., 2004, in press).

Groups for Mood Disorders

Depressive disorders. Burlingame et al.'s (2003) meta-analysis of 111 group psychotherapy studies concluded that patients suffering from depressive disorders posted higher levels of improvement than patients from several other diagnostic groupings (e.g., stress, medical, and adjustment disorders). In a related review, Burlingame et al. (2004) reported no differential effectiveness in the rate of improvement among depressed patients when CBT, process-oriented, and supportive group models were compared (although the support for CBT came from the most rigorous studies). The typical group is time limited (6 to 15 sessions) with a 90-minute average duration per session. Furthermore, group and individual treatment have been found to be equivalent, supporting the more cost-effective group modality (McRoberts, Burlingame, & Hoag, 1998).

On the other hand, four studies have found outcomes from self-help and nonprofessional groups (i.e., groups led by untrained college professors) to be equivalent to patient gains guided by formal change theories (CBT, existential, gestalt, and process-oriented; Burlingame et al., 2003). This finding raises an alternative explanation: that nonspecific therapeutic factors, inherent to groups and independent of theory of change, may account for patient improvement in these groups. If supported by future research, this finding suggests that therapists' awareness and facilitation of such factors might, in turn, increase the effectiveness of existing group models for depressive disorders.

Bipolar affective disorder (BAD). Three recent reviews of psychosocial interventions in treatment of BAD (Huxley, Parikh, & Baldessarini, 2000; Rothbaum & Astin, 2000; Swartz & Frank, 2001) indicate that group psychotherapy may be a useful adjunct to pharmacotherapy, particularly during the depressive and euthymic phase (Swartz & Frank, 2001). Still, this body of evidence is small and of questionable validity (Huxley et al., 2000; Rothbaum & Astin, 2000; Swartz & Frank, 2001).

Two reviews (Huxley et al., 2000; Swartz & Frank, 2001) describe a variety of PE group protocols for patients with BAD. The typical protocol is an outpatient, time-limited group that meets weekly or monthly, with treatment duration ranging anywhere from one taped lecture to 132 sessions. Pre- to posttreatment improvements have been reported in patients' general knowledge of their disease and treatment, decreased need for rehospitalizations, and self-reported sense of well-being. In addition, Huxley et al. (2000) reviewed three controlled trials and noted subjective improvements and increased patients' knowledge that were not reflected in objective clinical outcomes (Huxley et al., 2000; Swartz & Frank, 2001).

These reviews were followed by the first randomized blinded clinical trial that compared the efficacy of group PE and standard psychiatric treatment with a standard psychiatric treatment-only condition and a non-PE group condition. All subjects underwent prospective follow-up for at least 2 years prior to the study and were euthymic for at least 6 months prior to entering the study. The treatment consisted of 21 group sessions of 90 minutes each, with 8 to 12 patients per group. Each session aimed at improving four main areas: illness awareness, treatment compliance, early detection of prodromal symptoms and recurrences, and lifestyle regularity. The principal finding was that PE groups were efficacious in preventing recurrences and reducing days of hospitalization (Colom et al., 2003).

This finding is important because most group protocols have a significant PE component. For instance, CBT, interpersonal, psychodynamic, and supportive group treatments have been shown to increase a patient's ability to keep a full-time job, to decrease the rate and duration of hospitalizations, and to improve medication adherence and academic performance as well as socioeconomic functioning (Swartz & Frank, 2001).

Pathological grief. Two manualized, time-limited (12 sessions) therapeutic models dominate the research and treatment of pathological grief: an *interpretive* group model with psychodynamic focus and a *supportive* group model that focuses on adaptation to the patient's current life (Piper et al., 2002). Extensive and well-replicated evidence indicates that these two models are equally effective in a number of patient outcome areas, with similar attrition rates (Ogrodniczuk & Piper, 2003). Furthermore, research from the Vancouver/Edmonton team also has tested patient- and group process-related variables that may improve a therapist's ability to optimize treatment outcomes and predict early dropouts in these groups (Burlingame et al., 2004). For instance, patients with lower Quality of Object

Relations (QOR, an interview-based assessment of a person's relational functioning; Azim, Piper, Segal, Nixon, & Duncan, 1991) appear to be at a higher risk for early dropout in the interpretive model. Furthermore, high QOR scores predicted better outcome in the interpretive model and poorer outcome in the supportive model, while low QOR scores predicted better outcome in supportive treatment and poorer outcome in interpretive treatment (Piper et al., 1992).

Groups for Eating Disorders

Group treatment has played an integral role in the treatment of patients with eating disorders (Harper-Guiffre & MacKenzie, 1992). For instance, a recent meta-analysis (Burlingame et al., 2003) reports the magnitude of pre- to posttreatment improvement in this patient population as second only to that found in group treatment of depressive disorders. CBT is the dominant change theory in the recent empirical literature, although it is important to note that findings vary across different types of populations (Burlingame et al., in press).

Bulimia nervosa. Burlingame and colleagues (2003) note seven empirical and two meta-analytic studies that strongly support the efficacy of group CBT in treatment of bulimia nervosa. In general, greater improvements resulted when group was combined with other treatments (e.g., individual, pharmacotherapy). The typical group lasts from 9 to 15 sessions, and some evidence suggests a different effect for intensity and timing of interventions. Namely, more hours of therapy and early interruption of disordered eating behaviors, an approach that is rarely used in outpatient CBT protocols (Mitchell et al., 1993), may result in greater patient improvement.

While CBT protocols dominate recent empirical inquiries, there is little evidence to support their superiority over other formal change theories (Rosenvinge, 1990). In fact, two empirical studies have found CBT and interpersonal groups to be equivalent on measures of bingeing and emotional eating (cf. Burlingame et al., 2004). Also, a recent randomized trial (Chen et al., 2003) suggests equivalent efficacy between group and individual CBT treatment for bulimia. Finally, the contribution of group processes to the treatment success of (CBT) groups in the treatment of bulimia is an understudied topic.

Binge-eating disorder. Pendleton, Goodrick, Carlos Poston, Reeves, and Foreyt (2002) report promising results for CBT in treatment of binge eating. They report posttreatment abstinence rates of 50%, which are maintained at 6- to 12-month follow-up. They also report an augmentation effect for weight loss when exercise is coupled with CBT group treatment. The latter finding is important, because binge-eating disorder predominantly occurs in obese individuals (Spitzer et al., 1993, as cited by Pendleton et al., 2002).

The role of group processes in CBT group treatment for binge eating also is understudied (Burlingame et al., 2003). An exception is a study by Castonguay, Pincus, Agras, and Hines (1998), which found that early positive affect in the individual-level working atmosphere, early cohesion at a group level, and elevations in mid-session conflict scores predicted better outcome in binge-eating disorder groups.

Obesity. Empirical evaluations of group treatments for obesity have waxed and waned over the past three decades. However, exemplary investigations exist in the recent literature. For instance, a randomized controlled trial by Renjilan and colleagues (2001) found that group behavioral therapy for obesity produced greater weight loss than individual behavioral therapy. Interestingly, the results favoring group treatment persisted even among those patients who expressed a preference for individual treatment. However, poor maintenance of treatment-induced weight loss remains a major challenge. Participants often gradually abandon changes in diet and exercise and subsequently regain weight in the posttreatment period (Perri et al., 2001). For example, one study reported that in the year following behavioral therapy, obese people typically regain 30% to 50% of their initial weight loss (cf. Perri et al., 2001). However, the results of one randomized controlled trial (Perri et al., 2001) suggest that when problem-solving or relapse prevention groups are added to standard behavior therapy groups, patients may achieve better long-term maintenance of weight loss.

Anorexia nervosa. The use of homogeneous groups in treatment of anorexia nervosa is uncommon due to the lack of formal research support, insufficient skilled therapist manpower to run these groups, and the general clinical impression that such patients are difficult to treat in groups (Yellowlees, 1988). According to Polivy (1981, as cited by Mynors-Wallis, 1989), the important factors to be fostered in these groups are universality, family reenactment, interpersonal feedback, and increased self-esteem via the helping role. The presence of severe underweight and somatic complications that require medical attention appears to be a contraindication for group therapy (Rosenvinge, 1990). In addition, patients with excessive denial of their illness, lack of previous treatment, extreme social withdrawal, or a complicating disturbance (e.g., personality disorder or substance abuse) may not be the most suitable candidates for group therapy (Hall, 1985, cited by Mynors-Wallis, 1989). More recently, some have argued for heterogeneous blending of anorexic and bulimic patients in CBT groups to enhance diversity of opinion regarding body size (Bowers, 2000, as cited by Brabender, 2002).

Groups for Anxiety Disorders

Obsessive-compulsive disorder (OCD). The principal change theory in the treatment of OCD is a time-limited behavioral approach that emphasizes response prevention, via in vivo or imagined exposure and modeling; that is, exposure and response prevention (ERP). ERP protocols often include a PE component to help patients understand their symptoms as well as the cognitive and behavioral mechanisms of change underlying the treatment protocol (McLean et al., 2001). We have found only two controlled studies that have evaluated this approach, and both reported significant pre- to posttreatment symptom improvements.

Fals-Stewart, Marks, and Schafer (1993) found group and individual 12-week ERP treatments to be equivalent in significantly reducing members' levels of anxiety, depression, and obsessive-compulsive symptoms. McLean and colleagues (2001) compared ERP with a CBT protocol adapted from Salkovskis (1996; as cited by McLean et al., 2001). The latter focuses on identifying triggers that lead to intrusive thoughts and faulty appraisals. ERP was significantly more effective in reducing obsessive-compulsive symptoms than CBT, although both formats were more effective than a wait-list control condition. The advantage of ERP over CBT was maintained at 3-month follow-up. McLean and colleagues suggest that ERP may be better suited to the group format because it provides an optimal environment for modeling while also introducing group pressure for compliance with exposure requirements. They further suggest that, because of its complexity, CBT may be more suitable for individual treatment of OCD. These arguments are consistent with Van Noppen, Pato, Marsland, and Rasmussen's (1998) viewpoint, which emphasizes the advantage of universality, imparted information, instilled hope, imitative behavior, altruism, and competition in the group treatment of OCD.

Panic disorder/agoraphobia. The dominant change theory being tested in the most recent empirical literature for patients suffering from panic disorder is a CBT protocol consisting of (a) education regarding etiology and maintenance of the disease, (b) cognitive restructuring, (c) diaphragmatic breathing, and (d) interoceptive exposure to feared body cues. Three rigorously designed controlled studies have found consistently that patients treated in CBT groups showed significantly higher levels of improvement than wait-list controls at posttreatment assessment on measures of anxiety, fear, depression, frequency and severity of panic attacks, agoraphobic avoidance, and catastrophic thinking (Burlingame et al., 2003). CBT patients also demonstrate reliable posttreatment gains, with as many as 81% being classified as recovered.

On the other hand, two randomized controlled studies and one pre-to-post study indicate that self-help bibliotherapy, a 3-day CBT workshop, and process-oriented group treatment may result in equivalent patient improvement (cf. Burlingame et al., 2003). Such findings raise the possibility that improvement may be attributed to nonspecific elements of the group treatment, such as cohesion, interaction, and the like. Clearly, future research is needed that directly contrasts the effects of formal change theories and adequate measures of the effects of group processes.

Social phobia. The dominant group protocol in treatment of social phobia is a cognitive-behavioral group therapy (CBGT) protocol developed by Richard Heimberg and his colleagues (Heimberg & Becker, 2002). Burlingame and colleagues (2003) summarized five rigorous studies that were carried out at four sites using three different research teams and noted that all concluded that CBGT produced reliable improvement in salient symptoms of social phobia when compared with wait-list controls. Further support is found in a recent randomized, controlled trial by Furmark et al. (2002). Social phobia symptom severity was significantly and equally reduced after 9 weeks of either CBGT or citalopram treatment, whereas wait-list control subjects did not improve. Interestingly, symptom improvement was accompanied by significantly reduced cerebral blood flow bilaterally in the amygdala, hippocampus, and neighboring cortical areas in responders during a public speech task, regardless of treatment

approach, but not in treatment nonresponders and wait-list control subjects.

The strong evidence supporting the efficacy of CBGT is partially clouded by studies suggesting rival explanations. For instance, Heimberg's team also has reported significant and at times equivalent improvement for patients who are randomly assigned to unstructured discussion groups (Hope, Heimberg, & Bruch, 1995). These groups were designed as a credible placebo control to capture nonspecific group processes (e.g., cohesion, social support, etc.), and some of the findings from this team suggest that the nonspecific processes may play an important role in patient change. Furthermore, two randomized controlled studies suggest that exposure to group processes alone may be as potent as the entire CBGT treatment package (cf. Burlingame et al., 2003).

Groups for post-traumatic stress disorder (PTSD).[2] CBT interventions are the most researched and supported (Celano & Rothbaum, 2002) treatment in this area, and two main treatment paradigms dominate the PTSD literature. One is an exposure-based approach, where patients gradually confront their feared memories or avoided situations, whereas the other is an affect-management approach, where patients focus on managing their current symptoms. Both approaches have strong theoretical rationales and may be countertherapeutic if used alone or timed inappropriately (Celano & Rothbaum, 2002; Schein, Burlingame, Spitz, & Muskin, in press; Wolfsdorf & Zlotnick, 2001). Premature focus on traumatic memories in exposure may be retraumatizing, while avoidance of these memories through affect management may eventually worsen the symptoms of PTSD (Layne & Warren, in press). These findings lead many to recommend a stage approach to treatment, with first-stage treatments emphasizing safety and stabilization and creating a foundation for later treatment stages that involve exposure techniques (Wolfsdorf & Zlotnick, 2001).

The empirical knowledge on the exposure-based approach in treatment of veterans with chronic, combat-related PTSD recently was enriched by the VA Cooperative Study 420 (Schnurr et al., 2003), the largest PTSD randomized trial to date (Schnurr, Friedman, Lavori, & Hsieh, 2001) with 360 patients randomized to 60 groups across 10 sites. This rigorously designed study investigated the effectiveness of trauma-focused group therapy (Foy, Glynn, Ruzek, Riney, & Gusman, 1997; Unger, Wattemberg, Foy, & Glynn, in press), a manualized exposure-based group model specifically designed for patients who might not otherwise tolerate or comply with individual exposure therapy (Schnurr et al., 2003). Trauma-focused group therapy combines exposure with PE, cognitive restructuring, relapse prevention, and coping skills training. Manualized modification of a process-oriented model was used to control for the effects of nonspecific elements of the group process (Wattenberg, Foy, Unger, & Glynn, in press). The study failed to demonstrate the effectiveness of this form of therapy on standardized measures of PTSD severity and additional related measures (e.g., quality of life, service utilization, etc.), but it suggested that the patients who receive an adequate dose of treatment might significantly benefit from it.

Substance-Related Disorders

Multimodal substance abuse programs typically include individual, family, group, 12-step, pharmacotherapy, PE, and aftercare treatment components, and group is often a central component of these programs. Patients who participate in group treatment exhibit more improvement on typical measures of outcome (e.g., abstinence and use rates, urine drug screen) than those who refuse or drop out of treatment or those who receive standard care that does not involve group (Burlingame et al., 2004). However, differential effectiveness studies of formal change theories (psychodynamic groups vs. Hatha yoga, psychodynamic vs. CBT group, and behavioral vs. cognitive) suggest that

differences between theories of change are not sufficient to explain the effectiveness of these groups. Furthermore, cognitive and supportive-expressive group therapy (both alone and combined with individual therapy) have recently been found to be less effective than a combination of individual and group counseling based on a 12-step model, in a rigorous multicenter study conducted by Crits-Christoph et al. (1999). These authors concluded that the 12-step interventions might have been more successful because of their more supportive nature.

A limitation to the effectiveness of this literature was recently pointed out by Winters, Fals-Stewart, O'Farrell, Birchler, and Kelley (2002). They note that the majority of outcome studies have largely or exclusively relied on male participants. Interestingly, women constitute 30% of treatment admissions for drug use and 58% of drug users in the United States (Washington, 2001). Winters and colleagues opine that the treatment needs of substance-abusing men may be significantly different and suggest that women may respond better to an empathic treatment approach whereas men seem to respond better to a more utilitarian approach. In short, these authors argue that findings from the studies performed mainly on male subjects are not generalizable to women, and they call for more research that specifically targets substance-abusing women.

Personality Disorders

Many authors argue that the group format, either alone or combined with individual therapy, is a particularly appropriate form of psychotherapy for personality disorders (e.g., Budman, Cooley, et al., 1996; Clarkin, Marziali, & Munroe-Blum, 1991; MacKenzie, 2001). The basis of this argument is that because personality pathology is primarily reflected in interpersonal relationships, the group environment allows the member's interpersonal style to be revealed in a more spontaneous and less guarded fashion than in individual therapy (MacKenzie, 2001). The group format also provides reality testing from other group members, and the multiple targets for transference reactions can dilute the intensity when compared with the polarized interaction that takes place in individual therapy (Budman, Cooley, et al., 1996; Clarkin et al., 1991; Spitz, 1984).

Although promising, the empirical evidence for group treatment of personality disorders is restricted (Burlingame et al., 2003; Clarkin et al., 1991), with most research focusing on the individual format (MacKenzie, 2001). The existing group literature is characterized by diversity of the models, limited number of studies, and paucity of controlled studies.

The most promising outpatient group protocols include interpersonal group therapy (Marziali & Munroe-Blum, 1994) and dialectical behavior therapy (Linehan, 1993), with both having some empirical support (MacKenzie, 2001). Interpersonal group therapy is a time-limited modification of the process-oriented group model. Randomized controlled trials reviewed by MacKenzie (2001) indicate that patients with borderline personality disorder who received interpersonal group therapy achieved outcome benefits equivalent to those treated with individual psychodynamic therapy, and the former is clearly more cost-effective (Marziali & Munroe-Blum, 1994; Munroe-Blum & Marziali, 1995). Treatment benefits were reflected in patient-reported levels of depression, general symptoms, and social adjustment, as well as in objectively measured behavioral changes, with highly significant improvement at 1-year follow-up.

Dialectical behavior therapy is a modification of CBT designed specifically for treatment of borderline personality disorder. It primarily relies on weekly individual psychotherapy but also uses weekly psychosocial skills groups to supplement individual psychotherapy. The core feature of the therapist's approach in dialectical behavior therapy is constant validation and acceptance of the patient's present emotional states, behaviors, and thoughts, including their willingness to change. The main goals are to improve affect regulation and interpersonal skills using open-ended, 2½-hour weekly groups with rotating membership that continue for about 1 year (MacKenzie, 2001). Randomized controlled trials suggest that, in comparison with "treatment as usual," dialectical behavior therapy results in significantly greater decreases in suicidal ideation, hopelessness, and depression (Koons et al., 2001). Others have reported lower rates of suicide attempts, less attrition from individual therapy, fewer inpatient psychiatric days (Linehan, Armstrong, Suarez, Allmon, & Heard, 1991), lower rates of anger (Koons et al., 2001; Linehan et al., 1991), and better overall social adjustment (Linehan, Tutek, Heard, & Armstrong, 1994).

Group-oriented partial hospital programs. Patients with personality disorders typically represent a significant percentage of the patient population in day and evening treatment programs. Protocols focusing on this population are typically time-limited (e.g., 4–8 months) "milieu" treatments that involve a variety of small and large groups with different goals and theoretical orientations as well as family, individual, and pharmacotherapy. Groups typically have a heterogeneous membership, and an individual patient often attends more than one group per day. Treatment protocols with promising outcome data include Piper (e.g., Joyce, McCallum, & Piper, 1999; Piper et al., 2002) and Rosie, Azim, Piper, and Joyce (1995) programs. Both have been reviewed using randomized controlled trials with significant treatment effects on a wide range of variables assessing interpersonal functioning, symptoms, self-esteem, life satisfaction, and defensive functioning.

Special Populations and Settings

Schizophrenia and schizoaffective disorder. Group models in the treatment of schizophrenia are typically used as one component of a multimodal inpatient or outpatient treatment program that combines two or more treatment components (medication, individual, group, family therapy). The dominant model with very good evidence for effectiveness is the UCLA Social and Independent Living Skills program developed by Liberman and his co-workers (Roder, Zorn, Muller, & Brenner, 2001). Two meta-analytic studies (Benton & Schroeder, 1990; Mojtabai, Nicholson, & Carpenter, 1998) indicate significant pre-to-post treatment improvement on behavioral measures of social skills, assertiveness, and hospital discharge rates, with effect sizes of 0.76 and 0.41. Other models in use with less convincing research evidence are PE models; cognitive information-processing rehabilitation models that address specific information-processing deficits and remediation strategies; and CBT models that include belief modification and behavioral strategies for coping with positive symptoms of schizophrenia. Finally, preliminary research findings by Granholm, McQuaid, McClure, Pedrelli, and Jeste (2002) suggest that older patients with schizophrenia may benefit from a model (cf. Granholm et al., 2002) that combines CBT and social skills training.

Medical illness-oriented groups. There are a plethora of group treatments found in medical settings. These groups usually take place in medical settings, such as cancer wards. They may be led by a mental health professional or by other health care workers who specialize in working with patients who suffer from a particular medical illness (Vinogradov & Yalom, 1989). Two areas of practice and research, cancer and HIV, dominate the literature in this area of practice.

Group interventions for cancer patients treat a mix of diagnoses, with breast cancer being the most frequent. The most commonly used and researched group format is supportive-expressive treatment (Spiegel, Bloom, Kraemer, & Gottheil, 1989), which encourages affective expression and sharing concerns about life-threatening illness in the supportive group environment facilitated by the therapist. Spiegel et al. (1989) found that supportive-expressive treatment may improve survival rates in women with metastatic breast cancer; however, the majority of attempts to replicate these findings have failed to do so (Burlingame et al., 2003; Sherman, Leszcz, et al., in press), including two recent, large, multicenter randomized trials (Bordeleau et al., 2003; Goodwin et al., 2001). Still, there is growing evidence that supportive-expressive treatment improves psychological well-being and coping in women with metastatic breast cancer (e.g., Bordeleau et al., 2003; Goodwin et al., 2001; Sherman, Mosier, et al., in press).

Studies of group models for HIV/AIDS focus predominantly on gay men, with only one study involving more diverse group membership (i.e., heterosexuals and intravenous drug users constitute a significant portion of the population; Blanch et al., 2002). These group protocols have two main foci: prevention and treatment. *Prevention protocols*, with a predominantly PE focus, have been associated with decreases in unprotected sex, number of sexual partners, and new infections, with treatment dosage related to effects (Burlingame et al., 2004). Among treatment protocols, CBT and support models have the most promising, although modest (Sherman, Leszcz, et al., in press), empirical support on measures of depression and anxiety (Blanch et al., 2002), hostility, and somatization (Kelly et al., 1993; Mulder et al., 1994, 1995).

Conclusion

The evidence for selective diagnostic effectiveness is continuing to accumulate across a variety of contemporary applications of group treatment: as a primary form of treatment (e.g., social phobia), as an enhancement of individual therapy (e.g., borderline personality disorder), or as one component of multimodal treatment programs (e.g., substance-related disorders). In addition, group research is beginning to acknowledge the fact that psychotropic medications have become the rule rather than an exception in the treatment of a variety of disorders. This was reflected in studies that investigated the comparative effectiveness (e.g., CBGT vs. citalopram in social phobia; Furmark et al., 2002) or enhancement potential (e.g., PE groups and pharmacologic maintenance treatments for BAD; Colom et al., 2003) of these two forms of treatment. We are hoping to see more studies in the future that investigate the relationship between various psychopharmacologic and group treatments, as well as possible benefits of their combination.

Regardless of their diverse theoretical orientations and patient populations, most empirically validated group treatments seem quite alike, if viewed from the standpoint of their structural features: They are typically diagnosis- or problem-specific, homogeneous, time-limited, short-term, and manualized, with symptom reduction as their main goal. These managed care-friendly group treatments dominate contemporary group research. Studies investigating group treatments that are not necessarily focused on symptom reduction, such as nondirective group therapy or more traditional forms of interpersonal and psychodynamic group therapies (i.e., open-ended, heterogeneous) are only marginally represented. The exceptions are group treatments for personality disorders, which seem to require a longer-term time frame, often with a heterogeneous patient population, and, in the case of interpersonal group therapy (Marziali & Munroe-Blum, 1994), rely heavily on nonspecific group properties.

It is easy to imagine how the current health care climate may continue to favor theoretical models that incorporate managed care-friendly structural features by definition (e.g., CBT, behavioral therapy). Some other clinically viable models—where treatment goals are defined in terms of building a trusting therapeutic relationship that facilitates self-reflection, exploration, and personal growth rather than symptom-management (e.g., process-oriented, nondirective groups)—may become significantly modified to the point of nonrecognition

or reserved only for the most severe, chronic conditions, such as severe personality disorders. Concerns about the future of psychotherapies that rely primarily on nonspecific therapy factors have already been raised in the general psychotherapy literature. For example, Bohart, O'Hara, and Leitner (1998) opine that manualization, the requirement for diagnosis-specific treatments, and randomized-controlled study designs discriminate against humanistic therapies. It was, therefore, encouraging to see that several outcome studies reviewed in this chapter had leveraged their findings by highlighting the nonspecific group properties, including the ones that investigated theoretical models that traditionally do not rely on these properties (e.g., CBT in treatment of binge eating disorder; Castonguay et al., 1998). Some of these studies suggest the role of nonspecific properties as an agent of change that works in synergy with the formal theory of change (e.g., ERP in treatment of OCD; McLean et al., 2001) or independently of theory of change (e.g., substance use). These findings invite a more consistent and uniform empirical effort in investigating the role of the nonspecific group properties in the outcome studies across all patient populations and theories of change. The interested reader is directed to Burlingame et al. (in press) for a detailed discussion and study design recommendations for future research regarding the role of nonspecific elements of group treatment.

The emergence of empirically validated group models at the time when they were most needed (i.e., in the managed care era) is good news. Because of their cost-effectiveness, it would be reasonable to anticipate a "win-win-win" situation in the future where managed care organizations would be glad to reimburse for these relatively inexpensive treatments, providers would be allotted visits, and patients would get needed treatment. Yet, this scenario stands in contrast with findings from two recent surveys. The first survey, done by Taylor and colleagues (2001), indicates conflicting views regarding perceived effectiveness and preference for group treatment among managers of managed care organizations and providers (e.g., psychiatrists, social workers, and psychologists); the second survey (Fuhriman & Burlingame, 2001) found a discrepancy between available training in group therapy (it is diminishing) and predicted increased market demands for group psychotherapy. Findings from these two surveys are consistent with our clinical and research experience: For whatever reason (e.g., inadequate training, perception of group therapy as too complex, social anxiety, etc.), there may be variability in providers' comfort level when it comes to running groups.

Still, we are optimistic. First, we base our optimism on the growing empirical evidence for the effectiveness of group therapy. We believe that both providers and training programs will develop interest in group therapy as they become aware of this evidence. The second reason for our optimism is the evidence that nonspecific elements contribute to the effectiveness of group therapy. We find utilization of these nonspecific properties to be a creative act that many providers will find very gratifying as they begin to discover it. Finally, in today's society, where the family system does not provide as much emotional connection as it used to do, we believe that therapy groups have and will take over some of the functions of this system. They provide a safe place to communicate, talk, listen, and be heard. As such, groups meet a need that is built into every human being. We believe that the ability of therapy groups to empathically respond to this need can help channel this need into a growth-promoting therapeutic experience.

Notes

1. In the past decade, the psychotherapy literature has begun to group client-centered therapies together with other humanistic therapies (e.g., interpersonal therapy) under the name *experiential therapies* (Elliot, Greenberg, & Lietar, 2003). The research on these therapies was recently reviewed by Elliot et al. (2003),

including additional meta-analysis of more than 125 outcome studies.

2. Not to be confused with trauma-related groups, which typically focus on a broader range of short-term and long-term psychosocial consequences of a trauma, including PTSD as well as other psychiatric disorders. Examples of trauma-related groups are groups for adult survivors of childhood sexual trauma, groups for battered women, and domestic violence-related groups. Trauma-related groups often employ empirically supported treatment models developed for PTSD, although the transportability of these models has not been empirically supported (Celano & Rothbaum, 2002). Formal evidence for the effectiveness of existing group treatment models for trauma-related disorders is still limited (Burlingame et al., 2003).

References

Alonso, A. (2000). Group psychotherapy, combined individual and group psychotherapy. In B. J. Sadock & V. A. Sadock (Eds.), *Comprehensive textbook of psychiatry* (pp. 2146–2157). Philadelphia: Lippincott Williams & Wilkins.

Azim, H. F. A., Piper, W. E., Segal, P. M., Nixon, G. W. H., & Duncan, S. C. (1991). The Quality of Object Relations Scale. *Bulletin of the Menninger Clinic*, *55*, 323–343.

Barlow, S., Burlingame, G., & Fuhriman, A. (2000). Therapeutic application of groups: From Pratt's thought control classes to modern group psychotherapy. *Group Dynamics: Theory, Research & Practice*, *4*(1), 115–134.

Barlow, S. H., Burlingame, G. M., Nebeker, R. S., & Anderson, E. (2000). Meta-analysis of medical self-help groups. *International Journal of Group Psychotherapy*, *50*(1), 53–69.

Belfer, P. L., & Levendusky, P. (1985). Long-term behavioral group psychotherapy: An integrative model. In D. Upper & S. M. Ross (Eds.), *Handbook of behavioral group therapy* (pp. 119–144). New York: Plenum Press.

Benton, M. K., & Schroeder, H. E. (1990). Social skills training with schizophrenics: A meta-analytic evaluation. *Journal of Consulting and Clinical Psychology*, *58*(6), 741–747.

Blanch, J., Rousaud, A., Hautzinger, M., Martinez, E., Peri, J. M., Andres, S., Cirera, E., Gatell, J. M., & Gasto, C. (2002). Assessment of the efficacy of a cognitive-behavioural group psychotherapy programme for HIV-infected patients referred to a consultation-liaison psychiatry department. *Psychotherapy and Psychosomatics, 71*(2), 77–84.

Bohart, A. C., O'Hara, M., & Leitner, L. M. (1998). Empirically violated treatments: Disenfranchisement of humanistic and other psychotherapies. *Psychotherapy Research, 8*(2), 41–57.

Bordeleau, L., Szalai, J. P., Ennis, M., Leszcz, M., Speca, M., Sela, R., Doll, R., Chochinov, H. M., Navarro, M., Arnold, A., Pritchard, K. I., Bezjak, A., Llewellyn-Thomas, H. A., Sawka, C. A., & Goodwin, P. J. (2003). Quality of life in a randomized trial of group psychosocial support in metastatic breast cancer: Overall effects of the intervention and an exploration of missing data. *Journal of Clinical Oncology, 21*(10), 1944–1951.

Brabender, V. (2002). *Introduction to group therapy.* New York: John Wiley.

Budman, S. H., Cooley, S., Demby, A., Koppenaal, G., Koslof, J., & Powers, T. (1996). A model of time-effective group psychotherapy for patients with personality disorders: The clinical model. *International Journal of Group Psychotherapy, 46*(3), 329–355.

Budman, S. H., Demby, A., Soldz, S., & Merry, J. (1996). Time-limited group psychotherapy for patients with personality disorders: Outcomes and dropouts. *International Journal of Group Psychotherapy, 46*(3), 357–377.

Burlingame, G. M., & Davies, D. R. (2002). Self-help groups. In M. Heisen & G. Zimmer (Eds.), *The encyclopedia of psychotherapy* (Vol. 4, pp. 31–35). New York: Academic Press.

Burlingame, G. M., Earnshaw, D., Hoag, M., Barlow, S. H., Richardson, E. J., Donnell, A. J., & Villani, J. (2002). A systematic program to enhance clinician group skills in an inpatient psychiatric hospital. *International Journal of Group Psychotherapy, 32*(4), 555–587.

Burlingame, G. M., Fuhriman, A., & Mosier, J. (2003). The differential effectiveness of group psychotherapy: A meta-analytic perspective. *Group Dynamics: Theory, Research, and Practice, 7*(1), 3–12.

Burlingame, G., Lambert, M., Reisinger, C., Neff, W., & Mosier, J. (1995). Pragmatics of tracking mental health outcome in managed care settings. *Journal of Mental Health Administration, 22*(3), 226–235.

Burlingame, G. M., MacKenzie, K. R., & Strauss, B. (2004). Small group treatment: Evidence for effectiveness and mechanisms of change. In M. J. Lambert (Ed.), *Handbook of psychotherapy and behavior change* (5th ed., pp. 647–696). New York: John Wiley.

Burlingame, G. M., MacKenzie, K. R., & Strauss, B. (in press). *Evidence-based group treatment: Matching models with disorders and patients.* Washington, DC: American Psychological Association.

Burlingame, G., & Ridge, N. (in press). The development and maintenance of psycho-educational groups. In S. Hill (Ed.), *Psychologists desk reference.* Oxford, UK: Oxford University Press.

Castonguay, L. G., Pincus, A. L., Agras, W. S., & Hines, C. E. (1998). The role of emotion in group cognitive-behavioral therapy for binge eating disorder: When things have to feel worse before they get better. *Psychotherapy Research, 8*(2), 225–238.

Celano, M., & Rothbaum, B. O. (2002). Psychotherapeutic approaches with survivors of childhood trauma. *Seminars in Clinical Neuropsychiatry, 7*(2), 120–128.

Chen, E., Touyz, S. W., Beumont, P. J. V., Fairburn, C. G., Griffiths, R., Butow, P., Russell, J., Schotte, D. E., Gertler, R., & Basten, C. (2003). Comparison of group and individual cognitive-behavioral therapy for patients with bulimia nervosa. *International Journal of Eating Disorders, 33*, 241–254.

Clarkin, J. F., Marziali, E., & Munroe-Blum, H. (1991). Group and family treatment for borderline personality disorder. *Hospital and Community Psychiatry, 42*(10), 1038–1043.

Colom, F., Vieta, E., Martinez-Aran, A., Reinares, M., Goikolea, J. M., Benabarre, A., Torrent, C., Comes, M., Corbella, B., Parramon G., & Corominas, J. A. (2003). Randomized trial on the efficacy of group psychoeducation in the prophylaxis of recurrences in bipolar patients whose disease is in remission. *Archives of General Psychiatry, 60*, 402–407.

Crits-Christoph, P., Siqueland, L., Blaine, J., Frank, A., Luborsky, L., Onken, L. S., Muenz, L. R., Thase, M. E., Weiss, R. D., Gastfriend, D. R., Woody, G. E., Barber, J. P., Butler, S. F., Daley, D., Salloum, I., Bishop, S., Najavits, L. M., Lis, J., Mercer, D., Griffin, M. L., Moras, K., & Beck, A. T. (1999). Psychosocial treatments for cocaine dependence: National Institute on Drug Abuse collaborative cocaine treatment study. *Archives of General Psychiatry, 56*(6), 493–502.

Dyck, D. G., Hendryx, M. S., Short, R. A., Voss, W. D., & McFarlane, W. R. (2002). Service use among patients with schizophrenia in psychoeducational multiple-family group treatment. *Psychiatric Services, 53*(6), 749–754.

Elliot, R., Greenberg, L. S., & Lietar, G. (2003). Research on experiential psychotherapies. In M. J. Lambert (Ed.), *Bergin and Garfield's handbook of psychotherapy and behavior change* (5th ed., pp. 493–539). New York: John Wiley.

Fals-Stewart, W., Marks, A. P., & Schafer, J. (1993). A comparison of behavioral group therapy and individual behavior therapy in treating obsessive-compulsive disorder. *Journal of Nervous and Mental Disease, 181,* 189–193.

Foy, D. W., Glynn, S. M., Ruzek, J. I., Riney, S. J., & Gusman, F. D. (1997). Trauma focus group therapy for combat-related PTSD. *In Session: Psychotherapy in Practice, 3*(4), 59–73.

Fuhriman, A., & Burlingame, G. M. (1990). Consistency of matter: A comparative analysis of individual and group process variables. *The Counseling Psychologist, 18*(1), 6–63.

Fuhriman, A., & Burlingame, G. M. (1994). Group psychotherapy: Research and practice. In A. Fuhriman & G. M. Burlingame (Eds.), *Handbook of group psychotherapy: An empirical and clinical synthesis* (pp. 3–40). New York: John Wiley.

Fuhriman, A., & Burlingame, G. M. (2000). Group psychotherapy. In A. Kazdin (Ed.), *Encyclopedia of psychology* (pp. 31–35). Oxford, UK: Oxford University Press.

Fuhriman, A., & Burlingame, G. (2001). Group psychotherapy training and effectiveness. *International Journal of Group Psychotherapy, 51*(5), 399–416.

Furmark, T., Tillfors, M., Marteinsdottir, I., Fischer, H., Pissiota, A., Langstrom, B., & Fredrikson, M. (2002). Common changes in cerebral blood flow in patients with social phobia treated with citalopram or cognitive-behavioral therapy. *Archives of General Psychiatry, 59*(5), 425–433.

Ganzarain, R. C. (1989). *Object relations group psychotherapy: The group as an object, a tool, and a training base.* Madison, CT: International Universities Press.

Gelder, M. (1997). The future of behavior therapy. *The Journal of Psychotherapy Practice and Research, 6,* 285–293.

Goodwin, P. J., Leszcz, M., Ennis, M., Koopmans, J., Vincent, L., Guther, H., Drysdale, E., Hundleby, M., Chochinov, H. M., Navorro, M., Speca, M., & Hunter, J. (2001). The effect of group psychosocial support on survival in metastatic breast cancer. *The New England Journal of Medicine, 345*(24), 1719–1726.

Granholm, E., McQuaid, J. R., McClure, F. S., Pedrelli, P., & Jeste, D. V. (2002). A randomized controlled pilot study of cognitive behavioral social skills training for older patients with schizophrenia. *Schizophrenia Research, 53*(1–2), 167–169.

Harper-Guiffre, H., & MacKenzie, K. R. (Eds.). (1992). *Group psychotherapy for eating disorders.* Washington, DC: American Psychiatric Press.

Heimberg, R. G., & Becker, R. E. (2002). *Cognitive-behavioral group therapy for social phobia: Basic mechanisms and clinical strategies.* New York: Guilford Press.

Hope, D. A., Heimberg, R. G., & Bruch, M. A. (1995). Dismantling cognitive-behavioral group therapy for social phobia. *Behavior Research and Therapy, 33,* 637–650.

Huxley, N. A., Parikh, S. V., & Baldessarini, R. J. (2000). Effectiveness of psychosocial treatments in bipolar disorder: State of the evidence. *Harvard Review of Psychiatry, 8*(3), 126–140.

Joyce, A. S., McCallum, M., & Piper, W. E. (1999). Borderline functioning, work, and outcome in intensive evening group treatment. *International Journal of Group Psychotherapy, 49*(3), 343–368.

Kelly, J. A., Murphy, D. A., Bahr, G. R., Kalichman, S. C., Morgan, M. G., Stevenson, L. Y., Koob, J. J., Brasfield, T. L., & Bernstein, B. M. (1993). Outcome of cognitive-behavioral and support group brief therapies for depressed, HIV-infected persons. *American Journal of Psychiatry, 150*(11), 1679–1686.

Klein, R. H., Bernhard, H. S., & Singer, D. L. (Eds.). (1992). *Handbook of contemporary group psychotherapy: Contributions from object relations, self psychology, and social systems theories.* Madison, CT: International Universities Press.

Koons, C. R., Robins, C. J., Tweed, J. L., Lynch, T. R., Conzalez, A. M., Morse, J. Q., Bishop, G. K., Butterfield, M. I., & Bastian, L. A. (2001). Efficacy of dialectical behavioral therapy in women veterans with borderline personality disorder. *Behavior Therapy, 32,* 371–390.

Layne, C. M., & Warren, J. S. (in press). Influences on posttraumatic adjustment and recovery: Distressing reminders, secondary adversities, retraumatization, and the role of protective factors. In L. A. Schein, H. I. Spitz, G. M. Burlingame, & P. R. Muskin (Eds.), *Group approaches for psychological effects of catastrophic disaster and terrorist threats: Principles and methods.* New York: Hayworth Press.

Linehan, M. M. (1993). *Cognitive-behavioral treatment of borderline personality disorder.* New York: Guilford Press.

Linehan, M. M., Armstrong, H. E., Suarez, A., Allmon, D., & Heard, H. L. (1991). Cognitive-behavioral treatment of chronically parasuicidal borderline patients. *Archives of General Psychiatry, 48*(12), 1060–1064.

Linehan, M. M., Tutek, D. A., Heard, H. L., & Armstrong, H. E. (1994). Interpersonal outcome of cognitive behavioral treatment for chronically suicidal borderline patients. *American Journal of Psychiatry, 151*(12), 1771–1776.

MacKenzie, K. R. (2001). Group psychotherapy. In W. J. Livesley (Ed.), *Handbook of personality disorders* (pp. 497–526). New York: Guilford Press.

Marziali, E., & Munroe-Blum, H. (1994). *Interpersonal group psychotherapy for borderline personality disorder.* New York: Basic Books.

McLean, P. D., Whittal, M. L., Thordarson, D. S., Taylor, S., Sochting, I., Koch, W. J., Paterson, R., & Anderson, K. W. (2001). Cognitive versus behavior therapy in the group treatment of obsessive-compulsive disorder. *Journal of Consulting and Clinical Psychology, 69*(2), 205–214.

McRoberts, C., Burlingame, G. M., & Hoag, M. J. (1998). Comparative efficacy of individual and group psychotherapy: A meta-analytic perspective. *Group Dynamics, 2*(2), 101–117.

Mitchell, J. E., Pyle, R. L., Pomeroy, C., Zollman, M., Crosby, R., Seim, H., Eckert, E. D., & Zimmerman, R. (1993). Cognitive-behavioral group psychotherapy of bulimia nervosa: Importance of logistical variables. *International Journal of Eating Disorders, 14*(3), 277–287.

Mojtabai, R., Nicholson, R. A., & Carpenter, B. N. (1998). Role of psychosocial treatments in management of schizophrenia: A meta-analytic review of controlled outcome studies. *Schizophrenia Bulletin, 24*(4), 569–587.

Mulder, C. L., Antoni, M. H., Emmelkamp, P. M. G., Veugelers, P. J., Sandfort, T. G. M., van de Vijver, F. A. J. R., & de Vries, M. J. (1995). Psychosocial group intervention and the rate of decline of immunological parameters in asymptomatic HIV-infected homosexual men. *Psychotherapy and Psychosomatics, 63*(3–4), 185–192.

Mulder, C. L., Emmelkamp, P. M., Antoni, M. H., Mulder, J. W., Sandfort, T. G., & DeVries, M. J. (1994). Cognitive-behavioral and experiential group psychotherapy for HIV-infected homosexual men: A comparative study. *Psychosomatic Medicine, 56*, 423–431.

Munroe-Blum, H., & Marziali, E. (1995). A controlled trial of short-term group treatment for borderline personality disorder. *Journal of Personality Disorders, 9*, 190–198.

Mynors-Wallis, L. M. (1989). The psychological treatment of eating disorders. *British Journal Hospital Medicine, 41*(5), 470–475.

Ogrodniczuk, J. S., & Piper, W. E. (2003). The effect of group climate on outcome in two forms of short-term group therapy. *Group Dynamics: Theory, Research, and Practice, 7*(1), 64–76.

Patterson, C. H. (1974). *Relationship counseling and psychotherapy.* New York: Harper & Row.

Payson, A. A., Wheeler, K., & Wellington, T. A. (1998). Health teaching needs of clients with serious and persistent mental illness: Client and provider perspectives. *Journal of Psychological Nursing, 36*(2), 32–35.

Pendleton, V. R., Goodrick, G. K., Carlos Poston, W. S., Reeves, R. S., & Foreyt, J. P. (2002). Exercise augments the effects of cognitive-behavioral therapy in the treatment of binge eating. *International Journal of Eating Disorders, 31*, 172–184.

Perri, M. G., McKelvey, W. F., Renjilan, D. A., Nezu, A. M., Shermer, R. L., & Vieneger, B. J. (2001). Relapse prevention training and problem-solving therapy in the long-term management of obesity. *Journal of Consulting and Clinical Psychology, 69*(4), 722–726.

Piper, W. E., Joyce, A. S., McCallum, M., Azim, H. F., & Ogrodniczuk, J. S. (2002). *Interpretive and supportive psychotherapies: Matching therapy and patient personality.* Washington, DC: American Psychological Association.

Piper, W. E., McCallum, M., & Azim, H. F. A. (1992). *Adaptation to loss through short-term group psychotherapy.* New York: Guilford Press.

Piper, W. E., Rosie, J. S., Joyce, A. S., & Azim, H. F. A. (1996). *Time-limited day treatment for personality disorders: Integration of research design and practice in a group program.* Washington, DC: American Psychological Association.

Renjilan, D. A., Perri, M. G., Nezu, A. M., McKelvey, W. F., Shermer, R. L., & Anton, S. D. (2001). Individual versus group therapy for obesity: Effects of matching participants to their treatment preferences. *Journal of Consulting and Clinical Psychology, 69*(4), 717–721.

Roder, V., Zorn, P., Muller, D., & Brenner, H. D. (2001). Improving recreational, residential, and vocational outcomes for patients with schizophrenia. *Psychiatric Services, 52*(11), 1439–1441.

Rogers, C. R. (1951). *Client-centered therapy: Its current practice, implications, and theory.* Boston: Houghton Mifflin.

Rosenvinge, J. H. (1990). Group therapy for anorexic and bulimic patients: Some aspects on the conduction of group therapy and a critical review of some recent studies. *Acta Psychiatrica Scandinavica, 82*(Suppl. 361), 38–43.

Rosie, J. S., Azim, H. F. A., Piper, W. E., & Joyce, A. S. (1995). Effective psychiatric day treatment: Historical lessons. *Psychiatric Services, 46*(10), 1019–1026.

Rothbaum, B. O., & Astin, M. C. (2000). Integration of pharmacotherapy and psychotherapy for bipolar disorder. *Journal of Clinical Psychiatry, 61*(Suppl. 9), 68–75.

Rutan, J. S., & Stone, W. N. (2001). *Psychodynamic group psychotherapy* (3rd ed.). New York: Guilford Press.

Schein, L., Burlingame, G., Spitz, H., & Muskin, P. (in press). *Group approaches for psychological effects of catastrophic disaster and terrorist threats: Principles and methods.* New York: Hayworth Press.

Schnurr, P. P., Friedman, M. J., Foy, D. W., Shea, T., Hsieh, F. Y., Lavori, P. W., Glynn, S. M., Wattenberg, M., & Bernardy, N. C. (2003). Randomized trial of trauma-focused group therapy for posttraumatic stress disorder: Results from a Department of Veterans Affairs Cooperative Study. *Archives of General Psychiatry, 60*, 481–489.

Schnurr, P. P., Friedman, M. J., Lavori, P. W., & Hsieh, F. Y. (2001). Design of Department of Veterans Affairs Cooperative Study No. 420: Group treatment of posttraumatic stress disorder. *Controlled Clinical Trials, 22*(1), 74–88.

Sherman, A. C., Leszcz, M., Mosier, J., Burlingame, G. M., Cleary, T., Ulman, K. H., Simonton, S., Latif, U., Strauss, B., & Hazelton, L. (in press). Group interventions for patients with cancer and HIV disease: Part II. Effects on immune, endocrine, and disease outcomes at different phases of illness. *International Journal of Group Psychotherapy.*

Sherman, A. C., Mosier, J., Leszcz, M., Burlingame, G. M., Ulman, K. H., Cleary, T., Simonton, S., Latif, U., Hazelton, L., & Strauss, B. (in press). Group interventions for patients with cancer and HIV disease: Part I. Effects on psychosocial and functional outcomes at different phases of illness. *International Journal of Group Psychotherapy.*

Spiegel, D., Bloom, J. R., Kraemer, H. C., & Gottheil, E. (1989). Effect of psychosocial treatment on survival of patients with metastatic breast cancer. *Lancet, 2,* 888–891.

Spitz, H. I. (1984). Contemporary trends in group psychotherapy: A literature survey. *Hospital and Community Psychiatry, 35*(2), 132–142.

Sundel, M., & Sundel, S. S. (1985). Behavior modification in groups: A time-limited model for assessment, planning, intervention, and evaluation. In D. Upper & S. M. Ross (Eds.), *Handbook of behavioral group therapy* (pp. 3–24). New York: Plenum Press.

Swartz, H. A., & Frank, E. (2001). Psychotherapy for bipolar depression: A phase-specific treatment strategy? *Bipolar Disorders, 3,* 11–22.

Taylor, N. T., Burlingame, G. M., Kristensen, K. B., Fuhriman, A., Johansen, J., & Dahl, D. (2001). A survey of mental health care providers and managed care organization attitudes toward, familiarity with, and use of group interventions. *International Journal of Group Psychotherapy, 51*(2), 243–263.

Unger, W., Wattemberg, M. S., Foy, D. W., & Glynn, S. M. (in press). Trauma-focused group therapy (TFGT): An evidence based group approach to trauma with adults. In L. A. Schein, H. I. Spitz, G. M. Burlingame, & P. R. Muskin (Eds.), *Group approaches for psychological effects of catastrophic disaster and terrorist threats: Principles and methods.* New York: Hayworth Press.

Upper, D., & Ross, S. M. (1985). *Handbook of behavioral group therapy.* New York: Plenum Press.

Van Noppen, B. L., Pato, M. L., Marsland, R., & Rasmussen, S. A. (1998). A time-limited behavioral group for treatment of obsessive-compulsive disorder. *Journal of Psychotherapy Practice and Research, 7*(4), 272–280.

Vinogradov, S., & Yalom, I. D. (1989). *A concise guide to group psychotherapy.* Washington, DC: American Psychiatric Press.

Washington, O. G. (2001). Using brief therapeutic interventions to create change in self-efficacy and personal control of chemically dependent women. *Archives of Psychiatric Nursing, 15*(1), 32–40.

Wattenberg, M. S., Foy, D. W., Unger, W. M. & Glynn, S. M. (in press). Present-centered supportive group therapy for trauma survivors. In L. A. Schein, H. I. Spitz, G. M. Burlingame, & P. R. Muskin (Eds.), *Group approaches for psychological effects of catastrophic disaster and terrorist threats: Principles and methods.* New York: Hayworth Press.

Winters, J., Fals-Stewart, W., O'Farrell. T. J., Birchler, G. R., & Kelley, M. L. (2002). Behavioral couples therapy for female substance-abusing patients: Effects on substance use and relationship adjustment. *Journal of Consulting and Clinical Psychology, 70*(2), 344–355.

Wolfsdorf, B. A., & Zlotnick, C. (2001). Affect management in group therapy for women with posttraumatic stress disorder and histories of childhood sexual abuse. *Journal of Clinical Psychology, 57*(2), 169–181.

Yalom, I. D. (1995). *The theory and practice of group psychotherapy* (4th ed.). New York: Basic Books. (Original work published 1970)

Yellowlees, P. (1988). Group therapy in anorexia nervosa. *International Journal of Eating Disorders, 7*(5), 649–655.

22

Promoting Effective Team Performance Through Training

Dana E. Sims

Eduardo Salas

C. Shawn Burke

Our society constantly demands higher productivity, better performance, and greater profits. Teams offer an invaluable advantage in meeting these demands as they often provide more complex, innovative, adaptive, and comprehensive solutions than any other working structure (Hackman, 1987; Moreland & Levine, 1992; Sundstrom, De Meuse, & Futrell, 1990). Teams are capable of achieving more than the sum of their individual members' input in increasingly complex working environments (e.g., operating rooms, military combat, air traffic control). Through the past 20 years of team research, it has been determined that teamwork is a set of interrelated knowledge, skills, and attitudes (KSAs) that facilitate coordinated, adaptive performance to support one's teammates, objectives, and mission. However, not all teams achieve the high performance that is expected of them. In this chapter, team training will be discussed as one solution to ensuring that teams have the KSAs to meet performance goals.

Team training practices have progressed in the past decade and continue to evolve. In fact, the research and literature available to guide the design, implementation, and evaluation of training may be more theoretically, methodologically, and empirically comprehensive than ever before (Tannenbaum & Yukl, 1992). Training, whether focused on individual team members or the entire team, is concerned with developing instructional strategies for influencing trainee competencies and performance outcomes. A number of frameworks have been presented to assist in classifying the type of team, the task, and other factors that impact team training development (e.g., Fleishman, 1975; Hackman, 1969; O'Brien, 1967). We now know that effective training programs are those that (a) are systematically developed based on theory and a thorough needs analysis, (b) provide timely, diagnostic feedback, and (c) are supported by an organizational culture that encourages the transfer of the trained competencies to the task environment.

The overarching purpose of this chapter will be to discuss the factors that influence the design, delivery, and evaluation of team training strategies. Within this topic we will first discuss the construct of teamwork: that is, what makes teams effective? Then, we outline five steps in the training process: training needs analysis, defining training content, developing and implementing training, evaluating training effectiveness, and transfer of training, and we provide a number of literature-based tips that ensure effective team training. We conclude by discussing several of the most prominent team training strategies, including cross training, metacognition, team coordination training, team self-correction training, team building, and assertiveness training.

Teamwork Described

A team consists of two or more individuals who interact dynamically, interdependently, and adaptively toward a common and valued goal (Dyer, 1984; Salas, Dickinson, Converse, & Tannenbaum, 1992). These individuals are assigned specific functions to perform, and their interaction may be limited by the life span of the team's task. Teams often operate in complex and dynamic environments with rapidly evolving and ambiguous situations, intensified by information overload and severe time pressure. As a result, teams have unique task/work-flow interdependencies, contextual constraints, multilevel

influences, and temporal dynamics (Kozlowski & Bell, 2004), but they nevertheless enhance individual performance by using the input of other team members (Driskell & Salas, 1992). As such, effective teams require more than just task work; they also require the ability to coordinate with each other to facilitate task objectives (i.e., teamwork) (Bowers, Braun, & Morgan, 1997).

Teamwork is a blend of organized thoughts, feelings, and attitudes that facilitate coordinated, adaptive performance and task work objectives (see Figure 22.1).

Teamwork depends on the ability of each team member to (a) anticipate the needs of others and coordinate without overt communication, (b) adjust to each other's actions and the changing environment, and (c) create a shared understanding of the task in order to identify errors and correct them. There are a number of team performance models that depict the constructs related to teamwork (e.g., Cannon-Bowers, Tannenbaum, Salas, & Volpe, 1995; Fleishman & Zacarro, 1992); however, these models are inconsistent in defining the core constructs. In an effort to develop a parsimonious framework to guide more integrative work, Sims, Salas, and Burke (2004) have synthesized what is known about teamwork into a model reflecting five core teamwork competencies and three core teamwork-enabling processes (see Table 22.1).

Many team effectiveness models presume that a team will achieve its goals if members hold the appropriate competencies. Team goals include any number of tangible products or intangible solutions. Team researchers and practitioners tend to use the *outcomes* of the team's interactions (i.e., number of products, number of accidents) as criteria to determine training effectiveness. These outcomes are also used to measure *team effectiveness*. Although outcomes are easily observed and offer concrete evidence of change, they are not the most useful criteria; many factors outside the team's control can impact their performance. For instance, manufacturing teams cannot be solely responsible for failing to

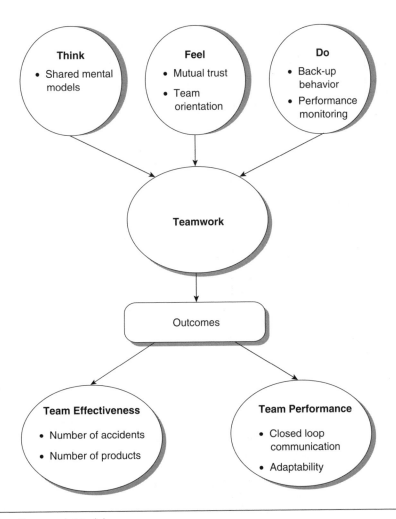

Figure 22.1   Teamwork Model

meet production quotas if they do not receive raw materials. For this reason, team training experts suggest examining team performance.

Team Performance

Team performance is the constellation of inputs and processes that result in particular team outcomes. Therefore, measurement may be more informative by focusing on the *processes* (e.g., coordination, communication, and cooperation) that enable or inhibit team members to perform together because the team has direct control over the processes that occur (Gladstein,

1984; Hackman, 1987; Tannenbaum, Beard, & Salas, 1992). Attention to the performance of a team will provide greater insight into the team's outcomes and the ability to give diagnostic feedback to improve overall team performance. One solution to address performance difficulties in the team is to offer team training to facilitate more effective teamwork.

Team Training

Team training is implemented to improve teamwork skills (e.g., communication, performance monitoring) so that both team performance and team effectiveness are enhanced.

Table 22.1   Core Teamwork Competencies and Teamwork-Enabling Competencies

Core Teamwork Competencies	Definitions	Selected Citations
Mutual performance monitoring	Tracking fellow team members' performance to ensure that everything is running as expected and to ensure procedures are followed	McIntyre & Salas, 1995
Adaptability	Being able to recognize deviations from expected action and readjust actions accordingly	Cannon-Bowers et al., 1995; Kozlowski et al., 1999
Back-up behavior	Providing feedback and coaching to improve performance, or when a lapse is detected, assisting the teammate in performing a task; completing a task for the team member when an overload is detected	McIntyre & Salas, 1995; Porter et al., 2003
Team leadership	Being able to direct/coordinate team members, assess team performance, allocate tasks, motivate subordinates, plan/organize, and maintain a positive team environment	Marks, Zaccaro, & Mathieu, 2000; Salas, Burke, & Stagl, in press; Zaccaro, Rittman, & Marks, 2001
Team orientation	Tending to enhance individual performance through the coordination, evaluation, and utilization of task inputs from other team members while performing team tasks	Driskell & Salas, 1992
Closed-loop communication	Performing actions including the initiation of a message by the sender, the receipt and acknowledgment of the message by the receiver, and the verification of the message by the initial sender	McIntyre & Salas, 1995
Shared mental models	Having a shared understanding of the team's goals, individual team member tasks, and how the team will coordinate to achieve common goals	Klimoski & Mohammed, 1994; Minionis, Zaccaro, & Perez, 1995
Mutual trust	Having an attitude among team members regarding the aura, mood, or climate of the team's internal environment	Bandow, 2001; Webber, 2002

Training is a theoretically based combination of tools, methods, and content that creates an instructional strategy. The science of training has taught researchers that there is more to devising a training program than ensuring that the program is content valid (e.g., training the knowledge, skills, and attitudes of interest) (Salas & Cannon-Bowers, 2001). Instead, training must be developed using sound instructional principles and a thorough needs analysis because team training is not (a) simply a location where individuals go to engage in task-relevant exercises, (b) necessarily a *single* program, or (c) simulation (Salas & Cannon-Bowers, 2001). This said, not only may the task and the environment act on team effectiveness; the team itself is in a constant state of flux, which means the training program must be flexible. Therefore, a team training program must consider the type of team, the task, and the environment (Cannon-Bowers & Salas, 1997).

Designing Team Training Systematically

Given the intricacy of team training, three over-arching steps have been suggested to ensure that team training is systematically designed, implemented, and evaluated. The first step is to conduct a thorough team task analysis to define the content and learning objectives of the training program. Next, a training strategy and method must be selected. Finally, a plan must be developed to evaluate the program. We will now provide a brief description of these steps and provide some lessons learned at each step.

Step 1: Training Needs Analysis

A team training analysis will identify the competencies and coordination demands required by the team task to determine the training objectives (what should be trained?). From this analysis, training objectives are created that describe what should be learned, the proficiency of the KSAs, and under what conditions those KSAs should be exhibited (Campbell & Kuncel, 2001). The answers to these questions will impact both the choice of delivery method and the instructional strategy chosen (how should it be trained?).

Tip 1: Consider the context. Conducting a team training analysis is a critical phase because team training does not exist in a vacuum. A team training analysis is much broader than a task analysis because it evaluates the skills needed as well as the organizational environment, the team context, and the individual characteristics of the trainees. In fact, many factors outside the training program can impact the success of training (e.g., organizational, individual, task, and motivational characteristics). This information should be gained from several sources (e.g., past job analyses, job incumbents, subject matter experts, critical incidents, supervisors) to gain a broad and accurate understanding of the needed KSAs (Goldstein, 1993).

Organization Context

Past empirical studies have indicated that organizational climate has a direct impact on the transfer of training (e.g., Rouiller & Goldstein, 1993; Tracey, Tannenbaum, & Kavanaugh, 1995). In answer to this, team task analyses have begun to examine the organizational context. An organizational analysis should include an evaluation of the organization's strategic goals, resources, climate/culture, and constraints (Goldstein, 1993) to determine what skills should be targeted (those needed now and in the future) and estimate the support of management.

Team Context

Team performance and team effectiveness are affected by a number of variables within the team (e.g., team task, structure, diversity, and the degree of interdependence). Likewise, these variables may influence the type of training that is most effective. For instance, the training must fit the stage of team development, as team processes may change as the team gains experience working together (e.g., Johnston, 1966; Kozlowski, Gully, Nason, & Smith, 1999). The structure or formality of the team can affect the type of training that is most appropriate. The structure of the team is defined by the flexibility of the individual team members to complete specific tasks (George, 1977). Thus, certain training strategies will be neither desired nor beneficial to a highly structured team. For instance, extensive cross training on other teammates' responsibilities would be of little benefit to highly structured team members who are not able to complete a task for another team member.

Individual Context

Individual characteristics of the trainees can also impact the effectiveness of any team training program. A training needs analysis should assess differences in team members' degrees of motivation, expectation, ability, experience, and learning preferences (e.g., Campbell,

McCloy, Oppler, & Sager, 1993; Gibson, 2001; Smith-Jentsch, Jentsch, Payne, & Salas, 1996; Tracey, Hinkin, Tannenbaum, & Mathieu, 2001).

Tip 2: Ensure that the KSAs targeted in training can be used on the job. The ability to perform a trained KSA does not ensure that the KSA will be used on the job. A variety of factors can impact whether employees use the KSAs that they learned during the training. These factors include, but are not limited to, how well the KSA was learned, employees' motivation to change typical behaviors, their ability to recognize when to use the skill, whether their manager supports the new KSAs, and whether the skill is (or is perceived to be) useful (Campbell & Kuncel, 2001; Lehman, Lempert, & Nisbett, 1988). These issues are referred to as the *transfer climate* (e.g., Baldwin & Ford, 1988; Ford & Weissbein, 1997; Tracey et al., 1995).

Another problem that may be encountered involves how often the new KSA is used on the job. Although the team may intend to use the new KSA, infrequent opportunities to do so may result in deterioration or loss of what was learned. Therefore, training programs should be targeted at frequently used KSAs, or refresher courses should be regularly offered to maintain the salience of the less frequently used KSAs.

Step 2: Defining Training Content

The training content covers a substantial portion of the KSA domain identified in the training objectives from Step 1 and guides the presentation of information to ensure that learning occurs (Gagne, Briggs, & Wager, 1988).

Tip 3: Determine if training is needed at the individual or team level. Teams are not an entity of their own but rather a collection of individuals that behave interactively. Therefore, attention has been drawn to the fact that the targeted KSAs may be individual or team-based skills

(e.g., Dyer, 1984; Kozlowski & Bell, 2004), as that will dictate whether individual or team-based training is more appropriate. An individual skill is one that can be performed independently, whereas a team skill is one that is a response to or an anticipation of the actions of a teammate (e.g., Kozlowski & Salas, 1997; Kozlowski, Brown, Weissbein, Cannon-Bowers, & Salas, 2000). For instance, if the team performs in a sequential structure (i.e., only one member works on the product at a given time and then hands off the task to the next team member), then individual training may be the most cost-effective and efficient method. Conversely, if the team works together simultaneously on the task (i.e., flying an aircraft), then a team-based training intervention may be most appropriate.

One comprehensive model that has been developed takes into account the team- and individual-level distinction, as well as the phases of team development (Kozlowski et al., 1999). The model includes four phases of team development including team socialization, skill acquisition, identification of each other's individual roles and their interdependencies, and adaptability to novel and challenging demands. Therefore, it is clear that for a team to improve its outcomes, team training must target the level at which the KSAs are lacking (individual/team) and consider the team's life cycle.

Tip 4: Decide on the purpose of the team training. The primary purpose of team training is to increase job knowledge or to gain or improve a particular skill that will improve team effectiveness. The purpose of training must be clearly articulated, as it is directly linked both to finding the most effective training strategy to implement and to evaluating the program's ultimate effectiveness. Team training may be developed to serve a variety of objectives including established, emergent (e.g., changes in the economy), or anticipated needs (e.g., changes in customer needs). Salas and Cannon-Bowers (1997) suggested that the team type and the team task should determine whether the task, team-specific skills, or generalizeable competencies (e.g., problem solving, communication) should be targeted.

Step 3: Developing and Implementing Training

As the science of training has developed, a number of tools, methods, and strategies have been designed for team training. Based on the information gained, the team task/cognitive analysis, tools, methods, and strategies should be carefully selected to align with the needs and constraints of the team and the organization. Although it may seem simple to design a training program, a number of factors must be considered before the training can be implemented.

Tip 5: Take time to decide who will present the training material. A subject matter expert within the team's domain is invaluable in determining the content of the training program. However, experts are not always the most appropriate trainers (Desimone, Werner, & Harris, 2002). The most appropriate trainer is one who is recognized as having the competencies targeted and the ability to communicate and motivate the trainees (Desimone et al., 2002).

Tip 6: The fidelity of the training program can affect the amount of learning that occurs. The fidelity of the training environment should be considered when conducting team training, especially if the targeted skills are performed under stressful conditions. This fidelity is often achieved through the use of simulators that create realistic task situations. Simulations are often scripted to guide the team through specific events that allow them to practice the targeted KSAs. In addition, training instructors can observe the situations under which performance degrades so that teams can receive specific feedback on their performance (or failure to perform) and additional training they need (George, 1977). Fidelity of the training environment has been suggested to include stimulus

fidelity, response fidelity, and equipment fidelity (Salas et al., 1992).

Tip 7: Use the information gained through the team task/cognitive analysis to choose the tools, methods, and strategies that will make up the team training program.

Implementing Training

Tools

Team training developers should not neglect the impact that tools, such as advance organizers (e.g., outlines, diagrams, and graphic organizers), preparatory information, and pre-practice briefs may have on maximizing practice during training (Cannon-Bowers, Rhodenizer, Salas, & Bowers, 1998). Media can vary in ability to maintain the interest of the trainees and the flexibility with which the trainer can adapt to the needs or questions posed by the trainees. For instance, a textbook writer cannot clarify information that the reader does not understand. Conversely, computer-adaptive learning environments can provide learners with additional assistance or remedial training when the information does not seem to be understood.

Methods

The methods chosen to present training material are important because they can impact the amount of learning that takes place. The methods used to present material can vary across topic area, the needs of the learner, and the constraints of the trainer. One method that has received a lot of empirical attention is practice: Does the trainee have an opportunity to rehearse the activity being learned during a training intervention. Researchers have suggested that practice (a) should be deliberate, interactive, and guided (Ericsson & Charnes, 1994); (b) should use appropriate levels of fidelity; (c) should use a variety of scenarios/ conditions to elicit the targeted KSAs; and (d) should provide a moderate amount of feedback (Campbell & Kuncel, 2001). Further evidence suggests that allowing trainees to make errors and providing corrective feedback increases the retention and transfer of the targeted KSAs to the workplace (e.g., Carlson, Lundy, & Schneider, 1992; Ivancic & Hesketh, 1995/1996).

Strategies

Training strategies are a systematic combination of tools, methods, and competency-based content. Each strategy has strengths and weaknesses; however, the choice of strategies will depend on the needs of the team. A number of team training strategies are provided in Table 22.2. Note that some training strategies are focused at either the individual or team level, whereas other strategies are effective for either level.

Tip 8: Determine how diagnostic feedback will be given to trainees. Without timely, constructive feedback, trainees will not be able to adjust their learning strategies to meet the expected level of effectiveness or performance (e.g., Baldwin & Ford, 1988; Schmidt & Bjork, 1992). Imagine a flight team that constantly crashes its simulator plane. Without an understanding of where the breakdowns occur and how best to resolve them, the team may never be allowed to fly. Team feedback will provide insight into where errors occur and how to fix them. Research suggests that timely and process-based feedback is most likely to improve overall learning and performance (e.g., Baldwin & Ford, 1988; Schmidt & Bjork, 1992). Depending on the type of data collected and the method used to collect it, the speed with which feedback can be provided will vary. Fortunately, as computers and technology continue to improve, data can be collected and analyzed at increasing speeds. The question then arises: Who receives the feedback, the team or the individual team member?

The question of who should receive team feedback (the team or the individual) is one issue that constantly arises in the team literature. Ultimately, this decision must be made based on the available feedback and whether the whole team would benefit. For instance, if an airport security team member is observed incorrectly identifying suspicious items, it may be beneficial for the whole team to receive additional feedback and training to bolster identification skills. Conversely, there are times when a single team member requires additional training, and then, the feedback should be provided at an individual level.

Step 4: Evaluation of Training Effectiveness

Evaluation of training is the third step in the training process. This step measures the effectiveness of the training and provides insight on whether the targeted KSAs were attained. A number of frameworks have been offered to guide the designing of an evaluation program (e.g., Bushnell, 1990; Galvin, 1983; Kirkpatrick, 1967; Kraiger, Ford, & Salas, 1993; Phillips, 1993), although the most widely accepted and cited of these evaluation frameworks was developed by Kirkpatrick (1967). The evaluation is often used to make adjustments in the training methods or strategies and to ensure "the greatest bang for the buck."

Training evaluation can be costly due to the physical resources (i.e., paper, software) and personnel (e.g., time of trainee, raters) required. As a result, training evaluation is often poorly planned, if it is conducted at all. Salas and Cannon-Bowers (1997) provide guidelines for effective training evaluation: (a) Design a clear link between the stated training objectives and what is measured during the evaluation, (b) provide timely and constructive feedback to the trainee and opportunities to practice the new KSAs, and (c) use measurement tools that are

Table 22.2   Individual and Team-Level Training Strategies

Strategy	Definition	Level	Sources
Assertiveness training	Uses behavioral modeling techniques to demonstrate both assertive and nonassertive behaviors. Provides multiple practice and feedback opportunities for trainees.	Individual	Smith-Jentsch, Salas, et al., 1996
Metacognitive training	Targets trainee's executive monitoring and self-regulatory cognitive processes for development. Develops metacognitive skills that regulate cognitive abilities such as inductive and deductive reasoning.	Individual	Ford et al., 1998; Schraw & Dennison, 1994
Stress exposure training	Provides information regarding links between stressors, trainee affect, and performance. Provides coping strategies for trainees in dealing with stressors.	Individual and team	Driskell & Johnston, 1998
Team dimensional training/ self-correction training	Teaches teams to review events, correct errors, discuss strategies, and plan for future events following a performance episode. This training is delivered through a combination of lecture, demonstration, practice, and feedback.	Individual and team	Smith-Jentsch et al., 1998; Blickensderfer et al., 1998
Scenario-based training	Used to enhance the performance of individuals and teams in technology-rich environments that are representative of actual operational conditions. Relies on scripted exercises or vignettes in which the trainee is presented with cues or trigger events that are similar to those that will be found in the actual task environment. Trainees are then given feedback regarding their responses.	Individual and team	
Sensitivity training	Aims to improve how team members interact, get along, trust, and communicate with others. May have impact on both work and personal relationships.	Team and individual	Wilson, Mullen, & Morton, 1968
Tactical team training	Intends to identify weaknesses in the team's tactical skills in order to correct them. Also called engagement simulation. The training program can range from completely unplanned as it would occur in combat to structured programs that have planned tactical situations.	Team	Shriver et al., 1975

(Continued)

Table 22.2 (Continued)

Strategy	Definition	Level	Sources
Fully immersive team training	Evaluates how best to train teams and ensure they transfer to the real combat environment. Designed to have realistic mission environments and interactions with teammates. Purpose of the training program is to provide mission planning and rehearsal as well as testing new equipment.	Team	Lampton & Parsons, 2001
Distributed mission training	Provides a dynamic, adaptive training environment to focus on teamwork skills such as communication, coordination, and decision making.	Team	Bell, 1999
Team coordination training	Improves team coordination, communication, and backup behavior. Provides practice opportunities for other KSAs that lead to effective coordination. Also known as crew resource management. Focuses on teaching team members about basic process underlying teamwork. Usually delivered through a combination of information, demonstration (e.g., video examples), and practice-based (e.g., role plays) methods over 2 to 5 days.	Team	Entin & Serfaty, 1999; Entin et al., 1994; Salas, Prince, et al., 1999
Team building	Targets role clarification, goal setting, problem solving, or interpersonal relations for improvement. However, recent meta-analytic evidence suggests team building only increases performance when targeting subjective criteria such as role clarification.	Team	Salas, Rozell, Mullen, & Driskell, 1999
Cross training	Exposes team members to the basic tasks, duties, and responsibilities of other team members in an effort to promote coordination, communication, and team performance. Intends to increase implicit coordination, interpositional knowledge, and shared mental models.	Team	Cannon-Bowers & Salas, 1998; Volpe et al., 1996
Verbal self-guidance training	Aims at improving the self-efficacy of the team by training team members to refrain from using negative statements about the team's functioning and to use more positive statements to guide their future actions.	Team	Brown, 2004

Strategy	Definition	Level	Sources
Team training	Provides trainees with the necessary competencies at both the individual and team levels to complete their assigned tasks safely and effectively, by providing interventions that facilitate (a) information presentation, (b) demonstration of teamwork behaviors and skills, (c) opportunities to practice, and (d) diagnostic feedback. This strategy may be more beneficial to newly formed teams.	Team	Salas & Cannon-Bowers, 2000; Kozlowski et al., 1999; Kozlowski, Gully, Salas, & Cannon-Bowers, 1996
Organizational training	Emphasizes team development, decision making, and problem solving. Uses work-related examples to assist team members in recognizing and resolving conflict within and outside of the team. Assists team members in gaining understanding about themselves and other teammates in a work-oriented context.	Team	Morton, 1965
Team Model Training (TMT)	A type of cross training in which the team is presented text and graphical information regarding an individual team member's tasks and then provides an event-based scenario situation so that the team can practice the skills. Found to significantly improve performance, communication, and interpositional knowledge.	Team	Duncan et al., 1996

adaptive/sensitive to changes as the task unfolds and the team gains experience working together.

Tip 9: Understand the pros and cons of the training evaluation tools used. Many new tools can be used to evaluate the effectiveness of training. However, tools should be chosen systematically. The measurement tool selected will depend greatly on what the researcher or practitioner wants to measure: processes (e.g., communication) or outcomes (e.g., accuracy) (see Table 22.3 or Goldstein, 1993, for a review) as well as the level of measurement (individual vs. team). For instance, the tools used to gather communication data may differ greatly from tools to collect data on a typist's accuracy.

The collection of process data will provide insight into why a certain level of performance was achieved. With no data regarding how the production team performs together, the leader is able to give little guidance beyond "Improve." If team members are also unable to diagnose where the problems occur, they have little chance of improving.

Tip 10: Pay attention to the level of collected data (individual vs. team). A factor in collecting multilevel data is how information is aggregated.

Table 22.3   Some Advantages and Disadvantages of a Selection of Data Collection Tools

Tool	Advantages	Disadvantages
Questionnaire	Larger sample size is possible Confidentiality is better Lower cost than other data collection measures (e.g., interviews) Results are easy to summarize and tabulate Can be self-administered	Response rate may be low Respondents may not understand questions No opportunity to follow up or clarify responses Cannot ensure who actual respondent is Unable to capture unexpected responses
Interview	If questions are unclear, interviewer can restate or clarify the question Improved response rates Can be adapted if additional information is available or offered	Requires skilled interviewer Higher cost than questionnaires Results are difficult to quantify Less confidentiality Time-consuming for the interviewees
Observation	Minimizes time away from the job tasks Provides opportunity to observe effective and ineffective behaviors	Requires skilled observer May alter typical behavior on the job Some tasks may not be observable (i.e., cognitive thought process)
Group discussion or focus groups	Opportunity for a variety of viewpoints Increases participation and support for decisions Opportunity to adapt questions to gather additional information	Requires skilled interviewer Time-consuming for the interviewees Difficult to quantify results Reduced confidentiality
Tests	Identifies gaps in knowledge, skills, and attitudes (KSAs) Easily quantifiable Offers normative data Flexibility in administration	Few validated tests for specific KSAs No indication of whether KSAs are being transferred to the workplace

Team researchers have begun to oppose blind aggregation without considering at what level the data is collected (individual vs. team) and whether interpretations of the data are consistent with the level collected (e.g., Kozlowski & Klein, 2000). A common example might be to collect individual perceptions of team efficacy, then average the individual perceptions and interpret them as the team's efficaciousness. Kozlowski and Klein (2000) have advocated against this procedure and provide suggestions for alternative methodologies.

Tip 11: Make sure your evaluation plan is sensitive to changes in team processes, and gather data at several points throughout the team's performance. The team and their environment are in constant flux, so any evaluation tool must be able to pinpoint when and why a change occurs in the team's performance. For instance, a team may perform the targeted skill by inadvertently choosing the correct response. This would only be identified if the team were given a number of opportunities to perform the skill and were only able to respond correctly once or were unable to explain the steps that led to their choice.

The training evaluation should also be sensitive to whether an error occurs because an individual team member lacks a particular skill or the team as a whole fails to perform appropriate teamwork behavior. The answer to this question will provide guidance as to how to rectify the situation. For this reason, team assessment should be sensitive enough to determine when team members are involved in a coordinated response or a simple individual response (Zalesney, Salas, & Prince, 1995).

Tip 12: Gather data to determine if there is a return on the investment due to the team training program. The training programs that have been discussed throughout this chapter have been designed and implemented for one ultimate purpose: to improve team performance and effectiveness. However, team training is often provided in an organizational setting that is also concerned with whether training provides a tangible (monetary) benefit. Therefore, one purpose of evaluating training is to be able to calculate changes that occurred as a direct result of the team training program and convert those changes into dollar amounts.

Step 5: Transfer of Training

There is no guarantee that teams that learn the targeted KSAs will transfer what they have learned to the workplace. In fact, factors before, during, and after team training can impact whether the learned material is transferred (for review, see Cannon-Bowers, Salas, & Milham, 2000). Due to space restrictions, we will limit this discussion to those factors that occur after the training has been provided.

Tip 13: Give team members a clear message that teamwork is valued. If employees are to behave as teammates, they must understand that the organization and upper management value teamwork. First and foremost, managers must support and reinforce teamwork behaviors (Tannenbaum & Yukl, 1992). This can be done not only by modeling teamwork behaviors but also by ensuring that performance appraisals and reward systems focus on team-level outcomes rather than just individual outcomes (Cannon-Bowers et al., 2000; Smith-Jentsch, Salas, & Brannick, 2001). If team-level outcomes are not attended to, trainees may assume that their individual behaviors or outcomes are of greater importance.

Which Team Training Strategies Are Effective?

Campbell and Kuncel (2001) aptly stated that "comparing instructional methods should only be for the purpose of developing optimal methods for meeting a particular training need" (p. 305). This suggests that there is no silver bullet of training. Although we provide a review of a number of training strategies and their effectiveness in this section, we do so only as a means of providing guidelines in selecting a training strategy. It must be understood that every opportunity to provide training is unique to the team, the organization, and the team task. The needs and constraints of the team, the deficiencies in skill bases, and the task requirements for the team must all be considered. Although there are many training strategies, only the six most prominent team-level strategies will be discussed here: cross training, metacognition, team coordination training, team self-correction training, team building, and assertiveness training.

Cross Training

Cross training generally involves training each individual member on the tasks of all other team members. The purpose of this team training strategy is to create shared task models and knowledge of task-specific role responsibilities to facilitate enhanced performance monitoring and backup behaviors (see Blickensderfer, Cannon-Bowers, & Salas, 1998; Volpe, Cannon-Bowers, Salas, & Spector, 1996). Some studies have found that teams given cross training outperform those that have not received cross training due to improved coordination, cooperation, and interpositional knowledge (Volpe et al., 1996). Team performance increases of 12% to 40% following the implementation of cross training have been reported.

Metacognitive Training

Metacognition "is the ability to reflect upon, understand, and control one's learning" (Schraw & Dennison, 1994, p. 460). It is proposed that the benefit of metacognitive training is that it teaches individuals to become more aware of the strategies they use to learn, to determine which strategies are the most appropriate, and to adjust accordingly. Past research has indicated that individuals will frequently use strategies that do not promote learning. For instance, left to their own learning strategies, students frequently terminate their practice sessions early because they underestimate their need for practice (Park & Tennyson, 1980; Tennyson & Rothen, 1979), or they choose items that are easier or more difficult than their true skill levels (Fisher, Blackwell, Garcia, & Greene, 1975; Snow & Peterson, 1980). Metacognitive skills are related to knowledge acquisitions, behavior acquisition, and increased self-efficacy (Ford, Smith, Weissbein, Gully, & Salas, 1998).

Team Coordination Training

Team coordination training creates a general understanding of teamwork skills to promote mutual performance monitoring and backup behavior (see Serfaty, Entin, & Johnston, 1998).

This team training technique was initially designed to assist teams that endure periods of high stress (Entin, Serfaty, & Deckert, 1994; Serfaty, Entin, & Volpe, 1993) (e.g., aviation and military settings). This strategy, also referred to as *crew resource management* training, is a family of instructional strategies that seek to improve teamwork by applying well-tested training tools (e.g., simulators, lectures, videos) targeted at specific content (i.e., teamwork KSAs) (Salas, Prince, et al., 1999). The unique aspect of this training strategy is that it teaches the team to adapt coordination strategies and reduce explicit communication under periods of high stress. In addition, the team is taught to use downtime to plan and strategize for future performances. Some studies have found performance increases of up to 15% due to this training strategy. Entin et al. (1994) found that improvements in performance resulted in reduced errors, better ability to adjust workloads within the team, and improved communication and coordination.

Self-Guided Correction Training

Another type of training that improves mutual performance monitoring as well as initiative, leadership, and communication is self-guided correction training. This training strategy teaches the team to diagnose, design, and implement solutions to their functional problems. The team directly drives this training, although the team leader may provide structure and guidance to the team members' exchanges. Success in training these skills and improving overall team performance has been found in both laboratory and field settings (Smith-Jentsch, Zeisig, Acton, & McPherson, 1998).

Team Building

Another technique that is used to increase team functioning and effectiveness is team building. Although team training and team building are seemingly similar, they approach teamwork from different perspectives. For instance, team training is generally intended to facilitate job-related KSAs whereas team building focuses on the processes of teamwork to assist individuals and groups in examining their own behavior and interrelationships.

It is important to note that team building has been found to have a larger impact on the attitudes, interpersonal skills, and problem solving of individuals than on overall team performance (e.g., Nicholas, 1982; Porras & Robertson, 1992). It has been suggested that this is due to the focus on interpersonal relations, communication, problem solving, goal setting, and decision making. Mixed results are reported as to the impact of team building on performance (DeMuse & Liebowitz, 1981; Nicholas, 1982; Woodman & Sherwood, 1980). Another possible explanation for the limited impact of team building on performance is that it is generally one-dimensional in its aim (i.e., problem solving, interpersonal skills) and therefore is only measurable in that instance, not in a global performance context. To the extent that additional facets of relevant team building interventions are added, the impact of team building interventions will rise. One meta-analysis found that the overall effect size of team building that used a combination of methods was 0.785, whereas individual aspects of team building had a smaller effect size (i.e., goal setting effect size = 0.622; interpersonal skills effect size = 0.622) (Svyantek, Goodman, Benz, & Gard, 1999). Finally, it should be noted that team building is not a one-shot deal. Observable improvements in cooperation may take time to appear and require ongoing attention to attain long-term effectiveness.

Assertiveness Training

Assertiveness training is designed to ensure that team members effectively communicate when they are (a) offering or requesting assistance, (b) offering a potential solution, or (c) providing feedback to other team members. This training is useful as it assumes that each team member is a resource who can provide unique perspectives and solutions to handle the team task (Smith-Jentsch, Salas, & Baker, 1996) and that learning to be assertive helps to ensure that each team member will be a confident communicator (Cannon-Bowers & Salas, 1998). Overall, assertiveness training targets the attitude that assertiveness is acceptable and offers the knowledge and skills to perform it through role modeling and active practice (Smith-Jentsch, Salas, et al., 1996).

Conclusion

Team training is one means of ensuring that work teams are provided the KSAs needed to work in a cooperative work environment. Throughout this chapter, it has been stressed that training must be systematically designed and implemented to achieve meaningful change. Quite a few choices must be made throughout the process of designing and implementing a training program, any of which can alter the overall effectiveness of the program. Therefore, these choices must be made intelligently and purposefully. There are many stories of a company that picks an off-the-shelf training program but fails to acquire the outcomes that were expected. Often, this is because the choice was made based on the cost or popularity of a particular training program rather than on the needs that exist in the organization. Because effective team training necessitates extensive planning and resources, it is in the company's best interest to pick (or develop) a program that meets its particular needs rather than one that is the latest fad.

References

Baldwin, T. T., & Ford, J. K. (1988). Transfer of training: A review and directions for future research. *Personnel Psychology, 41,* 63–105.

Bandow, D. (2001). Time to create sound teamwork. *The Journal for Quality and Participation, 24,* 41–47.

Bell, H. H. (1999). The effectiveness of distributed mission training. *Communications of the ACM, 42,* 72–79.

Blickensderfer, E., Cannon-Bowers, J. A., & Salas, E. (1998). Cross-training and team performance. In J. A. Cannon-Bowers & E. Salas (Eds.), *Making decisions under stress: Implications for individual and team training* (pp. 299–311). Washington, DC: American Psychological Association.

Bowers, C.A., Braun, C., & Morgan, B. B., Jr. (1997). Team workload: Its meaning and measurement. In M. T. Brannick, E. Salas, & C. Prince (Eds.), *Team performance assessment and measurement: Theory, research, and applications* (pp. 85–108). Hillsdale, NJ: Lawrence Erlbaum.

Brown, T. C. (2004). The effect of verbal self guidance training on collective efficacy and team performance. *Personnel Psychology, 56,* 935–964.

Bushnell, D. S. (1990). Input, process, output: A model for evaluating training. *Training and Development Journal, 44,* 41–43.

Campbell, J. P., & Kuncel, N. R. (2001). Individual and team training. In N. Anderson, D. S. Ones, H. K. Sinangil, & C. Viswesvaran (Eds.), *Handbook of industrial, work and organizational psychology* (pp. 278–312). London: Sage.

Campbell, J. P., McCloy, R. A., Oppler, S. H., & Sager, C. E. (1993). A theory of performance. In N. Schmitt & W. C. Borman (Eds.), *Performance selection in organizations* (pp. 35–70). San Francisco: Jossey-Bass.

Cannon-Bowers, J. A., Rhodenizer, L., Salas, E., & Bowers, C. A. (1998). A framework for understanding pre-practice conditions and their impact on learning. *Personnel Psychology, 51,* 291–320.

Cannon-Bowers, J. A., & Salas, E. (1997). Teamwork competencies: The interaction of team member knowledge, skills, and attitudes. In H. F. O'Niel (Ed.), *Workforce readiness: Competencies and assessment* (pp. 151–174). Mahwah, NJ: Lawrence Erlbaum.

Cannon-Bowers, J. A., & Salas, E. (Eds.). (1998). *Making decisions under stress: Implications for individual and team training.* Washington, DC: American Psychological Association.

Cannon-Bowers, J. A., Salas, E., & Milham, L. M. (2000). The transfer of team training: Propositions and preliminary guidance. In E. F. Holton, T. T. Baldwin, & S. S. Naquin (Eds.), *Advances in developing human resources: Managing and changing learning transfer systems* (Vol. 8, pp. 63–74). San Francisco: Berrett-Koehler.

Cannon-Bowers, J. A., Tannenbaum, S. I., Salas, E., & Volpe, C. E. (1995). Defining team competencies and establishing team training requirements. In R. Guzzo, E. Salas, & Associates (Eds.), *Team effectiveness and decision making in organizations* (pp. 333–380). San Francisco: Jossey-Bass.

Carlson, R. A., Lundy, D. H., & Schneider, W. (1992). Strategy guidance and memory aiding in learning a problem solving skill. *Human Factors, 32,* 129–145.

DeMuse, K. P., & Liebowitz, S. J. (1981). An empirical analysis of team building. *Group and Organizational Studies, 6,* 357–378.

Desimone, R. L., Werner, J. M., & Harris, D. M. (2002). *Human resource development* (3rd ed.). New York: Harcourt College.

Driskell, J. E., & Johnston, J. H. (1998). Stress exposure training. In J. A. Cannon-Bowers & E. Salas (Eds.), *Making decisions under stress: Implications for individual and team training* (pp. 191–217). Washington, DC: APA Press.

Driskell, J. E., & Salas, E. (1992). Can you study real teams in contrived settings? The value of small group research to understanding teams. In R. W. Swezey & E. Salas (Eds.), *Teams: Their training and performance* (pp. 101–124). Norwood, NJ: Ablex.

Duncan, P. C., Rouse, W. B., Johnston, J. H., Cannon-Bowers, J. A., Salas, E., & Burns, J. J. (1996). Training teams working in complex systems: A mental model-based approach. In W. B. Rouse (Ed.), *Human/technology interaction in complex systems* (Vol. 8, pp. 173–231). Greenwich, CT: JAI Press.

Dyer, J. L. (1984). Team research and team training: A state-of-the-art review. *Human Factors Review,* pp. 285–319.

Entin, E. E., & Serfaty, D. (1999). Adaptive team coordination. *Human Factors, 41,* 312–325.

Entin, E. E., Serfaty, D., & Deckert, J. C. (1994). *Team adaptation and coordination training* (TR-648-1). Burlington, MA: ALPHATECH.

Ericsson, K. A., & Charnes, N. (1994). Expert performance: Its structure and acquisition. *American Psychologist, 49,* 725–747.

Fisher, M. D., Blackwell, L. R., Garcia, A. B., & Greene, J. C. (1975). Effects of student choice on engagement in CIA arithmetic task in a low income school. *Journal of Educational Psychology, 67,* 776–783.

Fleishman, E. A. (1975). Toward a taxonomy of human performance. *American Psychologist, 30,* 127–149.

Fleishman, E. A., & Zacarro, W. J. (1992). Toward a taxonomy of team performance functions. In R. W. Swezey & E. Salas (Eds.), *Teams: Their training and performance* (pp. 31–56). Norwood, NJ: Ablex.

Ford, J. K., Smith, E. M., Weissbein, D. A., Gully, S. M., & Salas, E. (1998). Relationships of goal-orientation, metacognitive activity, and practice strategies with learning outcomes and transfer. *Journal of Applied Psychology, 83,* 218–233.

Ford, J. K., & Weissbein, D. (1997). Training of training: An updated review. *Performance and Instruction Quarterly, 10,* 22–41.

Gagne, R. M., Briggs, L. J., & Wager, W. W. (1988). *Principles of instructional design.* (3rd ed.). New York: Holt, Rinehart and Winston.

Galvin, J. C. (1983). What trainers can learn from educators about evaluating management training. *Training and Development Journal, 37,* 52–57.

George, C. E. (1977, March). *Team member coordination: Definition, measurement, and effect on performance.* Paper presented at the meeting of the Southeastern Psychological Association, New Orleans, LA.

Gibson, C. B. (2001). Me and us: Differential relationships among goal setting training, efficacy, and effectiveness at the individual and team level. *Journal of Organizational Behavior, 22,* 789–808.

Gladstein, D. L. (1984). Groups in context: A model of task group effectiveness. *Administrative Science Quarterly, 29,* 499–517.

Goldstein, I. L. (1993). *Training in organizations: Needs assessment, development, and evaluation* (3rd ed.). Monterey, CA: Brooks/Cole.

Hackman, J. R. (1969). Toward understanding the role of tasks in behavioral research. *Acta Psychologica, 31,* 125–128.

Hackman, J. R. (1987). The design of work teams. In J. Lorsch (Ed.), *Handbook of organizational behavior* (pp. 315–342). New York: Prentice Hall.

Ivancic, K., & Hesketh, B. (1995/1996). Making the best of errors during training. *Training Research Journal, 1,* 103–125.

Johnston, W. A. (1966). Transfer of team skills as a function of type of training. *Journal of Applied Psychology, 50,* 102–108.

Kirkpatrick, D. L. (1967). Evaluation of training. In R. L. Craig & L. R. Bittel (Eds.), *Training and development handbook* (pp. 87–112). New York: McGraw-Hill.

Klimoski, R., & Mohammed, S. (1994). Team mental model: Construct or metaphor? *Journal of Management, 20,* 403–437.

Kozlowski, S. W. J., & Bell, B. S. (2004). Work groups and teams in organizations. In W. C. Borman, D. R. Ilgen, & R. L. Klimoski (Eds.), *Comprehensive handbook of psychology: Vol. 12. Industrial and organizational psychology.* New York: John Wiley.

Kozlowski, S. W. J., Brown, K. G., Weissbein, D. A., Cannon-Bowers, J. A., & Salas, E. (2000). A multi-level perspective on training effectiveness: Enhancing horizontal and vertical transfer. In K. J. Klein & S. W. J. Kozlowski (Eds.), *Multilevel theory, research, and methods in organizations* (pp. 157–210). San Francisco: Jossey-Bass.

Kozlowski, S. W. J., Gully, S. M., Nason, E. R., & Smith, E. M. (1999). Developing adaptive teams: A theory of compilation and performance across levels and time. In D. R. Ilgen & E. D. Pulakos (Eds.), *The changing nature of work performance: Implications for staffing, personnel actions, and development* (pp. 240–292). San Francisco: Jossey-Bass.

Kozlowski, S. W. J., Gully, S. M., Salas, E., & Cannon-Bowers, J. A. (1996). Team leadership and development: Theory, principles, and guidelines for training leaders and teams. In M. Beyerlein, D. Johnson, & S. Beyerlein (Eds.), *Advances in interdisciplinary studies of work teams: Team leadership* (Vol. 3, pp. 251–289). Greenwich, CT: JAI Press.

Kozlowski, S. W. J., & Klein, K. J. (2000). A multilevel approach to theory and research in organizations: Contextual, temporal, and emergent processes. In K. J. Klein & S. W. J. Kozlowski (Eds.), *Multilevel theory, research, and methods in organizations: Foundations, extensions, and new directions* (pp. 3–90). San Francisco: Jossey-Bass.

Kozlowski, S. W. J., & Salas, E. (1997). An organizational systems approach for the implementation and transfer of training. In J. K. Ford, S. W. J. Kozlowski, K. Kraiger, E. Salas, & M. Teachout (Eds.), *Improving training effectiveness in work organizations* (pp. 247–287). Mahwah, NJ: LEA.

Kraiger, K., Ford, J. K., & Salas, E. (1993). Application of cognitive, skill-based, and affective theories of learning outcomes to new methods of training evaluation. *Journal of Applied Psychology, 78,* 311–328.

Lampton, D. R., & Parsons, J. B. (2001). The fully immersive team training (FITT) research system: Design and implementation. *Presence, 10,* 129–141.

Lehman, D. R., Lempert, R. O., & Nisbett, R. E. (1988). The effects of graduate training on reasoning: Formal discipline and thinking about every-day events. *American Psychologist, 43,* 431–442.

Marks, M. A., Zaccaro, S. J., & Mathieu, J. E. (2000). Performance implications of leader briefings and team interaction training for team adaptation to novel environments. *Journal of Applied Psychology, 85,* 971–986.

McIntyre, R. M., & Salas, E. (1995). Measuring and managing for team performance: Emerging principles from complex environments. In R. Guzzo & E. Salas (Eds.), *Team effectiveness and decision making in organizations* (pp. 149–203). San Francisco: Jossey-Bass.

Minionis, D. P., Zaccaro, S. J., & Perez, R. (1995). *Shared mental models, team coordination, and team performance.* Paper presented at the 10th Annual Meeting of the Society for Industrial and Organizational Psychology, Orlando, FL.

Moreland, R. L., & Levine, J. M. (1992). The composition of small groups. In E. J. Lawler, B. Markovsky, C. Ridgeway, & H. A. Walker (Eds.), *Advances in group processes* (Vol. 9, pp. 237–280). Greenwich, CT: JAI Press.

Morton, R. B. (1965). The organizational training laboratory—some individual and organization effects. *Advanced Management Journal, 30,* 58–67.

Nicholas, J. M. (1982). The comparative impact of organizational development interventions on hard criteria measures. *Academy of Management Review, 7,* 531–542.

O'Brien, G. (1967, January). *Methods of analyzing group tasks* (Technical Report No. 46). Urbana, IL: Department of Psychology, Group Effectiveness Research Laboratory. (DTIC No. AD 647 762)

Park, O., & Tennyson, R. D. (1980). Adaptive design strategies for selecting number and presentation of examples in coordinate concept acquisition. *Journal of Educational Psychology, 72,* 362–370.

Phillips, J. J. (1993). *Handbook of training evaluation and measurement methods.* Houston, TX: Gulf.

Porras, J. I., & Robertson, P. J. (1992). Organizational development: Theory, practice, and research. In M. D. Dunnette & L. M. Hough (Eds.), *Handbook of industrial organizational psychology* (2nd ed., Vol. 3, pp. 719–822). Palo Alto, CA: Consulting Psychologists Press.

Porter, C. O. L. H., Hollenbeck, J. R., Ilgen, D. R., Ellis, A. P. J., West, B. J., & Moon, H. (2003). Backup behaviors in teams: The role of personality and legitimacy of need. *Journal of Applied Psychology, 88,* 391–403.

Rouiller, J. Z., & Goldstein, I. L. (1993). The relationship between organizational transfer climate and positive transfer of training. *Human Resource Development Quarterly, 4,* 377–390.

Salas, E., Burke, C. S., & Stagl, K. C. (in press). Developing teams and team leaders: Strategies and principles. In D. Day, S. J. Zaccaro, & S. M. Halpin (Eds.), *Leader development for transforming organizations.* Mahwah, NJ: Lawrence Erlbaum.

Salas, E., & Cannon-Bowers, J. A. (1997). Methods, tools, and strategies for team training. In M. A. Quinones & A. Ehrenstein (Eds.), *Training for a rapidly changing workplace: Applications of psychological research* (pp. 249–280). Washington, DC: American Psychological Association.

Salas, E., & Cannon-Bowers, J. A. (2000). Designing training systems systematically. In E. A. Locke (Ed.), *The Blackwell handbook of principles of organizational behavior* (pp. 43–59). Malden, MA: Blackwell.

Salas, E., & Cannon-Bowers, J. A. (2001). The science of training: A decade of progress. *Annual Review of Psychology, 52,* 471–499.

Salas, E., Dickinson, T. L., Converse, S. A., & Tannenbaum, S. I. (1992). Toward an understanding of team performance and training. In R. J. Swezey & E. Salas (Eds.), *Teams: Their training and performance* (pp. 3–29). Norwood, NJ: Ablex.

Salas, E., Prince, C., Bowers, C., Stout, R., Oser, R. L., & Cannon-Bowers, J. A. (1999). A methodology for enhancing crew resource management training. *Human Factors, 41,* 161–172.

Salas, E., Rozell, D., Mullen, B., & Driskell, J. E. (1999). The effect of team building on performance: An integration. *Small Group Research, 30,* 309–329.

Schmidt, R. A., & Bjork, R. A. (1992). New conceptualizations of practice: Common principles in three paradigms suggest new concepts for training. *Psychological Science, 3,* 207–217.

Schraw, G., & Dennison, R. S. (1994). Assessing metacognitive awareness. *Contemporary Educational Psychology, 19,* 460–475.

Serfaty, D., Entin, E. E., & Johnston, J. (1998). Team adaptation and coordination training. In J. A. Cannon-Bowers & E. Salas (Eds.). *Decision making under stress: Implications for training and simulation*. Washington, DC: APA Press.

Serfaty, D., Entin, E. E., & Volpe, C. (1993). Implicit coordination in command teams. In *Proceedings of the Symposium on Command and Control Research, NDU* (pp. 53–57). Washington, DC: National Defense University Press.

Shriver, E. L., Mathers, B. L., Griffin, G. R., Jones, D. R., Word, L. E., Root, R. T., & Hayes, J. F. (1975, December). *REALTRAIN: A new method for tactical training of small units* (Technical Report S-4). Arlington, VA: U.S. Army Research Institute for the Behavioral and Social Sciences (NTIS No. AD-AO2403).

Sims, D. E., Salas, E., & Burke, C. S. (2004, April). *Is there a "Big Five" in teamwork?* Paper presented at the 19th annual meeting of the Society for Industrial and Organizational Psychology, Chicago.

Smith-Jentsch, K. A., Jentsch, F. G., Payne, S. C., & Salas, E. (1996). Can pretraining experiences explain individual differences in learning? *Journal of Applied Psychology, 81,* 110–116.

Smith-Jentsch, K., Salas, E., & Baker, D. P. (1996). Training team performance-related assertiveness. *Personnel Psychology, 49,* 909–936.

Smith-Jentsch, K. A., Salas, E., & Brannick, M. T. (2001). To transfer or not to transfer? Investigating the combined effects of trainee characteristics, team leader support, and team climate. *Journal of Applied Psychology, 86,* 279–292.

Smith-Jentsch, K. A., Zeisig, R. L., Acton, B., & McPherson, J. (1998). Team dimensional training. In J. A. Cannon-Bowers & E. Salas (Eds.), *Making decisions under stress: Implications for individual and team training*. Washington, DC: American Psychological Association.

Snow, R. E., & Peterson, P. (1980). Recognizing differences in student aptitudes. In W. McKeachie (Ed.), *New directions for teaching and learning, cognition, and college teaching* (No. 2, pp. 1–23). San Francisco: Jossey-Bass.

Sundstrom, E., De Meuse, K. P., & Futrell, D. (1990). Work teams: Applications and effectiveness. *American Psychologist, 45,* 120–133.

Svyantek, D. J., Goodman, S. A., Benz, L. L., & Gard, J. A. (1999). The relationship between organizational characteristics and team building success. *Journal of Business and Psychology, 14,* 265–283.

Tannenbaum, S. I., Beard, R. L., & Salas, E. (1992). Team building and its influence on team effectiveness: An examination of conceptual and empirical developments. In K. Kelley (Ed.), *Issues, theory, and research in industrial/organizational psychology* (pp. 117–153). Amsterdam: Elsevier.

Tannenbaum, S. I., & Yukl, G. (1992). Training and development in work organizations. *Annual Review of Psychology, 43,* 399–441.

Tennyson, R. D., & Rothen, W. (1979). Management of computer-based instruction: Design of an adaptive control strategy. *Journal of Computer-Based Instruction, 5,* 126–134.

Tracey, J. B., Hinkin, T. R., Tannenbaum, S., & Mathieu, J. E. (2001). The influence of individual characteristics and the work environment on varying levels of training outcomes. *Human Resource Development Quarterly, 12,* 5–23.

Tracey, J. B., Tannenbaum, S. I., & Kavanaugh, M. J. (1995). Applying trained skills on the job: The importance of work environment. *Journal of Applied Psychology, 80,* 239–252.

Volpe, C. E., Cannon-Bowers, J. A., Salas, E., & Spector, P. E. (1996). The impact of cross-training on team functioning: An empirical investigation. *Human Factors, 38,* 87–100.

Webber, S. S. (2002). Leadership and trust facilitating cross-functional team success. *Journal of Management Development, 21,* 201–214.

Wilson, J. E., Mullen, D. P., & Morton, R. B. (1968). Sensitivity training for individual growth: Team training for organizational development? *Training and Development Journal, 47,* 53.

Woodman, R. W., & Sherwood, J. J. (1980). The role of team development in organizational effectiveness: A critical review. *Psychological Bulletin, 88,* 166–186.

Zaccaro, S. J., Rittman, A. L., & Marks, M. A. (2001). Team leadership. *Leadership Quarterly, 12,* 451–483.

Zalesney, M. D., Salas, E., & Prince, C. (1995). Conceptual and measurement issues in coordination: Implications for team behavior and performance. In G. R. Ferris (Ed.), *Research in personnel and human resources management* (Vol. 13, pp. 81–115). Greenwich, CT: JAI Press.

23

Team Consultation

Felice Tilin

Joanne Broder Sumerson

Team consultation has been at the heart of organizational development interventions for the past half century (French, 1978/1999). It has grown in popularity as tasks became more complex, global competition intensified, and organizational successes became more closely intertwined with the outcomes of teams (Lawler, 2001). Individuals no longer can, by themselves, accomplish the complex tasks needed in today's organizations. The variety of knowledge and skills required for successful accomplishment of most organizational tasks is only possible by blending the expertise of individuals in the context of a team (Reich, 1987). Employees in industry must work together to solve common problems. Team development, consultation, and training are necessities in today's organizations, where the diversity and complexity of problems can no longer be tackled by one designated leader or a lone worker (Reich, 1987). Teams are established in organizations today as the main structure for accomplishing work, solving problems, and meeting productivity goals (Mohrman, Cohen, & Mohrman, 1995).

Effective team functioning is essential to the health and productivity of most organizations today. Team training methods have proliferated as a result (see Sims, Salas, & Burke, Chapter 22, this volume; Sunwolf & Frey, Chapter 26, this volume), and so have team consultation methods. This chapter will focus primarily on team consultation approaches with an eye toward determining the most effective consulting strategies for improving and maintaining high team performance.

Team consultation is most effective when it is closely tied to the development of the larger organizational system. In general, team consultation involves diagnosing or assessing the team's needs and then intervening, using methods that will benefit all the systems with which the team is involved, including individual group members, the group-as-a-whole, and the organization (Nevis, 1987; Weisbord, 1987). For the purposes of this chapter, however, we will focus primarily on the work consultants do with individual teams.

Defining Consultation

The dictionary defines consulting as "the provision of professional or expert advice" and a consultant as "one who gives professional advice or services" (Mish, 2001, p. 248). These definitions most accurately define technical consulting, for example, in the medical, financial, or technological arenas. For our purposes, a team consultant is defined as a "person in a position to have some influence over an individual, a group, or an organization but who has no direct power to make changes or to implement programs" (Block, 2000, p. 2). A team consultant's goal is to intervene so that group structure, policies, procedures, or processes change in a positive direction. The intervention is designed to promote group change and learning.

The consulting process requires a consultant to enter into an ongoing system for the purpose of helping members reach their goals. An intervention is an intentional strategy designed to reduce the gap between what is happening and what the client system decides should be happening. Intervention strategies are based on diagnosis. This requires a consultant to collect information about the group from group members via interviews, surveys, or questionnaires. Next, the consultant organizes and synthesizes the information and develops an intervention strategy designed to help group members to improve group functioning. Typically, the intervention includes feedback to group members about the results of the assessment and facilitation of a process in which group members develop a plan, based on the results of the assessment, to improve group effectiveness.

The primary goal of team consultation, then, is to improve the effectiveness and organizational productivity of the client team. To achieve this goal, it is important to explore what makes a team effective. Several reviews of the literature on work group or team effectiveness have been conducted, and they conclude that teams that are effective work well together by interacting cohesively and collaboratively while producing expected or better than expected results (Larson & LaFasto, 1989; Sundstrom, DeMeuse, & Futrell, 1990; Wheelan, 2005).

Sundstrom et al. (1990) stated that team effectiveness is a blend of two components: viability and performance. Team viability means that, at a minimum, team members are satisfied with the group and are willing to continue to work together to accomplish a task. In addition, a viable team is cohesive, and members have established clear norms, roles, and methods to coordinate tasks. Team performance means that the team is able to complete the ultimate goals and the tasks that result in positive organizational outcomes.

It is important for the consultant to recognize that although the team (and sometimes the consultant) may be hyperfocused on completing the task of the team, the dynamics that prevent tasks from being accomplished—or prevent the "right tasks at the right time" from being performed—are more related to team viability than to the capability of members to perform group tasks. After all, it is easier to say that a team should be cohesive, or that members should agree on group goals, than it is for team members to become cohesive and clear about goals.

Wheelan (2005) points out that groups have an overt goal that members may be quite capable of accomplishing, yet there are underlying covert goals that the group must accomplish as well. These covert goals often are not apparent to group members and can elude the consultant as well if he or she is not attentive to them. Wheelan maintains that a common example of this is group development. A group goes through stages of group development to reach productivity in much the same way that a child goes through developmental stages before he or she reaches full maturity. The research on group development contends that the task itself is not primarily responsible for derailing teams from accomplishing goals. Rather, these unconscious group dynamics add complications. Bion (1959) described two basic types of groups within a group: the basic assumption group and the work group. The work group describes the group, when it is working toward accomplishing the task. The basic assumption group describes the underlying emotional dynamics of the group, which take place in the group regardless of the task. He described these basic assumption groups as dependency, fight/flight, and pairing. Dependency is evident when the group depends on the leader to take action and does not take action on its own. Fight is characterized by unresolved conflict in the group. Flight, an outright avoidance of the task, is evident when the group engages in discussions or tasks totally unrelated to the group's tasks. Pairing emerges when two members of the group take on the work of the group by either arguing or solving problems while the other group members remain relatively uninvolved, allowing the pair to try to work on the group's problems.

In our consulting work, examples of these dynamic processes occur regularly. One of us worked with a team of highly educated human resource executives whose task was to make decisions about logistical planning for a leadership workshop. The designated team leader was away on vacation that day, and in her absence, the executives attempted to ask the consultant what to do. There was no lack of ability among members to make the necessary decisions, but because of the underlying dependency of the group, it was difficult for them to make these simple decisions without direction from the leader.

In essence, for the purposes of achieving consulting goals, the consultant needs to be aware of a variety of group dynamics. If a group is truly going to accomplish its goals, focusing on tasks alone will not suffice. The consultant and the group members must focus on the group's underlying dynamic processes as well (Bennis & Shepard, 1956; Sundstrom et al.,

1990; Urch-Druskat & Wolff, 2001; Wheelan, 1990). If groups pay attention to these group process variables, team effectiveness and productivity are much more likely to improve. Table 23.1 describes the characteristics of productive groups whose members have focused on process to ensure task accomplishment.

Success in team consultation is determined by the team's ability to meet its goals. Individual team goals will vary in nature but are most likely to be met when members have agreed about what the goals are and how they should be met (Wheelan, 2005). Typical team task goals include meeting the objectives dictated by the organization by producing a quality product or outcome on time and under budget. To accomplish team task goals, however, team process goals also must be met (Hoegl & Parboteeah, 2003; Jordan, Field, & Armendakis, 2002). These include developing a common language, restructuring systems and policies, determining interpersonal group boundaries, defining the means for obtaining status and power, developing criteria for member rewards and punishment, and defining a common ideology or value system (Goodman & Dean, 1989; Norton & Fox, 1997; Thierry, Koopman, & deGilder, 1998). These processes must be tailored to the requirements of the team's task goals to ensure task accomplishment and task quality.

Team Consultation Approaches

Because not all teams are successful in achieving task or process goals, organizations are beginning to recognize that it is worth investing in consultation to assist teams in reaching those goals. Consultants use a variety of approaches to help teams accomplish their goals. However, because the demand for team consultation has been high, many of the methods that have emerged in recent years to fill that demand have not been properly researched. As a result, designing interventions that work and are

Table 23.1 Group Process Variables Associated With Productivity

Process Variable	Examples of Studies
Members are clear about and agree with group goals	Guzzo, 1990; Weiss, 1984
Tasks are appropriate to group versus individual solution	Hackman, 1983; Latané, Williams, & Harkins, 1979
Members are clear about and accept their roles	Fisher & Gitelson, 1983; Kemery, Bedeian, Mossholder, & Touliatos, 1985
Role assignments match member abilities	Steiner, 1972
The leadership style matches the group's developmental level	Hershey & Blanchard, 1982; Vroom & Jago, 1978
The group has an open communication structure in which all members may participate	Goetsch & McFarland, 1980; Kano, 1971
The group gets, gives, and uses feedback about its effectiveness and productivity	Ketchum, 1984; Kolodny & Kiggundu, 1980
The group spends time defining and discussing problems it must solve or decisions it must make; members also spend time planning how they will solve problems and make decisions	Hackman & Morris, 1975; Harper & Askling, 1980; Laughlin, 1988
The group has effective decision-making strategies that were outlined in advance	Hirokawa, 1980; Vinokur, Burnstein, Sechrest, & Wortman, 1985
The group implements and evaluates its solutions and decisions	Lewin, 1951
Task-related deviance is tolerated	Hollander, 1960; Katz, 1982
The group norms encourage high performance and quality, success, and innovation	Bassin, 1988; Cummings, 1981; Hackman, 1987; Shea & Guzzo, 1987
Subgroups are integrated into the group-as-a-whole	Kolodny & Dresner, 1986; Mills, 1967
The group contains the smallest number of members necessary to accomplish its goal or goals	Gladstein, 1984; McGrath, 1984
The group has sufficient time together to develop a mature working unit and to accomplish its goals	Heinen & Jacobson, 1976
The group is highly cohesive and cooperative	Evans & Dion, 1991; Greene, 1989
Periods of conflict are frequent but brief, and the group has effective conflict management strategies	Bormann, 1975

cost- and time-effective can be extremely difficult (Buzaglo & Wheelan, 1999). The two most common categories of team interventions have been researched to some extent: team building and team consultation.

Team building or team training is one of the most commonly used techniques for improving team effectiveness (Freedman & Leonard, 2002). Typically, these training methods are aimed at developing self-awareness and teaching skills to individual team members that they can use to increase the effectiveness of their team. Communication skills, decision-making skills, and leadership skills are just some of the skills thought to be associated with team effectiveness. The assumption underlying team training is that if individuals are better equipped to work with others through learning more effective interpersonal skills, team performance will improve (see Axtell & Parker, 2003; Sims et al., Chapter 22, this volume; Sunwolf & Frey, Chapter 26, this volume). Because research on team building and team training are discussed in Chapters 22 and 26 of this volume, this chapter will focus on the second category of interventions, referred to as team consultation.

Team consultation approaches focus on the "group as a whole" in order to improve team performance. Team consultation involves assessing group processes and working with the group as a whole rather then focusing on individual or interpersonal behavior. An assumption underlying these approaches is that team members benefit from observing their own collective behavior within the context of the group (Weisbord, 1987). Working with the group as a whole, rather than individual members, is supported by research demonstrating that all groups go through similar developmental stages and experience similar dynamic processes, regardless of the individuals within them (Bennis & Shepard, 1956; Tuckman & Jensen, 1977; Wheelan, 2005). Thus, helping members to learn about group processes, identify their group's dynamics, and develop ways to improve

team processes is at the heart of team consultation approaches.

Kurt Lewin (1951) pioneered this approach, which he called the action research model. Action research has since been adopted and customized by consultants all over the world. The action research model requires the consultant to collect data, make an assessment of the team based on that data, provide feedback to the team about the assessment results, and work with the team to find solutions, new behaviors, or new frameworks by which to see their collective work. Strategies to monitor and evaluate team progress also are determined (Block, 2000; Schein, 1987; Wheelan & Tilin, 1999). One additional step in the process has been added over the years. Many consultants include an educational component in the consultation process to help team members understand how groups function and what they can do to facilitate their team's performance (Wheelan, 1999). The content of the educational component is derived from the assessment and, as a result, will vary from team to team.

It is important for the consultant to approach every project with the assumption that each team is unique. Intervention processes should be designed to meet the specific needs of a specific team, as opposed to using a standard methodology (Block, 2000; Koortzen & Cilliers, 2002). As a matter of fact, many consultants actually include the team members in the process of designing the intervention based on the assessment results. This practice is based on the foundational belief that the consultant is not "the expert" on what members should do to improve team performance. Consultants are, or should be, experts when it comes to team processes, theory and research on work groups, and the steps in the consulting process. Team members, however, are the ultimate decision makers in the consulting process. Team members are the best ones to interpret the assessment results and to develop plans to improve team performance.

The consultant is there to help the team grapple with the data and to make sure that the team is not misinterpreting the new information.

Assessment Strategies

Skills in devising assessment strategies are one of the core competencies required of consultants (Koortzen & Cilliers, 2002). Assessment data are collected to give the consultant a clear picture of the team's dynamics and needs so that an appropriate intervention can be created. Specific assessment strategies also should be customized for each team. Assessment strategies are both qualitative and quantitative in nature and often include a combination of both (Thierry et al., 1998). Common team assessment methods include interviews, surveys, and questionnaires.

Interviews

Interviews, although often time-consuming and costly, provide team members a private opportunity to share their personal views of the team with a consultant. If the consultant can gain the team member's trust, it is possible to gain an in-depth understanding of the team that members, at this point in the process, might not be willing to share as candidly in the group.

A common interviewing technique is the SWOT interview, in which team members identify the strengths and weaknesses of their team and opportunities and threats that the team must confront. The results of these interviews are collated, and a content analysis is performed to identify common issues and themes from the interviews.

Another interview technique is referred to as dynamic inquiry. This process uses more focused open-ended questions aimed at getting people to express their feelings about the group or other group members. Dynamic inquiry aims at uncovering the emotional reality of the group. A thematic analysis of the interviews is conducted, and the results are shared with the team (Boyatsis, 1998). Through the process of learning

about each other, group members can begin to create a shared language and agree on action steps to improve team performance. At the same time, this method can provide the consultant with a more thorough view of the emotional state of the group, which can help to inform the intervention that the consultant designs for that group (Goleman, Boyatsis, & McKee, 2002; McLeod & Kettner-Polley, 2004).

Surveys and Questionnaires

Team surveys and questionnaires are used to collect data that is more specifically targeted. For example, a consultant can develop a survey using specific questions to get a sense of how team members perceive their team meetings or how they feel about the group's performance. Surveys of this sort are inexpensive and quick ways of finding out very specific information about what group members think about a particular subject. Although surveys can provide useful information to group members, they are not designed to get at the bigger psychodynamic picture of the group and, therefore, may miss underlying issues or problems.

A more effective quantitative strategy for assessing the dynamics of the group as a whole is to use a questionnaire that has been researched and found to be reliable and valid. For example, the Group Development Questionnaire (GDQ) invites a team member to communicate his or her opinion of the team's effectiveness and performance (Wheelan & Hochberger, 1996). In this case, the instrument is used to measure a team's level of functioning according to the developmental stages of the integrated model of group development (Wheelan, 2005). The questions ask members to evaluate how the group is functioning with regard to group process variables associated with productivity (see Table 23.1). Each team member completes a questionnaire. Then, a group score is calculated. Results from the GDQ can clarify the underlying issues that may be barriers to group productivity. Team members are provided with a team profile, which identifies the team's developmental level and the issues that are inhibiting team performance. More information on this approach is provided in Chapter 7 of this volume by Wheelan).

Other forms of assessment data are considered secondary. Secondary forms of data include organizational documents, such as productivity reports and interteam memos. Benchmarking, which compares the team in question to other teams that are similar in purpose and nature, is another assessment strategy frequently used by consultants. The purpose of benchmarking is to gain insight into the processes, procedures, and practices employed by other teams. If these have been applied successfully and are relevant to the team, then team members may decide to incorporate some, or all, of these processes, procedures, and practices into their team's structure in order to improve their effectiveness and performance.

To gain an accurate snapshot of a team's dynamics and needs, the consultant should use a mix of assessment strategies. For instance, a qualitative, quantitative, and secondary strategy could be employed. Results of these assessment strategies are used to create an intervention strategy tailored specifically for the team in question.

Facilitating Interventions

Team interventions really begin during the data collection stage itself, as the team participants often gain heightened awareness of team issues and problems. Facilitation from the consultant continues at the feedback session and then carries on as the team plans ways to improve its own performance and resolve any problems that are getting in the way. This seems like a relatively simple process. However, the consultant who does not take dynamic processes into account will be surprised by the complexity of facilitation. For example, just giving people factual data from the assessment results can evoke less then straightforward responses from teams. There

often is a defensive response from participants about the assessment results. Defensiveness shows up in a variety of ways that range from silence to demands that the consultant give endless explanations or just "fix" the problem (Block, 2000). These are not rational responses. The complexity of individual and collective needs, as members try to cope with changing current behavior patterns, triggers these reactions. Because the group is dealing with issues that, in the collective emotions of the group, could be deeply disturbing and threatening, it is essential that the consultant build trust with the group. This means the consultant must be authentic about his or her own feelings while empathetic to group members' emotional situation.

A consultant must be prepared to give the group time to grapple with solutions that sometimes seem obvious and simple to an outsider. Block (2000) recommends that the consultant be highly attentive to inevitable resistance. He recommends that the consultant first look for clues about what the group is experiencing, then name the resistance, and finally—and most important—give the team members time to respond. Once the team can open up and recognize the problem, the consultant can focus on helping the team solve it.

Similarly, in the language of the Gestalt consulting model, the consultant can facilitate the group through the phases of an intervention by employing a technique referred to as the cycle of experience (Nevis, 1987). When used as a foundation for facilitation, the consultant observes the behaviors of the group that contribute to its difficulties and its successes. This live evidence should illustrate some of the data collected during the assessment. Then, the consultant can bring this into the group's awareness and compare it with the data at hand. As the members collectively begin to recognize these dynamics themselves, resistance breaks down, and the newfound collective clarity allows the group to make commitments and take actions. Ultimately, the group can put into practice new behaviors that alter the group's dynamics in a positive and more productive direction. The following case study provides the reader with a picture of how the steps in the team consulting process unfold in practice.

Rockin' and Rollin': From a Radio Station to a Cultural Institution

The project began when the radio station's executive director asked consultants to help him with a station that was at an apex of growth. It had started as a small college station with a mostly volunteer staff and was morphing into a bigger entity with membership contributions of about $2 million and a staff of 30, with another 15 or so interns and work study students. The executive director and the station's board members shared a collective vision to transform the station from a popular radio station to a cultural institution for alternative and classic rock music that would include a live venue facility. This would mean structuring the station for growth, identifying and developing leadership among the staff, and raising a great deal of money, which would require increasing the station's visibility in the community.

The consultant and the executive director agreed that the first step in the consulting process would be to take the "cultural pulse of the organization." This would be followed by a 2-day all-staff retreat. A dynamic inquiry interview was conducted with the senior team, the talent, and most of the full-time employees as well. The GDQ was administered to the senior team to determine how well that team was functioning. The results of the GDQ revealed that the senior team was overly dependent on the leader. There were, however, differences within the team. The people who had been with the station longer showed anti-authority tendencies, and the newer members to the staff (less than 2 years) were more dependent on the leader.

The dynamic inquiry revealed a common station story about its beginnings as a family and

"a hippie group" that was based on a collective worldview and a collective music view. Currently, people were deeply committed to the station, but the people themselves were changing. New people were being hired, and old-timers, who started as volunteers when they were young and single, were now managers with families to support and mortgages to pay. In addition, a more complex, competitive, technically advanced media world and a more diverse staff made it more difficult to discern common values. This created a haze among station leadership and staff. They were not clear what they were doing, and they were still using old inefficient systems. The staff was keeping up but also felt that they were burning out. In short, the station was already working beyond capacity.

The first stage of the intervention took place at the retreat and included both training interventions and process interventions. The group was encouraged to build ground with each other by sharing stories in small mixed groups about what they were most proud of and most concerned about during their past year with the station. By design, the small groups were a mix of long-term and short-term staff members. The themes from these group conversations were, of course, very similar to those identified by the dynamic inquiry process.

Next, the results of the dynamic inquiry and GDQ were revealed, along with some education about how teams develop. Small groups continued to discuss these themes. Then groups were formed to discuss solutions. This was met with resistance because people felt that the leader of the group, the executive director, should come up with these solutions. He stated that he was tired of bringing up solutions because they were for the most part rejected by the group and particularly by the senior staff members. At this point, the consultant froze the action and asked the team (including the executive director) to observe, using their new data, "what the group is doing now." Of course, once focused on it, the group members noticed that they were in a dependent mode as a group. Almost immediately, someone asked the consultant the following question: How do we get out of this mode? Someone in the group replied, "That question is a sign of dependency. We need to take responsibility for this as a team." This was a major shift in the team dynamic, and team members discussed, with the consultant's facilitation and support, ways to reduce their dependency and move toward interdependence.

Many complex operational and leadership challenges needed to be dealt with as part of this consultation. However, over the next few years, systems changed, the organization grew, and people learned to work together more effectively. The vision is now a reality. The station has more than tripled its membership contributions and is now living in a new home. This home is within the new cultural institution for alternative and classic rock music.

Researching the Effectiveness of Team Consultation

Team consultation is inherently difficult to study. These processes cannot be replicated in a laboratory setting. Also, like individuals in therapy, team members are not eager to be observed by outsiders or to have others know about their team's dynamics and secrets. As a result, most research in this area takes the form of case studies.

Team consultation interventions, designed to improve the performance of teams, have been investigated in a variety of case studies (e.g., Bassin, 1988; Cummings, 1981; Galagan, 1986; Gladstein, 1984; Manz & Sims, 1987; Seibold, 1995; Sundstrom et al., 1990; Wheelan, Brunner, Burchill, Craig, & Tilin, 1996; Wheelan & Furber, in press). Although these studies often report positive results (e.g., Halstead et al., 1986), most research reviews and meta-analyses report mixed or no effects of interventions on team performance or productivity (e.g., Druckman & Bjork, 1994; Hodgkinson & Wright, 2002; Salas,

Rozell, Driskell, & Mullen, 1999; Schultz, 1999; Sundstrom et al., 1990; Sunwolf & Seibold, 1999; Tannenbaum, Beard, & Salas, 1992).

One reason for the mixed results of research on intervention strategies designed to increase team effectiveness and productivity is that team training and team consultation are studied as if these two approaches were one and the same. Including approaches that target individual skill development with approaches that target the group as a whole in the same study invites ambiguous findings. Another reason for these mixed results is that underlying dynamic group processes and, in particular, group development, are not taken into account by consultants who design and facilitate interventions (Buzaglo & Wheelan, 1999; Sundstrom et al., 1990). If, to standardize the research protocol, all teams in a study are assessed using the same procedures and receive the same intervention, the results will be unclear. This is due to the fact that the dynamics and developmental level of teams mandate that interventions be tailored to address the particular needs of each group.

There are a number of practical hurdles to conducting research on real work teams. For example, to determine the success of an intervention, team results or productivity must be measured before and after the consultation. In some cases, however, team productivity cannot be measured because the organization does not track productivity to the team level. Instead, department and divisional productivity is monitored. Even if productivity can be tracked to the team level, it is difficult for team consultants to convince organizational representatives of the value of follow-up because it usually entails additional cost. Also, some consultants may feel that conducting research on teams that they have worked with may not be in their best interest. What if the findings are negative? How might that affect one's consulting practice? Here is another example of the need for researchers and practitioners to collaborate. A meeting of team researchers and practitioners to discuss ways to reduce the barriers to team consultation research and develop a shared research agenda would be a helpful first step.

In the meantime, based on our review of the literature and our experience as consultants, best team consulting practices should include the following:

- Collecting valid assessment data at the outset of the consultation
- Analyzing the data with attention given to the dynamic processes of the group, including the stage of group development
- Using the assessment results to design an intervention strategy targeting the intervention for a specific group
- Organizing the assessment results in a way that will help team members grapple with the meaning of those results
- Adding an educational component designed to help team members understand the dynamics of their team
- Developing a trusting relationship between the consultant and the group
- Focusing on the group as a whole as opposed to interpersonal dynamics
- Allowing sufficient time for members to develop specific plans to improve team processes and procedures
- Planning a follow-up whenever possible

References

Axtell, C., & Parker, S. (2003). Promoting role breadth self-efficacy through involvement, work design, and training. *Human Relations, 56*(1), 113–131.

Bassin, M. (1988). Teamwork at General Foods: New and improved. *Personnel Journal, 65*(5), 62–70.

Bennis, W. R., & Shepard, H. A. (1956). A theory of group development. *Human Relations, 9,* 415–437.

Bion, W. R. (1959). *Experiences in groups.* New York: Basic Books.

Block, P. (2000). *Flawless consulting* (2nd ed.). San Francisco: Jossey-Bass.

Bormann, E. G. (1975). *Discussion and group methods: Theory and practices* (2nd ed.). New York: Harper and Row.

Boyatsis, R. (1998). *Transforming qualitative information.* Thousand Oaks, CA: Sage.

Buzaglo, G., & Wheelan, S. (1999). Facilitating work team effectiveness: Case studies from Central America. *Small Group Research, 30*(1), 108–129.

Cummings, T. G. (1981). Designing effective work groups. In P. C. Nystrom & W. Starbuck (Eds.), *Handbook of organizational design* (Vol. 2, pp. 250–271). Oxford, UK: Oxford University Press.

Druckman, D., & Bjork, R. A. (Eds.). (1994). *Learning, remembering, believing: Enhancing human performance.* Washington, DC: National Academies Press.

Evans, C. R., & Dion, K. L. (1991). Group cohesion and performance: A meta-analysis. *Small Group Research, 22*(2), 175–186.

Fisher, C. D., & Gitelson, R. (1983). A meta-analysis of the correlates of role conflict and ambiguity. *Journal of Applied Psychology, 68,* 320–333.

Freedman, A. M., & Leonard, E. S. (2002). Organizational consulting to teams. In R. L. Lowman (Ed.), *Handbook of organizational consulting psychology* (pp. 27–53). San Francisco: Jossey-Bass.

French, W. L. (1999). *Organizational development: Behavioral science interventions for organizational improvements* (6th ed.). Saddle River, NJ: Prentice Hall. (Original work published 1978)

Galagan, P. (1986). Work teams that work. *Training and Development Journal, 40,* 33–35.

Gladstein, D. L. (1984). Groups in context: A model of task group effectiveness. *Administrative Science Quarterly, 29,* 499–517.

Goetsch, G. G., & McFarland, D. D. (1980). Models of the distribution of acts in small discussion groups. *Social Psychology Quarterly, 43,* 173–183.

Goleman, D., Boyatsis, R., & McKee, A. (2002). *Primal leadership.* Boston: Harvard Business Review.

Goodman, P., & Dean, J. (1989). Why productivity efforts fail. In W. French, C. Bell, & A. Zawacki (Eds.), *Organization development: Theory, research, and practice* (3rd ed., pp. 15–17). Homewood, IL: BPI Irwin.

Greene, C. N. (1989). Cohesion and productivity in work groups. *Small Group Behavior, 20,* 70–86.

Guzzo, R. A. (1990). Productivity research: Reviewing psychological and economic perspectives. In J. P. Campbell & R. J. Campbell (Eds.), *Productivity in organizations* (pp. 63–81). San Francisco: Jossey-Bass.

Hackman, J. R. (1983). *A normative model of work team effectiveness* (Tech. Rep. No. 2). New Haven, CT: Yale School of Organization and Management, Research Program on Group Effectiveness.

Hackman, J. R. (1987). The design of work teams. In J. W. Lorsch (Ed.), *Handbook of organizational behavior* (pp. 315–342). Englewood Cliffs, NJ: Prentice Hall.

Hackman, J. R., & Morris, C. G. (1975). Group tasks, group interaction process, and group effectiveness: A review and proposed integration. In L. Berkowitz (Ed.), *Advances in experimental social psychology* (Vol. 8, pp. 47–99). New York: Academic Press.

Halstead, L. S., Rintala, D. H., Kanellos, M., Griffin, B., Higgins, L., Rheinecker, S., Whiteside, W., & Healy, J. E. (1986). The innovative rehabilitation team: An experiment in team building. *Archives of Physical Medicine and Rehabilitation, 67,* 357–361.

Harper, N. L., & Askling, L. R. (1980). Group communication and quality of task solution in a media production organization. *Communication Monographs, 47,* 77–100.

Heinen, J. S., & Jacobson, E. J. (1976). A model of task group development in complex organizations and a strategy of implementation. *Academy of Management Review, 1,* 98–111.

Hershey, P., & Blanchard, K. H. (1982). *Management of organizational behavior: Utilizing human resources* (4th ed.). Englewood Cliffs, NJ: Prentice Hall.

Hirokawa, R. Y. (1980). A comparative analysis of communication patterns within effective and ineffective decision-making groups. *Communication Monographs, 47,* 312–321.

Hodgkinson, G., & Wright, G. (2002). Confronting strategic inertia in a top management team: Learning from failure. *Organization Studies, 23,* 949–977.

Hoegl, M., & Parboteeah, K. (2003). Goal setting and team performance in innovative projects: On the moderating role of team quality. *Small Group Research, 34*(1), 3–19.

Hollander, E. P. (1960). Competence and conformity in the acceptance of influence. *Journal of Abnormal and Social Psychology, 61,* 365–369.

Jordan, M., Field, H., & Armendakis, A. (2002). The relationship of group process variables and team performance: A team-level analysis in a field setting. *Small Group Research, 33*(1), 121–150.

Kano, S. (1971). Task characteristics and network. *Japanese Journal of Educational Social Psychology, 10,* 55–66.

Katz, G. M. (1982). Previous conformity, status, and the rejection of the deviant. *Small Group Behavior, 13,* 403–422.

Kemery, E. R., Bedeian, A. G., Mossholder, K. W., & Touliatos, J. (1985). Outcomes of role stress: A multisample constructive replication. *Academy of Management Review, 28,* 363–375.

Ketchum, L. (1984). How redesigned plants really work. *National Productivity Review, 3,* 246–254.

Kolodny, H. F., & Dresner, B. (1986). Linking arrangements and new work designs. *Organizational Dynamics, 14*(3), 33–51.

Kolodny, H. F., & Kiggundu, M. N. (1980). Towards the development of a sociotechnical systems model in woodlands mechanical harvesting. *Human Relations, 33,* 623–645.

Koortzen, P., & Cilliers, F. (2002). The psychoanalytic approach to team development. In R. Lowman (Ed.), *The California school of organizational studies handbook of organizational consulting psychology: A comprehensive guide to theory, skills, and techniques* (pp. 260–284). San Francisco: Jossey-Bass.

Larson, C., & LaFasto, F. (1989). *Teamwork: What must go right/what can go wrong.* Thousand Oaks, CA: Sage.

Latané, B., Williams, K., & Harkins, S. (1979). Many hands make light the work: The causes and consequences of social loafing. *Journal of Personality and Social Psychology, 37,* 822–832.

Laughlin, P. R. (1988). Collective induction: Group performance, social combination processes, and mutual majority and minority influence. *Journal of Personality and Social Psychology, 54,* 254–267.

Lawler, E. (2001). *Organizing for high performance: Employee involvement, TQM, re-engineering and knowledge management in the Fortune 1000.* San Francisco: Jossey-Bass.

Lewin, K. (1951). *Field theory in social science* (D. Cartwright, Ed.). New York: Harper.

Manz, C. C., & Sims, H. P. (1987). Leading workers to lead themselves: The external leadership of self-managing work teams. *Administrative Science Quarterly, 32,* 106–128.

McGrath, J. E. (1984). *Groups: Interaction and performance.* Englewood Cliffs, NJ: Prentice Hall.

McLeod, P. L., & Kettner-Polley, R. B. (2004). Contributions of psychodynamic theories to understanding small groups. *Small Group Research, 35*(3), 333–361.

Mills, T. M. (1967). *The sociology of small groups.* Englewood Cliffs, NJ: Prentice Hall.

Mish, F. C. (Ed.). (2001). *Merriman-Webster's collegiate dictionary* (10th ed.). Springfield, MA: Merriam-Webster.

Mohrman, S., Cohen, S., & Mohrman, A. (1995). *Designing team based organizations: New forms for knowledge work.* San Francisco: Jossey-Bass.

Nevis, E. (1987). *Organizational consulting: A gestalt appproach* (Gestalt Institute of Cleveland Press). New York: Gardner Press.

Norton, J., & Fox, R. (1997). *The change equation: Capitalizing on diversity for effective organizational change.* Washington, DC: American Psychological Association.

Reich, R. B. (1987). Entrepeneurship reconsidered: The team as hero. *Harvard Business Review, 65*(3), 77–83.

Salas, E., Rozell, D., Driskell, J. D., & Mullen, B. (1999). The effect of team building on performance: An integration. *Small Group Research, 30,* 309–329.

Schein, E. (1987). *Process consultation: Its role in organizational development.* Reading, MA: Addison Wesley.

Schultz, B. G. (1999). Improving group communication performance: An overview of diagnosis and intervention. In L. Frey (Ed.), *The handbook of group communication theory and research* (pp. 371–394). Thousand Oaks, CA: Sage.

Seibold, D. R. (1995). Developing the "team" in a team-managed organization: Group facilitation in a new plant design. In L. R. Frey (Ed.), *Innovations in group facilitation techniques: Case studies of applications in naturalistic settings* (pp. 282–298). Cresskill, NJ: Hampton Press.

Shea, G. P., & Guzzo, R. A. (1987). Group effectiveness: What really matters? *Sloan Management Review, 3,* 25–31.

Steiner, I. D. (1972). *Group process and productivity.* New York: Academic Press.

Sundstrom, E., DeMeuse, K. P., & Futrell, D. (1990). Work teams: Applications and effectiveness. *American Psychologist, 45*(2), 120–133.

Sunwolf & Seibold, D. R. (1999). The impact of formal procedures on group processes, members, and task outcomes. In L. Frey (Ed.), *The handbook of group communication theory and research* (pp. 395–431). Thousand Oaks, CA: Sage.

Tannenbaum, S. I., Beard, R. L., & Salas, E. (1992). Team building and its influence on team effectiveness: An examination of conceptual and empirical developments. In K. Kelly (Ed.), *Issues, theory and research in industrial/organizational psychology* (pp. 117–153). New York: Elsevier Science.

Thierry, H., Koopman, P., & deGilder, D. (1998). Assessment of organizational change. In P. Drenth, H. Thierry, & C. J. deWolff, *Handbook of organizational psychology* (2nd ed.). East Sussex, UK: Psychology Press.

Tuckman, B. W., & Jensen, M. A. C. (1977). Stages in small group development revisited. *Group and Organizational Studies, 2,* 419–427.

Urch-Druskat, V., & Wolff, S. (2001). Group emotional intelligence. In C. Cherniss & D. Goleman (Eds.), *The emotionally intelligent workplace* (pp. 146–148). San Francisco: Jossey-Bass.

Vinokur, A., Burnstein, E., Sechrest, L., & Wortman, P. M. (1985). Group decision making by experts: Field study of panels evaluating medical technologies. *Journal of Personality and Social Psychology, 63,* 70–84.

Vroom, V. H., & Jago, A. G. (1978). On the validity of the Vroom/Yetton model. *Journal of Applied Psychology, 63,* 151–162.

Weisbord, M. R. (1987). *Productive workplaces: Organizing and managing for dignity, meaning, and community.* San Francisco: Jossey-Bass.

Weiss, H. W. (1984). Contributions of social psychology to productivity. In A. P. Brief (Ed.), *Productivity research in the behavioral and social sciences* (pp. 143–173). New York: Praeger.

Wheelan, S. A. (1990). *Facilitating training groups.* New York: Praeger.

Wheelan, S. A. (1999). *Creating effective teams.* Thousand Oaks, CA: Sage.

Wheelan, S. A. (2005). *Group processes: A developmental perspective.* (2nd ed.). Boston: Allyn & Bacon.

Wheelan, S. A., Brunner, A., Burchill, C., Craig, R., & Tilin, F. (1996). The utility of group development theory in consulting with small, social service organizations: A case study. *Organization Development Journal, 14*(3), 4–15.

Wheelan, S., & Furber, S. (in press). Facilitating team development, communication, and productivity. In L. Frey (Ed.), *Innovations in group facilitation: Applications in natural settings.* Thousand Oaks, CA: Sage.

Wheelan, S., & Hochberger, J. (1996). Validation studies of the Group Development Questionnaire. *Small Group Research, 27*(1), 143–170.

Wheelan, S. A., & Kaeser, R. M. (1997). The influence of task type and designated leaders on developmental patterns in groups. *Small Group Research, 28,* 94–121.

Wheelan, S., & Tilin, F. (1999). The relationship between faculty group development and school productivity. *Small Group Research, 30*(1), 59–81.

24

Learning Groups

David W. Johnson

Roger T. Johnson

Groups have existed for as long as there have been humans (and even before). No matter what historical period, no matter what culture, no matter what geographical area humans live in, people form groups and resist the dissolution of their groups (Baumeister & Leary, 1995; Gardner, Pickett, & Brewer, 2000; Manstead & Hewstone, 1995). Groups have been the subject of countless books. Every human society has used groups to accomplish its goals and has celebrated when the groups were successful. Groups built the pyramids, constructed the Temple of Artemis at Ephesus, created the Colossus of Rhodes and the hanging gardens of Babylon, and built the temples of Angkor. It is obvious that groups outperform individuals, especially when performance requires multiple skills, judgments, and experiences. Many educators, however, overlook opportunities to use groups to enhance student learning and increase their own success, even though communities send children to be educated in large groups known as schools, and schools divide students into smaller groups called classes. In this chapter, we will define the nature of learning groups and the various methods of using groups in the classroom.

The implementation of cooperative learning (and the cooperative school) has flourished for numerous reasons (Johnson & Johnson, 1989, 1999):

- The amount of research validating cooperative learning's effectiveness (when there is discussion of "what works" in education, cooperative learning is always noted)
- The simultaneous accomplishment of multiple educational goals (increases academic learning and retention, improves relationships among students, and enhances students' social and cognitive development and psychological adjustment)

- The wide variety of ways in which cooperative learning has been operationalized and used, and its universality (has been used in many different countries and cultures throughout the world)

The theoretical principles underlying cooperative learning, furthermore, also have been applied in such diverse areas of education as communities of learners (Brown, 1994; Gamson, 1984), peer tutoring (Greenwood, Delquadri, & Hall, 1989; Simmons, Fuchs, Fuchs, Hodge, & Mathes, 1994), reciprocal teaching (Palinscar & Brown, 1984), and collaborative learning (Palinscar, Stevens, & Gavelek, 1988).

For these and many other reasons, the use of learning groups is one of the most important aspects of school life on all levels from preschool through graduate school and adult training programs. To discuss the educational use of small groups, it is first necessary to define the nature of group learning, discuss the goals of group learning, and review the history of the use of small groups for educational purposes.

Nature of Group Learning

On the surface, learning groups may be defined as students working together to learn. Yet, there is nothing magical about working in a group. Some groups are highly effective whereas other groups are highly ineffective. At least three types of groups may be distinguished: pseudo-learning groups, traditional learning groups, and cooperative learning groups (Johnson, Johnson, & Holubec, 1998; Katzenbach & Smith, 1993). A *pseudo-learning group* is a group whose members have been assigned to work together but who see each other as rivals, block or interfere with each other's performance, hide information from each other, attempt to mislead and confuse each other, and distrust each other. The result is that members would be more productive if they were working alone. A *traditional*

learning group is a group whose members are assigned to work together and accept that they have to do so, but members believe that they will be evaluated as individuals (not as members of the group) and structure the work so that very little joint work is required. The result is that most members benefit academically from working in the group, but the more hard-working and conscientious members would perform better if they worked alone. A *cooperative learning group* is a group whose members commit themselves to the common goal of maximizing their own and each other's learning. Members believe that their success depends on the efforts of all group members. Because most of the theorizing and research on learning groups has focused on cooperative learning, this chapter primarily focuses on cooperative learning groups, assuming that learning groups are organized around instructional goals so that members' goal achievements are positively correlated (Deutsch, 1962; Johnson & Johnson, 1975/2003; Johnson & Johnson, 1999).

A discussion of learning groups, therefore, must go beyond advocating the use of learning groups to a critical examination of the nature of effective learning groups. Learning groups are far more than a seating arrangement. Simply seating students together and instructing them to help each other can result in pseudo groups or traditional learning groups, neither of which maximizes the learning of all students. Only when a very clear cooperative structure is implemented in learning groups do they become fully effective (Johnson & Johnson, 1989, 1999, 1975/2003).

Goals of Group Learning

The effective use of cooperative learning groups can simultaneously accomplish multiple educational goals in the three major areas of academic learning and retention (including such aspects as intrinsic and continuing motivation to learn, higher level reasoning, and time on task), relationships among students (including diverse students in terms of ethnicity, culture, social class, disabilities, and gender), and students' social and cognitive development and psychological adjustment (including self-esteem, perspective taking, ability to cope with stress and adversity) (Johnson & Johnson, 1989, 1999). In addition, learning groups are commonly used to accommodate individual differences, solve current social problems, reduce risk factors associated with at-risk students (such as isolation, loneliness, and social rejection), prevent violence and bullying, enhance character development, inculcate values (including the democratic values required to be responsible citizens in society and the prosocial values needed for work and community life), and promote students' active involvement in learning situations.

History of Learning Groups

Cooperative learning has been around a long time. It will probably never go away. Its rich history makes it one of the most distinguished of all instructional practices. Thousands of years ago the *Talmud* stated that to understand its contents, one must have a learning partner. As early as the first century, Quintilian argued that students could benefit from teaching one another. The Roman philosopher Seneca advocated cooperative learning through such statements as *qui docet discet* (when you teach, you learn twice). Johann Amos Comenius (1592–1679) believed that students would benefit both by teaching and by being taught by other students. In the late 1700s, Joseph Lancaster and Andrew Bell made extensive use of cooperative learning groups in England, and the idea was brought to America when a Lancastrian school was opened in New York City in 1806. Within the Common School Movement in the United States in the early 1800s, there was a strong emphasis on cooperative learning. Certainly, the use of cooperative learning is not new to education.

There have been periods in which learning groups have had strong advocates, and this method was widely used to promote the educational goals of those times.

One of the most successful advocates of cooperative learning in America was Colonel Francis Parker. In the last three decades of the 19th century, Colonel Parker brought to his advocacy of cooperative learning enthusiasm, idealism, practicality, and an intense devotion to freedom, democracy, and individuality in the public schools. His fame and success rested on the vivid and regenerating spirit that he brought into the schoolroom and on his power to create a classroom atmosphere that was truly cooperative and democratic. When he was superintendent of the public schools at Quincy, Massachusetts (1875–1880), he averaged more than 30,000 visitors a year to examine his use of cooperative learning procedures (Campbell, 1965). Parker's instructional methods of structuring cooperation among students dominated American education through the turn of the century. Following Parker, John Dewey promoted the use of cooperative learning groups as part of his famous project method in instruction (Dewey, 1924). Dewey stressed the social aspects of learning and the role of cooperative experiences in school in preparing students for problem solving and democratic rational living. In the late 1930s, however, interpersonal competition began to be emphasized in public schools (Pepitone, 1980), and it dominated school life throughout the 1940s, 1950s, and early 1960s. Individualistic learning dominated classrooms in the late 1960s, the 1970s, and the early 1980s. In the 1980s, as part of the effective schools movement, the use of cooperative learning groups began to become more common. Cooperative learning groups are now used in schools and universities throughout most of the world in every subject area and from preschool through graduate school and adult training programs. Their use so pervades education that it is difficult to find a textbook on instructional methods, a teachers' journal, or instructional material that does not discuss cooperative learning.

In the mid-1960s at the University of Minnesota, the authors began training teachers to use learning groups effectively. The Cooperative Learning Center resulted from our efforts to synthesize and apply the existing knowledge concerning cooperative, competitive, and individualistic efforts to learning groups (Johnson, 1970; Johnson & Johnson, 1974, 1978, 1989; Johnson, Johnson, & Maruyama, 1983) and to translate the validated theory into a set of concrete strategies and procedures for using cooperative learning groups in classrooms and cooperative procedures in schools and school districts (Johnson & Johnson, 1994, 1999; Johnson et al., 1998). In the early 1970s, David DeVries and Keith Edwards at Johns Hopkins University developed teams-games-tournaments (TGT), and Shlomo and Yael Sharan in Israel developed the group investigation. In the late 1970s, Robert Slavin extended DeVries and Edwards's work at Johns Hopkins University by modifying TGT into student-team-achievement-divisions (STAD) and modifying computer-assisted instruction into team-assisted instruction (TAI). Spencer Kagan developed the Co-op Co-op procedure. In the 1980s, Kagan and Donald Dansereau developed cooperative structures and scripts, and many other individuals worked out further cooperative procedures.

The modern work on cooperative learning is in many ways a derivative of the group dynamics movement of the 1940s, 1950s, and 1960s (Johnson & Johnson, 1975/2003). The group dynamics movement had two interrelated goals. The first was the scientific study of group dynamics. Searching for ways to strengthen democracy, beginning in the late 1930s, social psychologists developed experimental methods of studying group dynamics and conducted studies of group discussion, group productivity, attitude change, and leadership. The second movement was the application of group dynamics theory and research to deriving methods for training leaders and group members in the

social skills needed to promote effective functioning of democratic groups. This movement began during World War II but gained considerable strength in the late 1940s and early 1950s. At the heart of both movements was Kurt Lewin, perhaps the greatest social psychologist who ever lived. He founded the Center for Group Dynamics at the Massachusetts Institute of Technology in the late 1940s. After his death in 1949, the center was eventually moved to the University of Michigan under the direction of Dorin Cartwright (Cartwright & Zander, 1968). The National Training Laboratories conducted most of the practical application of group dynamics research in the 1950s for applied behavioral science. Most of these efforts were focused on business, industry, and community development. A few social scientists—Alice Miel (1952), Matt Miles (1981) at Columbia University, and Richard Schmuck (Schmuck & Schmuck, 2001) at the University of Oregon, for example—focused on the dynamics of groups in educational settings. In addition, numerous researchers—Stuart Cook at the University of Colorado, Dean Tjosvold at Lingnan University, Hong Kong, and Norman Miller at the University of Southern California, for example—have contributed greatly to the understanding and implementation of cooperative learning, but they are not developers. The use of cooperative learning groups is based on practical procedures that have been operationalized from theory validated by research. What happened in cooperative learning is a textbook example of the relationships among theory, research, and practice (Johnson, 2003). Ideally, theory, research, and practice all interact with and enhance each other. Theory both summarizes existing research and guides future research. Research validates or disconfirms theory, thereby leading to its refinement and modification. Practice is guided by validated theory, and practical applications of the theory reveal inadequacies that lead to refining the theory. New research studies then need to be conducted, resulting in modifications and refinements in the theory and subsequently in the application procedures, so they may be more effectively and extensively used. In this chapter, therefore, the theoretical underpinnings of the use of learning groups will be reviewed, and the research validating the theory and the practical procedures for using learning groups will be discussed.

Theoretical Foundations

The use of cooperative learning groups is based solidly on a variety of theories in anthropology (Mead, 1936), sociology (Coleman, 1961), economics (Von Mises, 1949), political science (Smith, 1759/1976), psychology (Deutsch, 1949), and other social sciences. In psychology, where cooperation has received the most intense study, cooperative learning has its roots in social interdependence (Deutsch, 1949, 1962; Johnson & Johnson, 1989), cognitive developmental (Johnson & Johnson, 1979; Piaget, 1950; Vygotsky, 1978), and behavioral learning theories (Bandura, 1977; Skinner, 1968).

The *social interdependence perspective* began in the early 1900s, when one of the founders of the Gestalt School of Psychology, Kurt Kafka, proposed that groups were dynamic wholes in which the interdependence among members could vary. One of his colleagues, Kurt Lewin (1935, 1948), refined Kafka's notions in the 1920s and 1930s, stating that (a) the essence of a group is interdependence among members (created by common goals), which results in the group's being a "dynamic whole" so that a change in the state of any member or subgroup changes the state of any other member or subgroup; and (b) an intrinsic state of tension within group members motivates movement toward the accomplishment of the desired common goals. One of Lewin's graduate students, Morton Deutsch (1949, 1962), formulated a theory of cooperation and competition in the late 1940s. One of Deutsch's graduate students,

David Johnson (working with his brother, Roger Johnson), extended Deutsch's work into social interdependence theory (Johnson, 1970, 2003; Johnson & Johnson, 1974, 1989). The social interdependence perspective assumes that the way social interdependence is structured determines how individuals interact, and this, in turn, determines outcomes. Positive interdependence (cooperation) results in *promotive interaction* as individuals encourage and facilitate each other's efforts to learn. Negative interdependence (competition) typically results in *oppositional interaction* as individuals discourage and obstruct each other's efforts to achieve. In the absence of interdependence (individualistic efforts), there is *no interaction* as individuals work independently without any interchange with each other.

The *cognitive developmental perspective* is largely based on the theories of Jean Piaget (1950) and Lev Semenovich Vygotsky (1978). From Piaget's ideas and related theories comes the premise that when individuals cooperate on the environment, sociocognitive conflict occurs that creates cognitive disequilibrium, which in turn stimulates perspective-taking ability and cognitive development. Piagetians argue that during cooperative efforts, participants engage in discussions in which cognitive conflicts occur and are resolved, and inadequate reasoning is exposed and modified. The work of Vygotsky and related theorists is based on the premise that knowledge is social, constructed from cooperative efforts to learn, understand, and solve problems. Group members exchange information and insights, discover weak points in each other's reasoning strategies, correct one another, and adjust their understanding on the basis of others' understanding.

Two groups are related to developmental theorists. Controversy theorists (Johnson & Johnson, 1979, 1995) posit that being confronted with opposing points of view creates uncertainty or conceptual conflict, which creates a reconceptualization and an information search, which results in a more refined and thoughtful conclusion.

Cognitive restructuring theorists state that for information to be retained in memory and incorporated into existing cognitive structures, the learner must cognitively rehearse and restructure the material (Wittrock, 1978). An effective way of doing so is explaining the material to a collaborator.

The *behavioral learning theory* perspective focuses on the impact of group reinforcers and rewards on learning. The assumption is that actions followed by extrinsic rewards are repeated. Skinner (1968) focused on group contingencies, Bandura (1977) focused on imitation, and Homans (1974), as well as Thibaut and Kelley (1959), focused on the balance of rewards and costs in social exchange among interdependent individuals. More recently, Slavin (1983) has emphasized the need for extrinsic group rewards to motivate efforts to learn in cooperative learning groups.

There are basic differences among the three theoretical perspectives. Social interdependence theory assumes that cooperative efforts are based on intrinsic motivation generated by interpersonal factors in working together and joint aspirations to achieve a significant goal. The behavioral social perspective assumes that cooperative efforts are powered by extrinsic motivation to achieve group rewards. Social interdependence theory is made up of relational concepts dealing with what happens among individuals (e.g., cooperation is something that exists only among individuals, not within them), whereas the cognitive developmental perspective is focused on what happens within a single person (e.g., disequilibrium, cognitive reorganization). The differences in basic assumptions among the three theoretical perspectives create theoretical conflicts and disagreements that have yet to be fully explored or resolved. These three theoretical perspectives have, however, generated a considerable body of research to confirm or disprove their predictions. Although all three theoretical perspectives underlie the use of cooperative learning, Vygotsky's social constructionism underlies the related group procedure.

Collaborative Learning

Cooperative learning is sometimes differentiated from *collaborative learning*, which has its roots in the world of Sir James Britton and others in England in the 1970s (Britton, 1990). Quoting Vygotsky (1978), Britton notes that just as the individual mind is derived from society, a student's learning is derived from the community of learners. Britton is quite critical of educators who wish to provide specific definitions of the teacher's role. He recommends placing students in groups and letting them generate their own culture, community, and procedures for learning. Britton believed in *natural learning* (learning something by making intuitive responses to whatever our efforts throw up) rather than *training* (the application of explanations, instructions, or recipes for action). The source of learning is interpersonal; learning is derived from dialogues and interactions with other students and sometimes the teacher. Britton viewed any structure provided by teachers as manipulation that creates training, not learning; therefore, teachers should assign students to groups, provide no guidelines or instructions, and stay out of their way until the class is over. As an educational procedure, therefore, collaborative learning has historically been much less structured and more student directed than cooperative learning, with only vague directions given to teachers about its use. The vagueness in the role of the teacher and students results in a vagueness in the definition of the nature of collaborative learning. More recently, Bruffee (1993) described collaborative learning as "a reculturative process that helps students become members of knowledge communities whose common property is different from the common property of the knowledge communities they already belong to" (p. 3). Roschelle and

Behrend (1995) describe collaborative learning as "the mutual engagement of participants in a coordinated effort to solve a problem together" (p. 70). While there is a clear definition of cooperative learning, there is considerable ambiguity about the meaning of collaborative learning. For all practical and theoretical purposes, however, cooperative learning and collaborative learning are usually seen as synonymous and used interchangeably. In this chapter, cooperative learning will be used to signify both.

Overall Research Support for Learning Groups

Over the course of the past 100 years, numerous outcomes of cooperative, competitive, and individualistic efforts have been studied. The wide variety of variables may be subsumed within the three broad and interrelated outcomes of efforts exerted to achieve quality of relationships among participants, and participants' psychological adjustment and social competence.

When students work together cooperatively, it is in their best interests that other members of their group learn, and, therefore, they promote each other's learning and success. Promotive interaction occurs as individuals encourage and facilitate each other's efforts to reach the group's goals (such as maximizing each member's learning). Group members promote each other's success by giving and receiving help and assistance, exchanging resources and information, and providing feedback on academic progress and responsible group behavior. In addition, when group members challenge each other's reasoning, encourage increased efforts to learn, and mutually influence each other's reasoning and behavior, success is more likely. Finally, striving for mutual benefit, building and maintaining high levels of trust, and coping effectively with anxiety and stress have a positive influence on individual and group learning (Johnson & Johnson, 1989, 1999). When students compete with each other, it is in their best interests that other students do not learn, and therefore, they tend to interfere with each other's learning. Negative interdependence typically results in students opposing and obstructing each other's learning. Oppositional interaction occurs as students discourage and obstruct each other's efforts to achieve. Students focus both on increasing their own achievement and on preventing any classmate from achieving higher than they do. When students work individualistically, they tend to ignore each other. No interaction exists when students work independently without any interaction or interchange with each other. Students focus only on increasing their own achievement and ignore as irrelevant the efforts of others.

More than 375 experimental studies on achievement were conducted between 1898 and 1989 (Johnson & Johnson, 1989). A meta-analysis of all studies indicates that cooperative learning results in significantly higher achievement and retention than do competitive and individualistic learning (effect sizes = 0.67 and 0.64, respectively) (see Table 24.1). When only the methodologically high-quality studies are included in the analysis, the superiority of cooperative over competitive or individualistic efforts was still pronounced (effect sizes = 0.88 and 0.61, respectively).

Some cooperative learning procedures contained a mixture of cooperative, competitive, and individualistic efforts whereas others contained pure cooperation. The original jigsaw procedure (Aronson, Blaney, Stephan, Sikes, & Snapp, 1978), for example, is a combination of resource interdependence and an individualistic reward structure. TGT (DeVries & Edwards, 1973) and STAD (Slavin, 1978) are mixtures of cooperation and intergroup competition. TAI (Slavin, Leavey, & Madden, 1982) is a mixture of individualistic and cooperative learning. When the results of pure and mixed operationalizations of cooperative learning were compared, the pure operationalizations produced higher achievement

Table 24.1 Results of Social Interdependence Meta-analysis

Conditions	Achievement	Interpersonal Attraction	Social Support	Self–Esteem
Total studies				
Coop vs. Comp	0.67	0.67	0.62	0.58
Coop vs. Ind	0.64	0.60	0.70	0.44
Comp vs.Ind	0.30	0.08	−0.13	−0.23
High-quality studies				
Coop vs. Comp	0.88	0.82	0.83	0.67
Coop vs. Ind	0.61	0.62	0.72	0.45
Comp vs. Ind	0.07	0.27	−0.13	−0.25
Mixed operationalizations				
Coop vs. Comp	0.40	0.46	0.45	0.33
Coop vs. Ind	0.42	0.36	0.02	0.22
Pure operationalizations				
Coop vs. Comp	0.71	0.79	0.73	0.74
Coop vs. Ind	0.65	0.66	0.77	0.51

SOURCE: Reprinted from Johnson, D. W., & Johnson, R. (1989). *Cooperation and competition: Theory and research*. Edina, MN: Interaction Book Company.

NOTE: Coop = Cooperation, Comp = Competition, Ind = Individualistic.

(effect sizes: cooperative vs. competitive, pure = 0.71, mixed = 0.40, cooperative vs. individualistic, pure = 0.65, mixed = 0.42).

Besides higher achievement and greater long-term retention of what is learned, cooperation, compared with competitive or individualistic efforts, tends to result in more of the following (Johnson & Johnson, 1989, 1999):

Higher level reasoning (critical thinking) and metacognitive thought. Cooperative efforts promote a greater use of higher level reasoning strategies and critical thinking than do competitive or individualistic efforts (effect sizes = 0.93 and 0.97, respectively).

Even writing assignments show an increase in higher level thought when they are done cooperatively.

Process gain. In cooperative groups, members more frequently generate new ideas, strategies, and solutions than they would think of on their own.

Transfer of what is learned within one situation to another (group to individual transfer). What students learn in a group today, they are able to do alone tomorrow.

Positive attitudes toward the subject being studied. Cooperative efforts result in more positive attitudes toward the subject area and greater continuing motivation to learn more about it. The positive attitudes extend to the instructional experience.

Time on task. Cooperators spend more time on task than do competitors (effect size = 0.76) or students working individualistically (effect size = 1.17).

The more students learn in cooperative groups, the more they like each other. Since 1940, more than 180 studies have compared the impact of cooperative, competitive, and individualistic efforts on interpersonal attraction. Cooperative efforts, compared with competitive and individualistic experiences, promote considerably more liking among individuals (effect sizes = 0.66 and 0.60, respectively). When only the high-quality studies were included in the analysis, the effect sizes were 0.82 (cooperative vs. competitive) and 0.62 (cooperative vs. individualistic). The effect sizes are higher for the studies using pure operationalizations of cooperative learning than for studies using mixed operationalizations (cooperative vs. competitive, pure = 0.79 and mixed = 0.46; cooperative vs. individualistic, pure = 0.66 and mixed = 0.36). These positive feelings extend to the teacher and the principal, both of whom tend to be liked better by cooperators than by students working competitively or individualistically.

Cooperators tend to like each other when they are homogeneous and also when they differ in intellectual ability, disabilities, ethnic membership, social class, and gender (Johnson & Johnson, 1989). Heterogeneity is a great resource when individuals work cooperatively. The positive impact of heterogeneity results from frequent and accurate communication, accurate perspective taking, mutual inducibility, multidimensional views of each other, feelings of psychological acceptance and self-esteem, psychological success, and expectations of rewarding and productive future interaction (Johnson & Johnson, 1989). Cooperative learning has been demonstrated to be an essential prerequisite for managing diversity within the school.

Besides liking each other, cooperators give and receive considerable social support, both personally and academically. Since the 1940s, 106 studies have compared the relative impact of cooperative, competitive, and individualistic efforts on social support. Cooperative experience promoted greater social support than did competitive or individualistic experiences (effect sizes = 0.62 and 0.70, respectively). Social support has been found to promote achievement and productivity, physical health, psychological health, and successful coping with stress and adversity.

Working cooperatively with peers and valuing cooperation result in greater psychological health (and greater social competencies and higher self-esteem) than does competing with peers or working independently (Johnson & Johnson, 1989, 1999). Cooperation is positively related to a number of indices of psychological health such as emotional maturity, well-adjusted social relations, strong personal identity, ability to cope with adversity, social competencies, and basic trust in and optimism about people. Personal ego-strength, self-confidence, independence, and autonomy are all promoted by being involved in cooperative efforts. Individualistic attitudes tend to be related to a number of indices of psychological pathology such as emotional immaturity, social maladjustment, delinquency, self-alienation, and self-rejection. Competitiveness is related to a mixture of healthy and unhealthy characteristics. Cooperative experiences are not a luxury. They are an absolute necessity for healthy development.

Since the 1950s, more than 80 studies have compared the relative impact of cooperative, competitive, and individualistic experiences on self-esteem (Johnson & Johnson, 1989, 1999). Cooperative experiences promoted higher self-esteem than did competitive or individualistic experiences (effect sizes = 0.58 and 0.44, respectively). Our research demonstrated that cooperative experiences tended to be related to beliefs that one is intrinsically worthwhile, that others see one in positive ways, that one's attributes compare favorably with those of one's peers, and that one is a capable, competent, and successful person. In cooperative efforts, students (a) realize that they are accurately known, accepted, and liked by their peers; (b) know that they have contributed to their own, others', and group success; and (c) perceive themselves and others in a differentiated and realistic way that allows for multidimensional comparisons based on complementarity of own and others' abilities. Competitive experiences tended to be related to conditional self-esteem based on whether one wins or loses. Individualistic experiences tended to be related to basic self-rejection.

An important aspect of psychological health is social perspective-taking—the ability to understand how a situation appears to other people. The opposite of social perspective-taking is egocentrism (being unaware of perspectives other than your own). Cooperative experiences increase perspective-taking ability whereas competitive and individualistic experiences tend to promote egocentrism (Johnson & Johnson, 1989, 1999). Individuals working cooperatively learn more social skills and become more socially competent than do people competing or working individualistically (Johnson & Johnson, 1989, 1999). Finally, through cooperative efforts, many of the attitudes and values essential to psychological health and learning are adopted (Johnson & Johnson, 1989, 1999). Students need to develop a love of learning, a commitment to high-quality work, respect for other people and their property, the value of diversity, a commitment to being a responsible citizen, and so forth. Through interpersonal influences in cooperative endeavors, such attitudes are developed.

This body of research has considerable generalizability because the included studies have been conducted by many researchers, with markedly diverse orientations, working in different settings and countries, in 11 different

decades. Research participants have varied as to cultural background, economic class, age, and gender, and a wide variety of research tasks and measures of the dependent variables have been used (Johnson & Johnson, 1989). The research on cooperative efforts, furthermore, has unusual breadth; that is, it has focused on a wide variety of diverse outcomes. Over the past 100 years, researchers have focused on such outcomes as achievement, higher level reasoning, retention, time on task, transfer of learning, achievement motivation, intrinsic motivation, continuing motivation, social and cognitive development, moral reasoning, perspective-taking, interpersonal attraction, social support, friendships, reduction of stereotypes and prejudice, valuing differences, psychological health, self-esteem, social competencies, internalization of values, the quality of the learning environment, and many others. Many of these studies have focused on preventing and treating a wide variety of social problems such as bigotry (racism, sexism, exclusion of people with disabilities), antisocial behavior (delinquency, drug abuse, bullying, violence, incivility), lack of prosocial values and egocentrism, alienation and loneliness, psychological pathology, and low self-esteem (see reviews by Cohen, 1994; Johnson & Johnson, 1974, 1989, 1999; Johnson et al., 1983; Kohn, 1992; Sharan, 1980; Slavin, 1991). A strength of cooperative learning is that it simultaneously achieves such diverse outcomes. These outcomes can be accomplished, however, only if cooperative learning is carefully structured to include five basic elements.

Basic Elements of Cooperative Learning

For a lesson to be cooperative, five basic elements are essential (Johnson & Johnson, 1989; Johnson et al., 1998). They are described here.

1. Positive interdependence. Positive interdependence is the perception that you are linked with others in such a way that you cannot succeed unless they do (and vice versa); that is, their work benefits you, and your work benefits them. It promotes a situation in which students work together in small groups to maximize the learning of all members, sharing their resources, providing mutual support, and celebrating their joint success. Positive interdependence is the heart of cooperative learning. Students must believe that they sink or swim together. Within every cooperative lesson, positive goal interdependence must be established through mutual learning goals (learn the assigned material and make sure that all members of your group learn the assigned material).

To strengthen positive interdependence, joint rewards (if all members of your group score 90% correct or better on the test, each will receive 5 bonus points), divided resources (giving each group member a part of the total information required to complete an assignment), and complementary roles (reader, checker, encourager, elaborator) may also be used. For a learning situation to be cooperative, students must perceive that they are positively interdependent with other members of their learning group. Positive interdependence creates the overall superordinate goals that unite diverse students into a common effort.

It also results in a joint superordinate identity. Students need to develop unique identities as individuals, social identities based, among other things, on their ethnic, historical, and cultural background, and a superordinate identity that unites them with all the other members of their society. At the same time, they need to understand the social identity of classmates and respect them as collaborators and friends. Positive interdependence, furthermore, underlies a common culture that defines the values and nature of the society in which the students live.

2. Individual accountability. Individual accountability exists when the performance of each individual student is assessed, and the results are given back to the group and the individual. It is important that the group knows who needs more assistance, support, and encouragement in completing the assignment. It is also important that group members know that they cannot "hitchhike" on the work of others. The purpose of cooperative learning groups is to make each member a stronger individual in his or her right. Students learn together so that they can subsequently perform higher as individuals. To ensure that each member is strengthened, students are held individually accountable to do their share of the work. Common ways to structure individual accountability include (a) giving an individual test to each student, (b) randomly selecting one student's product to represent the entire group, or (c) having each student explain what they have learned to a classmate.

3. Face-to-face promotive interaction. Once teachers establish positive interdependence, they need to maximize the opportunity for students to promote each other's success by helping, assisting, supporting, encouraging, and praising each other's efforts to learn. There are cognitive activities and interpersonal dynamics that occur only when students get involved in promoting each other's learning. This includes orally explaining how to solve problems, discussing the nature of the concepts being learned, teaching one's knowledge to classmates, and connecting present with past learning. Accountability to peers, ability to influence each other's reasoning and conclusions, social modeling, social support, and interpersonal rewards all increase as the face-to-face interaction among group members increases. In addition, the verbal and nonverbal responses of other group members provide important information concerning a student's performance. Silent students are uninvolved students who are not contributing to the learning of others as well as themselves. Promoting each other's success results both in higher achievement and in getting to know each other on a personal as well as a professional level. To obtain meaningful face-to-face interaction, the size of groups needs to be small (two to four members). Finally, although positive interdependence creates the conditions for working together, the actual face-to-face interaction in which students work together and promote each other's success builds the personal relationships that are essential for developing pluralistic values.

4. Social skills. Contributing to the success of a cooperative effort requires interpersonal and small group skills. Placing socially unskilled individuals in a group and telling them to cooperate does not guarantee that they will be able to do so effectively. People must be taught the social skills for high-quality cooperation and be motivated to use them. Leadership, decision making, trust building, communication, and conflict-management skills have to be taught just as purposefully and precisely as academic skills. Procedures and strategies for teaching students social skills may be found in Johnson and Johnson (1999, 2003). Finally, social skills are required for interacting effectively with peers from other cultures and ethnic groups.

5. Group processing. Group processing exists when group members discuss how well they are achieving their goals and maintaining effective working relationships. Groups need to describe what member actions are helpful and unhelpful and make decisions about what behaviors to continue or change. Students must also be given the time and procedures for analyzing how well their learning groups are functioning and the extent to which students are employing their social skills to help all group members to achieve and to maintain effective working relationships within the group.

Such processing (a) enables learning groups to focus on group maintenance, (b) facilitates the learning of social skills, (c) ensures that members receive feedback on their participation, and (d) reminds students to practice collaborative skills consistently. Some of the keys to successful processing are allowing sufficient time for it to take place, making it specific rather than vague, maintaining student involvement in processing, reminding students to use their social skills while they process, and ensuring that clear expectations as to the purpose of processing have been communicated. Finally, when difficulties in relating to each other arise, students must engage in group processing and identity to define and solve the problems they are having as they try to work together effectively.

To effectively use cooperative learning, teachers must understand the nature of cooperation and the essential components of a well-structured cooperative lesson. When teachers understand what positive interdependence, promotive interaction, individual accountability, social skills, and group processing are and when they develop skills in structuring them, they are able to (a) adapt cooperative learning to their unique circumstances, needs, and students and (b) fine-tune their use of cooperative learning to solve problems students are having in working together.

Key Cooperative Learning Methods

The widespread use of cooperative learning is due partially to the variety of cooperative learning methods available for teacher use, ranging from very concrete and prescribed to very conceptual and flexible. Cooperative learning is actually a generic term that refers to numerous methods for organizing and conducting classroom instruction. Almost any teacher can find a way to use cooperative learning that is congruent with his or her philosophies and practices. So many teachers use cooperative learning in so many different ways that all the operationalizations cannot be listed here. In assessing the effectiveness of specific cooperative learning methods, however, there are a number of researcher-developers who have developed cooperative learning procedures, conducted programs of research and evaluation of their

Table 24.2   Modern Methods of Cooperative Learning

Researcher-Developer	Method	Developed
Johnson & Johnson, 1999	Learning Together	Mid-1960s
DeVries & Edwards, 1973	Teams-Games-Tournaments (TGT)	Early 1970s
Sharan & Sharan, 1976, 1992	Group Investigation	Mid-1970s
Johnson & Johnson, 1979, 1995	Constructive Controversy	Mid-1970s
Aronson et al., 1978	Jigsaw Procedure	Late 1970s
Slavin, 1978	Student Teams Achievement Divisions (STAD)	Late 1970s
Cohen, 1994	Complex Instruction	Early 1980s
Slavin et al., 1982	Team-Assisted Instruction (TAI)	Early 1980s
Kagan, 1985	Cooperative Structures	Mid-1980s
Stevens et al., 1987	Cooperative Integrated Reading and Composition (CIRC)	Late 1980s

SOURCE: Adapted from Johnson & Johnson (2002).

method, and then involved themselves in teacher-training programs. The 10 people and programs listed in Table 24.2 are commonly credited as the creators of modern-day cooperative learning.

In the late 1960s, Learning Together was developed by the authors (Johnson & Johnson, 1999; Johnson et al., 1998) as a conceptual system for teachers to use to re-plan their existing lessons for cooperative learning. There are three types of cooperative learning: (a) formal cooperative learning, which is used for assignments that last from one class period to several weeks; (b) informal cooperative learning, which is used with direct teaching for quick, intermittent discussions that last for a few minutes; and (c) cooperative base groups, which last for a semester or year and provide each member with the support, help, encouragement, and assistance he or she needs to progress academically. The three types of cooperative learning may be used in an integrated way to form an overall instructional program.

TGT was developed by DeVries and Edwards (1973) as a combination of cooperative learning, intergroup competition, and an instructional game format. Students are assigned to cooperative groups of four that are heterogeneous in terms of performance level (one high-, two middle-, and one low-performing student in each group). The teacher presents a lesson. Students then work in their groups to make sure that all members have mastered the lesson. Next, a competitive tournament is conducted to determine which cooperative group best learned the assigned material. The cooperative group with the most tournament points "wins" the class intergroup competition and is recognized with certificates and other forms of group rewards.

Group Investigation was developed by Sharan and Sharan (1976, 1992) as a refinement of John Dewey's (1924) group project method and consists of having cooperative groups complete projects that require planning, inquiry, and discussion. After a general area of study is presented to the entire class, students form groups of three to six members to study a topic related to that general area. Each group makes a plan as to what aspects of the class topic they will investigate as a group and what each member will contribute. Each group makes a presentation or display to communicate its findings to the entire class. One member of each group is appointed to a steering committee that coordinates the presentations.

Constructive or Academic Controversy was developed in the mid-1970s by the authors (Johnson & Johnson, 1979, 1995) to structure intellectual conflicts into cooperative learning groups. In academic controversies, students are required to (a) produce a group report detailing the group members' best reasoned judgment about an issue and (b) individually take a test on both sides of the issue. The controversy procedure consists of six stages. First, students are assigned to groups of four. Each group is divided into two pairs. One pair is assigned the "pro" position on the issue, and the other pair is assigned the "con" position. Students research, learn, and prepare their assigned position on the topic being studied. Second, students present the best case possible for their assigned position and listen carefully to the opposing position. Third, students engage in an open discussion where they refute the opposing position, rebut the attacks on their position, and continue to advocate their position and learn the opposing position. Fourth, students reverse perspectives and present the opposing position accurately, sincerely, and forcefully. Fifth, students drop all advocacy and strive to reach consensus about their best reasoned judgment on the issue by synthesizing or integrating the best reasoning from both sides. Finally, students' learning is assessed, and the groups process how well they carried out the procedure.

Jigsaw was developed by Aronson and his associates (1978) as a combination of cooperative learning and individualistic grading and consists of subdividing the group task and resources so that each member has unique information required by all group members. Each member is given access to only one part of the materials required to complete the assignment, and each member is responsible for thoroughly learning the material and then teaching it to all other members of the group. The only way students can learn the other sections is to listen carefully to their group members. Students are tested on the material and graded individually.

STAD was developed by Slavin (1978) as a combination of cooperative learning and intergroup competition. Students are assigned to four-member heterogeneous groups and work to make sure that all members have mastered the lesson. Students take individual quizzes on the material, their test scores are compared with their own past average performance, and points are awarded based on the degree to which students met or exceeded their own earlier performance. Members' points are added together to form team scores, and the teams are ranked from the highest to the lowest. The winning team is recognized in a newsletter.

Complex Instruction was developed by Elizabeth Cohen (1994) to integrate cooperative learning into a specific curriculum that involves students in hands-on science activities directed toward the discovery of important scientific principles. Students are assigned to heterogeneous small groups at learning centers. Each member is assigned a role (facilitator, checker, safety officer, cleanup coordinator, reporter), and the roles are rotated with each lesson. The tasks are structured so that input from other members is required (no single individual is likely to solve the problem or accomplish the task objectives without at least some input from others). Groups rotate learning centers until each student has completed every task from each learning center. Learning is assessed, but no individual grades are assigned.

TAI was developed by Slavin et al. (1982) as a combination of cooperative and individualistic learning. A curriculum-based procedure with a specific set of instructional materials, it uses cooperative learning to teach mathematics classes for Grades 2 through 8. Students are assigned to cooperative groups of four members of mixed performance levels. Students take a placement test and are placed at the appropriate point in the individualized mathematics program and assigned a sequence of math lessons. Students work alone completing the lessons, ask members of their group for help when they need it, have a group member check their answers (using an answer sheet) every time they complete four problems, and take a formative test (which is scored by a group member) when the last block of four questions is completed correctly.

Cooperative Structures were developed by Spenser Kagan (1985) as specific cooperative learning techniques teachers may use. Many dozens of structures were specified, such as various ways to use pairs, triads, and groups of four to have students work together while completing an aspect of a lesson. Teachers can select the structures they wish to use in a lesson and sequence various structures to create a complete lesson.

CIRC was developed in the mid-1980s by Stevens et al. (1987) as a comprehensive curriculum and program that uses cooperative learning to teach reading and writing for Grades 1 through 8. Students are assigned to homogeneous reading groups according to reading level, assigned to pairs or triads, and teamed with another pair or triad from a different-level reading group. Students engage in cross-group team practice, verify that assignments are done correctly, and make sure each member is ready to take the tests. Students take a test after every three lessons and receive points based on their individual performance; the cross-group teams receive certificates.

In addition to these procedures, numerous other ways have been proposed to structure cooperative learning. Examples are collaborative learning, which was developed in England by Sir James Britton and others in the 1970s as a way to give students the power to govern their own learning (Britton, 1990; Bruffee, 1993), tribes

(developed by Jeanne Gibbs, 1987, to promote the social development of children), cooperative scripts (developed primarily at the college level by Dansereau and his associates, 1979), think-pair-share (developed by Frank Lyman; see McTighe & Lyman, 1988), and many others. They are all valuable teaching procedures.

Research on Cooperative Learning Methods

Of all the numerous ways that cooperative learning is used, only eight methods have been subjected to empirical validation in a way that a relevant effect size could be computed (Johnson & Johnson, 2002). The authors found 164 studies on specific cooperative learning methods, a substantial number, especially considering that 28% of them have been conducted since 1990 and 100% have been conducted since 1970. The studies were done at all levels of schooling (46%, elementary schools; 20%, middle schools; 11%, high schools; and 24%, postsecondary and adult settings), and the majority lasted for considerable time (46%, 30 sessions or more; 52%, 2 to 29 sessions; and 2%, for only one session). Most of the studies used good to excellent methodology (45% randomly assigned participants to conditions, 25% randomly assigned groups to conditions, and only 30% did not randomly assign participants or groups to conditions). The research has been conducted in North America, Europe, the Middle East, Asia, and Africa and has involved minority as well as majority populations. Thus, there is considerable research on specific cooperative learning methods, and the research has considerable validity and generalizability.

The results for the different methods of cooperative learning appear in Table 24.3 (Johnson & Johnson, 2002). In all cases, cooperation promotes higher achievement than competition and individualistic efforts do.

The results for the averaged effect sizes were very similar, somewhat higher for Learning

Table 24.3 Meta-analysis Results for Cooperative Learning Methods

	Average Effect Sizes			Weighted Effect Sizes				
	Effect	SD	k	Effect	SE	k	Cld 95%	fsn
Learning Together								
Cooperation vs. Competition	0.82	0.50	25	0.70	0.06	25	±0.12	62
Cooperation vs. Individualistic	1.03	0.69	56	0.91	0.04	56	±0.08	200
Competition vs. Individualistic	0.06	0.47	10	0.08	0.10	10	±0.19	0
Teams-Games-Tournaments (TGT)								
Intergroup Cooperation vs. Competiton	0.48	0.69	9	0.47	0.05	9	±0.10	12
Intergroup Cooperation vs. Individualistic	0.58	0.43	5	0.55	0.11	5	±0.22	9
Group Investigation								
Cooperation vs. Competition	0.37	1.19	2	0.86	0.14	2	±0.27	7
Cooperation vs. Individualistic	0.62	0.00	1	0.62	0.44	1	±0.86	2
Academic Controversy								
Cooperation vs.Competition	0.59	0.44	16	0.61	0.07	16	±0.14	32
Cooperation vs. Individualistic	0.91	0.59	11	0.86	0.10	11	±0.19	36
Jigsaw								
Cooperation vs. Competition	0.29	0.78	9	0.41	0.05	9	±0.11	9
Cooperation vs. Individualistic	0.13	0.29	5	0.09	0.11	5	±0.21	0
Student Teams Achievement Divisions (STAD)								
Intergroup Cooperation vs. Competition	0.51	0.72	15	0.46	0.05	15	±0.09	19
Intergroup Cooperation vs. Individualistic	0.29	0.71	14	0.28	0.07	14	±0.14	6
Team-Assisted Instruction (TAI)								
Cooperation vs. Competition	0.25	0.14	7	0.19	0.04	7	±0.09	0
Cooperation vs. Individualistic	0.33	0.26	8	0.19	0.06	8	±0.12	0
Competition vs. Individualistic	−0.08	0.52	2	−0.32	0.13	2	±0.25	0
Cooperative Integrated Reading and Composition (CIRC)								
Cooperation vs. Competition	0.18	0.23	7	0.20	0.04	7	±0.07	0
Cooperation vs. Individualistic	0.18	0.00	1	0.18	0.00	1	±0.22	0

SOURCE: Adapted from Johnson & Johnson (2002).

NOTE: SD = standard deviation; k = the number of averaged effect sizes in the meta-analysis; SE = standard error; Cld 95% = the value of the 95% confidence interval around the weighted effect size; fsn = fail safe N (the number of additional studies needed to change the significance of the results below 0.20).

Together and TAI and somewhat lower for Group Investigation and Jigsaw. No studies were found for Cooperative Learning Structures. Studies of Complex Instruction (see Cohen & Lotan, 1997) compared complex instruction with other group instructional procedures (rather than comparing them with competitive or individualistic instruction), and therefore, relevant effect sizes could not be derived.

It should be noted that a previous meta-analysis of the research on cooperative learning methods conducted by Bak (1992) found similar results. The effect sizes were Jigsaw, 0.29; Learning Together, 0.67; student team learning, 0.28; Group Investigation, 0.13; subject-oriented methods, 0.13; and others, 0.21.

The cooperative learning methods may be ranked by the size of the effect they have on achievement and by the number of comparisons available. When the impact of cooperative lessons is compared with competitive learning, Group Investigation promoted the greatest effect, followed by Learning Together, Constructive Controversy, STAD, Jigsaw, TAI, CIRC, and finally, TGT. When the impact of cooperative lessons is compared with individualistic learning, Learning Together promotes the greatest effect, followed by Constructive Controversy, Group Investigation, STAD, TAI, CIRC, Jigsaw, and TGT. There are reasons, however, why these rankings should be suggestive only. Because few studies have been conducted on several of the methods, the effect sizes are very tentative. The fewer the number of studies, the more likely the same investigator conducted the studies, the less the variety of achievement measures used, the more homogeneous the participants, and the more similar the subject matter studied. In addition, different measures of achievement were used in different studies. The confidence educators can have in the effect sizes, furthermore, is inversely related to the number of studies that have been conducted on the method. When the methods are ranked by the number of effects associated with each finding for the cooperative

versus competitive comparison, the ranking of the methods is Learning Together, Academic Controversy, STAD, Jigsaw, TGT, TAI, CIRC, and Group Investigation. For the cooperative versus individualistic comparison, the ranking is Learning Together, Academic Controversy, STAD, TAI, TGT, Group Investigation, and CIRC.

The methods of cooperative learning may be evaluated on five dimensions: (a) ease of learning the method, (b) ease of initial use in the classroom, (c) ease of long-term maintenance of use of the method, (d) robustness of the method (applicability to a wide variety of subject areas and grade levels), and (e) adaptability of the method to changing conditions (Johnson & Johnson, 2002). Each cooperative learning method may be classified on a 5-point scale (*easy* to *difficult*) on these dimensions. When the resulting score is correlated with the effect sizes for each method, the results indicate that the more conceptual the cooperative learning method, the higher the achievement of cooperative compared with competitive, $r(197) = 0.32$, $p < .001$, and individualistic learning, $r(197) = 0.46$, $p < .001$.

Finally, the direct-conceptual rating and the characteristics of the studies (whether participants were randomly assigned to conditions, age of participants, type of cooperative learning, whether cooperation is contrasted with competition or individualistic efforts, duration of the study, mixed vs. homogeneous groups in terms of gender, and year published) were placed in a linear regression analysis using weighted effect sizes (Johnson & Johnson, 2002). The only significant predictor of the impact of cooperative learning on achievement was the direct-conceptual rating, $t = 6.78$, $p < .0001$.

The diversity of the eight cooperative learning methods provides additional validation of the effectiveness of cooperative learning. The methods range from specific procedures (such as Jigsaw and CIRC) to conceptual frameworks educators use to build their own cooperative lessons (such as Learning Together and Group

Investigation), curriculum packages in which cooperative learning is central (such as TAI and STAD), and rather complex procedures that require some sophistication to use (such as Constructive Controversy). That all of these methods are effective in increasing achievement is a tribute to the power of cooperation.

There is no reason to expect the different methods of cooperative learning to interfere with each other's effectiveness. All the methods may be used in the same classroom and school. A teacher, for example, may use TAI in math, Learning Together in science and language arts, and Group Investigation in social studies, with the expectation that the different methods will enhance and enrich each other's effectiveness. There is currently, however, no research on the ways in which the different methods of cooperative learning may enhance or interfere with each other's effectiveness.

The results of this meta-analysis provide evidence that (a) considerable research has been conducted on cooperative learning methods, (b) eight diverse methods have been researched, (c) all methods have produced higher achievement than competitive and individualistic learning, and (d) the more conceptual approaches to cooperative learning may produce higher achievement than the direct methods. These conclusions are all the stronger due to the diversity of the research on which they are based, ranging from controlled field experimental studies to evaluative case studies.

Conclusion

We know a great deal about the effective use of learning groups. We know that they must be structured cooperatively, not competitively or individualistically. There are a variety of major theories that underlie their use. The theory that has inspired the most research and application to learning groups is social interdependence theory. The basic premise of the theory is that the structure of learning goals largely determines how students interact, and those interaction patterns largely determine outcomes. Hundreds of studies indicate that the use of cooperative learning groups results in greater effort to achieve, more positive relationships among students, and greater student psychological health than do competitive or individualistic efforts. These outcomes are most easily accomplished, however, when positive interdependence, individual accountability, promotive interaction, appropriate use of social skills, and group processing are present. There are multiple operationalizations of cooperative learning, of which eight have been empirically validated. The results of the research indicate that all eight methods are effective. The more studies that have been conducted on a cooperative learning method, and the more conceptual the method, the more effective it seems to be. Despite the breadh and diversity of operationalizations of cooperative learning, current evidence indicates that educators may use almost any method and be successful as long as the five basic elements are included in the procedure.

Despite the considerable body of evidence on the effectiveness of learning groups, numerous issues about the use of learning groups need to be clarified by future research. First, although cooperative learning is one of the most powerful and effective instructional procedures available to teachers, it is underutilized in most schools. More research needs to be conducted on why the discrepancy between research and practice exists and how teachers can be influenced to implement learning groups and institutionalize their use.

Second, there are many problems in education that need to be solved, such as the high percentage of students who drop out before completing high school or college, many students performing below what is expected academically for their age and grade level, and the number of students who are prejudiced toward others. More research needs to be conducted to clarify how the use of learning groups may help solve these problems.

Third, there are other theories, such as Thibaut and Kelley's (1959) social exchange theory of cooperation and competition and Bandura's (1977) theory of group agency, that need to be related to the use of learning groups in the future.

Fourth, when students cooperate they must build and maintain trust, resolve conflicts constructively, ensure that benefits are distributed justly, and induce motivation to achieve goals. These aspects of working together have not been directly related to the use of learning groups. Because they affect learning, perception, cognition, motivation, and self-development, they should be investigated further.

Fifth, in school, goals are imposed on students. Students are required to learn to read and write whether they want to or not. The issue of inducing commitment to imposed goals is of considerable importance in schools, and the role of learning groups in doing so needs to be better understood.

Sixth, most discussions of instructional methods assume there is only one goal—to learn academic material. The role of education in society, however, is much broader than the mastery of academic learning measured by standardized tests. Students are supposed to develop all the competencies, attitudes, and values needed to be productive members of society. Thus, the ways in which instructional procedures (such as learning groups) affect multiple goals simultaneously needs to be studied.

The use of learning groups is one of the most powerful tools available to educators. Their use is solidly based on theory and validated by hundreds of research studies conducted over 11 decades. Learning groups require that students work together to achieve joint goals. By definition, learning groups have to be cooperative, and to be most effective, the implementation of learning groups should include positive interdependence, individual accountability, promotive interaction, the appropriate use of social skills, and group processing. The more educators learn to use the power of cooperative learning groups, the more effective and successful they will be. These results provide strong validation for the effectiveness of learning groups. The use of learning groups is one of the most successful and widespread applications of group dynamics theory and research.

References

Aronson, E., Blaney, N., Stephan, C., Sikes, J., & Snapp, M. (1978). *The jigsaw classroom.* Beverly Hills, CA: Sage.

Bak, B. (1992). *Meta-analytic integration of the relationship between learning and cooperative achievement.* Ann Arbor, MI: UMI Dissertation Services.

Bandura, A. (1977). *Principles of behavioral modification.* New York: Holt, Rinehart, & Winston.

Baumeister, R., & Leary, M. (1995). The need to belong: Desire for interpersonal attachment as a fundamental human motivation. *Psychological Bulletin, 117,* 497–529.

Britton, J. (1990). Research currents: Second thoughts on learning. In M. Brubacher, R. Payne, & K. Richett (Eds.), *Perspectives on small group learning: Theory and practice* (pp. 3–11). Oakville, Ontario: Rubicon.

Brown, A. (1994). The advancement of learning. *Educational Researcher, 23*(8), 4–12.

Bruffee, K. (1993). *Collaborative learning.* Baltimore: Johns Hopkins University Press.

Campbell, J. (1965). *The children's crusader: Colonel Francis W. Parker.* Doctoral dissertation, Teachers College, Columbia University.

Cartwright, D., & Zander, A. (Ed.). (1968). *Group dynamics* (3rd ed.). New York: Harper & Row.

Cohen, E. (1994). *Designing groupwork* (2nd ed.). New York: Teachers College Press.

Cohen, E., & Lotan, A. (Eds.). (1997). *Working for equity in heterogeneous classrooms: Sociological theory in action.* New York: Teachers College Press.

Coleman, J. (1961). *The adolescent society.* New York: Macmillan.

Deutsch, M. (1949). A theory of cooperation and competition. *Human Relations, 2,* 129–152.

Deutsch, M. (1962). Cooperation and trust: Some theoretical notes. In M. R. Jones (Ed.), *Nebraska symposium on motivation* (pp. 275–319). Lincoln: University of Nebraska Press.

DeVries, D., & Edwards, K. (1973). Learning games and student teams: Their effects on classroom process. *American Educational Research Journal, 10,* 307–318.

Dewey, J. (1924). *The school and society.* Chicago: University of Chicago Press.

Gamson, Z. (1984). *Liberating education.* San Francisco: Jossey-Bass.

Gardner, W., Pickett, C., & Brewer, M. (2000). Social exclusion and selective memory: How the need to belong influences memory for social events. *Personality and Social Psychology Bulletin, 26,* 486–496.

Gibbs, J. (1987). *Tribes.* Santa Rosa, CA: Center Source Publications.

Greenwood, C., Delquadri, J., & Hall, R. (1989). Longitudinal effects of classwide peer tutoring. *Journal of Educational Psychology, 81,* 371–383.

Homans, G. C. (1974). *Social behavior: It's elementary forms.* San Diego: Harcourt Brace Jovanovich.

Johnson, D. W. (1970). *Social psychology of education.* New York: Holt.

Johnson, D. W. (2003). Social interdependence: Interrelationships among theory, research, and practice. *American Psychologist, 58*(11), 934–945.

Johnson, D. W., & Johnson, R. (1974). Instructional goal structure: Cooperative, competitive, or individualistic. *Review of Educational Research, 44,* 213–240.

Johnson, D. W., & Johnson, R. (1978). Cooperative, competitive, and individualistic learning. *Journal of Research and Development in Education, 12,* 3–15.

Johnson, D. W., & Johnson, R. (1979). Conflict in the classroom: Controversy and learning. *Review of Educational Research, 49,* 51–70.

Johnson, D. W., & Johnson, R. (1989). *Cooperation and competition: Theory and research.* Edina, MN: Interaction Book Company.

Johnson, D. W., & Johnson, R. (1994). *Leading the cooperative school* (2nd ed). Edina, MN: Interaction Book Company.

Johnson, D. W., & Johnson, R. (1995). *Creative controversy: Intellectual challenge in the classroom* (3rd ed.). Edina, MN: Interaction Book Company.

Johnson, D. W., & Johnson, R. (1999). *Learning together and alone: Cooperative, competitive, and individualistic learning* (5th ed.). Boston: Allyn & Bacon.

Johnson, D. W., & Johnson, R. (2002). Cooperative learning methods: A meta-analysis. *Journal of Research in Education, 12*(1), 5–24.

Johnson, D. W., & Johnson, R. (2003). *Joining together: Group theory and group skills* (8th ed.). Boston: Allyn & Bacon. (Original work published 1975)

Johnson, D. W., Johnson, R., & Holubec, E. (1998). *Cooperation in the classroom* (6th ed.). Edina, MN: Interaction Book Company.

Johnson, D. W., Johnson, R., & Maruyama, G. (1983). Interdependence and interpersonal attraction among heterogeneous and homogeneous individuals: A theoretical formulation and a meta-analysis of the research. *Review of Educational Research, 53,* 5–54.

Kagan, S. (1985). *Cooperative learning resources for teachers.* Riverside: University of California at Riverside.

Katzenbach, J., & Smith, D. (1993). *The wisdom of teams.* Cambridge, MA: Harvard Business School Press.

Kohn, A. (1992). *No contest* (2nd ed.). Boston: Houghton Mifflin.

Lewin, K. (1935). *A dynamic theory of personality.* New York: McGraw-Hill.

Lewin, K. (1948). *Resolving social conflicts.* New York: Harper.

Manstead, A., & Hewstone, M. (Eds.). (1995). *The Blackwell encyclopedia of social psychology.* Oxford, UK: Blackwell.

McTighe, J. & Lyman, F. (1988). Cueing thinking in the classroom: The promise of theory-embedded tools. *Educational Leadership, 45*(7), 18–24.

Mead, M. (Ed.). (1936). *Cooperation and competition among primitive peoples.* New York: McGraw-Hill.

Miel, A., et al. (1952). *Cooperative procedures in learning.* New York: Teachers College Press.

Miles, M. (1981). *Learning to work in groups* (2nd ed.). New York: Teachers College Press.

Palinscar, A., & Brown, A. (1984). Reciprocal teaching of comprehension-fostering and monitoring activities. *Cognition and Instruction, 1,* 117–175.

Palinscar, A., Stevens, D., & Gavelek, J. (1988, April). *Collaborating in the interest of collaborative learning.*

Paper presented at the Annual Meeting of the American Educational Research Association, New Orleans.

Pepitone, E. (1980). *Children in cooperation and competition.* Lexington, MA: D. C. Heath.

Piaget, J. (1950). *The psychology of intelligence.* New York: Harcourt.

Roschelle, J., & Behrend, S. (1995). The construction of shared knowledge in collaborative problem solving. In C. O'Malley (Ed.), *Computer-supported collaborative learning* (pp. 69–97). Berlin: Springer-Verlag.

Schmuck, R., & Schmuck, P. (2001). *Group processes in the classroom* (8th ed.). Boston: McGraw-Hill.

Sharan, S. (1980). Cooperative learning in teams: Recent methods and effects on achievement, attitudes, and ethnic relations. *Review of Educational Research, 50,* 241–272.

Sharan, S., & Sharan, Y. (1976). *Small group teaching.* Englewood Cliffs, NJ: Educational Technology.

Sharan, S., & Sharan, Y. (1992). *Group investigation: Expanding cooperative learning.* New York: Teacher's College Press.

Simmons, D., Fuchs, D., Fuchs, L., Hodge, J., & Mathes, P. (1994). Importance of instructional complexity and role reciprocity to classwide peer tutoring. *Learning Disabilities Research and Practice, 9,* 203–212.

Skinner, B. (1968). *The technology of teaching.* New York: Appleton-Century-Crofts.

Slavin, R. (1978). Student teams and achievement divisions. *Journal of Research and Development in Education, 12,* 39–49.

Slavin, R. (1983). *Cooperative learning.* New York: Longman.

Slavin, R. (1991). Group rewards make groupwork work. *Educational Leadership, 5,* 89–91.

Slavin, R., Leavey, M., & Madden, N. (1982). *Team-assisted individualization: Mathematics teacher's manual.* Baltimore: Johns Hopkins University, Center for Social Organization of Schools.

Smith, A. (1976). *The theory of moral sentiments* (D. Raphael & A. Macfie, Eds.). Oxford, UK: Clarendon. (Original work published 1759)

Stevens, R., Madden, N., Slavin, R., & Farnish, A. (1987). Cooperative integrated reading and composition: Two field experiments. *Reading Research Quarterly, 22,* 433–454.

Thibaut, J. W., & Kelley, H. H. (1959). *The psychology of groups.* New York: John Wiley.

Von Mises, L. (1949). *Human action: A treatise on economics.* New Haven, CT: Yale University Press.

Vygotsky, L. (1978). *Mind in society.* Cambridge, MA: Harvard University Press.

Wittrock, M. C. (1978). The cognitive movement in instruction. *Educational Psychologist, 13,* 15–19.

25

Mediating Intragroup and Intergroup Conflict

Tricia S. Jones

M ost contemporary organizations depend on groups to secure organizational goals. Groups are an organizational fact of life, as are the conflicts that arise from intragroup and intergroup interaction. As previous chapters in this volume attest, there is considerable knowledge about causes and consequences of group conflicts. Unfortunately, much less is known about how to manage group conflict effectively for the good of the disputing parties and the larger organization, especially when the disputants cannot manage the conflict on their own. This area of group practice has been neglected, especially in regard to the application of third-party interventions like mediation.

Mediation of group conflict has received little attention from conflict theorists or researchers. Messick and Mackie (1989) noted that scholars in intergroup conflict and negotiation processes rarely draw on both literatures to inform theory, practice, or research. Jeffrey Polzer (1996), a prominent theorist in multiparty negotiation,

reflected that the conflict and negotiation literature is heavily oriented toward interpersonal negotiation processes and that very little work has been done to articulate the challenges and opportunities for effectively negotiating between and within groups. The research that has been conducted is too often acontextual (outside a real-world context) (Frey, 1995). Researchers rarely attend to the interaction between parties in group conflict (Couch & Murabito, 1986), often relying on laboratory experiments involving student subjects to investigate dynamics of multiparty negotiation (Crump, 2003; Crump & Glendon, 2003). The field research on mediating in multiparty or group conflicts comes from environmental and public policy venues (Dukes, in press) or from international relations (Greig, 2001)—contexts that have somewhat limited relevance to the workplace.

This chapter discusses mediation of intragroup and intergroup conflicts in the workplace.

The first section defines mediation, contrasts it with other forms of third-party intervention, and presents a basic model of mediation. The second section identifies some common challenges of intragroup conflicts and suggests mediation strategies to meet these challenges. In this section, the primary emphasis is on matching mediation style and strategy to the type of conflict experienced. The third section addresses the application of mediation to intergroup conflict, with special emphasis on issues of timing, ripeness for mediation, and influence on the worldview of the groups. The last section suggests fruitful areas for theory development, research, and practice in this relatively unexplored, but important, conflict management arena.

The Nature of Mediation

Mediation is a form of third-party intervention in which an impartial third party becomes involved in an existing dispute between two or more disputants in order to facilitate communication and help the parties to resolve conflict constructively. Constructive resolution may mean solving problems, making decisions on contested issues, or repairing relational tensions.

In the past two decades, mediation has been defined and explored from a variety of disciplinary backgrounds (McEwen, 1999). Critics argue there have been so many variations of mediation that the term is in danger of becoming meaningless (Deutsch, 1991). Initially, mediation was used almost exclusively in labor management and international contexts. However, with the advent of the alternative dispute resolution movement, mediation has been applied to community, family, court, educational, judicial, and organizational contexts (Hedeen, in press; Jones, 1994; Karrambayya & Brett, 1994; Kelly, in press; Slaikeu & Hasson, 1998). With each new context of application, the form and function of mediation have expanded.

In this chapter, mediation will be discussed in terms of the elements that appear common across these contexts. Those elements include the presence of an impartial third party who assists disputants in their negotiation without usurping decision-making control.

Mediators are neutral or impartial third parties having no vested interest in the outcome of the mediation. There has been a great deal of debate in the mediation field about the definition of impartiality (Mayer, 2004), with some arguing that no mediator can be truly impartial or unbiased—*neutral* in the pure sense of the term. Still, a hallmark of mediation is the assumption that the mediator comes to the dispute without an intent to pursue the interests of one party over the other. A corollary is that mediators eschew active advocacy on behalf of certain disputants. Much of the mediation practice literature helps mediators identify and counteract potential biases that may challenge their impartiality (Lang & Taylor, 2000). One of the more problematic aspects of organizational mediation is the extent to which impartiality can be assumed when a long-term prior relationship exists between mediators and disputants who are members of the same organization (Costantino & Merchant, 1996; Kolb & Sheppard, 1985).

Most scholar practitioners consider mediation a form of facilitated interests-based negotiation (Fisher, Ury, & Patton, 1991; Moore, 2003). The mediator is invited into an ongoing dispute by the disputants (or at least becomes involved with their approval). Usually, when the mediator enters the process, the disputants have attempted to resolve their conflict and have been unable to do so; their initial negotiations have resulted in an impasse or failure to manage all critical issues in the conflict.

The primary distinction between mediation and other forms of third-party intervention is the degree to which the mediator is involved in substantive discussion without making decisions about the conflict. This is in direct contrast to

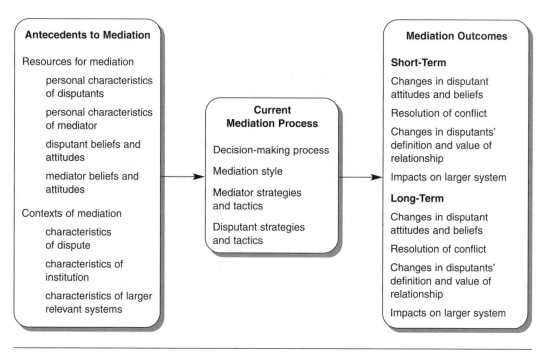

Figure 25.1   Model of Mediation

adjudication and arbitration, in which the third party is given the right and the responsibility (either through contractual, legal, or statutory means) to render a decision with which the disputants are expected to comply. A mediator's involvement in substantive discussions is one characteristic that distinguishes mediation from facilitation or conciliation, two other forms of third-party intervention (Jones, 1985). Facilitation, discussed in detail by (Sunwolf and Frey (Chapter 26, this volume), helps groups engage in constructive decision-making processes or dialogues. Facilitators and conciliators rarely become involved in the substantive issues but rely on process tools to construct and manage a framework for effective communication.

The application of mediation to challenges in intragroup and intergroup conflict requires a basic understanding of the process of mediation and factors that influence efficacy. Given the variety of approaches to mediation, the model presented in Figure 25.1 pulls liberally from Herrman, Hollett, and Gale's (2004) model of

interpersonal mediation, Bercovitch's model of international mediation (Bercovitch & Houston, 2000), and Greig's (2001) analysis of international mediation.

Antecedents to Mediation

A number of antecedent factors are brought to the mediation or underlie the mediation. These are distinguished as *resources for mediation* and *contexts of mediation*. Resources for mediation include the personal characteristics, beliefs, and attitudes of both the disputants and the mediator. Contexts of mediation include characteristics of the dispute, the institution, and relevant larger systems.

Resources for mediation. A great deal of research has examined how personal characteristics of disputants, such as gender, race, age, experience, and knowledge, impact interpersonal or family mediation (Kressel, 2000; Kressel & Pruitt, 1989).

No workplace research exists, however, concerning the relationship between characteristics of group composition or group members and the mediation process. Similarly, research, including the Mediator Skills Program studies (Herrman et al., 2004), has examined personal characteristics of mediators and how those characteristics are related to interpersonal and family mediation and to labor mediation (Kochan & Jick, 1978). In environmental or international mediation, the research on mediator characteristics is limited to discussions of the importance of mediator rank, status, or experience (Bercovitch & Houston, 2000).

Disputants' beliefs and attitudes involve the disputants' orientations to and understanding of mediation. As Herrman et al. (2004) indicate, this includes the disputants' willingness to participate, their perceptions of whether participation is voluntary (Lipsky, Seeber, & Fincher, 2003), their expectations, and their motivations to resolve the dispute. In the optimal scenario, disputants are willing to mediate, perceive their participation as truly voluntary, see no retaliation or negative consequence for refusing to mediate, have positive expectations for the mediation process and outcome, and are highly motivated to resolve the dispute (Bingham, in press). Although one may assume that similar relationships apply when disputants are groups rather than individuals, or individuals within a group, there is no research confirming this assumption.

A mediator's beliefs and attitudes encompass the mediator's ideology about mediation, its purposes, and appropriate goals. Considerable attention has been given to mediator ideology and its manifestation in mediation styles and strategies (Bush & Folger, 1994; Picard, 2004). There are strong factions aligned with certain mediation ideologies and against others (Mayer, 2004; Winslade & Monk, 2000). A mediator's ideology is most germane in its impact on mediation strategies and tactics. Yet, mediator ideology also influences mediation by predisposing a mediator to become involved in certain disputes, to encourage or allow involvement of parties in addition to the direct disputants, and to frame the goals of the mediation for disputants.

Contexts of mediation. All disputes are profoundly influenced by the immediate historical, cultural, and institutional contexts in which they occur. Mediation is no exception. The immediate context of the dispute includes characteristics such as the intensity, degree of hostility, and seriousness of the dispute. Very intense conflicts are considered high-conflict situations (Cloke & Goldsmith, 2000) that require distinct interventions to handle the emotionality of the disputants (Jones, 2001; Jones & Bodtker, 2001). In her model of workplace dispute resolution systems, Jameson (1999) outlined several characteristics of workplace disputes that impact the type of dispute resolution mechanism most likely to be successful.

The historical context of the dispute concerns what has happened prior to mediation. Disputes differ in terms of the length of time the parties have been in conflict, the number of attempts previously made to resolve the dispute, and the success of those attempts (Greig, 2001). New conflicts that are being referred to mediation for the first time require different interventions than long-term, embedded, and seemingly intractable conflicts that have resisted earlier attempts at mediation.

An infinite number of cultural contexts may influence mediation; however, in workplace conflicts, the organizational culture deserves special attention (Conrad & Poole, 2002). Organizational culture dictates what people have conflicts about, how they are expected to manage those conflicts, and what recourse is preferred or possible when their attempts fall short (Lipsky et al., 2003). Groups may have idiosyncratic work cultures, but they are usually variations on the organizational culture.

Institutional context refers to the overall dispute system design of the organization. Ury, Brett, and Goldberg (1993), in the first dispute system design treatise, identified interests-based, rights-based, and power-based approaches, which are coordinated to deal with workplace conflict. Mediation, an interests-based approach, is influenced by the other dispute resolution mechanisms available and how well those are used. With the recent federal mandates to have alternative dispute resolution systems in all federal agencies—a mandate closely paralleled by emerging dispute resolution systems in state governments and private corporations—there has been considerable interest in institutional contexts for dispute resolution (Costantino & Merchant, 1996; Lipsky et al., 2003; Slaikeu & Hasson, 1998). Yet, this scholarship almost exclusively focuses on individuals in disputes with other individuals or with the larger system. Organizational dispute system design has not satisfactorily addressed intragroup and intergroup conflict or its management.

Current Conflict Management Process

The second stage of the mediation model concerns what happens during the mediation itself. Herrman et al. (2004) identify four areas of process: factors that prime readiness (e.g., mediator empathy, feeling heard, ability to talk and voice concerns, perceived self-efficacy, and hostility of environment), procedural factors (e.g., mediation conditions such as procedural clarity), problem-solving behavior, and decision-making process. Bercovitch and Houston (2000) simplify their description and identify the decision-making process used as well as the mediator strategies and tactics.

The meat of the mediation process is the specific strategies and tactics that the mediator employs. Some scholars have developed taxonomies of strategies and tactics (Jones, 1988; Kochan & Jick, 1978; Simkin, 1971). Most identify some variation of three basic strategies: communication-facilitation, substantive-directive, and procedural.

Beyond the discussion of mediator behaviors is the larger issue of style, or the underlying logic

that provides some coherence to the individual tactics used.

Kressel (2000) says mediator style "refers to a cohesive set of strategies that characterize the conduct of a case" (p. 535). Unlike some authors who argue that mediation styles or orientations cannot be mixed (Bush & Folger, 1994), Kressel feels that mediators can employ a large range of styles and strategies, analogous to Frank Sander's famous admonition to "fit the forum to the fuss" (Sander & Goldberg, 1994). According to Kressel, mediators can and should fit the style to the situation.

Gulliver (1979), in his cross-cultural study of mediation, argues that mediator styles can be viewed on a continuum from passive to active (see also Merry, 1982). In their qualitative study of mediation process, Silbey and Merry (1986) found that bargaining (active) mediation roles are more effective than therapeutic (passive) roles, especially in more functional and less intimate relationships. Kolb (1983) identified two mediator roles: the *dealmaker*, who has a directive or active mediator role, and the *orchestrator*, who manages the pattern of interaction but leaves substantive issues to the disputants.

Most mediator-style taxonomies reflect a key distinction made by Leonard Riskin (1994), who argued that there are two basic styles: facilitative and evaluative. Facilitative mediation, as the name suggests, involves a nondirective, passive mediator role where the primary focus of the mediator is on facilitating communication between the parties. An evaluative mediator is much more active and inclined "to argue the merits" of various options, make recommendations for solutions, and raise questions about the acceptability of other options on the table.

But mediators are not the only participants in the mediation process. The disputants' strategy and tactics are equally important (Folger & Jones, 1994). Although some research investigates disputant behavior in mediation (Jones, 1985, 1988), this is the exception rather than the rule. There are no studies of disputant behavior in mediated group conflict.

Mediation Outcomes

Mediation outcomes can be either short-term or long-term (Herrman, 1993). Changes in disputants' attitudes and beliefs may involve their orientations to issues in dispute, perceptions of the conflict and/or the other disputant, or personal understanding and personal growth (Moore, 2003). A central outcome is the resolution of the conflict itself: whether the conflict is resolved or made more intense (Benjamin & Irving, 1995). Changes in the disputants' definition of their relationship with the other party (Cloke, 2001) are also possible, and the outcome of mediation can extend beyond the dispute proper to reinforce or challenge larger system or institutional dynamics (Bingham, in press).

Challenges of Mediating Intragroup Conflict

What are the special challenges of intragroup conflict in the workplace where mediation may be effective? In this section, some of these challenges are outlined in terms of practice implications for mediation.

Differential Treatment of Different Kinds of Conflict

It is incorrect to assume that all group conflict needs to be treated in the same way. Mediators knowledgeable about intragroup conflict dynamics realize that not all conflict is equal in terms of its impacts on the group. In fact, just as there is "good cholesterol" and "bad cholesterol," there is both good and bad group conflict. The mediator needs to intervene to promote, and even generate, the good conflict and to de-emphasize or remove the bad conflict.

The good conflict, which requires enhancement, is task conflict, and the bad conflict, which requires reduction, is relationship conflict and

process conflict. As Karen Jehn (2000) explains, task conflict is about work that is being done or being proposed; relationship conflict is about personal and social issues that are not related to work; and process conflict is about task strategy and the delegation of duties and responsibilities.

Research links task and relationship conflicts with performance in ongoing work teams (Jehn, 1995, 1997; Simons & Peterson, 2000). Moderate task conflict is related to positive group performance whereas relationship conflict is associated with negative group performance (Peterson & Behfar, 2003). Recent research (Jehn, Northcraft, & Neale, 1999) suggests that process conflict negatively affects performance and morale. Jehn (2000) compared the relative proportion of task, relationship, and process conflict in management teams and found that proportional relationship conflict and proportional process conflict were negatively related to commitment, cohesiveness, satisfaction, and individual performance. Proportional task conflict was positively related to performance and member attitudes. However, Jehn (2000) also found that the absence of all three kinds of conflict was not good for groups; groups need to have relatively high task conflict and low relationship and process conflict.

Why is task conflict positive? Sambamurthy and Poole (1992) note that effective decision making depends on the group's ability to extract a range of competing interpretations of the situation and synthesize these diverse interpretations into a decision acceptable to the entire group. Task conflict management needs to be handled carefully so that diversity of interpretation isn't stifled or group cohesion challenged. When task conflict is managed well, the group is superior to individuals in the quality of problem solving (Lewicki & Litterer, 1985).

Why is relationship and process conflict negative? Peterson and Behfar (2003) argue that relationship conflict is destructive for groups for three reasons: (a) it limits the information processing ability of the group because it focuses attention on relational problems rather than task problems; (b) it increases stress and anxiety, which decreases ability to think critically (Jones & Bodtker, 2001); and (c) it often causes hostile attributions and conflict escalation, which eclipse other aspects of group function. Process conflict is detrimental because it similarly distracts the group from focus on task and often masks interpersonal power struggles (Jehn, 2000).

The mediator can help groups address task conflict and decrease relational and process conflict in a variety of ways: surfacing the task conflict, encouraging certain types of dialogue, engaging substantive task issues through evaluative style, and addressing relational and process conflict in private. Although some groups can do this for themselves, other groups need third-party intervention to accomplish this end. In fact, it should be assumed the group has already experienced some level of dysfunctional conflict prior to the decision to bring in a mediator. The length and severity of this dysfunctional conflict will impact the effectiveness of mediation.

Surfacing the task conflict. Often, groups are reluctant to engage in open conflict because conflict is unpleasant for them, even when it is important for group functioning (Smith & Berg, 1987). When conflict does arise, groups try to suppress it or seek quick but inferior resolutions. The mediator can play a critical role by raising the task conflict issues and encouraging the group to attend to them fully. In this capacity, the mediator can help the group retain focus on its task conflicts (thus deflecting attention from relational and process conflict).

Mediators typically rank certain issues through their agenda setting. In the case of group conflict, the mediator can build an agenda that privileges task conflict as the initial focus of full group discussion. Of course, mediators must be sensitive to the fact that in some cases, surfacing task conflict may not have the desired results. When the task under discussion is routine, task conflict can actually be counterproductive (DeChurch & Marks, 2001; Jehn, 1995). The optimal intervention for the mediator is to surface task conflict on nonroutine to complex task issues.

Promoting dialogue and constructive controversy. Surfacing task conflict alone is not sufficient. Groups often lack the ability to engage in dialogue over task issues. Mediators can present and facilitate task-related discussion using techniques, like Constructive Controversy developed by David and Roger Johnson, that have improved cognitive reasoning, problem solving, and creativity (Johnson, Johnson, & Tjosvold, 2000). Any dialogue-based process (Pearce & Littlejohn, 1997; Schweiger, Sandberg, & Rechner, 1989) aims to help the group uncover the assumptions they are making about the task, identify critical information needs, and then exchange that information. Even when the dialogue or discussion feels competitive, group research suggests that unearthing assumptions and arguments is critical to creating patterns of communication that reinforce more integrative decision-making cycles later in the group process (Franz & Jin, 1995).

The only study of mediation in intragroup conflict in an organizational setting sheds additional light on the importance of increasing members' understanding of peer positions and assumptions. Christa Arnold (1995) studied the relationship of co-orientational accuracy (the extent to which members share and understand each other's perceptions of a situation) and mediation on group process and satisfaction. As an experiment, she manipulated co-orientational accuracy (high versus low) and mediation (the presence or absence of a mediator) in problem-solving groups. She studied 24 decision-making groups and found that groups with high co-orientational accuracy (HCA), whether or not they were mediated, made better decisions and used friendlier and less aggressive interaction strategies than either of the low co-orientational accuracy (LCA) groups. In HCA groups, a mediator increased the quality of decision making and facilitated friendlier interaction strategies among group members. However, members of HCA-mediated groups were less satisfied with the discussion than members of HCA-nonmediated groups. It seems that groups are more satisfied with their own discussion when they are in control.

Engaging substantive task issues through evaluative style. Although some mediation scholars adhere to a "one best style" philosophy (Bush & Folger, 1994), there is a time and place for both evaluative and facilitative styles (Riskin, 1994). Mediators can and should embrace an evaluative style when discussing task conflict issues in a conflicted group. As labor management mediators have long understood (Simkin, 1971), mediators can make arguments and suggestions and point out the weaknesses in options that disputants cannot present with impunity. Mediators can frame task-related issues in ways that help group members make better decisions (Putnam & Holmer, 1992). Mediators can challenge suggestions made by group members and can engage in highly directive behaviors in terms of focusing on specific issues or facts. In highly contentious groups, a more evaluative style may be required, at least initially, to encourage the group back to productive patterns of behavior.

Addressing relational and process conflict in private. In the later stages of relational and process conflict, the entire group may be embroiled in the issues that began as disputes between individuals. Yet, mediators must resist the temptation to allow the entire group to remain involved as support agents in a conflict they do not own. It is important for the mediator to remove the discussion of the relational or process conflict to a private meeting of the involved parties (Moore, 2003). Once those involved are removed from the full group, the escalatory potential of the conflict will decrease, much as a flame falters when deprived of oxygen. The group acts as an audience for the relational conflicts, an audience that stimulates face-saving and more extreme behaviors.

In addition to privacy, the use of a more facilitative mediation style is important when mediating relational conflict. Here, the relational nature of the conflict suggests mediators should be more concerned with helping parties to understand each other and share their feelings in a way that helps them have voice and recognition (Bush & Folger, 1994). For relational and process problems, an evaluative style is likely to be unproductive or counterproductive.

Groups suffering from process conflict that has not developed into secondary relational conflict may also benefit from techniques used in the mediation and facilitation of very large groups (Bunker, 2000). Usually reserved for groups of 50 or more (to as large as a thousand), methods for work design have been developed that help groups create templates for task responsibilities, task coordination, task assignment, and oversight procedures. Mediators trained in the use of work design methods can transfer these to smaller organization groups experiencing process conflict.

Balancing Diversity and Cohesion

Smith and Berg (1987), in their excellent analysis of dialectical tensions in groups, identified three sources of conflict in groups: (a) the bringing together of individuals with different interests, skills, and values; (b) the perceptual tendency of individuals to polarize as a way of handling confusion and ambiguity; and (c) the ambivalence group members feel toward the group as a whole when they feel their individual identity is being subjugated to the group identity. They note the tendency for groups to become stuck in paralyzing "we-they" dynamics that are rapidly escalatory.

Other researchers support the argument that poorly managed group diversity can erupt in destructive conflict (Franz & Jin, 1995; Murphy, 1995). Jehn, Chadwick, and Thatcher (1997) used a quasi-experimental field study to investigate diversity, conflict, and work performance. They found that, without intervention, higher levels of diversity in teams (operationalized as differences in sex, age, and nationality) increased relational conflict in groups, whereas value congruence decreased relational conflict, even in highly diverse groups. Similarly, Sheehan and Martin (2003) reported that intragroup conflict mediates the relationship between diversity and group effectiveness: When diversity is allowed to create relational conflict, the group performance suffers, but when diversity is managed to avoid relational conflict, group performance benefits.

Mediators can balance diversity and cohesion to prevent and intervene in dysfunctional conflict. In terms of prevention, mediators can help develop superordinate goals, develop positive conflict styles that become normative, make diversity issues transparent, and guard against coalition formation. Once diversity-related conflict has become relational, the mediator can manage it through strategies discussed in the earlier section.

Develop superordinate goals. Diversity often leads to relational conflicts because of perceived disrespect for the values, behaviors, or attitudes of someone easily categorized as "different" (Ting-Toomey, 1985). Mediators can encourage groups to identify and establish superordinate goals that supersede an individual's value system but do not conflict with it. Not only are these goals likely to prevent relational conflict, but if conflict does erupt, these goals can serve as a touchstone for realigning the group around less contentious issues (Rothman, 1997).

Mediators can aid groups in creating and reinforcing social norms relevant to a newly created superordinate goal. Larson (2003) suggests that in multiparty negotiations, invoking social norms about how the group expresses and enacts value systems is a critical shift in the flow from antagonism to collaboration.

Develop positive conflict styles that become normative. An important function of mediation is to educate the parties in more constructive ways of engaging in conflict (Jones, 1985; Moore, 2003). Group members may not realize that their conflict styles or negotiation behaviors are ineffective. Mediators can coach group members individually or as a whole in developing more agreeable styles. Agreeable conflict styles, defined as a blend of collaborative and accommodative styles, are strongly related to group satisfaction with conflict management (DeChurch & Marks, 2001).

When groups work through conflict, they are not just dealing with the current situation but also reenacting old patterns of conflict management and creating or reinforcing new scripts or norms for dealing with conflict (Bettenhausen & Murnigham, 1985). Kuhn and Poole's (2000) study of naturally interacting groups demonstrates that conflict styles established early in a group's life influence later conflict activities. Thus, the more a mediator can coach group members to use constructive conflict behavior, the more these constructive scripts become an implicit mode of functioning when conflict occurs.

Make diversity issues transparent. Many groups fall into a dangerous trap by ignoring diversity-related issues. Mediators are effective at helping groups make diversity issues transparent. The core value of transparency is to provide groups a better understanding of the members' differences and to encourage perspective taking (Ting-Toomey, 1985).

W. Barnett Pearce, a specialist in communication and conflict, uses the process of circular reasoning—a technique of asking questions that focus on differences and involve comparisons—and encourages members to adopt a variety of perspectives (Pearce, 1995). Circular reasoning clarifies for group members how they are constructing the social reality of the group, and, thus, how they can deconstruct it if needed. Other general dialogue processes can also be used to address assumptions about others and uncover potential areas for more intensive work on diversity-related conflict (Gurin, Peng, Lopez, & Nagda, 1999).

Guard against coalition formation. Multiparty negotiation theory provides insight about the dangers of coalition formation (Polzer, Mannix, & Neale, 1995). Coalitions occur when two or more parties cooperate to obtain a mutually desired outcome that satisfies the interests of the coalition but not the whole group (Polzer, Mannix, & Neale, 1998). In multiparty negotiations, coalitions are considered short-term, self-interested, and politically motivated. Prevailing wisdom in multiparty negotiation is that once the issue has been dealt with, the coalition dissolves. But, in the context of intragroup conflict, coalitions leave a residue of distrust that can poison future group process.

Smith and Berg (1987) refer to this phenomenon as *splitting*. According to their theory, subgroup formation (coalitions), or splitting, occurs in response to the emotional aspects of ongoing conflicts. Splitting is often exacerbated by diversity-related (i.e., ethnic) differences.

Mediators may not be able to prevent coalition formation, but they can try to discourage coalitions. Some of the ways to do this are establishing group discussion patterns that prevent people from speaking for factions, engaging group members in collaborative tasks that reduce the chance of splitting, and concentrating first on issues that build collaboration rather than emphasize differences relevant to coalitions. International mediators refer to this last technique as the *gradualism sequencing strategy* (Weiss, 2003).

Coalitions also form in response to dynamics in the larger organization that influence the group (Takacs, 2001). Mediators may be able to help the group negotiate its own boundaries of influence, in other words, make explicit the degree to which pressures outside the group are allowed to affect group processes (Smith & Berg, 1987).

Mediation can reduce dysfunctional intragroup conflict. An added advantage of effective mediation is the relationship between constructive intragroup conflict and intergroup conflict. The degree of cooperation or competition in intragroup interaction is a good predictor of how the group is likely to behave in intergroup conflicts (Keenan & Carnevale, 1989; Louis & Terry, 2003). Whether the converse is true is empirically unconfirmed. Still, improving cooperative tendencies within a group, which increases cooperative tendencies in their interactions with other groups, is especially valuable in the workplace.

Challenges of Mediating Intergroup Conflict

Much of the theory and research concerning intergroup conflict has been reported in earlier chapters of this volume. Dutifully acknowledged is the powerful insight of Sherif's realistic group conflict theory (Jackson, 1993; Sherif, 1966, 1998) and Tajfel's social identity theory (Tajfel, 1969, 1978; Tajfel & Turner, 2001). Equally noted is the research on intergroup contact processes (Pettigrew & Tropp, 2000) and recategorization programs (Kessler & Mummendey, 2001) that have proven surprisingly effective in overcoming intergroup bias and prejudice.

The negotiation literature reports the destructive potential of groups in conflict with other groups. Groups are more competitively oriented in negotiations than their individual members (McCallum et al., 1985). This competitiveness may be a function of ethnocentrism and bias (Kinzel & Fisher, 1993), decreased trust between groups (Brewer, 1979), the salience of group identity over optimal gains (Peterson, 1997), or all these factors combined. The corpus of intergroup conflict research proves that intergroup conflict is characterized by self-perpetuating and escalatory competitive cycles that increase the likelihood of destructive outcomes (Keashley, Fisher, & Grant, 1993).

This section will not repeat discussion of ways to reduce intergroup conflict through bias reduction or reduction of in-group/out-group hostilities. Instead, the section will concentrate on other ways that mediators can improve intergroup conflict through selecting the "ripe" time for intervention, using selective sequencing strategies in concert with multiple mediators and communication technologies, and working to change the worldview of group members to reduce social hostility.

Picking the "Ripe" Time for Mediation

When mediation happens is as important as how mediation happens, especially in intergroup conflict. In their research, Regan and Stamm (2000) found a curvilinear relationship between the timing of mediation during a dispute and dispute duration. They found that when mediation was attempted early or late in a dispute, it reduced dispute duration. By contrast, when mediation was attempted in the middle of the dispute cycle, it lengthened the duration. Mediation can be successful early in a conflict, before the parties have built up high levels of hostility that make cooperation difficult. Also, mediation can be successful late in a conflict, after disputants have expended significant resources and realize it may be better to engage in settlement than incur further costs.

Greig (2001) studied issues of ripeness and timing in mediation in international conflict. Although his analyses concern international rivalries, the implications for workplace intergroup conflict are apparent. While Regan and Stamm (2000) looked at the effect of timing of mediation intervention on duration of dispute, Greig (2001) examined a range of negative outcomes that occur with mediation attempts in "unripe" circumstances. Poorly timed mediation has little chance of success and, therefore, wastes physical and emotional effort and organizational resources. Using mediation

in unripe circumstances increases negative group interaction and increases the tendency for destructive conflict management; "unsuccessful mediations may teach rivals that management of their conflict is unlikely, forcing the adoption of more coercive, aggressive strategies by both sides" (Greig, 2001, p. 692).

How can a mediator spot the ripe opportunities for intervention or help organizations understand when mediation will be most beneficial for this intergroup dispute? Four contextual factors influence the prospects for mediation success:

1. Degree of costs and pain that develop throughout the intergroup conflict

2. Perception among parties that they are unlikely to unilaterally affect the situation in their favor

3. The level of threat to the groups if settlement or resolution does not happen

4. The belief that a constructive resolution, or the basis for a settlement, exists

The intergroup conflict has to have lasted long enough to create discomfort at some recognizable level for one or ideally both groups. The parties cannot assume that they have the power to craft and implement a solution without the agreement of the other group. There has to be some influential threat to the groups if the conflict is not settled. In organizational situations, this threat would probably come from higher levels of organizational leadership. Also, the groups have to think there is a reasonable solution or package of solutions to address this conflict.

A mediator can use these contextual factors to encourage and schedule entrée to a conflict. The mediator can also focus on these factors when persuading groups to make a sincere attempt at mediation. Sincerity is important. Mediation can be used manipulatively, as Richmond (1998) has suggested in his study of international mediation. Rather than using mediation to reduce the level of conflict in the rivalry, the party might use mediation to gain breathing space and regroup resources, improve their bargaining position, gain legitimacy for the position, or avoid making concessions by prolonging dispute.

Detailing costs. The mediator can convince a group it has incurred sufficient costs to warrant mediation. Zartman (1985) suggests that financial and emotional expense can encourage disputants to change their strategies toward one another. In these ripe moments, disputants are locked in "mutually hurting stalemates" in which unilateral solutions become blocked but mutual solutions become more possible. A mediator can help groups see these stalemates and convince the groups to move past them. These discussions should be held in private with each group to reduce the embarrassment that might occur in open discussion.

Reinforcing operative interdependence. Mediators can dissuade a group from making the incorrect assumption that they can handle the situation without the cooperation of the other group. Tinged with bravado, these group denials of interdependence can seriously block conflict management.

Securing pressure from leadership. A mediator may enlist organizational leadership to support a perceived threat or sanction if the conflict is not resolved. Depending on the organizational dispute system design, the mediator may be able to truthfully explain that failure to settle in negotiation or mediation will require referral to a rights- or power-based method of dispute resolution that can be far more costly (Ury et al., 1993).

Discovering possibilities for resolution. Perhaps most important, the mediator can help groups see possibilities for resolution that were not obvious in the din of conflict. Serious or intractable conflicts continue because the parties see no way out. They assume they have no choice but to defeat the opponent (Rothman, 1997). As long as groups believe this, there is no motivation to attempt collaboration. Mediators will be more successful in these endeavors when they are realistic about the possibilities for resolution—not promising a rosier picture than actually exists (Larson, 2003).

Sequencing Strategies, Communication Technologies, and Multiple Mediators

Once the mediator is engaged in intergroup conflict, a determining factor is the agenda setting or sequencing strategies employed. Joshua Weiss (2003) discusses advantages and disadvantages of three sequencing strategies used in intractable multiparty conflicts: gradualism, the boulder-in-the-road technique, and the committee approach.

Gradualism is a strategy in which the mediator tries to move the parties slowly and incrementally from simpler to more complex issues. The basic logic is that initial trust is low, and tackling easier issues first builds trust and cooperative momentum. There are some weaknesses to this strategy: It requires patience, it doesn't work as well when there is turnover among or within parties, and it is vulnerable to "spoilers" or those who want to prevent resolution. Gradualism also assumes that parties believe no single issue is a deal breaker—especially if all other issues have been handled. Gradualism is less effective in intergroup conflicts than in dyadic conflicts. In intergroup conflicts, there is a greater chance of group composition changing over time and a greater probability that at least some group members are not resigned to the need to resolve the conflict.

The boulder-in-the-road strategy is the opposite of gradualism. It proposes to address the most complex issue first. Once the boulder is removed, the rest of the process is easier. Of course, there are some challenges with this approach. If the boulder cannot be resolved, the strategy preempts the possibility of handling other issues. Having a breakdown early in the process can have more dramatic consequences; people feel more justified to use escalatory responses. If the strategy fails, it may be very difficult to start the process again because parties assume the boulder is still there, thus calling into question the utility of the entire effort. Unless the mediator has reasonable expectations of success, this sequencing strategy is not a good idea for intergroup conflict.

The committee approach involves taking the difficult issues, dividing the parties into committees, and assigning each committee an issue to discuss. The committees work simultaneously on their issues. This can work well in very large groups (which may have more difficulty in process on any conflict) (Bunker, 2000), especially if the issues are of relatively equal importance. Of course, assignment of parties to committees should be done carefully. Also, reporting between committees on contingent issues is critical. A disadvantage of this approach is that parties may feel they cannot support the decision of a committee because they did not have a voice in that committee. There is also less ability to link or package issues in the negotiation.

Communication technologies can be used to assist the committee approach to mediation. Mediators have found that electronic meeting systems and similar technologies can increase participation and decrease destructive interaction patterns in intense intergroup conflict (Harmon, 1998). Some methods help groups develop shared mental models, or general perspectives, that enhance cooperation (Swaab, Postmes, Neijens, Kiers, & Dumay, 2002). Given the rapid growth in online dispute resolution practice, mediators are becoming more knowledgeable and sophisticated about the use of these technologies (Rule, 2002). The use of computer-mediated communication for mediation process has shown a tendency to increase process and relational conflict, at least initially; this tendency would have to be monitored carefully by the mediator (Hobman, Bordia, Irmer, & Chang, 2002).

The multiple mediator model is used almost exclusively in the mediation of international conflicts (Crocker, Hampson, & Aall, 2001), but it can be applied in workplace conflicts. International mediators have argued that using multiple mediators in the same dispute can create unique incentives and processes for conflict management that are not possible with a single mediator model (Iji, 2001). Certainly, if a committee sequencing approach is used, you need multiple mediators to oversee simultaneous committee processes. If multiple mediators are used, they must clarify their roles, coordinate their processes, and avoid internal conflicts in the mediation team (Crocker, Hampson, & Aall, 2000; McCallum, 2001; Metcalfe, 2000). The use of multiple mediators poses an additional advantage specific to organizational mediation; the mediators are not likely to have the same familiarity or previous history with the disputing groups. As Kolb and Sheppard (1985) suggested, one of the most serious disadvantages of using internal mediators for workplace conflict is that they are not truly impartial third parties because they have too much relational history and vested interest in their connections with disputants.

Changing the Group's Worldview to Reduce Hostility

Groups create a social reality through discourse and behavior, and the social reality becomes self-fulfilling, especially in group conflict. How groups perceive the symbolic or realistic threats of external parties has significant influence on cognitive, affective, and behavioral consequences (Dovidio, Maruyama, & Alexander, 1998). The same dynamic is seen in interpersonal conflict (Gottman, 1994) where defensive orientations based on hostile worldviews are a prime predictor of destructive, aggressive, and retaliatory conflict behavior. Thus, one task for a mediator is to assess and counteract hostile worldviews held by competing groups.

Roy Eidelson and Judy Eidelson (2003) wrote a summary piece that details five worldviews, or "belief domains," that are critical in the development of intergroup conflict: superiority, injustice, vulnerability, distrust, and helplessness. Mediators can intervene in certain ways to reduce each of these worldviews.

Superiority is a group's assumption that, in some way, it is better than others outside the group. Obviously, this contempt dynamic relates strongly to the bases of realistic group conflict theory and social identity theory. A group may feel superior to the group with which it is in conflict or to some general "other." It is unrealistic to assume that mediation can make significant impacts in this dynamic in short-term intervention. However, mediators can attempt various intergroup contacts that have proven effective in the reduction of contempt and prejudice (Pettigrew & Tropp, 2000). Mediators can also play on a perception of superiority by calling on the group to take more responsibility or initiative to resolve the conflict.

Injustice is a core belief that the group has been mistreated by specific others or the world at large. This mind-set results in groups seeing injustice where it may not exist and responding defensively or retaliating against an imagined threat. Leaders often play an important role in promoting a group's adoption of the injustice worldview. An effective leader (or mediator) can alter the group's perceptions of justice. For example, a mediator can work with a group privately to unearth its assumptions of injustice, identify opportunities for factually dispelling those notions, and indicate how the erroneously perceived injustice has tainted their relationship with the other group. Compared with opposing groups, mediators are much more likely to be believed when they present evidence that an injustice has not been committed.

Vulnerability is the belief that the individual or group is perpetually in harm's way. This perception produces high levels of anxiety that stimulate aggressive and preemptive action. Mediators may use one of two general strategies to help the group deal with perceived vulnerability. First, a mediator may agree that the group is indeed vulnerable and may intervene to help empower the group (Cloke, 2001; Jones & Bodtker, 2001). Empowering the group involves working with the group to clarify the group's goals and resources and to identify possible sources of additional influence. Second, a mediator may assess the group as already powerful, or at least much less vulnerable than the group assumes. In this case, the mediator can help articulate the sources of strength already possessed by the group. In this process, a mediator may be aided by the ability to take a larger systems-oriented focus—to see the bigger picture of the group in relation to the organization. When groups feel vulnerable, their perception of their fit with the surrounding social system may be distorted.

Helplessness is similar to vulnerability but requires slightly different mediation intervention. Helplessness is the conviction that even carefully planned and executed actions will fail to produce desired outcomes. At a group level, it is a collective sense of powerlessness and dependency. The group can focus so much on its own weaknesses that it feels unable to address other issues. Mediators can reduce perceptions of helplessness using the empowerment and systems-perspective strategies just discussed. In addition, and more specific to this worldview weakness, the mediator can help the group test its efficacy on incremental interventions. In other words, the mediator can guide the group to detail exactly what goal they want to accomplish, specify the tasks necessary to accomplish that goal, select measurable indicators that the goal has been achieved, establish contingency plans for potential failure of task completion, enact the attempt, and evaluate the group's effectiveness. The mediator can help create tests of success, tasks designed to prove to the group that it is more able than anticipated.

The final problematic worldview is distrust, an obstacle to any constructive, collaborative conflict management. Group distrust is rarely generalized but usually specific to the other group involved in the conflict. Issues of distrust require long-term interventions. Conflict managers know all too well how quickly trust can be destroyed and how difficult it is to rebuild (Moore, 2003). Mediators dealing with a distrustful group may attempt to lay groundwork for incremental processes that allow the groups to rebuild trust.

But realistically, the mediation is likely to be much shorter term. In this case, a mediator can still help the group discuss necessary implications of distrust and the resolutions possible with a distrusted other. The mediator can clarify whether the source of the distrust has to affect all areas of resolution. Perhaps the group has good reason to distrust the other group in terms of its goodwill but has little reason to distrust the group in terms of its probability of complying with the law or policy that impacts the issue in conflict. Groups tend to generalize sources of distrust and allow distrust of "something" to become distrust of "everything." Mediators can fit the group with a more discerning lens.

Mediators can also help groups craft livable solutions with untrustworthy parties. If all conflict resolution required high levels of trust, few conflicts would be resolved. The art of mediation in this instance is identifying areas of risk that are excessive and not allowing those to be a part of an agreement. Mediators can help groups define agreements that are too risky—that depend too much on the other group for success. Mediators can also help the groups identify enforcement or accountability structures that can be approached, should the other party fail to uphold the agreement.

Eidelson and Eidelson (2003) conclude that four of these five worldviews act as triggers to destructive intergroup conflict: superiority, injustice, vulnerability, and distrust. Thus, mediation interventions that reduce these perceptions will de-escalate conflict situations.

Future Directions

Given the infancy of this area of scholarship, there are many fruitful directions to explore in terms of theory, research, and practice on mediating intragroup and intergroup conflict. Some of the more pressing are presented here.

Mediating Emotion in Group Conflict

Issues of emotion and conflict have only recently begun to receive the attention deserved in the general conflict literature. There are strong arguments for the centrality of emotion in conflict and the need to revise our theories of conflict to appreciate these influences (Jones, 2001; LeBaron, 2002). Also, initial theories suggest that the emotionality of a conflict has consequences for mediation practice (Jones & Bodtker, 2001). In terms of practice implications, perhaps the most sophisticated work has been done in terms of shame cycles in interpersonal conflicts (Retzinger, 1993).

Little theory development and few practice applications have explored the emotional experiences of groups in conflict. Better understanding of how groups construct emotional realities and how those realities can be influenced would provide mediators with possible interventions. Identifying ways to generate constructive emotions in groups may be instrumental for mediators to turn high conflicts to low conflicts. Also, understanding the residual emotional experiences of groups after conflict may provide insights about recurring dispute cycles and ways to interrupt them.

Understanding Group Mediation as Part of a Larger Dispute Design System

In workplace conflict, the ideal is to have a well-designed, comprehensive dispute system that coordinates structures of prevention, intervention, and postvention (Lipsky et al., 2003). Hallmarks of successful systems are proportional use of interests-based, rights-based, and power-based interventions in which "loopback" functions allow disputants to take the dispute back to an interests-based process whenever possible (Slaikeu & Hasson, 1998).

How mediation of group conflict can and should fit within larger dispute systems design is almost completely unexplored. Critical questions for exploration include the following:

- Under what conditions should group conflict be referred to mediation rather than an alternative dispute resolution procedure?
- What are the characteristics of intragroup or intergroup conflict that heighten the chance for mediation success?
- When is it ineffective or even dangerous to use mediation rather than a rights-based or power-based approach?
- How can mediators be selected and assigned for maximum effectiveness in intragroup and intergroup conflict?
- How can an organization balance the use of internal, but uninvolved mediators to maximize the mediator's knowledge of the organizational context and culture without challenging the mediator's impartiality?
- What loopback procedures are most effective with group mediation?
- Are there certain points in the referral of the dispute to rights- and power-based processes where looping back to mediation should be discouraged or disallowed?
- Are there certain kinds of group conflicts where loopback structures are more important?

More Longitudinal Appreciation of the Structure of Group Conflict

As in most organizational conflict scholarship, the conflict episode is punctuated in a way that reinforces concentration on the current conflict reality rather than the arc of the conflict trajectory (Kusztal, 2002). This is especially true in group conflicts. Looking at the complete scope of the conflict dynamic would improve mediation practice. The more a mediator understands about the emergence of the conflict, the micropatterning of the conflict, and larger cycles of engagement in the conflict, the better able he or she is to select appropriate styles and interventions.

Looking longitudinally also increases the mediator's ability to ascertain conditions of ripeness or help create them. There may be different ripeness conditions for different kinds of group conflict in organizations. Or there may be different conditions of ripeness in which one group is primed for mediation but the other is not, due to group or organizational influences.

A longer term perspective may also help mediators and organizational leaders understand when the needs of the group may be outweighed by the needs of the larger organization. In some situations, allowing a group conflict to escalate (i.e., withholding mediation that might ameliorate the conflict) might hurt the group but engender conditions that are beneficial to the organization, as in situations of social justice concerns (Hedeen, in press).

Finally, taking a longer term perspective also helps us to understand the impact of the changing nature of group members on the cycles of conflict and attempted resolution. Putnam and Stohl (1990) discussed the idea of bona fide groups with permeable boundaries and changing members that were highly influenced by the environment. How groups change creates conflict. Change in membership affects responses to conflict and conflict management orientations. The interplay of environment, group change, and conflict intervention through mediation is a complex puzzle waiting to be solved.

References

Arnold, C. L. (1995). Small group conflict management in organizational setting: Mediation and coorientational accuracy in decision-making groups. *Dissertation Abstracts International, Section A: Humanities and Social Sciences, 55*(7-A), 1741.

Benjamin, M., & Irving, H. H. (1995). Research in family mediation: Review and implications. *Mediation Quarterly, 13*(1), 53–82.

Bercovitch, J., & Houston, A. (2000). Why do they do it like this? An analysis of the factors influencing mediation behavior in international conflicts. *Journal of Conflict Resolution, 44*(2), 170–202.

Bettenhausen, K. L., & Murnigham, J. K. (1985). The emergence of norms in competitive decision-making groups. *Administrative Science Quarterly, 30,* 350–372.

Bingham, L. B. (in press). Employment dispute resolution: The case for mediation. *Conflict Resolution Quarterly, 22*(1, 2).

Brewer, M. B. (1979). In-group bias in the minimal intergroup situation: A cognitive-motivational analysis. *Psychology Bulletin, 86,* 307–324.

Bunker, B. B. (2000). Managing conflict through large group methods. In M. Deutsch & P. Coleman (Eds.), *The handbook of conflict resolution* (pp. 546–567). San Francisco: Jossey-Bass.

Bush, R. A. B., & Folger, J. P. (1994). *The promise of mediation.* San Francisco: Jossey-Bass.

Cloke, K. (2001). *Mediating dangerously: The frontiers of conflict resolution.* San Francisco: Jossey-Bass.

Cloke, K., & Goldsmith, J. (2000). *Resolving personal and organizational conflict: Stories of transformation and forgiveness.* San Francisco: Jossey-Bass.

Conrad, C., & Poole, M. S. (2002). *Strategic organizational communication: Toward the 21st century* (5th ed.). Orlando, FL: Harcourt-Brace.

Costantino, C. A., & Merchant, C. S. (1996). *Designing conflict management systems.* San Francisco: Jossey-Bass.

Couch, C. J., & Murabito, J. (1986). Mediating intergroup negotiations. In C. Couch & S. Saxton (Eds.), *Studies in symbolic interaction: A research annual: The Iowa School* (Supplement 2, Part B, pp. 365–374). Stamford, CT: JAI Press.

Crocker, C. A., Hampson, F. O., & Aall, P. (Eds.). (2000). *Herding cats: Multiparty mediation in a complex world.* Washington, DC: U.S. Institute of Peace Press.

Crocker, C. A., Hampson, F. O., & Aall, P. (2001). A crowded stage: Liabilities and benefits of multiparty mediation. *International Studies Perspectives, 2,* 51–67.

Crump, L. (2003). Multiparty negotiation and the management of complexity. *International Negotiation, 8*(2), 189–196.

Crump, L., & Glendon, I. (2003). Towards a paradigm of multiparty negotiation. *International Negotiation, 8*(2), 197–235.

DeChurch, L. A., & Marks, M. A. (2001). Maximizing the benefits of task conflict: The role of conflict management. *International Journal of Conflict Management, 12*(1), 4–23.

Deutsch, M. (1991). Subjective features of conflict resolution: Psychological, social, and cultural influences. In Raimo Vayrynen (Ed.), *New directions in conflict theory: Conflict resolution and conflict transformation* (pp. 26–56). London: Sage.

Dovidio, J. F., Maruyama, G., & Alexander, M. G. (1998). A social psychology of national and international group relations. *Journal of Social Issues, 54*(4), 831–846.

Dukes, E. F. (in press). What we know about environmental conflict resolution: An analysis based upon research. *Conflict Resolution Quarterly, 22*(1, 2).

Eidelson, R. J., & Eidelson, J. I. (2003). Dangerous ideas: Five beliefs that propel groups toward conflict. *American Psychologist, 58*(3), 182–192.

Fisher, R., Ury, W., & Patton, B. (1991). *Getting to yes: Negotiating agreement without giving in* (2nd ed.). New York: Penguin Books.

Folger, J. P., & Jones, T. S. (Eds.). (1994). *New directions in mediation: Communication research and perspectives.* Beverly Hills, CA: Sage.

Franz, C. R., & Jin, K. G. (1995). The structure of group conflict in a collaborative work group during information systems development. *Journal of Applied Communication Research, 23,* 108–127.

Frey, L. (1995). Introduction: Applied communication research on group facilitation in natural settings. In L. Frey (Ed.), *Innovations in group facilitation: Applications in natural settings* (pp. 1–24). Cresskill, NJ: Hampton Press.

Gottman, J. M. (1994). *What predicts divorce? The relationship between marital processes and marital outcomes.* Hillsdale, NJ: Lawrence Erlbaum.

Greig, J. M. (2001). Moments of opportunity: Recognizing conditions of ripeness for international mediation between enduring rivals. *Journal of Conflict Resolution, 45*(6), 691–718.

Gulliver, P. H. (1979). *Disputes and negotiation: A cross-cultural perspective.* New York: Academic.

Gurin, P., Peng, T., Lopez, G., & Nagda, B. A. (1999). Context, identity, and intergroup relations. In D. Prentice & D. Miller (Eds.), *Cultural divides: The social psychology of intergroup contact* (pp. 133–170). New York: Russell Sage Foundation.

Harmon, J. (1998). Electronic meetings and intense group conflict: Effects of a policy-modeling performance support system and an audio communication support system on satisfaction and agreement. *Group Decision & Negotiation, 7*(2), 131–155.

Hedeen, T. (in press). A case for the field of community mediation. *Conflict Resolution Quarterly, 22*(1, 2).

Herrman, M. S. (1993). On balance: Promoting integrity under conflicted mandates. *Mediation Quarterly, 11*(2), 123–138.

Herrman, M., Hollett, N., & Gale, J. (2004). *Mediation from beginning to end: A testable theory.* Unpublished manuscript, University of Georgia, Athens.

Hobman, E. V., Bordia, P., Irmer, B., & Chang, A. (2002). The expression of conflict in computer-mediated and face-to-face groups. *Small Group Research, 33*(4), 439–466.

Iji, T. (2001). Multiparty mediation in Tajikistan: The 1997 Peace Agreement. *International Negotiation, 6*(3), 357–386.

Jackson, J. W. (1993). Realistic group conflict theory: A review and evaluation of the theoretical and empirical literature. *Psychological Record, 43*(3), 395–405.

Jameson, J. K. (1999). Toward a comprehensive model for the assessment and management of intraorganizational conflict: Developing the framework. *International Journal of Conflict Management, 10*(3), 268–294.

Jehn, K. A. (1995). A multimethod examination of the benefits and detriments of intragroup conflict. *Administrative Science Quarterly, 40,* 256–282.

Jehn, K. A. (1997). A qualitative analysis of conflict types and dimensions in organizational groups. *Administrative Science Quarterly, 42,* 530–557.

Jehn, K. A. (2000). The influence of proportional and perceptual conflict composition on team performance. *International Journal of Conflict Management, 11*(1), 56–74.

Jehn, K. A., Chadwick, C., & Thatcher, S. M. B. (1997). To agree or not to agree: The effects of value congruence, individual demographic dissimilarity, and conflict on workgroup outcomes. *International Journal of Conflict Management, 8,* 287–305.

Jehn, K. A., Northcraft, G. B., & Neale, M. A. (1999). Why differences make a difference: A field study of diversity, conflict, and performance in workgroups. *Administrative Science Quarterly, 44,* 741–763.

Johnson, D. W., Johnson, R. T., & Tjosvold, D. T. (2000). Constructive controversy: The value of intellectual opposition. In Morton Deutsch & Peter Coleman (Eds.), *The handbook of conflict resolution* (pp. 65–85). San Francisco: Jossey-Bass.

Jones, T. S. (1985). *"Breaking up is hard to do": An exploratory investigation of communication behaviors and phases in child-custody divorce mediation.* Unpublished doctoral dissertation, The Ohio State University.

Jones, T. S. (1988). Phase structures in agreement and no-agreement mediation. *Communication Research, 15,* 470–495.

Jones, T. S. (1994). A dialectical reframing of mediation process. In J. Folger & T. Jones (Eds.), *New directions in mediation: Communication research and perspectives* (pp. 26–47). Beverly Hills, CA: Sage.

Jones, T. S. (2001). Emotional communication and conflict: Essence and impact. In W. Eadie & P. Nelson (Eds.), *The language of conflict and resolution* (pp. 81–104). Thousand Oaks, CA: Sage.

Jones, T. S., & Bodtker, A. (2001). Mediating with heart in mind. *Negotiation Journal, 17*(3), 217–244.

Karrambayya, R., & Brett, J. (1994). Organizational mediation. In Joseph Folger & Tricia Jones (Eds.), *New directions in mediation: Communication research and perspectives* (pp. 143–162). Beverly Hills, CA: Sage.

Keashley, L., Fisher, R. J., & Grant, P. R. (1993). The comparative utility of third party consultation and mediation within a complex simulation of intergroup conflict. *Human Relations, 46*(3), 371–393.

Keenan, P. A., & Carnevale, P. (1989). Positive effects of within-group cooperation on between-group negotiation. *Journal of Applied Social Psychology, 19*(12), 977–992.

Kelly, J. B. (in press). Family mediation research: Is there empirical support for the field? *Conflict Resolution Quarterly, 22*(1, 2).

Kessler, T., & Mummendey, A. (2001). Is there any scapegoat around? Determinants of intergroup conflicts at different categorization levels. *Journal of Personality and Social Psychology, 81*(6), 1090–1102.

Kinzel, R., & Fisher, R. J. (1993). Ethnocentrism, group cohesion, and constituent pressure on negotiators in intergroup conflict. *International Journal of Conflict Management, 4*(4), 323–336.

Kochan, T. A., & Jick, T. (1978). The public sector mediation process: A theory and empirical examination. *Journal of Conflict Resolution, 22*, 209–240.

Kolb, D. M. (1983). *The mediators.* Cambridge: MIT Press.

Kolb, D. M., & Sheppard, B. H. (1985). Do managers mediate or even arbitrate? *Negotiation Journal, 1*(4), 379–388.

Kressel, K. (2000). Mediation. In M. Deutch & P. Coleman (Eds.), *Handbook of conflict resolution* (pp. 522–545). San Francisco: Jossey-Bass.

Kressel, K., & Pruitt, D. (Eds.). (1989). *Mediation research.* San Francisco: Jossey-Bass.

Kuhn, T., & Poole, M. S. (2000). Do conflict management styles affect group decision making? *Human Communication Research, 26*(4), 558–592.

Kusztal, I. (2002). Discourses in the use and emergence of organizational conflict. *Conflict Resolution Quarterly, 20*(2), 231–248.

Lang, M., & Taylor, A. (2000). *The making of a mediator: Developing artistry in practice.* San Francisco: Jossey-Bass.

Larson, M. J. (2003). Low-power contributions in multilateral negotiations: A framework analysis. *Negotiation Journal, 19*(2), 133–150.

LeBaron, M. (2002). *Bridging troubled waters: Conflict resolution from the heart.* San Francisco: Jossey-Bass.

Lewicki, R., & Litterer, J. (1985). *Negotiation: Readings, exercises, and cases.* Homewood, IL: Irwin.

Lipsky, D. B., Seeber, R. L., & Fincher, R. D. (2003). *Emerging systems for managing workplace conflict: Lessons from American corporations for managers and dispute resolution professionals.* San Francisco: Jossey-Bass.

Louis, W., & Terry, D. (2003). Whom to fight when about what: Social identity and strategic decisions in multi-group conflicts. *Australian Journal of Psychology, 55*, 51–56.

Mayer, B. (2004). *Beyond neutrality: Confronting the crisis in conflict resolution.* San Francisco: Jossey-Bass.

McCallum, D. M., Harring, K., Gilmore, R., Drenan, S., Chase, J. P., Insko, C., & Thibaut, J. (1985). Competition and cooperation between groups and between individuals. *Journal of Experimental Social Psychology, 21*, 301–320.

McCallum, J. S. (2001). Herding cats [Book review]. *Parameters: US Army War College, 31*(2), 144–146.

McEwen, C. A. (1999). Toward a program-based ADR research agenda. *Negotiation Journal, 15*(4), 325–338.

Merry, S. E. (1982). Defining success in the neighborhood justice movement. In R. Tomasic & M. Feeley (Eds.), *Neighborhood justice: An assessment of an emerging idea* (pp. 134–156). New York: Longman.

Messick, D. M., & Mackie, D. M. (1989). Intergroup relations. *Annual Review of Psychology, 40*, 45–81.

Metcalfe, D. (2000). OECD agreement to criminalize bribery: A negotiation analytic perspective. *International Negotiation, 5*(1), 129–156.

Moore, C. (2003). *The mediation process: Practical strategies for resolving conflict* (3rd ed.). San Francisco: Jossey-Bass.

Murphy, B. O. (1995). Promoting dialogue in culturally diverse workplace environments. In L. Frey (Ed.), *Innovations in group facilitation: Applications in natural settings* (pp. 77–93). Cresskill, NJ: Hampton Press.

Pearce, W. B. (1995). Bringing news of difference: Participating in a systemic social constructionist communication. In L. Frey (Ed.), *Innovations in group facilitation: Applications in natural settings* (pp. 94–116). Cresskill, NJ: Hampton Press.

Pearce, W. B., & Littlejohn, S. (1997). *Moral conflict: When social worlds collide.* Thousand Oaks, CA: Sage.

Peterson, E. A. (1997). Majority influence in negotiation. *Dissertation Abstracts International: Section B: The Sciences & Engineering, 57*(12-B), June, pp. 77–78.

Peterson, R. S., & Behfar, K. J. (2003). The dynamic relationship between performance feedback, trust, and conflict in groups: A longitudinal study. *Organizational Behavior & Human Decision Processes, 92*(1–2), 102–112.

Pettigrew, T. F., & Tropp, L. R. (2000). Does intergroup contact reduce prejudice? Recent meta-analytic findings. In S. Oskamp (Ed.), *Reducing prejudice and discrimination* (pp. 93–114). Mahwah, NJ: Lawrence Erlbaum.

Picard, C. (2004). Exploring an integrative framework for understanding mediation. *Conflict Resolution Quarterly, 21*(3), 295–312.

Polzer, J. T. (1996). Intergroup negotiations: The effects of negotiating teams. *Journal of Conflict Resolution, 40*(4), 678–698.

Polzer, J. T., Mannix, E. A., & Neale, M. A. (1995). Multiparty negotiation in its social context. In R. M. Kramer & D. M. Messick (Eds.), *Negotiation as a social process: New trends in theory and research* (pp. 123–142). Thousand Oaks, CA: Sage.

Polzer, J. T., Mannix, E. A., & Neale, M. A. (1998). Interest alignment and coalitions in multiparty negotiation. *Academy of Management Journal, 41*(1), 42–54.

Putnam, L. L., & Holmer, M. (1992). Framing, reframing, and issue development. In L. L. Putnam & M. E. Roloff (Eds.), *Communication and negotiation* (pp. 128–155). Newbury Park, CA: Sage.

Putnam, L. L., & Stohl, C. (1990). Bona fide groups: A reconceptualization of groups in context. *Communication Studies, 41*(3), 248–265.

Regan, P., & Stamm, A. (2000). In the nick of time. *International Studies Quarterly, 44,* 239–260.

Retzinger, S. M. (1993). *Violent emotions: Shame and rage in marital quarrels.* Newbury Park, CA: Sage.

Richmond, O. (1998). Devious objectives and the disputants' view of international mediation: A theoretical framework. *Journal of Peace Research, 35,* 707–722.

Riskin, L. L. (1994). Mediator orientations, strategies, and techniques: Alternatives to the high cost of litigation. *Mediation Quarterly, 12*(9), 111–114.

Rothman, J. (1997). *Resolving identity-based conflict in nations, organizations, and communities.* San Francisco: Jossey-Bass.

Rule, C. (2002). *On-line dispute resolution.* San Francisco: Jossey-Bass.

Sambamurthy, V., & Poole, M. S. (1992). The effects on variations in capabilities of GDSS designs on management of cognitive conflicts in groups. *Information Systems Research, 3,* 224–251.

Sander, F. E. A., & Goldberg, S. B. (1994). Fitting the forum to the fuss: A user-friendly guide to selecting an ADR procedure, *Negotiation Journal, 10*(1), 49–67.

Schweiger, D., Sandberg, W., & Rechner, P. (1989). Experiential effects of dialectical inquiry, devil's advocacy, and consensus approaches to strategic decision making. *Academy of Management Journal, 32,* 745–772.

Sheehan, A. L., & Martin, R. (2003). Understanding diversity to maximize work team effectiveness: Field studies designed to unravel the complex relationship between diversity and team effectiveness. *Australian Journal of Psychology, 55,* 144–148.

Sherif, M. (1966). *In common predicament: Social psychology of intergroup conflict and cooperation.* Boston: Houghton-Mifflin.

Sherif, M. (1998). Experiments in group conflict. In J. M. Jenkins & K. Oatley (Eds.), *Human emotions: A reader* (pp. 245–252). Malden, MA: Blackwell.

Silbey, S. S., & Merry, S. E. (1986). Mediator settlement strategies. *Law and Policy, 8,* 7–32.

Simkin, W. E. (1971). *Mediation and the dynamics of collective bargaining.* Washington, DC: Bureau of National Affairs.

Simons, T. L., & Peterson, R. S. (2000). Task conflict and relationship conflict in top management teams: The pivotal role of intragroup trust. *Journal of Applied Psychology, 85,* 102–111.

Slaikeu, K. A., & Hasson, R. H. (1998). *Controlling the costs of conflict: How to design a system for your organization.* San Francisco: Jossey-Bass.

Smith, K. K., & Berg, D. N. (1987). *Paradoxes of group life: Understanding conflict, paralysis, and movement in group dynamics.* San Francisco: Jossey-Bass.

Swaab, R. I., Postmes, T., Neijens, P., Kiers, M., & Dumay, A. C. M. (2002). Multiparty negotiation support: The role of visualization's influence on the development of shared mental models. *Journal of Management Information Systems, 19*(1), 129–150.

Tajfel, H. (1969). Cognitive aspects of prejudice. *Journal of Social Issues, 25,* 79–97.

Tajfel, H. (1978). *Differentiation between social groups: Studies in the social psychology of intergroup relations.* London: Academic Press.

Tajfel, H., & Turner, J. (2001). An integrative theory of intergroup conflict. In M. A. Hogg & D. Abrams (Eds.), *Intergroup relations: Essential readings* (pp. 94–109). Philadelphia: Psychology Press.

Takacs, K. (2001). Structural embeddedness and intergroup conflict. *Journal of Conflict Resolution, 45*(6), 743–770.

Ting-Toomey, S. (1985). Toward a theory of conflict and culture. In W. Gudykunst, L. Stewart, & S. Ting-Toomey (Eds.), *Communication, culture, and organizational processes* (pp. 71–86). Beverly Hills, CA: Sage.

Ury, W., Brett, J., & Goldberg, S. B. (1993). *Getting disputes resolved: Designing systems to cut the costs of conflict.* Cambridge, MA: PON Books.

Weiss, J. (2003). Trajectories toward peace: Mediator sequencing strategies in intractable communal conflicts. *Negotiation Journal, 19(2)*, 109–116.

Winslade, J., & Monk, G. (2000). *Narrative mediation: A new approach to conflict resolution.* San Francisco: Jossey-Bass.

Zartman, W. (1985). *Ripe for resolution: Conflict and intervention in Africa.* New York: Oxford University Press.

26

Facilitating Group Communication

Sunwolf

Lawrence R. Frey

> *fa·cil·i·tate, v.t. 1. to make easier or less difficult; help forward, 2. to assist in the progress of.*
>
> —Adapted from Merriam-Webster Dictionary (2004)

Communication may be the "lifeblood that flows through the veins of groups" (Frey, 1994a, p. x), but unfortunately, all too often, when groups are left on their own, those veins become clogged, communication ceases to flow, and the result is that groups flounder and perform less effectively than possible (Frey, 1995a). As Sunwolf and Seibold (1999) documented in some detail, naturally occurring (free) group discussion (e.g., communication processes of groups that have not been required or encouraged to use formal group process techniques) too often negatively affects group practices, processes, and products in several interconnected ways. For instance, free-discussion groups demonstrate ineffective use of time resources, with real-time distortions occurring as members perceive that the time available is shorter than it really is (Holsti, 1971) and that they must find solutions quickly (Poole, 1991). Free-discussion groups also tend to skip important group phases, engaging in premature idea evaluation (Collaros & Anderson, 1969) or jumping to the choice phase during decision making and disregarding problem analysis (Maier, 1970). The unmanaged social interaction in such groups can result in conformity pressure or discussion loafing, with a minority of members dominating discussions (Chung & Ferris, 1971), opposing views being stifled (Schacter, 1968), and majorities frequently determining final outcomes (MacCoun & Kerr, 1988). Conflict may also go unmanaged, with free-discussion groups becoming trapped in escalating conflict spirals or cycles of conflict avoidance (Folger, Poole, & Stutman, 1993) and high-status members dominating discussions as other members become reluctant to contribute conflicting ideas (Janis, 1972, 1989). Useful information is often not shared between members of free-discussion groups, especially relevant noncommon knowledge (Stasser, 1992), and biased information sampling often emerges during group discussions (Stasser & Titus, 1985). Members of such groups too often experience difficulty balancing both task and social needs. They feel unable to contribute wholeheartedly to the content of a decision discussion while working on group relationships (Hewes, 1986) and adopt the first available solution to avoid social tensions resulting from disagreement (Hall & Watson, 1970). Finally, members of free-discussion groups experience difficulty in listening to relevant information during group discussion, and members are unable to recall the remarks of those who spoke just before them, the "next-in-line effect" (Brenner, 1973).

As these and other documented problems demonstrate, groups often need help enacting effective communication practices and processes; in short, they need *group facilitation,* defined by Frey (1995a) as "any meeting tecshnique, procedure, or practice that makes it easier for groups to interact and/or to accomplish their goals" (p. 4). *Meeting procedures* are "sets of rules or guidelines which specify how a group should organize its process to achieve a particular goal" (Poole, 1991, p. 55). In this case, the group process that is being facilitated is *communication,* "the processes by which verbal and nonverbal messages are used to create and share meaning" (Frey, Botan, & Kreps, 2000, p. 28).

In this chapter, we provide an overview of meeting procedures that scholars and practitioners have designed to structure and improve group communication processes in various ways. We start by offering a brief historical overview of group communication facilitation. We then examine procedures that have been developed to facilitate two types of communication that correspond to the two major dimensions of group life that scholars have traditionally identified: relational and task group communication. Throughout that discussion, we offer examples of group communication facilitation procedures but focus on those procedures that have received research attention. We conclude the chapter by pointing out gaps in the research literature and suggesting profitable directions for future research on facilitating group communication.

A Brief History of Group Communication Facilitation

Frey (1995a) divided research about group communication facilitation into three historical time periods. The first period, from about 1890 to 1945, was largely focused on whether the presence of others in a group had facilitative and inhibitive effects on individuals (e.g., Allport, 1920; Pessin & Husband, 1933; Travis, 1925, 1928; Triplett, 1897; Weston & English, 1926) and whether group discussion was superior when compared with individual problem solving (e.g., Barton, 1926; Dashiell, 1935; Gurnee, 1937; Jenness, 1932; Marston, 1924; Shaw, 1932; Thorndike, 1938; Timmons, 1939; Watson, 1928).

Perhaps the most important work during that time period was that of educators, who, during the 1920s and 1930s, adopted Dewey's (1910) *reflective thinking process,* a systematic pattern of thinking proposed for solving complex problems in a democratic manner that involved five steps:

1. A felt difficulty

2. Its location

3. Suggestion of possible solution

4. Development by reasoning of the bearing of suggestions

5. Further observation and experiment leading to its acceptance or rejection; that is the conclusion of belief or disbelief. (p. 72)

Variations on this model were subsequently incorporated into the first textbooks on group discussion (e.g., Baird, 1927; Elliott, 1927; McBurney & Hance, 1939; Sheffield, 1927). Although these pedagogical writings offered this and other prescriptive methods for facilitating group communication, it wasn't until the second historical period, from 1945 to 1970, that research was directed toward studying the facilitative and inhibitive effects of these methods. Researchers demonstrated that using reflective thinking did, in fact, lead to higher quality group decisions (e.g., Sharp & Millikin, 1964) and differentiated effective from ineffective group participants (Pyron, 1964; Pyron & Sharp, 1963). Osborn (1957) developed the discussion technique of *brainstorming*—generating as many ideas as possible, "piggybacking" on previous ideas, and withholding criticism—to facilitate idea generation in groups, with researchers finding that brainstorming groups produced more ideas than nonbrainstorming groups (for a review, see Lamm & Trommsdorff, 1973).

Other researchers showed the facilitative effects of imposing on groups various communication networks, "the arrangement or pattern of communication channels among the members of a group" (Shaw, 1981, p. 453), such as the wheel, circle, chair, or Y; these networks restricted how group members could communicate with one another. The effects found for networks depended on the type of task that groups confronted (Hirokawa & Gouran, 1989). Researchers also examined the facilitative effects

of communication enacted by group leaders, such as the studies by Lewin and his associates (e.g., Lewin & Lippitt, 1938; Lewin, Lippitt, & White, 1939; Lippitt, 1939, 1940; Lippitt & White, 1952), which experimentally exposed groups to three leadership styles (authoritarian, democratic, and laissez-faire) and assessed the impact on group productivity and member satisfaction. Blake and Mouton (1968) also identified some specific leadership communicative behaviors that group members could engage in to facilitate group interaction and task accomplishment.

During this period, whole-group formats for facilitating group communication were created and investigated. Merton (1946) and Merton, Fiske, and Kendall (1956), for instance, developed the *focused interview*, later called the *focus group*, which involved "8 to 12 individuals who discuss a particular topic under the direction of a moderator who promotes interaction and assures that the discussion remains on the topic of interest" (Stewart & Shamdasani, 1990, p. 109). Scholars also discovered that metacommunication (communication about communication) could be effectively employed to facilitate groups, leading to the development of T-groups (training groups), in which members focused directly on their communication processes (e.g., Benne, 1964; Cooper & Mangham, 1971); these were later adapted for promoting personal growth (e.g., sensitivity and encounter groups; Golembiewski & Blumberg, 1977; Lieberman, Yalom, & Miles, 1973; Rogers, 1970).

The third historical period, from about 1970 to 1990, saw researchers intensify the study of group communication facilitation practices at the same time that they began to recognize group facilitation itself as an important form of communication. From such a constitutive perspective, communication is "not just an act that someone does to another; more importantly, it is the process by which people attribute meaning, form relationships, make decisions, and so forth" (Frey, 1995a, p. 11). One line of research during that period continued to explore the facilitative effects of various group discussion procedures, especially for generating ideas and making decisions. The techniques of reflective thinking and brainstorming received considerable attention, along with other techniques such as ideal solution and single question, often pitted against one another, against nominal groups (where individuals work alone and then pool their efforts), or against free-discussion groups to see their relative effects (for a review, see Frey, 1995a). Training or educating individuals about these and other group communication meeting procedures also received attention (e.g., Firestien, 1990), as did the facilitative effects of offering feedback to groups about their interaction and performance (for a review, see Nadler, 1979). The modalities of communication that groups use also received considerable attention, especially new group communication technologies, such as teleconferencing, computer conferencing, and electronic meeting systems (for a review, see Scott, 1999).

In addition to the three historical periods that Frey (1995a) identified, we would add a fourth period, starting around 1990 and continuing today, which has focused on facilitating group communication in context. Most of the previous lines of research on group communication facilitation (with some notable exceptions, such as the studies of group communication leadership styles by Lewin and colleagues) have been conducted in the laboratory, employing student participants who have little investment in the process working together in a single meeting for a truncated time period to solve an artificial task created by the researcher (see Frey, 1994b). Surprisingly, these laboratory studies have included few replications, leading to a disparate, rather than coherent body of scholarship about group communication facilitation procedures. As evidence for this claim, Sunwolf and Seibold (1999), in their cross-disciplinary review of 33 studies conducted from 1957 to 1997, found that of the 56 procedures developed for facilitating communication processes in groups, only 9 had been investigated by more than one of the articles reviewed.

Most important, the almost exclusive reliance on such groups has resulted in what Farris (1981) called a *social psychological error:* the tendency to explain group communication (in this case, about facilitation) from observations independent of their context. To counter this tendency, researchers have begun to move out into the world of natural groups and study the process of facilitating communication in them (see the studies in Frey, 1995b, in press). In doing so, as shown in the next section, they have investigated a wider array of group facilitation techniques and communication processes facilitated by those techniques.

Group Communication Facilitation Techniques

The facilitation of communication in groups potentially covers a wide variety of techniques; indeed, it could be said that all techniques, in one way or another, are designed to facilitate communication in groups. For the purposes of this review, we categorize group communication facilitation techniques with respect to whether they are primarily designed to facilitate relational or task group communication, although we recognize the inherent overlap and interdependence of these two forms of group communication. The facilitation techniques reviewed sometimes involve whole-group designs but more often constitute particular procedures that can be used in any group by an outside facilitator, by a group's designated leader, or by group members themselves. Although these facilitation techniques certainly affect individual members (e.g., producing changes in individuals' communication styles), we concentrate on explaining the effects that they have at the group level. We also feature some relatively new group communication facilitation techniques with which readers may not be familiar, in addition to traditional procedures that have received significant attention.

Facilitating Relational Communication in Groups

Although the relational dimension of groups is traditionally acknowledged as one of the two primary dimensions of group life (e.g., Keyton, 1999), the facilitation of relational communication in groups has received far less attention than the facilitation of task group communication. This lack of attention to facilitating relational communication in groups is probably due to the tendency of laboratory researchers to privilege the study of problem-solving and decision-making processes and groups over relational processes (e.g., socialization practices) and groups (e.g., families and support groups; Frey, 1994b); indeed, it is difficult to even talk about relationship development when a collection of people meets only once for a limited period of time. However, as researchers have moved into the field to study natural groups, they have begun to investigate, primarily via qualitative methods resulting in case reports, facilitation techniques designed to affect relational communication with respect to (a) forming groups, (b) promoting relationships in diverse groups, (c) offering members social support, and (d) managing conflict within and between groups.

Facilitating Group Formation

Numerous scholars have focused on the developmental phases of group life, with the most important task during the formative stage seen as members needing to orient themselves to the group (Tuckman, 1965). This orientation phase (Fisher, 1970) creates a primary tension of social unease and inhibition among members (Bormann, 1990), characterized by group interaction that tends to be tentative and polite (Wheelan, 1994). To facilitate this phase, icebreakers are typically used at the initial meeting of a group to introduce members to one another, usually by saying their name and sharing some personal information. Although numerous icebreakers have been developed and are recommended by practitioners (e.g., Booth, 2000; Christian, 1997; Forbess-Greene, 1980; Pike & Solem, 2000; West, 1999), to our knowledge, no research exists regarding the facilitative effects of using them. Some group communication textbooks actually suggest that traditional icebreakers may cause problems, such as perceived status differences emerging from the information shared as members engage in self-comparison (one-upping or one-downing themselves) and compete for status in a newly formed group, thereby creating further tensions during this initial stage (e.g., Beebe & Masterson, 1997; Brilhart, Galanes, & Adams, 2001).

Recently, Sunwolf (in press) offered a new technique, called *empathic attunement,* for facilitating communication during the initial stage of zero-history training groups of professional helpers. Specifically, it was used for facilitating groups of capital defense lawyers appointed by the court to represent indigent, incarcerated defendants facing the death penalty, who were attending a week-long trial advocacy program to learn how to successfully defend a capital case. The technique was designed to help these attorneys to advocate more successfully as they communicated their clients' life stories to jurors weighing the issue of whether to impose a life or death sentence. Each lawyer was asked to sit in the center of a circle and become his or her client, adopting the client's voice, behaviors, and attitudes. The facilitator then asked the person, "Who are you and what are you most afraid of?" followed by "Tell me about the lawyer you have on your case." Sunwolf provided qualitative evidence that this facilitation technique had important outcomes both at the individual level, enabling lawyers to become more attuned to their most problematic clients, and at the group level, helping group members to bond with one another based on shared values. A supportive group culture was created for talking about difficult professional challenges that established participation norms for speaking, listening, and offering feedback. Those who facilitated these groups acknowledged that this technique stood in stark contrast to the get-acquainted icebreaker activities they typically used, which took longer, were attended sporadically, and resulted in only nominal groups with little group cohesion.

Facilitating Relationships in Diverse Groups

Although groups are becoming more diverse as a result of U.S. domestic demographic changes and globalization trends (e.g., Earley, 1993; Kirchmeyer & Cohen, 1992; Larkey, 1996; Triandis, 1995), the study of cultural diversity in groups continues to be a relatively underexplored area (Frey, 2000; Ketrow, 1999; Oetzel, 2003). What research does exist suggests that although diversity can often benefit group problem solving and decision making (e.g., Kirchmeyer & Cohen, 1992; Larkey, 1996; McLeod, Lobel, & Cox, 1996; Watson, Kumar, & Michaelsen, 1993), especially when groups confront creative, innovative, and rapidly changing tasks (Eisenhart & Schoonhoven, 1990; Kono, 1988; Nemeth, 1986; Pelz & Andrews, 1976), diversity also can produce significant problems in group members' communication and relationships (Earley, 1993; Kirchmeyer, 1993; Kirchmeyer & Cohen, 1992; Larkey, 1996; Ruhe & Eatman, 1977; Triandis, 1960; Triandis, Hall, & Ewen, 1965; Vaid-Raizada, 1985; Watson et al., 1993). As Oetzel's (2003) review of the relevant literature concluded, "Culturally diverse groups have more group process difficulty (e.g., more tension and conflict) than do culturally homogeneous groups," and the promised "benefits occur only if diversity is managed properly" (p. 121).

Unfortunately, there have been few attempts to design and document the facilitation of relational communication in culturally diverse groups. One exception is Kawakami's (in press) research on the facilitation of communication in diverse groups comprising members from "high-context" cultures (also called collectivist or interdependent self-construal cultures), which emphasize relationships over tasks and nonverbal behavior over verbal behavior, and those from "low-context" cultures (also called individualistic or independent self-construal cultures), which emphasize tasks over relationships and value verbal behavior over nonverbal behavior (Hall, 1976, 1983). Kawakami argued that in groups including members from both orientations, attention needs to be paid, both at the start of group formation and over the course of a group's life, to relational communication, as high-context cultural members cannot fully attend to group problem solving or decision making until they build personal relationships with other group members. Moreover, Kawakami pointed out that relational communication, especially for those from high-context cultures, is accomplished largely through nonverbal interaction (Ketrow, 1999). To facilitate groups including high- and low-context members, Kawakami designed a set of nonverbal communication facilitation techniques involving kinetics (body movements, including gestures, facial expressions, posture, and touch) that employ four phases: (a) introduction to the theme for which the kinetic exercise is designed, (b) engagement in the kinetic exercise (e.g., passing objects around in a circle in various patterns), (c) individual reflection about the exercise, and (d) facilitated group reflection and debriefing about the exercise. Kawakami showed, via qualitative data, how the use of kinetic facilitation techniques helped members of three task groups to manage the tensions associated with diversity by promoting productive relational communication among members that subsequently enabled them to accomplish their group tasks.

Facilitating Social Support

The growth of social support or self-help groups, "small groups formed for the specific purpose of providing mutual aid among members who share a common dilemma" (Cline,

1999, p. 516), has been so dramatic that Wuthnow (1994) declared them as constituting a "small-group movement" that has redefined our sense of community (p. 2). The evidence appears to support that claim, as support groups for people coping with illnesses have become a source of information and comfort for more than 25 million Americans (Kessler, Mickelson, & Zhao, 1997); they are the most common means by which individuals in this country attempt to change health behaviors (Davison, Pennebaker, & Dickerson, 2000).

Social support groups work by structuring members' communicative behavior in some important ways (Cline, 1999; Wright & Frey, in press). First, such groups encourage discussion of topics (especially health-related topics) that are generally discouraged in other group contexts. Second, a high degree of personal disclosure is demanded, which, itself, can be therapeutic (e.g., Droge, Arnston, & Norton, 1986; Katz, 1993). Third, such disclosure most often takes the form of "telling one's story" because narratives help to "organize the relevant symbols in one's environment, making it possible to gain meaning from the past, give meaning to the present, and reduce uncertainty about the future" (Arnston & Droge, 1987, p. 161). By engaging in these communicative practices, group participants experience four types of support: (a) informational support, which "provides recipients with information to help deal with stressful situations"; (b) emotional support, which "deals with individuals' feelings, primarily in terms of relieving negative emotions and sometimes supplementing them with positive emotions"; (c) esteem support, which "is used to make others feel good about themselves by demonstrating respect through compliments, validation of opinions and beliefs, alleviation of guilt felt by others, and offers of encouragement"; and (d) tangible assistance, which "provides recipients with direct help by offering to lend a helping hand in the form of, for instance, money, babysitting, or meals" (Alexander, Peterson, & Hollingshead, 2003, pp. 313–314).

Facilitating Group Conflict Management

Conflict among group members is a ubiquitous feature of group life, and in fact, a certain amount of conflict can be functional in groups, increasing, for instance, members' involvement in a group or their ability to engage in creative group problem solving. The successful management of conflict in groups, however, is critical if members are to emerge from conflict relationally satisfied and ready to accomplish the task (Schweiger, Sandberg, & Ragan, 1986; Schwenk & Cosier, 1993). It is not surprising, therefore, that practitioners and scholars have devoted attention to developing and studying facilitation techniques designed to manage conflicts within and between groups. Given that the mediation of conflict within groups is addressed in the previous chapter (Jones, Chapter 25, this volume), we focus here on those techniques designed to facilitate communication between two or more groups experiencing conflict. These facilitation techniques typically involve whole-group formats, with specific techniques embedded within those formats, and they are designed primarily to manage affective conflict (relationally based conflict) and secondarily to manage procedural conflict (process-based conflict about how to work on a task) or task conflict (Nicotera, 1997).

One approach to managing intergroup conflict communication involves the use of dialogue groups, in which members of groups in conflict are brought together in a facilitated single group (usually with two facilitators, one from each "side") to tell the story of their personal (rather than collective) experience for the purpose of "working through" the conflict on an interpersonal level. Bar-On's (1993, 1995) To Reflect and Trust (TRT) dialogue groups, for instance, have brought together descendants of Holocaust survivors and descendants of Nazi perpetrators, British ex-militaries and people from Northern Ireland (Catholic and Protestant), Israeli-Jews and Palestinians (Maoz & Ellis, in press), and Jews and Arabs living in the United States. Facilitators make sure that participants in these dialogue groups do not engage in intellectualized and politically polarized arguments about relevant issues but, instead, share narratives of how the conflict has affected them and their families personally. In documenting the nature and effects of TRT groups, Albeck, Adwan, and Bar-On (in press) claimed that

> such sharing does more than simply juxtapose differing perspectives as they are told separately; it allows for gradual integration of those perspectives, especially when the members of the various groups and generations recount them in each other's presence.

Telling one's life story in such a TRT historical circle encounter can facilitate the evolution of a new, shared narrative among participants. Telling one's personal story to those from the "other side" also seems to help improve participants' subsequent ability to listen more deeply to the stories of those others.

Another communication approach to managing group conflict is the public dialogue sessions sponsored by the Public Dialogue Consortium (for an overview, see Spano, 2001; for information on the consortium, see www.publicdialogue.org). The format of these sessions consists of a series of facilitated small and large group activities designed to enable participants, usually members of the same community, to discuss openly the most pressing issues facing them so that they can "produce a coherent set of communicative practices and an accompanying theoretical discourse that enables community members to engage in positive social change" (Spano, in press). The sessions are grounded in the theoretical perspectives of social constructionism (e.g., Gergen 1999; Shotter, 1993; Shotter & Gergen, 1994) and the coordinated management of meaning (Cronen, 1995; Pearce, 1989; Pearce & Pearce, 2000a). They are designed to promote dialogic communication (Littlejohn & Domenici, 2001; Pearce & Pearce, 2000b; Spano, 2001), which encourages relational interactants to stay

in the tension between holding their own ground and being profoundly open to others (Buber, 1958; Pearce & Pearce, 2000a). The sessions typically involve six stages: (a) issue identification, (b) eliciting different views, (c) framing the issue, (d) generating options for action, (e) deliberating and deciding, and (f) implementing public agreements (Spano, in press). Spano (2001, in press) has documented how this facilitation technique enables community members to confront and do something about some of the most contentious conflicts facing them.

A third communication facilitation technique for managing group conflict is demonstrated in the work of Walker, Daniels, and Cheng (in press), who have employed collaborative learning to help manage communication between groups involved in environmental and natural resource conflicts. The collaborative learning workshops that they conduct involve facilitated groups in conflict working in both large and small groups through five phases—assessment, training, design, implementation and facilitation, and evaluation—and nine stages—introducing the process, identifying the situation (problem), describing the situation, dialoguing about interests and concerns, developing improvements (transformative model), comparing models (improvements) with collective reality, deliberating about desirable and feasible change, implementing change, and taking stock (evaluation) (Daniels & Walker, 2001). Walker et al. provided quantitative data from questionnaires completed by participants to demonstrate the value of this technique, especially in comparison to alternative facilitation techniques that had been tried for managing contentious environmental conflicts.

As a final example, Sline (in press) used a combination of process consultation (Schein, 1969) and an action research model. Process consultation involves helping groups and organizations to solve their own problems by teaching members about communication processes, the consequences of those processes, and how to change them if needed; it stands in contrast to other forms of consulting, such as expert resource consulting. Combined with an action research model (Lewin, 1946), this format was used to facilitate the affective conflict occurring between two organizational groups that claimed ownership of the International Jazz Festival held each year in Park City, Utah. Sline detailed how he facilitated the first four steps of the action research model—making a preliminary diagnosis of the conflict, gathering data about it, feeding back the data to the organization, and leading a group composed of key stakeholders through a process of data exploration in a day-long confrontation meeting. A call-out procedure was used, with participants stating their ideas in free-form fashion in maximum-mix "buzz groups," a means of dividing a large group into smaller subgroups to maximize members' participation in discussion and decision making (Seibold & Krikorian, 1997). A general group discussion followed, which subsequently led the two groups to engage in creating a newly constituted Jazz Foundation that has successfully resolved the conflict.

Facilitating Task Communication in Groups

In contrast to the facilitation of relational communication in groups, task group communication facilitation has received considerable attention from researchers. Most of this research, as previously explained, has been conducted in a laboratory setting, although, as we highlight below, some researchers have moved into the field to study task group communication facilitation. In line with a functional approach to group task accomplishment, which argues that to be successful, task groups must fulfill particular functions (e.g., Hollingshead et al., in press; Wittenbaum et al., 2004), we organize this review with regard to four major interrelated task group functions that facilitations are designed to effect, as identified by Sunwolf and Seibold (1999): structuring, analyzing, creating, and agreeing (see Table 26.1). We conclude

with an overview of the facilitation of team communication, which effectively brings together both the facilitation of task and relational group communication.

Facilitating Structure

At the start of their deliberations, many task groups adopt, either explicitly or implicitly, particular facilitation practices that structure their communication. These facilitation practices include (a) Robert's Rules of Order (a written guide for the conduct of group meetings); (b) parliamentary procedure (a rigid structure for large group meetings that requires a formal leader and provides for the regimented introduction of old and new business); (c) agendas (a written document that identifies issues to be considered in a meeting, as well as the order in which they will be discussed); and (d) standard agenda performance (an agenda format that uses a plan to evaluate relevant events as they are implemented by the group); (e) various discussion formats (formats that allow groups to interact with outsiders to gather information or ideas, such as a symposium, panel, colloquy, forum, or roundtable).

Perhaps, agendas are the most typical of these structuring techniques. For example, Plott and Levine (1978) reported that the use of agendas by task groups tended to produce the decisions they were designed to influence. Research on the interaction between agendas and decision rules on group communication by Thompson, Mannix, and Bazerman (1988) found that three-person group negotiations that used an explicit structuring agenda, as well as a majority decision rule, produced more unequal distribution of member resources and more often relied on two-person coalitions than groups that used no agenda with majority rule, an explicit agenda with unanimity rule, or no agenda with unanimity rule.

The structuring of group communication occurs not only through the use of particular facilitation practices such as agendas but also with regard to the medium of communication

Table 26.1   Techniques for Facilitating Task Group Communication

Structuring	Analyzing	Creating	Agreeing
Agenda	6M analysis	6 thinking hats	Consensus rules
Communication technologies	Cognitive map	Analogy storm	Decision rules
Discussion formats	Delphi method	Brainstorming and reverse brainstorming	Negotiation
Parliamentary procedure	Devil's advocacy	Brainwriting	Problem-centered leadership
Robert's Rules of Order	Dialectical inquiry	Buzz groups	Straw poll
Standard agenda performance	Expert approach	Bug list	Voting procedures
	Fishbone diagram	Collective notebook	Weighting system
	Flowchart	Consensus mapping	
	Focus groups	Creative problem solving	
	Force field analysis	Crystal ball	
	Incrementalism	Excursion	
	Interpretive structural modeling	Five W's and H	
	Ideal-solution format	Ideals method	
	Is/is not analysis	Idea needlers	
	Journalist's 6 questions	Idea writing	
	Mixed scanning	Imaginary world	
	Multiattribute decision analysis	Lateral thinking	
		Left-right brain alternation	
	Multidimentional scaling	Lions' den	
	Nominal group technique	Lotus blossom	
	Pareto analysis	Manipulative verbs	
	Problem census	Mess finding	
	Program evaluation and review technique	Morphological analysis	
	Reflective thinking	Object stimulation	
	Risk procedure	Picture tour	
	Single-question format	Problem reversal	
	Stepladder technique	Progressive abstraction	
		Role storming	
		Semantic intuition	
		Synectics	
		Visioning	
		Wildest idea	
		Wishful thinking	

NOTE: Expansion and adaptation of Sunwolf (2002, Table 11.1, pp. 208–210) and Sunwolf and Seibold (1999, Table 15.1, pp. 400–403). For a description of these techniques, see Sunwolf (2002).

that group members employ. The early research on group communication networks has evolved into the study of the wide variety of communication technologies—ranging from electronic meeting systems (e.g., desktop videoconferencing) to computer-supported groupware (e.g., Lotus Notes)—that are employed to facilitate group meetings (Scott, 1999). Poole and DeSanctis (1992) pointed out that these communication technologies can be facilitative for groups not only because of the structural communication features that are built into a particular technology (e.g., technologies that allow individual members to contribute ideas simultaneously and then pool those ideas in useful ways, such as reporting the ideas mentioned most often) but also because of the spirit or general goals and attitudes that a particular technology promotes (e.g., democratic decision making). Documenting their facilitation of teams that were part of an ongoing quality enhancement effort at a large U.S. service organization, using a group decision support system (which combines communication, computer, and decision technologies to facilitate group decision making), Poole, DeSanctis, Kirsch, and Jackson (1995) found that this helped the teams to structure their communication in useful ways (with members referring to the technology as an "organizer") that contributed to an improved group spirit (with members saying they felt "empowered" by the sharing of control that the technology provided). In general, however, the use of these communication technologies with groups has yielded mixed results when compared with groups that meet face-to-face: Group performance and member satisfaction are generally enhanced by the technologies, but more communication problems are evidenced, and groups take longer to accomplish tasks (for a review, see Scott, 1999).

Facilitating Analysis

To be successful, members of task groups must analyze the nature of the task/issue/problem that

confronts them. It is not surprising, therefore, that researchers and practitioners have developed numerous facilitation techniques that help group members to engage in such analysis. Indeed, in contrast to the five primary facilitation formats for helping groups to structure communication, Sunwolf and Seibold (1999) found 26 facilitations that help groups to analyze, although they also reported that group analysis facilitations have undergone limited comparisons when contrasted with procedures that help groups to structure, create, or agree.

The first step involved in analyzing a task/issue/problem is to get group members to focus on it. Perhaps the exemplar of such facilitation is focus groups, which, as previously explained, are a whole-group format in which a facilitator focuses members on a particular topic, primarily to accomplish the goals of the researcher/facilitator, often for the purpose of developing subsequent communication campaigns and interventions. Kreps (1995), for instance, employed focus groups with community members to generate data for directing two health promotion campaigns: one to increase public acceptance, support, and utilization of an urban substance abuse center and the other to develop and refine media messages for preventing the spread of sexually transmitted diseases within a university community. Chapel, Peterson, and Joseph (1999) conducted focus groups with gang members and at-risk youth to develop anti-gang television advertisements. Plax, Kearney, Allen, and Ross (in press) employed them with undergraduate and graduate student borrowers, parents who borrowed money, financial aid professionals, and internal staff involved in the collection of student loans to develop and implement a nationwide educational program designed to assist students with debt management in college and beyond. An interesting variation on focus groups, offered by Shields (1981), is informed by symbolic convergence theory, which focuses on symbolic processes that create a shared reality that binds people together into a group (Bormann, 1985, 1996). Focus groups based on this theory encourage group members to share their fantasies (a *fantasy* is a "creative and imaginative shared interpretation of events that fulfills a group psychological or rhetorical need"; Bormann, Bormann, & Harty, 1995, p. 201) for the purpose of discovering their *rhetorical visions* (a coherent view of group members' experience). Bormann et al. (1995) employed this approach to discover the rhetorical vision of a group of teenage tobacco users regarding smoking and chewing tobacco, using the results to make recommendations regarding media messages designed to promote a tobacco-free life sponsored by the Center for Nonsmoking and Health of the Minnesota Department of Health. Cragan and Shields (1995) used focus groups based on symbolic convergence theory to assess consumers' reactions to suggested improvements in their local newspaper, refine a plaintiff attorney's persuasive opening and closing statements, and generate a qualitative database to develop quantitative research instruments to assess the law enforcement training provided to recent police academy graduates.

Once group members focus on a topic, a variety of specific group communication facilitation techniques can be used to help them analyze that topic. Two strategies are the previously explained reflective thinking technique, which has generally been found to result in higher quality group decisions than some other techniques (Schultz, Ketrow, & Urban, 1995; for exceptions, see Brilhart, 1966; Larson, 1969), and the nominal group technique (e.g., Van de Ven & Delbecq, 1974). Many other procedures can be used to help groups to analyze topics (see Table 26.1), although only a few of these procedures have been studied by researchers. Those procedures that have consistently produced superior group decision making have been (a) devil's advocacy (in which a member is assigned to critique other members' contributions) (e.g., Murrell, Stewart, & Engel, 1993; Schweiger et al., 1986; Schweiger, Sandberg, & Ragan, 1989; Schwenk & Cosier, 1993; Schwenk & Valacich, 1994; Valacich & Schwenk, 1995a, 1995b); (b) dialectical inquiry (in which two subgroups each analyze a problem

and develop a plan, then meet and debate their plans, reach consensus on the most important issues, and develop a course of action) (e.g., Schweiger et al., 1986, 1989; Schwenk & Valacich, 1994; Valacich & Schwenk, 1995a, 1995b); and (c) stepladder (in which two group members first analyze a problem, then a third member joins them, and then a fourth, until all group members have participated) (e.g., Rogelberg, Barnes-Farrell, & Lowe, 1992).

Facilitating Creativity

Task groups often confront tasks that require the devotion of at least part of the discussion time to creative idea generation; consequently, many group communication facilitation techniques have been developed to help groups to engage in creative thinking (Table 26.1). Many of these facilitation techniques are designed to counter five self-imposed constraints on creativity that Jarboe (1999) contended limited groups: (a) fear of breaking the norm, (b) fear of rejection, (c) lack of motivation, (d) inadequate cognitive models, and (e) a reluctance to engage in play that seems frivolous. Of the 35 facilitations listed, however, only brainstorming and creative problem solving have received significant scholarly attention (Sunwolf, 2002).

When a group's goal is to generate the maximum number of creative solutions to a problem, brainstorming techniques trigger creativity and block premature idea evaluation. Scholars have been surprised, however, by substantial research showing that interacting members of brainstorming groups generate fewer ideas, as well as fewer quality ideas, compared with nominal groups that don't use brainstorming (Sunwolf & Seibold, 1999). The inferior performance of brainstorming groups has been attributed either to communication apprehension among members (Jablin, Seibold, & Sorenson, 1977) or to premature idea evaluating, social loafing, or free riding (Diehl & Strobe, 1987). Facilitated brainstorming, however, in comparison to nonfacilitated brainstorming, has been shown to positively affect communication in groups and to produce superior performance (Offner, Kramer, & Winter, 1996). Group members and leaders may perceive that they understand how to facilitate brainstorming in a general sense but have insufficient training and authority to effectively enforce the rules of brainstorming (such as no premature judgment of offered ideas). In addition to the presence of a facilitator, brainstorming success may be related to the diversity of the group members; some evidence suggests that ethnic diversity may enhance the productivity of brainstorming groups. McLeod et al. (1996), for instance, found that ethnically diverse brainstorming groups produced more effective and feasible ideas than homogeneous brainstorming groups did.

In addition to brainstorming, facilitation training in creative problem-solving techniques appears to make a difference in helping groups to create new ideas. Creative problem solving is a facilitation that contains some components of rational problem solving (e.g., data gathering, problem definition, solution generation, and evaluation) but differs by also motivating members' efforts, allowing for incubation phases where task work ceases, designating specific imagination phases, and giving attention to the social dimensions of a group (Sunwolf & Seibold, 1999). Firestien (1990) reported that groups trained in creative problem-solving techniques increased their positive communication contributions to the group, decreased their negative comments, and produced more ideas than members in untrained groups.

As scholars have moved into the field, they have also begun to study other types of group communication facilitation techniques that are designed to help groups analyze problems and develop creative solutions to them. For instance, one of the most innovative techniques is that of interactive management, a method based on Warfield's (1994) science of generic design, which aims to help groups solve complex problems by integrating contributions from individuals with diverse views, backgrounds, and perspectives (Warfield & Cardenas, 1994). Interactive management uses a set of methodologies matched to the stage of group development and the requirements of the situation; typically, these methodologies include the nominal group technique (explained previously), idea writing (a five-step technique for developing and discussing ideas in four- to six–person groups), interpretive structural modeling (a computer-assisted methodology to help groups to identify relationships among ideas that impose order on the complexity of an issue), and field and profile representations (visual portrayals of complex ideas and their relationships). Interactive management has been applied in a number of situations to help groups generate creative ideas for complex problems. Broome (1995), for example, employed it to create an action plan for promoting greater participation in Comanche tribal governance. Broome (in press) also used the technique to promote creative citizen peace-building efforts among Greeks and Turks concerning the protracted conflict situation in Cyprus. The method was particularly useful in helping these combatants to collaboratively produce new ideas and plans about peace building by viewing the situation as a systemic whole rather than through the prism of their individual or group worldviews.

Facilitating Agreement

The effective accomplishment of group tasks ultimately involves group members reaching agreement regarding the task/issue/problem confronting them and the decisions/solutions needed. A variety of group communication facilitation techniques, therefore, have been designed to help groups reach agreement. Voting procedures, for example, offer structures based on a predetermined criterion for decisional agreement (e.g., majority rules or unanimity); the primary objective of a particular voting method may be to reach closure (group agreement) or to provide an opportunity for diverse viewpoints to be acknowledged. How group members communicate their agreement or lack of agreement also appears to affect decisional outcome. For example, Kerr and MacCoun (1985) found that public polling in juries reduced the likelihood of deadlock in 3-person groups, although in 6-person and 12-person groups, open polling actually increased the frequency of deadlock. Furthermore, pre-voting preferences of group members are influenced by whether voting occurs simultaneously (e.g., raising of hands) or sequentially (going around the circle to express individual member opinions), with Davis, Kameda, Parks, Stasson, and Zimmerman (1989) reporting that sequential polling, where members who had not yet voted perceived certain opinion trends from votes cast, was more likely to change the pre-polling opinions of individual members.

Facilitating Communication in Teams

Perhaps the most important conceptual development in the study of groups in the last 10 to 20 years has been the conception of groups as teams. Significant changes in contemporary organizations have led to the flattening of organizational hierarchy and to decision making by relatively autonomous work groups. Thus, the concept of teamwork "reflects [both] the group's task successes and the development of positive interpersonal relationships" (Rosen, 1989, p. 42), and LaFasto and Larson's (2001) empirical study of 6,000 team members and leaders bears out the need to integrate these two dimensions if teams are to be successful.

Teams, of course, flounder just as much as other task-oriented groups, perhaps even more, given the need to successfully integrate task and relational dimensions, with 80% to 90% of teams demonstrating difficulties achieving their performance goals (Wheelan & Furbur, in press). As a result, significant attention has been directed toward facilitating teams, with those facilitations invariably focusing on teaching members of teams about a wide variety of task and relational communication processes. Seibold (1995), for instance, described the team facilitation he engaged in with a U.S. manufacturing plant: "Although some emphasis was placed in enhancing individuals' skills, primary attention was directed to working with members collectively to understand the team processes involved in problem solving, integrating resources, sharing information, and dealing with interpersonal difficulties" (p. 261). This process facilitation included teaching team members about a variety of meeting planning, structuring, and problem-solving techniques (including many of those examined in this chapter), as well as skill-building sessions focused on listening, communicating criticism, and mediating conflict, then providing members with opportunities to put into practice their new knowledge of task group communication and relational communication skills to create, as Seibold claimed, a "process within a process" (p. 262). Seibold subsequently documented the positive effects of this process facilitation on team accomplishment in that manufacturing plant.

Part of what made Seibold's (1995) facilitation successful was that he built in "feedback phases" where teams were provided with evaluative information about their behavior. As pointed out previously, the provision of feedback as a facilitative procedure has demonstrated much success over the years, especially when that feedback focuses directly on communication processes being enacted (or lack thereof). Bales's (1950) interaction process analysis, a methodology for coding the function served by the communication exchanged during group discussion into 12 categories (six task and six relational functions), is a popular technique taught in group communication classes for making observations of groups and feeding back the information to them (Keyton, 1997), although there is little research on its use as a facilitation/consultation procedure. Bales and Cohen (1979) later developed the System for the Multiple Level Observation of

Groups (SYMLOG), a method that has group members retrospectively rate their own and other members' communicative behaviors with regard to dominance-submissiveness, friendliness-unfriendliness, and instrumentally controlled-emotionally expressive dimensions to see the extent to which a group is unified or polarized. Keyton (1995) employed SYMLOG as a facilitation procedure with a team of medical residents and nursing staff, showing how the feedback provided about their intergroup communication helped to enact changes that strengthened residents' relationships with the nursing staff.

Much of the purpose of providing feedback to teams involves helping members to come to new understandings about their situation: in this case, to make sense of themselves as a team. A team is an ephemeral concept, a metaphor or figure of speech in which a word or phrase that denotes one object is applied to another; in that sense, it is more a way of thinking about a group than a way of structuring it. Group members, however, often have overly rigid or dysfunctional conceptions of what a team means, often applying, for instance, the notion of a sports team to reference their organizational work team (e.g., Keidel, 1987, 1988). Such a conception, as Gribas and Sims (in press) pointed out, can have potentially negative effects, leading to the problem that "groups comprised of individuals working together often believe that they are having team problems when, in fact, they are merely functioning with an inappropriate metaphor (mental model) or set of metaphors." To counter that problem, Gribas and Sims developed a three-phase facilitative procedure that involves instructing group members about the team concept as a metaphor, illuminating the meaning of that metaphor as understood by the members, and then engaging in strategic symbolic reorientation to promote symbolic ambiguity regarding the team metaphor to encourage members to "explore all possibilities for ways of 'being a team' that can facilitate effective and harmonious functioning." They showed

how this facilitation procedure helped office workers who provide social services to university students to achieve a broader understanding of the team concept and themselves as a team, with follow-up interviews conducted a year later showing that participants continued to value the intervention and that it had affected their conceptions of teamwork. As Gribas and Sims concluded, this study "reinforces the value of group communication facilitation focused on perceptual reorientation—that is, on the development of collective sensemaking through a focus on symbolic practices."

Not all facilitations of team communication, however, demonstrate such success, as many research studies and meta-analyses report mixed, poor, or no effects of interventions on team performance (e.g., Salas, Rozell, Mullen, & Driskell, 1999; Schultz, 1999; Sundstrom, De Meuse, & Futrell, 1990; Sunwolf & Seibold, 1999; Tannenbaum, Beard, & Salas, 1992). One reason such facilitations may not succeed is indicated by Wheelan and Furbur (in press): "Group development typically is not taken into consideration by those who design and facilitate interventions." The authors described a facilitation procedure taking group development into account that they employed with 10 multidisciplinary teams of a U.S. insurance company. Members of these teams first completed the Group Development Questionnaire (GDQ; Wheelan & Hochberger, 1996), which assesses work team development with respect to four stages that have emerged from the research literature: (a) inclusion and dependency, (b) counterdependency and conflict, (c) development of trust and open communication among members, and (d) work. Across the next 8 months, the teams received four 8-hour days of training that involved members learning about teams and the task and relational communication skills needed to participate in them. The GDQ was completed before the training began, between Days 2 and 3, and between Days 3 and 4, and the results were fed back to the teams with subsequent training to deal with any problems noted. The quantitative data showed that compared with the initial GDQ results, at the end of the facilitation, the team members perceived themselves to be significantly more focused on the third and fourth stages, more effective, and more productive; moreover, the teams' actual productivity—as measured by objective standards (e.g., the number of days it took to generate an insurance bill) and by customer ratings of the teams' service, accessibility, knowledge, and turnaround time—remained constant or increased during the year following the facilitation in comparison to the previous year.

The State and Fate of Facilitating Group Communication

As this review of the literature reveals, a wealth of techniques have been designed to facilitate communication in groups, with the findings from both laboratory and field studies generally showing the positive effects that these facilitation techniques can have on relational, task, and team communication and outcomes. Poole (1991, pp. 75–80) offered nine reasons why these communication facilitation procedures demonstrate such positive effects on groups:

1. Procedures coordinate members' thinking

2. Procedures provide a set of objective ground rules

3. Procedures protect groups against their own bad habits

4. Procedures capitalize on the strengths of groups

5. Procedures balance member participation

6. Procedures surface and help manage conflicts

7. Procedures give groups a sense of closure in their work

8. Procedures make groups reflect on their meeting process

9. Procedures empower groups

However, despite our understanding of the conceptual reasons for the positive effects of employing group communication facilitation procedures and the mounting empirical evidence documenting those effects, significant problems and gaps in the research literature remain to be addressed. First, we still know relatively little about the facilitation of relational communication in groups. Although some scholars have begun to address this issue, there are few facilitation procedures for helping group members to form positive relationships. There are also many group tasks, apart from problem solving and decision making, that deserve attention, many of which involve facilitating relational communication, such as group formation and socialization of new members. As one example, scholars have documented the role of communication practices such as rituals ("organized symbolic practices and ceremonial activities which serve to define and represent the social and cultural significance of particular occasions, events or changes"; O'Sullivan, Hartley, Saunders, Montgomery, & Fiske, 1994, p. 267) in helping group members to cope with the loss of a member or the ending of their group (e.g., Adelman & Frey, 1997; Keyton, 1993), but there has been no research of which we are aware that has studied the process of facilitating such important group communicative practices.

Second, the majority of the research on group communication facilitation has studied adult groups, ignoring children's groups. This is unfortunate, for a significant portion of children's lives develops and unfolds in the context of small groups, as children are born into a primary group (family), learn in classroom groups, socialize in play groups, compete on athletic teams, identify territorially with neighborhood groups, worship in both peer and mixed-age groups, collaborate as youthful citizens in scout troops, and reproduce social structures in cliques, among many other groups (Sunwolf & Leets, in press). Moreover, scholars argue that experiences in children's groups carry over to their behavior in adult groups (Keyton, 1994; Socha, 1997, 1999). What research does exist on facilitating communication in children's groups suggests that when given such help, children can learn to manage interactional problems and engage in the type of collaborative group decision-making that will serve them well in adult groups (e.g., Socha & Socha, 1994).

Practitioners and scholars have also tended to facilitate and study groups that have many resources at their disposal, such as those in for-profit organizations, undoubtedly because those organizations pay financially for research and consultation. Underresourced groups, especially those that are at the margins of society, however, clearly have a great need for the benefits that group communication facilitation potentially offers (for some relevant studies of such communication activism, see Frey & Carragee, 2004).

Third, although many group communication facilitation techniques are available, these techniques are often not grounded in group and/or (group) communication theory. What research does exist demonstrates the value of using theory to guide group communication facilitation. Wheelan and Furbur's (in press) research, for instance, clearly shows the value of using group developmental theory to facilitate team communication, and Poole et al.'s (1995) research demonstrates how structuration theory offers guidelines for structuring mediated group communication. There remain, however, many important and potentially useful theories of groups and (group) communication (Poole, 1999; Poole & Hollingshead, 2004a, 2004b, in press) that have not yet been translated into group communication facilitation practice.

Fourth, there is a need for multimethodological research that combines quantitative and qualitative approaches to studying group communication facilitation. The majority of the research conducted on group communication facilitation in the laboratory has relied on quantitative methods, whereas the majority of research conducted in the field (with some notable exceptions) has used qualitative methods. In addition, much of the research that has been conducted has focused on the immediate, short-term effects of group communication facilitation, ignoring the long-term effects that accrue. Using both methods longitudinally would go a long way toward broadening and deepening our knowledge of group communication facilitation.

Finally, despite the evidence regarding the positive effects of employing group communication facilitation procedures, group members simply do not consistently use these procedures, even when they are taught to do so (Jarboe, 1999). Poole and DeSanctis (1990), for instance, reported that 50% of the groups in their studies did not follow the facilitation procedures they were taught. The challenge, therefore, for scholars and practitioners alike is helping group members to accept what they often see as "bad-tasting medicine" (Poole, 1991, p. 66). Perhaps some of this resistance is due to the ways in which practitioners and scholars employ and study group communication facilitation procedures, often in a noncollaborative, top-down manner (Frey, 1995a). Ultimately, we must realize that group communication facilitation itself is a prescriptive form of communication that sends a message about how individuals and groups ought to communicate; accordingly, our message ought to mirror the communication processes we promote.

References

Adelman, M. B., & Frey, L. R. (1997). *The fragile community: Living together with AIDS.* Mahwah, NJ: Lawrence Erlbaum.

Albeck, J. H., Adwan, S., & Bar-On, D. (in press). Dialogue groups: TRT's guidelines for working through intractable conflicts by personal storytelling in encounter groups. In L. R. Frey (Ed.), *Innovations and applications with natural groups: Facilitating group creation, conflict, and conversation* (Facilitating Group Communication in Context, Vol. 1). Cresskill, NJ: Hampton Press.

Alexander, S. C., Peterson, J. L., & Hollingshead, A. B. (2003). Help is at your keyboard: Support groups on the Internet. In L. R. Frey (Ed.), *Group communication in context: Studies of bona fide groups* (2nd ed., pp. 309–334). Mahwah, NJ: Lawrence Erlbaum.

Allport, F. H. (1920). The influence of the group upon association and thought. *Journal of Experimental Psychology, 3,* 159–182.

Arnston, P., & Droge, D. (1987). Social support in self-help groups: The role of communication in enabling perceptions of control. In T. L. Albrecht, M. B. Adelman, & Associates (Eds.), *Communicating social support* (pp. 148–171). Newbury Park, CA: Sage.

Baird, A. C. (1927). *Public discussion and debate.* Boston: Ginn.

Bales, R. F. (1950). *Interaction process analysis.* Cambridge, MA: Addison-Wesley.

Bales, R. F., & Cohen S. P. (1979). *SYMLOG: A system for the multiple level observation of groups.* New York: Free Press.

Bar-On, D. (1993). First encounter between children of survivors and children of perpetrators of the Holocaust. *Journal of Humanistic Psychology, 33*(4), 6–14.

Bar-On, D. (1995). Encounters between descendants of Nazi perpetrators and descendants of Holocaust survivors. *Psychiatry, 58,* 225–245.

Barton, W. A., Jr. (1926). The effect of group activity and individual effort in developing ability to solve problems in first-year algebra. *Educational Administration and Supervision, 12,* 412–518.

Beebe, S. A., & Masterson, J. T. (1997). *Communicating in small groups: Principles and practices* (5th ed.). New York: Longman.

Benne, K. D. (1964). History of the play group in the laboratory setting. In L. P. Bradford, J. R. Gibb, & K. D. Benne (Eds.), *T-group theory and laboratory method: Innovation in re-education* (pp. 80–135). New York: John Wiley.

Blake, R. R., & Mouton, J. S. (1968). *Corporate excellence through grid organization development.* Houston, TX: Gulf.

Booth, N. (2000). *75 icebreakers for great gatherings: Everything you need to bring people together.* St. Paul, MN: Brighton.

Bormann, E. G. (1985). Symbolic convergence theory: A communication formulation. *Journal of Communication, 35,* 128–138.

Bormann, E. G. (1990). *Small group communication: Theory and practice* (3rd ed.). New York: Harper & Row.

Bormann, E. G. (1996). Symbolic convergence theory and communication in group decision making. In R. Y. Hirokawa & M. S. Poole (Eds.), *Communication and group decision making* (2nd ed., pp. 81–113). Thousand Oaks, CA: Sage.

Bormann, E. G., Bormann, E., & Harty, K. C. (1995). Using symbolic convergence theory and focus group interviews to develop communication designed to stop teenage use of tobacco. In L. R. Frey (Ed.), *Innovations in group facilitation: Applications in natural settings* (pp. 200–232). Cresskill, NJ: Hampton Press.

Brenner, M. (1973). The next-in-line effect. *Journal of Verbal Learning and Verbal Behavior, 12,* 320–323.

Brilhart, J. K. (1966). An experimental comparison of three techniques for communicating a problem-solving pattern to members of a discussion group. *Speech Monographs, 33,* 169–177.

Brilhart, J. K., Galanes, G. J., & Adams, K. (2001). *Effective group discussion: Theory and practice* (10th ed.). Boston: McGraw-Hill.

Broome, B. J. (1995). The role of facilitated group process in community-based planning and design: Promoting greater participation in Comanche tribal governance. In L. R. Frey (Ed.), *Innovations in group facilitation: Applications in natural settings* (pp. 27–52). Cresskill, NJ: Hampton Press.

Broome, B. J. (in press). The role of facilitation in protracted conflict situations: Promoting citizen peace-building efforts in Cyprus. In L. R. Frey (Ed.), *Innovations and applications with natural groups: Facilitating group creation, conflict, and conversation* (Facilitating Group Communication in Context, Vol. 1). Cresskill, NJ: Hampton Press.

Buber, M. (1958). *I and thou* (R. G. Smith, Trans., 2nd ed.). New York: Scribner.

Chapel, G., Peterson, K. M., & Joseph, R. (1999). Exploring anti-gang advertisements: Focus group discussions with gang members and at-risk youth. *Journal of Applied Communication Research, 27,* 237–247.

Christian, S. S. (1997). *Instant icebreakers: 50 powerful catalysts for group interaction and high-impact learning.* Duluth, MN: Whole Person Associates.

Chung, K. H., & Ferris, M. J. (1971). An inquiry of the nominal group process. *Academy of Management Journal, 14,* 520–524.

Cline, R. J. W. (1999). Communication in social support groups. In L. R. Frey (Ed.), D. S. Gouran, & M. S. Poole (Assoc. Eds.), *The handbook of group communication theory and research* (pp. 516–538). Thousand Oaks, CA: Sage.

Collaros, P. A., & Anderson, L. R. (1969). The effect of perceived expertness upon creativity of members of brainstorming groups. *Journal of Applied Psychology, 53,* 159–163.

Cooper, C. L., & Mangham, I. L. (1971). *T-groups: A survey of research.* London: Wiley-Interscience.

Cragan, J. F., & Shields, D. C. (1995). Using SCT-based focus group interviews to do applied communication research. In L. R. Frey (Ed.), *Innovations in group facilitations: Applications in natural settings* (pp. 233–256). Cresskill, NJ: Hampton Press.

Cronen, V. E. (1995). Coordinated management of meaning: The consequentiality of communication and the recapturing of experience. In S. J. Sigman (Ed.), *The consequentiality of communication* (pp. 16–75). Mahwah, NJ: Lawrence Erlbaum.

Daniels, S. E., & Walker, G. B. (2001). *Working through environmental conflict: The collaborative learning approach.* Westport, CT: Praeger.

Dashiell, J. F. (1935). Experimental studies of the influence of social situations on the behavior of individual human adults. In C. Murchison (Ed.), *Handbook of social psychology* (pp. 1097–1158). Worchester, MA: Clark University Press.

Davis, J. H., Kameda, T., Parks, C., Stasson, M., & Zimmerman, S. (1989). Some social mechanics of group decision making: The distribution of opinion, polling sequence, and implications for consensus. *Journal of Personality and Social Psychology, 57,* 1000–1012.

Davison, K. P., Pennebaker, J. W., & Dickerson, S. S. (2000). Who talks? The social psychology of illness support groups. *American Psychologist, 55,* 205–217.

Dewey, J. (1910). *How we think.* Boston: D. C. Heath.

Diehl, M., & Strobe, W. (1987). Productivity loss in brainstorming groups: Toward the solution of a riddle. *Journal of Personality and Social Psychology, 53,* 497–509.

Droge, D., Arnston, P., & Norton, R. (1986). The social support function in epilepsy self-help groups. *Small Group Behavior, 17,* 139–163.

Earley, P. C. (1993). East meets West meets Mideast: Further explorations of collectivist and individualist work groups. *Academy of Management Journal, 36,* 319–348.

Eisenhart, K., & Schoonhoven, C. (1990). Organizational growth: Linking founding team, strategy, environment and growth among U.S. semiconductor ventures, 1978–1988. *Administrative Science Quarterly, 35,* 504–529.

Elliott, H. S. (1927). *The why and how of group discussion.* New York: Association Press.

Farris, G. F. (1981). Groups and the informal organization. In R. Payne & C. L. Cooper (Eds.), *Groups at work* (pp. 95–117). New York: John Wiley.

Firestien, R. L. (1990). Effects of creative problem-solving training on communication behaviors in small groups. *Small Group Research, 21,* 507–521.

Fisher, B. A. (1970). Decision emergence: Phases in group decision making. *Speech Monographs, 37,* 53–66.

Folger, J. P., Poole, M. S., & Stutman, R. (1993). *Working through conflict: A communication perspective* (2nd ed.). Glenview, IL: Scott, Foresman.

Forbess-Greene, S. (1980). *The encyclopedia of icebreakers: Structured activities that warm-up, motivate, challenge, acquaint, and energize.* St. Louis, MO: Applied Skills Press.

Frey, L. R. (1994a). The call of the field: Studying communication in natural groups. In L. R. Frey (Ed.), *Group communication in context: Studies of natural groups* (pp. ix-xiv). Hillsdale, NJ: Lawrence Erlbaum.

Frey, L. R. (1994b). The naturalistic paradigm: Studying small groups in the postmodern era. *Small Group Research, 25,* 551–577.

Frey, L. R. (1995a). Applied communication research on group facilitation in natural settings. In L. R. Frey (Ed.), *Innovations in group facilitation: Applications in natural settings* (pp. 1–23). Cresskill, NJ: Hampton Press.

Frey, L. R. (Ed.). (1995b). *Innovations in group facilitation: Applications in natural settings.* Cresskill, NJ: Hampton Press.

Frey, L. R. (2000). Diversifying our understanding of diversity and communication in small groups: Dialoguing with Clark, Anand, and Roberson. *Group Dynamics: Theory, Research, and Practice, 4,* 222–229.

Frey, L. R. (Ed.). (in press). *Innovations and applications with natural groups* (Facilitating Group Communication in Context, 2 vols.). Cresskill, NJ: Hampton Press.

Frey, L. R., Botan, C. H., & Kreps, G. L. (2000). *Investigating communication: An introduction to research methods* (2nd ed.). Boston: Allyn & Bacon.

Frey, L. R., & Carragee, K. (Eds.). (2004). *Communication activism* (2 vols.). Manuscript in preparation.

Gergen, K. J. (1999). *An invitation to social constructionism.* Thousand Oaks, CA: Sage.

Golembiewski, R., & Blumberg, A. (Eds.). (1977). *Sensitivity training and the laboratory approach: Readings about concepts and applications* (3rd ed.). Itasca, IL: F. E. Peacock.

Gribas, J., & Sims, J. (in press). Metaphoric illumination and symbolic ambiguity: Applying the team metaphor for perceptual reorientation. In L. R. Frey (Ed.), *Innovations and applications with natural groups: Facilitating group task and team communication* (Facilitating Group Communication in Context, Vol. 2). Cresskill, NJ: Hampton Press.

Gurnee, H. (1937). Maze learning in the collective situation. *Journal of Experimental Psychology, 11,* 348–368, 437–464.

Hall, E. T. (1976). *Beyond culture.* Garden City, NY: Anchor Press.

Hall, E. T. (1983). *The dance of life: The other dimension of time.* Garden City, NY: Anchor Press/ Doubleday.

Hall, J., & Watson, W. H. (1970). The effects of a normative intervention on group decision making performance. *Human Relations, 23,* 299–317.

Hewes, D. E. (1986). A socio-egocentric model of group decision-making: An amplification of socio-egocentric theory. In R. Y. Hirokawa & M. S. Poole (Eds.), *Communication and group decision-making* (pp. 265–291). Beverly Hills, CA: Sage.

Hirokawa, R. Y., & Gouran, D. S. (1989). Facilitation of group communication: A critique of prior research and an agenda for future research. *Management Communication Quarterly, 3,* 71–92.

Hollingshead, A. N., Wittenbaum, G. M., Paulus, P. B., Hirokawa, R. Y., Ancona, D. G., Peterson, R. S., Jehn, K. A., & Yoon, K. (in press). The functional perspective. In M. S. Poole & A. B. Hollingshead (Eds.), *Theories of small groups: An interdisciplinary perspective.* Thousand Oaks, CA: Sage.

Holsti, O. (1971). Crises, stress, and decision-making. *Interactional Social Science Journal, 23,* 53–67.

Jablin, F. M., Seibold, D. R., & Sorenson, R. L. (1977). Potential inhibitory effects of group participation on brainstorming performance. *Central States Speech Journal, 28,* 113–121.

Janis, I. L. (1972). *Victims of groupthink: Psychological studies of foreign policy decisions and fiascoes.* Boston: Houghton Mifflin.

Janis, I. L. (1989). *Crucial decisions: Leadership in policymaking and crisis management.* New York: Free Press.

Jarboe, S. (1999). Group communication and creativity processes. In L. R. Frey (Ed.), D. S. Gouran, & M. S. Poole (Assoc. Eds.), *The handbook of group communication theory and research* (pp. 335–368). Thousand Oaks, CA: Sage.

Jenness, A. (1932). The role of discussion in changing opinion regarding a matter of fact. *Journal of Abnormal and Social Psychology, 27,* 29–34.

Katz, A. H. (1993). *Self-help in America: A social movement perspective.* New York: Twayne.

Kawakami, H. (in press). Kinetic facilitation techniques for diverse groups. In L. R. Frey (Ed.), *Innovations and applications with natural groups: Facilitating group creation, conflict, and conversation* (Facilitating Group Communication in Context, Vol. 1). Cresskill, NJ: Hampton Press.

Keidel, R. W. (1987). Team sports models as a generic organizational framework. *Human Relations, 40,* 591–612.

Keidel, R. W. (1988). *Corporate players: Designs for working and winning together.* New York: John Wiley.

Kerr, N. L., & MacCoun, R. J. (1985). The effects of jury size and polling method on the process and product of jury deliberations. *Journal of Personality and Social Psychology, 48,* 349–363.

Kessler, R. C., Mickelson, K. D., & Zhao, S. (1997). Patterns and correlates of self-help group membership in the United States. *Social Policy, 27,* 27–46.

Ketrow, S. M. (1999). Nonverbal aspects of group communication. In L. R. Frey (Ed.), D. S. Gouran, & M. S. Poole (Assoc. Eds.), *The handbook of group communication theory and research* (pp. 251–287). Thousand Oaks, CA: Sage.

Keyton, J. (1993). Group termination: Completing the study of group development. *Small Group Research, 24,* 84–100.

Keyton, J. (1994). Going forward in group communication research may mean going back: Studying the groups of children. *Communication Studies, 45,* 40–51.

Keyton, J. (1995). Using SYMLOG as a self-analytic group facilitation technique. In L. R. Frey (Ed.), *Innovations in group facilitation: Applications in natural settings* (pp. 148–176). Cresskill, NJ: Hampton Press.

Keyton, J. (1997). Coding communication in decision-making groups. In L. R. Frey & J. K. Barge (Eds.), *Managing group life: Communicating in decision-making groups* (pp. 236–269). Boston: Houghton Mifflin.

Keyton, J. (1999). Relational communication in groups. In L. R. Frey (Ed.), D. S. Gouran, & M. S. Poole (Assoc. Eds.), *The handbook of group communication theory and research* (pp. 192–222). Thousand Oaks, CA: Sage.

Kirchmeyer, C. (1993). Multicultural task groups: An account of the low contribution levels of minorities. *Small Group Research, 24,* 127–148.

Kirchmeyer, C., & Cohen, A. (1992). Multicultural groups: Their performance and reactions with constructive conflict. *Group & Organization Management, 1,* 153–170.

Kono, T. (1988). Factors affecting the creativity of organizations: An approach from the analysis of new product development. In K. Urabe, J. Child, & T. Kagano (Eds.), *Innovation and management: International comparisons* (pp. 105–144). New York: Walter de Gruyter.

Kreps, G. L. (1995). Using focus group discussions to promote organizational reflexivity: Two applied communication field studies. In L. R. Frey (Ed.), *Innovations in group facilitation: Applications in natural settings* (pp. 177–199). Cresskill, NJ: Hampton Press.

LaFasto, F., & Larson, C. (2001). *When teams work best: 6,000 team members and leaders tell what it takes to succeed.* Thousand Oaks, CA: Sage.

Lamm, H., & Trommsdorff, G. (1973). Group versus individual performance on tasks requiring ideational proficiency (brainstorming): A review. *European Journal of Social Psychology, 3,* 361–388.

Larkey, L. K. (1996). Toward a theory of communicative interactions in culturally diverse work groups. *Academy of Management Review, 21,* 463–491.

Larson, C. E. (1969). Forms of analysis and small group problem-solving. *Speech Monographs, 36,* 452–455.

Lewin, K. (1946). Action research and minority problems. *Journal of Social Issues, 2,* 34–46.

Lewin, K., & Lippitt, R. (1938). An experimental approach to the study of autocracy and democracy: A preliminary note. *Sociometry, 1,* 292–300.

Lewin, K., Lippitt, R., & White, R. K. (1939). Patterns of aggressive behavior in experimentally created "social climates." *Journal of Social Psychology, 10,* 271–299.

Lieberman, M. A., Yalom, I. D., & Miles, M. B. (1973). *Encounter groups: First facts.* New York: Basic Books.

Lippitt, R. (1939). Field theory and experiment in social psychology: Autocratic and democratic group atmosphere. *American Journal of Sociology, 45,* 26–49.

Lippitt, R. (1940). An experimental study of the effect of democratic and authoritarian group atmospheres. *University of Iowa Studies in Child Welfare, 16,* 43–195.

Lippitt, R., & White, R. K. (1952). An experimental study of leadership and group life. In G. E. Swanson, T. M. Newcomb, & E. L. Hartley (Eds.), *Readings in social psychology* (pp. 340–355). New York: Holt.

Littlejohn, S. W., & Domenici, K. (2001). *Engaging communication in conflict: Systemic practice.* Thousand Oaks, CA: Sage.

MacCoun, R., & Kerr, N. L. (1988). Asymmetric influence in mock jury deliberations: Jurors' bias for leniency. *Journal of Personality and Social Psychology, 54,* 21–33.

Maier, N. R. F. (1970). *Problem solving and creativity in individuals and groups.* Belmont, CA: Brooks/Cole.

Maoz, I., & Ellis, D. G. (in press). Facilitating groups in severe conflict: The case of transformational dialogue between Israeli-Jews and Palestinians. In L. R. Frey (Ed.), *Innovations and applications with natural groups: Facilitating group creation, conflict, and conversation* (Facilitating Group Communication in Context, Vol. 1). Cresskill, NJ: Hampton Press.

Marston, W. M. (1924). Studies in testimony. *Journal of Criminal Law & Criminology, 15,* 5–31.

McBurney, J. H., & Hance, K. G. (1939). *The principles and methods of discussion.* New York: Harper and Brothers.

McLeod, P. L., Lobel, S. A., & Cox, T. H., Jr. (1996). Ethnic diversity and creativity in small groups. *Small Group Research, 27,* 248–264.

Merton, R. K. (1946). The focused interview. *American Journal of Sociology, 51,* 541–557.

Merton, R. K., Fiske, M., & Kendall, P. L. (1956). *The focused interview.* Glencoe, IL: Free Press.

Murrell, A. J., Stewart, A. C., & Engel, B. T. (1993). Consensus versus devil's advocacy: The influence of decision process and task structure on strategic decision making. *Journal of Business Communication, 30,* 399–414.

Nadler, D. (1979). The effects of feedback on task group behavior: A review of the experimental literature. *Organizational Behavior and Human Performance, 23,* 309–338.

Nemeth, C. (1986). Differential contributions of majority vs. minority influence. *Psychological Review, 93,* 23–32.

Nicotera, A. M. (1997). Managing conflict communication in groups. In L. R. Frey & J. K. Barge (Eds.), *Managing group life: Communicating in decision-making groups* (pp. 104–130). Boston: Houghton Mifflin.

Oetzel, J. G. (2003). The effects of culture and cultural diversity on communication in work groups: Synthesizing vertical and cultural differences with a face-negotiation perspective. In L. R. Frey (Ed.), *New directions in group communication* (pp. 121–137). Thousand Oaks, CA: Sage.

Offner, A. K., Kramer, T. J., & Winter, J. P. (1996). The effects of facilitation, recording, and pauses on group brainstorming. *Small Group Research, 27,* 283–298.

Osborn, A. (1957). *Applied imagination: Principles and procedures of creative thinking* (Rev. ed.). New York: Scribner.

O'Sullivan, T., Hartley, J., Saunders, D., Montgomery, M., & Fiske, J. (1994). *Key concepts in communication and cultural studies* (2nd ed.). London: Routledge.

Pearce, W. B. (1989). *Communication and the human condition.* Carbondale: Southern Illinois Press.

Pearce, W. B., & Pearce, K. A. (2000a). Combining passions and abilities: Toward dialogic virtuosity. *Southern Communication Journal, 65,* 161–175.

Pearce, W. B., & Pearce, K. A. (2000b). Extending the theory of coordinated management of meaning (CMM) through a community dialogue process. *Communication Theory, 10,* 405–423.

Pelz, D. C., & Andrews, F. M. (1976). *Scientists in organizations: Productive climates for research and development* (Rev. ed.). Ann Arbor: University of Michigan, Institute for Social Research.

Pessin, J., & Husband, R. W. (1933). Effects of social stimulation on human maze learning. *Journal of Abnormal and Social Psychology, 28,* 148–154.

Pike, B., & Solem, L. (2000). *50 creative training openers and energizers: Innovative ways to start your training with a bang!* San Francisco: Jossey-Bass/Pfeiffer and Creative Training Techniques Press.

Plax, T. G., Kearney, P., Allen, T. H., & Ross, T. (in press). Using focus groups to design a nationwide debt-management educational program. In L. R. Frey (Ed.), *Innovations and applications with natural groups: Facilitating group task and team communication* (Facilitating Group Communication in Context, Vol. 2). Cresskill, NJ: Hampton Press.

Plott, C. R., & Levine, M. E. (1978). A model of agenda influence on committee decisions. *American Economic Review, 68,* 146–160.

Poole, M. S. (1991). Procedures for managing meetings: Social and technological innovation. In R. A. Swanson & B. O. Knapp (Eds.), *Innovative meeting management* (pp. 53–109). Austin, TX: 3M Meeting Management Institute.

Poole, M. S. (1999). Group communication theory. In L. R. Frey (Ed.), D. S. Gouran, & M. S. Poole (Assoc. Eds.), *The handbook of group communication theory and research* (pp. 37–70). Thousand Oaks, CA: Sage.

Poole, M. S., & DeSanctis, G. (1990). Understanding the use of group decision support systems: The theory of adaptive structure. In J. Fulk & C. Steinfield (Eds.), *Organizations and communication technology* (pp. 175–195). Newbury Park, CA: Sage.

Poole, M. S., & DeSanctis, G. (1992). Microlevel structuration in computer-supported group decision-making. *Human Communication Research, 19,* 5–49.

Poole, M. S., DeSanctis, G., Kirsch, L., & Jackson, M. (1995). Group decision support systems as facilitators of quality team efforts. In L. R. Frey (Ed.), *Innovations in group facilitation techniques: Applications in natural settings* (pp. 299–320). Cresskill, NJ: Hampton Press.

Poole, M. S., & Hollingshead, A. B. (Eds.). (2004a). Theoretical perspectives, part 1 [Special issue]. *Small Group Research, 35*(1).

Poole, M. S., & Hollingshead, A. B. (Eds.). (2004b). Theoretical perspectives, part 2 [Special issue]. *Small Group Research, 35*(3).

Poole, M. S., & Hollingshead, A. B. (Eds.). (in press). *Theories of small groups: An interdisciplinary perspective.* Thousand Oaks, CA: Sage.

Pyron, H. C. (1964). An experimental study of the role of reflective thinking in business and professional conferences and discussions. *Speech Monographs, 31,* 157–161.

Pyron, H. C., & Sharp, H., Jr. (1963). A quantitative study of reflective thinking and professional conferences and discussions. *Speech Monographs, 31,* 157–161.

Rogelberg, S. G., Barnes-Farrell, J. L., & Lowe, C. A. (1992). The stepladder technique: An alternative group structure facilitating effective group decision making. *Journal of Applied Psychology, 77,* 730–737.

Rogers, C. (1970). *Carl Rogers on encounter groups.* New York: Harper & Row.

Rosen, N. (1989). *Teamwork and the bottom line: Groups make a difference.* Hillsdale, NJ: Lawrence Erlbaum.

Ruhe, J., & Eatman, J. (1977). Effects of racial composition on small work groups. *Small Group Research, 8,* 479–486.

Salas, E., Rozell, D., Mullen, B., & Driskell, J. E. (1999). The effect of team building on performance: An integration. *Small Group Research, 30,* 309–329.

Schacter, S. (1968). Deviation, rejection, and communication. In D. Cartwright & A. Zander (Eds.), *Group dynamics: Theory and research* (3rd ed., pp. 165–181). Beverly Hills, CA: Sage.

Schein, E. H. (1969). *Process consultation.* Reading, MA: Addison-Wesley.

Schultz, B. G. (1999). Improving group communication performance: An overview of diagnosis and intervention. In L. R. Frey (Ed.), D. S. Gouran, & M. S. Poole (Assoc. Eds.), *The handbook of group communication theory and research* (pp. 371–394). Thousand Oaks, CA: Sage.

Schultz, B., Ketrow, S. M., & Urban, D. M. (1995). Improving decision quality in the small group: The role of the reminder. *Small Group Research, 26,* 521–451.

Schweiger, D. M., Sandberg, W. R., & Ragan, J. W. (1986). Group approaches for improving strategic decision making: A comparative analysis of dialectical inquiry, devil's advocacy, and consensus. *Academy of Management Journal, 29,* 51–71.

Schweiger, D. M., Sandberg, W. R., & Ragan, J. W. (1989). Experiential effects of dialectical inquiry, devil's advocacy, and consensus approaches to strategic decision-making. *Academy of Management Journal, 32,* 745–772.

Schwenk, C. R., & Cosier, R. A. (1993). Effects of consensus and devil's advocacy on strategic decision-making. *Journal of Applied Social Psychology, 23,* 126–139.

Schwenk, C. R., & Valacich, J. S. (1994). Effects of devil's advocacy and dialectical inquiry on individuals versus groups. *Organizational Behavior and Human Decision Processes, 59,* 210–222.

Scott, C. R. (1999). Communication technology and group communication. In L. R. Frey (Ed.), D. S. Gouran, & M. S. Poole (Assoc. Eds.), *The handbook of group communication theory and research* (pp. 432–472). Thousand Oaks, CA: Sage.

Seibold, D. R. (1995). Developing the "team" in a team-managed organization: Group facilitation in a new-design plan. In L. R. Frey (Ed.), *Innovations in group facilitation: Applications in natural settings* (pp. 259–281). Cresskill, NJ: Hampton Press.

Seibold, D. R., & Krikorian, D. H. (1997). Planning and facilitating group meetings. In L. R. Frey & J. K. Barge (Eds.), *Managing group life: Communicating in decision-making groups* (pp. 270–305). Boston: Houghton Mifflin.

Sharp, J., Jr., & Millikin, J. (1964). Reflective thinking ability and the product of problem-solving discussion. *Speech Monographs, 31,* 124–127.

Shaw, M. E. (1932). Comparison of individuals and small groups in the rational solution of complex problems. *American Journal of Psychology, 44,* 491–504.

Shaw, M. E. (1981). *Group dynamics: The psychology of group behavior* (3rd ed.). New York: McGraw-Hill.

Sheffield, A. D. (1927). *Creative discussion: A statement of method for leaders and members of discussion groups and conferences* (2nd rev. ed.). New York: Association Press/Womans Press.

Shields, D. C. (1981). Dramatistic communication-based focus group interviews. In J. F. Cragan & D. C. Shields (Eds.), *Applied communication theory and research* (pp. 313–319). Prospect Heights, IL: Waveland Press.

Shotter, J. (1993). *Conversational realities: Constructing life through language.* Thousand Oaks, CA: Sage.

Shotter, J., & Gergen, K. J. (1994). Social construction: Knowledge, self, others, and continuing the conversation. In S. A. Deetz (Ed.), *Communication yearbook* (Vol. 17, pp. 3–33). Thousand Oaks, CA: Sage.

Sline, R. W. (in press). Who owns the jazz festival? A case of facilitated intergroup conflict management. In L. R. Frey (Ed.), *Innovations and applications with natural groups: Facilitating group creation, conflict, and conversation* (Facilitating Group Communication in Context, Vol. 1). Cresskill, NJ: Hampton Press.

Socha, T. J. (1997). Group communication across the life span. In L. R. Frey & J. K. Barge (Eds.), *Managing group life: Communicating in decision-making groups* (pp. 1–28). Boston: Houghton Mifflin.

Socha, T. J. (1999). Communication in family units: Studying the first "group." In L. R. Frey (Ed.), D. S. Gouran, & M. S. Poole (Assoc. Eds.), *The handbook of group communication theory and research* (pp. 475–492). Thousand Oaks, CA: Sage.

Socha, T. J., & Socha, D. M. (1994). Children's task-group communication: Did we learn it all in kindergarten? In L. R. Frey (Ed.), *Group communication in context: Studies of natural groups* (pp. 227–246). Hillsdale, NJ: Lawrence Erlbaum.

Spano, S. (2001). *Public dialogue and participatory democracy: The Cupertino community project.* Cresskill, NJ: Hampton Press.

Spano, S. (in press). Theory, practice, and public dialogue: A case study in facilitating community transformation. In L. R. Frey (Ed.), *Innovations and applications with natural groups: Facilitating group creation, conflict, and conversation* (Facilitating Group Communication in Context, Vol. 1). Cresskill, NJ: Hampton Press.

Stasser, G. (1992). Information salience and the discovery of hidden profiles by decision making groups: A "thought experiment." *Organizational Behavior and Human Decision Processes, 52,* 156–181.

Stasser, G., & Titus, W. (1985). Pooling of unshared information in group decision making: Biased information sampling during discussion. *Journal of Personality and Social Psychology, 48,* 1467–1478.

Stewart, D. W., & Shamdasani, P. N. (1990). *Focus groups: Theory and practice.* Newbury Park, CA: Sage.

Sundstrom, E., De Meuse, K. P., & Futrell, D. (1990). Work teams: Applications and effectiveness. *American Psychologist, 45,* 120–133.

Sunwolf. (2002). Getting to "GroupAha!": Provoking creative processes in task groups. In L. R. Frey (Ed.), *New directions in group communication* (pp. 203–217). Thousand Oaks, CA: Sage.

Sunwolf. (in press). Empathic attunement facilitation: Stimulating immediate task engagement in zero-history training groups of helping professionals. In L. R. Frey (Ed.), *Innovations and applications with natural groups: Facilitating group creation, conflict, and conversation* (Facilitating Group Communication in Context, Vol. 1). Cresskill, NJ: Hampton Press.

Sunwolf & Leets, L. (in press). Being left out: Rejecting outsiders and communicating group boundaries in childhood and adolescent peer groups. *Journal of Applied Communication Research.*

Sunwolf & Seibold, D. R. (1999). The impact of formal problem-solving procedures on group processes, members, and task outcomes. In L. R. Frey (Ed.), D. S. Gouran, & M. S. Poole (Assoc. Eds.), *The handbook of group communication theory and research* (pp. 395–431). Thousand Oaks, CA: Sage.

Tannenbaum, S. I., Beard, R. L., & Salas, E. (1992). Team building and its influence on team effectiveness: An examination of conceptual and empirical developments. In K. Kelley (Ed.), *Issues, theory, and research in industrial/organizational psychology* (pp. 228–252). Amsterdam: Elsevier Science.

Thompson, L. L., Mannix, E. A., & Bazerman, M. H. (1988). Group negotiation: Effects of decision rule, agenda, and aspiration. *Journal of Personality and Social Psychology, 54,* 86–95.

Thorndike, R. L. (1938). The effect of discussion upon the correctness of group decisions, when the factor of majority influence is allowed for. *Journal of Social Psychology, 9,* 343–464.

Timmons, W. M. (1939). *Decisions and attitudes as outcomes of the discussion of a social problem* (Contributions to Education, No. 777). New York: Columbia University, Teachers College, Bureau of Publications.

Travis, L. E. (1925). The effect of a small audience upon eye-hand coordination. *Journal of Abnormal and Social Psychology, 20,* 142–146.

Travis, L. E. (1928). The influence of the group upon the stutterer's speed in free association. *Journal of Abnormal and Social Psychology, 23,* 45–51.

Triandis, H. C. (1960). Cognitive similarity and communication in a dyad. *Human Relations, 13,* 175–183.

Triandis, H. C. (1995). The importance of contexts in studies of diversity. In S. E. Jackson & M. N. Ruderman (Eds.), *Diversity in work teams: Research paradigms for a changing workplace* (pp. 225–233). Washington, DC: American Psychological Association.

Triandis, H. C., Hall, E. R., & Ewen, R. B. (1965). Member heterogeneity and dyadic creativity. *Human Relations, 18*, 33–35.

Triplett, N. (1897). The dynamogenic factors in peacemaking and competition. *American Journal of Psychology, 9*, 507–533.

Tuckman, B. W. (1965). Developmental sequence in small groups. *Psychological Bulletin, 63*, 384–399.

Vaid-Raizada, V. K. (1985). Management of interethnic conflict in an Indian manufacturing organization. *Group and Organization Studies, 2*, 419–427.

Valacich, J. S., & Schwenk, C. (1995a). Devil's advocacy and dialectical inquiry effects on face-to-face and computer-mediated group decision making. *Organizational Behavior and Human Decision Processes, 63*, 158–173.

Valacich, J. S., & Schwenk, C. (1995b). Structuring conflict in individual, face-to-face, and computer-mediated group decision making: Carping versus objective devil's advocacy. *Decision Sciences, 26*, 369–392.

Van de Ven, A. H., & Delbecq, A. L. (1974). The effectiveness of nominal, Delphi, and interacting group decision-making processes. *Academy of Management Journal, 17*, 605–621.

Walker, G. B., Daniels, S. E., & Cheng, A. S. (in press). Facilitating dialogue and deliberation in environmental conflict: The use of groups in collaborative learning. In L. R. Frey (Ed.), *Innovations and applications with natural groups: Facilitating group creation, conflict, and conversation* (Facilitating Group Communication in Context, Vol. 1). Cresskill, NJ: Hampton Press.

Warfield, J. N. (1994). *A science of generic design: Managing complexity through systems design* (2nd ed.). Salinas, CA: Intersystems.

Warfield, J. N., & Cardenas, A. R. (1994). *A handbook of interactive management* (2nd ed.). Ames: Iowa State University Press.

Watson, G. B. (1928). Do groups think more efficiently than individuals? *Journal of Abnormal and Social Psychology, 23*, 328–336.

Watson, W. E., Kumar, K., & Michaelsen, L. K. (1993). Cultural diversity's impact on interaction process and performance: Comparing homogeneous and diverse task groups. *Academy of Management Journal, 36*, 590–602.

West, E. (1999). *The big book of icebreakers: 50 quick, fun activities for energizing meetings and workshops.* New York: McGraw-Hill.

Weston, S. B., & English, H. B. (1926). The influence of the group on psychological test scores. *American Journal of Psychology, 37*, 600–601.

Wheelan, S. A. (1994). *Group processes: A developmental perspective.* Boston: Allyn & Bacon.

Wheelan, S. A., & Furbur, S. (in press). Facilitating team development, communication, and performance. In L. R. Frey (Ed.), *Innovations and applications with natural groups: Facilitating group task and team communication* (Facilitating Group Communication in Context, Vol. 2). Cresskill, NJ: Hampton Press.

Wheelan, S., & Hochberger, J. (1996). Validation studies of the Group Development Questionnaire. *Small Group Research, 27*, 43–170.

Wittenbaum, G. M., Hollingshead, A. B., Paulus, P. B., Hirokawa, R. Y., Ancona, D. C., Peterson, R. S., Jehn, K. A., & Yoon, K. (2004). The functional perspective as a lens for understanding groups. *Small Group Research, 35*, 3–16.

Wright, K. B., & Frey, L. R. (in press). Communication and support groups for people living with cancer. In D. O'Hair & G. L. Kreps (Eds.), *Cancer care and communication.* Cresskill, NJ: Hampton Press.

Wuthnow, R. (1994). *Sharing the journey: Support groups and America's new quest for community.* New York: Free Press.

27

Psychoeducational Groups

Nina W. Brown

Psychoeducational groups encompass a wide range and variety of group topics and structures. Many groups that fall under this category are covered in other chapters in this book; learning groups, skills training groups, team building and training, and conflict mediation. This chapter will focus on personal development, support and therapy-related, and life transitions psychoeducational groups. Included in this review are groups for children, adolescents, and adults.

The literature search for this chapter was limited to the keywords *psychoeducational groups research, support groups research,* and *therapy-related groups research* and the years 1990 to the present. Search engines consulted included PubMed, Ovid, PsycLIT, Incarta, MedLine, and ERIC. This produced more than 1,000 entries. The criteria for inclusion in this review were quasi-experimental or qualitative research designs, publication in a national or international peer-refereed journal from 1990 to the present, specific outcomes identified, and statistical analyses of results. Not included were articles that describe models of psychoeducational

groups, where outcomes were presented in vague and nonspecific language, and those that did not use any analyses in reporting results. Also eliminated were dissertations, books and book chapters, conference presentations, and unpublished manuscripts.

Definitions and Descriptions

Psychoeducational groups are a hybrid of an academic class and a counseling/therapy group, and they have many characteristics of each (Brown, 2003). Gladding (1995) considers these groups to be similar to guidance groups. The Association for Specialists in Group Work (1990), a division of the American Counseling Association, defines psychoeducational groups as those used to educate people who are facing a potential threat to understand developmental life events or to learn to cope with immediate life crises. Corey (2001) defines psychoeducational groups by their structure, which is designed to develop specific skills, understand themes, or deal with life transitions.

Types of Psychoeducational Groups

Table 27.1 presents an overview of the types of groups described in this chapter: personal development, support and therapy-related, and life transitions. Examples are provided for each type, but these are just a few of the wide range of possible groups, and they are listed to highlight the extent to which psychoeducational groups are used. The extensive use of psychoeducational groups points out the necessity for continuing research to guide and direct their use.

Table 27.1   Types and Examples of Development, Support, and Transitions

Personal Development		
Prevention	*Development*	*Remediation*
Violence	Life skills	Conflict resolution
Substance abuse	Self-esteem issues	Anger management
Teen pregnancy	Communication skills	Relationship issues
HIV-AIDS	Psychological boundaries	
Spirituality		
Emotional expression		
Support and Therapy-Related		
Medical	*Psychological/Emotional*	*Recovery*
Cancer	Post-traumatic stress disorder	Addiction
Cardiac	Attention-deficit/hyperactivity disorder	Substance abuse
Diabetes	Depression/other mood disorders	Gambling
Intestinal disorders	Physical and emotional abuse	Sex
Ulcers	Anxiety	Eating
Sexually transmitted disease	Eating disorders	Work
Life Transitions		
General	*Specific Populations*	
Parenting	Divorce	
Dating	Grief	
Career	Loss	
Existential issues	Crises	
Grandparents as parents	Displaced homemaker	
Deployment (military)		
Unemployment		

The first type of group is categorized as *personal development* and can be divided into three areas: prevention, developmental, and remediation. Prevention psychoeducational groups are focused on trying to prepare participants for possible future situations and circumstances they may encounter. Some groups target specific at-risk populations whereas others use a more broad-brush approach.

Developmental groups have a major focus on assisting participants to understand and develop their inner resources, to develop skills, and to address their relationship to the larger culture. These groups tend not to be problem focused, nor are they targeted for at-risk populations. The concerns and issues are general, common, and shared.

Remediation groups are problem focused, although they may not be provided for a specific audience, that is, one that exhibits the particular problem, for example, anger management. They tend to be narrowly focused, and emphasize behavior change.

The second type of group is categorized as *support and therapy-related*. These are combined as a category because considerable recent literature refers to support therapy groups. However, some support groups continue to exist that are not connected to therapy. Therapy-related groups are those that run concurrently with other treatment for participants. The concurrent treatment can be medical or psychological. Support groups may be part of the treatment plan, or they may be selected by the participants. Three types of support- and therapy-related psychoeducational groups are medical, psychological/emotional, and recovery. These are focused on a specific disorder for which treatment by medical and mental health professionals also is provided.

The third type of group is categorized as *life transitions*. These groups focus on the varied situations and circumstances that often occur for many people. Some are expected for almost everyone, such as existential issues, and these are categorized as general. Other situations and circumstances happen to some people, such as divorce, and are categorized as specific.

General Elements for Psychoeducational Groups

The psychoeducational groups used in this review have certain elements that define them. These are

- An identifiable body of information to be presented
- An instructional/educational component
- Both cognitive and affective learning
- A relatively short time-frame
- No emphasis on group process
- Minimal theory

All groups reviewed seemed to have a specific body of information that was presented. Self-care was the primary focus, but reducing ambiguity and uncertainty and fostering the therapeutic group factor of universality (Yalom, 1995) also were emphasized in the reviewed studies.

With an emphasis on information, it follows that psychoeducational groups have an instructional/educational component. Indeed, this is the most important and defining characteristic of these groups. Methods for delivery of instruction may differ, but this identifiable characteristic is always present.

Participants' cognitive and affective learning were expectations in psychoeducational groups. Group members were expected to express feelings and to become more personally aware in addition to gaining more information about the particular concern, issue, condition, or problem. Exploration of feelings often was identified specifically in the descriptions of the groups. These groups are relatively brief, ranging from 4 to 12 sessions, and even the support groups described in the literature tended to be time bound. Support groups of longer duration were, for the most part, not led by a mental health professional and could be categorized as self-help groups. The perception of and definition for support groups seems to have shifted to become more clearly differentiated from self-help groups.

The structure for psychoeducational groups de-emphasizes process as it is defined by Brown (2003). That is, the group leader is less attuned to the here and now interactions among group members than would be the case in therapy and psychotherapy groups. Process does have a role, but other components and factors tend to be highlighted and emphasized more than process.

Theories, such as learning, developmental, personality, or counseling/therapy, do not appear to have much of a role in psychoeducational groups. They are not used to structure group experiences or to foster learning. This, too, is very different from the approaches generally associated with therapy and psychotherapy groups.

Key Methods

Table 27.2 lists and categorizes methods used in psychoeducational groups. The categories are instructional, experiential, and evaluation. The proportions for each category could not be determined for the studies that were reviewed, as most articles limited their descriptions of these factors.

Instructional methods are designed for educating. Usually, these are methods similar to those used in classrooms for students of all ages, and they are used the same way in psychoeducational groups. That is, they are used to present information. No studies were located on the efficacy of these methods for psychoeducational groups, and it appears that they are used because they are the usual modes for teaching, and there is some evidence of their effectiveness in classroom settings. It is not established that the same applies to their use in psychoeducational groups, although this does seem to be intuitively possible.

Some therapies use a particular mode, such as art therapy, music therapy, and dance therapy, and leaders are trained in its use. These leaders generally are certified after training and supervision. However, the *experiential methods* used in the reviewed psychoeducational groups studies were not used in the same ways or in as much depth as is done in those therapies. For example, art exercises call for participants to draw, but the product is not analyzed. Participants use drawing to anchor feelings, experiences, and the like, but they do not explore

Table 27.2   Methods Used in Psychoeducational Groups

Instructional	Experiential	Evaluation
Media: video, PowerPoint, tapes, movies	Art	Self-report
Writing/journals	Music	Author-constructed scales
Readings	Movement, e.g., dance	Commercial tests
Lectures	Imagery	Semantic differential
Discussions	Games, toys, play	
Expert presentations	Unique and special, e.g., sweat lodge	

hidden meanings in them, nor does the leader encourage this. Experiential methods are used to give participants a nonverbal way to express what they are remembering, experiencing, and the like because words are not always adequate.

Experiential methods help to increase awareness in participants who lack verbal facility or use words to effectively mask important feelings. They also can be used to focus attention on a particular point, to relieve tension and anxiety, and to demonstrate a concept for participants. The research literature has little to report on the efficacy of these methods.

Evaluation methods are not well described in the literature. Also, few studies used follow-up to determine retention of learning. Most surprising is that many studies do not report any assessment of the educational component. This can be considered a major oversight because one of the major goals of psychoeducational groups is to educate participants about the particular problem, issue, concern, or condition.

Many articles were rejected for this review because they did not report any evaluation at all. As a result, their effectiveness could not be judged due to lack of evidence. A considerable number of studies only described participants' self-reported satisfaction with the group, but the means for arriving at that conclusion were not described. Some studies used objective instruments in evaluation. These instruments had some evidence of validity and reliability.

Conditions and Topics for Studies

Table 27.3 presents an overview of the conditions or topics covered in the reviewed studies. About 58% of all studies reviewed were about groups whose focus was psychiatric conditions. About 39% of those studies focused on psychiatric conditions, patients, and families of people with schizophrenia. The other two most prevalent categories were eating disorders (10 studies) and caregivers of Alzheimer's patients (12 studies).

Other psychiatric conditions included general psychiatric disabilities, bipolar disorder, depression, affective disorder, personality disorders, and post-traumatic stress disorder (PTSD).

Physical illness was the category with the next highest number of studies ($n = 28$). The illnesses that were the focus for this group of studies included asthma, dialysis, cystic fibrosis, sickle cell anemia, cardiac, HIV-AIDS, fibromyalgia, diabetes, and epilepsy.

In the life transitions and personal adjustment category, 24 studies covered grief, divorce, working mothers, parenting, and grandparents as parents. Two studies did not fall into any of these categories and were labeled "other."

In about 30% of the studies, the target audiences were the families or caregivers for patients and clients. Only eight could be classified as prevention groups, and three of the eight were relapse prevention groups. These are separated, as target audiences in the first category did not exhibit the symptom, action, or condition, whereas the second category included follow-up groups to reduce or eliminate the possibility of recurrence. In about 20% ($n = 14$) of the reviewed studies, adolescents were the target audience, and children were the target audience in about 8% ($n = 9$).

Review of Studies

Each condition or category embraces a wide variety of target audiences, and this variety makes it difficult to draw conclusions from the results of the studies. The topics and target audiences for each research category in this review are described next.

Alzheimer's/Dementia

The vast majority of these studies focused on the caretakers/relatives, with only a few that also included the patient. The studies that did include the patient tended to report the results

Table 27.3   Conditions and Topics for Studies on Psychoeducational Groups

Condition/topic	n of Studies	Percentage of Total
Physical illness	28	22
Cancer	10	
All other combined	18	
Psychiatric conditions	61	57
Alzheimer's	12	
Depression	8	
Eating disorders	10	
Schizophrenia	24	
Substance abuse	7	
All other combined	12	
Other	26	21
Personal adjustment	12	
Life transitions	12	
Combined	2	
TOTAL	127	100

for the caretakers, as did the studies that focused only on the caretakers. Studies in this category were Buckwalter et al., 1999; Cummings, Long, Peterson-Hazen, and Harrison, 1998; Gallagher-Thompson, Arean, Rivera, and Thompson, 2001; Gerdner, Buckwalter, and Reed, 2002; Haupt, Karger, and Jaenner, 2000; Hebert et al., 2003; McFarland and Sanders, 2000; Monahan, Greene, and Coleman, 1992; Morano & Bravo, 2002; Ostwald, Hepburn, Caron, Burns, and Mantell, 1999; Printz-Feddersen, 1990; Sorenson, Pinquart, and Duberstein, 2002; and Whitlatch, Zarit, and von Eye, 1991.

Jenkins, & Lockwood, 1995; Edgar, Rosberger, & Collet, 2001), breast cancer patients (Edelman, Craig, & Kidman, 2000; Helgeson, Cohen, Schulz, & Yasko, 1999; Rosberger, Edgar, Collet, & Fournier, 2002; Taylor et al., 2003), cancer patients and their families (Gagon et al., 2002; Roberts, Piper, Denny, & Cuddeback, 1997), partners of breast cancer patients (Bultz, Speca, Brasher, Geggie, & Page, 2000), children of parents who have cancer (Landry-Dattee, Gauvain-Piquard, & Cosset-Delaigue, 2000), and males with prostate cancer (Coreil & Behal, 1999; Gregoire, Kalogeropoulos, & Corcos, 1997).

Cancer

Studies in this category focused on cancer patients in general (Cunningham, Edmonds,

Depression

The nine studies in this category focused on adolescents (Fine, Forth, Gilbert, & Haley, 1991), adults in general (Free, Oei, & Sander, 1991), females (Lara, Navarro, Rubi, & Mondragon, 2003), postpartum mothers (Chen, Tseng, Chou, & Wang, 2000; Honey, Bennett, & Morgan, 2002; Okano, Nagata, Hasegawa, Nomura, & Kumar, 1998), the elderly (Rokke, Tomhave, & Jocic, 2000), and prevention (Beardslee et al., 1997; Rice & Meyer, 1994).

Eating Disorders

Ten studies in this category focused on adolescent females only (Rocco, Ciano, & Balestrieri, 2001), adults (Ciano, Rocco, Angarano, Biasin, & Balestrieri, 2002; Peterson et al., 2001; Weiss & Orysh, 1994; Wiseman, Sunday, Klapper, Klein, & Halmi 2002), adult prevention (Sapia, 2001; Stice & Ragan, 2002), at-risk females (Kaminski & McNamara, 1996), adolescents and their families (Geist, Heinmaa, Stephens, Davis, & Katzman, 2000), and families of patients (Uehara, Kawashima, Goto, Tasaki, & Someya, 2001).

Schizophrenia

The vast majority of these studies were focused on the families of patients with schizophrenia. These studies can be categorized as follow-ups (Basan, Pichel-Walz, & Bauml, 2000; Hornung, Feldmann, Kingberg, Buchkremer, & Reker, 1999; McFarland, Link, Dushay, Marchal, & Crilly, 1995), studies with patients as the target audience (Eguiluz, Gonzalez, Munoz, Guadilla, & Gonzalez, 1998; Hornung, Kieserg, Feldmann, & Buchkremer, 1996; Hornung, Klingberg, Feldmann, Schonauer, & Schulze, 1998; Hornung, Northoff-Helling, Vogel-Helleberg, & Feldmann, 2000), studies with relatives and caregivers as audiences (Cassidy, Hill, & O'Callaghan, 2002; Dyck, Hendryx, Short, Voss, & McFarlane, 2002; Dyck et al., 2000; Feldmann, Hornung, Buchkremer, & Arolt, 2001; Kane, DiMartino, & Jimenez, 1990; McFarland,

Link, et al., 1995; Posner, Wilson, Kral, Lander, & Mcllwraith, 1992; Ran et al., 2003; Shimodera et al., 2000; Tomaras et al., 2000; Vallina-Fernandez, Lemos-Giraldez, Roder, & Gutierrez-Perez, 2001), and reviews (Pekkala & Merinder, 2000, 2002).

Physical Illnesses

Numerous physical illnesses were addressed in the reviewed studies. Devine (1996) conducted an analysis of psychoeducational groups used with asthma patients. Other studies were focused on dialysis (Devins et al., 2000), cystic fibrosis (Goldbeck & Babka, 2001), sickle cell anemia (Kaslow et al., 2000), cardiac concerns (Lenz & Perkins, 2000; Mayou, Springings, Birkhead, & Price, 2002), HIV-AIDS (Malow, West, Corrigan, Penna, & Cunningham, 1994; Pomeroy, Kiam, & Green, 2000; Sorensen et al., 1994), fibromyalgia (Nicassio et al., 1997), diabetes (Olmstead, Daneman, Rydall, Lawson, & Rodin, 2002; Sarkidi & Rsenqvist, 1999), dialysis (Devins et al., 2000), and epilepsy (Helgeson, Mittan, Tan, & Chayasirisobhon, 1990; Olley, Osinoso, & Brieger, 2001).

Psychiatric Conditions

These studies also varied in terms of target audience and condition. Conditions addressed included affective disorder (Beardslee, Wright, Rothberg, Salt, & Versage, 1996; Keller & Schuler, 2002), bipolar disorder (Colom et al., 2003; Fristad, Goldberg-Arnold, & Gavazzi, 2002), trauma (Carbonell & Parteleno-Barehmi, 1999; Lubin, Loris, Burt, & Johnson, 1998; Trowell et al., 2002), psychiatric disabilities in general (Bullock, Ensing, Alloy, & Weddle, 2000; Cuijpers & Stam, 2000; Heller, Roccoforte, Hsieh, Cook, & Pickett, 1997; Pollio, North, & Osborne, 2002; Shin & Lukens, 2002; Solomon, Draine, & Mannion, 1996), and personality disorders (Rice & Meyer, 1994). One study focused on children who had a parent with a disorder (Beardslee et al., 1993), and another described the family of a child with a disorder (Fristad et al., 2002). One study each focused on relapse prevention (Colom et al., 2003), children and adolescents (Carbonell & Parteleno-Barehmi, 1999), and families of patients with a disorder (Cuijpers & Stam, 2000; Heller et al., 1997; Pollio et al., 2002; Stam & Cuijpers, 2001).

Substance Abuse

It was somewhat unexpected to find so few studies on the use of psychoeducational groups with substance abuse treatment and prevention. These, too, varied in target audience and focus: adults (Burge et al., 1997), adolescents and prevention (Botvin, Baker, Dusenbury, Tortu, & Botvin, 1990; Botvin, Schinke, Epstein, & Diaz, 1994), adolescents (Caplan et al., 1992; Kaminer, Burleson, & Goldberger, 2002), adult males (Bartholomew, Hiller, Knight, Nucatola, & Simpson, 2000), and adult relapse prevention (Sandahl & Ronnbers, 1990).

Other

All other studies were categorized as "other." These were varied in topic or condition addressed and in target audience. There was no consistency, even among studies for the same topic and audience.

Topics and audiences included children and conflict (Aber, Jones, Chaudry, & Samples, 1998), Asian families and adjustment (Bentel-spacher, De Silva, Goh, & LaRowe, 1997), female athletes' adjustment (Constatine, 1995), male adolescent adjustment (Franklin & Pack-Brown, 2001), college adjustment (Harris, Altekruse, & Engles, 2003; Nosanow, Hage, & Levin, 1999), incarcerated adolescents (Claypoole, Moody, & Peace, 2000), incarcerated adults (Morgan & Flora, 2002), bereavement for families (Goldstein, 1996), bereavement for adults

(Lieberman & Yalom, 1992), bereavement for children (Mulcahey & Young, 1995), self-acceptance for adults (Hurley, 1991), self-concept for adolescents (Wells, Miller, Tobacyk, & Clanton, 2002), couples (Kaiser, Hahlweg, Fehm-Wolfsdorf, & Groth, 1998), anger management for adults (McWhirter & Page, 1999), anger management for children (Shectman, 2001), working mothers (Morgan & Hensley, 1998), well-being (Palmer & Braud, 2002), male batterers (Rosenbaum, Gearan, & Ondovic, 2002), patient care (Schwiebert & Myers, 1994), ill relatives (Solomon et al., 1996), parenting (Shelton et al., 2000; Solis-Camara, Fox, & Nicholson, 2000), grandparents (Vacha-Hasse, Ness, Dannison, & Smith, 2000), in vitro fertilization (McNaughton-Cassill, Bostwick, Arthur, Robinson, & Neal, 2002), and aging parents (Smith, Majeski, & McClenny, 1996).

Meta-analysis, Evaluation, and Reviews

Although there were few studies in some categories, some were meta-analyses, evaluations, and reviews that incorporated large numbers of subjects or studies. The results of these studies are helpful in understanding the efficacy of psycho-educational groups for the particular condition or topic. These are briefly reported and summarized by topic.

Cancer

Edgar et al. (2001) randomly assigned 225 breast and colon cancer patients to four treatment conditions: individual sessions, group sessions, a nondirective support group, or a no-intervention control. The treatment was Nucare, a short-term psychoeducational coping skills intervention. Patients attending the individual sessions intervention showed more improvement than did those attending the other two intervention groups. The author noted that the groups were too small and difficult to schedule to provide valid findings.

Roberts, Black, and Todd (2002) conducted an evaluation of an education and support program for cancer patients and their families and friends. Data from 152 programs with 1,460 participants (1994 to 2000) showed significant improvement for coping ability, knowledge, communication, and relationships.

Asthma

Devine (1996) did a meta-analysis of 31 studies on the effect of psychoeducational groups for adults with asthma. Beneficial effects were found for occurrence of asthmatic attacks, dynamic respiratory volume, peak expiratory flow rate, functional status, adherence to treatment regime, use of health care, use of PRN medications, psychological well-being, and psychomotor knowledge of inhaler use.

Primary Prevention

Durlak and Wells (1997) conducted a meta-analytic review of 177 primary prevention mental health programs for children and adolescents. This is discussed here because the primary setting for most interventions in the review was the school, and most were group interventions focused on providing information. They classified the programs as environment centered, transition, person centered, and other. Only 36% of the programs had identifiable goals, and the outcomes for the interventions were mixed, although most were positive.

Incarcerated Offenders

Morgan and Flora (2002) found positive effects for treatment in a meta-analysis of 26 empirical studies on group psychotherapy with incarcerated offenders. Although the term *psychotherapy* was applied, the majority of studies used in the analyses had structure alone or a mixture of structure and psychotherapy. The groups focused on substance abuse, mental health, and anger.

Eating Disorders

Rocco et al. (2001) used a psychoeducational experimental approach to the prevention of eating disorders for 106 adolescent girls, 63 in the experimental group and 43 in the control group. The experimental group received three psychoeducational sessions over a 3-month period. These sessions were focused on presenting information about eating disorders. The experimental group showed a significant improvement in bulimic attitudes, asceticism, ineffective feelings, maturity fears, and better management of anxiety.

Alzheimer's/Dementia and Schizophrenia Studies

What follows are some examples of studies conducted on families, caretakers, and patients with schizophrenia, Alzheimer's, and dementia that is a result of aging. All studies had positive outcomes for patients, although patients were not participants in the groups. These are termed secondary gains. Primary gains were reduced stress and better coping skills for family members and caretakers.

Ostwald et al. (1999) conducted a study on the outcomes of a 3-year psychoeducational group for 94 primary caregivers and families of Alzheimer's patients. The group sessions consisted of seven weekly 2-hour multimedia training sessions. Repeated measures analysis of variance showed significant differences between the members that received the training and the control group in reducing caregivers' negative reactions and feelings of burden over time.

Sorenson et al. (2002) conducted a meta-analysis of 78 studies of family caregivers of older adults, involving six interventions with six outcome variables. Psychoeducational and psychotherapeutic interventions showed the most consistent effects on all measures.

Schizophrenia

The findings from the studies on psychoeducational groups for families or caregivers and patients with schizophrenia present the clearest results. That is, multifamily psychoeducational groups have positive outcomes for participants and patients. This conclusion is further supported by the meta-analysis of Pekkala and Merinder (2002). An additional finding is that there are similar results for multicultural and global use of multifamily psychoeducational groups for this audience.

Hornung et al. (1999) conducted a 5-year follow-up for schizophrenic outpatients and their key persons assigned to an intervention involving psychoeducation, cognitive behavioral therapy, or both or to standard care or a control group. Rehospitalization was lower for patients who participated in the combined psychoeducational group and cognitive-behavioral intervention.

Pekkala and Merinder (2002) reviewed 10 studies of randomized controlled trials of psychoeducational groups for schizophrenia and/or serious mental illness. Major findings were that any kind of psychoeducational intervention significantly decreased relapse or readmission rates at 9 to 18 months follow-up compared with standard care.

Ran and colleagues (2003) used a cluster randomized controlled study for three treatment groups of 326 patients with schizophrenia and their family members. The treatments were psychoeducational family groups, medication alone, and a control group. The psychoeducational family group demonstrated more knowledge, increased positive attitudes toward the schizophrenic family member, and an increase in treatment compliance. The patients whose families participated in the psychoeducational group demonstrated less relapse.

Similar results were found for multifamily psychoeducational groups for patients with schizophrenia in Switzerland (Feldmann et al., 2001), France (Cassidy et al., 2002), Germany (Basan et al., 2000; Hornung et al., 1998; Tomaras et al., 2000), Japan (Shimodera et al., 2000), and Spain (Eguiluz et al., 1998).

Conclusion

These studies point out the wide range of topics that psychoeducational groups address and their popularity across the globe. These groups cover the spectrum of conditions and topics with variations in audiences, methods, number of sessions, time periods, benefits, and outcomes. Psychoeducational groups are popular and have many strengths as well as some drawbacks and weaknesses as evidenced by these studies.

The major constraint when discussing the studies reviewed in this chapter is the lack of consistency, even within a category of studies. That alone makes comparisons difficult and provides insufficient evidence for valid conclusions. The exceptions are the multifamily psychoeducational groups for families and caretakers of people with schizophrenia, Alzheimer's, or dementia related to aging. These studies were consistent in reporting positive outcomes for participants and for patients.

The overall weaknesses for the studies were

- The lack of systematic controlled studies
- Measured outcomes inconsistent with the stated goal of the group
- Vague goals for the group
- A broad focus for short-term groups that was unrealistic
- Failure to assess the educational component although it was a primary goal for the group

- Lack of theory base for methods and group facilitation
- Failure to describe or assess leader training/ education

The most significant weakness was the paucity of systematically controlled studies. Studies where the participants were used as their own controls also were minimal. It is difficult to generalize about outcomes when the basic research design is flawed or major components are missing.

In numerous studies, what was assessed was not consistent with the stated purpose or intent of the group. For example, some studies had a stated purpose of providing information, but they measured affective outcomes or psychological functioning. These outcomes are also important, but they should be an integral part of the purpose or goal for the group.

Vague goals, a broad focus, and lack of theory-based methods also were prevalent. Most groups were short-term, and the goals stated were unrealistic for the available time. It would be more helpful if the goals were narrow, specific, and realistic, and methods were selected and used within a theoretical framework. Some studies noted the use of cognitive behavioral strategies, but most studies did not report any theoretical framework at all.

Although these were psychoeducational groups and the educational component was of primary importance, few studies directly assessed it. Studies could be enhanced by assessing participants' knowledge gains and the efficacy of instructional methods. Some studies used published tests and scales, but these usually were focused on psychological and emotional factors. Most studies, however, used participants' self-report as the assessment.

Scant evidence was provided about the level and training or education for group leaders, particularly their expertise in leading psychoeducational groups. This is a glaring omission, as it cannot be assumed that leaders are prepared to conduct groups by virtue of their professional preparation programs or experience. These weaknesses do not allow for the generalizability of findings across studies. The exceptions to this conclusion are the few carefully designed and controlled studies included in the review.

Conclusions can be drawn only about the efficacy of these multifamily groups for patients with schizophrenia and groups for families and caregivers of Alzheimer's or dementia patients. The meta-analyses for incarcerated offenders and asthma patients also allow for conclusions as these had sufficient numbers of subjects and were analyzed empirically. The other conditions had either too few subjects, inadequate or no controls, lack of assessment or other valid measures, and/or inadequate or missing statistical analyses.

Strengths

There also were some strengths in the reviewed studies that should be mentioned.

- Most indicated positive outcomes for participants
- There were efforts to serve a broad audience
- There seemed to be a realization that fear and anxiety could be reduced when valid information was given to participants
- Attempts were made to have members capitalize on unused personal strengths and resources
- It seems possible to help clients and victims via psychoeducational groups for their caretakers and family members
- There was an increased use of psychoeducational groups for physical illnesses and other conditions
- These groups are short-term and can be used with people of all ages
- There appears to be an acceptance that simply providing information is not sufficient; the affective realm also needs attention
- The groups provided an opportunity and place for members to express uncomfortable and negative feelings

Some psychoeducational groups did not have positive outcomes for participants in terms of what was assessed or was simply reported. However, most outcomes were positive, and only a few studies showed mixed or negative outcomes.

The broad application of these groups is readily seen in the list of studies for each category. The majority of studies had a unique focus, such as the target audience, topic, or condition. Also, global use of psychoeducational groups is further evidence that these groups are useful for people of various ages, with different conditions, and from different cultures.

An unstated assumption underlying these groups is that valid information can reduce fear and anxiety. This notion seems intuitively obvious; however, it could be a stated major goal and could be assessed more frequently to validate this assumption. Even if this was the only accomplishment for these groups, it would be a major one, and it should be pursued.

The findings were mixed on capitalizing on group members' strengths. Some studies did mention coping and other skills increases, but it was unclear if these were taught or if members were encouraged to identify unused or unrecognized personal strengths. This, too, could be a valuable focus for psychoeducational groups.

The studies on conducting multifamily and caregiver groups for patients who had schizophrenia and Alzheimer's or dementia point out the secondary gains that can result for the patients themselves. Although patients were not members of the groups in most of these studies, the outcomes that were most frequently assessed were the patients' rehospitalization, compliance, and relapse. It appears that some audiences can benefit indirectly from psychoeducational groups. There also seems to be a trend in this direction as similar approaches were used in groups for eating disorders, physical illness, and other psychological/emotional disorders.

The increasing use of psychoeducational groups for physical illnesses is a positive development. This use points out the realization and acceptance of the mind/body connection and an understanding that the affective realm also is important when treating physical illnesses. These groups were used to reduce confusion and ambiguity, to promote a realistic perspective for the person about the illness or disease, and to assist participants in developing better coping skills.

Decided advantages of psychoeducational groups are their brief time frame and their usefulness to people of all ages. Positive effects were found for a psychoeducational group experience as short as one day (Rosberger et al., 2002), and most groups were only 8 to 12 sessions long. This is an advantage in terms of time and money. The use of psychoeducational groups with people of all ages, from kindergarten to the elderly, also increases their impact and utility.

A strength that was not addressed in the majority of studies was that the group context could provide an opportunity and a safe place to express uncomfortable and negative feelings. This strength should not be underestimated or minimized because people with physical or mental conditions or other life problems carry emotional burdens that can seldom be openly expressed. The cost to the individual of suppressed feelings can be high, lead to other complications, and negatively affect relationships.

Recommendations

Both qualitative and quantitative research is needed on the structure, process, efficacy, and design for psychoeducational groups. Although carefully designed and controlled studies are most desirable, descriptive, evaluative, and all forms of qualitative research could do much to add to the body of knowledge. Examples of qualitative research that could yield valuable information include case studies where the group is the case, field research, narrative analysis, and synthesis of qualitative research.

Descriptive studies can be helpful, especially when they provide rich illustrations, case and clinical examples, and enough data so that the studies can be replicated. The diverse nature of psychoeducational groups lends itself to studies where the numerous variables are not subject to control or may even defy systematic manipulation. Studies could focus on planning, training for group leaders, group process, group dynamics, emphases such as content versus process, instructional strategies for the varied audiences, and other group topics. Of particular interest may be culture and other diversity issues and how these affect the design and outcomes for psychoeducational groups.

Evaluative studies are also necessary, particularly those that assess the structure and organization for groups, materials, delivery of information, quality of information, leadership styles, and activities such as exercises. Even simple informal assessments of participants' perceptions of these components would be helpful for future groups. Group leaders and organizers need to learn how to construct instruments, such as Likert scales, and how to use assessment techniques, such as the semantic differential.

Issues such as countertransference, therapeutic factors, and group stages are not relevant only for therapy groups. They also apply to psychoeducational groups and are deserving of discussion and research. These should not be neglected as they play major roles in outcomes for participants, affecting them in ways that may not be directly observed or measured. Leaders could benefit from a better understanding of what is taking place in the group and how to constructively use their countertransference for the groups' benefit as well as minimizing its potential negative impact.

Carefully designed and controlled studies should be a top priority for future research. Such studies would enhance our understanding of effective group methods and strategies. Research is needed on instructional methods and on how group processes and development affect these short-term groups. Also, investigations into the best way to train and educate leaders in effective facilitative skills are necessary.

Psychoeducational support and therapy groups are increasing in number and range. Thus, it is even more critical that research be conducted in a rigorous manner so that the effectiveness and impact of psychoeducational groups can be evaluated objectively.

References

Aber, J., Jones, M., Chaudry, N., & Samples, F. (1998). Resolving conflict creatively: Evaluating the developmental effects of a school-based violence prevention programming neighborhood and classroom context. *Development & Psychopathology, 10*(2), 187–213.

Association for Specialists in Group Work. (1990). *Ethical guidelines for group counselors and professional standards for the training of group workers.* Alexandria VA: Author.

Bartholomew, N., Hiller, M., Knight, K., Nucatola, D. C., & Simpson, D. (2000). Effectiveness of communication and relationship skills training for men in substance abuse treatment. *Journal of Substance Abuse Treatment, 18*(3), 217–225.

Basan, A., Pichel-Walz, G., & Bauml, J. (2000). Psychoeducational intervention for schizophrenic patients and subsequent long-term ambulatory care: A four-year follow-up (in German). *Fortschr. Neural. Psychiatr, 68*(12), 537–545.

Beardslee, W., Salt, P., Porterfield, K., Rothberg, P., van de Velde, P., Swatling, S., Hoke, L., Moilanen, D., & Wheelock, I. (1993). Comparison of preventive interventions for families with parental affective disorder. *Journal of the American Academy of Child Adolescent Psychiatry, 32*(2), 254–263.

Beardslee, W., Versage, E., Wright, E., Salt, P., Rothberg, P., Drezner, K., & Gladstone, T. (1997). Examination of preventive interventions for families with depression: Evidence of change. *Development of Psychopathology, 9*(1), 109–130.

Beardslee, W., Wright, E., Rothberg, P., Salt, P., & Versage, E. (1996). Response of families to two preventive intervention strategies: Long-term differences in behavior and attitude change. *American Academy of Child and Adolescent Psychiatry, 35*(6), 774–782.

Bentelspacher, C., De Silva, E., Goh, T., & LaRowe, K. (1997). A process evaluation of the cultural compatibility of psychoeducational family group treatment with ethnic Asian clients. *Social Work With Groups, 19*(3–4), 41–55.

Botvin, G., Baker, E., Dusenbury, L., Tortu, S., & Botvin, E. (1990). Preventing adolescent drug abuse through multimodal cognitive-behavioral approach: Results of a 3-year study. *Journal of Consulting & Clinical Psychology, 58*(4), 437–446.

Botvin, G., Schinke, S., Epstein, J., & Diaz, T. (1994). Effectiveness of culturally focused and generic skills training approaches to alcohol and drug abuse prevention among minority youth. *Psychology of Addictive Behavior, 8*(2), 116–127.

Brown, N. (2003). *Psychoeducational groups: Process and practice.* New York: Brunner-Routledge.

Buckwalter, K., Gerdner, L., Kohout, F., Hall, G., Kelly A., Richards, B., & Sime, M. (1999). A nursing intervention to decrease depression in family caregivers of persons with dementia. *Archives of Psychiatric Nursing, 13*(2), 80–81.

Bullock, W., Ensing, D., Alloy, V., & Weddle, C. (2000). Leadership education: Evaluation of a program to promote recovery in persons with psychiatric disabilities. *Psychiatric Rehabilitation, 24*(1), 3–12.

Bultz, B., Speca, M., Brasher, P., Geggie, P., & Page, S. (2000). A randomized controlled trial of a brief psychoeducational support group for partners of early stage breast cancer patients. *Psycho-Oncology, 9*(4), 303–313.

Burge, S., Amodei, N., Elkin, B., Catala, S., Andrew, S., Lane, P., & Seale, J. (1997). An evaluation of two primary care interventions for alcohol abuse among Mexican-American patients. *Addiction, 92*(12), 1705–1716.

Caplan, M., Weissberg, R., Grober, J., Sino, P., Grady, K., & Jacoby, C. (1992). Social competence promotion with inner-city and suburban young adolescents: Effects on social adjustment and alcohol use. *Journal of Consulting & Clinical Psychology, 60*(1), 56–63.

Carbonell, D., & Parteleno-Barehmi, C. (1999). Psychodrama groups for girls coping with trauma.

International Journal of Group Psychotherapy, 49(3), 285–306.

Cassidy, E., Hill, S., & O'Callaghan, E. (2002). Efficacy of a psychoeducational intervention in improving relatives' knowledge about schizophrenia and reducing hospitalization. *European Psychiatry, 16*(8), 446–450.

Chen, C., Tseng, Y., Chou, F., & Wang, S. (2000). Effects of support group intervention in postnatally distressed women: A controlled study in Taiwan. *Journal of Psycho-somantic Research, 49*(6), 395–399.

Ciano, R., Rocco, P., Angarano, A., Biasin, E., & Balestrieri, M. (2002). Group-analytic and psychoeducation therapies for binge-eating disorders: An exploratory study on efficacy and persistence of effects. *Psychotherapy Research, 12*(2), 231–239.

Claypoole, S., Moody, E., & Peace, S. (2000). Moral dilemma discussions: An effective group intervention for juvenile offenders. *Journal for Specialists in Group Work, 25*(4), 394–411.

Colom, F., Vieta, E., Martinez-Aran, A., Reinares, M., Goikolea, J., Benabarre, A., Torrent, C., Comes, M., Carbella, B., Parramon, G., & Corominas, J. (2003). A randomized trial on the efficacy of group psychoeducation in the prophylaxis of recurrences in bipolar patients whose disease is in remission. *Archives of General Psychiatry, 60*(4), 402–407.

Constatine, M. (1995). Retired female athletes in transition: A group counseling intervention. *Journal of College Student Development, 36*(6), 604–605.

Coreil, J., & Behal, R. (1999). Man to man prostate cancer support groups. *Cancer Practice, 7*(3), 122–129.

Corey, G. (2001). *Theory and practice of counseling and psychotherapy* (5th ed.). Pacific Grove, CA: Brooks-Cole.

Cuijpers, P., & Stam, H. (2000). Burnout among relatives of psychiatric patients attending psychoeducational support groups. *Psychiatric Services, 51*(3), 375–379.

Cummings, S., Long, J., Peterson-Hazen, S., & Harrison, J. (1998). The efficacy of a group treatment model in helping spouses meet the emotional and practical challenges of early stage caregiving. *Clinical Gerontologist, 20*(1), 29–45.

Cunningham, A., Edmonds, C., Jenkins, G., & Lockwood, G. (1995). A randomized comparison of two forms of a brief, group psychoeducational program for cancer patients: Weekly sessions versus a "weekend intensive." *International Journal of Psychiatry Medicine, 25*(2), 173–189.

Devine, E. (1996). Meta-analysis of the effects of psychoeducational care in adults with asthma. *Research in Nursing & Health, 19*(5), 367–376.

Devins, G., Hollomby, D., Barre, P., Mandin, H., Taub, K., Paul, L., Gutterman, R., & Binik, Y. (2000). Long-term knowledge retention following predial-ysis psycho-educational intervention. *Nephron, 86*(2), 129–134.

Durlak, J., & Wells, A. (1997). Primary prevention mental health programs for children and adoles-cents: A meta-analytic review [Special issue]. *American Journal of Community Psychology, 25*(2), 115–144.

Dyck, D., Hendryx, M., Short, R., Voss, W., & McFarlane, W. (2002). Service use among patients with schizophrenia in psychoeducational multi-ple-family group treatment. *Psychiatric Service, 53*(6), 749–754.

Dyck, D., Short, R., Hendryx, M., Norell, D., Myers, M., Patterson, T., McDonnell, M., Voss, W., & McFarlane, W. (2000). Management of negative symptoms among patients with schizophrenia attending multiple-family groups. *Psychiatric Services, 51*(4), 513–519.

Edelman, S., Craig, A., & Kidman, A. (2000). Group interventions with cancer patients: Efficacy of psychoeducational versus support groups. *Journal of Psychosocial Oncology, 18*(3), 67–85.

Edgar, L., Rosberger, Z., & Collet, J. (2001). Lessons learned: Outcomes and methodology of a coping skills intervention trial comparing individual and group formats for patients with cancer. *International Journal of Psychiatry Medicine, 31*(3), 289–304.

Eguiluz, I., Gonzalez, T., Munoz, P., Guadilla, M., & Gonzalez, G. (1998). Evaluation of the efficacy of psychoeducative groups in schizophrenic patients (Article in Spanish). *Actas Luso Esp Neurol Psiquiatr Cienc Afines, 26*(1), 29–34.

Feldmann, R., Hornung, W., Buchkremer, G., & Arolt, V. (2001). The influence of familial loading on the course of schizophrenic symptoms and the success of psychoeducational therapy. *Psychopathology, 34*(4), 192 –197.

Fine, S., Forth, A., Gilbert, M., & Haley, G. (1991). Group therapy for adolescent depressive disorder:

A comparison of social skills and therapeutic support. *Journal of the American Academy of Child and Adolescent Psychiatry, 30*(1), 79–85.

Franklin, R., & Pack-Brown, S. (2001). Team brothers: An Africentric approach to group work with African-American male adolescents. *Journal for Specialists in GroupWork, 26*(3), 237–245.

Free, M., Oei, T., & Sander, M. (1991). Treatment outcome of a group cognitive therapy program for depression. *International Journal of Group Psychotherapy, 41*(4), 533–547.

Fristad, M., Goldberg-Arnold, J., & Gavazzi, S. (2002). Multifamily psychoeducation groups (MFPG) for families of children with bipolar disorder. *Bipolar Disorders, 4*(4), 254–262.

Gagon, P., Charbonneau, C., Allard, P., Soulard, C., Dumont, S., & Fillon, L. (2002). Delirium in advanced cancer: A psychoeducational intervention for family caregivers. *Journal of Palliative Care, 18*(4), 253–261.

Gallagher-Thompson, D., Arean, P., Rivera, P., & Thompson, L. (2001). A psychoeducational intervention to reduce distress in Hispanic family caregivers: Results of a pilot study. *Clinical Geron-tologist, 23*(1–2), 17–32.

Geist, R., Heinmaa, M., Stephens, D., Davis, R., & Katzman, D. (2000). Comparison of family therapy and family group psychoeducation in adolescents with anorexia nervosa. *Canadian Journal of Psychiatry, 45*(2), 173–178.

Gerdner, L., Buckwalter, K., & Reed, D. (2002). Impact of a psychoeducational intervention on caregiver response to behavioral problems. *Nursing Research, 51*(6), 363–374.

Gladding, S. (1995). *Group work: A counseling specialty* (2nd ed.). Englewood Cliffs, NJ: Prentice Hall.

Goldbeck, L., & Babka, C. (2001). Development and evaluation of a multi-family psychoeducational program for cystic fibrosis. *Patient Education & Counseling, 44*(2), 187–192.

Goldstein, M. (1996). Psychoeducation and relapse prevention. *International Journal of Clinical Psycho-pharmacology, 9*(5), 59–69.

Gregoire, I., Kalogeropoulos, D., & Corcos, J. (1997). The effectiveness of a professionally led support group for men with prostate cancer. *Urology Nursing, 17*(2), 58–66.

Harris, H., Altekruse, M., & Engles, D. (2003). Helping freshmen student athletes adjust to college life using psychoeducational groups. *Journal for Specialists in Group Work, 28*(1), 64–81.

Haupt, M., Karger, A., & Jaenner, M. (2000). Improvement of agitation and anxiety in demented patients after psychoeducative group intervention with their caregivers. *International Journal of Geriatric Psychiatry, 15*(12), 1125–1129.

Hebert, R., Levesque, L., Vezina, J., Lavoie, J., Ducharme, F., Gendron, C., Preville, M., Voyer, L., & Dubois, M. (2003). Efficacy of a psychoeducative group program for caregivers of demented persons living at home: A randomized controlled trial. *Journal of Gerontology, 58*(1), S58–S67.

Helgeson, D., Mittan, R., Tan, S., & Chayasirisobhon, S. (1990). Sepulveda Epilepsy Education: The efficacy of a psychoeducational treatment program in treating medical and psychosocial aspects of epilepsy. *Epilepsia, 31*(1), 75–82.

Helgeson, V., Cohen, S., Schulz, R., & Yasko, J. (1999). Education and peer discussion group interventions and adjustment to breast cancer. *Archives of General Psychiatry, 56*(4), 340–347.

Heller, T., Roccoforte, J., Hsieh, K., Cook, J., & Pickett, S. (1997). Benefits of support groups for families of adults with severe mental illness. *American Journal of Orthopsychiatry, 67*(2), 187–198.

Honey, K., Bennett, P., & Morgan, M. (2002). A brief psycho-education group intervention for post-natal depression. *British Journal of Clinical Psychology, 41*(4), 405–409.

Hornung, W., Feldmann, R., Kingberg, S., Buchkremer, G., & Reker, T. (1999). Long-term effects of a psychoeducational psychotherapeutic intervention with schizophrenic outpatients and their key persons: Results of a five-year follow up. *European Archives of Psychiatry Clinical Neuroscience, 249*(3), 162–167.

Hornung, W., Kieserg, A., Feldmann, R., & Buchkremer, G. (1996). Psychoeducational training for schizophrenic patients: Background, procedure, and empirical findings. *Patient Education & Counseling, 29*(3), 257–268.

Hornung, W., Klingberg, S., Feldmann, R., Schonauer, K., & Schulze, M. (1998). Collaboration with drug treatment by schizophrenic patients with and without psychoeducational training: Results of a 1-year follow up. *Acta Psychiatrica Scandinavica, 97*(3), 213–219.

Hornung, W., Northoff-Helling, U., Vogel-Helleberg, P., & Feldmann, R. (2000). Early rehabilitation for schizophrenia in-patients. A pilot study of a combined psycho-educational-psychotherapeutic group therapy program. *Krankenhauspsychiatrie, 11*(2), 44–48.

Hurley, J. (1991). FIRO-B's disassociation from two central dimensions of interpersonal behavior. *Psychological Reports, 68*(2), 2443–2454.

Kaiser, A., Hahlweg, K., Fehm-Wolfsdorf, G., & Groth, T. (1998). The efficacy of a compact psycho-educational group training program for married couples. *Journal of Consulting and Clinical Psychology, 66*(5), 753–760.

Kaminer, Y., Burleson, J., & Goldberger, R. (2002). Cognitive behavioral coping skills and psychoeducation therapies for adolescent substance abuse. *Journal of Nervous & Mental Disease, 190*(1), 737–745.

Kaminski, P., & McNamara, K. (1996). A treatment for college women at risk for bulimia: A controlled evaluation. *Journal of Counseling & Development, 74*(3), 288–294.

Kane, C., DiMartino, E., & Jimenez, M. (1990). A comparison of short-term psycho-educational and support groups for relatives coping with chronic schizophrenia. *Archives of Psychiatric Nursing, 4*(6), 343–353.

Kaslow, N., Collings, M., Rashid, F., Baskin, M., Griffith, J., Hollins, L., & Eckman, J. (2000). The efficacy of a pilot family psychoeducational intervention for pediatric sickle cell disease (SCD). *Families, Systems & Health, 18*(4), 381–404.

Keller, F., & Schuler, B. (2002). Psychoeducational groups for families of in-patients with affective disorder. *Psychiatric Prax, 29*(3), 130–135.

Landry-Dattee, N., Gauvain-Piquard, A., & Cosset-Delaigue, M. (2000). A support group for children with one parent with cancer: Report on 4-year experience of a talking group. *Bulletin of Cancer, 87*(4), 355–362.

Lara, M., Navarro, C., Rubi, N., & Mondragon, L. (2003). Two levels of intervention in low-income women with depressive symptoms: Compliance and program assessment. *International Journal of Social Psychiatry, 49*(1), 43–57.

Lenz, E., & Perkins, S. (2000). Coronary artery bypass graft surgery and their family member caregivers: Outcomes of a family-focused staged psychoeducational intervention. *Applied Nursing Research, 13*(3), 142–150.

Lieberman, M., & Yalom, I. (1992). Brief group psychotherapy for the spousally bereaved: A controlled study. *International Journal of Group Psychotherapy, 42*(2), 117–132.

Lubin, H., Loris, M., Burt, J., & Johnson, D. (1998). Efficacy of psychoeducational group therapy in reducing symptoms of post traumatic stress disorder among multiply traumatized women. *American Journal of Psychiatry, 155*(9), 1172–1177.

Malow, R., West, J., Corrigan, S., Penna, J., & Cunningham, S. (1994). Outcome of psychoeducational of HIV risk reduction. *AIDS Education Prevention, 6*(2), 113–125.

Mayou, R., Springings, D., Birkhead, J., & Price, J. (2002). A randomized controlled trial of a brief educational and psychological intervention for patients presenting to a cardiac clinic with palpitation. *Psychological Medicine, 32*(4), 699–706.

McFarland, P., & Sanders, S. (2000). Educational support groups for male caregivers of individuals with Alzheimer's disease. *American Journal of Alzheimer's Disease, 15*(6), 367–373.

McFarland, W., Link, B., Dushay, R., Marchal, J., & Crilly, J. (1995). Psychoeducational multiple family groups: Four-year relapse outcome in schizophrenia. *Family Process, 34*(2), 127–144.

McFarland, W., Lukens, E., Link, B., Dushay, R., Deakins, S., Newmark, M., Dunne, E., Horen, B., & Toran, J. (1995). Multiple-family groups and psychoeducation in the treatment of schizophrenia. *Archives of General Psychiatry, 52*(8), 679–687.

McNaughton-Cassill, M., Bostwick, J., Arthur, N., Robinson, R., & Neal, G. (2002). Efficacy of brief couples support groups developed to manage the stress of in vitro fertilization treatment. *Mayo Clinic Proceedings, 77*(10), 1060–1066.

McWhirter, B., & Page, G. (1999). Effects of anger management and goal setting group intervention on state-trait anger and self-efficacy beliefs among high risk adolescents. *Current Psychology: Developmental, Learning, Personality, Social, 18*(2), 223–237.

Monahan, D., Greene, V., & Coleman, P. (1992). Caregiver support groups: Factors affecting use of services. *Social Work, 37*(3), 254–260.

Morano, C., & Bravo, M. (2002). A psychoeducational model for Hispanic Alzheimer's disease caregivers. *Gerontologist, 42*(1), 122–126.

Morgan, B., & Hensley, L. (1998). Supporting working mothers through group work. *Journal of Specialists in Group Work, 23*(3), 298–311.

Morgan, R., & Flora, D. (2002). Group psychotherapy with incarcerated offenders: A research synthesis. *Group Dynamics, 6*(3), 203–218.

Mulcahey, A., & Young, M. (1995). A bereavement support group for children: Fostering communication about grief and healing. *Cancer Practice, 3*(3), 150–156.

Nicassio, P., Radojenic, V., Weisman, M., Schuman, C., Kim, J., Schoenfeld-Smith, K., & Krall, T. (1997). A comparison of behavioral and educational interventions for fibro-myalgia. *Journal of Rheumatology, 24*(10), 2000–2007.

Nosanow, M., Hage, S., & Levin, J. (1999). Group intervention with college students from divorced families. *Journal of College Student Psychotherapy, 14*(1), 43–57.

Okano, T., Nagata, S., Hasegawa, M., Nomura, J., & Kumar, R. (1998). Effectiveness of antenatal education about postnatal depression: A comparison of two groups of Japanese mothers. *Journal of Mental Health, 7*(2), 191–198.

Olley, B., Osinoso, H., & Brieger, W. (2001). Psychoeducational therapy among Nigerian adult patients with epilepsy: A controlled outcome study. *Patient Education and Counseling, 42*(1), 25–33.

Olmstead, M., Daneman, D., Rydall, A., Lawson, M., & Rodin, G. (2002). The effects of psychoeducation on disturbed eating attitudes and behavior in young women with type 1 diabetes mellitus. *International Journal of Eating Disorders, 32*(2), 230–239.

Ostwald, S., Hepburn, K., Caron, W., Burns, T., & Mantell, R. (1999). Reducing caregiver burden: A randomized psychoeducational intervention for caregivers of persons with dementia. *Gerontologist, 39*(3), 299–309.

Palmer, G., & Braud, W. (2002). Exceptional human experiences, disclosure, and a more inclusive view of physical, psychological, and spiritual well being. *Journal of Transpersonal Psychology, 34*(1), 29–61.

Pekkala, E., & Merinder, L. (2000). Psychoeducation for schizophrenia. *Cochrane Database System Review, 4*, CD002831.

Pekkala, E., & Merinder, L. (2002). Psychoeducation for schizophrenia. *Cochrane Database System Review, 2*, CD002831.

Peterson, C., Mitchell, J., Engbloom, S., Nugent, S., Pederson, M., Crow, S., & Thuras, P. (2001). Self-help versus therapist-led group cognitive-behavioral treatment of binge eating disorder at follow-up. *International Journal of Eating Disorders, 30*(4), 363–374.

Pollio, D., North, C., & Osborne, V. (2002). A family-responsive psychoeducation group for families with an adult member with mental illness: Pilot results. *Community Mental Health Journal, 38*(5), 413–421.

Pomeroy, E., Kiam, R., & Green, D. (2000). Reducing depression, anxiety, and trauma of male inmates: An HIV/AIDS psychoeducational group intervention. *Social Work Research, 24*(3), 156–167.

Posner, C., Wilson, K., Kral, M., Lander, S., & Mcllwraith, R. (1992). Family psycho-education support groups in schizophrenia. *American Journal of Orthopsychiatry, 62*(2), 206–218.

Printz-Feddersen, V. (1990). Group process effect on caregiver burden. *Journal of Neuroscience Nursing, 22*(3), 164–168.

Ran, M., Xiang, M., Chan, C., Leff, J., Simpson, P., Huang, M., Shan, Y., & Li, S. (2003). Effectiveness of psychoeducation intervention for rural Chinese families experiencing schizophrenia: A randomized controlled trial. *Social Psychiatry & Psychiatric Epidemiology, 38*(2), 69–75.

Rice, K., & Meyer, A. (1994). Preventing depression among adolescents: Preliminary process results of a psychoeducational intervention program. *Journal of Counseling and Development, 73*(2), 145–152.

Roberts, C., Piper, L., Denny, J., & Cuddeback, G. (1997). A support group intervention to facilitate young adults' adjustment to cancer. *Health and Social Work, 22*(2), 133–141.

Roberts, S., Black, C., & Todd, F. (2002). The Living with Cancer Education Program II. Evaluation of an Australian education and support programme for cancer patients and their family and friends. *European Journal of Cancer Care, 11*(4), 280–289.

Rocco, P., Ciano, R., & Balestrieri, M. (2001). Psychoeducation in the prevention of eating disorders: An experimental approach in adolescent school girls. *British Journal of Medical Psychology, 74*(4), 351–358.

Rokke, P., Tomhave, J., & Jocic, Z. (2000). Self-management therapy and educational group therapy for depressed elders. *Cognitive Therapy & Research, 24*(1), 99–119.

Rosberger, Z., Edgar, L., Collet, J., & Fournier, M. (2002). Patterns of coping in women completing treatment for breast cancer. *Journal of Psychosocial Oncology, 20*(3), 19–37.

Rosenbaum, A., Gearan, P., & Ondovic, C. (2002). Completion and recidivism among court and self-referred batterers in a psychoeducational group treatment program: Implications for intervention and public policy. *Journal of Aggression, Maltreatment & Trauma, 5*(2), 199–220.

Sandahl, C., & Ronnbers, S. (1990). Brief group therapy in relapse prevention for alcohol dependent patients. *International Journal of Group Psychotherapy, 40*(4), 453–476.

Sapia, J. (2001). Using groups for the prevention of eating disorders among college women. *Journal for Specialists in Group Work, 26*(3), 256–266.

Sarkidi, A., & Rsenqvist, U. (1999). Study circles at the pharmacy—a new model for diabetes education in groups. *Patient Education Counseling, 37*(1), 89–96.

Schwiebert, V., & Myers, J. (1994). Midlife caregivers: Effectiveness of a psychoeducational intervention for midlife adults with parent-care responsibilities. *Journal of Counseling and Development, 72*(6), 627–632.

Shectman, Z. (2001). Prevention groups for angry and aggressive children. *Journal for Specialists in Group Work, 26*(3), 228–236.

Shelton, R., Barkley, R., Crosswait, C., Moorehouse, M., Fletcher, K., Barrett, S., Jenkins, L., & Metevia, L. (2000). Multimodal psychoeducational intervention for preschool children with disruptive behavior: Two year post-treatment follow-up. *Journal of Abnormal Child Psychology, 28*(3), 253–266.

Shimodera, S., Inove, S., Mino, Y., Tanaka, S., Kii, M., & Metoki, Y. (2000). Expressed emotion and psychoeducational intervention for relatives of patients with schizophrenia: A randomized controlled study in Japan. *Psychiatry Research, 96*(2), 141–148.

Shin, S., & Lukens, E. (2002). Effects of psychoeducation for Korean-Americans with chronic mental illness. *Psychiatric Services, 53*(9), 1125–1131.

Smith, G., Majeski, R., & McClenny, B. (1996). Psychoeducational support groups for aging parents: Development and preliminary outcomes. *Mental Retardation, 34*(3), 172–181.

Solis-Camara, R., Fox, R., & Nicholson, B. (2000). Parenting young children: Comparison of a psychoeducational program in Mexico and the United States. *Early Childhood Development & Care, 163*, 115–124.

Solomon, P., Draine, J., & Mannion, E. (1996). The impact of individualized consultation and group workshop family education intervention on ill relatives' outcomes. *Journal of Nervous and Mental Disease, 184*(4), 252–255.

Sorensen, H., London, J., Heitzmann, C., Gibson, D., Morales, E., Dumont, R., & Acree, M. (1994). Psychoeducational group approach: HIV risk reduction in drug users. *AIDS Education Prevention, 6*(2), 95–112.

Sorenson, S., Pinquart, M., & Duberstein, P. (2002). How effective are interventions with caregivers? An updated meta-analysis. *Gerontologist, 42*(3), 356–372.

Stam, H., & Cuijpers, P. (2001). Effects of family intervention on burden of relatives of psychiatric patients in the Netherlands: A pilot study. *Community Mental Health Journal, 37*(2), 179–187.

Stice, E., & Ragan, J. (2002). A preliminary controlled evaluation of an eating disturbance psychoeducational intervention for college students. *International Journal of Eating Disorders, 31*(2), 159–171.

Taylor, K., Lamdan, R., Siegel, J., Shelby, R., Moran-Klimi, K., & Hrywna M. (2003). Psychological adjustment among African American breast cancer patients: One-year follow-up results of a randomized psychoeducational group intervention. *Health Psychology, 22*(3), 316–323.

Tomaras, V., Mavreas, V., Economou, M., Ioannovich, E., Karydi, V., & Stefanis, C. (2000). The effect of family intervention on chronic schizophrenics under individual psychosocial treatment: A 3-year study. *Social Psychiatry & Psychiatric Epidemiology, 35*(11), 487–493.

Trowell, J., Kolvin, I., Weeramanthri, T., Sadowski, H., Berelowitz, M., Glasser, D., & Leitch, I. (2002). Psychotherapy for sexually abused girls: Psychopathological outcome findings and patterns of change. *British Journal of Psychiatry, 180*(3), 234–246.

Uehara, T., Kawashima, Y., Goto, M., Tasaki, S., & Someya, T. (2001). Psychoeducation for the families of patients with eating disorders and changes in expressed emotion: A preliminary study. *Comprehensive Psychiatry, 42*(2), 132–138.

Vacha-Hasse, T., Ness, C., Dannison, L., & Smith, A. (2000). Grandparents raising grandchildren: A psychoeducational approach. *Journal for Specialists in Group Work, 25*(1), 67–78.

Vallina-Fernandez, O., Lemos-Giraldez, S., Roder, V., & Gutierrez-Perez, A. (2001). Controlled study of an integrated psychological intervention in schizophrenia. *European Journal of Psychiatry, 15*(3), 167–179.

Weiss, C., & Orysh, L. (1994). Group counseling for eating disorders: A two-phase treatment program. *Journal of College Student Development, 35*(6), 487–488.

Wells, D., Miller, M., Tobacyk, J., & Clanton, R. (2002). Using a psychoeducational approach to increase the self-esteem of adolescents at high risk for dropping out. *Adolescence, 37*(146), 431–434.

Whitlatch, C., Zarit, S., & von Eye, A. (1991). Efficacy of interventions with caregivers: A reanalysis. *The Gerontologist, 31*(1), 9–14.

Wiseman, C., Sunday, S., Klapper, F., Klein, M., & Halmi, K. (2002). Short-term CBT versus psychoeducation on an inpatient eating disorder unit. *Eating Disorders: The Journal of Treatment & Prevention, 10*(4), 313–320.

Yalom, I. (1995). *The theory and practice of group psychotherapy*. New York: Basic Books.

28

Skills Training Groups

Miguel A. Quiñones

Kelly de Chermont

A plethora of methods are available to train individuals and groups on a number of skills. Despite recent interest in the use of electronic media for instruction via the Internet (e.g., e-learning), a recent report by the American Society for Training and Development found that 72% of training in organizations is still conducted in a traditional instructor-led classroom setting (Sugrue, 2003). One training method that has not received much attention in the traditional organizational training literature is skills training groups. As evidence of this lack of attention, the most recent review of the training literature makes no mention of skills training groups (see Salas & Cannon-Bowers, 2001).

The reason for this apparent lack of attention is that skills training groups have grown out of the clinical and therapy-oriented traditions and have been used to teach individuals more fundamental life skills. However, as Wheelan (1990) points out, skills training groups can be an effective method for teaching job-relevant skills such

as decision making, supervision, and customer relations. The purpose of this chapter is to introduce readers to the key methods used in skills training groups as well as to review the literature assessing their effectiveness. Finally, areas in need of further research attention are identified.

Wheelan (1994) defines skills training groups as a group-based method of instruction aimed at giving participants basic life skills that will help them function more effectively in social contexts including work and home. Prior to the advent of skills training groups, individuals had few options for improving these skills and received help only when functioning deteriorated to the point where they required psychotherapy or other forms of counseling. The increased pace of work life, coupled with the complexity of family life in our constantly changing, technology-driven world, has increased the need for individuals to improve their ability to cope. Thus, skills training groups have started to move out of the realm of psychotherapy and treatment and into the mainstream.

A variety of names have been used to refer to these groups, but all share the goal of improving a person's ability to cope with life's challenges (Corey & Corey, 1992). For example, one can find skills training groups aimed at helping spouses deal with the stresses of marriage. Others can focus on anger management, active listening, relaxation techniques, time management, communication skills, effective decision making, and leadership (Wheelan, 1994). However, the overwhelming majority of studies using skills training groups have focused on what can generically be called interpersonal or social skills (cf. Lane et al., 2003; Lieberman & Snowden, 1993). The focal populations in these studies have included psychiatric patients (Weingardt & Zeiss, 2000), federal workers (McNamara, Schwandt, Goldstein, & Medlin, 1982), medical students (May, 1984), and counseling professionals (May, 1986), to name a few.

Other examples of skills training groups are

- Parents of teenagers interested in improving the quality of their communications
- Recently laid off individuals learning interviewing skills
- Retail salespersons improving their customer service behaviors
- Doctors improving their bedside manner
- Couples learning how to be better listeners

The focus of skills training groups is the individual. Thus, these groups can be differentiated from group training interventions such as team training (cf. Salas & Cannon-Bowers, 1997), where the focus is on improving the performance of the entire team. Furthermore, team training interventions deal with skills such as coordination, backup behaviors, and shared mental models. These skills are relevant only at the team level of analysis. By contrast, skills training groups use the group setting to impart skills to the individual. There is no expectation that participants will work together as a team in the future.

Key Methods

The theoretical rationale for the use of skills training groups comes from Bandura's social learning theory (cf. Bandura, 1991). This theory argues that a large portion of learning happens when people observe the behavior of others (referred to as models). However, the amount of learning is dependent on a number of model, observer, and situational factors. For example, if the model's behavior results in positive outcomes, the likelihood that the observer will repeat that behavior increases. If the observer does not identify with the model, learning will be diminished. However, when the model's behavior is novel and distinctive and draws the observer's attention, learning will be enhanced.

The concept of self-efficacy, or a person's belief in his or her capacity to perform a given task, also is important in this theory. Self-efficacy beliefs are influenced by several factors including previous performance, physiological factors such as anxiety and fatigue, and situational factors such as task difficulty and availability of important resources (see Gist & Mitchell, 1992). Self-efficacy has been consistently found to predict motivation to learn as well as actual learning (Quiñones, 1997). It has also been found to predict trainees' attempts to transfer their newly learned skills (Ford, Smith, Sego, & Quiñones, 1993). Thus, one key goal of a skills training group is to provide the proper environment (models, practice, feedback, support) to foster learning and increase self-efficacy levels.

In a training context, behavioral modeling has proven to be one of the most effective methods for teaching a number of skills, including interpersonal skills (Trimble, Nathan, & Decker, 1990). Bednar, Corey, Evans, and Gazda (1987) describe the typical sequence of a skills training group based on behavioral modeling principles. These steps include (a) theoretical instruction, (b) leader modeling, (c) demonstration using simulation, (d) personally relevant interactions, and (e) transfer of training. Two important factors in behavioral modeling are the nature of the models used and the amount and spacing of practice given. For example, Douglas and Mueser (1990) found that the number of role plays used in a skills training group aimed at teaching conflict resolution skills to the mentally ill was a significant predictor of learning. In terms of the sequencing of practice, research has found that spacing practice events and allowing for variability in the type of practice used increases learning (Holladay & Quiñones, 2003). Finally, it is important that trainees are exposed to models exhibiting both correct and incorrect behaviors (Baldwin, 1997) and that feedback is provided.

It could be said that the group context itself represents the key method for improving skills in skills training groups. However, within that context, a number of decisions have to be made when designing an effective skills group. Wheelan (1990) recommends that designers of skills groups adopt a systematic development process that begins with a thorough needs assessment (see also Nelson-Jones, 1992). Additional steps in the development process include developing behavioral objectives, identifying evaluation criteria, selecting media and behavioral models, and ensuring that the leader has the necessary skills to lead the group (cf. Goldstein & Ford, 2002). Each of these steps is discussed in more detail below.

Needs Assessment

The process of needs assessment is typically divided into person, task, and organizational analyses (see Goldstein & Ford, 2002). Person analysis is the process by which the current skill levels of training participants are assessed, and their psychological readiness for training is determined. Specifically, Wheelan (1990) recommends developing an accurate profile of the skills group, including information about participants' desired outcomes and previous training experience and the extent to which their attendance is voluntary. In fact, research by Quiñones (1995) has documented the negative effects

of forcing individuals to attend training for remediation.

Other important factors that should be assessed during the person analysis phase include personality, values, and motivation of trainees. Research has clearly demonstrated the importance of trainee motivation for the success of training interventions (Quiñones, 1997; Salas & Cannon-Bowers, 2001). Thus, ensuring that trainees are coming to training with positive attitudes and high motivation is critical for any training program.

In skills training groups, person factors are even more critical because participants are acting as models for each other and provide feedback throughout the sessions. Thus, trainee characteristics will have a large influence on the level of trust and support as well as other critical group processes (Wheelan, 1994). These group processes must be carefully managed, and gathering information about group members is an important first step. Illustrating the importance of considering a training group's composition, a meta-analysis by Ang and Hughes (2002) found that skills training groups aimed at antisocial youths were more effective when they consisted of a mix of prosocial and antisocial individuals.

In addition to the person analysis, a comprehensive needs analysis also includes a thorough task analysis. The purpose of the task analysis is to identify the specific skills and behaviors a person must possess to perform in a given setting. The end result of a task analysis is a list of behavioral objectives that form the foundation for training program design and evaluation criteria (cf. Quiñones & Tonidandel, 2003). Behavioral objectives should be observable and measurable and describe the end goal of the training program. For example, a skills training group aimed at improving communication skills may have the following behavioral objectives:

- Be able to listen without interruption
- Empathize with another's point of view
- Speak audibly and clearly
- Structure thoughts in a logical manner

These objectives make clear the specific behaviors that group participants must exhibit for the program to be considered a success. In addition to specifying the new behaviors that will be learned, it is also important to identify inappropriate behaviors that trainees will have to unlearn (Wheelan, 1994). Skills group designers and leaders should rely on behavioral objectives to make decisions about which specific training method should be used. The decisions should be based on the extent to which a specific training method is appropriate for teaching a particular skill within a group context. More will be said about this later.

A good example of how to conduct a task analysis is provided by Mehaffey and Sandberg (1992). They present a methodology for identifying the specific skills that should be targeted in a social skills training group for elementary school children. Several program development tools are described, including a social skill scale that teachers, parents, and other trained observers can use to rate children on dimensions such as participation, communication, and cooperation. Mehaffey and Sandberg also propose the use of sociograms to determine the degree of peer acceptance among target children. The information gathered through these instruments is used to develop an eight-session skills training program, with each session focused on a specific skill such as sharing and cooperating.

The final stage of a typical needs assessment is the organizational analysis (see Goldstein & Ford, 2002). The purpose of the organizational analysis is to ensure that there are appropriate resources and a positive climate in the environment to which the skills are supposed to transfer (e.g., work, family, school, etc.). There is a growing body of evidence that a positive transfer climate where the trainee receives support and encouragement to try out new skills is critical for the effective transfer of these skills (Rouiller & Goldstein, 1993). Within the context of the types of skills typically taught in skills training groups (e.g., interpersonal skills), this means

receiving support from a spouse, supervisor, friends, or colleagues (Wheelan, 1990).

Develop Evaluation Criteria

The behavioral objectives identified during the needs assessment phase should be used to develop criteria by which the success of the program will be evaluated (Kraiger & Jung, 1997). Evaluation methods can range from ratings of skill attainment by trainees and others to standardized role plays and observations in the transfer setting. To evaluate the program adequately, an untrained control group and random assignment of participants to trained and untrained groups are critical (Quiñones & Tonidandel, 2003). Statistical comparisons between the two groups can be used to gather evidence about the effectiveness of the skills group (Arvey & Cole, 1989).

Select Media and Behavioral Models

Only after the content of the skills group is identified and appropriate criteria for judging success are chosen should the specific media for presenting the training material be selected. Options can include having the group leader (trainer) demonstrate effective and ineffective behaviors, showing videotaped images of these behaviors, and having participants read descriptions of the proper way to execute a given skill (Nelson-Jones, 1992). The participants themselves can serve as models, but care must be taken to ensure that at least some of the participants can perform the skills effectively (Ang & Hughes, 2002). The optimum ratio of positive and negative models has yet to be determined, but research shows that displaying both is critical for learning new skills (Baldwin, 1997).

Another aspect of training design that has received very little attention in the skills training literature is the use of transfer-enhancing interventions both during and after training. For example, Marx (1982) describes the application in a training context of techniques developed to minimize relapse among substance abusers. Some of the recommendations include making participants aware of situational cues that could trigger undesirable behavior, coping strategies for dealing with relapse, and strategies for selecting situations that will support the use of newly learned skills. These and other interventions aimed at increasing transfer, such as goal setting and self-management, have proven to be successful in enhancing the application of learned skills (Richman-Hirsch, 2001). However, to date, there are no studies examining these interventions in the context of skills training groups.

Group Leader Skills

The group leader, or trainer, plays a critical role in the success of a skills training group. Wheelan (1990) cites the following roles played by the trainer: (a) providing support, (b) creating psychological safety, (c) providing direction, (d) presenting an empathetic and likable demeanor, (e) creating awareness of current skill levels, (f) demonstrating new skills, (g) providing opportunities for practice, (h) enhancing likelihood for transfer of learning, and (i) encouraging confidence and independence.

Bednar et al. (1987) describe the process by which prospective trainers can prepare themselves to lead a skills group. First, the leader must be proficient in the skill being taught. Also, the prospective leader might participate in a group similar to the one he or she is proposing to lead. This could be followed by some time co-leading a group before the trainer leads a group alone. Critical leader skills include having empathy, using effective communication, giving feedback, resolving conflict effectively, and managing group dynamics.

Nelson-Jones (1992) identifies two general styles that group leaders tend to adopt. The didactic style is task oriented, directive, and goal driven; it provides few opportunities for discussion. By contrast, the facilitative leader tends to focus more on the dynamics, feelings, and psychological well-being of the group participants. The environment is more participative, and the participants have more freedom. In reality, most trainers employ both facilitative and didactic elements throughout the life of the group. The critical skill for the trainer is being adaptable and perceptive enough to know when to use a particular approach.

A Case Example

A critical and fundamental skill that managers must possess is self-awareness (Whetten & Cameron, 2005). Skills training groups can be an effective method for developing this skill among business students or managers. This case example illustrates how the steps described here would be applied to the development and execution of a skills training group for developing self-awareness.

1. *Needs assessment.* The goal of this step is to determine the current level of self-awareness skill among participants and identify barriers to the implementation of learned skills. Specific behaviors that lead to greater self-awareness are also documented and used to develop evaluation criteria and instructional protocols such as behavioral models.

- A series of self-assessments are administered to participants asking them to rate themselves on a number of dimensions such as social skills, learning style, personality characteristics, and values.
- The same ratings can be collected about the participants from individuals who know them well (e.g., co-workers, peers, parents, friends) and compared with the self-ratings to develop a measure of self-awareness. Similarity between self-ratings and the ratings of others can be considered an indication of higher levels of self-awareness.

- Barriers to implementing learned skills can also be assessed either in a group format or individually through ratings or interviews. Factors such as lack of support from peers and others to change their level of self-awareness can be investigated.
- Specific behaviors that have been found to be related to higher levels of self-awareness are self-disclosure and feedback seeking. Self-disclosure involves sharing aspects of our self-knowledge with others to get verbal or nonverbal feedback concerning the accuracy of our self-perceptions. Feedback seeking is a more general behavior that includes asking others about our behaviors such as our level of performance on the job or social interaction skills in a group.

2. *Develop evaluation criteria.* The purpose of this step is to develop measurable indicators that can be used to determine changes in self-awareness skills. Some criteria used in a skills training group aimed at improving self-awareness skills are ratings by self and others of self-awareness behaviors (e.g., self-disclosure and feedback seeking) and role-play exercises designed to elicit key behaviors.

- Ideally an evaluation design should consist of a comparison group that does not participate in the skills training group (see Quiñones & Tonidandel, 2003). Scores on the evaluation measures are collected from both groups and compared. If the skills group was successful, the trained group will show greater increases in scores on the criteria measures when compared with the comparison group.

3. *Select media and behavioral models.* The goal of this step is to develop the actual content of the training group. In a self-awareness skills training group, the content includes leader demonstrations, videotaped models, and participant role-play exercises.

- At the beginning of the program, the leader/instructor introduces the general topic of self-awareness and describes its importance for managerial performance. Behaviors leading to higher self-awareness such as self-disclosure and feedback seeking are emphasized.
- Videotaped models demonstrating proper and improper behaviors leading to self-awareness are presented to the members of the skills group. At this point, the leader facilitates a discussion of the models presented and points out the correct and incorrect behaviors if the participants are not able to distinguish them for themselves.
- Participants role-play the demonstrated behaviors in front of the group and receive feedback on their behavior. It is critical that the leader establish a climate of trust and cooperation so that participants feel comfortable performing the role-play exercises and receiving feedback from the other participants.

Conclusion

Skills training groups are an effective method for teaching a number of life skills. Their use has expanded from clinical domains to more mainstream arenas such as students, managers, executives, and couples. However, although there are studies showing the effectiveness of skills training groups for improving a number of skills, a comprehensive research agenda that identifies the various factors that are likely to impact the effectiveness of skills training groups has yet to be proposed. Thus, it is difficult to draw general conclusions and recommendations for forming and conducting skills training groups that are based on empirical evidence.

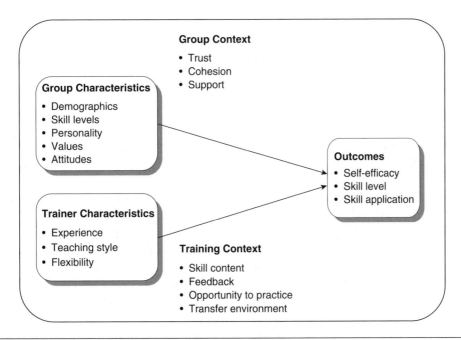

Figure 28.1   A Framework for Research on Skills Training Groups

Figure 28.1 presents a first attempt to develop such a framework. Four categories of variables proposed to influence the effectiveness of the skills group are presented. These include group characteristics, trainer characteristics, group context, and training context. All of these factors are hypothesized to influence three key outcomes of skills training groups: self-efficacy, skill level, and skill application. This framework is not intended to be exhaustive in terms of all of the factors that can affect the success of a skills training group. Rather, the framework presents variables that have been shown to influence other types of groups and can be reasonably expected to have an influence in skills training groups. It is intended to serve as a catalyst for more programmatic research into this powerful method of instruction.

Group Characteristics

The composition of a skills training group, including demographic characteristics, skill level,

personality, values, and attitudes, is hypothesized to influence training effectiveness. In terms of demographics, homogeneous groups will probably be more cohesive and engender more trust among participants (Porter, 1997). Also, because research has demonstrated that the more a person identifies with a behavioral model, the better he or she learns (cf. Bandura, 1976), one can reasonably expect that homogeneous groups will lead to more rapid learning during training. On the other hand, trainees are likely to encounter diverse others when they leave the training group. Therefore, practicing their skills within a heterogeneous group is likely to increase transfer.

The composition of the group in terms of skill level is also likely to influence the effectiveness of the skills training group (Ellis et al., 2003). The most obvious reason is that low performers need to see the correct way to perform a skill. Thus, having high performers in the group provides positive models from whom to learn. In fact, Ang and Hughes (2002) found that mixed skill level training groups were more successful than homogeneous ones. In addition, variety in skill level among trainees can also increase the variability of practice, which is related to transfer (Holladay & Quiñones, 2003). The downside is that those who perform the skills the best may not benefit as much from the training intervention. However, the group leader, through demonstrations and videotaped examples, should be able to boost those trainees' skill levels as well.

Personality, values, and attitudes will also influence the dynamics of a skills training group. For example, past research has demonstrated that individuals who have high levels of openness to experience (one of the big-five personality dimensions) benefit more from training (Barrick & Mount, 1991). Furthermore, Jehn, Northcraft, and Neale (1999) found that value diversity was associated with decreased satisfaction, intent to remain in the group, and commitment to the group. Clearly, the composition of a skills training group will influence its dynamics and ultimate success.

Trainer Characteristics

Three trainer characteristics hypothesized to influence the success of skills training groups are presented in Figure 28.1. These include trainer experience, teaching style, and flexibility. Although there is little research on trainer characteristics, a few studies suggest that they may influence skills group outcomes. For example, Quiñones, Ford, and Teachout (1995) found that trainer experience was positively related to performance across many jobs. Specifically, they found that the relationship was strongest when experience was measured using specific, task-based counts such as the number of times a task was performed. Thus, it could reasonably be expected that trainers who lead more training groups will be more effective. Similarly, trainers with more charismatic styles have been found to be more successful (Towler & Dipboye, 2001). Finally, because skills group participants are likely to vary in their learning styles and training

needs, trainers who are more flexible can be hypothesized to lead in ways that produce better training outcomes.

Group Context

Skills training groups must have a high level of trust, cohesion, and support in order to promote learning (Wheelan, 1994). Although this contention has not been empirically demonstrated in this context, a large body of research demonstrates the critical role of these factors on overall group performance. For example, a meta-analysis by Mullen and Copper (1994) found a positive relationship between group cohesion and performance. Cohesive skills groups are more likely to encourage each other to attempt the modeled behaviors. Spreitzer, Nobel, Mishra, and Cooke (1999), in a study of process improvement teams in the automotive industry, found support for the link between trust and performance. Consistent with the framework proposed in Figure 28.1, Jones and George (1998) hypothesized that the values and attitudes of group members would be related to the level of trust that develops. When trust is present in a skills training group, trainees are more likely to try to perform the new skills without fear of being ridiculed. Trust also allows group members to give each other feedback about their behavior. Wheelan (1994) suggests that support from the group leader and other group members is important for skills training groups.

Training Context

The final variables presented in Figure 28.1 are skill content, feedback, opportunity to practice, and transfer environment. The importance of these training design and context variables has been well established in the training literature (Goldstein & Ford, 2002). For example, Ford, Quiñones, Sego, and Sorra (1992) suggest that transfer of training is enhanced when individuals are given the opportunity to practice the skills acquired in training. Trainees will also learn more if they are given feedback on their performance from the group leader as well as their peers. In addition, Rouiller and Goldstein (1993) found that certain organizational environments were more conducive to promote transfer of training than others. Finally, the content of the training has to be well designed and relevant for improving the skills targeted by the skills group (Goldstein & Ford, 2002). Although the skills training literature recognizes these factors as being important, there is no research examining their impact on skill development and transfer.

In summary, what is needed is a systematic research program that begins to examine these and other factors that have been identified by the training literature but have not been studied within the context of skills training groups. Studies are needed that manipulate these variables and compare the skills groups on outcomes such as skill learning, transfer and self-efficacy. More meta-analytic research that empirically summarizes the existing literature and categorizes studies based on the variables identified in Figure 28.1 will also move the field forward.

In conclusion, skills training groups represent an underresearched and underutilized technique for teaching important life skills. As the method becomes more widely used, the empirical evidence needs to keep up with their popularity.

References

Ang, R. P., & Hughes, J. N. (2002). Differential benefits of skills training with antisocial youth based on group composition: A meta-analytic investigation. *Social Psychology Review, 31,* 164–185.

Arvey, R. D., & Cole, D. A. (1989). Evaluating change due to training. In I. L. Goldstein (Ed.), *Training and development in organizations* (pp. 89–117). San Francisco: Jossey-Bass.

Baldwin, T. T. (1997). Effects of alternative modeling strategies on outcomes of interpersonal-skills training. In D. F. Russ-Eft, H. S. Preskill, & C. Sleezer (Eds.), *Human resource development review: Research and implications* (pp. 11–30). Thousand Oaks, CA: Sage.

Bandura, A. (1976). *Social learning theory.* Upper Saddle River, NJ: Prentice Hall.

Bandura, A. (1991). Social cognitive theory of self-regulation. *Organizational Behavior & Human Decision Processes, 50,* 248–287.

Barrick, M. R., & Mount, M. K. (1991). The Big Five personality dimensions and job performance: A meta-analysis. *Personnel Psychology, 44,* 1–26.

Bednar, R. L., Corey, G., Evans, N. J., & Gazda, G. M. (1987). Overcoming obstacles to the future development of research on group work. *Journal for Specialists in Group Work, 12,* 98–111.

Corey, M. S., & Corey, G. (1992). *Groups: Process and practice* (4th ed.). Belmont, CA: Brooks/Cole.

Douglas, M. S., & Mueser, K. T. (1990). Teaching conflict resolution skills to the chronically mentally ill: Social skills training groups for briefly hospitalized patients. *Behavior Modification, 14,* 519–547.

Ellis, A. P., Hollenbeck, J. R., Ilgen, D. R., Porter, C., West, B. J., & Moon, H. (2003). Team learning: Collectively connecting the dots. *Journal of Applied Psychology, 88,* 831–835.

Ford, J. K., Quiñones, M. A., Sego, D. J., & Sorra, J. (1992). Factors affecting the opportunity to perform trained tasks on the job. *Personnel Psychology, 45,* 511–527.

Ford, J. K., Smith, E. M., Sego, D. J., & Quiñones, M. A. (1993). Impact of task experience and individual factors on training-emphasis ratings. *Journal of Applied Psychology, 78,* 583–590.

Gist, M. E., & Mitchell, T. R. (1992). Self-efficacy: A theoretical analysis of its determinants and malleability. *Academy of Management Review, 17,* 183–211.

Goldstein, I. L., & Ford, J. K. (2002). *Training in organizations: Needs assessment, development, and evaluation* (4th ed.). Belmont, CA: Wadsworth/Thomson Learning.

Holladay, C. L., & Quiñones, M. A. (2003). Practice variability and transfer of training: The role of self-efficacy generality. *Journal of Applied Psychology, 88,* 1094–1103.

Jehn, K., Northcraft, G., & Neale, M. (1999). Why differences make a difference: A field study of diversity, conflict, and performance in workgroups. *Administrative Science Quarterly, 44,* 741–763.

Jones, G. R., & George, J. M. (1998). The experience and evolution of trust: Implications for cooperation and teamwork. *Academy of Management Review, 23,* 531–546.

Kraiger, K., & Jung, K. M. (1997). Linking training objectives to evaluation criteria. In M. A. Quiñones & A. Ehrenstein (Eds.), *Training for a rapidly changing workplace: Applications of psychological research* (pp. 151–175). Washington, DC: American Psychological Association.

Lane, K. L., Wehby, J., Menzies, H. M., Doukas, G. L., Munton, S. M., & Gregg, R. M. (2003). Social skills instruction for students at risk for antisocial behavior: The effects of small-group instruction. *Behavior Disorders, 28,* 229–248.

Lieberman, M. A., & Snowden, L. R. (1993). Problems in assessing prevalence and membership characteristics of self-help group participants. *Journal of Applied Behavioral Science, 29,* 166–180.

Marx, R. D. (1982). Relapse prevention for managerial training: A model for maintenance of behavior change. *Academy of Management Review, 7,* 433–441.

May, R. J. (1984). Achieving long-term gains in interpersonal skill training with medical students: Ideas for the second decade. *Professional Psychology: Research & Practice, 15,* 9–17.

May, R. J. (1986). Evaluation of a clinical assessment seminar for interns. *Professional Psychology: Research & Practice, 17,* 27–30.

McNamara, J. R., Schwandt, D. R., Goldstein, J. H., & Medlin, S. (1982). A multilevel evaluation of interpersonal skill training in a federal agency. *Group & Organization Studies, 7,* 35–49.

Mehaffey, J. I., & Sandberg, S. K. (1992). Conducting social skills training groups with elementary school children. *School Counselor, 40,* 61–67.

Mullen, B., & Copper, C. (1994). The relation between group cohesiveness and performance: An integration. *Psychological Bulletin, 115,* 210–227.

Nelson-Jones, R. (1992). *Group leadership: A training approach.* Belmont, CA: Brooks/Cole.

Porter, G. (1997). Trust in teams: Member perceptions and the added concern of cross-cultural interpretations. In M. M. Beyerlein & D. A. Johnson (Eds.), *Advances in interdisciplinary studies of work teams* (pp. 45–77). Burlington, MA: Elsevier Science/JAI Press.

Quiñones, M. A. (1995). Pre-training context effects: Training assignment as feedback. *Journal of Applied Psychology, 80,* 226–238.

Quiñones, M. A. (1997). Contexual influences on training effectiveness. In M. A. Quiñones & A. Ehrenstein (Eds.), *Training for a rapidly changing workplace: Applications of psychological research* (pp. 177–199). Washington, DC: American Psychological Association.

Quiñones, M. A., Ford, J. K., & Teachout, M. S. (1995). The relationship between work experience and job performance: A conceptual and meta-analytic review. *Personnel Psychology, 48,* 887–910.

Quiñones, M. A., & Tonidandel, S. (2003). Conducting training evaluation. In J. Edwards, J. Scott, & N. Raju (Eds.), *The human resources program-evaluation handbook* (pp. 225–243). Newbury Park, CA: Sage.

Richman-Hirsch, W. L. (2001). Posttraining interventions to enhance transfer: The moderating effects of work environments. *Human Resource Development Quarterly, 12,* 105–119.

Rouiller, J. Z., & Goldstein, I. L. (1993). The relationship between organizational transfer climate and positive transfer of training. *Human Resource Development Quarterly, 4,* 377–390.

Salas, E., & Cannon-Bowers, J. A. (1997). Methods, tools, and strategies for team training. In M. A. Quiñones & A. Ehrenstein (Eds.), *Training for a rapidly changing workplace: Applications of psychological research* (pp. 249–279). Washington, DC: American Psychological Association.

Salas, E., & Cannon-Bowers, J. A. (2001). The science of training: A decade of progress. *Annual Review of Psychology, 52,* 471–499.

Spreitzer, G. M., Nobel, D. S., Mishra, A. K., & Cooke, W. N. (1999). Predicting process improvement team performance in an automotive firm: Explicating the roles of trust and empowerment. In R. Wageman (Ed.), *Research on managing groups and teams: Groups in context* (pp. 71–92). Burlington, MA: Elsevier Science/JAI Press.

Sugrue, B. (2003). *State of the industry report.* Alexandria, VA: American Society for Training and Development.

Towler, A., & Dipboye, R. L. (2001). Effects of trainer expressiveness, organization of lecture, and goal orientation on training outcomes. *Journal of Applied Psychology, 86,* 664–673.

Trimble, S. K., Nathan, B. R., & Decker, P. J. (1990). The effect of positive and negative models on learning in behavior modeling training: Testing for proactive and retroactive interference. *Journal of Human Behavior & Learning, 7,* 1–12.

Weingardt, K. R., & Zeiss, R. A. (2000). Skills training groups on a psychiatric intensive care unit: A guide for group leaders. *Cognitive & Behavioral Practice, 7*, 385–394.

Wheelan, S. A. (1990). *Facilitating training groups: A guide to leadership and verbal intervention skills.* New York: Praeger.

Wheelan, S. A. (1994). *Group processes: A developmental perspective.* Needham Heights, MA: Allyn & Bacon.

Whetten, D. A., & Cameron, K. S. (2005). *Developing management skills.* Upper Saddle River, NJ: Prentice Hall.

PART VI

Conclusion:
Charting the Future

29

Integrating Group Research and Practice

George Anderson

Susan A. Wheelan

I n fields such as medicine, therapy, and education, recent discussions have centered on the gap that exists between those who practice in their professional field and those who conduct research in that field. Gruman (2003) told the story of an Australian researcher who discovered that stomach ulcers, which doctors had thought resulted from factors such as stress and diet, were often caused by bacteria treatable with antibiotics. However, "in spite of articles published in scientific journals and endorsement of the researcher's work by the NIH panel, many primary-care providers still have not changed the way they treat ulcers to conform to current medical knowledge" (p. 20). A similar divide is seen in the field of psychotherapy. Tavris (2003) cited numerous examples of subjective clinical opinions held by therapists that have been proven false by researchers. For example, a common belief that low self-esteem causes aggressiveness, drug use, and low achievement in children is simply not borne out by research.

This aptly named *researcher-practitioner gap* is very much in evidence in the group field as well (Hyatt et al., 1997). In this chapter, we will examine why this gap continues to exist. We also will describe a more ideal state of affairs and offer suggestions on how to close the gap so that group researchers and practitioners can begin to engage in increasingly collaborative work. By way of example, we will focus on the field of group and organizational psychology. However, the discussion is equally applicable to all the disciplines represented in this volume.

In addition to identifying opportunities for mutually beneficial collaboration, there may be other pragmatic reasons for examining the researcher-practitioner gap. Farr (1997) wrote,

Since I/O (Industrial and Organizational) psychologists look at organizations and their effectiveness, it seems to make sense that we should do this periodically in relation to our own professional organization to see how well we are meeting the needs of our most important stakeholders, our members. . . . Such reflection and self-observation may provide insights for desired change. (p. 1)

This examination is exactly what practitioners recommend to clients who desire increased effectiveness or productivity. As practitioners and researchers, our credibility may well depend on our ability to practice what we preach.

The Researcher-Practitioner Gap

A discussion of integrating group research and practice must begin by examining the current level of collaboration between practitioners and researchers. Although the gap is obvious to both groups currently engaged in either research or practical endeavors, investigations have taken place to demonstrate that such a divide actually exists. Amabile et al. (2001) noted that between January 1994 and June 1999, only 4% of the articles published in the *Academy of Management Journal*, and less than 1% of the articles published in *Administrative Science*, listed academics and practitioners as coauthors. McIntyre (1990) contended that this lack of collaboration is a result of fundamentally differing goals. He stated,

The university naturally expects industrial and organizational faculty, because they view themselves as scientists, to generate journal articles, to acquire external grant or contract funds, and to teach. Yet, the workplace, the focal point of our field, expects from industrial/organizational psychology nothing more than quick, simple answers to profit-relevant questions without all the

niceties so characteristic of university-spawned products. Because their goals differ, the workplace and the university are fundamentally incompatible. (p. 42)

When organizations value different things, reward systems for those operating within those organizations will inevitably vary. In industry, rewards are based on quick solutions to problems, solutions that can somehow be related to the organization's short-term goals. In academia, rewards are based on the conduct of research and the publication of that research. This fundamental incompatibility has led to actions by both scientists and practitioners that have perpetuated the schism. Brice and Waung (2001) outline the pattern well. At the turn of the last century, academics within the field of psychology believed that investigating psychological principles outside of the laboratory was inconsistent with the goals of developing rigorous science. They wrote, "Since the inception of I/O psychology, there has been a debate about whether the field has been fueled by the 'academic camp' which emphasizes the importance of scientific rigor versus the 'applied camp' which emphasizes the need for research to be useful in everyday workplace settings" (p. 1). Although World War I represented the first successful large-scale application of psychology in this country, it nevertheless generated little interest in solving applied problems. Murphy and Saal (1990) noted that after the war, Bruce V. Moore, thought to be the first person to receive a PhD in I/O psychology, was reputed to have said, "Now we can get back to the real business of psychology."

This gap is hardly shrinking. Murphy and Saal (1990) studied trends in academic journals and discovered that in the 1950s and 1960s, nonacademics contributed about 30% to 40% of the published research articles in the I/O psychology literature. In the 1990s, nonacademic I/O psychologists contributed only 15% of the published research articles, and the gap continues. Academics and practitioners—who are working toward parallel goals, with insights to share with each other, yet distrustful of each other—appear to be moving even farther apart.

Instead of fostering collaboration with academic institutions, business organizations have generally been much more comfortable hiring consultants to do unproven team building, for example, than funding research on that topic. Even the occasional research that points to increased collaboration between the two camps still acknowledges a dangerous separation (Brice & Waung, 2001). Evidence of the existence of this gap also can be seen in the extensive interest and effort that is being expended to close that gap (Hyatt et al., 1997). Thus, despite varying views on the cause of, or remedy for, the researcher-practitioner gap, there is little doubt that the schism is real.

Fundamentally, closing the divide will require the integration of two distinct value systems. Academia, which emphasizes rigor and scientific caution, does not necessarily support the emphasis on action and solution of practical problems, which at times, can be overvalued by industry. This divide can be illustrated by the initial questions each group poses. For example, after new research findings have been validated, academicians may ask: How can I get this published? Practitioners, when faced with new research findings, may not be as concerned with validation and will most certainly ask: How can I use this to solve a problem? In any field, what the primary stakeholders value determines the direction of that field. However, in the group field, there are two distinct sets of values, and this makes collaboration difficult and rare.

Stakeholder influence affects all aspects of an organization. Murphy and Saal (1990) remind us of a curious organizational phenomenon that happens to I/O psychologists who become practitioners. Inevitably, the practitioners will be required to give up their status as psychologists once they join an organization. They will be called "manager of human resources," "director of organizational development," or "corporate training and development specialist." And, while

a title needn't define a person, it certainly can point to his or her status within the organization. Engineers, lawyers, and chemists, for much of their career, maintain their scientific and professional status within an organization. However, organizational psychologists, for the most part, do not. Murphy and Saal suggest that in industry settings, psychologists are not thought to possess any unique specialized knowledge. Other organizational members feel that they also know a good deal about human behavior. In addition, the knowledge held by a psychologist is unlikely to be perceived as essential for organizational success.

In terms of organizational competencies and talent development, successful integration of science and practice requires that a person be skilled in research design and the practice of psychology in an organization. Research skills include designing experiments, operationalizing variables, and collecting, analyzing, and interpreting data. Practice skills also include problem definition and diagnosis, but these must be complemented by skill in selling these services within an organization while functioning as an operational manager. Skill development is limited by the infrequent opportunities that researchers or practitioners have to use each other's skills or to understand the intricacies of both sides of the field. Practitioners simply don't have the time or opportunity to do research, and researchers often don't have the opportunity to test data and hypotheses in the real world. Until these various skills are fully recognized, valued, and taught, and opportunities are made available to apply these learnings, the integration of research and practice may remain stymied.

Examining the Gap

Given the reality of the researcher-practitioner gap, which has been attributed to differing stakeholders with disparate goals, other questions follow. First, why does the gap remain despite efforts to close it? Second, why should we make an effort to close it? Although several models have been developed to explain the gap, Anderson, Herriot, and Hodgkinson (2001) also have attributed the root cause of the gap to the divergent stakeholders of each group. They presented a compelling model to explain their point of view. These authors explained the divide by describing four types of science, using the two dimensions of practical relevance and methodological rigor: *popularist* science, which is high in relevance and low in methodological rigor; *pragmatic* science, which is high in both relevance and rigor; *pedantic* science, which is high in rigor but low in relevance; and *purile* science, which is low in both relevance and methodological rigor.

The authors contend that stakeholders have pushed practitioners toward popularist science while academic stakeholders have pushed researchers into pedantic science. Practitioners' stakeholders are generally their internal client groups, and their effectiveness is measured by speed, easily implemented and tailored solutions, and cost competitiveness. These interests lend themselves to high relevance and low rigor, defined as popularist science. Researchers' stakeholders are tenured academics who seek to gain research grants and enhance the reputation of their institution. These interests lend themselves to high rigor and low relevance, defined as pedantic science. These powerful and divergent stakeholder groups push their fields to opposing points on the model, and there is generally no incentive for movement to a more desirable state of high relevance and rigor, the pragmatic quadrant.

Although this framework is eye-opening and useful to both groups with regard to why the schism exists, additional explanation is needed to understand why these stakeholders push their respective groups to a quadrant that maintains division. Murphy and Saal (1990) offered prerequisites for integrating science and practice. In doing so, they offered additional insights into the motivations of these varying stakeholders to maintain the divide. Until behavior that

recognizes scientific rigor can be related to an organization's goals, there will be little incentive for practitioners to move toward pragmatic science. Until researcher and practitioner stakeholders can move to common or, at the very least, overlapping ground, it is doubtful that movement to close the gap will occur. Although this may be difficult, it is not impossible. Consider Six Sigma methodology. This set of tools for statistical process control, developed by Harry (1994), has been adopted by many organizations as an alternative to Total Quality Management. Industry, desperate to improve organizational process and reduce inefficiencies, embraced the methodological rigor necessary to implement Six Sigma. Organizations saw the value of Six Sigma in terms of improving manufacturing processes, customer service procedures, and decision-making ability. Because these could be easily linked to immediate goals, organizations developed infrastructure and reward systems that encouraged the use of Six Sigma tools.

Why, then, is movement toward pragmatic science the ultimate goal? Simply put, the answer is that researchers, practitioners, and the field of study stand to benefit. These benefits can be explained best by the problems that could be solved by collaboration. Researchers, who constantly battle funding and access to real-world situations, could find themselves with new venues in which to test their hypotheses and see their findings implemented. Researchers also would see additional sources of funding to support their endeavors. Practitioners, who find themselves implementing untested theories, battling staffing constraints, and lacking the necessary skills to conduct meaningful research and analysis, would find themselves with informed research collaborators serving as extensions of their departments. As already discussed in the Six Sigma example, adoption of research and rigor in organizations can solve real contemporary organizational problems.

Leonard and Freedman (2000) traced how in the past collaboration between research and practice solved real and compelling social problems. During the years 1945 to 1961, considered by many to be "the Golden Age of Group Dynamics," Kurt Lewin (1947a, 1947b) shifted from highly controlled laboratory research to applied research. Prior to Lewin, standard experimental designs had been used to study groups. Researchers were primarily interested in manipulating key variables and studying the effects. During World War II, however, Lewin collaborated with other social psychologists and his graduate students to support the war effort. For example, his collaboration with Margaret Mead to change the food habits of Americans was particularly successful.

In 1946, when the unifying effect of the war effort was fading, racial tensions in the United States were exacerbated due to housing shortages and soaring unemployment. Lewin, his students, associates, and several public and private agencies convened a conference on intergroup relations, which focused on discrimination in housing, education, and employment. Leonard and Freedman (2000) cite this as "one of the earliest, if not the earliest applications of action research to achieve social change" (p. 3). Incidentally, this also was the first known use of interpersonal feedback to influence participants' behavior. Although participant involvement is the standard today, it was revolutionary then.

The impact of this event was staggering. Social psychologists, working collaboratively, began to use social psychology to improve the human condition and to develop a social behavioral science. The 1946 conference spawned the National Training Labs (NTL), a nonprofit educational institution that continues to this day. Unfortunately, Lewin died suddenly and was never able to participate in NTL programs. Yet, he is credited with being one of the first to have endorsed and pursued the integration of theory, research, and social action.

Despite the loss of Lewin, the NTL thrived, and its participants went on to generate innovative research and application methods. Rogers (1970), Luft (1984), Schutz (1971), and others

adapted existing group models to develop personal growth workshops. Tannenbaum (1961) conducted T-groups, and McGregor (1960) introduced Theory X and Theory Y. Harris conducted survey feedback with Proctor and Gamble. Sheperd and Blake, in their work with an Esso refinery, developed a managerial grid and labeled their approach *organizational development*. Independently, in 1959, McGregor and Beckhard also described their efforts to bring cultural change at General Mills as *organizational development* (French & Bell, 1989; Leonard & Freedman, 2000).

Throughout the 1950s and 1960s, business and organizational leaders allowed behavioral scientists to work with subordinate teams. The scaling back of social change goals in the late 1960s and early 1970s was accompanied by the maturation of team-based techniques. As a result, Leonard and Freedman (2000) wrote, "Many participants experienced team building as enjoyable, enlightening and useful in improving intragroup relations but much less effective in accomplishing significant personal or team transformations" (p. 3). In short, participants became skeptical that these approaches could affect group or individual change. Some of these experiences, immortalized in the comic strip *Dilbert*, were the beginning of a renewed widening of the research-practitioner gap. For a variety of reasons, researchers and practitioners withdrew from each other during this time period. The result was that approaches to group work became less and less linked to solid theory and research. Collaboration between researchers and practitioners all but disappeared during that time.

The field of industrial and organizational psychology, and group psychology in general, risks becoming irrelevant and obsolete if science and practice remain disconnected. As was stated previously, the schism remains in all the disciplines that make up group psychology. However, there are some indications that the gap is narrowing. Closing the gap, as we have seen, requires that researchers and practitioners work together to solve significant social problems.

Fruitful Paths

Researchers and practitioners have devoted themselves to finding methods to help teams be effective and productive, although as has been the case in the past, the two groups are not always working together. The gap remains, but the chance to close it is at hand. This book is an example of one small attempt to increase collaboration among researchers and practitioners. Instead of the traditional tome in which only academics are chapter authors, this book contains the work of both group researchers and practitioners, some of whom wrote chapters together. Some of the researchers also work and conduct research in the field. Some of the practitioners also teach, participate in research, and write from time to time. This provides evidence that some researchers have moved from the lab to study groups in their natural context, and some practitioners are conducting research and writing scholarly articles and chapters. The question now is how to engage more researchers in field research and more practitioners in the research endeavor.

For group researchers, gaining access to real-world groups is necessary to validate the results of laboratory research. Experimental studies conducted in the laboratory are more tightly controlled, but the groups are contrived (McGrath, Arrow, & Berdahl, 1999). Experimental research alone is insufficient. Testing theories and research in the real world of groups is necessary as well to establish external validity (see Hoyle, Chapter 12, this volume, for an expanded discussion of these issues). Ultimately, researchers need to determine whether their findings hold up in the real world, in different contexts, with different group members, at different times. Group researchers need access to real groups in order to answer these questions.

At the same time, practitioners and the organizations of which they are a part need simple, cost-effective strategies that work. In this case, they need to know how groups function, what makes groups effective and productive, and what methods are best to help work groups improve their effectiveness and productivity. Practitioners need access to solid research that has been field-tested, so to speak, to determine the best and most cost-effective strategies to support their teams.

Although we agree that the organizations, researchers, and practitioners value different things, we do not think that researchers and practitioners are driven only by organizational values. Group researchers and practitioners are driven by the desire to solve problems and to help groups—and group members—reach their goals. Researchers go about this by trying to discover how groups operate and how groups can improve their results, whether those results are therapeutic, educational, or business oriented. Practitioners go about this by trying to discover the best and most cost-effective ways to help groups to improve their performance. Although the researcher-practitioner gap is real, this researcher-practitioner connection is equally real.

For example, the cost of team training and consultation in U.S. companies is very high, and return on investment is quite low (Casio, 1991; Salas, Rozell, Mullen, & Driskell, 1999). More research is needed to determine which training and consultation approaches improve team performance and how to increase the effectiveness of promising approaches. Organizations have a stake in this effort. Instead of funding untested team training and consultation approaches, it seems more logical for companies to invest in research in this area as they would invest in product development. Researchers have a stake as well. Access to real-world groups helps to test the external validity of experimental research and theoretical concepts. Practitioners also have a stake in the research process because they would become more valuable to their organization as the methods they use produce more reliably positive effects on the bottom line.

Some group researchers and practitioners have already moved in this direction, as is evidenced in this text. Collaborative relationships have been developed in the study not only of work groups but also of psychotherapy groups, psychoeducational groups, and other group contexts. More collaboration is needed, however, to close the gap for good. Developing collaborative researcher-practitioner relationships in which research questions relevant to both are defined and explored benefits not only the collaborators but also the organizations they belong to and the society at large.

Some steps that could be taken to increase collaboration are described next.

1. Convene a working conference of group practitioners and researchers to explore strategies to increase collaboration.

2. Include representative researchers and practitioners from all segments of group research and practice (group therapy, work groups, psychoeducational groups) and all disciplines that study and work with such groups.

3. Invite representatives from the public, private, and nonprofit sectors who have a stake in strengthening collaborative researcher-practitioner relationships and in the outcomes of group research and practice (corporations, health care, education, government, community development, and the like).

4. Encourage conference members to develop strategies not only to increase collaboration but also to fund the proposed strategies.

Although these steps would take a good deal of effort to implement, it would be well worth it. We live, learn, develop, work, and heal in groups. The effectiveness of those groups is important not only to the quality of individual human life but also to the duration of the human species. Working collaboratively on something so crucial to us all would be a privilege.

References

Amabile, T., Patterson, C., Mueller, J., Wojcik, T., Odomirok, P., Marsh, M., & Kramer, S. (2001). Academic-practitioner collaboration in management research: A case of cross-profession collaboration. *Academy of Management Journal, 44,* 418–431.

Anderson, N., Herriot, P., & Hodgkinson, G. (2001). The practitioner-researcher divide in industrial, work and organizational (IWO) psychology: Where are we now and where do we go from here? *Journal of Occupational and Organizational Psychology, 74,* 391–411.

Brice, T. S., & Waung, M. (2001). Is the science-practice gap shrinking? Some encouraging news from an analysis of SIOP programs. *The Industrial-Organizational Psychologist, 38,* 29–37.

Casio, W. F. (1991). Using utility analysis to assess training outcomes. In I. L. Goldstein (Ed.), *Training and development in organizations* (pp. 63–88). San Francisco: Jossey-Bass.

Farr, J. (1997). Organize IO psychology: Past, present, future. *The Industrial-Organizational Psychologist, 35,* 6–13.

French, W. L., & Bell, C. H. (1989). A history of organizational development. In W. L. French, C. H. Bell, & R. A. Zawacki (Eds.), *Organizational development: Theory, practice, and research* (pp. 18–32). Homewood, IL: BPI/Irwin.

Gruman, J. (2003, March 28). Basic vs. applied research: Finding a balance. *Chronicle of Higher Education,* p. B20.

Harry, M. (1994). *The vision of six sigma.* Phoenix, AZ: Sigma.

Hyatt, D., Cropanzano, R., Finfer, L., Levy, P., Ruddy, T., Vandaveer, V., & Walker, S. (1997). Bridging the gap between academics and practice: Suggestions from the field. *The Industrial-Organizational Psychologist, 35,* 14–24.

Leonard, H., & Freedman, A. (2000). From scientific management through fun and games to high-performing teams: A historical perspective on team-based organizations. *Consulting Psychology Journal: Practice and Research, 52,* 3–19.

Lewin, K. (1947a). Frontiers in group dynamics, I. *Human Relations, 1,* 5–41.

Lewin, K. (1947b). Frontiers in group dynamics, II. *Human Relations, 1,* 143–158.

Luft, J. (1984). *Group processes: An introduction to group dynamics.* Palo Alto, CA: Mayfield.

McGrath, J. E., Arrow, H., & Berdahl, J. L. (1999). Cooperation and conflict in interacting groups. *Polish Psychological Bulletin, 30*(1), 1–14.

McGregor, D. (1960). *The human side of enterprise.* New York: McGraw-Hill.

McIntyre, R. M. (1990). Our science-practice: The ghost of industrial-organizational psychology. In K. R. Murphy & F. E. Saal (Eds.), *Psychology in organizations: Integrating science and practice* (pp. 41–48). Hillsdale, NJ: Lawrence Erlbaum.

Murphy, K., & Saal, F. (1990). What should we expect from scientist-practitioners? In K. R. Murphy &

F. E. Saal (Eds.), *Psychology in organizations: Integrating science and practice* (pp. 49–66). Hillsdale, NJ: Lawrence Erlbaum.

Rogers, C. (1970). *On encounter groups.* New York: Harper & Row.

Salas, E., Rozell, D., Mullen, B., & Driskell, J. E. (1999). The effect of team building on performance: An integration. *Small Group Research, 30,* 309–329.

Schutz, W. C. (1971). *Here comes everybody.* New York: Harper & Row.

Tannenbaum, R. (1961). *Bob Tannenbaum: An unfolding life.* Bethel, ME: National Training Laboratories.

Tavris, C. (2003, February 28). Mind games; Psychological warfare between therapists and scientists. *Chronicle of Higher Education,* pp. B7–B9.

Index

About the Editor

Susan A. Wheelan (PhD, University of Wisconsin, 1974) is president of GDQ Associates, Inc., and an adjunct professor at the Massachusetts School of Professional Psychology. Until recently, she was professor of psychological studies and faculty director of the Training and Development Center at Temple University, where she received the university's Great Teacher Award in 1992. Dr. Wheelan has written seven books, edited three more, and published scores of journal articles. She has provided consultation to a wide variety of organizations. Both her research and consultation focus on work teams and groups.

About the Contributors

Dominic Abrams (PhD, University of Kent, 1984) is Director of the Centre for the Study of Group Processes at the University of Kent, UK, and his research interests include social identity, intergroup relations, deviance, prejudice, and group decision processes. He is coeditor of the journal *Group Processes and Intergroup Relations* and has written or edited several books in the area of social identity and group processes. He has been Secretary of the European Association of Experimental Social Psychology and is currently chair of the Research Board of the British Psychological Society.

Yvonne Agazarian (EdD, FAGPA, Temple University, 1968) is the developer of the theory of Living Human Systems and its Systems-Centered™ practice, founder of the Systems-Centered™ Training and Research Institute, and an international consultant on that method. She is a Clinical Professor at Adelphi University and is in private practice in Philadelphia. Author and coauthor of several books, she received the Group Psychologist of the Year award from Division 49 of the American Psychological Association in 1997.

Deborah G. Ancona (PhD, Columbia University, 1982) is the Seley Distinguished Professor of Management at the Sloan School of Management at MIT. She does small group research, in particular about how teams manage both their internal and external dynamics to obtain high performance. She taught at the Amos Tuck School of Business, Dartmouth College, before joining the faculty at MIT.

George Anderson (PhD, University of Louisville, 1994) is Manager of Executive & Customer Education at Crotonville, General Electric's corporate university in Ossining, New York, where he manages a team that designs and administers GE's executive education, strategic customer programming, change management education, and acquisition cultural integration workshops. He has a wide range of experience in occupational development, including managerial positions with GE's Answer Center and its Appliances' Leadership Development Center.

Holly Arrow (PhD, University of Illinois at Urbana-Champaign, 1996) is a member of both the Psychology Department and the Institute for Cognitive and Decision Sciences at the University of Oregon. She is coauthor of a book on small groups as complex systems and is widely published in books and journals. Trained in complexity theory at the Santa Fe Institute Complex Systems Summer School, class of 1995, she has served two terms as president of the Society for Chaos Theory in Psychology & Life Sciences (2002–2004).

Sally H. Barlow (PhD, University of Utah, 1978) is Professor of Psychology at Brigham Young University in Utah. She is also an Adjunct Professor in Psychiatry at the University of Utah Medical School, a consultant to the Utah State Hospital, and a member of the staff of the Utah Valley Regional Medical Center in Provo. She is coauthor of a book on psychotherapy and has refereed numerous journal articles and publications, including *Journal of the Specialists in Group Work*.

Jennifer L. Berdahl (PhD, University of Illinois, 1999) is an Assistant Professor of Management and Psychology at the University of Toronto. Her research investigates the social psychology of power in groups and organizations, and its recent focus is on the effects of power on perceptions, emotions, and behaviors in small groups and on sex harassment as a mechanism for enforcing sex-based distinctions and power inequalities in organizations.

Nina W. Brown (PhD, College of William and Mary, 1973) is a Professor and Eminent Scholar of Counseling at Old Dominion University in Norfolk, Virginia. She is also a licensed professional counselor and a nationally certified counselor. Her primary specialties are group counseling/therapy, counseling theories, and destructive narcissism. She is the author of 15 books and numerous articles.

C. Shawn Burke (PhD, George Mason University, 2000) is a Research Scientist at the University of Central Florida, Institute for Simulation and Training in Orlando, Florida. She has presented at numerous peer-reviewed conferences, has published in several scientific journals and books on the topics of teams and team training, and serves as an ad hoc reviewer for the *Human Factors* journal and *Quality Safety in Health Care.*

Gary M. Burlingame (PhD, University of Utah, 1983) is Professor of Clinical Psychology at Brigham Young University. He regularly contributes to the group psychotherapy and measurement literature: more than 90 books, book chapters, and peer-reviewed articles and more than 150 international, national, and regional presentations. He has served as a consultant to more than 20 federal, state, and private entities including the White House, Department of Labor, Food & Drug Administration, and health maintenance organizations.

Jeni L. Burnette is a PhD student at Virginia Commonwealth University and holds an undergraduate degree from the University of North Carolina at Chapel Hill. She is studying group dynamics and interpersonal relationships, with a focus on performance in collective endeavors and implicit theories of relationships and forgiveness. She teaches undergraduate social psychology and graduate-level statistics labs.

Damon M. Centola is a Fellow of the National Science Foundation-funded IGERT program on Non-linear Dynamics and Chaos at Cornell University. His dissertation research concerns the effects of network structure on the dynamics of collective action, and his recent work on computational models of unpopular norms has been accepted for publication in the *American Journal of Sociology.* He has bachelor's and master's degrees in philosophy.

Jonathon N. Cummings (PhD, Carnegie Mellon University, 2001) is Assistant Professor of Management at the Sloan School of Management at MIT. Supported by a National Science Foundation Early Career Award, he conducts research on ways that organizations can foster innovation through geographically dispersed teams and networks.

Kelly de Chermont is a doctoral candidate at Rice University, where she received her master's degree. Based on her research about broad issues of group functioning and organizational diversity, she has published in *Psychological Bulletin* and has presented papers at professional conferences. She consults with public and private organizations on various issues including training, leadership, and team development.

Janice L. DeLucia-Waack (PhD, Pennsylvania State University, 1987) is an Associate Professor in the Department of Counseling, School of Educational Psychology at the University at Buffalo, SUNY. She is the author or coauthor of several books in the areas of multicultural counseling and group work, including a session-by-session manual on the use of music in group therapy.

Georgina Randsley de Moura (PhD, University of Kent, 2004) is a postdoctoral researcher working with Emanuele Castano and Dominic Abrams on a project on collective responsibility, funded by the Economic and Social Research Council. She has published in the areas of organizational identity, collective action, and intergroup deviance.

Amanda Dykema-Engblade is a doctoral student in the Applied Social Psychology Program at Loyola University Chicago. Her dissertation looks at the roles of redundancy and expertise in group decision-making and performance. She teaches Social Psychology and Industrial/Organizational Psychology at Loyola. Her research interests include minority influence, transactive memory, and individual versus group decision-making.

Donelson R. Forsyth (PhD, University of Florida, 1978) is Professor of Psychology at Virginia Commonwealth University. He has written and edited several books and was the founding editor of the journal *Group Dynamics.* He is a social psychologist whose research interests include group processes, reactions to success and failure, individual differences in moral thought, and applications of social psychology in clinical settings.

Lawrence R. Frey (PhD, University of Kansas, 1979) is Professor and Associate Chair of the Department of Communication at the University of Colorado at Boulder. He is the author/editor of 12 books, three journal special issues, and 55 book chapters and journal articles. He has received 10 distinguished scholarship awards, including the 2000 Gerald M. Phillips Award for Distinguished Applied Communication Scholarship from the National Communication Association (NCA) and the 2003 and 2000 Ernest Bormann Research Award from NCA's Group Communication Division.

Daniel Frings is a graduate student at the University of Kent, funded by a scholarship from the Economic and Social Research Council. His research interests include deviance and intergroup emotions. He graduated from Cardiff University in 2003.

Addie J. Fuhriman (PhD, University of Minnesota, 1969) is Professor Emeritus of Psychology, former Dean of Graduate Studies, and Assistant to the President for Planning and Assessment at Brigham Young University. Previously, she was Chair and Professor of Educational Psychology at the University of Utah. Her teaching and research interests are in counseling psychology, specifically group psychotherapy process and outcome. She is active in the American Psychological Association and the American Group Psychotherapy Association.

Susan Gantt (PhD, Georgia State University, 1984) is a Diplomate in Group Psychology, ABPP, and a licensed psychologist in private practice in Atlanta, Georgia. She is the Director of the Systems-Centered™ Training and Research Institute and works for the Department of Psychiatry and Behavioral Sciences of the Emory University School of Medicine. She is coauthor of a book and author of several articles on the systems-centered approach.

Marvin H. Geller (PhD, Massachusetts Institute of Technology, 1969) is a practicing psychoanalyst, an organizational consultant, and Codirector of the Organizational Program at the William Alanson White Institute. Previously, he was Director of Counseling Services at Princeton University, where he taught psychoanalytic theory and group and organizational process. He has published numerous articles and book reviews.

Stephen J. Guastello (PhD, Illinois Institute of Technology, 1982) is an Associate Professor of Psychology at Marquette University in Milwaukee. He has written more than 100 journal articles and book chapters pertaining to personality theory, computer-based test interpretations, and applications of nonlinear dynamics. He is a Past President of the Society for Chaos Theory in Psychology & Life Sciences and currently serves as its Treasurer and Trustee.

Terry R. Halfhill (PhD, University of Tennessee, 2001) is Assistant Professor of Management with the business and economics division, Commonwealth College, at the Pennsylvania State University–New Kensington campus. Previously, he was a member of the Industrial/Organizational Psychology faculty at the University of North Texas and an associate with its Center for the Study of Work teams (CSWT). He has served as an organizational consultant to a variety of academic, governmental, and military organizations.

Kelly Bouas Henry (PhD, University of Illinois, 1997) is Assistant Professor of Psychology at Missouri Western State College. Her research focuses on a variety of group processes, with special emphasis on developmental patterns and the dynamics of group structure.

Michael A. Hogg (PhD, Bristol University, 1983) is Professor of Social Psychology at the University of Queensland and an Australian Research Council Professorial Fellow. He is also a Visiting Professor of Psychology at the University of California, Santa Barbara. The founding journal editor (with Dominic Abrams) for *Group Processes and Intergroup Relations,* he serves on the editorial board of several publications. He has written more than 200 books, book chapters, and journal articles.

Rick H. Hoyle (PhD, University of North Carolina, 1988) is a Senior Research Scientist in the Terry Sanford Institute of Public Policy and the Department of Psychology: Social and Health Sciences at Duke University. He also serves as Associate Director for Data Services in the Center for Child and Family Policy and Director of the Data Core in the Trans-disciplinary Prevention Research Center, funded by the National Institute on Drug Abuse. He is a Fellow of the Society for the Psychological Study of Social Issues and editor of the *Journal of Social Issues.*

David W. Johnson (PhD, Columbia University, 1966) is a Professor of Educational Psychology at the University of Minnesota, where he holds the Emma M. Birkmaier Professorship in Educational Leadership. He is Codirector of the Cooperative Learning Center and past Editor of the *American Educational Research Journal.* He has written more than 350 research articles and book chapters, as well as more than 40 books. An organizational consultant to schools and businesses, he is a recognized authority on experiential learning and a practicing psychotherapist.

Roger T. Johnson (EdD, University of California at Berkeley, 1969) is a Professor in the Department of Curriculum and Instruction with an emphasis in Science Education at the University of Minnesota. He has broad experience teaching in public schools and is an authority on inquiry teaching and science education. He is the Codirector of the Cooperative Learning Center, which conducts research on cooperative educational strategies, and author of several articles and book chapters.

Tricia S. Jones (PhD, Ohio State University, 1985) is Professor in the Department of Psychological Studies in the College of Education at Temple University. She has published more than 40 articles and book chapters on conflict and has coedited several volumes. She is the Editor-in-Chief of *Conflict Resolution Quarterly* (formerly *Mediation Quarterly*) and the recipient of the 2004 Jeffrey Z. Rubin Theory to Practice Award from the International Association for Conflict Management.

Cynthia R. Kalodner (PhD, Pennsylvania State University, 1988) is Professor in the Department of Psychology at Towson University, where she is Director of the master's program in Counseling Psychology and works closely with post-master's students seeking licensure. She is author of a book and author or coauthor of more than 40 book chapters and journal articles and is coeditor of a handbook on group counseling.

Suad Kapetanovic (MD, University of Zagreb School of Medicine, Croatia, 1995) completed his psychiatry residency and fellowship in child and adolescent psychiatry in 2004 at the University of Utah's Department of Psychiatry.

He is a licensed physician in the states of Utah and California. His areas of interest include child, adolescent, and young adult psychiatry and process-oriented group psychotherapy for young adults.

Michael W. Macy (PhD, Harvard University, 1985) is Professor and Chair of Sociology at Cornell University. His research team uses computational models and laboratory experiments with human subjects to look for elementary principles of self-organization, hoping to find clues as to how simple and predictable local interactions might account for familiar but highly enigmatic global patterns. Recent articles have appeared in *American Sociological Review, American Journal of Sociology,* and the *Proceedings of the National Academy of Sciences.*

Randy H. Magen (PhD, University of Wisconsin, Madison, 1992) is Associate Professor in the School of Social Work at the University of Alaska, Anchorage. Previously, he was on the faculty at the Columbia University School of Social Work. His scholarly interests and publications have been in group work and in the co-occurrence of domestic violence and child maltreatment.

Eugene Mangiardi (MSW, Smith College, 1998) is Clinical Assistant Professor at the University of Alaska's School of Social Work. His area of focus is the application of clinical social work theory and direct practice skills in mental health, family services, child welfare, and substance abuse.

Tjai M. Nielsen (PhD, University of Tennessee, 2001) is Assistant Professor in the School of Business at George Washington University. He has written multiple articles, book chapters, and technical reports on executive development, work teams, and corporate citizenship. An international consultant, he previously spent 3 years as a consultant at RHR International Company in the areas of executive selection and development, succession planning, team development, and executive coaching.

Marshall Scott Poole (PhD, 1979, University of Wisconsin) is Professor of Communication and of Information and Operations Management at Texas A&M University. His articles have appeared in leading journals, and he has coauthored or edited 10 books. His research interests include group and organizational communication, information systems, conflict management, and organizational innovation.

Miguel A. Quiñones (PhD, Michigan State University, 1993) is Associate Professor of Management and Policy and Lesk Faculty Fellow at the Eller College of Management at the University of Arizona. Previously, he was Assistant and then Associate Professor of Psychology and Management at Rice University. He has published in a range of journals and is coeditor of a book applying research to workplace training. He has consulted with public and private organizations, including several Fortune 500 companies.

Maria T. Riva (PhD, University of Pittsburgh, 1990) is Associate Professor of Counseling Psychology at the University of Denver and has experience facilitating many types of counseling and psychotherapy groups. In 2001, she was awarded the University of Denver's Distinguished Teaching Award. She has numerous publications on group counseling and psychotherapy, and she is Associate Editor of the *Journal for Specialists in Group Work,* after serving on its editorial board for 6 years.

Steven Ross (PhD, University of Utah, 1970) is Associate Professor and Associate Residency Training Director in the Department of Psychiatry at the University of Utah's School of Medicine. He is a Diplomate in Counseling Psychology and holds the Certificate of Proficiency in the Treatment of Alcohol and Other Psychoactive Substance Use Disorders from the American Psychological Association. He coedited four volumes on behavioral group therapy.

Eduardo Salas (PhD, Old Dominion University, 1984) is Trustee Chair and Professor of

Psychology at the University of Central Florida, where he directs the Applied Experimental & Human Factors Program. He is also Program Director for the Human Systems Integration Research Department at the Institute for Simulation and Training. He is coauthor of more than 200 journal articles and book chapters and coeditor of 13 books. He is designing tools and techniques to minimize human errors in aviation, law enforcement, and medical environments.

Dana E. Sims is a doctoral student in Industrial/Organizational (I/O) Psychology at the University of Central Florida, where she earned her master's degree in 2003. Her research interests include teamwork, team training, mentoring, patient safety, and trust in organizational settings. She has presented and published extensively on these topics.

Joanne Broder Sumerson (PhD, Temple University, 2004) is Adjunct Professor at Temple University, St. Joseph's University, and Walnut Hill College. She also works for the School District of Philadelphia in the Office of Research and Evaluation and was Associate Director of the Training and Development Center at Temple University, which provides training and consultation to public and private sector organizations.

Eric D. Sundstrom (PhD, University of Utah, 1973) is Professor of Psychology at the University of Tennessee and has combined a career as a university professor and private consultant in research and development focused on effectiveness of teams and organizations. His research on work team effectiveness, physical working environments, and related topics has generated more than 70 professional publications, including two books and articles in more than a dozen refereed scientific journals.

Sunwolf (PhD, University of California–Santa Barbara, 1998; JD, University of Denver College of Law, 1976) is an Associate Professor of Communication at Santa Clara University. A former trial attorney and Training Director for

Colorado's Public Defender Office, she facilitates training groups of attorneys nationally. Her coauthored research on jury deliberations received the 2000 Dennis S. Gouran Research Award from NCA's Group Communication Division.

Felice Tilin (PhD, Temple University, 1997) is a Senior Consultant with the Teleos Leadership Institute and President of GroupWorks Consulting. Recently, she served as the Academic Director for the Corporate Learning Program at the University of Pennsylvania's Graduate School of Education. Previously, she was the Director of the Center for Professional Development at the University of Pennsylvania and a Director of Organizational Development at the Cigna Corporation.

R. Scott Tindale (PhD, University of Illinois at Urbana-Champaign, 1984) is Chair of the Department of Psychology at Loyola University Chicago. He is an Associate Editor for the *Journal of Personality and Social Psychology* and *Group Processes and Intergroup Relations*, and he coedited a book on social psychology. His research focuses on the social and cognitive processes associated with small group decision-making and problem-solving.

Maximillian Wachtel (PhD, University of Denver, 2001) leads psychotherapy groups with a wide range of clients and training groups for a small business. His dissertation research was a field study on group co-leadership development. He directed the Group Therapy Institute at the Mental Health Corporation of Denver, a group dedicated to group therapy training and practice with individuals who have severe and persistent mental illness.

Erin Wittkowski is a graduate student in the Applied Social Psychology Program at Loyola University Chicago. She is currently completing her course work and finishing her thesis, which examines subjective norms and the theory of reasoned action. She also works as a research assistant for Dr. Scott Tindale, examining small group decision-making. She is a graduate of the University of Northern Iowa.

Huiyan Zhang is a PhD candidate at Texas A&M University. Her research interests include organizational communication, communication technologies used in work groups, and culture's impacts on health and organizational life. She has presented her work at several national conferences and is currently working on empirical case studies of interaction in virtual teams in partial fulfillment of her PhD.